THE INTERNATIONAL LESSON ANNUAL 1992–93

September–August

A Commentary and Teacher's Guide on the International Sunday School Lessons
Uniform Series

Edited by
William H. Willimon and Patricia P. Willimon

Lesson Analysis by
LLOYD R. BAILEY
WILLIAM H. WILLIMON
PAT McGEACHY
WILLIAM H. SMITH
and
Enrichment Articles by Fred B. Craddock,
William H. Willimon, and Patricia P. Willimon

ABINGDON PRESS
Nashville

THE INTERNATIONAL LESSON ANNUAL—1992-93

Copyright © 1992 by Abingdon Press

ISBN 0-687-19156-4

Library of Congress ISSN 0074-6770

Editors' Preface

It is difficult for us to believe that we wrote our first material for *The International Lesson Annual* back in 1984. With this edition, we celebrate our tenth year of work with the *Annual,* first as writer, then as editor-writer, now as a husband-wife team of editors and writers.

Your warm response has brought us great satisfaction in our work. We have been deeply gratified by your thoughtful letters and telephone calls. Through this work, we have made many new friends in many different places.

One of you called to tell us about your class discussion of one of the lessons from the Old Testament in last year's *Annual.* Another one of you was good enough to share the written responses of your class to our series on the Epistles last year. We value your reactions, even when they are critical of what we do. It is good for us to know that you care about the work we do. It is especially good to hear the ways in which you think we can serve you better as editors and as writers.

Lessons within this year's series will take us from Genesis, the very first book of our Bible, into Luke's beloved Gospel, then through Romans and Galatians, some of Paul's greatest work. Our writers have been selected because of their previous work with the *Annual* and for their expertise with the biblical material.

The International Lesson Annual has enjoyed many years of success, bringing the fruits of in-depth Bible study to millions of Christians around the world. Today more than ever in our history we need to encounter the Bible. We need to study Scripture in such a way that it speaks to us in our daily lives. Your adult class, where you teach each Sunday, is a great place for people to meet God's word.

If you are new to *The International Lesson Annual,* you will note that each of the four quarters (with thirteen lessons per quarter) is divided into five sections. These sections guide the teacher through the lesson in such a way that the adult teacher is enabled to present the lesson in a relevant, engaging manner. Each lesson begins with "The Main Question," which presents the basic question that is at the forefront of that lesson. Both the King James and the New Revised Standard Version treatments of the biblical text are printed to make study of the passages easier for you. The third section, "As You Read the Scripture," explores the scriptural passage, verse by verse, highlighting important exegetical details. The fourth section, "The Scripture and the Main Question," has a detailed exposition of the text and its everyday significance for Christian living today. You will probably find more material here than you can use in one class session. Feel free to adapt it with your class in mind. Finally, "Helping Adults Become Involved" gives you a step-by-step lesson plan to adapt for use in your class.

In addition to this every-Sunday teaching guide, we have also included a few special spiritual enrichment articles that will help to increase your effectiveness as an adult Bible teacher.

Welcome to another year with the Bible and *The International Lesson Annual!*

William H. Willimon and Patricia P. Willimon, *Editors*

Contents

FIRST QUARTER

Old Testament Personalities

UNIT I: GOD CHOOSES AND RELATES TO A PEOPLE (SEPT. 6–27)

LESSON   PAGE

Introduction.. 11

1. God's Call and Promise to Abram..12
   Sept. 6—*Genesis 11:27–12:9*

2. God's Call to Moses.. 18
   Sept. 13—*Exodus 3:1–4:17*

3. God's Choice of Joshua to Succeed Moses..........................26
   Sept. 20—*Joshua 1*

4. God's Provision of Leadership Through Deborah..............34
   Sept. 27—*Judges 4–5*

UNIT II: THE PEOPLE CHOOSE A MONARCHY (OCT. 4–25)

Introduction.. 42

5. Samuel, the Last Judge.. 42
   Oct. 4—*1 Samuel 7:15–8:22*

6. David: King over All the People.. 49
   Oct. 11—*1 Samuel 16:1-13; 2 Samuel 2:1-7; 5:1-5*

7. Solomon: Wise King..57
   Oct. 18—*1 Kings 1:28-37; 2:1-4; 3:3-14*

8. Josiah: King of Reforms..64
   Oct. 25—*2 Chronicles 34*

UNIT III: THE PROPHETS' ROLES IN A DIVIDED KINGDOM (NOV. 1–29)

Introduction.. 72

9. Elijah: Prophet of Courage..73
   Nov. 1—*1 Kings 17:1-7; 18*

10. Amos: Prophet of Justice.. 81
    Nov. 8—*Amos 2:6–3:2; 5:24*

11. Hosea: Prophet of God's Love..88
    Nov. 15—*Hosea 1:1-3; 3:1-2; 6:4-6; 11:1-4*
    Spiritual Enrichment Article: "Meeting and Being Met
    by the Bible in Your Adult Class".................................. 95
    William and Patricia Willimon

12. Micah: Prophet of Righteousness.................................... 99
    Nov. 22—*Micah 6*

13. Jeremiah: Persistent Prophet.. 106
    Nov. 29—*Jeremiah 1:1-10; 8:22–9:3; 20:7-13*

SECOND QUARTER
Good News for All

UNIT I: COMING OF THE GOOD NEWS
(DEC. 6–27)

LESSON   PAGE

Introduction.. 115
1. God's Purpose Through Love................................115
   Dec. 6—*Hebrews 1:1-4; Ephesians 1:3-14*
2. God's Promise to Zechariah................................. 123
   Dec. 13—*Luke 1:1-25*
3. God's Promise to the Gentiles.............................130
   Dec. 20—*Luke 2:1-40*
4. Jesus Filled with the Spirit...................................138
   Dec. 27—*Matthew 3:1–4:11*

UNIT II: LIVING THE GOOD NEWS
(JAN. 3–31)

Introduction.. 144
5. The Coming of the Holy Spirit............................. 145
   Jan. 3—*Acts 2*
6. A Call to Holy Living.. 152
   Jan. 10—*1 Peter 1:13-25*
7. The Church Is for All People............................... 159
   Jan. 17—*Acts 11*
8. Learning God's Wisdom.. 166
   Jan. 24—*1 Corinthians 1:1–2:13*
9. One Body in Christ... 174
   Jan. 31—*Ephesians 4:1-16*

UNIT III: SHARING THE GOOD NEWS
(FEB. 7–28)

Introduction.. 181
10. Commissioned to Witness.....................................181
    Feb. 7—*Luke 24:13-53*
11. Proclaim the Gospel...188
    Feb. 14—*Romans 10*
12. Serve and Honor... 196
    Feb. 21—*Romans 15:1-13*
13. Teach the Truth...203
    Feb. 28—*2 Timothy 2:14-26; Titus 2*

THIRD QUARTER
Believing in Christ
(The Gospel of John)

UNIT I: JOHN: THE WORD BECAME FLESH
(MAR. 7–28)

LESSON		PAGE
	Introduction	210
1.	Life in Christ	211
	Mar. 7—*John 1:1-18*	
2.	Necessity of the New Birth	218
	Mar. 14—*John 3:1-21*	
3.	Light of the World	225
	Mar. 21—*John 9*	
4.	Coming to Life	232
	Mar. 28—*John 11:1-44*	

UNIT II: JOHN: THE GREAT LOVE
(APR. 4–25)

	Introduction	240
5.	Do as I Have Done	241
	Apr. 4—*John 13:1-20*	
	Spiritual Enrichment Article: "He's Back!"	248
	William H. Willimon	
6.	I Have Seen the Lord	250
	Apr. 11—*John 20:1-18*	
7.	To Love Is to Serve	258
	Apr. 18—*John 21*	
8.	The Bread of Life	265
	Apr. 25—*John 6*	

UNIT III: JOHN: BELIEVE IN JESUS
(MAY 2–30)

	Introduction	272
9.	The Witness of John the Baptist	273
	May 2—*John 1:19-34*	
10.	We Have Found Him	280
	May 9—*John 1:35-40*	
11.	Encountering Christ	286
	May 16—*John 4:1-42*	
12.	Confronting the Galilean	294
	May 23—*John 7:37-52*	
13.	The Promise of the Spirit	300
	May 30—*John 14*	

FOURTH QUARTER
Following God's Purpose

UNIT I: JOY IN SERVING CHRIST
(JUNE 6–27)

LESSON   PAGE

Introduction 308

1. A Worthy Life 309
   June 6—*Philippians 1:3-14, 27-30*

2. Christ, Our Model 317
   June 13—*Philippians 2:1-18*

3. Keep On Keeping On 324
   June 20—*Philippians 3:1-16*

4. Rejoice in the Lord 332
   June 27—*Philippians 4*
   Spiritual Enrichment Article:
   "Paul's Letter to the Philippians" 339
   Fred B. Craddock

UNIT II: CHRIST ABOVE ALL
(JULY 4–25)

Introduction 342

5. The Preeminent Christ 343
   July 4—*Colossians 1*

6. The Sufficient Christ 351
   July 11—*Colossians 2*

7. Life in Christ 358
   July 18—*Colossians 3*

8. Christ Unites 366
   July 25—*Philemon*

UNIT III: NEWNESS THROUGH CHRIST
(AUGUST 1–29)

Introduction 373

9. New Life 374
   August 1—*Ephesians 1:15–2:10; 3:14-19*

10. New Fellowship 381
    August 8—*Ephesians 2:11–3:6*

11. New Behavior 389
    August 15—*Ephesians 5:1-20*

12. New Family Order 397
    August 22—*Ephesians 5:21–6:4*

13. New Strength 404
    August 29—*Ephesians 6:10-20*

FIRST QUARTER
Old Testament Personalities

UNIT I: GOD CHOOSES AND RELATES TO A PEOPLE
Lloyd R. Bailey

FOUR LESSONS   **SEPTEMBER 6–27**

To begin this quarter's study of Old Testament personalities, these four sessions focus on the highlights of God's initial relationship with the primal community that will ultimately produce both Synagogue and Church. The necessity for that relationship is spelled out in Genesis 1–11: The ideal world that God had created (Genesis 1–2) has been terribly disrupted by human pride and disobedience (Genesis 3–4). The response of God was then twofold: on the one hand, the establishment of limits on the human lifespan (6:1-4) and ability to interact (11:1-9), and the cleansing of the earth by means of the great flood (6:5–9:17); on the other hand, acts of graciousness and commitment to the future, such as the birth of the Sethite line (4:25-26), the preservation of Noah and his family (6:13-18), the covenant with humankind after the flood (9:8-11), and the multiplication of the race thereafter (10:1-32; 11:10-32) in keeping with the divine promise (1:27-28; 9:1).

The transition from chapter 11 to chapter 12 changes the focus of the divine action. Whereas the "primeval story" was concerned with the beginnings and failures of the human race, the "patriarchal story" (Genesis 12–50) focuses on God's interaction with the single genealogical line through which "shall all the families of the earth be blessed" (12:3 KJV;.see also GNB). Thus the overall flow of the narrative suggests that the call of Abraham's clan to be an obedient and exemplary community is God's new initiative in the struggle to rehabilitate an errant humanity.

In this unit we explore the implications of God's call.

This Quarter's Writer:
To lead us through our first quarter's study of Old Testament personalities, we are fortunate to have as our guide an internationally renowned biblical scholar, Dr. Lloyd R. Bailey, Sr.

Lloyd Richard Bailey, Sr., is a native of Burnsville, North Carolina. He is an ordained United Methodist minister (Western North Carolina Conference) who served in the parish in Iowa before joining the faculty of Union Theological Seminary (New York) and of Duke Divinity School in 1971 as professor of Hebrew Bible (Old Testament). A graduate of Hebrew Union College-Jewish Institute of Religion, his areas of publication include biblical studies, preaching, and such life crises as aging, dying, and death.

Dr. Bailey will challenge us to grapple with the historical background of Old Testament personalities. Under his leadership, your class will grow in its ability to apply the witness of past leaders in the faith to our present attempts to be faithful.

God's Call and Promise to Abram

Background Scripture: Genesis 11:27–12:9

The Main Question

Is there any realistic hope for a time when the earth will not be "filled with violence" (Genesis 6:11) and when "every imagination of the thoughts" of the human heart will not be "only evil continually" (v. 5)? If such violence and thoughts have characterized human history from its beginnings (Genesis 1–11), are things likely to change in the future? If so, wherein does such hope reside? What role might human beings play? Is there hope beyond the possibility of their failure?

The story of Abram's call, obedience, betrayal of the promise, and of God's ultimate intervention may serve as an illustration of the question and an indication of the answer. This is especially the case in the light of the fact that Abram (Abraham) is often considered to be the "father of the Faith" (Isaiah 51:2; Romans 4:12; James 2:21), whom members of the Synagogue and the Church should imitate. For the full range of the question and answer to be grasped, however, Abram's call must be understood in the context of the "primeval story" (Genesis 1–11, see above), and the "background Scripture" must be expanded to include the entirety of chapter 12. To end the reading at verse 9 is to focus attention entirely on the human element (Abram)—and it is, after all, the problem! That is made clear when we read that Abraham forsakes the "promised land" (disbelieves the promise?) and goes down to Egypt (vv. 10-16). Only later does the true hero of the account emerge, and thus the ultimate source of hope becomes clear (vv. 17-20).

Selected Scripture

King James Version	New Revised Standard Version
Genesis 11:31-32	*Genesis 11:31-32*
31 And Terah took Abram his son, and Lot the son of Haran his son's son, and Sarai his daughter in law, his son Abram's wife; and they went forth with them from Ur of the Chaldees, to go into the land of Canaan; and they came unto Haran, and dwelt there.	31 Terah took his son Abram and his grandson Lot son of Haran, and his daughter-in-law Sarai, his son Abram's wife, and they went out together from Ur of the Chaldeans to go into the land of Canaan; but when they came to Haran, they settled there. 32 The days of Terah were two hundred five years; and Terah died in Haran.
32 And the days of Terah were two hundred and five years: and Terah died in Haran.	
Genesis 12:1-9	*Genesis 12:1-9*
1 Now the Lord had said unto Abram, Get thee out of thy country,	Now the Lord said to Abram, "Go from your country and your kin-

and from thy kindred, and from thy father's house, unto a land that I will shew thee:

2 And I will make of thee a great nation, and I will bless thee, and make thy name great; and thou shalt be a blessing:

3 And I will bless them that bless thee, and curse him that curseth thee: and in thee shall all families of the earth be blessed:

4 So Abram departed, as the LORD had spoken unto him; and Lot went with him: and Abram was seventy and five years old when he departed out of Haran.

5 And Abram took Sarai his wife, and Lot his brother's son, and all their substance that they had gathered, and the souls that they had gotten in Haran; and they went forth to go into the land of Canaan; and into the land of Canaan they came.

6 And Abram passed through the land unto the place of Sichem, unto the plain of Moreh. And the Canaanite was then in the land.

7 And the LORD appeared unto Abram, and said, Unto thy seed will I give this land: and there builded he an altar unto the LORD, who appeared unto him.

8 And he removed from thence unto a mountain on the east of Bethel, and pitched his tent, having Bethel on the west, and Hai on the east: and there he builded an altar unto the LORD, and called upon the name of the LORD.

9 And Abram journeyed, going on still toward the south.

dred and your father's house to the land that I will show you. 2 I will make of you a great nation, and I will bless you, and make your name great, so that you will be a blessing. 3 I will bless those who bless you, and the one who curses you I will curse; and in you all the families of the earth shall be blessed." 4 So Abram went, as the LORD had told him; and Lot went with him. Abram was seventy-five years old when he departed from Haran. 5 Abram took his wife Sarai and his brother's son Lot, and all the possessions that they had gathered, and the persons whom they had acquired in Haran; and they set forth to go to the land of Canaan. When they had come to the land of Canaan, 6 Abram passed through the land to the place at Shechem, to the oak of Moreh. At that time the Canaanites were in the land. 7 Then the LORD appeared to Abram, and said, "To your offspring I will give this land." So he built there an altar to the LORD, who had appeared to him. 8 From there he moved on to the hill country on the east of Bethel, and pitched his tent, with Bethel on the west and Ai on the east; and there he built an altar to the LORD and invoked the name of the LORD. 9 And Abram journeyed on by stages toward the Negeb.

Key Verses: **Get thee out of thy country, and from thy kindred, and from thy father's house, unto a land that I will shew thee: And I will make of thee a great nation, and I will bless thee, and make thy name great; and thou shalt be a blessing. (Genesis 12:1-2)**

Key Verses: **Go from your country and your kindred and your father's house to the land that I will show you. I will make of you a great nation, and I will bless you, and make your name great, so that you will be a blessing. (Genesis 12:1-2)**

As You Read the Scripture

Genesis 11:27-32. This is the conclusion of the "primeval story," whereby Abram's family is placed in the context of the spread of the human race following the flood of Noah's time. From a great range of possibilities (Genesis 10), one clan emerges as the instrument for God's interaction with humankind.

Verse 27. "Abram" is a variation of the name "Abraham" (which will not emerge until 17:5).

Verse 28. Several locations for "Ur of the Chaldeans" have been proposed, but the traditional (and likely) one is in southern Iraq, near the Persian Gulf. The Chaldeans were a part of the Babylonian Empire.

Verse 29. For a similar change of name from "Sarai" to "Sarah," see 17:15.

Verse 31. Haran is in southern Turkey, six hundred miles from Ur.

Genesis 12:1-20. The complete, initial story of Israel's goals and beginnings.

Verse 3. The Church has traditionally read the text in the universal sense (Galatians 3:8) and apparently so did the early Synagogue (to judge from Matthew 23:15). No text in the Bible is more central to the self-understanding of the two communities than this one.

Verse 7. It is important, from the point of view of appraising Abram's faith, to realize that he will not live to see this part of the promise realized ("to your *descendants* . . . ").

Verse 9. The Negeb is the southern termination of the "promised land," bordering on the Sinai Peninsula.

Verse 10. Scarcity and irregularity of rainfall in southern Canaan produced famine with some frequency, causing inhabitants to seek food in Egypt, where fertility was determined by the more regular flooding of the Nile.

The Scripture and the Main Question

Biblical literature has many forms, each one meant to elicit a given response from the hearers or readers. For example, there is legislation that presupposes obedience (Exodus 21:1–23:19), and there are proverbs that evoke reflection. The story of Abram, by contrast, is a saga of national beginnings, wherein the ancestor personifies the group. Hearers are drawn into the story, and it is presupposed that they will identify with the hopes of the ancestors, see their own failures enacted, and imitate the admirable aspects of the hero or heroine. What happened to Abram, then, was not merely an event that remained in the past, but was a paradigm of what happens to the community in every age. Thus we read it, in the present, as the people of God, in order to have our identity defined, corrected, or encouraged.

Go from Your Country

The response asked of Abram is a demanding one. His family is to forsake clan and friends, realizing that they may never see one another again. Such disruptions of the family were far less frequent then than they are now, and thus the divine command must have seemed particularly harsh and saddening. Furthermore, the journey would take Abram's family across national borders where they would not be subject to protection. The threat of exploitation, compounded by the harshness of the geographical environment, would have engendered a measure of anxiety. Finally, the realization that citizens of a "high" culture, like that of Canaan, would not necessarily welcome a foreigner who proclaimed a new god and who expected to become "a great nation" (v. 2), must have raised doubts in Abram's mind about the success of the venture. Thus one can only be filled with admiration at the faith and courage of the man and his family when the text records, as if it were a quick decision, "So Abram went, as the LORD had told him" (v. 4). Not without reason, therefore, would future generations both in the Synagogue and in the Church cite him as an admirable person to be imitated. "Abraham believed God, and it was reckoned to him as righteousness" (Romans 4:3, citing Genesis 15:6). This is all the more the case when we realize that aspects of the threefold promise could not be fulfilled in Abram's own lifetime ("I will make of you a great nation"; "To your descendants I will give this land"). Abram's family members thus devote their lives to a cause they will not live to see to fruition. Indeed, late generations within Israel would understand the promise to have been fully realized only at the time of the formation of the State during the reigns of David and Solomon (after more than five hundred years had passed).

Now, There Was a Famine . . .

Famine or not, residence in Egypt had not been a part of the divine commission. The "promised land," where God intended to "make your name great" (v. 2), was Canaan, and not the land of the pharaohs. From this perspective, Abram's departure to the Nile Valley may be viewed as an act of faithlessness, and this following "hard on the heels" of the glowing report that he had built an altar "and called on the name of the LORD" (v. 8). Hope for a positive resolution of "The Main Question" (above) begins to fade as the hero of the national saga is revealed to have clay feet, just like ordinary folks. Did he not believe that God could or would keep the promise?

Our estimation of Abram's faintness of heart is compounded when we read his request of Sarai. He is afraid that the Egyptians will kill him, and thus he asks her to deny their true relationship and then allows her to enter the harem of the pharaoh. From the standpoint of the storyline, the problem here is not of violation of personal relationship, but rather risk to the future of the promise. Abram now does more than forsake the "promised land"; he is willing to destroy the promise in the interest of his own safety. Without Sarai as his wife, there will be no Isaac, and without Isaac there can be no Israel. Surely Abram must have been aware of this, but preservation of one's life is a high priority with most humans and not with Abram alone. The writer observes, perhaps in derision, that Abram was subsequently blessed by Pharaoh with "sheep, oxen, male donkeys, male and female servants, female donkeys, and camels" (v. 16), but not with the mother of Israel-to-be!

But the LORD Afflicted Pharaoh . . .

If either Abram or his servants expressed recognition of the danger of the situation, it is not recorded in the story. Nonetheless, "all is well that ends well," no thanks to human beings! The deity now becomes the hero of the tale, affirming the viability of the solution to the situation that the "primeval story" has depicted. Is there hope for a different future, in which the social ideals of creation will be realized? God continues to see the necessity for an "Israel" (ultimately, for a Synagogue and a Church) even if Abram has temporarily lost sight of the vision.

Unease with the situation is first articulated, not by the "chosen community" (as we might have supposed), but by a foreigner. The pharaoh, having learned of Sarai's marital status (and apparently prompted by "great plagues" of divine origin, according to v. 17), castigates Abram for what he has done, returns his wife, and directs him to leave the country. Regardless of Pharaoh's motives, it is unsettling to realize that the Bible's first lecture on ethics comes from an "outsider," and that it is directed toward the hero of the national saga, who typified the community in every age! One may have the sinking feeling, upon hearing this, that the story was directed toward the reality of the community both past and present!

The sacred story, then, relates realities both human and divine so that may they be clear right from the beginning. There is the possibility of a world at peace rather than filled with violence (Genesis 6:11), of humans whose hearts desire justice and humaneness rather than "only evil continually" (6:5). That possibility rests, in part, upon Abram and those who believe God and obey as Abram did, thus producing a community whose ideals for ethics and liturgy are those outlined in the Bible. It rests, ultimately, however, in the knowledge of the deity that such a community can be effective, and even more in the power of the deity to redeem its failures and transform it into an instrument of salvation.

Helping Adults Become Involved

Preparing to Teach

It will be helpful to place the account of Abraham's call in the context of the larger narrative. Read the first eleven chapters of Genesis with two emphases in mind: (1) attitudes or events that have contributed to the disruption of God's design (for example, Lamech's escalation of violence in Genesis 4:23-24) and (2) attempts by the deity to limit or overcome the disruption (for example, by establishing various speech patterns in Genesis 11:1-9). This enables the reader to sense the gospel in the subsequent account of God's redemptive action, which begins at 12:1.

Presentation to the class might follow the outline below.

    I. The geographical situation
    II. Abraham's call in the context of the larger story (Genesis 1–11)
    III. The biblical account and its implications for the reader

Introducing the Main Question

Everyone in your class will be aware that the world is a discouraging and frustrating place in which to hope for a better future. Be it at the international, national, state, or local level, can things ever be better than they are now in terms of justice, humaneness, and love for others? This was a fundamental problem that faced the biblical thinkers right from the beginning of the story. It is a more pressing problem when one observes how much things are the same after more than three thousand years. Their proposal was that God's ultimate approach to the problem was the election of an obedient community that would, by word and example, be "a blessing to all the families of the earth." Will it yet succeed, where prior approaches (massive punishment, as in the great flood of Noah's time) failed?

Developing the Lesson

I. The geographical situation

Class members will be helped by a quick overview of political realities at the time of Abraham, and of the long and dangerous route his family took in obedience to God's call. If maps are not available in the classroom, then look for suitable ones in Bibles or Bible dictionaries or related books (for example, GNB's "Ancient World," p. 379; *The Interpreter's One-Volume Commentary on the Bible*, ed. Charles M. Laymon [Nashville: Abingdon Press, 1971], Map 2, hereafter referred to as *IOCB*; or best of all, "The Ancient World at the Time of the Patriarchs," a map that is less cluttered than the others and has the route Abraham took clearly marked, in *The Interpreter's Dictionary of the Bible, Supplementary Volume*, eds. Keith Crim et al. [Nashville: Abingdon Press, 1976], hereafter referred to as *IDBS*. One or more of these resources probably will be in your church library). It may be equally helpful to draw a rough map on a chalkboard. Mention should be made of the distance involved, the crossing of borders and lack of protection, and so on.

II. Abraham's call in the context of the larger story (Genesis 1–11)

The importance of this material for understanding today's lesson has been outlined above. Your own reading of those chapters will clarify the matter even more. If a copy of *IDBS* is available, you might want to read the article on "Genesis" (Section A, "Primeval History," pp. 356-58).

III. The biblical account and its implications for the reader

Genesis 12 may be divided into three episodes, and these have been adequately discussed above under the heading "The Scripture and the Main Question." You might proceed by presenting this material in your own words.

Helping Class Members Act

The following topics may be helpful in enabling the class members to think about the implications of the text for their own lives.

The reality of the present world

Ask members of the class to list those aspects of life that they have found to be discouraging and that diminish their hope for a better future for humanity. Such items might be listed on a chalkboard or large paper.

Individuals or groups who have made a difference

Obedience to God's call sometimes involves loneliness, doubt, hardship, and danger, as did the long journey of Abraham to a new land. Are there persons or groups in the history of the Church, or in the local community, who have endured hardship in order to be obedient to God? What have been some positive consequences, however large or small, for others?

17

Failure even with good intentions

Are there other persons in the biblical tradition who, while otherwise obedient, have sometimes evidenced human weakness and yet were used by the deity for ultimate good? The episode of David and Bathsheba would be a good example. Are there illustrations in more recent times? We need to realize that all humans are fallible, and yet remain within the realm of usefulness for God's purposes.

Maintaining the faith even in view of failure

Discussion of this possibility can involve such possibilities as drawing faith from others through communal worship; reading the Scriptures and other literature concerning God's redemptive action; and realizing that one may not be able to see, at the moment, the good that may come from one's current faithfulness, witness, and endurance. Obedience to God may produce consequences long after one's own lifetime ("To your descendants I will give this land," God said to Abram). Consider the case of Methodist circuit riders in the wilderness of North America two hundred years ago. They were often hungry, at the point of collapse from fatigue, infirm from exposure to the weather, and were threatened by wild beasts and inhospitable settlers. Could they have imagined the present number of churches, agencies, colleges, and membership that have resulted from their hardship and devotion? What are some illustrations on the local scene or from the observation of class members?

Planning for Next Sunday

The study of the Old Testament personalities continues with Moses' call to obedience and service. We will be moving ahead in the history of the chosen community approximately five hundred years. In order for the class members to gain a historical orientation, they might read Exodus 1:1–4:17.

LESSON 2   SEPTEMBER 13

God's Call to Moses

Background Scripture: Exodus 3:1–4:17

The Main Question

Having chosen a community through which "shall all families of the earth be blessed" (Genesis 12:3 KJV; see Lesson 1), will God now deliver that community from life-threatening distress? The migration of Jacob's family to Egypt in order to escape a terrible famine (Genesis 42:1-2; 43:1-2; 46:1-7), undertaken with high expectation and with the understanding that it was the will of God (45:1-11), has become the occasion for bondage to the pharaoh (Exodus 1:8-14), a situation that persisted for a generation. God's promises to the patriarchs (see, for example, Genesis 12:1-3; 15:1-21;

18

17:1-8) must now have seemed but a delusion. After a long a time of apparent silence, would the deity now act? Did God even continue to act in history in the way that the traditions that had been handed down for generations reported had once been the case? Did human beings still experience a divine call to provide leadership in such uncertain and dangerous times as had previously been the case at the time of Abraham? If so, was there any reasonable chance of success, given the weakness and oppression of the descendants of Jacob and the power and ruthlessness of the Egyptian government?

Yet, the day arrived when Israel escaped (Exodus 12) and survived in the barren wilderness (chaps. 13–18). At a sacred mountain, the people reflected upon the cause and meaning of what had happened and pledged to become a community that would be identified as the Lord's possession and holy nation (19:1-7).

When later generations of believers, Christians and Jews, heard or read this astonishing story, they found not only parallels to their doubts and of their own time, but also courage to hope for a different future and to trust God's call to obey or to provide leadership for others. God will preserve his people. May today's lesson give us encouragement as well.

Selected Scripture

King James Version

Exodus 3:1-7, 10-14

1 Now Moses kept the flock of Jethro his father in law, the priest of Midian: and he led the flock to the backside of the desert, and came to the mountain of God, even to Horeb.

2 And the angel of the LORD appeared unto him in a flame of fire out of the midst of a bush: and he looked, and, behold, the bush burned with fire, and the bush was not consumed.

3 And Moses said, I will now turn aside, and see this great sight, why the bush is not burnt.

4 And when the LORD saw that he turned aside to see, God called unto him out of the midst of the bush, and said, Moses, Moses. And he said, Here am I.

5 And he said, Draw not nigh hither: put off thy shoes from off thy feet, for the place whereon thou standest is holy ground.

6 Moreover he said, I am the God of thy father, the God of Abraham, the God of Isaac, and the God of

New Revised Standard Version

Exodus 3:1-7, 10-14

Moses was keeping the flock of his father-in-law Jethro, the priest of Midian; he led his flock beyond the wilderness, and came to Horeb, the mountain of God. 2 There the angel of the LORD appeared to him in a flame of fire out of a bush; he looked, and the bush was blazing, yet it was not consumed. 3 Then Moses said, "I must turn aside and look at this great sight, and see why the bush is not burned up." 4 When the LORD saw that he had turned aside to see, God called to him out of the bush, "Moses, Moses!" And he said, "Here I am." 5 Then he said, "Come no closer! Remove the sandals from your feet, for the place on which you are standing is holy ground." 6 He said further, "I am the God of your father, the God of Abraham, the God of Isaac, and the God of Jacob." And Moses hid his face, for he was afraid to look at God.

Jacob. And Moses hid his face; for he was afraid to look upon God.

7 And the LORD said, I have surely seen the affliction of my people which are in Egypt, and have heard their cry by reason of their taskmasters; for I know their sorrows. . . .

7 Then the LORD said, "I have observed the misery of my people who are in Egypt; I have heard their cry on account of their taskmasters. Indeed, I know their sufferings. . . .

....

....

10 Come now therefore, and I will send thee unto Pharaoh, that thou mayest bring forth my people the children of Israel out of Egypt.

11 And Moses said unto God, Who am I, that I should go unto Pharaoh, and that I should bring forth the children of Israel out of Egypt?

12 And he said, Certainly I will be with thee; and this shall be a token unto thee, that I have sent thee: When thou hast brought forth the people out of Egypt, ye shall serve God upon this mountain.

13 And Moses said unto God, Behold, when I come unto the children of Israel, and shall say unto them, The God of your fathers hath sent me unto you; and they shall say to me, What is his name? what shall I say unto them?

14 And God said unto Moses, I AM THAT I AM: and he said, Thus shalt thou say unto the children of Israel, I AM hath sent me unto you.

10 So come, I will send you to Pharaoh to bring my people, the Israelites, out of Egypt." 11 But Moses said to God, "Who am I that I should go to Pharaoh, and bring the Israelites out of Egypt" 12 He said, "I will be with you; and this shall be the sign for you that it is I who sent you: when you have brought the people out of Egypt, you shall worship God on this mountain."

13 But Moses said to God, "If I come to the Israelites and say to them, 'The God of your ancestors has sent me to you,' and they ask me, 'What is his name?' what shall I say to them?" 14 God said to Moses, "I AM WHO I AM." He said further, "Thus you shall say to the Israelites, 'I AM has sent me to you.' "

Key Verse: **Come now therefore, and I will send thee unto Pharaoh, that thou mayest bring forth my people the children of Israel out of Egypt. (Exodus 3:10)**

Key Verse: **So come, I will send you to Pharaoh to bring my people, the Israelites, out of Egypt. (Exodus 3:10)**

As You Read the Scripture

Exodus 3:1. Midian is possibly in northwest Arabia, on the eastern shore of the Gulf of Aqabah. Moses had fled there after killing an oppressive Egyptian (2:11-21). The sacred mountain is alternatively called Horeb and Sinai (compare Chicago and the Windy City).

Verse 6. At a time when many gods were believed to exist, it was important that Moses understand that he was being addressed by the deity who had guided and made promises to the patriarchs. This, then, is no chance encounter, but rather the continuation of an ancient relationship. This becomes even clearer when, in the next verse, Israel is referred to as "my people."

Verse 8. "Milk and honey," an oft-repeated phrase (for example, Deuteronomy 6:3), symbolizes the fertility of the land of Canaan, in contrast both to Midian, where Moses now dwells, and to the dependence on the Egyptians of the slaves in Egypt.

Verse 12. The response, "I will be [with you]" is not merely a promise to assist Moses; it is also a linguistic reference (play on words) to the divine name; compare verse 14 in the alternative form found in the NRSV footnote ("I will be what I will be"). That is, the divine name (rendered in the NRSV as "the LORD") has consonants similar to those of the expression, "I will be." Even the name of the deity is here interpreted as indicating a commitment to deliver the chosen community.

The identification of the "sign" that authenticates Moses as God's messenger has long been a subject of debate. Is it that the freed slaves will later worship the deity on this same mountain (as the punctuation in NRSV suggests)? If so, it would hardly help Moses at the time when he most needs confirmation—namely, when he seeks to exhort the people to follow him out of Egypt—since it would still lie in the future. The other possibility is that the sign refers to the encounter at the miraculously "burning bush," an extraordinary event that indicates the power of the One who now commissions Moses. (For yet a third possibility, see the footnote in JB. The sign that authenticated Moses has been lost from the present text.)

Verse 13. The fact that various ancestors of Israel had worshiped multiple deities is evident from such passages as Joshua 24:2, 15. It would not be surprising, then, if Moses were to speak of "the God of your fathers," for him to be asked, "Which one?"

Verse 14. The unclarity of the deity's answer is indicated by the footnote in the NRSV and by a vast scholarly literature. Is this a statement of divine freedom, equivalent to a refusal to answer (compare 33:19)? Does it mean, "I am the Creator" (rendering the verb as "cause to be")? Or is the meaning the same as in verse 12 (equivalent to "I am really here, ready to act as Savior")? In the story as it now stands, in view of Moses' question in verse 13, the last of these possibilities seems most likely. This is supported by verse 15 (see the NRSV footnote).

Verse 15. The modern English rendering "the Lord" follows an ancient and respectful substitution of this title for the divine name, which actually stands in the Hebrew text (sometimes Anglicized as "Yahweh"). The consonants of the divine name are y-h-w-h, allowing a word play on the consonants of the third-person singular verb ("he is" or "he will be," y-h-y-h). When the deity participates in this word play, the subject must be changed to the first person: "I am" or "I will be."

The Scripture and the Main Question

The main question (see the opening paragraph of the present lesson) is not openly asked in the text before us, and yet it clearly forms its background. The descendants of Jacob have now been away from their promised homeland for 430 years (Exodus 12:40), and their brutal treatment by the pharaoh has grown increasingly worse (chap. 1). The deity, in initiating the process of deliverance, cannot assume that the enslaved Israelites will know who the patriarchal deity is, to say nothing of worshiping that deity. Neither will they understand that this is a deity who keeps promises, even if long delayed by the family's decision to forsake the "promised land." This is a deity who, in just seeing their affliction, promises to act on their behalf. Their communal failure to be of one mind, to remember the promises and the divine nature, and their skepticism about a better future are perhaps projected upon Moses by the inspired formulator of the account as it now stands.

Who Am I That I Should Go?

Moses' question reflects the typical reluctance of biblical prophets to accept the divine call (for example, Jeremiah 1:6). At the same time, it is an indication of the enormously difficult task to which he is being summoned (pharaohs being reluctant to lose their work force) and also the fact that he is a fugitive from Egyptian justice. He can scarcely show his face in order to announce God's deliverance without risking his life. The deity, in typical fashion, brushes the objection aside, since success does not depend on the ability of the messenger alone ("I will be with you"). The deity is committed to the survival, renewal, and vitality of the people of the promise (they will "serve God upon this mountain").

"If I . . . Say to Them . . . They [Will] Ask Me . . .

Moses' reluctance and uncertainty continue with a second objection. The people will certainly want more information and assurance before they literally risk their lives in the pursuit of freedom. The deity gives what may be a twofold answer. On the one hand, God is not reducible to a simple definition, but perhaps the immediate future will help to clarify the matter ("I will be what I will be"). On the other hand, a comforting assertion is made through a folk explanation of the divine name: "I will be with you." Furthermore, this is the same deity whom the ancestors have worshiped. What is now about to be done is in continuity with ancient tradition and promises. The traditional faith is a viable one, to which one can make a commitment. This is never again to be forgotten ("Thus I am to be remembered throughout all generations"). Furthermore, God has confidence in the willingness of the people to risk and to act, even if Moses does not ("And they will hearken to our voice"), even in the face of adversity ("I know that the king of Egypt will not let you go unless compelled").

Suppose They Do Not Believe Me

Despite the previous assurances, Moses' reluctance to lead continues. Such apparent realism on his part underscores the difficulty of believing that God will act in history in a decisive fashion. Not without reason did Moses continue to hesitate, because he would be the first to experience the wrath of Pharaoh, and because the courage of the community is not automatically to be presumed. See, for example, the violent reaction of the people to Jeremiah's acceptance of God's call (Jeremiah 26). Nonetheless, God promises to convince the people that Moses speaks the truth and is to be followed. Moses will find support and a following far in excess of his expectations. The real problem will not be so much lack of faith on the part of the Hebrews as it will be the entrenched evil of the governmental structures. Such structures, however, will not have the last word.

I Have Never Been Eloquent

Moses' objections continue to pile up, now totaling four. This one resides, not in exterior realities, but in the messenger's perceived lack of qualification. It is an excuse that implies that the deity has been mistaken as to the ability of the one chosen, as if the creature had better judgment in this regard than does the Creator. The deity's response is now a direct but patient refutation. God, the Creator of all human abilities, certainly should know the capabilities of each and does not require more than has been made possible. Even if humans do not know what they can accomplish, the deity is well aware of it. As if that were not enough, special assistance is to be given Moses at the crucial moments. After all, this is not his plan that is being put into operation, but that of the One who "Is."

Please Send Someone Else

All of Moses' objections have been answered, and yet his faintness of heart (perhaps understandably) continues. It is not a callous refusal, but one that springs from Moses' innermost being. He is aware of the potential for terrible events ahead, however the demand for freedom may turn out. Death and suffering are the sure result, as even the deity has acknowledged ("I will stretch out my hand and smite Egypt . . . "). Once the process has begun, there will be no turning back.

The patience of God is now at an end ("The anger of the LORD was kindled"), but not the determination that something be done about the future of the people of God. If Moses will not be the chief spokesperson, then the deity will simply choose and empower another. The least that Moses can do is to support his brother, Aaron, in the desperate situation at hand, and to that, at least, Moses apparently agrees. Time has run out for Moses. He has no more excuses for delay.

As for Aaron, it is not recorded that he made a single objection. His role is accepted, and the fateful events are set into motion. Had that not happened, there would have been no Israel, and thus no Church or Synagogue in the present, and thus no class today to study this story!

Helping Adults Become Involved

Preparing to Teach

It will be helpful to the class to hear a brief summary of the biblical story from the time of Abraham's call (Genesis 12; Lesson One) to that of Moses. In order to do this, one need not get bogged down in the details of the patriarchal lives that consume the remaining thirty-eight chapters of Genesis. It will be sufficient to mention two major developments: (1) *The promise* "I will make of you a great nation" (Genesis 12:2) is kept despite the barrenness of the patriarchal wives: Isaac was born when his mother was well beyond the age of child bearing (Genesis 16–17; 21:1-3); Jacob and Esau were born after a period of barrenness by their mother, Rebekah

(25:19-26); then Jacob becomes the father of a multitude of sons, ancestors of the twelve tribes of Israel (29:31-35; 30:1-24; 35:16-18); and (2) *the journey* of Jacob's clan to Egypt in order to escape a great famine (42:1-2; 43:1-2; 45:26-28; 46:1-7), where they remain even after the death of Joseph (50:22-26), and are thus there when a new and hostile dynasty comes to power (Exodus 1:8-22).

Some historical background may also be of interest to the class in understanding the story. Egyptian records tell us that nomads from Syro-Palestine (Canaan) regularly came to the Nile Delta in search of grazing areas or in need of food (just as did Jacob's group). A painting of such a group from about 1900 B.C. is reproduced in the following sources and would be useful for the class to see: *The Westminster Historical Atlas to the Bible*, revised edition (p. 23); *Everyday Life in Bible Times* (National Geographic Society, pp. 108-9).

The "new king over Egypt, who did not know Joseph" (Exodus 1:8, possibly meaning that he did not respect the old agreement that Joseph had made) may reflect the rise to power of the nineteenth dynasty around the year 1300 B.C. Thus the usual candidate for the pharaoh who oppressed the Israelites is Rameses II, one of the most energetic and able rulers Egypt ever produced. Brief remarks about this fact may be found in *The Interpreter's Bible*, 12 vols., ed. George A. Buttrick (Nashville: Abingdon Press, 1952–1957), vol. 1, p. 836; hereafter referred to as *IB*. Photos of his statues may be seen in *IOCB*, p. 36. See also the article "Rameses" in *The Interpreter's Dictionary of the Bible*, 5 vols., eds. George A. Buttrick and Keith R. Crim (Nashville: Abingdon Press, 1976), vol. 4, pp. 10-12; hereafter referred to as *IDB*.

Presentation of the lesson material to the class might take place under the following headings.

    I. Bridging the gap between Abraham and Moses: the biblical story between Lessons 1 and 2
    II. The historical background: how material outside the Bible sheds light on the events
    III. The biblical account and its implications for us today

Introducing the Main Question

The main question of whether God will now deliver the community from life-threatening distress must have been in the minds of the oppressed Israelites in Egypt, and it is a question that has arisen many times in the life of Synagogue and Church. Indeed, it is one that history poses regularly for those who would take the Faith seriously: Can the Community of faith survive amid the challenges posed by the modern world? Does God work concretely in the life of a society, or is all that merely the quaint faith of one's naive ancestors? Does God still single out persons for leadership and expect them to take risks in order to help provide the opportunity for justice and freedom?

Developing the Lesson

It might be interesting to see how much of the biblical story from Abraham to Moses that the class members can reconstruct from their own knowledge. See if they can sketch the genealogy involved: Abraham-Isaac-Jacob-Joseph, in terms of the major actors; Abraham-Isaac-Jacob-Levi-(after this it gets a bit difficult; see Exodus 6:16-20)-Kohath-Amram-Aaron and Moses. You can fill in the blanks of the story as outlined under "Preparing to Teach."

See, as well, if the class can fill in any historical background: What century are we talking about in the case of Moses? (The thirteenth?) Who might the pharaoh be? (Rameses II?) Did the pharaohs actually use foreign slaves in their massive building projects? (Yes.) Where might the sacred mountain (Horeb/Sinai) have been located? (Several locations have been suggested. Read the article "Sinai, Mount," in *IDB*, vol. 4, pp. 376-78; or "The Location of Sinai," in *IB*, vol. 1, pp. 836-37, with the map on p. 832 for the traditional location.)

Discussion of the text can proceed under the divisions as outlined above under "The Scripture and the Main Question."

Helping Class Members Act

The following questions may help to guide the class members as they think about the implications of the text for their own lives.

1. Does it sometimes appear that there is a gap between the way the deity is supposed to act (based on the stories that have come down to us in the Bible) and the way life actually is? That is, may we rightfully share the uncertainties of Moses and the community in Egypt as to whether and how the deity is involved in the world? What are some things that lead us to doubt? Is God's activity limited to producing a change in human nature (conversion), or does it extend to more direct transformation of the social order? Can you cite instances where the latter might have happened in our own society or community? Would you agree, for example, with the religious interpretation of history that is found (and that you likely have sung) in "The Battle Hymn of the Republic" (wherein victories of the Union Army during the Civil War are understood as God's justice at work)?

Mine eyes have seen the glory of the coming of the Lord;
He is trampling out the vintage where the grapes of wrath are stored;
He hath loosed the fateful lightning of his terrible swift sword; . . .
In the beauty of the lilies Christ was born across the sea . . .
as he died to make men holy, let us die to make men free, while God is marching on.

2. What are the implications of the fact that God's name is understood to indicate, not a static, eternal presence, but a being who is known from specific, disruptive historical moments? It is as if one did not think so much of what God *is* as what God *does*. Does this imply that Christian life should be characterized more by orthopraxy ("right action") than by orthodoxy (right belief? What are the dangers of one without the other?

3. God's self-disclosure was, in the case of Moses, not mere information about the present and future, but a call to service. Nonetheless, were Moses' doubts ones with which we can identify? Have there been situations in your own life when, on a level great or small, you might have provided leadership but declined to do so and made excuses similar to those of Moses ("Let someone else do it!" "What will I say?" "Nobody will listen!")? Have we

observed situations in which leaders, initially reluctant and timid, had a telling effect on their family, neighbors, or community? Do we know of cases where God persisted with the call of a reluctant spokesperson, as was the case with Moses? What positive characteristics of humans can contribute to a greater potential for a positive effect than a person may realize?

Planning for Next Sunday

Our study of Old Testament personalities continues with the account of God's choice of Joshua to succeed Moses. Although we will be moving ahead only a single generation, we will skip some of the great events in Israel's history: the period of wandering in the wilderness, the giving of guidelines for ethics and worship at Mt. Sinai, and arrival at the borders of the "promised land," where Moses gives his long farewell speech. We will be leaping from the beginning of the book of Exodus, across Leviticus, Numbers, and Deuteronomy, to land in the first chapter of Joshua. It might be well for the class to consider the highlights of the deleted material, perhaps by skimming the topical headings in their NRSV Bibles.

LESSON 3   SEPTEMBER 20

God's Choice of Joshua to Succeed Moses

Background Scripture: Joshua 1

The Main Question

At a time of transition in the communal life of the People of God, *what are the bases of hope for a positive future?* Are there promises in Scripture that have potential for realization, generation after generation? What shape should the life of faith now take? How important is it that humans respond in a given way, in addition to trusting that God will act? What sort of leader is important under the changed circumstances? New occasions demand new duties and new leaders to guide us in our new duties.

These are questions that concerned readers of the book of Joshua at the time for which it was written: exiles from Judah in the alien land of Babylonia in the sixth century B.C. Although there are radical differences between their situation and our own, there are enough similarities to provide insight for transitional moments in the present.

Selected Scripture

King James Version	New Revised Standard Version
Joshua 1:1-11	*Joshua 1:1-11*
1 Now after the death of Moses the servant of the LORD it came to	After the death of Moses the servant of the LORD, the LORD spoke

26

pass, that the LORD spake unto Joshua the son of Nun, Moses' minister, saying,

2 Moses my servant is dead; now therefore arise, go over this Jordan, thou, and all this people, unto the land which I do give to them, even to the children of Israel.

3 Every place that the sole of your foot shall tread upon, that have I given unto you, as I said unto Moses.

4 From the wilderness and this Lebanon even unto the great river, the river Euphrates, all the land of the Hittites, and unto the great sea toward the going down of the sun, shall be your coast.

5 There shall not any man be able to stand before thee all the days of thy life: as I was with Moses, so I will be with thee: I will not fail thee, nor forsake thee.

6 Be strong and of a good courage: for unto this people shalt thou divide for an inheritance the land, which I sware unto their fathers to give them.

7 Only be thou strong and very courageous, that thou mayest observe to do according to all the law, which Moses my servant commanded thee: turn not from it to the right hand or to the left, that thou mayest prosper whithersoever thou goest.

8 This book of the law shall not depart out of thy mouth; but thou shalt meditate therein day and night, that thou mayest observe to do according to all that is written therein: for then thou shalt make thy way prosperous, and then thou shalt have good success.

9 Have not I commanded thee? Be strong and of a good courage; be not afraid, neither be thou dismayed: for the LORD thy God is with thee whithersoever thou goest.

10 Then Joshua commanded the officers of the people, saying,

11 Pass through the host, and command the people, saying, Prepare you victuals; for within three

to Joshua son of Nun, Moses' assistant, saying, 2 "My servant Moses is dead. Now proceed to cross the Jordan, you and all this people, into the land that I am giving to them, to the Israelites. 3 Every place that the sole of your foot will tread upon I have given to you, as I promised to Moses. 4 From the wilderness and the Lebanon as far as the great river, the river Euphrates, all the land of the Hittites, to the Great Sea in the west shall be your territory. 5 No one shall be able to stand against you all the days of your life. As I was with Moses, so I will be with you; I will not fail you or forsake you. 6 Be strong and courageous; for you shall put this people in possession of the land that I swore to their ancestors to give them. 7 Only be strong and very courageous, being careful to act in accordance with all the law that my servant Moses commanded you; do not turn from it to the right hand or to the left, so that you may be successful wherever you go. 8 This book of the law shall not depart out of your mouth; you shall meditate on it day and night, so that you may be careful to act in accordance with all that is written in it. For then you shall make your way prosperous, and then you shall be successful. 9 I hereby command you: Be strong and courageous; do not be frightened or dismayed, for the LORD your God is with you wherever you go."

10 Then Joshua commanded the officers of the people, 11 "Pass through the camp, and command the people: 'Prepare your provisions; for in three days you are to

27

days ye shall pass over this Jordan, to go in to possess the land, which the Lord your God giveth you to possess it.

cross over the Jordan, to go in to take possession of the land that the Lord your God gives you to possess.' "

Key Verse: **Have not I commanded thee? Be strong and of a good courage; be not afraid, neither be thou dismayed: for the Lord thy God is with thee whithersoever thou goest. (Joshua 1:9)**

Key Verse: **Be strong and courageous; do not be frightened or dismayed, for the Lord your God is with you wherever you go. (Joshua 1:9)**

As You Read the Scripture

Joshua 1:1. The death of Moses is recorded in the previous chapter (Deuteronomy 34), and thus the story is set in the thirteenth century B.C., a generation after the clan of Jacob ("Israel") had escaped from Egypt.

Verse 2. The people are still in Transjordan, looking over into the "promised land." Although Moses has given them his final blessing (Deuteronomy 33), further directions and encouragement are necessary before they undertake their hazardous journey across the Jordan River.

Verse 3. The journey is not undertaken in a vacuum, but as the continuation and realization of previous divine promises, as is then made clear in verse 5 (echoing the promise to Moses at Exodus 3:12): "I will be with you; I will not fail you or forsake you."

Verse 6. The oath to "their ancestors" refers back to the oath sworn to the patriarchs (Abraham, Isaac, and Jacob), as for example in Genesis 12:1-3, 7 and 13:14-17.

Verse 7. The "law that my servant Moses commanded" refers in a general way to the contents of Exodus–Deuteronomy, but more specifically to Moses' final warnings and advice in Deuteronomy, as is made clear by verse 8.

Verse 8. "This book of the law" is the language by which Deuteronomy refers to itself (see, for example, 17:18; 28:58, 61; 29:20-21, 27; 30:10). Thus if one wants to understand Joshua's story, suggests the author, one must place it within the religious ideas of the book of Deuteronomy.

Verse 9. The phrase "wherever you go" is intended to give comfort to the readers during the time of national exile. God's promise applies to any location, and not merely to the generation standing in the Plains of Moab at the time of Joshua.

Verses 12-15. The previous arrangement that these tribes be allowed to settle in Transjordan is related in Numbers 32.

In general, notice the tone of this chapter, which serves as an introduction to the account of Israel's settlement in the land of Canaan. Rather than focusing on geography, military statistics, or battle plans, as might a document that is concerned to relate "just the facts," it consists of a series of speeches that are heavily theological in nature (by the deity in verses 1-9, by Joshua in verses 10-15, and by the people in verses 16-18). The crucial issue is, therefore, the action of God (past and the impending future) and what an appropriate response by the people ought to be.

The Scripture and the Main Question

One may distinguish the time at which a document is written from the time of the period it describes. For example, a book about the American Revolution (in the late eighteenth century) may be written in the 1990s with the interests of late twentieth-century readers in mind. Just so, the book of Joshua concerns characters and events in the thirteenth century B.C., but its author lives in and writes for an audience in the sixth century. In fact, Joshua through 2 Kings was written with that audience in mind: exiles from Judea, carried to Babylon as the result of the conquest of the former by King Nebuchadnezzar of Babylon in the year 587 B.C. (2 Kings 25; Jeremiah 52).

The problem faced by the exiles was not merely social disruption, economic ruin, and political termination, but also a religious crisis of unparalleled proportions. The "promised land" had been lost to the enemy, and the ruling members of the Davidic Dynasty (believed to have been chosen by God for perpetual leadership) had been reduced to prisoners of war. Indeed, it looked as if the entire promise to the patriarchs (for example, in Genesis 12:1-3) was but a delusion. Under such circumstances of change and disruption, how is faith to be kept alive, and what hope is there for a different future? This is the main question behind today's lesson.

With land, Temple, and royal family lost as a source of the people's identity, attention now focused with renewed intensity on the sacred story (the scriptures then in the process of formation). The newest, and as yet unofficial, document was the so-called Former Prophets or History Books, Joshua–2 Kings (which modern interpreters have come to call the Deuteronomic History because of its use of terminology and religious ideas from the book of Deuteronomy). It seeks to summarize the faithlessness that led the people to their present desperate condition and, at the same time, to cite the divine promises and model leadership roles that could serve as the basis for a renewed community. Thus Israel, standing on the borders of the land of Canaan (in the thirteenth century), becomes an analogy of the Judean exiles in the sixth: both in need of comfort, courage, and strong leadership at a time of danger and discouragement.

Into the Land That I Am Giving

Following the lead of Deuteronomy 9:4-7, the deity stresses the fact that residence in the land of Canaan is not a right or a reward to which the people are entitled. Their future resides entirely within the discretion, the mercy, and the graciousness of the deity. Even the previous promise to the patriarchs (to which the deity will now be faithful) rests upon the same basis. The exilic audience would have been especially appreciative of the present-tense description: "that I am [now] giving," suggesting that it is a present-day possibility rather than something that happened long ago. Thus God's promise is constantly at work for the well-being of the people wherever they are, even in exile: "God is with you wherever you go" (v. 9).

Being Careful to Act in Accordance

While the future depends on God's graciousness and gift, there is nonetheless a human component. Repeatedly, Joshua is told, "Be strong

29

and courageous" (vv. 6, 9, 18). This is not a proposal to manifest natural will and strength, however, but is a call to faithfulness to the sacred traditions of the community (the lack of which, it may be implied, led the people to their present exilic situation).

It must be clearly understood that obedience to "all the law that my servant Moses commanded" (v. 7) is not a legalism by which reward or punishment is affected. The term *law* is an inaccurate and misleading translation of the Hebrew word *torah*, which denotes "revelation," "instruction," and "sacred story." Otherwise put, it is not a collection of legalisms but is rather the sacred story (scripture) that reveals God's gracious actions and that instructs the community as to the appropriate response. It answers the question: For those who have experienced God's unmerited goodness, what form should the life of faith take? The answer does not leave one uncertain or with such subjective modern directions as "love God and do as you please." Rather, it issues detailed, but workable, guidelines for the particularities of life: "There shall be . . . "; "You shall not . . . "; "If there is among you . . . then . . ."; and so on.

Such attention to detail may itself be regarded as a manifestation of divine graciousness, because it does not leave members of the community in a quandary amid the ambiguities of life. Furthermore, it is not to be considered a burden (contrary to Christian misunderstanding), because the sensitive and grateful recipient of God's goodness will acknowledge the deity's right to command. Such commands, and obedience to them, help to ensure the life-giving quality (in the realms of economics, sociology, psychology, and government) that is to be the very definition of what it means to be "Israel."

Note that there are no warnings of negative consequences of disobedience here (in contrast to other places in Scripture—for example, Deuteronomy 8:11-20). It is as if the exiles, hearing the opening scenes of the Deuteronomic History, needed to realize that residence in the land does not ultimately depend on their own efforts; God's graciousness transcends human frailties. (This is a point of view that is crucial to the New Testament: "But God proves his love for us in that while we still were sinners Christ died for us" [Rom. 5:8].)

The Lord Spoke to Joshua

God's agenda, as outlined under the headings above, is not addressed to the assembled congregation, but to Moses' successor (v. 1). It is now Joshua's responsibility to relay such information to the people and to direct their subsequent actions (vv. 10-11). It is he whom the deity will empower ("I will be with you; I will not fail you or forsake you"; v. 5). He will be instrumental in the success of the people's attaining their proper destiny ("For you shall put this people in possession of the land" (v. 6). And he receives the promise for the congregation to act in a way that is appropriate for those of their status: "All that you have commanded us we will do, and wherever you send us we will go" (v. 16).

It is clear, then, as the people face the uncertainties of the future, that God will continue to work through human leaders and will provide for a succession of them. Nonetheless, while such leadership is another of God's gifts, this does not remove the element of vulnerability and faintness of heart ("Be strong and courageous") nor does it remove the obligation to adhere strictly to the divine agenda (". . . being careful to act in accordance . . . ").

Helping Adults Become Involved

Preparing to Teach

Although the theological reflections of the lesson may be understood in the context of Joshua's preparation to lead the people across the Jordan River (late thirteenth century B.C.), it is helpful to set it in the context for which it was proposed: the exilic situation of the Judeans in the sixth century B.C.. First, acquaint yourself with the former situation by reading articles about Joshua and the conquest of Canaan in *IDBS*, vol. 2, pp. 751-54 (sections 2 and 3) and 995-96. If this seems a bit compact and technical, try *IOCB*, pp. 122-24 and 1020-21. Material on the Deuteronomic History may be found in *IDBS*, pp. 226-28. Information about the exile may be found in *IDB*, vol. 2, pp. 186-88, or less compactly in *IOCB*, pp. 1025-26, and in *IB*, vol. 1, pp. 285-88.

A map may be useful in enabling the class to see how far removed the exiles were from their homeland. Most Bibles usually have such maps at the back.

To gain an appreciation of *torah* as defined above (rather than as "law"), see the article "Torah" in *IDBS*, pp. 909-11.

Presentation to the class might take place under the following headings.

    I. What we know about Joshua's setting.
    II. What we know about the historian's (author's) setting.
    III. A brief summary of the goal of the Deuteronomic History.
    IV. The text of the lesson.

Introducing the Main Question

As a religious group (Synagogue, Church, denomination, local congregation) moves into a new situation or period of its history, there is the possibility that it will lose contact with its roots and thus that traditional values will perish. The values and practices of a new age may so contaminate the group that it will lose its identity. At such a moment, the choice of the right leadership is crucial: a person of courage and of commitment to the ideals upon which the community was founded. Such a situation faced the Israelites after the death of Moses as they stood on the borders of the "promised land," then in the hands of the Canaanites.

Religious groups face a related crisis when they have long been under oppressive governments, have become discouraged about affecting their society, or are slowly losing membership and facing extinction. It may be helpful to realize that such crises are not unique and to learn how our spiritual ancestors during biblical times handled them. Such a situation was faced by the Judeans, exiled to a far distant land in the sixth century B.C. They survived, in part, by studying their own past and being reminded of God's graciousness and expectations. Might our church survive in the same way?

31

FIRST QUARTER

Developing the Lesson

I. What we know about Joshua's setting.

Present a brief review of Israel's history from the exodus out of Egypt to the borders of the "promised land," with the aids of the resources presented above. A map showing the long and perilous route will be helpful (Oxford Annotated NRSV, Map 2; Oxford Study Edition of REB, Map 2). Help the class to realize that crossing the Jordan and settling in the land was a precarious undertaking (a) militarily—there were well-organized and defended city-states that would not welcome intruders who were inclined to think of the land as their own; and (b) religiously—the worship of the Canaanites, tied as it was to the fertility of nature, would have a strong appeal to the former Egyptian slaves (Israelites), who might not know how to succeed in an agricultural environment and thus assume that adoption of Canaanite religion was a necessary ingredient. For drawings (based on excavations) of what a city from a slightly later period might have looked like, see the article "Megiddo" in *IDB*, vol. 3, pp. 335-42.

II. What we know about the historian's setting.

A preliminary stage of exile took place in 598 B.C. (2 Kings 24). The city was spared physical destruction, but the Temple was plundered and ten thousand captives taken from its environment, including the royal family. The more extensive stage of exile took place in 587, when cities throughout Judea were besieged and destroyed, including the Temple in Jerusalem. The reigning king was slain, and vast numbers of captives were taken (see 2 Kings 25; Jeremiah 52).

Use a map (Map 6 in NRSV and REB) to show the class the extent of the exiles' march. Use the material presented under "The Scripture and the Main Question" to describe the condition and mentality of the exiles: in small villages, bereft of Temple, leadership, and festivals that had customarily nurtured their faith and identity; wondering why God had failed to keep the promise of land, many offspring, and blessing to others (Genesis 13:14-17); wondering if God has forgotten them and thus they would never return home; beginning to suspect that perhaps God, as they had perceived the deity, did not exist and thus accepting both the culture and religion of their captors. (Isaiah chapters 40–55 is much concerned with these problems and how to overcome them.)

III. A brief summary of the goal of the Deuteronomic History.

The scope of this history (Joshua–2 Kings) is Israel's existence in the "promised land," from the entry of the Israelites at the time of Joshua to the loss of the land at the time of exile (560 B.C.).

The whole may be understood under two headings: (1) Why has the present lamentable situation come about, in view of the promises to the patriarchs? In fact, that question is directly raised by Deuteronomy 29:24 and 1 Kings 9:8, with the answer supplied immediately thereafter: "It is because they abandoned the covenant of the LORD . . . and served other gods" (Deuteronomy 29:24-26). The situation is of Israel's own making, then, and should not raise the question of God's justice or providence. The issue is simply one of disloyalty, something warned against in the first of the Ten Commandments. (See also Joshua 23:15-16; 2 Kings 17:7-40.) (2) Wherein does hope reside for the future? The answer focuses on the record of God's graciousness, initiatives, and unconditional promises (2 Samuel 7:4-17). Forgiveness is always available to those of contrite heart (1 Kings 8), and rehabilitation often takes the form of a refining judgment (Judges 2-4), comparable to the exile in which the original readers now found themselves. Thus the work opens with exhortations to be faithful and have courage (Joshua 1) and closes with the observation that the Davidic Ruler yet lives, even if in exile (2 Kings 25:27-30).

IV. The text of the lesson.

You might proceed under the divisions of the biblical text that were outlined above ("The Scripture and the Main Question").

Helping Class Members Act

Discussion might include the following issues as the class members think about the implications of the lesson for times of change and disruption in their own lives.

1. The comparison of the Israelites at the time of Joshua with people of our own time does not lie in our entry into a new geographical setting, but rather in the rapid pace of change in our time. Are there new elements in our age, comparable perhaps to the lure of Canaanite religion, that have the potential to lead the churches away from their traditional values? What can be done about the situation?

2. Israel's leadership was encouraged to be "careful to do according to all the *torah*" (v. 7). How important do you think the Bible is, or should be, in the life of the contemporary church (and of your denomination)? What evidence is there that it is (or is not) being taken seriously? What substitute sources of identity are being proposed for it?

3. The major point of the Deuteronomic History is that Israel has neglected the first of the Ten Commandments ("You shall have no other gods before me"). If one's ultimate concern may be defined as "God" (financial security, political power, sexual satisfaction, reputation, or whatever), how well do you think that your own society is doing in this regard?

4. Given the political realities ("hard-ball politics") and the economic realities ("dog eat dog") of our society, do you think there are any potential leaders who would take the Christian faith seriously in those realms at a disadvantage? Is there evidence that the electorate holds such values in low regard?

Planning for Next Sunday

The lesson concerns Deborah the Prophetess, in the period of the Judges (Judges 4–5), and thus roughly the same historical background as today's story of Joshua. In order to set the Prophetess in her context, suggest that the class read Judges 1:1–5:31.

God's Provision of Leadership Through Deborah

Background Scripture: Judges 4–5

The Main Question

The community that God had chosen to be a blessing to all the families of the earth (Genesis 12:3; see Lesson 1) and a "kingdom of priests and a holy nation" (Exodus 19:6) retained the freedom to depart from that calling. This led to alternating periods of apostasy and of fidelity after the death of Joshua, as recorded by the Deuteronomic Historian in Joshua–2 Kings (see Lesson 3). Either response to God's enduring initiative was, the historian suggests, within the divine sovereignty. During periods of infidelity, in the absence of a centralized government to provide security (Lesson 5), enemies round-about were allowed to oppress Israel. When the Israelites were again ready to assume their obedient identity, the deity provided a charismatic military savior-hero ("judge") who helped them regain their independence.

Among the military savior-heroes was one whom many modern readers might find surprising, especially if they have assumed that the Bible (and the Old Testament in particular) is a male-oriented document in which women play passive and subordinate roles. (Indeed, the Bible is sometimes condemned by some readers for this alleged tendency.) However, in no way is Deborah's leadership depicted as unusual or unexpected. She is not treated in passing, nor are the events with which she is connected of minor importance. Her leadership was so central at a crucial moment in the history of Israel that she has been lauded in Israel's worship ever since.

We live in an age when increasing numbers of women are being given the opportunity to lead in the church. Today's study of Deborah reminds us that inspired women have always led God's people.

Selected Scripture

King James Version	New Revised Standard Version
Judges 4:4-10, 14-16	*Judges 4:4-10, 14-16*
4 And Deborah, a prophetess, the wife of Lapidoth, she judged Israel at that time.	4 At that time Deborah, a prophetess, wife of Lappidoth, was judging Israel. 5 She used to sit under
5 And she dwelt under the palm tree of Deborah between Ramah and Bethel in mount Ephraim: and the children of Israel came up to her for judgment.	the palm of Deborah between Ramah and Bethel in the hill country of Ephraim; and the Israelites came up to her for judgment. 6 She
6 And she sent and called Barak the son of Abinoam out of Kedesh-naphtali, and said unto him, Hath not the Lord God of Israel com-	sent and summoned Barak son of Abinoam from Kedesh in Naphtali, and said to him, "The Lord, the God of Israel, commands you, 'Go, take position at Mount Tabor, bringing

manded, saying, Go and draw toward mount Tabor, and take with thee ten thousand men of the children of Naphtali and of the children of Zebulun?

7 And I will draw unto thee to the river Kishon Sisera, the captain of Jabin's army, with his chariots and his multitude; and I will deliver him into thine hand.

8 And Barak said unto her, If thou wilt go with me, then I will go: but if thou wilt not go with me, then I will not go.

9 And she said, I will surely go with thee: notwithstanding the journey that thou takest shall not be for thine honour; for the LORD shall sell Sisera into the hand of a woman. And Deborah arose, and went with Barak to Kedesh.

10 And Barak called Zebulun and Naphtali to Kedesh; and he went up with ten thousand men at his feet: and Deborah went up with him.

....

14 And Deborah said unto Barak, Up; for this is the day in which the LORD hath delivered Sisera into thine hand: is not the LORD gone out before thee? So Barak went down from mount Tabor, and ten thousand men after him.

15 And the LORD discomfited Sisera, and all his chariots, and all his host, with the edge of the sword before Barak; so that Sisera lighted down off his chariot, and fled away on his feet.

16 But Barak pursued after the chariots, and after the host, unto Harosheth of the Gentiles: and all the host of Sisera fell upon the edge of the sword; and there was not a man left.

Key Verse: **[Deborah] sent and called Barak . . . and said unto him, Hath not the LORD God of**

ten thousand from the tribe of Naphtali and the tribe of Zebulun. 7 I will draw out Sisera, the general of Jabin's army, to meet you by the Wadi Kishon with his chariots and his troops; and I will give him into your hand.' " 8 Barak said to her, "If you will go with me, I will go; but if you will not go with me, I will not go." 9 And she said, "I will surely go with you; nevertheless, the road on which you are going will not lead to your glory, for the LORD will sell Sisera into the hand of a woman." Then Deborah got up and went with Barak to Kedesh. 10 Barak summoned Zebulun and Naphtali to Kedesh; and ten thousand warriors went up behind him; and Deborah went up with him.

....

14 Then Deborah said to Barak, "Up! For this is the day on which the LORD has given Sisera into your hand. The LORD is indeed going out before you." So Barak went down from Mount Tabor with ten thousand warriors following him. 15 And the LORD threw Sisera and all his chariots and all his army into a panic before Barak; Sisera got down from his chariot and fled away on foot, 16 while Barak pursued the chariots and the army to Harosheth-ha-goiim. All the army of Sisera fell by the sword; no one was left.

Key Verse: **[Deborah] sent and summoned Barak . . . and said to him, "The LORD, the God of Israel,**

Israel commanded, saying, Go and draw toward mount Tabor. (Judges 4:6)

commands you, 'Go, take position at Mount Tabor.' " (Judges 4:6)

As You Read the Scripture

Judges 4:1. The historian introduces yet another cycle in Israel's history of relationship with God, each with four stages: apostasy, punishment, repentance, and deliverance (for example, 3:7-11 and 3:12-30). The present cycle is described first in prose (chap. 4) and then in poetry (chap. 5).

Verse 5. Trees were sometimes used in deriving oracular decisions in the ancient Near East, and it may be that the place where Deborah was consulted was beneath just such a sacred tree. (For mention of a "diviner's oak," see Judges 9:37.)

Verse 6. Mount Tabor was an ancient sanctuary and thus an appropriate place for rally and consultation prior to battle.

Verse 7. The site of battle—the plain of a river that would be muddy during the rainy season—was carefully chosen in view of the enemy's use of chariots. This is made explicit at 5:21. The river Kishon was still treacherous in 1903 when horses pulling supply wagons for nearby archaeological excavations drowned in it.

Verse 11. The importance of this event does not appear until verse 17. The Kenites were normally allies of Israel, but this separated group was apparently friendly with the Canaanites, and thus the fleeing general would feel safe in their presence.

5:1-2. The poem is one of the most ancient compositions in the Bible and one of the most difficult to translate (English versions differ widely). Whether or not Deborah and Barak composed it "on that day," it was meant for recitation in the cult thereafter. Note that someone (a priest?) exhorts others (congregation?) to "bless the Lord" (vv. 2, 9), there is mention of melody (v. 3), and the deity is addressed (v. 31). Evidence of careful crafting emerges in the balanced number of syllables (in Hebrew) for sections of the song (for example, 108 concerning Jael in vv. 24-27 and 106 concerning Sisera's mother in vv. 28-30).

Verses 4-5. A historical flashback in which the deity's previous military power is recalled: when the people marched out of Sinai on their way to conquer the land from the Canaanites.

Verses 6-9. Events just before the time of Deborah. This includes the plundering of caravans, worship of "new" (Canaanite) gods, and intertribal warfare by poorly armed troops.

Verses 10-11. Caravaneers, the wealthy, and other travelers are invited to inspire troops to Deborah's cause by reciting old songs of victory.

Verses 12-13. The previous call to arms is successful, and the army sets out.

Verses 14-18. A list of those who responded, or failed to respond, to Deborah's call. Zebulun and Naphtali formed the core of the army (4:6).

Verses 19-27. An account of the battle and its aftermath, including a detail that the prose account (chap. 4) does not mention—the flooding river creates a mire that the chariots cannot negotiate. At its midpoint is a bitter reminder that Meroz (a town?) did not come to the aid of the heroes of Israel. The "stars" (v. 20) possibly refer to the heavens, which supplied rain and produced the fatal torrent.

Verses 28-30. There may be an intended contrast between the mother of Sisera, destined to weep, and the celebration for Deborah, "a mother in Israel" (v. 7).

Verse 31. "Forty years" is a "round number," symbolizing something like "a long time" or "a generation." Note its use for other "Judges" in 3:11, 8:28; 13:1, and the use of 80 (40 x 2) in 3:30.

The Scripture and the Main Question

The emerging Israelite community at the time of Joshua (Lesson 3) faced a problem of near insurmountable odds. The land in which they desired to settle (Canaan) was already occupied by an ancient and formidable society. Its cities were strongly fortified, and its soldiers were well armed. This was especially true of the most desirable area for settlement, the coastal plain where the Canaanites and Philistines could use their chariots with great effectiveness.

Joshua's group, therefore, was forced to concentrate in the hill country, where life would be far more difficult for both agriculture and shepherding; the forests had not been cleared, and the soil was comparatively poor. Even so, Canaanite cities were there also, and the territory would be hotly contested. As if this were not trouble enough, the mountains were not all of one piece; they were broken in half by a wide valley (Jezreel/Esdraelon) that stretched from the Mediterranean Sea on the west to the Jordan Valley on the east. Consequently, Israelite settlements would be in two separate areas (north and south of the valley), with an area of solid Canaanite control in between. The unhappy result was that the Canaanites could prevent a united Israel and were easily able to dominate the latter. Consequently, "the Israelites lived among the Canaanites . . . and they took their daughters as wives for themselves . . . and they worshiped their gods" (Judges 3:5-6).

While God raised up charismatic military leaders who achieved some success in providing the scattered Israelites with security (Othniel, 3:7-11; Ehud, 3:12-30; Shamgar, 3:31), still the overall picture remained unchanged. The balance of power was not tipped, and the disunity of the tribes of Israel remained. A decisive action might be taken by defeating the Canaanites in the valley, but it was so precarious a venture that no one had dared to undertake it. Those who might have been expected to attempt such a campaign, or might have supposed that God would inspire to arrange it, were not confident (foolish?) enough to undertake it. It was a time that demanded an extraordinary leader, one with amazing courage and belief in the vision of what Israel was supposed to be and could be. At the proper moment, God inspired that leader to act. Her name was Deborah, and her exploits were such that they gave rise to both a prose and a poetic (liturgical) account that were recited throughout succeeding generations. More than that, they inspired a writer who lived a thousand years later to pen a story modeled after the other heroine in Deborah's story: Jael, the wife of Heber the Kenite. That inspiring account played its own role in enabling the community to keep its faith amid persecution, and it consequently found its way into the Bible of the Roman Catholic Church (namely, the book of Judith).

Again Did What Was Evil

It has been the tendency of societies, ancient and modern, to fluctuate in their devotion to the ideals upon which they were founded. The conviction of Scripture is that the deity is so committed to the community as an instrument for the achievement of those goals that, in moments of failure, steps must be taken to chasten, restore, and revitalize it. Human nature being what it is, however, such restorations are temporary and thus the deity must repeatedly act on behalf of creation.

Deborah, a Prophetess . . . Was Judging Israel

Among the topics that Deborah was consulted about, apparently, was when, where, and how God might act to deliver the people from their oppressors. (Exactly how she served as this channel of communication is unclear.) Thus when she came to an understanding of the will of God—that the moment of salvation was at hand—she immediately informed Barak and exhorted him to action.

If You Will Go with Me, I Will Go

Deborah's awareness of military tactics may be suggested by the fact that she made her appeal during the rainy season (November–March), when the soggy soil of the valley would impede the mobility of the chariot wheels. Indeed, the fact that she is said to have "judged" Israel (not necessarily to be identified with her function as a prophetess) may indicate that she had a role in previous conflicts. (The earliest meaning of the term *judge* seems to be that of a charismatic savior-hero rather than a purely judicial figure; compare the activities of "Judge" Samson in Judges 13–16.)

In any case, confidence in Deborah is shown by what Barak now says: If she leads, he will muster the troops. Otherwise, he will not risk it. This is a surprising turn in the story and one that will give God's chosen instrument the opportunity to fulfill her role as savior. Her response is seemingly instantaneous and bold: "I will surely go with you." Whether her statement that "the LORD will sell Sisera into the hand of a woman" reflects confidence in her own role, or whether it anticipates the activity of Jael (vv. 17-22), is unclear.

Now Heber . . . Had Separated from the Other Kenites

This seemingly meaningless detail will later make it possible for Jael to strike the decisive blow. Thus the reader is driven to ask: Was it merely an accident that Heber thus departed from his kin and settled precisely where he did? Or was there, even in that, a divine providence at work that no human could foresee at the time? No certain answer can be made apart from the eyes of faith as guided by the account in Scripture.

The Lord Has Given Sisera into Your Hand

Ultimately, neither Deborah nor Barak will save Israel. It is the Lord who will be the Savior, as Deborah states from the very beginning and as the narrator states in conclusion (4:23).

SEPTEMBER 27 LESSON 4

Lord, When You Went Out from Seir . . .

Expectation in the present crisis, and then the celebration of success, is not treated in liturgical and historical isolation. It is recalled and celebrated that, from the beginnings of Israel (as the people journeyed in the wilderness of Sinai toward the "promised land"), God had been the Savior. This is expressed in poetic language concerning the granting of covenant at Mt. Sinai: "the earth trembled. . . . The mountains quaked." That amazing event now forms the backdrop of what God has arranged through Deborah and Jael. At appropriate moments, as the story is told, praise for the deity wells up: "Bless the LORD" (Judges 5:2, 9).

Most Blessed of Women Be Jael

Jael's conclusive role in the event is apparently accidental. She enters the scene only because Sisera, in his panicked flight, just "happens" to enter her tent. She knows, however, of the battle and recognizes the general at sight. Thus when the reader (and the general!) least expect it, a decisive blow is struck. Jael knows what is at stake in the success of her decision to act, and she knows that she will pay with her life if she fails. Yet, she does not hesitate to act for the welfare of Israel. Most blessed of women, indeed! Her situation is not unlike that of others in the tradition who "just happened" to be at the right place at the right time. Compare, for example, the maiden Esther, from a pious Jewish family, who accepts the unusual role of entry into the harem of the king of Persia and likewise ends up as the savior of her people. She was advised by her kinsman Mordecai, "Who knows? Perhaps you have come to royal dignity for just such a time as this" (Est. 4:14). Thus tyrants can never feel entirely secure even in the presence of the seemingly powerless, and the oppressed should never lose hope that a savior resides in the least likely place and moment.

Helping Adults Become Involved

Preparing to Teach

Helpful background information may be found in the following articles in *IDB*, "Deborah" (vol. 1, pp. 808-9); "Barak" (vol. 1, pp. 353-54); and "Sisera" (vol. 4, pp. 380-81). The text itself is discussed in *IOCB* (pp. 139-42), which has a small map of the area of the battle.

You may want to remind yourself (and the class) that this story is part of the Deuteronomic History (see Lesson 3), and thus you should think about its impact on the intended audience: the Judean exiles in Babylonia in the sixth century B.C.

The skill of the lyricist (poet) in chapter 5, should you decide to mention it briefly, is discussed in detail in *Judges*, Anchor Bible Series, vol. 6-A (pp. 105-16).

Presentation to the class might take place under the following headings.

I. Deborah's situation
II. The exilic audience
III. The author (of chapter 5) as poet
IV. The text of the lesson

39

FIRST QUARTER

Introducing the Main Question

Biblical episodes contain many surprising turns of event, from the point of view of both the participants and the modern reader. These surprises are, for example, the unexpected conclusion of an episode; the mysterious providence of the deity, which allows a seemingly insignificant event ultimately to become decisive; and the fact that the least likely of leaders sometimes becomes the hero. This last type of surprise is especially evident in the period of the judges in the choice of pre-monarchical leadership. Thus Saul could object, "I am only a Benjaminite, from the least of the tribes of Israel, and my family is the humblest of all the families of the tribe of Benjamin" (1 Samuel 9:21). Unexpected also, even to the prophet Samuel, was the choice of David, the youngest of the sons of an obscure Judean family, to succeed Saul (1 Samuel 16:1-13; see Lesson 5).

Sometimes the surprise is only that of the modern reader and not that of persons in the period of the Bible. Such is the case of the prophetess Deborah in the present lesson. She is lauded as few persons in the Bible are, and for a role that is quite unusual (if not without parallel) in our own society, that of military leadership in the service of the religious community. Because of her courage and faith, she is praised in a long liturgical composition that is not accorded any other of the Judges.

While the Bible (and the Old Testament in particular) is sometimes condemned by modern readers for being "patriarchal" (male dominated) in authorship and outlook, it will be noted when the text is read that Deborah and Jael are not treated as aberrations. Nor are they alone in being recognized as saviors of the chosen community. (See, for example, the crucial role played by the prophetess Huldah in 2 Chronicles 34:22-28; see also Lesson 8.) Deborah's story, therefore, warns us against a hasty generalization of the Bible's attitude toward women. It helps us to anticipate the point of Lesson 6, that God (unlike humans) "looks upon the heart" rather than upon external appearances. Perhaps, as well, it may caution us about mistaken and inappropriate attitudes toward women in the present.

Developing the Lesson

I. Deborah's situation

Outline Israel's situation both geographically (tribes separated by the Valley of Jezreel) and politically (oppressed by the militarily superior Canaanites), with the aid of the information given above (and in the readings if more is desired). You may need to provide a map for further clarity. If one is not available in the classroom, pass one around from the sources mentioned above or draw one on the blackboard (using those sources as a model).

II. The exilic audience

Review for the class the situation and goals of the Deuteronomic Historian (Lesson 3). The situation of this audience is comparable to that of the oppressed Israelites at the time of Deborah: outnumbered, isolated, and without discernible leadership.

III. The author (of chapter 5) as poet

Your ability to discuss this optional topic will depend entirely on the availability of Anchor Bible Series volume 6-A to provide information. It

40

will speak of inclusion, chiastic structure, meter, syllable balance, and so on. (It might help to read the article "Poetry, Hebrew," in *IDB*, vol. 3, pp. 829-38.) An example of syllable balance is given above under "As You Read the Scripture," at 5:1-2. (The point is to demonstrate that this poem is not a spontaneous composition for private use, but rather is a finely honed liturgy for use across the ages.)

IV. The text of the lesson
You might proceed under the divisions of the biblical text outlined above in "The Scripture and the Main Question."

Helping Class Members Act

Discussion might include the following issues as the class members think about the implications of the lesson for their own lives.

1. In view of the fact that God is often depicted in Scripture as a warrior, and remembering that military leaders such as Deborah were memorialized in liturgical materials like Judges 5, is it fitting that church hymnals contain such songs as "The Battle Hymn of the Republic" and "Onward, Christian Soldiers"? (This was a vigorous item of discussion when one denomination recently revised its hymnal.) If the singing of such hymns is inappropriate, is the reading of such texts as Judges 5 inappropriate as well? (Should one ever use the term *inappropriate* to characterize a Scripture text?)

2. Since God's mighty deeds for salvation of the community, on the magnitude of Deborah's victory, are sometimes few and far between, how is the faith of the community to be kept alive in the meanwhile? Is the role of such liturgical pieces as Judges 5 and of liturgy in the present to make the story "present" again?

3. What is your evaluation of the historian's theological interpretation of Israel's history (in chaps. 3–4, that is, of the four stages)? Do you believe God chastens and delivers the church as need be?

4. Given that the Deborah-Jael story (and the Huldah story; Lesson 8) has the status of Scripture, what are the implications for the recognition of leadership by women in the present? In what way might today's texts speak to those contemporary Christian denominations who are currently debating the issue of women's ordination to the ministry?

Planning for Next Sunday

Good leaders are essential for good community. Next Sunday we begin a series on the monarchy in Israel. Ask class members to read 1 Samuel 7:15–8:22 in preparation for this new series and to ask themselves as they read, "What are the qualities of a good leader?"

UNIT II: THE PEOPLE CHOOSE A MONARCHY

FOUR LESSONS   OCTOBER 4–25

The next four sessions in our study of Old Testament personalities focuses on kingship. First, the reasons for the transition from informal guidance by "judges" (such as Deborah and Samuel) to rigid ongoing management by monarchs at the time of Saul; second, consideration of the reigns of three of the most famous kings: David, Solomon, and Josiah. The monarchy was a transition of fateful consequence, both for good and ill. On the one hand, it helped to ensure the security and prosperity of the people. On the other hand, it fostered oppression, class divisions, and nationalism, none of which was compatible with the old ideals of the Mosaic Age. For reasons both internal (as just stated) and external (opposition by Persia), monarchy came to an end during the period of exile (587–539 B.C.) and was not restored thereafter. It left an enduring legacy, however, in the idea that Davidic descendants were a divinely anointed form of leadership ("messianism," a concept that would later be central to Christianity.)

LESSON 5   OCTOBER 4

Samuel, the Last Judge

Background Scripture: 1 Samuel 7:15–8:22

The Main Question

How should a society govern itself during a time of change? What new structures will ensure economic stability and political security, and yet protect traditional values (especially religious ones) from the pressures that are sure to be placed upon them? Is there the possibility that, in the pressing demand for security, the unique heritage of the group will be sacrificed and thus its identity will be totally transformed? In order to preserve the past, should a diversified power structure be maintained, leaving authority in the hands of as many groups as possible? Or, in order to survive the future as an independent group, should power be centralized in the interests of efficiency, flexibility, and effectiveness?

These kinds of questions were thrust upon Israel late in the eleventh century B.C. as the people sought to grapple with unavoidable threats to their security and independence. The obvious alternative to their present system of governance would be, on the one hand, effective, but on the other hand it was a potentially fatal threat to the very theology and sociology that was the essence of Israel. The old system had been characterized by *ad hoc* leadership of judges. The proposed new system was dynastic leadership by kings.

42

At this crucial moment, God's instrument of transitional leadership was the aged Samuel, whose experience included that of priest (1 Samuel 1:1-28; 3:1), prophet ("seer," chap. 9), and judge (7:15-17). He forged a compromise that functioned well in the short run and that remained an ideal long after.

We live in a time of change. What is the best way to order our society during this time? That question is behind today's lesson.

Selected Scripture

King James Version

New Revised Standard Version

1 Samuel 7:15-17

15 And Samuel judged Israel all the days of his life.

16 And he went from year to year in circuit to Bethel, and Gilgal, and Mizpeh, and judged Israel in all those places.

17 And his return was to Ramah; for there was his house; and there he judged Israel; and there he built an altar unto the LORD.

1 Samuel 8:1-9, 19-22

1 And it came to pass, when Samuel was old, that he made his sons judges over Israel.

2 Now the name of his firstborn was Joel; and the name of his second, Abiah: they were judges in Beersheba.

3 And his sons walked not in his ways, but turned aside after lucre, and took bribes, and perverted judgment.

4 Then all the elders of Israel gathered themselves together, and came to Samuel unto Ramah,

5 And said unto him, Behold, thou art old, and thy sons walk not in thy ways: now make us a king to judge us like all the nations.

6 But the thing displeased Samuel, when they said, Give us a king to judge us. And Samuel prayed unto the LORD.

7 And the LORD said unto Samuel, Hearken unto the voice of the people in all that they say unto thee: for they have not rejected thee, but

1 Samuel 7:15-17

15 Samuel judged Israel all the days of his life. 16 He went on a circuit year by year to Bethel, Gilgal, and Mizpah; and he judged Israel in all these places. 17 Then he would come back to Ramah, for his home was there; he administered justice there to Israel, and built there an altar to the LORD.

1 Samuel 8:1-9, 19-22

When Samuel became old, he made his sons judges over Israel. 2 The name of his firstborn son was Joel, and the name of his second, Abijah; they were judges in Beersheba. 3 Yet his sons did not follow in his ways, but turned aside after gain; they took bribes and perverted justice.

4 Then all the elders of Israel gathered together and came to Samuel at Ramah, 5 and said to him, "You are old and your sons do not follow in your ways; appoint for us, then, a king to govern us, like other nations." 6 But the thing displeased Samuel when they said, "Give us a king to govern us." Samuel prayed to the LORD, 7 and the LORD said to Samuel, "Listen to the voice of the people in all that they say to you; for they have not rejected you, but they have rejected me from being king over them. 8 Just as they have done

they have rejected me, that I should not reign over them.

8 According to all the works which they have done since the day that I brought them up out of Egypt even unto this day, wherewith they have forsaken me, and served other gods, so do they also unto thee.

9 Now therefore hearken unto their voice: howbeit yet protest solemnly unto them, and shew them the manner of the king that shall reign over them.

....

19 Nevertheless the people refused to obey the voice of Samuel; and they said, Nay; but we will have a king over us;

20 That we also may be like all the nations; and that our king may judge us, and go out before us, and fight our battles.

21 And Samuel heard all the words of the people, and he rehearsed them in the ears of the LORD.

22 And the LORD said to Samuel, Hearken unto their voice, and make them a king. And Samuel said unto the men of Israel, Go ye every man unto his city.

Key Verse: **And the LORD said unto Samuel, Hearken unto the voice of the people in all that they say unto thee: for they have not rejected thee, but they have rejected me, that I should not reign over them. (1 Samuel 8:7)**

to me, from the day I brought them up out of Egypt to this day, forsaking me and serving other gods, so also they are doing to you. 9 Now then, listen to their voice; only—you shall solemnly warn them, and show them the ways of the king who shall reign over them."

....

19 But the people refused to listen to the voice of Samuel; they said, "No! but we are determined to have a king over us, 20 so that we also may be like other nations, and that our king may govern us and go out before us and fight our battles." 21 When Samuel had heard all the words of the people, he repeated them in the ears of the LORD. 22 The LORD said to Samuel, "Listen to their voice and set a king over them." Samuel then said to the people of Israel, "Each of you return home."

Key Verse: **And the LORD said to Samuel, "Listen to the voice of the people in all that they say to you; for they have not rejected you, but they have rejected me from being king over them." (1 Samuel 8:7)**

As You Read the Scripture

1 Samuel 7:16. Persons who had legal problems would bring them to these designated places for resolution.

8:5. The demand for a king does not begin here. See, for example, the invitation extended to Gideon in Judges 8:22-23 and the self-proclaimed rulership of Abimelech in Judges 9. It is not merely kingship that is proposed, but an office modeled after that of "the other nations."

Verse 7. The title "king" is one of Israel's oldest designations for the deity, reflecting a belief that there was no higher authority. Note Gideon's

rejection of the office in Judges 8:23, "[Only] the LORD will rule over you."
At an earlier time, the Canaanites had used the title "lord" for their deities.
In even earlier Assyrian belief, the title, once reserved for deity only, came
to be applied to human rulers.

Verse 10. By using the verb *asking*, the narrator likely alludes to the
future office holder (*sha'al* means "he asked"; the name Saul means "the
one asked for," *sha'ul*). Sophisticated hearers in ancient Israel would have
understood this clever anticipatory pun.

Verse 11. Samuel's warnings are not projections in a vacuum, but are
based on observation of royal practice in neighboring societies. The people
desire a king "to judge us" (NRSV: "govern"), but they must understand
that the consequence will be a mixture of justice and injustice.

Verse 22. Samuel is not immediately ready to act, and the narrator must
set the stage for the emergence of the future king (in chap. 9). The people
are dismissed, to be reassembled at 10:17.

Israel's traditions about the emergence of the monarchy are complex and
seemingly reflect differing perspectives. In chapter 8, on the one hand,
Samuel (and the deity) are negatively inclined toward the institution and
only reluctantly agree to allow it. In chapter 9, on the other hand, the deity
sees in Saul one who will "save my people from the hand of the Philistines;
for I have seen the suffering of my people" (v. 16); the attitude is positive
and continues through 10:16. At 10:17, however, the negative attitude
resumes. Modern interpreters have traditionally assumed that multiple
sources are in evidence here: an early pro-monarchical source and a later
anti-monarchical one. (The latter supposedly had its origin only during the
monarchical period when the flaws of kingship had become evident.
After-the-fact warnings were then placed in Samuel's mouth, as at 8:10-18,
in order to absolve the deity and prophet Samuel from misjudgment.)
Recent interpreters have been inclined to think that both perspectives are
equally old, reflecting a division of the community about the merits of
kingship from its very beginnings. Samuel thus represents both sides of the
debate.

Note also possible alternative accounts of how candidate Saul came to the
prophet's attention: (1) Saul arrived, seeking lost donkeys (9:1-17); (2) he
was chosen by lot from all Israel (10:20-24); and (3) he was chosen as a
consequence of his earlier successful military activity as well (11:1-15).

The Scripture and the Main Question

In the early post-Mosaic age there was no sustained military leadership in
Israel. In a moment of crisis, it was believed, a charismatic leader ("judge")
would arise at the Lord's bidding and vanquish the enemy. This leader
would then return to ordinary life. An example of such leadership may be
found in the book of Judges, in which Gideon is informed of a Midianite
invasion. He leaves the wheat harvest, organizes successful resistance to the
intruders, and then returns to finish the harvest (chaps. 6–8).

For a long time, this form of non-government served Israel rather well.
Its flaws, however, are evident as early as the fifth chapter of Judges (the
"song of Deborah"). The various tribes, sworn to come to mutual defense,
did not always do so. There was no power of enforcement, no standing
army, no assurance of when or if the charismatic leader would arise. Hence,
the people approached Gideon for a more permanent arrangement: "Rule

over us, you and your son and your grandson" (Judges 8:22). Gideon refused the honor and reminded them that there would be but one unlimited ruler in Israel—God.

The arrival of the Sea Peoples, however, changed the magnitude of the external threat. These settlers from the Aegean Sea (related to the later Greeks) formed strong city-states on the southern coast, and with the aid of weapons and chariots made of iron they began to press toward Israelite settlements in the hill country. (Foremost among them were the Philistines, who eventually gave their name to the area: Palestine.) They were able to capture Israel's most sacred religious emblem in battle (1 Samuel 4–6) and thereafter pressed relentlessly across the plain and into the hills (1 Samuel 13, 17–18, 23, 27). Eventually, they were able to kill King Saul and three of his sons in a resounding defeat (chap. 31).

Under such sustained attack, a standing army, training, organized supply chains, and indeed the whole bureaucracy of monarchy were demanded anew.

He Administered Justice There

This well-chosen phrase by the biblical narrator sets the background for the debate concerning kingship that is to follow. Whatever the organizational and military faults of the old system may be, at least there were leaders who insisted on justice as defined in the old religious traditions: "[He] built there an altar to the LORD" (7:17). There were exceptions, of course, as the beginning of chapter 8 makes quite clear.

A King to Govern Us

In their panic and their desire for a short-term expedient solution, the people saw only the advantages of the dynastic monarchies that characterized the surrounding nations. They seemingly had forgotten that they had lived under such a regime previously, and with disastrous results: For 430 years they had been reduced to slavery by the pharaoh of Egypt. Because, in that system, authority was focused on a single individual who was undergirded by "divine" sanction, slavery was not only an instrument of state but also the social structure willed by the gods. The king (Pharaoh) was the gods' instrument, and thus obedience to his directives was a matter not only of civil law but also of religious piety; indeed, the two could scarcely be distinguished. Therefore, disobedience was far more than a criminal act; it was blasphemy tantamount to atheism.

Such memories and dangers, however, were cast aside. Drastic measures, even ones rejected previously (for example, by Gideon) seemed necessary. Why quibble about traditional freedoms and values if the entire society is in danger of collapse? After all, is not survival the primary value?

You Shall Solemnly Warn Them

Samuel apparently sought to enact some modification of traditional monarchical autonomy and unchecked power by reminding the people of the disadvantages of having a monarchy. His warnings of what would come to pass apparently were based on well-known practice in neighboring states. Those who "run before [the king's] chariots" apparently are to be identified with the palace guard (compare Genesis 41:43). By "horsemen" and "commanders of thousands" is meant military service in general (compare the modern idea of conscription). The king's "officer and his courtiers" (v. 15) are military officers, high officials, or others whom he might choose to honor. This he would do by seizing the ancestral property of families and transferring it to others. This practice was commonly done in the ancient Near East, and the best illustration of it in Israel (reflecting the reality of Samuel's warnings) is to be found in 1 Kings 21, where King Ahab, with the assistance of Queen Jezebel, murders Naboth and appropriates his vineyard. Further evidence of Samuel's correct perception is to be found in the oracles of the prophets, who frequently object to royal abuses. See, for example, Solomon's use of forced labor in 1 Kings 9, Jeroboam's failures in 1 Kings 13–14, the succession of evil kings, Jeremiah's rejection of King Jehoiakim (22:18-19), Hosea's characterization of the king and his advisers (7:3-7), and many others.

In effect, Samuel is asking the people, who have traditionally been governed by the Mosaic perspectives and values, the following questions:

"Have you thought about taxation, forced labor, and conscription, which will be necessary to support the bureaucracy?"

"Have you checked with your neighbors to learn how the system you propose has worked out in practice?"

"Do you know that power corrupts and that absolute power corrupts absolutely?"

"Do you not know that humans ultimately cannot serve two masters, or give both God and humans the title 'king' and all that it implies?"

"Do you not foresee the conflict between the ethical and the legal, and do you not realize that the latter cannot become an end in itself?"

But the People Refused to Listen

Religious ideals apparently are fine during a time of relative security, but they are expendable in moments of crisis (when one talks about "the real world"). Kingship there will be, but Samuel's warnings were apparently part of a compromise of checks-and-balances whereby traditional monarchy was modified, at least temporarily. The deceased monarch was not automatically to be succeeded by his son so as to establish a dynasty. Note how a different family was chosen to succeed Saul when the deity picked the king through the office of the prophet (1 Samuel 16). The king must be held accountable to traditional values, or else he can be replaced (15:17-23).

Helping Adults Become Involved

Preparing to Teach

In order to place Samuel in his historical context, it might be helpful to read the article "Samuel" in *IDB*, vol. 4, pp. 201-2 (esp. sect. 2: "Historical Reconstruction"). You may also want to read the article "Philistines" in *IDB*, vol. 3, pp. 791-95, and/or part of the article "The History of Israel," in *IB*, vol. 1 (sect. IV, "The United Monarchy"). Especially helpful in understanding Samuel's fears is the article "King, Kingship," in *IDB*, vol. 3, pp. 11-17.

Presentation to the class might take place under the following headings.

47

I. What we know about Samuel's setting
II. First Samuel as part of the Deuteronomic History
III. The text of the lesson and our own situation

Introducing the Main Question

One of the most famous statements in the Bible is Paul's advice to the Christians at Rome: "Let every person be subject to the governing authorities; for there is no authority except from God, and those that exist have been instituted by God. Therefore whoever resists authority resists what God has appointed" (Romans 13:1-2). This text is deeply ingrained in the American religious consciousness, and it has helped to enforce the idea that a "good" Christian is always an obedient citizen.

There is, however, another perspective on the matter, attributed to Peter "and the apostles" in response to a governmental order: "We must obey God rather than any human authority" (Acts 5:29). When these two perspectives are brought into conversation (argument?), a lively debate is likely to result concerning the "rightful" place of government and the ultimate authority for Christian behavior. The debate about that matter, in the history of Synagogue and Church, began during the period of the judges and reached a crucial moment at the time of the prophet Samuel.

Developing the Lesson

I. What we know about Samuel's setting
Sketch briefly the chronology that ties Lesson Four with the present one: Deborah, 1100 B.C. (1 Samuel 1–4); Saul and the beginning of Israelite monarchy, 1020 B.C. Summarize the system of government that was operative in the pre-monarchical period—namely, that of the judges (see above under "The Scripture and the Main Question." Outline the problem presented for Israel's security by the arrival of the Philistines.

II. First Samuel as part of the Deuteronomic History
Joshua–2 Kings forms a grand theological history of Israel. The setting and goals of the final product are sketched in Lesson Three (under "Developing the Lesson," sect. II), and you may want to review them with the class. Why would the Judean exiles, centuries later, be interested in Samuel's warnings about the dangers of kingship? Would this help to explain why, once the Exile was over, monarchy was not restored?

III. The text of the lesson and our own situation
You might proceed under the divisions of the biblical text that were outlined above in "The Scripture and the Main Question."

Helping Class Members Act

Today, your class discussion might include the following issues as class members think about the implications of the lesson for their own society.
1. Did biblical prophets ever go beyond mere criticism of the state to indulge in activities that led to its overthrow? [Yes, occasionally, especially in the early period. See, for example, 1 Kings 19:15-18, where Elijah is instructed by the deity to appoint successors to the current kings of Syria

and Israel, who are then to use their swords to eradicate enemies. See also 2 Kings 8:7-15, where the command is carried out and the Syrian designate then assassinates his master. Then see 9:1-10, where a similar procedure is carried out in Israel.] What theological and ethical value, if any, do such stories in Scripture have for the Church in the present? Is the same idea, with a secular orientation, to be found in the Declaration of Independence of the American Colonies?

2. A well-known theologian, speaking of the tendency of governments to claim the ultimate allegiance of their citizens, has said that such an attempt "belongs to the devil precisely because it claims to be God" (Reinhold Neibuhr, *Do the State and the Nation Belong to God or to the Devil?* [London: SCM Press, 1937], p. 10). From the point of view of the Bible (and the first of the Ten Commandments in particular, Exodus 20:3), is this a valid warning for Christian citizens to keep in mind?

3. Is there a parallel between the fears that Samuel had concerning unbridled kingship and the fears that the founders of the United States had concerning European monarchy as the model for their government? In both instances, it has been argued by a modern analyst, monarchy was the prevailing model, and the solution was to limit it by establishing checks and balances. Was the president, then, a modified version of King George III? In the case of the Bible, the limited guidelines failed to check royal power for very long. (Note, for example, that David was succeeded by his son Solomon, thus establishing dynastic succession [1 Kings 2], something that Samuel never intended.) Are there parallels to this in our own governmental history? Aside from the legal issues involved, is this a theological issue for Christians? Is it a matter of Christian morality to obey the policies of "the Sovereign"? If so, under what conditions? If not, why?

Planning for Next Sunday

Of all of Israel's kings, King David was the greatest. Ask the class to try to recall their most vivid memories of stories they've heard about David.

David: King over All the People

Background Scripture: 1 Samuel 16:1-13; 2 Samuel 2:1-7; 5:1-5

The Main Question

In the compromise that was worked out at the inception of kingship in Israel (Lesson 5), the prophet Samuel retained for himself (and presumably for his successors) the right to choose each succeeding monarch. Thereby, he believed, the traditional values of the "chosen people" (Lesson 1) would be safeguarded in the choice of leader. Presumably, the prophet (as spokesperson for the deity, and as one upon whom the "Spirit of the Lord" rested) would be able to make a more reliable choice than would the population at large (who had, after all, thoughtlessly clamored for a "king like all the nations"). In any case, choice of any kind would be preferable to the automatic inheritance of the office, which dynastic succession would bring.

It should surprise us, then, as it must have the prophet himself, that Samuel's judgment in the matter of Saul's successor was repeatedly rejected by God. The prophet had, in one sense, used very good judgment in rejecting the descendants of Saul, for whom there was a public clamor. On the other hand, he relied on common-sense surface criteria, as might have the average person of his time. God rejected his choices until the seemingly least likely candidate arrived for scrutiny. God then delivered an immortal description of the contrast between divine and human perception in such matters.

Since the same criteria for the selection of leaders often appeal to voters in our own society (the vast majority of whom understand themselves to be "born-again Christians") it is in order for them today to ponder the account of the selection of David to guide Israel in the struggle to actualize God's agenda for human society.

What are the criteria for a godly leader?

Selected Scripture

King James Version	New Revised Standard Version
1 Samuel 16:1, 6-7, 11-13	*1 Samuel 16:1, 6-7, 11-13*
1 And the LORD said unto Samuel, How long wilt thou mourn for Saul, seeing I have rejected him from reigning over Israel? fill thine horn with oil, and go, I will send thee to Jesse the Bethlehemite: for I have provided me a king among his sons.	1 The LORD said to Samuel, "How long will you grieve over Saul? I have rejected him from being king over Israel. Fill your horn with oil and set out; I will send you to Jesse the Bethlehemite, for I have provided for myself a king among his sons."
....	....
6 And it came to pass, when they were come, that he looked on Eliab, and said, Surely the LORD's anointed is before him.	6 When they came, he looked on Eliab and thought, "Surely the LORD's anointed is now before the LORD." 7 But the LORD said to
7 But the LORD said unto Samuel, Look not on his countenance, or on the height of his stature; because I have refused him: for the LORD seeth not as man seeth; for man looketh on the outward appearance, but the LORD looketh on the heart.	Samuel, "Do not look on his appearance or on the height of his stature, because I have rejected him; for the LORD does not see as mortals see; they look on the outward appearance, but the LORD looks on the heart."
....	....
11 And Samuel said unto Jesse, Are here all thy children? And he said, There remaineth yet the	11 Samuel said to Jesse, "Are all your sons here?" And he said, "There remains yet the youngest,

youngest, and, behold, he keepeth the sheep. And Samuel said unto Jesse, Send and fetch him: for we will not sit down till he come hither.

12 And he sent, and brought him in. Now he was ruddy, and withal of a beautiful countenance, and goodly to look to. And the LORD said, Arise, anoint him: for this is he.

13 Then Samuel took the horn of oil, and anointed him in the midst of his brethren: and the spirit of the LORD came upon David from that day forward. So Samuel rose up, and went to Ramah.

2 Samuel 5:1-5

1 Then came all the tribes of Israel to David unto Hebron, and spake, saying, Behold, we are thy bone and thy flesh.

2 Also in time past, when Saul was king over us, thou wast he that leddest out and broughtest in Israel: and the LORD said to thee, Thou shalt feed my people Israel, and thou shalt be a captain over Israel.

3 So all the elders of Israel came to the king to Hebron; and king David made a league with them in Hebron before the LORD: and they anointed David king over Israel.

4 David was thirty years old when he began to reign, and he reigned forty years.

5 In Hebron he reigned over Judah seven years and six months: and in Jerusalem he reigned thirty and three years over all Israel and Judah.

Key Verse: Then Samuel took the horn of oil, and anointed him in the midst of his brethren: and the spirit of the LORD came upon David from that day forward. So Samuel rose up, and went to Ramah. (1 Samuel 16:13)

but he is keeping the sheep." And Samuel said to Jesse, "Send and bring him; for we will not sit down until he comes here." 12 He sent and brought him in. Now he was ruddy, and had beautiful eyes, and was handsome. The LORD said, "Rise and anoint him; for this is the one." 13 Then Samuel took the horn of oil, and anointed him in the presence of his brothers; and the spirit of the LORD came mightily upon David from that day forward. Samuel then set out and went to Ramah.

2 Samuel 5:1-5

Then all the tribes of Israel came to David at Hebron, and said, "Look, we are your bone and flesh. 2 For some time, while Saul was king over us, it was you who led out Israel and brought it in. The LORD said to you: It is you who shall be shepherd of my people Israel, you who shall be ruler over Israel." 3 So all the elders of Israel came to the king at Hebron; and King David made a covenant with them at Hebron before the LORD, and they anointed David king over Israel. 4 David was thirty years old when he began to reign, and he reigned forty years. 5 At Hebron he reigned over Judah seven years and six months; and at Jerusalem he reigned over all Israel and Judah thirty-three years.

Key Verse: Then Samuel took the horn of oil, and anointed him in the presence of his brothers; and the spirit of the LORD came mightily upon David from that day forward. Samuel then set out and went to Ramah. (1 Samuel 16:13)

As You Read the Scripture

1 Samuel 16:1. The rejection of Saul is related in chapter 15. The oil is to be used to anoint the new monarch (9:16; 10:1). The Hebrew verb meaning "to anoint" is *mashah,* and one anointed is a *mashiah,* from which derives the title (in English) "Messiah."

Verse 2. Samuel's fear derives from Saul's expectation of dynastic succession, and thus to anoint someone else would be an act of sedition. The road from Samuel's residence to Bethlehem would pass through Saul's hometown, and might therefore arouse suspicion. The deity provides the prophet with a justifiable excuse for the journey.

Verse 4. The anxious reaction of the elders at Samuel's arrival may reflect the tension between the prophet and the king (as related in chap. 15). They do not want to become embroiled in the controversy.

Verse 5. Worshipers "consecrated" themselves by performing certain rites as preparation for worship (sacrifice).

Verse 6. Jesse's sons come before Samuel in the order of their birth, beginning with Eliab, the oldest. This is made clear in 1 Chronicles 2:13-15.

Verse 10. Here, David is the eighth son, whereas in 1 Chronicles 2:13-15 he is the seventh. It was a common belief in the ancient Near East (and in folklore in general) that the seventh son possessed special powers. See the article "Generation, Seventh," in the *IDBS,* pp. 354-56.

2 Samuel 2:1. Saul's conflicts with David (beginning at 1 Samuel 18) have forced the latter to flee from one place to another (see, for example, 22:1). Now that Saul is dead (2 Samuel 1:1), David begins to seek the office to which Samuel had already appointed him. First, he seeks to determine the city that will be his base of operation.

Verse 2. David's wives are not Judeans, as he was, but were from the northern tribes (who showed a tendency to prefer a descendant of Saul for king). Such marriages may have been an astute political move on David's part to secure allies among the northern tribes.

Verse 4. David's plan is apparently twofold: first, recognition as king by his Judean kinsmen, then getting the northerners to "come around."

Verse 5. Jabesh-gilead was within the territory of the northern tribe of Manasseh, and its inhabitants had particular fondness for King Saul (1 Samuel 11). By sending them a message of gratitude for burying Saul, David not only honors the deceased king (whom God had, after all, anointed; see 1 Samuel 9–10), but he also seeks friendship with those who might otherwise be his opponents. He urges them to accept him as Saul's rightful successor.

2 Samuel 5:1. With the death of Abner (3:30; a general of Saul's army and an advocate of dynastic succession; see 2:8-9) and of Ishbosheth the son of Saul (2:8; 4:5-8), northern opposition to David's kingship has collapsed. Thus "all the tribes of Israel" now acknowledge David's right to the office.

Verse 4. David's total life span is seventy years, a traditional symbolic number for completion and accomplishment. For other instances of its use, see Genesis 5:24; 46:27; 50:3; Exodus 15:27; 24:1; 2 Kings 10:1; Isaiah 23:15; Jeremiah 25:11; Luke 10:1.

The Scripture and the Main Question

The proposal to establish kingship like that in other nations in response to the military threat of the Philistines and the Canaanites (1 Samuel 1–11) had posed a serious threat to the traditional identity and values of Israel. The prophet Samuel was able to forge a compromise: modification of the office of king so as to bring it under traditional sanctions, without diminishing its effectiveness to deal with external enemies (see Lesson 5). Above all else, the future monarchs would be expected *to rely on the prophetic office for determination of the divine will in the implementation of public policies.* Consequently, Samuel felt free to initiate and to direct a military campaign against the Amalekites (1 Samuel 15:1-3). King Saul, however, soon found it expedient (if not profitable in the present instance) to go his own way, and this led to stormy conflict with the prophet. Thus Samuel announces, "Surely, to obey is better [to the Lord] than sacrifice. . . . For rebellion is no less a sin than divination, and stubbornness is [as bad as] iniquity and idolatry" (15:22-23). Nonetheless, although the prophet then announces that God has "rejected you from being king" (v. 23), he was not able to relieve Saul of that office.

It is clear, then, that a crisis in authority would be precipitated by the death of the first monarch: would he be succeeded by a son (and thereby a dynasty initiated), or would the prophet maintain the power to pick a successor? If the latter, by what criteria?

I Have Provided for Myself a King

The choice of one of Jesse's sons to succeed Saul is a rejection of dynastic kingship, and thereby God indicates that *absolute power is not to be concentrated in human hands.* In Israel, monarchs are not to have unlimited, self-appointed, and self-perpetuating authority. They are to rule (and be respected) only for so long as they uphold what is right in the eyes of the Lord. The two families (Saul's and Jesse's) do not even belong to the same tribe: Saul is from Benjamin (1 Samuel 9:1-2), whereas Jesse is from Judah. Thus the prophet, sensing divine guidance, removes himself from the sphere of influence by Saul's partisans and seeks a traditional, pious family (who will have brought up its children to respect traditional values and who presumably will respect the directions of the prophet).

Surely the Lord's Anointed Is Now Before the Lord

The prophet has sensed which family is the proper one, but apparently not the particular son. Therefore, he begins in a common-sense way, with the oldest. After all, biblical tradition allowed certain rights to the firstborn (see the story of Esau and Jacob, where the latter deprives the former of his "birthright," Genesis 25). Furthermore, this son should have more experience with life and possibly be the strongest physically, and thus perhaps be more able to govern. As if that were not enough, he may have been the tallest, even tall for the society as a whole ("Do not look . . . on the height of his stature," v. 7). This was often a criterion for kingship in the ancient Near East, and the narrator has been careful to point out that Saul met this expectation (1 Samuel 9:2, " . . . he stood head and shoulders above everyone else") In any case, in the art of the time the monarch can usually be spotted by his unusual height. Not surprisingly, therefore, Samuel concluded that this surely must be the leader whom the Lord had in mind! After all, are not human conventions and desires, our stereotypes of the "right people," likely to have divine approval?

But the Lord Said to Samuel . . .

It is characteristic of Israel's God, with mysterious providence, to sometimes do the unexpected, including the choice of whom to bless or to select for leadership. Recall how the "father" of Israel turns out to be the younger Jacob, a trickster, and not the older, more admirable Esau (Genesis 25:23; 27:1-40). The aged and blind Jacob suddenly crosses his hands on the heads of his grandsons and blesses the "wrong" one, even as their father, Joseph, vigorously protests that he has mistakenly put his right hand on the head of the younger boy (Genesis 48:8-22). Nonetheless, Jacob proceeds, knowing precisely what he is doing.

It is not without precedent then, that God turns a deaf ear to human standards and conventions. In the present case, the deity, no doubt to the growing consternation of the prophet, runs through the entirety of Jesse's sons then present without approving any of them as Saul's successor. (How "picky" can one get?) The reason for this has been indicated at the rejection of the oldest, in one of the more memorable verses in the entire Bible.

> But the LORD said to Samuel, "Do not look on his appearance or on the height of his stature, because I have rejected him; for the LORD does not see as mortals see; they look on the outward appearance, but the LORD looks on the heart." (1 Samuel 16:7)

There Remains Yet the Youngest

Since, in the tested experience of ancient Israel, wisdom resided with the aged (see Job 12:12), the remaining young son should be the least likely possibility for God's choice. Indeed, he apparently is so young that his father has not thought to include him in the sacrificial service that the prophet has come to perform. Nonetheless, at David's appearance, God urges Samuel, "Rise and anoint him; for this is the one" (v. 12). It is not inappropriate here to make comparison with Paul's remarks about the lowly status of the followers of Jesus at Corinth:

> Consider your own call, brothers and sisters: not many of you were wise by human standards, not many were powerful, not many were of noble birth. But God chose what is foolish in the world to shame the wise; God chose what is weak in the world to shame the strong; God chose what is low and despised in the world . . . to reduce to nothing things that are.
> (1 Corinthians 1:26-28)

The last phrase of this quotation is more helpfully rendered by the Revised English Bible: " . . . to overthrow the existing order."

And the Spirit of the Lord Came Mightily upon David

The Bible and Christian history are filled with astonishing reports of the transformation of humans that has taken place as the result of religious experience. One thinks, for example, of the physical exploits of Samson (Judges 14:5-6) and of even of Elijah (1 Kings 18:46; see Lesson 9); of the proclamations of (the so-called Second) Isaiah (61:1-4); of the power of apostolic preaching (Acts 10:44); of the transformation of sinful lives; and so on. Do such dramatic transformations occur today?

Then All the Tribes of Israel Came

It was an extended period of time before David became king of all of Israel after having led the people of Judah (more than seven years). His suitability to lead the people and his nearness to the ideal anointed one (Messiah) ultimately became evident to all. Repeatedly thereafter he is the standard against which the Deuteronomic Historian measured his successors in office (see, for example, 2 Kings 16:1-2; 18:1-3). Thereby *the goodness and providence of God, even in surprising actions, is acknowledged.* God often chooses unusual people to do his work.

Helping Adults Become Involved

Preparing to Teach

The historical situation in the present lesson is not much different from that of the previous one (Lesson 5). Armed conflict between Israel and its neighbors (Canaanites and Philistines) has continued, with both successes (1 Samuel 14; 17; 23:1-5) and failure (1 Samuel 31). Details may be found in the article "Saul, Son of Kish," in *IDB*, vol. 4, pp. 228-33. Continue, if you desire, with the article "David," in *IDB*, vol. 1, pp. 771-82. Should you desire to understand the concept of the "anointed one" (messiah) and the role David played as the ideal, read "Messiah, Jewish" in *IDB*, vol. 3, pp. 360-65, although this is not essential.

A map showing the boundaries of the tribes may be useful in locating the supporters of Saul's descendant versus those of David. See the following maps: GNB, p. 381; *IDB*, vol. 4, p. 702 (rather confusing; see the "key" on p. 703); NRSV, Map 3. Almost any Bible atlas will be helpful.

Presentation to the class might take place under the following headings.

    I. The historical situation
   II. The danger of dynastic succession
 III. The text of the lesson and its implications for today's leaders

Introducing the Main Question

The political climate in our country is one in which *image is more important than substance.* Thus commercials by popular entertainers in support of a candidate "carry weight" with the electorate. It is important to "look presidential." It has been suggested that Richard Nixon lost one of his televised debates with John Kennedy in part because Nixon looked as if he needed a shave. Convictions fluctuate with the findings of the latest poll. It is important to be photographed with the family, to wear a flag on the lapel, to appear at the "right" functions, and to speak the current "in" clichés. What chance would Abraham Lincoln have in a presidential election today? (Too tall, gaunt, ungainly, unkempt hair, rumpled clothing, "country" to the core.) Consequently, the modern electorate is sometimes astonished to find out (rather slowly) that it may have been "had." Even more serious is the fact that persons of great potential and character have been passed over or felt that it was futile for them to campaign.

Things have not changed in this regard over the centuries. As far as humans are concerned in the choice of leadership, it is "once a chump, always a chump." Fortunately for Israel and the Church, however, the deity sometimes arranges for the "obvious" candidate to be bypassed and provides a savior in the unexpected person. Thus when the prophet Samuel would have chosen the oldest son of Jesse as the next king of Israel, God instructed him instead to anoint the seemingly least likely of the brothers. God then outlined an approach to choosing leaders that Christians might well keep in mind: "Pay no attention to his outward appearance and stature. . . . Mortals see only appearances but the LORD sees into the heart" (1 Samuel 16:7 REB).

Developing the Lesson

I. The historical situation

Mention the continuing conflict between Israel and its neighbors, even after the victory of Deborah (Lesson 4) and the inauguration of the kingship under Saul, which was supposed to provide security (Lesson 5). Brief mention of particulars is made above and in the readings. The situation becomes so serious that Saul is killed in battle against the Philistines (1 Samuel 31). The choice of the next leader is, therefore, crucial, not only militarily but also religiously (note how Saul often disobeyed the prophet Samuel and set himself up as an ultimate authority; 1 Samuel 15).

II. The danger of dynastic succession

Dynastic succession was the usual ancient Near Eastern practice, thus concentrating power in the hands of a single family and making reformation rather unlikely. Review the situation at Saul's death: the desire to appoint Saul's son Ishbosheth as king, promoted by the powerful and popular general Abner. That desire is evident in opposition to David among the northern tribes, an opposition that continued for seven years while David was king in Judah.

III. The text of the lesson and its implications for today's leaders

You might proceed under the division of the biblical text that was outlined above in "The Scripture and the Main Question."

Helping Class Members Act

Discussion might include the following issues as class members think about the implications of the lesson for their own lives.

1. Are there instances in your own experience where a most unlikely candidate for leadership (at the national, state, and local levels; either secular or religious office) has emerged and served with courage, if not accomplishment? Are there, on the other hand, instances where humans, as usual, looked only on the external appearance and chose a less than adequate person?

2. When the text tells us that humans tend to look on external appearance, whereas God looks at the heart (1 Samuel 16:7), what sort of characteristics do you think are being lauded? Have you looked for those characteristics in leaders whom you have helped to choose?

3. How does God's "rule of thumb" for the selection of leaders reflect the traditional practice of hiring employees by such external appearances as sex, race, age, or physical ability? How does it reflect the current practice

of quota hiring and equal opportunity employment (if the latter involves "reverse discrimination")?

Planning for Next Sunday

Good leaders are wise people. But how does one define that difficult word *wisdom*?

LESSON 7   OCTOBER 18

Solomon: Wise King

Background Scripture: 1 Kings 1:28-37; 2:1-4; 3:3-14

The Main Question

The danger of a centralized (monarchical) government for ancient Israel, when the idea was first proposed, was that a concentration of power would undermine many of the society's traditional values (see Lesson 5). The validity of such warnings by the prophet Samuel was borne out by the rebellion of the first monarch, Saul, and thus the prophet sought to avoid dynastic succession by choosing one of the sons of Jesse as the next ruler (see Lesson 6). Thanks to David's piety and general success, royal theologians then proposed that a dynasty was God's will; God had entered into a covenant with the Davidic line as a means of fostering traditional religious values and protecting the community from external threats (2 Samuel 7). That is, from a practical point of view, if dynastic succession is inevitable sooner or later (given the ancient Near Eastern pattern and the human desire for power), it was better that it be David's descendants than some other family. Perhaps David's good example and influence would live on in the attitude and values of his descendants in office.

A crucial test for this bold departure from Samuel's warnings came, therefore, at David's death. Even if the best of his sons were chosen to succeed him, it would be possible for power, prestige, and wealth to so seduce him that he would be little more than a king like all the nations have (as the people had initially proposed at 1 Samuel 8:5). How might the new monarch prepare himself for this awesome task so that, while facing an uncertain future, he might be guided by the wisdom of the past? What are the biblical standards for wise leadership?

Selected Scripture

King James Version	Revised Standard Version
1 Kings 2:1-4	*1 Kings 2:1-4*
1 Now the days of David drew nigh that he should die; and he	1 When David's time to die drew near, he charged his son Solomon,

charged Solomon his son, saying,

2 I go the way of all the earth: be thou strong therefore, and shew thyself a man;

3 And keep the charge of the Lord thy God, to walk in his ways, to keep his statutes, and his commandments, and his judgments, and his testimonies, as it is written in the law of Moses, that thou mayest prosper in all that thou doest, and whithersoever thou turnest thyself:

4 That the Lord may continue his word which he spake concerning me, saying, If thy children take heed to their way, to walk before me in truth with all their heart and with all their soul, there shall not fail thee (said he) a man on the throne of Israel.

1 Kings 3:5-12

5 In Gibeon the Lord appeared to Solomon in a dream by night: and God said, Ask what I shall give thee.

6 And Solomon said, Thou hast shewed unto thy servant David my father great mercy, according as he walked before thee in truth, and in righteousness, and in uprightness of heart with thee; and thou hast kept for him this great kindness, that thou hast given him a son to sit on his throne, as it is this day.

7 And now, O Lord my God, thou hast made thy servant king instead of David my father: and I am but a little child: I know not how to go out or come in.

8 And thy servant is in the midst of thy people which thou hast chosen, a great people, that cannot be numbered nor counted for multitude.

9 Give therefore thy servant an understanding heart to judge thy people, that I may discern between good and bad: for who is able to judge this thy so great a people?

10 And the speech pleased the Lord, that Solomon had asked this thing.

saying, 2 "I am about to go the way of all the earth. Be strong, be courageous, 3 and keep the charge of the Lord your God, walking in his ways and keeping his statutes, his commandments, his ordinances, and his testimonies, as it is written in the law of Moses, so that you may prosper in all that you do and wherever you turn. 4 Then the Lord will establish his word that he spoke concerning me: 'If your heirs take heed to their way, to walk before me in faithfulness with all their heart and with all their soul, there shall not fail you a successor on the throne of Israel.' "

1 Kings 3:5-12

5 At Gibeon the Lord appeared to Solomon in a dream by night; and God said, "Ask what I should give you." 6 And Solomon said, "You have shown great and steadfast love to your servant my father David, because he walked before you in faithfulness, in righteousness, and in uprightness of heart toward you; and you have kept for him this great and steadfast love, and have given him a son to sit on his throne today. 7 And now, O Lord my God, you have made your servant king in place of my father David, although I am only a little child; I do not know how to go out or come in. 8 And your servant is in the midst of the people whom you have chosen, a great people, so numerous they cannot be numbered or counted. 9 Give your servant therefore an understanding mind to govern your people, able to discern between good and evil; for who can govern this your great people?"

10 It pleased the Lord that Solomon had asked this. 11 God said to him, "Because you have asked this,

11 And God said unto him, Because thou hast asked this thing, and hast not asked for thyself long life; neither hast asked riches for thyself, nor hast asked the life of thine enemies; but hast asked for thyself understanding to discern judgment;

12 Behold, I have done according to thy words: lo, I have given thee a wise and an understanding heart; so that there was none like thee before thee, neither after thee shall any arise like unto thee.

and have not asked for yourself long life or riches, or for the life of your enemies, but have asked for yourself understanding to discern what is right, 12 I now do according to your word. Indeed I give you a wise and discerning mind; no one like you has been before you and no one like you shall arise after you."

Key Verse: **Give therefore thy servant [Solomon] an understanding heart to judge thy people, that I may discern between good and bad: for who is able to judge this thy so great a people? (1 Kings 3:9)**

Key Verse: **Give your servant [Solomon] therefore an understanding mind to govern your people, able to discern between good and evil; for who can govern this your great people? (1 Kings 3:9)**

As You Read the Scripture

1 Kings 1:28. Bathsheba, formerly the wife of Uriah the Hittite, whom David arranged to have killed in battle (2 Samuel 11), is now married to David and is the mother of Prince Solomon (2 Samuel 12:24).

Verse 30. David's oath concerning Solomon was suggested to him previously by Bathsheba as part of a plot by the prophet Nathan (1 Kings 1:11-14). Possibly they have "put words in the king's mouth" during a period of failing mental powers (1:1-3). Nathan's motivations may have been the supposition that he could influence Solomon more than Adonijah (who had laid claim to the throne, according to 1:5).

Verse 32. Zadok would be needed to consecrate the new king; Nathan might issue an oracle of divine support; and Benaiah was a military commander whose support would be crucial in case of opposition.

Verse 33. A mule was the animal of choice for riding by kings and for the trip to be crowned in particular. (See Zechariah 9:9; Matthew 21:5; and the article "Ass" in the *IDBS*, pp. 72-73.) The common idea that riding a mule was a sign of humility is a misunderstanding.

Verse 34. The "law of Moses" probably is a reference to the book of Deuteronomy, since it in particular contains regulations for the conduct of Israel's monarchs (17:14-20).

1 Kings 2:4. This conditional warning would be of interest to the audience of the Deuteronomic Historian (see Lesson 3), the exiles in Babylonia during the sixth century B.C. The failure of subsequent kings to heed it would justify the punishment that had befallen the community.

1 Kings 3:3-14. This preamble to Solomon's reign is seemingly based on an Egyptian pattern: revelation in a dream (3:5-15a), the offering of sacrifice (3:15b), and communication with his officials (3:15c). Such literary influence may have resulted from Solomon's marriage to a daughter of the king of Egypt (3:1).

Verse 3. "High places" were open-air sanctuaries such as the Canaanites often used to worship fertility and astral deities. Although the Temple in Jerusalem had not yet been built, the historian condemns the practice.

Verse 4. The reason for the journey to worship at Gibeon is not stated, other than that is "the principal high place." According to later history (1 Chronicles 16:39; 21:29; 2 Chronicles 1:3), the Mosaic portable sanctuary had been stored there. In any case, Solomon may have desired, in keeping with ancient practice, to obtain divine communication by means of a dream.

Verse 7. Solomon's description of himself as "a little child" is exaggeration prompted by the humility that is appropriate in prayer. In fact, he is old enough to be married and to assume the throne (3:1) as well as to purge his opponents (1 Kings 2). There are Egyptian parallels (the pharaoh as a child shielded by a statue of a deity).

The Scripture and the Main Question

The account of Solomon's assumption of the leadership of Israel begins with intrigue and brutality of the very type that the prophet Samuel had feared (Lesson 5). Prince Adonijah, David's fourthborn son (2 Samuel 3:1-4) and apparently the oldest living one, had a legitimate claim to the throne. David did not denounce his desire to assume that role, and Adonijah had the support of significant members of the court (1 Kings 1:5-7; 2:15). Others, however, plotted to undermine his claim, possibly by giving the elderly (and apparently senile) David false information about a previous promise. In any case, they appealed to David's pride by suggesting that Adonijah had acted "behind his back." Bathsheba is encouraged to join the plot when it is pointed out to her that Adonijah had a different mother than did her son, Solomon (see 1:11; rivalry between wives?), and Nathan assures her that "I will come in after you and confirm your words" (1:14).

Your Son Solomon Shall Succeed Me as King

The plan was successful, and David instructed them that Solomon would be anointed as his successor (coregent). Even so, Adonijah retained powerful supporters, and after the death of David he continued to press his claim. Consequently Solomon put him to death (2:13-25) along with his cousin Joab, who had commanded the army (2:28-35), and he banished the priest Abiathar (2:26-27).

After such a ruthless beginning (however justifiable it may have seemed to some), it may have appeared to others that Samuel's worst nightmare had come true and that leadership of the chosen community had degenerated into a matter of "dog eat dog" and "the survival of the fittest." Indeed, they now *were* governed (in the words of their request) "like all the other nations."

When David's Time to Die Drew Near

In the midst of the crisis, Solomon is given deathbed advice by his father, not about how to survive political intrigue, but about the necessity to follow traditional guidelines and to perpetuate the values of the society. "Keep the charge of the LORD your God, walking in his ways and keeping his statutes . . . as it is written in the law of Moses. . . . Then the LORD will establish his word" (2:3-4).

Such deathbed charges or blessings are rather common in the Bible (Genesis 27:1-4; 48:1-9; Deuteronomy 33) and in intertestamental literature. Eighteenth-century Methodists in particular paid close attention to deathbed scenes for whatever edification they might impart.

At the end of a person's life, what does that person wish for posterity?

That I May Discern Between Good and Evil

Solomon is now depicted as having taken his father's deathbed advice to heart. He visits a sanctuary where the granting of revelation by the deity is apparently well known. His prayer for an understanding mind indicates that he intends to serve as the ultimate arbiter of justice and that he desires to govern the people fairly. It is something God grants in response to earnest petition, and not something that is intrinsic to human nature. This establishment of Solomon's fitness for administration may be intended to serve as the model for future rulers as the Davidic dynasty sets out on its course through history.

The actualization of the ideal is illustrated in the initial accomplishments of Solomon's reign: judicial astuteness (3:16-28), construction of the central sanctuary (5:1–6:38; 7:13–8:66), and visits by foreign leaders who desire to learn his wisdom (10:1-13). As his forty-year reign progressed, however, the deterioration of the ideal became manifest: the worship of foreign deities whom he had allowed for his wives (11:1-8) and attempts to execute those whom he perceived to be a threat (11:40). Troubles at the end of his reign (11:14, 23) are attributed to divine displeasure ("The LORD was angry with Solomon, because his heart had turned away from the LORD"; 11:9). Equally serious and indicative of his insensitivity and oppressiveness is the attitude of his son and successor, Rehoboam, likely learned from his father. When a group of citizens requested that he "lighten the hard service of your father and his heavy yoke that he placed on us" (12:1-4), Rehoboam replied with arrogance and contempt, "My father disciplined you with whips, but I will discipline you with scorpions" (12:14). As a consequence, the ten northern tribes rebelled and renounced Davidic leadership, never to be restored, thus weakening the identity and security of the chosen community and contributing to the ultimate defeat and exile of each part.

Helping Adults Become Involved

Preparing to Teach

Background information for understanding the struggle to succeed David as king may be found in the following articles in *IDB:* "Adonijah," vol. 1, p. 47; "Abiathar," vol. 1, pp. 6-7; "Benaiah," vol. 1, pp. 380-81; "Nathan," vol. 3, p. 511; and "Zadok," vol. 4, pp. 928-29. Solomon's accomplishments are well discussed in the article "Solomon," vol. 4, pp. 399-408.

Because Solomon's story is ultimately a part of the much larger Deuteronomic History (Lesson 3), you may wish to review the goals of that work. Why would its authors have been interested in the reasons for Solomon's successes and failures?

For the idea that dreams were a medium of communication between gods and humans and that persons (especially leaders) might sleep at a sanctuary so as to enhance this possibility, see the article "Dream" in *IDB*, vol. 1, pp. 868-69.

Brief commentary on the text of the lesson may be found in *IOCB*, pp. 183-84.

Presentation to the class might take place under the following headings.

     I. The situation as David's death approached
    II. The method of resolution
   III. The text of the lesson and its contemporary application

Introducing the Main Question

It has been observed that, given human nature, "power tends to corrupt, and absolute power tends to corrupt absolutely." Thus elected officials, initially sensitive to the needs of their constituency, may become increasingly callous (especially since incumbents are likely to be reelected). After all, certain classes are "out of sight, out of mind"! Initially honest representatives, surrounded by a sea of cash (in the form of contributions and appropriations), may become increasingly convinced that they deserve more than they are getting and thus may help themselves (especially if that is the way "the game is played"). If the word *legal* can be stretched to new lengths to cover their action, if it is in that "gray area," that is good enough! After all, if something is not illegal, it is moral, isn't it? Once persons become accustomed to power and substantial compensation, then they are vulnerable to the desires of those who might be able to deprive them of that power, and thus "enlightened self-interest" may take the form of carefully disguised favoritism. For these and other reasons, is it desirable that there be limitations on terms of office?

This issue was faced in early Israel as King David's death approached. Should the people heed the warnings of the prophet Samuel, who not only had envisioned checks and balances on the dangerous new office of king, but also had sought to prohibit dynastic succession by turning from Saul's family to that of David? Or should they "go for it," since David had been close to ideal, and it might be that his values and procedures would be passed on to his descendants in office? Given the reality of ancient practice (dynastic succession) and human nature, it was almost inevitable that power would be increasingly concentrated in a single individual and that bureaucracy would be self-perpetuating.

Given those realities, how does the religiously sensitive leader, about to assume office, counter them? The story of King Solomon is that of a ruler who recognized the difficulty of office and dealt with it admirably—at least for a while.

Developing the Lesson

I. The situation as David's death approached

This is a complicated matter, and it is difficult to reconstruct the motives of participants because we are so far removed from them. Therefore, the situation can be discussed in general terms only, using 1 Kings 1, the information provided above, and the *IDB* articles. Mention should be made of Adonijah's legitimate and open claim, of the groups that supported and opposed him, and of the fact that dynastic succession had been thus far resisted. The fact that David allows it (regardless of which son succeeds him) is a radical departure from the procedure that brought him to the throne after the death of Saul. This shows the near inevitable centralization of power in human governments.

II. The method of resolution

This topic includes both the plot of Nathan with Bathsheba and Solomon in chapter 1 and the execution of Adonijah and Joab in chapter 2. Thus Solomon's assertiveness in killing both a brother and a cousin may be contrasted with David's reaction when his son Absalom sought to overthrow him (2 Samuel 15–18). This illustrates *the growing power and ruthlessness of monarchy in Israel,* which will later lead to deterioration of the traditional social and economic values of the society (see Lessons 8–13). Thus the importance of the religious tone with which Solomon will begin his reign (the present lesson) is underlined.

III. The text of the lesson and its contemporary application

You might proceed under the divisions of the biblical text that were outlined above in "The Scripture and the Main Question."

Helping Class Members Act

Discussion might include the following issues as the class members think about the implications of the lesson for their own lives.

1. David's deathbed charge to his son Solomon apparently affected the latter in the desired way. Are such scenes important or desirable in the transmission of Christian values? Do you know of any modern examples of it? Would you consider doing so with your own children?

2. In general, do you think that limitation of term of office is a good idea (comparable to dynastic change in ancient Israel)? Why or why not?

3. Is "wisdom" (for which Solomon prayed) an innate ability limited to some persons? Is it acquired by experience? Or is it a "spiritual gift" for which one might pray, as did Solomon? Do you think there are any contemporary leaders who understand it in the latter sense? Is it important, before setting out on a crucial venture, for any Christian (leader or not) to pray for guidance and strength, or is this mere piety with no realistic consequence?

Planning for Next Sunday

Often, great leaders are great reformers. Make a list of the ills in our society which need reform today.

Josiah: King of Reforms

Background Scripture: 2 Chronicles 34

The Main Question

The stated reasons for Israel's existence, according to the sacred stories that were recited to the people, were to be a blessing to all the families of the earth (see Lesson 1 in this unit) and to be the Lord's "priestly kingdom and a holy nation" (Exodus 19:6). Consequently, they were to have a distinctive social structure and form of governance (Lesson 5). The difficulty in maintaining this identity as the people of God, given the lure of the alien cultures in the "promised land" (Canaan), was anticipated by Moses in his farewell address (Deuteronomy 29–33) and in God's charge to Joshua (Lesson 3). Deterioration of the people's desire to maintain their distinctiveness and traditional values became evident at the time of Samuel: "We will have a king over us" (Lesson 5) and was even clearer by the time of Elijah (Lesson 9) and the prophets who came after him (Lessons 10–13).

The popularity of the fertility cults (centralized around the god known as Baal) and the vested interest of the bureaucracy in maintaining the governmental status quo slowed efforts to reform the society in accordance with its ancient ideals. Had Israel so accommodated itself to the prevailing (and alien) cultures of its neighbors that it was now impossible to recover? If not, what was the best hope of doing so? Prophetic exhortation to repent? A national collapse as divine discipline, leading to a purified remnant for a new beginning (Hosea; Lesson 11)? Or should there be a king who would use the power of the central government to purge the problems from its midst? This was the issue that faced the pious citizens of Judah in the mid-seventh century B.C. and that reached a resolution during the reign of King Josiah. How do these governmental crises of ancient Israel relate to the challenge of human governance in our time?

Selected Scripture

King James Version	New Revised Standard Version
2 Chronicles 34:2, 8, 14b-16a, 19, 21, 30-32	*2 Chronicles 34:2, 8, 14b-16a, 19, 21, 30-32*
2 And [Josiah] did that which was right in the sight of the LORD, and walked in the ways of David his father, and declined neither to the right hand, nor to the left.	2 [Josiah] did what was right in the sight of the LORD, and walked in the ways of his ancestor David; he did not turn aside to the right or to the left.
8 Now in the eighteenth year of his reign, when he had purged the land, and the house, he sent Shaphan the son of Azaliah, and Maa-	8 In the eighteenth year of his reign, when he had purged the land and the house, he sent Shaphan son of Azaliah, Maaseiah the governor

seiah the governor of the city, and Joah the son of Joahaz the recorder, to repair the house of the LORD his God.

of the city, and Joah son of Joahaz, the recorder, to repair the house of the LORD his God.

....

. . . Hilkiah the priest found a book of the law of the LORD given by Moses.

15 And Hilkiah answered and said to Shaphan the scribe, I have found the book of the law in the house of the LORD. And Hilkiah delivered the book to Shaphan.

16 And Shaphan carried the book to the king. . . .

. . . the priest Hilkiah found the book of the law of the LORD given through Moses. 15 Hilkiah said to the secretary Shaphan, "I have found the book of the law in the house of the LORD"; and Hilkiah gave the book to Shaphan. 16 Shaphan brought the book to the king. . . .

....

19 And it came to pass, when the king had heard the words of the law, that he rent his clothes.

19 When the king heard the words of the law he tore his clothes.

....

21 Go, inquire of the LORD for me, and for them that are left in Israel and in Judah, concerning the words of the book that is found: for great is the wrath of the LORD that is poured out upon us, because our fathers have not kept the word of the LORD, to do after all that is written in this book.

21 "Go, inquire of the LORD for me and for those who are left in Israel and in Judah, concerning the words of the book that has been found; for the wrath of the LORD that is poured out on us is great, because our ancestors did not keep the word of the LORD, to act in accordance with all that is written in this book."

....

30 And the king went up into the house of the LORD, and all the men of Judah, and the inhabitants of Jerusalem, and the priests, and the Levites, and all the people, great and small: and he read in their ears all the words of the book of the covenant that was found in the house of the LORD.

31 And the king stood in his place, and made a covenant before the LORD, to walk after the LORD, and to keep his commandments, and his testimonies, and his statutes, with all his heart, and with all his soul, to

30 The king went up to the house of the LORD, with all the people of Judah, the inhabitants of Jerusalem, the priests and the Levites, all the people both great and small; he read in their hearing all the words of the book of the covenant that had been found in the house of the LORD.

31 The king stood in his place and made a covenant before the LORD, to follow the LORD, keeping his commandments, his decrees, and his statutes, with all his heart and all his soul, to perform the words of the covenant that were written in this

perform the words of the covenant which are written in this book.

32 And he caused all that were present in Jerusalem and Benjamin to stand to it. And the inhabitants of Jerusalem did according to the covenant of God, the God of their fathers.

book. 32 Then he made all who were present in Jerusalem and in Benjamin pledge themselves to it. And the inhabitants of Jerusalem acted according to the covenant of God, the God of their ancestors.

Key Verse: **And Josiah took away all the abominations out of all the countries that pertained to the children of Israel, and made all that were present in Israel to serve, even to serve the Lᴏʀᴅ their God. And all his days they departed not from following the Lᴏʀᴅ, the God of their fathers. (2 Chronicles 34:33)**

Key Verse: **Josiah took away all the abominations from all the territory that belonged to the people of Israel, and made all who were in Israel worship the Lᴏʀᴅ their God. All his days they did not turn away from following the Lᴏʀᴅ the God of their ancestors. (2 Chronicles 34:33)**

As You Read the Scripture

2 Chronicles 34:1. Josiah's dates are 640–609 B.C. and thus he was well after the time of Solomon (Lesson 7), two centuries after Elijah (Lesson 9), and was a contemporary of Jeremiah (Lesson 13). He became king when his father was murdered (2 Kings 21:23; 2 Chronicles 33:24).

Verse 2. That he did "what was right" contrasts him with many of his predecessors who did "what was evil" (for example, his father, 33:22).

Verse 3. "To seek the God of his ancestor David" means that Josiah relied exclusively on the Lord as opposed to the fertility deities of Canaan and the gods of the Assyrians to whom his ancestors had become vassals. "Asherim" are cult objects associated with the worship of the Canaanite fertility goddess Asherah, sometimes described as the mother of Baal.

Verse 5. Jerusalem, as the capital city, was the place where altars to foreign deities, a part of diplomatic procedure, would be concentrated. Burning someone's bones deprived that person of burial and subsequent funerary rites, thus depriving him or her of rest in the underworld (realm of all dead). It was thus the ultimate act of contempt for an enemy.

Verse 6. That he carried out such reforms in the territory of Manasseh (and other tribes mentioned) shows Josiah's expanding power. These tribes were part of neighboring Israel, conquered by the Assyrians and incorporated into their empire in 733–721 B.C. A period of Assyrian weakness allowed Josiah to bring these tribes of Israel under Judean control.

Verse 8. The Temple in Jerusalem was sometimes described as the "house" where the deity resided. According to 2 Kings 22:3, Shaphan was the royal secretary. According to 2 Kings 22:4, the money had been collected at the Temple gates. Here all of Israel is depicted as having been solicited, and thereby the chronicler develops his theme that there is but one true Temple.

Verse 12. For Merarites and Kohathites as sub-groups of the Levites see Exodus 6:16. Yet another group (Gershonites) is not mentioned here. The use of musical instruments to create a coordinating rhythm for workers is well known in antiquity and in more recent times.

Verse 14. Here, much of Josiah's reform precedes the finding of "the book" in the Temple. In the earlier parallel account (2 Kings 22), the book inspires the reformation. Modern interpreters generally assume that the account in Kings (the Deuteronomic History, for which see Lesson 3) is the more reliable. The book is usually assumed to be the legislative "core" of what is now known as Deuteronomy 12–26. Part of the reason for this identification is that Josiah's subsequent actions correspond to the demands of that book.

Verse 22. It is remarkable, since this is the time of Jeremiah and Zephaniah, that they were passed over in favor of the prophetess Huldah. The reason is unclear. In any case, she must have been a person held in high respect. The "quarters" of Jerusalem reflect its geographical expansion.

Verse 24. The "curses" presumably are those outlined in Deuteronomy 27–28, upon those who have been disobedient to the traditional values.

The Scripture and the Main Question

The books of Kings and Chronicles, surveying the history of Israel and Judah from the beginning of monarchy onward, are nearly unrelieved in their condemnation of society. There has been a steady deterioration of the traditional social and religious values that had their beginnings in the Mosaic age at Mt. Sinai.

The major portion of blame is laid at the door of the monarchs, and that for several reasons. (1) Royal building projects (Temple, palace, fortifications, irrigation, and so on) necessitated taxation and sometimes involved forced labor, the latter especially of non-Israelite population elements (see 1 Kings 9:15-22). The indebtedness for building the Temple alone was 120 talents of gold (9:14). (2) The success of Solomon in the realms of diplomacy, economics, and education ("wisdom") led to an influx of ambassadors, caravaneers, and resident aliens, bringing with them the ethical values of their own societies and necessitating cultic facilities for them. Note how Solomon erected sanctuaries so that his "seven hundred princesses [wives] and three hundred concubines" could observe their ancestral religions (1 Kings 11:1-8). The problem would become especially severe during the reign of King Ahab because of the values of his foreign queen, Jezebel (see Lesson 9). (3) The development of international commerce, along with an emerging governmental bureaucracy, fostered the development of social and economic classes with attendant oppression of the poor (see Lessons 10 and 12). (4) When either Israel or Judah lost its autonomy by becoming the vassal of Assyria or Babylonia (see Lesson 13 for the latter), this necessitated oaths of allegiance to the gods of the conquerors and local cultic facilities for their officials and soldiers. See, for example, the actions of King Ahaz when he decided to seek Assyrian help against his local enemies.

> Ahaz sent messengers to King Tiglath-pileser of Assyria, saying, "I am your servant and your son. Come up, and rescue me. . . . " When King Ahaz went to Damascus to meet King Tiglath-pileser . . . he saw the altar that was at Damascus. King Ahaz sent . . . a model of the altar [back to Jerusalem]. (2 Kings 16:7, 10)

It is little wonder, then, that Josiah, as part of his reform, could

> bring out of the temple of the Lord all the vessels made for Baal, for Asherah, and for all the host of heaven. . . . He deposed the idolatrous priests whom the kings of Judah had ordained. . . . He broke down the houses of the male temple prostitutes that were in the house of the Lord. . . . [And] he removed the horses that the kings of Judah had dedicated to the sun [god]. (2 Kings 23:4-11)

It is little wonder as well that the author of 2 Chronicles, ever concerned to elevate his own country (Judah) at the expense of neighboring Israel, makes no mention of the fact that such abominations actually existed in the Temple in Jerusalem!

David, despite a few ugly lapses of his own (see, for example, 2 Samuel 11), became the historians' ideal, and Jeroboam I (who fostered the schism of the Davidic-Solomonic State) became the arch-villain. Thus there is the constant refrain that King So-and-so "did not do . . . as his father David had done" (see, for example, 2 Kings 16:2) or that King So-and-so "walked in the sins of Jeroboam" (see for example, 1 Kings 16:31). Few are the exceptions, given the self-evident necessity for the current practices. Even in those instances, one often reads an evaluation such as the following: "[Azariah] did what was right in the sight of the Lord. . . . Nevertheless the high places were not taken away" (2 Kings 15:3-4).

While some of the prophets likewise denounced such cultic apostasy (for example, Hosea; see Lesson 11), others concentrate on the social, economic, and judicial failures of the society (for example, Amos and Micah; see Lessons 10 and 12). Indeed, things became so serious that Jeremiah characterized the entire country as "a den of robbers" (Jeremiah 7:8-11). Even to criticize the government might subject one to the death penalty (Jeremiah 26:20-23).

It is doubtful that the majority of the citizens of Judah saw the need for reform—certainly not the large foreign population; not the diplomats who desired to promote the welfare of the state; not religious leaders who valued ecumenicity; not an educated elite who lauded "enlightenment"; not the bureaucrats who understandably desired to preserve their status and income; not the upwardly mobile whose advancement depended on "networking," which change would disrupt.

Those who desired thorough change must have had little realistic expectation of its coming to pass. After all, those who were capable of bringing it about were the very persons who had the greatest investment in the status quo. Even the few kings who had tried it found the results to be partial and of limited duration (for example Hezekiah, whose reign was interrupted by Assyrian invasion; see 2 Kings 18). Clearly, then, the slight and only hope was a ruler of unusual piety and determination, presented with an extraordinary circumstance that would rally public support, and this combined with a period of weakness by the Assyrian Empire to which allegiance had been sworn. Just such a happy configuration of events was the case when Josiah came to the throne of Judah.

While He Was Still a Boy

In contrast to the account in 2 Kings 22, which knows nothing of Josiah prior to his eighteenth year of reign, the chronicler records that Josiah's devotion to the Lord began to be manifest in his eighth year (that is, at age sixteen; see verse 3). How we are to account for this remains a mystery. Of his father (Amon) it is recorded, "He did what was evil in the sight of the LORD, as his father Manasseh had done" (33:22). Some positive influence may have been derived nonetheless from his grandfather Manasseh, who late in life humbled himself before the Lord (33:14-20). (This surprising reversal, of which the author of 2 Kings knows nothing, has given rise to the late intertestamental book known as The Prayer of Manasseh.) Any role played by Josiah's mother is also uncertain. According to 2 Kings 22:1, her name was Jedidah, daughter of Adaiah. This grandfather's name means "the Lord has adorned himself," possibly reflecting the fact that his family were pious worshipers of Israel's traditional deity. In any case, Josiah's name reflects such worship as well, since it means "the Lord gives (the child birth)." The fact that names reflect the faith of a parent is clear from the case of Solomon (see 2 Samuel 12:24-25). David chose the name *Solomon*, connected with the worship of a Canaanite deity, causing the prophet Nathan to propose instead that he be called Jedidiah, "the one whom the Lord loves."

In the Twelfth Year

The chronicler suggests that Josiah's famous reform began when he was twenty years old. This was six years before the scroll was found in the Temple (in his eighteenth year, verse 8). This also contrasts with the account in 2 Kings 22, wherein the discovery of the scroll plays a (the?) formative role in the king's motivation to transform his country. The chronicler apparently wants to depict Josiah's spiritual formation as being well advanced before that accidental discovery and as being rooted in his personal nature.

As Far As Naphtali . . . He Broke Down the Altars

Since this territory (and others listed) is not in Judah but in the former state of Israel (which had been incorporated into the Assyrian Empire in 733 B.C.; see 2 Kings 15:29; Isaiah 9:1), Josiah could not have so acted if the Assyrians had been vigilant in the maintenance of their provinces. Fortunately, they had entered into a period of neglect following the death of the energetic King Assurbanipal in 629 (627?) B.C., when Josiah was no more than thirteen years old. A revolt and the establishment of independence by Babylonia in 626 B.C. so preoccupied and weakened the Assyrians that they were forced to neglect their territories in Palestine.

Although the author of 2 Kings (23:12) alludes to actions against Assyrian cult objects ("the altars . . . of Ahaz"; see also 16:7-10), the chronicler does not do so, concentrating instead only on Canaanite religious influences. While this may reflect prudence on the part of Josiah, it is more likely that the chronicler does not wish to complicate his portrait of Josiah's character by introducing the extraneous element of Assyrian weakness. Thereby, the reform becomes entirely a matter of Josiah's character and the Lord's providence, apart from the fluctuations of ancient Near Eastern power groups.

To Repair the House of the Lord

It was customary practice for kings in the ancient Near East to repair temples near the beginning of their reign. This signalled to the citizenry that these kings were pious and worthy of obedience. (Notice such action by Solomon soon after his coronation, 1 Kings 5–8). The chronicler, by placing the reform prior to such construction, suggests that even the recovery of the "lost" book of Moses resulted from Josiah's piety.

I Have Found the Book of the Law

The scroll, found in the process of Temple repair, is likely the core of the book of Deuteronomy (chaps. 12–26, to which sermonic material based upon it as part of the reform was then added as chaps. 1–11; see above, "As You Read the Scripture"). Modern interpreters are inclined to believe that the scroll was composed from old Mosaic (and later) traditions that had been gathered during the reign of a previous (and less successful) reforming monarch, Hezekiah (715–687 B.C.). It had remained hidden (or neglected) in the Temple during the reigns of Manasseh and Amon, both of whom "did what was evil in the sight of the LORD" (2 Chronicles 33:2, 22). There it awaited the proper ruler, Josiah, who would make it into an instrument of national policy for reformation.

He Read in Their Hearing All the Words of the Book

The scroll was more than an instrument of royal policy: it was part of the sacred tradition (scripture), which the people in theory acknowledge as normative for their liturgical and ethical life. Josiah thus sought to mobilize the entire society to take seriously the implications of the story of God's gracious acts that brought Israel into existence and gave them "the promised land." (See William and Patricia Willimon's discussion of this episode in their enrichment article, "Meeting and Being Met by the Bible in Your Adult Class."

Helping Adults Become Involved

Preparing to Teach

Much information concerning the background of Josiah's reform has been presented above. If you desire to learn more, the following articles in *IDB* will be helpful: "Hezekiah," vol. 2, pp. 598-600; "Josiah," vol. 2, pp. 996-99); "Deuteronomy," vol. 1, pp. 831-38, especially section 8, "King Josiah and Deuteronomy." On the book of which our lesson is a part, see "Chronicles, I and II," vol. 1, pp. 572-80, which has several maps, or the *IB* on Chronicles, vol. 3.

Since this account has a parallel in 2 Kings 22–23, which is part of the Deuteronomic History, you might want to review what that history is all about (see Lesson 3).

Presentation of the lesson material to the class might take place under the following headings.

    I. The biblical story from Solomon to Josiah
   II. The historical setting of Josiah's reform
  III. The chronicler and his book
  IV. The text of the lesson

Introducing the Main Question

"The more things change, the more they stay the same" is commonly said of our society (and perhaps of others). Regardless of which political party came to power in the last election, the amount of significant change in policies, foreign and domestic, is usually small. Indeed, the system is so arranged that dramatic change (such as a new party might bring) is almost impossible.

Today's lesson is about a time in the history of Israel when drastic reformation was badly needed in order to preserve the identity of the "believing community." However, it was also one in which such change, because of political realities, seemed most unlikely. It turned out, however, that a single leader could indeed make a significant difference, provided that the people were willing to take their faith seriously, even if it were costly to do so.

Those of us who now hear the story, although we live in a radically different world, may ponder anew the issues of qualified leadership of "a Christian nation" and of our obligation as voters.

Developing the Lesson

I. The biblical story from Solomon (Lesson 7) to Josiah (Lesson 8)

Sketch, in broad outline, the major developments, including the following: Solomon becomes king (961 B.C.); the kingdom is divided at his death, forming Israel (the north) and Judah (the south) (922 B.C.); the prophet Elijah opposes Ahab and Jezebel (about 860 B.C.; Lesson 9); the ministry of Amos and Hosea begins (about 760 B.C.; Lessons 10 and 11); Israel loses Galilee and Transjordan to the Assyrians (733 B.C.; time of the prophet Isaiah); the end of the northern kingdom (Israel) because of Assyrian conquest (721 B.C.); the Assyrians attack Judah, but withdraw before capturing the city of Jerusalem (701 B.C.); the reign of King Josiah (640–609 B.C.).

II. The historical setting of Josiah's reform

Describe the religious and political situations, based on the information presented above and in the readings. Mention the influence of Canaanite fertility religions; the necessity to honor Assyrian gods as part of diplomacy and vassal status at the time; multiple sanctuaries around the country, which allowed uncontrollable departures from the traditional faith; groups that would be opposed to departure from the status quo; the general tendency of monarchs and bureaucrats to avoid religious values; and so on.

III. The chronicler and his book

Prior to this topic, you might say a few words about the other great history of the period: the Deuteronomic History (written to explain to the exiles in Babylonia why this fate had befallen them and to give them hope for the future). Reflect on 2 Kings 22:14-20 in this light.

You might want to outline briefly the organization of 1 and 2 Chronicles (see *IDB*, vol. 1, p. 572). Mention that it is post-exilic (the precise date often debated by modern interpreters; see *IDB*, vol. 2, p. 580), then say a few words about its purpose and theology (using the *IDB* article).

IV. The text of the lesson

You might proceed under the divisions of the biblical text that were outlined above in "The Scripture and the Main Question."

Helping Class Members Act

Discussion might include the following issues as the class members think about the implications of the lesson for their own lives.

1. How important is it that a child be taught to revere the Bible and to attend church regularly? Is it preferable to "go easy" in these matters until the child becomes an adult and can make her or his own "intelligent" choice? Is it possible that a parent's (or grandparent's) conscientiousness in the former case will not "bear fruit" until many years later, when the parent may not be alive to see it? Does God's providence sometimes have a long-term agenda that humans cannot perceive at the time?

2. Should Christian voters in the United States take into consideration (among other factors) the religious faith of candidates—not their mere use of religious language in campaign speeches or their cynical manipulation of religious issues in order to attract votes, but their "hard" commitment over the years? Why or why not? Is it your impression that voters actually are concerned about candidates from a religious point of view?

3. Should the Church seek to use the legislative power of the State to promote its socioeconomic agenda, just as Josiah used his power to purge his society of dangerous elements? Are some practices so detrimental to society that their advocates should be eliminated at any cost?

Planning for Next Sunday

Ask class members to think about the question "Who is a real prophet of God?"

UNIT III: THE PROPHETS' ROLES IN A DIVIDED KINGDOM

FIVE LESSONS   November 1–29

Kingship was inaugurated in Israel with high expectation that it would help to ensure justice within and security without (Unit II). In these regards there was some success (Lessons 6–7), although there were limitations so severe that King Josiah carried out a thorough reform (Lesson 8). Ultimately, participation in foreign intrigue and violation of loyalty oaths to superpowers Assyria and Babylonia led to the defeat and exile of both parts of the Davidic Kingdom—northern Israel and southern Judah.

The primary critics of social values during the monarchical period (if not of the monarchs themselves and their policies) were the prophets, persons (male and female) summoned by the deity in order to call attention to departure from Israel's ancient ideals, to urge reformation (repentance), to announce God's impending discipline (judgment), and to reflect on whatever hope there might be for the future beyond that judgment (usually exile). Their proclamation of what ought to be and of what the deity might do in order to bring it about was derived primarily from the sacred traditions (an early form of Genesis–Deuteronomy).

LESSON 9   NOVEMBER 1

Elijah: Prophet of Courage

Background Scripture: 1 Kings 17:1-7; 18

The Main Question

A standard theme of prophetic literature is the allure and the danger of the forces of nature, which the Canaanites designated by the divine title *ba'al* ("Lord," "Owner"). Since it was on these powers that human life depended, it is perhaps understandable that they were perceived as deities and thus to be treated with reverence, each with temples, liturgies, cultic personnel, ethical guidelines, and sacred traditions. Israel's normative thinkers, however, regarded such powers as nothing other than impersonal forces of nature, even if controlled by the one transcendent deity. It was unfitting, therefore, that humans, created "in the image of God" (Genesis 1:27), should make acquisition of the benefits of nature their ultimate concern—that is, functionally making them their "gods." The famous story of the contest between Elijah and the prophets of Baal on Mount Carmel is one of the basic texts in which that issue is presented. At the same time, Elijah is a paradigm of the strength of character that is sometimes necessary to resist the natural appeal and the societal desire for the blessings that Baal provides.

The worship of false gods continues even in our own day. How can we find the wisdom to resist idolatry?

Selected Scripture

King James Version	New Revised Standard Version
1 Kings 18:17-18, 20-24, 36-39	*1 Kings 18:17-18, 20-24, 36-39*
17 And it came to pass, when Ahab saw Elijah, that Ahab said unto him, Art thou he that troubleth Israel?	17 When Ahab saw Elijah, Ahab said to him, "Is it you, you troubler of Israel?" 18 He answered, "I have not troubled Israel; but you have, and your father's house, because you have forsaken the command-ments of the Lord and followed the Baals.
18 And he answered, I have not troubled Israel; but thou, and thy father's house, in that ye have for-saken the commandments of the Lord, and thou hast followed Baalim.	

20 So Ahab sent unto all the children of Israel, and gathered the prophets together unto mount Carmel.

21 And Elijah came unto all the people, and said, How long halt ye between two opinions? if the LORD be God, follow him: but if Baal, then follow him. And the people answered him not a word.

22 Then said Elijah unto the people, I, even I only, remain a prophet of the LORD; but Baal's prophets are four hundred and fifty men.

23 Let them therefore give us two bullocks; and let them choose one bullock for themselves, and cut it in pieces, and lay it on wood, and put no fire under: and I will dress the other bullock, and lay it on wood, and put no fire under:

24 And call ye on the name of your gods, and I will call on the name of the LORD: and the God that answereth by fire, let him be God. And all the people answered and said, It is well spoken.

....

36 And it came to pass at the time of the offering of the evening sacrifice, that Elijah the prophet came near, and said, LORD God of Abraham, Isaac, and of Israel, let it be known this day that thou art God in Israel, and that I am thy servant, and that I have done all these things at thy word.

37 Hear me, O LORD, hear me, that this people may know that thou art the LORD God, and that thou hast turned their heart back again.

38 Then the fire of the LORD fell, and consumed the burnt sacrifice, and the wood, and the stones, and the dust, and licked up the water that was in the trench.

39 And when all the people saw it, they fell on their faces: and they

20 So Ahab sent to all the Israelites, and assembled the prophets at Mount Carmel. 21 Elijah then came near to all the people, and said, "How long will you go limping with two different opinions? If the LORD is God, follow him; but if Baal, then follow him." The people did not answer him a word. 22 Then Elijah said to the people, "I, even I only, am left a prophet of the LORD; but Baal's prophets number four hundred fifty. 23 Let two bulls be given to us; let them choose one bull for themselves, cut it in pieces, and lay it on the wood, but put no fire to it; I will prepare the other bull and lay it on the wood, but put no fire to it. 24 Then you call on the name of your god and I will call on the name of the LORD; the god who answers by fire is indeed God." All the people answered, "Well spoken!"

....

36 At the time of the offering of the oblation, the prophet Elijah came near and said, "O LORD, God of Abraham, Isaac, and Israel, let it be known this day that you are God in Israel, that I am your servant, and that I have done all these things at your bidding. 37 Answer me, O LORD, answer me, so that this people may know that you, O LORD, are God, and that you have turned their hearts back." 38 Then the fire of the LORD fell and consumed the burnt offering, the wood, the stones, and the dust, and even licked up the water that was in the trench. 39 When all the people saw it, they fell on their faces and said, "The LORD indeed is God; the LORD indeed is God."

said, The LORD, he is the God; the
LORD, he is the God.

Key Verse: And Elijah came unto
all the people, and said, How long
halt ye between opinions? if the
LORD be God, follow him: but if
Baal, then follow him. And the
people answered him not a word.
(1 Kings 18:21)

Key Verse: Elijah then came near
to all the people, and said, "How
long will you go limping with two
different opinions? If the LORD is
God, follow him; but if Baal, then
follow him." (1 Kings 18:21)

As You Read the Scripture

1 Kings 17:1. Ahab was ruler of the Northern Kingdom (Israel) during
the period 968–860 B.C.. He was an able and energetic leader.

Verse 4. Literature from many lands relates that a hero was fed by beasts
or birds, as Elijah is here by ravens.

18:2. Samaria is the capital city, the residence of the monarch.

Verse 4. Jezebel is the daughter of the king of Tyre (an ancient domain to
the north). A devotee of her nation's traditional religions, she is hence
hostile to the religion of Israel.

Since caves in the area are rather small, it seems unlikely that such groups
of prophets could be separated securely in a single location. The Hebrew
word can be understood in a generic sense, however, and hence the REB's
"caves."

Verse 5. Concern for the horses and mules is due to their value to the
military.

Verse 12. Obadiah's fear is that since Elijah's travels have been
unpredictable (". . . whither I know not"), it will do no good to report to the
king that he has been spotted.

Verse 19. Asherah is a Canaanite goddess, and in some ancient texts she is
the mother of Baal.

Verse 21. "Limping" may be a reference to a cultic dance performed by
the worshipers of Baal. Note the use of the term in verse 26.

Verse 27. The fact that Elijah taunts the priests of Baal at noon has led
some modern interpreters to suspect that the "baal" involved was a solar
deity who would then be directly overhead.

The exact nature of the references to Baal's absence is obscure. Some
modern interpreters see cultic allusions, for example to the Baal of Tyre as
the originator of practical wisdom and invention ("he is musing"). Others
suspect a euphemism for defecation ("he has gone aside").

Verse 28. The practice of self-laceration as part of worship is otherwise
attested in the ancient Near East and in some sects of modern Islam (the
dervishes). In some ancient rites, it was used to induce an ecstatic state that
led to prophetic utterance.

Verses 32-35. Presumably, the saturation of the area with water was to
prevent fraud in the ignition of fire, although some modern interpreters
have suggested that a rite of imitative magic (to induce rain) was intended
by Elijah.

Verse 36. "The time of the offering of the oblation" may refer to the practice of the Temple in Jerusalem. In the much later Second Temple, this was about three P.M.

Verse 39. The cry of the people ("The LORD indeed is God") is likely not a spontaneous composition, but an ancient traditional liturgical chant.

Verse 43. The servant looks toward the sea (Mediterranean) because it lies directly west, the direction from which the fall rains come. Sevenfold repetition is a staple of ancient Near Eastern literature.

Verse 45. "Jezreel," rather than designating the great and fertile valley, here indicates the town where King Ahab had a residence (see 1 Kings 21).

Verse 46. While it is possible that a runner, by direct route, might outdistance a chariot that would follow a winding road, the real intent of the text is to show the effect of Elijah's euphoric state after his triumph. The prophet apparently wished to be the first to break the "bad news" to Queen Jezebel and to be there to support Ahab in the latter's newfound trust in the traditional faith (Yahwism).

The Scripture and the Main Question

In time of crisis, people tend to reach for gods who promise to deliver. King Ahab, for reasons both economic and political, sought an alliance with the successful Phoenician coastal cities to his north. Ahab hoped to overcome his royal troubles with a marriage to Jezebel, daughter of King Itto-baal of Tyre and Sidon. (The marriage may well have been arranged by Ahab's energetic and able father, Omri. See 1 Kings 16:29-31.) She was astute, strong willed (chap. 21), and utterly devoted to the religion of her family. Hence Ahab erected a sanctuary in which she might worship (16:32-33), and she financed an extensive cultic apparatus (18:19). Such royal patronage undoubtedly facilitated a willingness, at all levels of the society, to forsake the traditional religion of Israel in favor of ecumenicity.

Baal, for the Canaanites (including their northern branch, the Phoenicians), was the god of rainfall, called also "the Thunderer" and "the Cloud Rider." Thus he was the personification of that force of nature upon which agricultural fertility and hence human well-being depended.

Biblical Hebrew has no equivalent for "It is raining." One could say only, "The Lord (Yahweh) makes it rain." The easiest way to demonstrate this reality, suggested Elijah, is for the annual cycle of rainfall, which is attributed to an annual struggle between Baal and his enemies, to be interrupted and then reinstituted by the word of a prophet of Yahweh. Otherwise put, there is no Baal, and humans who center their lives on the acquisition of his benefits are deluded, irreligious, and dangerous to the values of Israel's traditional faith.

Neither Dew Nor Rain . . . Except by My Word

Nothing could make it clearer than this that there is no divine force in the realm of nature that affects human welfare apart from God, in whose name Elijah speaks. The resultant drought was of unparalleled proportions, so much so that even the brook to which Elijah had been sent dried up. This drought is recorded in other sources; therefore, there is reason to believe in the historicity of the text at this point.

Go, Present Yourself to Ahab; I Will Send Rain

To remove any doubt, Elijah announces not only the beginning of the great drought but also its termination. Again he seeks to end the false religion that Queen Jezebel fosters. In the meanwhile, Elijah has had to hide for his life, lest his execution remove the final demonstration of the lesson the deity has in mind.

Is It You, You Troubler of Israel?

The king now reveals his ultimate concern: the economic collapse that the famine is producing. From his point of view, then, it is Elijah who is to blame. Thus he has failed to see the deeper problem that his tolerance for Canaanite religion has fostered. Note how, a bit later, he will be able to seize the property of one of his subjects (and execute an innocent man in the process), something that previous kings of Israel did not have the power to do. The entire socioeconomic fabric of the society is being changed, and Elijah's evaluation of the king is "I have not troubled Israel; but you have, and your father's house, because you have forsaken the commandments of the LORD and followed the Baals" (18:18). God's prophet will not allow the king to look for a scapegoat for national troubles.

Limping with Two Different Opinions

The populace, ever desirous of playing it safe, wants to "have their cake and eat it too." What if there is actually something to Baalism. Suppose my crops fail as a consequence of my neglect of the liturgical practices of my Canaanite neighbors? The ideals of Yahwism are one thing, but taking chances on my economic status is quite another! When the prophet reminds them that the two religious systems are opposites (one cannot hold them both at one time; to accept Baalism is automatically to reject Yahwism), they maintain a discreet, noncommittal, and cautious silence. It is better not to choose sides unless one is absolutely forced to do so, apparently. In this discouraging circumstance, the prophet stands resolute: "I, even I only, am left . . . "). His life is possibly on the line if he loses the contest, and yet the stakes for his society are high enough that he does not flinch. The people remain noncommittal until they see how things turn out, and then they begin to chant traditional liturgical confessions, turning in a frenzy against those whom they previously followed.

But the Hand of the Lord Was on Elijah

Elated by the implications of the event for the rejuvenation of the traditional faith and values, Elijah is capable of an extraordinary physical feat. He desires to be present when Queen Jezebel learns what has happened. Little does he know that she will be unmoved by it and in fact will threaten his life (19:2), and that shallow public support for him will not suffice to prevent it. This plunges him into great despair and sends him to the sacred mountain (Horeb/Sinai) in order to examine the foundations of his faith (19:4-18).

What was the significance of this story to the exiles in Babylonia who heard it as part of the Deuteronomic History? (For a review of the purposes of that history, see Lesson 3 of this unit.) They lived at a time when the faithful were few, when they were under a hostile government (comparable to that of Jezebel), when the official religion was opposed to their own, and when leaders of courage were almost nonexistent. Yet, even though some exiles must have felt (as Elijah did) that they were alone, surely there were others who maintained the faith (comparable to those whom Obadiah hid in the caves). The future may depend on a single courageous individual of the Elijah-type, thus causing self-examination among the audience. A return to the homeland would seem like a miracle, and yet, suggests the story, miracles do happen! Such a miracle came to be forty-eight years after the Exile began, when the Babylonians, masters of the world, were defeated by the Persians, and King Cyrus issued his famous edict allowing the exiles to go free (2 Chronicles 36:22-23; Ezra 1:1-4).

What are the idolatries in our own day for which courageous prophets may be needed?

Helping Adults Become Involved

Preparing to Teach

It may be helpful to familiarize yourself with the religion of Jezebel's ancestors. Useful will be the following articles in the *IDB:* "Canaanites," section 6 ("Literature and Religion") in vol. 1, pp. 497-98; "Asherah" in the same volume, pp. 250-52; and "Baal" in the same volume, pp. 328-29.

Seek to understand Elijah's place within the developing prophetic movement by reading section VI.B.1 in the article "The History of the Religion of Israel," in *IDB*, vol. 1, pp. 315-17, or preferably by reading the article "Elijah the Prophet" in *IDB*, vol. 2, pp. 88-90.

The lesson might proceed under the following headings.

  I. Elijah in the context of Israelite history
 II. The threat of Baalism and its modern parallels
III. The text of the lesson in relation to idolatrous temptations
     in our own day

Introducing the Main Question

Begin today's class with the question, "Do you believe in God?" This is a common question and one asked in a national poll a few years ago. I suspect that the question was understood largely in rational terms: "How do you think that it all began? Does creation demand a Creator?" It may be argued, however, that one's "god" is more than the answer to intellectual speculation. In actuality, it is that which determines our values and actions "when the chips are down." If *god* may be defined as a person's "ultimate concern," then such "gods" include social status, power over others, sexual pleasure, wealth, and a number of other realities that the class members can name (and have enjoyed!).

Now tell the class how, in the religion of Israel's Canaanite neighbors, overwhelming desire for economic security and power was represented by Baal, the supposed god who was manifest in the rains upon which the fertility of nature depended. Baal was, therefore, a power that, if properly worshiped, increased the crops and ultimately "put two chariots in every garage." To worship Baal was to make the acquisition of his benefits into the paramount goal of one's life and to allow their accumulation to determine one's ethical values.

The increasing prevalence of Baalism in ancient Israel was a mortal threat to the social, economic, and judicial aspects of the traditional religion (Yahwism). Thus the prophets often denounced this Canaanite value system and those who allowed it to make inroads into their faith. In today's lesson, we will see that conflict at work in the confrontation between King Ahab and the prophet Elijah.

Developing the Lesson

I. Elijah in the context of Israelite history

The rise to power of the dynasty of King Omri of Israel brought a period of stability and prosperity. (The dates of this dynasty of four kings are 876–842 B.C.) The primary external danger was the expansion of Assyrian power from the east (around the so-called "Fertile Crescent"; see the Oxford Annotated NRSV, Map 6). Omri's goal was to forge an alliance of small kingdoms in Syria and Palestine which would be capable of holding the Assyrians at bay. In the case of the king of Tyre (Phoenicia) the alliance included the marriage of the children of the two kings: Ahab of Israel and Jezebel of Tyre. This alliance was effective enough that in 853 B.C. the two nations turned back the Assyrian army at the famous battle of Qarqar. King Ahab contributed two thousand chariots and ten thousand foot soldiers on that occasion.

II. The threat of Baalism and its modern parallels

The alliance with Tyre brought with it official patronage of Baalism, thus encouraging the local citizens who were already attracted to it by their Canaanite neighbors. The problems with this situation, from an orthodox Yahwistic point of view, included the following: (1) Alleged "gods" had played no role in Israel's history of salvation and thus were irrelevant to the existence of "the people of God." Loyalty to them was, furthermore, disloyalty to the deity who *had* acted on their behalf. In any case, worship of many gods (polytheism) rather than of one (monotheism) is an unnecessary fragmentation of one's life and values. (2) Baalism included liturgical celebrations and ethical practices that were the opposite of Israel's traditional values (for example, sexual activity as part of some worship services). (3) Since rainfall is a mere natural process, it is not appropriate that humans regard it as a deity. All such processes have been brought into being and are under the governance of a single Creator.

To worship Baal was to put the desire for security above all else, to desire to possess and to prosper at any cost and at the sacrifice of other values. It is to confuse the Creator with the benefits of creation, to confuse the Giver with the gifts of nature.

III. The text of the lesson in relation to idolatrous temptations in our own day

You might proceed under the divisions of the biblical text as outlined above in "The Scripture and the Main Question."

FIRST QUARTER

Helping Class Members Act

Discussion might include the following issues as class members think about the implications of the lesson for their lives.

1. In a desperate national crisis (for example, invasion, famine, or epidemic), Canaanites would occasionally practice human sacrifice as a means of indicating devotion to the deity. Thereby, it was hoped, the lot of society as a whole would be improved. Our society seeks to promote prosperity through lax pollution controls, relaxation of safety features in the construction of automobiles, raising the speed limit, and so on, even if in doing so lives will be lost. Being cost-effective is the rationale. "Isn't it better a few people die than the economy be retarded?" Does this mean that Baal, rather than being an ancient superstition, is alive and well under the guise of Gross National Product?

2. What are some of the instances in our society in which a monetary value is placed on human life?

3. Elijah demonstrated to ancient Israel that Baal was fallible (no rain for three years) and thus those persons whose ultimate faith was in Baal's benefits faced a crisis of meaning. Is this comparable to an economic crisis in our own society? Is it cruel for the Church to expose our false gods?

4. Is the old saying true that times of prosperity (comparable to that of Ahab's time) lead to a relaxation of traditional values (for example, insensitivity to the poor)? "If persons cannot succeed in this 'Land of Opportunity,' then it is their own fault!" In order to reduce the budget for school lunches for disadvantaged children, let catsup count as one of their vegetables. Take away the Social Security benefits of the sick and the elderly, and then force them to go to court for years at their own expense to prove that they are entitled. Believe that, under such circumstances, no truly needy person will be harmed. In such circumstances, has Baal become God?

As the Teacher from Nazareth would put it later, ultimate loyalty belongs to God alone, and that excludes Baal: "No one can serve two masters" (Matthew 6:24).

We shall be known by our "gods."

Planning for Next Sunday

We move forward about a century to the time of the prophet Amos. His concerns are related to those of Elijah, although they are more specific: economic and judicial injustice, perhaps springing in part from the values of Canaanite society (worship of Baal). Perhaps the class can read the entirety of his little book (nine chapters), noting his passionate concern for the poor and the oppressed.

Amos: Prophet of Justice

Background Scripture: Amos 2:6–3:2; 5:24

The Main Question

Who are God's people? How is a community that identifies itself historically with the biblical faith to be recognized as such? Is it because of a certain ethnic or racial membership? Is it a given liturgical style? Is it mental assent to and recitation of a distinctive creed (for example, "Jesus Christ is Lord")? Is it adherence to specific social, economic, and political ideals? Is it possible for such a community to so adopt the agenda of the world that it is externally indistinguishable from its neighbors?

What are the proper implications of such a community's sense of "election" in terms of accountability? Does such a status guarantee moral sensitivity? Does it presuppose a greater tolerance of its fallibilities on God's part? Is its status a perpetual commitment to historical continuity, so that there will always be an "Israel" (Church or Synagogue)?

The book of Amos does not address these questions abstractly, but only in terms of the Israel of its day. Therein, the prophet has very clear ideas about what the answers must be. Parallels between his time and our own make it possible to bridge the gap between the past and the present and thus bring his analysis and criticism to bear on modern churches and their members. This will be your challenge as you lead today's class.

Selected Scripture

King James Version	New Revised Standard Version
Amos 2:6-12	*Amos 2:6-12*

6 Thus saith the Lord; For three transgressions of Israel, and for four, I will not turn away the punishment thereof; because they sold the righteous for silver, and the poor for a pair of shoes;	6 Thus says the Lord:
	For three transgressions of Israel,
	   and for four, I will not revoke
	   the punishment;
	because they sell the righteous
	   for silver,
	   and the needy for a pair of
	   sandals—

7 That pant after the dust of the earth on the head of the poor, and turn aside the way of the meek: and a man and his father will go in unto the same maid, to profane my holy name:	7 they who trample the head of
	   the poor into the dust of
	   the earth,
	   and push the afflicted out of
	   the way;
	father and son go in to the same
	   girl,
	   so that my holy name is
	   profaned;

8 And they lay themselves down upon clothes laid to pledge by every altar, and they drink the wine of the condemned in the house of their god.

9 Yet destroyed I the Amorite before them, whose height was like the height of the cedars, and he was strong as the oaks; yet I destroyed his fruit from above, and his roots from beneath.

10 Also I brought you up from the land of Egypt, and led you forty years through the wilderness, to possess the land of the Amorite.

11 And I raised up of your sons for prophets, and of your young men for Nazarites. Is it not even thus, O ye children of Israel? saith the LORD.

12 But ye gave the Nazarites wine to drink; and commanded the prophets, saying, Prophesy not.

Amos 3:2
2 You only have I known of all the families of the earth: therefore I will punish you for all your iniquities.

Key Verse: **But let judgment run down as waters, and righteousness as a mighty stream. (Amos 5:24)**

8 they lay themselves down beside every altar
on garments taken in pledge;
and in the house of their God they drink
wine bought with fines they imposed.

9 Yet I destroyed the Amorite before them,
whose height was like the height of cedars,
and who was as strong as oaks;
I destroyed his fruit above,
and his roots beneath.

10 Also I brought you up out of the land of Egypt,
and led you forty years in the wilderness,
to possess the land of the Amorite.

11 And I raised up some of your children to be prophets
and some of your youths to be nazirites.
Is it not indeed so, O people of Israel?
says the LORD.

12 But you made the nazirites drink wine,
and commanded the prophets, saying, "You shall not prophesy."

Amos 3:2
2 You only have I known
of all the families of the earth;
therefore I will punish you
for all your iniquities.

Key Verse: **But let justice roll down like waters, and righteousness like an everflowing stream. (Amos 5:24)**

As You Read the Scripture

Amos 2:6. The introductory phrase, "Thus says the LORD," makes it clear that the prophet is not issuing his private social criticism, but rather is bringing the sacred tradition with its ideals to bear on contemporary society. This distinction is then reinforced with sporadic statements, "says the LORD" (2:11, 16).

"Israel" here means the Northern Kingdom (the ten tribes who broke away at Solomon's death; see 1 Kings 12), rather than the entirety of Jacob's (Israel's) twelve descendants. For the Southern Kingdom (Judah), see 2:45.

The "punishment" is not here stated, but begins to be spelled out in 2:13-16 and especially elsewhere in the book.

Verse 9. The Amorites were a major population element in Canaan prior to the Israelite settlement there.

Verse 11. Nazirites were an order of persons, usually young males, who dedicated themselves to a period of special, strict conduct. Avoidance of wine (v. 12) was not because the drink was innately harmful (as in modern prohibition) but as a form of discipline.

Amos 3:1. That a separate prophetic speech begins here (perhaps given at a different time and place than the previous one) is made clear by the opening phrase, "Hear this word. . . . " In recognition of this, the chapter division was placed here by medieval interpreters (beginning with the Latin Bible), and the NRSV translation committee has left a wide space before it.

Verse 2. Some modern interpreters think that the first part of the verse was originally intended as a question: "[You say that] you only have I known of all the families of the earth?" With that self-understanding, the people should then accept the judgment that follows.

The word *known* means more than acquaintance here, suggesting affection (see Jeremiah 1:5). The wording of the NRSV inadvertently implies that the deity has concern for Israel only. Equally accurate grammatically and preferable in terms of God's providence is the NAB's: "You alone have I favored, more than all the families of the earth."

The Scripture and the Main Question

Who are God's people?

According to the sacred traditions handed down from antiquity at the time of the prophet Amos (in the eighth century B.C.), God had chosen a community through which "shall all families of the earth be blessed" (Genesis 12:3 KJV), with the expectation that "you shall be for me a priestly kingdom and a holy nation" (Exodus 19:6).

God's expectation of this people, in terms of liturgical and ethical behavior, had then been spelled out at great length in the revelation at Mt. Sinai (Exodus 20–Numbers 6). So important were these expectations—and especially the ones concerning economic, social, and governmental behavior—that Moses, standing on the border of the "promised land," reminds the people of them at great length (Deuteronomy 12–26), including sermonic exhortation (chaps. 1–11), reflections on obedience and disobedience (chaps. 27–28), and final advice (chaps. 29–34).

To maintain the faith while the community is young and struggling is one thing; to do so in the long run, in times of security and prosperity, is quite another. Carelessness and a false sense of identity become especially likely if the purpose of one's election begins to shift. Whereas formerly that election might be understood in terms of obedience, service, and distinctiveness from one's neighboring states, now it could come to be understood in terms of privilege, pride, and security. Such a time of misunderstanding was that of the prophet Amos, for whom the question to be posed of Israel is "How well are we doing in terms of the ancient ideals of the people of God, and what is the deity to do if it appears that those ideals cannot be recovered?"

FIRST QUARTER

For Three Transgressions . . . and for Four

Israel is singled out for evaluation by the deity only after a series of denunciations of surrounding states (1:3–2:5), most of whom have traditionally been enemies and whom Israelites would have considered immoral by comparison to themselves. This is the prophet's way of making clear that Israel is not distinguishable from its neighbors in terms of humanity and justice. This would be especially reprehensible in view of the long history of warnings by God's spokespersons that the chosen community must not adopt the callous policies of other groups (for example, see Leviticus 18:24-30).

The introductory formula ("For three . . . and for four . . . "; see also 1:3, 6, 9, 11, 13; 2:1, 4) is not a literal count of transgressions, but rather means something like "For offenses without number. . . . "

This, the prophet's initial indictment (with many more to follow in the book) concerns taking unfair advantage of the needy through the judicial system. The "righteous" (a term here more akin to the legally innocent who have not broken any law) are sold into servitude for indebtedness, even for minimal sums. (Slavery, as in the pre-Civil War South, is not intended.) The judicial system is then utilized (or perverted) in a way that favors the powerful; rather than being used to protect the powerless, it is being used to exploit them ("they . . . turn aside the way of the afflicted"; NAB, "they . . . force the lowly out of the way").

The basis for the prophet's objection to a man and his father's going in to have intercourse with the same girl is unclear. Such a situation is not prohibited in Israelite legal traditions—at least as they survive in the Bible. Is this an indentured servant of whom they take advantage? In any case, special sensitivity to women who are powerless in sexual matters is called for.

So callous has become the population, so adept are they at separating the legal from the moral (from justice as outlined in the ancient ideals), that one can go to worship in garments taken as security for a loan. (Debtors would use other items for security if they had them, and thus the present situation denotes the seriousness of their need. Israelite law forbade the retention of such items overnight, lest the debtor suffer because of their loss during the evening chill; see Exodus 22:26-27.) Spreading such garments beside the altar clearly indicates an intention of spending the night, and thus presumably a violation of the regulation. Apparently, those unable to pay a fine in cash might do so with wine, and this financial status is of such little concern to the creditor that the beverage would be consumed at the sanctuary. The incongruity of such worship is so striking to the prophet that he can describe it only by making an analogy to the crime of rebellion by a servant against the master (NRSV, "transgression").

Yet I Destroyed the Amorite

A brief account of God's gracious and unmerited action on behalf of Israel at the time of settlement in Canaan under the leadership of Joshua is now given. That land might well have remained in the possession of its earlier inhabitants (including the Amorites), or indeed the descendants of Jacob could have remained slaves in Egypt as they had been for a long time. Nonetheless, deliverance from bondage and the gift of "a good and broad land, a land flowing with milk and honey" (Exodus 3:8) were granted them although they had done nothing to deserve them. A proper sense of gratitude for this kindness should have produced obedience to the traditional norms of the community, but the result has been, instead, the perverse behavior outlined in verses 6-8. Prior voices of opposition to such ingratitude have been ignored or suppressed ("[You] commanded the prophets, saying, 'You shall not prophesy' "). The society should be under no illusion, therefore, that its policies are proper and in conformity with the ideals for which it was founded. Rather, it is now openly and knowingly in rebellion and has set itself up as an authority in the definition of what is "right."

So, I Will Press You Down

The indictment of rebellion and failure to be the true Israel is now finished. The deity, speaking through the prophet, now moves to a sentencing of punishment. This pronouncement uses the language of invasion by an enemy, resulting in terror and flight by the local population. The ultimate cause of such an impending event is stated clearly, in theological terms, from the outset. It will not be just one of those things that happen, but rather will reflect the judgment of God. This is reinforced by the formal way in which the pronouncement ends (" . . . says the LORD"), thereby making it clear that the prophet is not speaking on his own authority or giving a private societal analysis.

Hear This Word . . . O People

God's vested interest in the activity of the community is here made clear: " . . . the whole family that I brought up out of the land of Egypt." God, therefore, has a right to be concerned about the present and to take responsive action in the immediate future.

In what ways might God be leading our churches to be more faithful today?

Helping Adults Become Involved

Preparing to Teach

As is usually the case, it will be helpful to understand the situation to which the biblical text was originally addressed. Amos's proclamations seem to have taken place during a short period of time around the year 760 B.C. This was during a period of great prosperity under one of Israel's most able monarchs, Jeroboam II (786–746 B.C.). Brief information about him may be found in the article "Jeroboam" in IDB, vol. 2, p. 842. (Note: Do not confuse him with the prior discussion of Jeroboam I.) It will also be useful to have a general idea of Amos's background, the form of the book, and his overall thought, which may be obtained in IDB, vol. 1, pp. 116-21. Or you might want to read the general introduction to the book of Amos in IB, vol. 6. Less information is available in the "Introduction" in IOCB, p. 465.

Presentation to the class might take place under the following headings.

FIRST QUARTER

    I. The prophet's historical situation
   II. What we know about Amos the person
  III. The biblical account and its implications for the church today

Introducing the Main Question

Your introduction can take place in a straightforward fashion, using the materials presented above as the lesson opens. You might begin by asking, Who are God's people? How do we identify the "people of God"? Write the class members' responses on the chalkboard or newsprint. Their responses can serve as a catalyst for today's lesson.

Developing the Lesson

I. The prophet's historical situation

Remind the class of the division of the Davidic-Solomonic Kingdom, which took place in 922 B.C., resulting in Israel (the Northern Kingdom) and Judah (the Southern Kingdom). Beginning with the dynasty of Jehu in 842 B.C., a period of security and prosperity began for Israel, reaching a pinnacle during the reign of Jeroboam II. We all know that periods of prosperity often lead to competition for resources, the widening of social and economic classes, materialism, and a neglect of traditional values. This was the situation in which Amos found himself, and he was a pioneer in thinking through the implications of such faithlessness for the future of the community God had called.

II. What we know about Amos the person

From your background reading, you might learn (and want to point out) that:

A. Amos was a Judean, preaching across the border in Israel. Criticism from "outsiders" is often resented, and this is reflected in the confrontation reported in 7:10-13.

B. Amos was not called as a prophet when he was a child, in contrast to Jeremiah (see Jeremiah chapter 1). Rather, he was an adult layman who felt compelled to provide insight and leadership during a time of declining spiritual values (see 7:14-15).

C. Amos's prior profession consisted of harvesting an inferior variety of fig that grew on the coastal plain ("sycamore trees," 7:14; you might want to read the article "Sycamore" in IDB, vol. 4, pp. 470-71), and in caring for sheep in the barren semi-desert of Judah near Tekoa (1:1). He was thus what would now be called a migrant farmer, working part of the year in agriculture near the coast and part of the year with flocks in the mountains. His low socioeconomic status may be reflected as well in the fact that his father's name is not given when he is introduced at 1:1 (contrast Hosea 1:1; Jeremiah 1:1; Isaiah 1:1). This may have contributed to his passion for social justice, which is perhaps the strongest among the biblical prophets. One who has experienced injustice and an economic struggle is uniquely qualified to speak to those realities from a theological perspective.

III. The biblical account and its implicatins for the church today

You might proceed under the divisions of the biblical text that have been outlined above under the heading "The Scripture and the Main Question."

Helping Class Members Act

Discussion might focus on parallels between Amos's society and our own. Since these parallels are so numerous, class members will have little difficulty in pointing them out, provided that the self-indictment in doing so does not make them uncomfortable (but then, it should!). The first segment of discussion might focus on the wall that our society tries to erect between what is allowable and legal (especially in the realm of economics) versus the values taught by the Church. Since it is sometimes said (even by a recent president of the United States) that people are poor because they want to be poor—that is, anybody can "get ahead" in this "land of opportunity" if he or she wants to—need one feel an obligation to assist the poor? Should we avoid telling merchants what we will pay for their products, since they might be willing to sell it for much less than it is worth, and we can give them a good "skinning"? Have we ever justified a "shady deal" or taken advantage of a person in commerce by saying, "Business is business"? Recall some basic rules of American life: When the going gets tough, the tough get going! Thou shalt not interfere with thy neighbor's God-given right to make a buck (even if it destroys the quality of a neighborhood with pollution, traffic, or even eviction for construction). If we don't do this, someone else will!

Are Christians often indistinguishable from others in these regards (as was ancient Israel from its neighbors)? Have we not so adapted the values of the Bible to those of the surrounding culture that not even attendance at worship causes a twinge of conscience? It is reported that many of the guards and other employees at Nazi death camps were "practicing" Christians in the sense that they regularly were present in church to hear the gospel proclaimed and to receive the sacraments.

The second segment of discussion might focus on Amos's assumption about the basis for moral action: Because of what God had previously done for Israel—gracious actions that were undeserved ("Yet I destroyed the Amorite . . . I brought you up out of the land of Egypt"), the people ought to respond with gratitude and obedience. Therefore, should members of the Church in the present be moral in the hope of reward or punishment: "God will bless you real good!" and give you life after death. Or should they think about what the Church and the Synagogue have contributed to the quality of life of their country and community and to their personal development (God still at work for "Israel") and resolve to repay their indebtedness to divine graciousness with gracious acts of their own?

Planning for Next Sunday

Next week's topic will be the thought of Amos's contemporary, the prophet Hosea. Amos and Hosea share the same historical situation, so you will already have learned that background. Ask the class to read the book of Hosea and think about the ways the two prophets are alike and different.

Hosea: Prophet of God's Love

Background Scripture: Hosea 1:1-3; 3:1-2; 6:4-6; 11:1-4

The Main Question

What is the relationship between God's graciousness (love, mercy) and judgment? Are they, as the Church has often sought to depict, at opposite ends of the spectrum? (This point of view is most often a basis for contrasting the supposed portrait of God in the Old Testament with that supposed for the New Testament: the former supposedly characterized by unrelenting legalistic judgment and the latter supposedly characterized by sentimental forgiveness.)

When God's judgment is evident, what is its purpose? Vindictiveness (seeking revenge)? Retribution (just punishment)? Deterrence (an example to discourage others)? Rehabilitation (growth through educational suffering)?

Is it possible to view these supposedly opposite attributes of God (love and judgment) as *aspects of a single process*? May they be two manifestations of the same divine reality? Has the religious community, from time to time, seen God at work from both perspectives in a single episode in its history? Is it helpful for individuals to reflect upon misfortunes in their lives from the point of view of such a twofold divine nature?

These are today's questions as we study Hosea.

Selected Scripture

King James Version	New Revised Standard Version
Hosea 1:1-3	*Hosea 1:1-3*
1 The word of the LORD that came unto Hosea, the son of Beeri, in the days of Uzziah, Jotham, Ahaz, and Hezekiah, kings of Judah, and in the days of Jeroboam the son of Joash, king of Israel.	1 The word of the LORD that came to Hosea son of Beeri, in the days of Kings Uzziah, Jotham, Ahaz, and Hezekiah of Judah, and in the days of King Jeroboam son of Joash of Israel.
2 The beginning of the word of the LORD by Hosea. And the LORD said to Hosea, Go, take unto thee a wife of whoredoms and children of whoredoms: for the land hath committed great whoredom, departing from the LORD.	2 When the LORD first spoke through Hosea, the LORD said to Hosea, "Go, take for yourself a wife of whoredom and have children of whoredom, for the land commits great whoredom by forsaking the LORD." 3 So he went and took Gomer daughter of Diblaim, and she conceived and bore him a son.
3 So he went and took Gomer the daughter of Diblaim; which conceived, and bare him a son.	
Hosea 3:1-2	*Hosea 3:1-2*
1 Then said the LORD unto me, Go	1 The LORD said to me again, "Go,

yet, love a woman beloved of her friend, yet an adulteress, according to the love of the LORD toward the children of Israel, who look to other gods, and love flagons of wine.

2 So I bought her to me for fifteen pieces of silver, and for an homer of barley, and an half homer of barley.

Hosea 6:4-6

4 O Ephraim, what shall I do unto thee? O Judah, what shall I do unto thee? for your goodness is as a morning cloud, and as the early dew it goeth away.

5 Therefore have I hewed them by the prophets; I have slain them by the words of my mouth: and thy judgments are as the light that goeth forth.

6 For I desired mercy, and not sacrifice; and the knowledge of God more than burnt offerings.

Hosea 11:1-4a

1 When Israel was a child, then I loved him, and called my son out of Egypt.
2 As they called them, so they went from them: they sacrificed unto Baalim, and burned incense to graven images.
3 I taught Ephraim also to go, taking them by their arms; but they knew not that I healed them.

4 I drew them with cords of a man, with bands of love. . . .

***Key Verse:* For I desired mercy, and not sacrifice; and the knowledge of God more than burnt offerings. (Hosea 6:6)**

love a woman who has a lover and is an adulteress, just as the LORD loves the people of Israel, though they turn to other gods and love raisin cakes." 2 So I bought her for fifteen shekels of silver and a homer of barley and a measure of wine.

Hosea 6:4-6

4 What shall I do with you,
    O Ephraim?
  What shall I do with you,
    O Judah?
Your love is like a morning cloud,
  like the drew that goes away early.
5 Therefore I have hewn them by
    the prophets,
  I have killed them by the
    words of my mouth,
  and my judgment goes forth
    as the light.
6 For I desire steadfast love and
    not sacrifice,
  the knowledge of God rather
    than burnt offerings.

Hosea 11:1-4a

1 When Israel was a child, I
    loved him,
  and out of Egypt I called my son.
2 The more I called them,
  the more they went from me;
they kept sacrificing to the Baals,
  and offering incense to idols.
3 Yet it was I who taught
    Ephraim to walk,
  I took them up in my arms;
  but they did not know that I
    healed them.
4 I led them with cords of human
    kindness,
  with bands of love. . . .

***Key Verse:* For I desire steadfast love and not sacrifice, the knowledge of God rather than burnt offerings. (Hosea 6:6)**

As You Read the Scripture

Hosea 1:1. The kings of both nations are listed in order that hearers (or readers) in either one may be able to locate Hosea chronologically.

Verse 2. Although interpreters have long sought to take the term *harlotry* in a figurative sense (e.g., religious apostasy), there is no reason not to take it literally in the case of Hosea's wife.

Hosea 3:1. Considerable time has passed since the first passage. Note the remainder of chapter 1, where three children are born.

"Raisin cakes" were apparently used in cultic ceremonies of a Canaanite fertility deity.

The woman mentioned here is Hosea's now unfaithful wife, the Gomer of 1:3. Interpreters have sometimes sought to deny this fact, but chapter 2 does not make sense otherwise (see esp. 2:2).

Verse 2. Why it was necessary to "buy" the woman's time is a matter of conjecture. Had she become a common prostitute, and thus it was necessary for him to hire her services? This seems likely, in view of the explicit wording of 1:2.

The inclusion of barley (using two standard dry measures) may indicate that Hosea could not raise the price in cash.

Hosea 6:4. Ephraim was often the predominant tribe in the Northern Kingdom and thus serves as a designation for Israel (in contrast to the Southern Kingdom's Judah).

Verse 5. "Hewn them by the prophets" is an unusual idiom for addressing society with penetrating words of judgment. These words have, in effect, been death-dealing, although the judgment itself has not yet come to reality. It is apparent, however, that it will not be long delayed; it is as certain as the "going forth of light" at dawn (see v. 3, where the people use a similar experience for their faith in God's restoration of the society).

Verse 6. Modern interpreters are divided as to whether the prophet here rejects the sacrificial cult ("not sacrifice, . . . rather than . . . ") or whether he means that it is an empty procedure, given the current moral climate.

Hosea 11:1. The "child" is the group that Moses led out of Egypt, which had its liturgical beginnings at the time of the Sinai legislation. God is here depicted as a parent, a shift from the husband-wife imagery of previous chapters (1–3, for example).

Verse 4. The image is suddenly that of the farmer who cares for his animals, a surprising departure from the parental analogy of verses 1-3. By contrast, the REB continues the parental portrait: "I lifted them like a little child to my cheek, that I bent down to feed them." Such a difference in translation is made possible by the fact that the earliest form of the Hebrew text consisted of consonants only, vowels not being included in a shorthand version. Later, ambiguity might arise as to what vowels might have been intended at certain points. Here, the consonant '-l can be vocalized either as 'ol ("yoke" as in RSV) or as 'ul ("little child" as in REB). Other ambiguities are involved in the differing translations.

The Scripture and the Main Question

Amos (Lesson 10) and Hosea are contemporaries in the sense that each began his ministry around the year 760 B.C. and both within the same society (the Northern Kingdom, Israel). However, while Amos's prophetic career apparently was of short duration (within a decade, if not much less), that of Hosea apparently extended to the time immediately preceding the fall of that nation to the Assyrians in 721 B.C. The turbulent changes that the society underwent in those intervening years helps to explain the theological differences of the two prophets.

Amos's ministry seems to have opened with some optimism that the society might right itself and recover its status as the family whom the Lord had chosen (3:1). Hence there are pleas for the people to repent (5:4-7) and for the deity to relent (7:1-3). When those pleas fell on deaf ears, the prophet announced God's unrelenting judgment tantamount to an end of the elect status (8:11-14; 9:1-4). (Note: The so-called happy ending, 9:11-15, is usually attributed to Amos's disciples in a later generation.)

Whereas Amos's ministry was confined to the stable reign of a single king (Jeroboam II), that of Hosea saw several dynastic changes, which made it clear that the religious quality of the country would ever remain the same: Leaders, both political and religious, are just as guilty as is the population at large (4:4-6; 5:1-4; 7:1-7). No amount of hearing the proclamation of the sacred traditions (the scripture of the time) will have any effect (8:11-12), and thus an unrelenting judgment by the deity is inevitable (5:8-14; 7:11-16; 10:7-8).

Unlike Amos, who seems to have envisioned judgment as God's final word on the situation, Hosea came to believe that God's judgment may ultimately be redemptive and thus that it is an act of grace. For that society, at that time, a dismantling of the existing social, economic, and political institutions was the only way the deity could raise the question of ultimate priorities and provide for a renewal of the ancient ideals. The prophet was thus a short-term pessimist but a long-term optimist as he sought to understand what the deity must do with an errant community and to locate God's sovereignty amid the terrible crisis through which Israel must pass.

Two major factors contributed to the prophet's pioneering thought in this regard: (1) the sacred tradition that proclaimed that God had previously sought to cleanse the earth through a great flood at the time of Noah, thus providing for a new beginning; (2) the experience of the prophet as spouse and parent, which provided an analogy by which to describe the divine nature.

Go, Take for Yourself a Wife

Hosea's initial prophetic act is to enter into a marriage that will serve, by way of analogy, to disclose the sinfulness of his society. This he does under the belief that it is the will of God. The woman's tendency will be toward unfaithfulness, just as is the tendency of Israel in its relationship to God (that is, it will always feel the lure of Canaanite religion, with its promise of fertility of flock and soil). The symbolism continues in the names the prophet gives to their three children, indicating the end of the Israelite kingdom (1:4-9).

Presumably, this strange call to the prophetic office came to the prophet when he was a young man of marriageable age (that is, in his teens). Even if he realized the symbolic nature of the marriage before it took place, he grew to love the woman intensely (to judge from 2:1-2; 3:1-3).

Go, Love a Woman Who . . . Is an Adulteress

Some modern interpreters have questioned whether this is the same woman as the one in Hosea 1, but there is no good reason for doing so, because it would destroy the analogy between Hosea's situation and that of God. Gomer's exact situation ("I bought her . . . ") is not stated in the text. What is clear is that the prophet continues to love his errant spouse and takes costly steps to restore their relationship. He has rejected the option of a divorce and condemning her to death (Deuteronomy 22:22).

The analogy continues, when God is described also as a wronged spouse, something spelled out in greater detail in 2:1-13. Just as the prophet desires, contrary to justice, that their marriage relationship continue, so also the deity will take concrete steps to rehabilitate the errant people and restore them to the ideal passionate commitment of former days (2:14-23). It is apparent, however, that reconciliation will not be easy; the prophet anticipates a period of isolation from God comparable to the period of oppression in Egypt (2:15; 3:3).

What Shall I Do with You?

Prophetic proclamation of the need to change priorities, or of misfortunes that should lead to such change, have but a temporary effect on Israelite society. Even passionate, and perhaps serious, announcement in the liturgy that the prophetic call has been accepted (6:1-3) is soon forgotten. National days of mourning, perhaps precipitated by national calamity, have evidenced only shallow and temporary change of heart, and it is soon "business as usual." Reformation is no more permanent than the dew of the morning, which vanishes with the heat of the rising sun (6:4). This is the case, despite a long tradition of prophetic protest (6:5), and thus when the deity takes more drastic action the people cannot fault the deity for not striving for reconciliation and not giving them fair warning: "My judgment goes forth [as surely] as the light [of day]" (6:5).

The nature of the judgment and its devastating totality are not mentioned here, but are clear elsewhere in the book (see, for example, 7:16; 8:14; 9:3). The purpose of such an ultimate divine action may be gathered from 5:14-15:

> For I will be like a lion. . . .
> until they acknowledge their
> guilt and seek my face.

Presumably, the catastrophic judgment (national exile) that still lies in the future will bring about true and lasting reformation and the recovery of ancient ideals. Thus what is perceived to be a terrible act of divine judgment will ultimately be seen as an act of God's graciousness and commitment to the idea of "a priestly kingdom and a holy nation" (Exodus 19:6).

When Israel Was a Child

The prophet's mode of perception of the divine nature now switches from marital analogy (chaps. 1–3) to that of parenting. Presumably, he has been left with three small children for whom to provide care when his spouse abandons him. Rather than turn them over to grandparents (or whomever else was available in the extended family), he seems to have loved them, cared for them personally, and thereby perceived a new dimension of

God's attitude toward an errant "son." Note the tenderness and accuracy of emotion in the following description (REB; see also above under "As You Read the Scripture"):

> It was I who taught Ephraim to walk,
>   I who took them in my arms . . .
>   that I lifted them like a little child to my cheek,
>   that I bent down to feed them.

The "child," however, rather than having responded to loving parental care with proper spiritual formation, has become rebellious and even rejects the parent: "The more I called them, the more they went from me" (11:2). Consequently, the "parent" will let them go their own way and learn a few things from the school of hard knocks: "They shall return to the land of Egypt, and Assyria shall be their king" (11:5).

Helping Adults Become Involved

Preparing to Teach

Review the changing historical events from the beginning of Hosea's ministry to the fall of the Northern Kingdom (with the assistance of the articles on Hosea in *The Interpreter's Bible, The Interpreter's One-Volume Commentary on The Bible,* or *The Interpreter's Dictionary of the Bible.*

It will also be useful to have an idea of the organization of Hosea's book and overall thought, and this may be obtained from the aforementioned sources as well.

Presentation to the class might take place under the following headings.

    I. What we know about the prophet's historical setting
   II. What we know about Hosea the person
  III. What we know about the book of Hosea
  IV. The biblical account

Introducing the Main Question

> But, oh, the things I learned from her
> I walked a mile with Pleasure,
>   She chattered all the way,
> But left me none the wiser
>   For all she had to say.
>
> I walked a mile with Sorrow,
>   And ne'er a word said she;
> But, oh, the things I learned from her
>   When Sorrow walked with me!
>   (Robert Browning Hamilton)

No doubt what the poet says here will reflect the experience of many adults. The difficult question for the person of faith is this: Is God ever involved in such a process? Does God's sovereignty manifest itself in the process of communal and personal transformation that arises from calamity? Do God's concern, love, and desire for renewal ever take the form of misfortune, so that divine graciousness and judgment are two facets of the same reality? This difficult question about judgment as it pertained to the society of his time is addressed by the prophet Hosea.

Developing the Lesson

I. What we know about the prophet's historical setting

The following are the main events from the cessation of Amos's ministry (Lesson 10) to the end of that of Hosea. Such changing circumstances helped to convince the prophet that, apart from a catastrophic interruption of national life, transformation of the society would not take place.

786–746 B.C.: Israelite king Jeroboam II restores the power and prosperity of his nation (2 Kings 14:24-25; Amos 6:2, 13-14). At the death of his successor, Zechariah, in 745, a period of rapid dynastic change and instability begins.

745 B.C.: The beginning of Assyrian design to capture Syro-Palestine, under the energetic new king, Tiglath-pileser III. This is understood by the prophet Hosea as God's impending judgment on an errant society.

740 B.C.: Assyria receives tribute from Syria (Isaiah 10:9; 37:13). Thus the judgment that the prophet anticipates draws near.

738 B.C.: King Menahem of Israel pays tribute to the Assyrians rather than try to repel them by force (2 Kings 15:17-22).

737 B.C.: Pekah assassinates Menahem and tries to affirm the independence of Israel (2 Kings 15:25-31; compare Hosea 8:4).

734 B.C.: Assyria attacks Syro-Palestine and incorporates the majority of Israel (Galilee and Gilead) into its empire (2 Kings 15:29; compare Isaiah 9:1). Only the southern portion, including the capital city, remains independent. Still, this was not sufficient to bring about any religious reformation and convinced the prophet that destruction of the remainder was necessary.

726 B.C.: The king of Israel refuses further tribute to Assyria, in the belief that Egyptian aid will be sufficient to escape retribution (2 Kings 17:4; Hosea 7:11; 12:1).

725–722 B.C.: A three-year siege by the Assyrians ends the kingdom of Israel (2 Kings 17:5-6).

II. What we know about Hosea the person

Hosea's marital situation, including the rearing of small children, has been mentioned above. He is the only canonical prophet who is an Israelite by birth (the others being Judeans), and this is reflected in peculiarities of his speech and in his fondness for agricultural idioms (whereas Judeans tend to use pastoral ones). He was skilled in rhetoric, knew the history of his people in depth, and exercised considerable influence on such subsequent works as Deuteronomy. His innovative thought is evident in the idea of judgment as divine discipline.

III. What we know about the book of Hosea

His speeches have been preserved (by disciples?) in less complete form than those of most of the other prophets, and their arrangement is often difficult to decipher. This has given the book a fragmentary appearance and makes it difficult to discover the "flow" of the argument.

IV. The biblical account

You might proceed under the divisions of the biblical text that have been outlined above in "The Scripture and the Main Question."

Helping Class Members Act

The prophet was correct in his belief that his society would not reform as the consequence of internal dynamics (prophetic speeches, popular sentiment, and so on), but rather only as the result of external coercion. Could his observation be generalized concerning secular institutions in the present ("We don't need new laws. We can regulate ourselves!")? Are there examples in our society where disruption (civil disobedience) has brought about needed change?

Does the Bible tend to depict God as favoring the status quo or involved in radical societal change or both? In what aspects of contemporary society do you think God may be at work in "the winds of change"?

Ask class members: If Hosea is right that God's discipline may be a form of graciousness, would you want to generalize that claim and say that all misfortune was engineered by God for that purpose? If not, why? What is the role of religious faith in those calamities that may not be of divine origin?

Are there illustrations in your community or in your own life of God's graciousness taking the form of discipline?

Planning for Next Sunday

The location of prophetic activity now switches from the Northern Kingdom (Israel) to the South (Judah) as one studies the sayings of Micah. A different historical situation thus forms the background, and you may want to begin by reading the article "Judah" in *IDB*, vol. 2, pp. 1003-4.

Read Micah 6.

Meeting and Being Met by the Bible in Your Adult Class

WILLIAM AND PATRICIA WILLIMON

"Well look," he said, "I'm a Baptist, you're a Methodist, but the main thing is not so much what you believe as long as you are sincere, right?"

This opinion, although held by lots of people, just happens to be wrong. Believing whatever seems right to you personally has little to do with believing as a Christian, and a belief is not right simply because somebody sincerely believes it. Adolph Hitler was as "sincere" as John Wesley, except that one man lived and died by what was true, whereas the other lived and died by a lie. While clear thinking isn't the answer to every problem in life, it is possible for people to be in misery, not because their hearts are not right or because they are bad people, but because they are confused. If people

95

become confused at a cloverleaf intersection, think how much more confused they are apt to be about God.

As Christians we are those who think about God. Thinking about God is called *theology,* and all of us do it even if we don't know that's what we are doing. Everybody tries to make sense out of life, wonders what he or she is doing here, would like to know where we will be tomorrow, and the real name of the person who lives next door. So there are no non-theologians, there is just good theology and bad theology. One of the major reasons why adults are in your class (whether they know it or not) is to think about God, to do theology. You are all theologians! But where do you begin? On what basis do you make theological judgments?

I take as my text Nehemiah 8:1-10. A strange, long-forgotten scroll has been found in the walls at Jerusalem during renovation. It is a Torah scroll, a collection of "the law of Moses, which the LORD had given to Israel." Ezra assembled the whole nation at the Water Gate (stop snickering, please), and at the Water Gate, Ezra stood in a special pulpit and read aloud the whole law. Most had never heard it. It had been lost during years of turmoil and exile. The people heard again those ancient words, "Hear, O Israel: The LORD is our God, the LORD alone. You shall love the LORD your God with all your heart, and with all your soul, and with all your might" (Deuteronomy 6:4).

The people wept when they heard the law, when they heard again what God wanted of them. They wept tears of repentance and confession. This is God's Chosen People at their best—hearing the law of God, listening, aligning their lives accordingly. (See Lloyd Bailey's extensive discussion of this episode in "The Scripture and the Main Question," Lesson 8, Unit 2, First Quarter.)

You get this biblical religion in Luke 4. Jesus returns to his hometown synagogue and what does he do? What Israelites do every Sabbath—he picks up Torah, God's law, and he reads and interprets.

Israel's faith is a religion of speaking and listening. God speaks. We listen. As Paul once said, "Faith comes from hearing."

Torah—law, the gospel—represents for the Israelites, for us, the "overagainstness" of God. Judaism and Christianity are not religions we find in our hearts or discover in nature walks in the woods or stumble upon by thinking long thoughts in our study. This kind of religion comes to us as *a word from the outside*—in an ancient scroll found buried in a wall, in the sermon of a young Nazarene prophet back home from college for the weekend. In such movements we are reminded that our God is a real God, not some projection of our collective imagination. Our God stands over against us, outside us, beyond us. Our God's ways are higher than our ways; God's thoughts are deeper than our thoughts. We have to be told what this God wants from us. Somebody has to speak it to us. Luther called this the *verbum externum,* the "external word."

This word coming from God through people is not always a comforting, pleasing, easy word. When this external, over against, divine word came upon the people that day at the Water Gate, they wept. They wept at the gap, the great chasm between our ways and God's ways.

As Christians, we have come forth from the mass of humanity to listen to the word of God, as revealed by and contained within the Bible, and to align our lives accordingly. Dietrich Bonhoeffer asserts in his famous *The Cost of Discipleship* that every "revival of Church life always brings in its train a richer understanding of the Scriptures. Behind all the slogans and catchwords . . . there arises a quest . . . for Jesus Christ himself. What did Jesus mean to say to us? What is his will for us today? How can he help us to be good Christians in the modern world? . . . Let us get back to Scriptures, to the word and call of Jesus Christ himself" (*The Cost of Discipleship* [New York: Macmillan, 1966], pp. 29-30).

Now it sounds all well and good that we should be people who read, study, and honor the Bible. Being for the Bible is much like being for motherhood and apple pie. Who wouldn't be for the Bible? Yet, in placing the Bible at the center of our theology, we are engaging in risky, dangerous, countercultural activity.

One year, in early December, I was in my office, talking to one of my parishioners about some problems in her life. She told me about the conflict she was feeling over what to do with her life. Should she turn this way or that way? What should she do? "Preacher," she asked, "what should I do?"

Fortunately for her, I am a seminary-trained pastor and have had courses in pastoral counseling. So I responded to her as I had been taught, displaying my great sophistication and good pastoral counseling technique, "Well, what do *you* think you ought to do?"

Isn't this the purpose of counseling? You come to me as your pastor, and I try to help you find the answer to what ails you in you. I'm not here to preach or to scold; I'm not even here to give answers. I'm here only as a kind of therapeutic midwife to help you find the answers to what ails you in you. Right?

Then it hit me: In just a couple of weeks I was going to stand in front of a congregation and tell a familiar, but still odd, story of how, after waiting for thousands of years for us to cure what ails us through our own devices, God finally resorted to his own devices. One night at Bethlehem, God stole into human history and laid an "answer" on our back doorstep. The story of Christ's nativity is *not* an account of how we finally got ourselves together, got organized, and worked out our own salvation—you have the answer to what ails you in you. The story is about how what God wanted to do for us was so great, so loving, so completely beyond the bounds of human striving or imagination that God had to come here and do it for us, resorting to virgin birth, angels, and the like—or it would not have gotten done.

At last the Holy Spirit got my attention, grabbed me by the collar, shook me up and down. "Are you all right, Preacher?" the woman asked. The difference between going to your preacher for help and going to your local psychiatrist is not just that one charges you an arm and a leg while the other does it for free. The difference is that your preacher offers help in the light of a strange story called the gospel, which is witnessed to by a strange book called the Bible.

You may think that the toughest task of a Christian is serving on your church's finance committee without losing your faith. No, the toughest task of a Christian is to hold your life and your church accountable to this peculiar, odd, not-made-for-television story called the gospel.

I'm sorry—you heard it here first—the solution to what ails you is not found first in you. It is found wrapped in swaddling cloths and lying in a manger. And every day you have to jump out of bed, turn off the alarm, brush your teeth, and remind yourself that you live in the light of this peculiar story and not some other. The world has a stock of competing stories, alternative saviors, and rival accounts of how we live and move and have our being. As Christians, we live by a story called the gospel. This doesn't mean that the Bible is a rule book. On many issues in life, the Bible will not tell you exactly what to do. But the Bible is helpful in placing us in the right context in which we can begin to ask and to answer our questions as Christians, as believers who feel that our lives are supported by and held accountable to the purposes of God.

By merely turning to the Bible you will not find an easily identifiable, one-to-one "answer" to modern ethical problems like abortion or homosexuality or nuclear power. But you will find something better even than answers: the context, the vantage point from which Christians move to answer our questions.

We like to think of ourselves as open-minded. In reality, the modern mind has flattened the universe to a one-dimensional, human-centered reality in which what might be is usually defined on the basis of what already is, and the primary human task is adjustment to the status quo rather than open-minded imagining of a new heaven and a new earth. At its best, our dealing with Scripture is mind-blowing.

Come to us, to your adult class, where we study the International Lesson. We will open up your heart and mind and slap you with possibilities you won't hear about on the evening news or that you cannot read about in the morning paper.

We can only act within a world we can envision. The modern world, with its rather myopic worldview, tends to produce people who make small, cautious moves in life because their vision isn't much further than the limits of their own egos. So most of us settle down, keep low. Even little moves scare us.

Jesus preaches a sermon that begins, "Blessed are you poor . . . blessed are you hungry . . . blessed are you persecuted . . . blessed are you unemployed. . . . oh, how fortunate are those of you going through marital distress. . . . "

The congregation does a doubletake. Blessed? Fortunate? What is this? In our world, when you are poor, you are treated like a nobody, a failure.

When you are unemployed, people avoid you as if you had some kind of social disease.

The preacher says, "Oh, excuse me, I should have been more clear. I'm not necessarily talking about the American way. I am talking the kingdom of God way. In this new, inbreaking kingdom, the poor shall be royalty; those whom you consider outcasts and failures are at the center."

How shall they and we hear of this kingdom without a preacher, a biblical preacher? How shall they and we see without a teacher, a biblical teacher?

That's *you!* You are the means by which God touches peoples' lives through scripture.

God be with you as you teach your class this Sunday. We are all counting on you to help us be confronted by this bracing, mind-expanding word from the outside. We are all counting on you to help us meet the Bible.

Micah: Prophet of Righteousness

Background Scripture: Micah 6

The Main Question

Just as prophets in Israel (the Northern Kingdom, after 922 B.C.) observed the difference between the "actual" and the "ideal" (see Lessons 9–11), so also did prophets in Judah (the Southern Kingdom; see Lesson 13). By the "ideal" is meant the chosen community as defined and anticipated in the sacred traditions of its founding and early history (Genesis–Deuteronomy). By the "actual" is meant society as observed by the prophets whose oracles have come down to us.

Seldom was that difference more clearly and bluntly drawn than by Micah of Moresheth in Judah, a contemporary and possibly a disciple of Isaiah (in the last third of the eighth century B.C.). In addition to pointing, with an annoying specificity, to the failure of his society to be God's "priestly kingdom and a holy nation" (Exodus 19:6), Micah poses what are perhaps the ultimate theological questions: What is it that God expects of creatures? As far as the welfare of the individual is concerned, as well as the health of society, what is "the good"?

We receive an answer in the form of one of the most memorable passages in all of Scripture:

> And what does the LORD require of you
> but to do justice, and to love kindness,
> and to walk humbly with your God?
>
> (Micah 6:8)

What does God expect of us? That is today's question.

Selected Scripture

King James Version	New Revised Standard Version
Micah 6:1-8	*Micah 6:1-8*
1 Hear ye now what the LORD saith; Arise, contend thou before the mountains, and let the hills hear thy voice.	1 Hear what the LORD says: Rise, plead your case before the mountains, and let the hills hear your voice.
2 Hear ye, O mountains, the LORD's controversy, and ye strong foundations of the earth: for the LORD hath a controversy with his people, and he will plead with Israel.	2 Hear, you mountains, the controversy of the LORD, and you enduring foundations of the earth; for the LORD has a controversy with his people, and he will contend with Israel.
3 O my people, what have I done	3 "O my people, what have I done

unto thee? and wherein have I wearied thee? testify against me.

4 For I brought thee up out of the land of Egypt, and redeemed thee out of the house of servants; and I sent before thee Moses, Aaron, and Miriam.

5 O my people, remember now what Balak king of Moab consulted, and what Balaam the son of Beor answered him from Shittim unto Gilgal; that ye may know the righteousness of the LORD.

6 Wherewith shall I come before the LORD, and bow myself before the high God? shall I come before him with burnt offerings, with calves of a year old?

7 Will the LORD be pleased with thousands of rams, or with ten thousands of rivers of oil? shall I give my firstborn for my transgression, the fruit of my body for the sin of my soul?

8 He hath shewed thee, O man, what is good; and what doth the LORD require of thee, but to do justly, and to love mercy, and to walk humbly with thy God?

Key Verse: **He hath shewed thee, O man, what is good; and what doth the LORD require of thee, but to do justly, and to love mercy, and to walk humbly with thy God? (Micah 6:8)**

to you? In what have I wearied you? Answer me!

4 For I brought you up from the land of Egypt, and redeemed you from the house of slavery; and I sent before you Moses, Aaron, and Miriam.

5 O my people, remember now what King Balak of Moab devised, what Balaam son of Beor answered him, and what happened from Shittim to Gilgal, that you may know the saving acts of the LORD."

6 "With what shall I come before the LORD, and bow myself before God on high? Shall I come before him with burnt offerings, with calves a year old?

7 Will the LORD be pleased with thousands of rams, with ten thousands of rivers of oil? Shall I give my firstborn for my transgression, the fruit of my body for the sin of my soul?"

8 He has told you, O mortal, what is good; and what does the LORD require of you but to do justice, and to love kindness, and to walk humbly with your God?

Key Verse: **He has told you, O mortal, what is good; and what does the LORD require of you but to do justice, and to love kindness, and to walk humbly with your God? (Micah 6:8)**

As You Read the Scripture

Micah 6:1-2. Mountains, hills, and foundations of the earth are addressed as if they had been witnesses long ago to the covenant between God and Israel, wherein the latter agreed to be an obedient and witnessing community. Now that the covenant has not been kept, the witnesses are summoned as part of God's case against Israel. *Controversy* and *content* are legal terms, making an analogy to a court of law; the REB's "case against" and "argue" are clearer in this regard.

Verse 5. The Balak-Balaam episode is found in Numbers 22–24. The former is a king of Moab who hired the latter to place a curse on the Israelites who were on their way from Egyptian bondage to the "promised land." The gracious intervention of the deity prevented it.

On the journey across the Jordan into that land, Shittim was the last camp on the far side and Gilgal the first one after the crossing. Thereby God's continuing presence at crucial moments is called to mind.

Verse 6. The scene shifts from courtroom to temple as a member of the congregation (on behalf of the people) asks a question of the priest. The question continues through verse 7, with the response in verse 8.

Verse 7. "Give my firstborn" refers to infant sacrifice, which was sometimes carried out in the ancient Near East. (Please do not try to make it apply to abortion!)

Verses 9-16. This speech is separate from verses 1-8. The two may have been editorially placed in their present order so that the abuses listed in verses 9-16 illustrate the basis of God's lawsuit in verses 1-8.

Verse 9. "Tribe" and "city" are not named and thus the terms may be used in the general sense. They are all the same; take your pick; the nearest one to whomever hears the text.

Verse 10. "The scant measure that is accursed" is clarified by the GNB: "They use false measures, a thing that I hate."

Verses 14-15. The implication is that these various actions by the people will be frustrated as a means of punishment for breaking the covenant. Parallels may be found in the book of Deuteronomy, where the consequences of disobedience are listed (28:30-31, 38-42).

Verse 16. To keep "the statutes of Omri" must mean that, in general, his unjust practices (and those of his son Ahab) have been adopted by the society at large. Such an accusation would be especially galling to the prophet's Judean audience, because Omri was a king in the neighboring state of Israel (often Judah's enemy) and because Ahab had committed several unflattering acts (for example, seizing the vineyard of Naboth; 1 Kings 21).

To "hiss" at someone (forcing breath from the mouth) was a sign of astonishment or derision (Lamentations 2:15-16; Ezekiel 27:35-36).

The Scripture and the Main Question

Israel's theologians, following the exodus from Egypt, came to the conclusion that this amazing event of liberation from slavery was further evidence of God's graciousness and election (see Lessons 1–2) and that gratitude should lead the community to bring God's requirements to reality. They then sought some analogy whereby these conclusions could be clearly and compellingly expressed. (Later, various prophets would use the analogy of marriage or parenting for the Exodus, suggesting love, forgiveness, and accountability as fitting response to the actions of God. See especially Lesson 11.) The analogy that they chose was that of international diplomacy. It was as if God were a great king who had entered into a treaty or alliance (covenant) with smaller surrounding states. In return for the gracious acts of the great king, the vassal states were expected to be loyal, supportive, and accountable to one another. If the treaty were broken, then the great king had the right to take punitive measures, including forcing the rebellious state to return to the alliance.

Rise, Plead Your Case

The prophet continues the aforementioned analogy of God as the wronged party in the broken treaty, now summoning the rebel Israel to trial. Indulging in a bit of legal fiction, the prophet calls the mountains and hills as witnesses; they will have observed both Israel's ancient promises and its failure to keep them.

The plaintiff opens by playing the role of defendant. What could possibly have led the people of Israel to act in the way they have? After all that the deity has done for them (summarized in vv. 4-5), how could they possibly act with such ingratitude? Openly, before a global forum, God asks how this can be possible and receives only silence for an answer. Forced self-examination does not lead to a defensible justification for failure. No justification is possible, since God's saving acts have been substantial, repeated, and unmerited.

With What Shall I Come Before the Lord?

In the process of a legal case, a charge must be lodged as to what the defendant has done, failed to do, or ought to do. The question now asked provides the plaintiff with the opportunity to make that charge. The question continues with a series of logical possibilities, each of which will be rejected by the deity. Will a costly sacrificial animal, a year-old calf, entirely to be consumed by fire, suffice? Will a thousand rams, which only a king could provide? Vast amounts of olive oil, an essential item for cooking and skin care, upon which all life depended? Even the ultimate sacrifice, one's firstborn child? There is an earnestness in the questioner's progression of possibilities, a willingness to offer everything in total surrender, that makes it possible for God to provide an answer.

He Has Told You, O Mortal . . .

The answer will be nothing new. Indeed, it has been revealed and expected of the people of God all along, throughout history. In the sacred traditions (in the nucleus of what we now call the Bible), the requirements have long been made clear. As Jesus would later say to the inhabitant of hell who pleaded that a warning be sent to his relatives who were yet alive so that they might avoid the place: "They have Moses and the prophets; they should listen to them. . . . If they do not listen to Moses and the prophets, neither will they be convinced even if someone rises from the dead" (Luke 16:29, 31). The future of God's people, therefore, lies only in taking our past seriously.

It is significant that the question is depicted as having been posed by a single individual and that the answer is directed to an individual. Every person in Israel must keep this question and its proper answer in mind, pondering its implications.

To Do Justice

Rather than an abstraction whose meaning might be debated, this phrase means to actualize, to put into practice in one's environment the commandments that have come down from Sinai (not merely the famous Ten Commandments, either). The phrase has an aspect of "acting according to precedent," and thus one's life is to be governed by the tradition rather than by personal advantage. (See vv. 10-12 for the reverse of what this requirement has in mind.)

And to Love Kindness

The Hebrew word that the NRSV has rendered as "kindness" has several nuances and cannot adequately be translated by any one English word. The REB translates it as "to love loyalty" (fidelity of one's oath to God's covenant). Another rendering is "solidarity [with one's fellow members of the community of faith]." Thus "kindness" is rather bland and nonspecific. It is God's *hesed* ("steadfast love") that keeps the community in existence despite its failures. It is human *hesed* that makes shared community possible and allows justice to flourish. It is *hesed* that necessitates that hostility between community members be overcome and makes it possible to speak of the "household of faith" (Galatians 6:10). There must be (to return to the analogy from international diplomacy) communal solidarity among the clients of the great king.

And to Walk Humbly with Your God

Again, the NRSV's "humbly" does not convey the entire picture of the original meaning. The word has aspects of close attention and thoughtful preservation, akin to the term *piety*. The implication is that one must look with attention as one "walks with" God through the journey of life. Such attention is mandated by respect and gratitude for God's gracious acts in the past (outlined here in vv. 3-5). It is an ethical posture, grounded in the realization that we are creatures who depend on God for everything meaningful. It is also to realize that one is always a sinner.

Can I Forget the Treasures of Wickedness?

Verses 10-12 give a specificity to the legal case that the deity has called for trial. They concern life in its ordinary sense, as humans naturally like to live, life as it naturally is when people have no concern for "justice . . . kindness . . . walking humbly with God." The focus is on economic life and gain, thus hitting at the heart not only of the initial hearers but of the modern reader as well. When the religious community so orients itself to the values the Canaanite Baal represents (see Lesson 9) that it loses its identity as the people of the Lord, then drastic action must be taken to restore it. Micah's opinion about the lengths to which the great king would go to reform the errant vassal are among the most severe in the Bible (3:12, a text that was cited by Jeremiah's friends as a precedent for his own message when he was on trial for his life; 26:16-20).

God's love leads to God's judgment.

Helping Adults Become Involved

Preparing to Teach

Familiarity with the prophet and his teaching can be obtained by reading the article "Micah the Prophet" in *IDB,* vol. 3, pp. 369-72, or in *IB,* vol. 6, or in *IOCB,* pp. 483-90.

On the analogy of international diplomacy/treaty for expressing Israel's relationship to God (and thus how gratitude is emphasized as the motivation for obedience), see the article "Covenant, Mosaic," in *IDBS,* pp. 192-97, especially Section 4.

See also the *IDB* articles entitled "Righteousness in the OT," vol. 4, pp. 80-85; "Love in the OT," vol. 3, pp. 164-68; and "Humility," vol. 2, pp. 659-60.

The lesson might proceed under the following headings.

     I. God's covenant: its form and implications
    II. Micah: the man and his message
   III. The text of the lesson and its implications for today

Introducing the Main Question

When James Earl ("Jimmy") Carter took the oath of office as President of the United States in January 1977, he placed his hand on a Bible that had been opened, at his request, to the sixth chapter of the book of Micah. He read aloud verse 8, which he described as a "timeless passage," and then remarked that a change of presidents was a milestone in the life of a nation.

The very question of the essence of God's requirement of creatures, and of those who would identify themselves with the Church and the Synagogue in particular, is at the center of today's lesson. It is the ultimate question of the religious life: "With what shall I come before the LORD, and bow myself before God on high?" The prophet then attempts to sum up the faith, to crystallize the divine requirements in a few succinct phrases: "do justice . . . love . . . kindness . . . walk humbly with your God."

It is our task to understand those compact requirements, not only within the context of Micah's message, but also as they might apply to our own lives.

Developing the Lesson

I. God's covenant: its form and implications

The idea of "covenant" not only gives form to Micah's message (the summons to trial in vv. 1-5) but also explains the basis of his condemnation of Judah. It may be well to outline to the class the form that treaties between monarchs took in the ancient Near East, with the aid of the *IDBS* article "Covenant, Mosaic." The formal parts are (1) *Preamble:* the great king introduces himself and gives his titles; (2) *Historical Review:* the great king recites his gracious acts on behalf of the proposed vassals; (3) *Requirement:*

perpetual expectations of the vassals, in view of what the great king has done and will continue to do for them; (4) *List of Witnesses:* usually the deities in whose name each side has sworn to keep the treaty; and (5) *Blessings and Curses:* the good that will result from fidelity and the terrible consequences of disobedience.

Israel's adaptation of this form as a means of expressing its faith in God may be found (at least the first three elements) in Exodus 20. *Preamble:* "I am the LORD your God. . . ." *Historical Review:* " . . . who brought you out of the land of Egypt, out of the house of slavery." *Requirements:* Loyalty only to the great king (vv. 3-11) and obligations to one's fellows in covenant, the other vassals (vv. 12-17).

A *List of Witnesses* is presupposed by Micah's call to the "mountains, hills, and foundations of the earth" to come into court and attest to the arrangement. *Blessings and Curses* are outlined as part of Moses' final address in Deuteronomy 27–28 and may be behind Micah's threats in 6:14-15.

God, as a great king, has acted graciously for Israel throughout the history of the community, and this should have inspired gratitude that led to obedience. Instead, there had been disobedience, infidelity to the covenant oath, and ingratitude. Thus God inquires, "O my people, what have I done to you?" (See Lesson 10 for similar thoughts from Amos.)

II. Micah: the man and his message

Locate Micah chronologically in relation to the other prophets who have been studied in this unit. He prophesied during the days of Jotham (750–735 B.C.), Ahaz (735–715), and Hezekiah (715–687), according to Micah 1:1. He is, then, a contemporary of Isaiah, a century later than Elijah (Lesson 9), a bit later than Amos (Lesson 10), possibly overlaps slightly with the end of Hosea's ministry (Lesson 11), and is roughly a half-century earlier than Josiah (Lesson 8) and Jeremiah (Lesson 13).

Details of Micah's life and message, such as you care to present, may be found in the sources recommended above. You might mention the fact that he is concerned about injustice with an intensity rivaling that of Amos; that he believes that God will destroy his country as do Amos, Hosea, and Jeremiah; and that his book contains passages of hope beyond the destruction, as do those of the same three prophets.

III. The text of the lesson and its implications for today

You might proceed under the divisions of the biblical text that were outlined above in "The Scripture and the Main Question."

Helping Class Members Act

Discussion might include the following issues as the class members think about the implications of the lesson for their own lives.

1. In view of the goodness that God has shown to us (individually or collectively), is there any possible justification for the rebellious ways in which we conduct ourselves? Or must we, like those to whom the deity addressed the question (v. 3), stand in silence?

2. In search of an answer to the question "With what shall I come?" the prophet points to the past: "He has shown you. . . . " Is it your impression

that the churches and their members rely on Scripture as an authoritative guide for their ethical behavior? If not, on what do they rely?

3. Is the society in which we live characterized by justice (whether biblical or legal), or is it characterized by arbitrariness, inequality, complacency, and fraud? Can you list instances where individuals or groups have striven for justice? Conversely, are there instances where injustice is carried out in the name of justice?

4. When Christian groups denounce each other, are they practicing the communal solidarity that Micah had in mind when he spoke of "kindness"? Do you feel any obligation to help other Christians, even if you do not know them, just because they belong to "the household of faith"? What ought to be the consequence (if any) of remembering that God loved and loves *me*, when I have not done and cannot do anything to deserve it?

5. Is it your impression, observing how Christians denounce each other and how self-confidently they proclaim that their denomination alone has the way to heaven, that all Christians are "walking humbly" with their God? Is it your impression that, in our society's workplaces from nine to five, Christians are attentive to the gospel in the way that they "walk"? What agenda is really operative?

6. The prophet condemns economic abuse: "scant measure . . . wicked scales . . . deceitful weights" (6:10-11). What forms does such abuse now take, such that the prophet (and the Bible) would now condemn it? Misleading advertising? Price fixing? Hidden charges? Shoddy merchandise? Double billing? Exorbitant interest? Customer and employee theft?

Planning for Next Sunday

List the characteristics of "God's prophet." These assumptions and preconceptions will be confirmed or questioned as we study the prophet Jeremiah.

LESSON 13 NOVEMBER 29

Jeremiah: Persistent Prophet

Background Scripture: Jeremiah 1:1-10; 8:22–9:3; 20:7-13

The Main Question

Biblical prophets were sent to announce both God's graciousness and God's judgment (and indeed the two are often aspects of a single process; see Lesson 11 of this unit). The consequences of such a proclamation, of bringing a religious community into conversation with its sacred traditions, can be disillusioning, frustrating, and occasionally physically dangerous. Nonetheless, persons called to such a task may correctly sense that what is at stake for their society is a matter of life and death. Thus they will feel compelled to continue despite all opposition, even if their efforts are ineffective in the short run. It is in the speeches of Jeremiah, and in his so-called confessions in particular, that subsequent generations are best able to grasp the inner turmoil of a biblical prophet. Present generations, therefore, may feel a particular kinship with him as they ponder their own ethical dilemmas, uncertainties, and convictions.

What does Jeremiah—prophet of God's judgment and graciousness—have to say to us today?

Selected Scripture

King James Version	New Revised Standard Version

Jeremiah 1:9-10

9 Then the LORD put forth his hand, and touched my mouth. And the LORD said unto me, Behold, I have put my words in thy mouth.

10 See, I have this day set thee over the nations and over the kingdoms, to root out, and to pull down, and to destroy, and to throw down, to build, and to plant.

Jeremiah 20:7-11

7 O LORD, thou hast deceived me, and I was deceived: thou art stronger than I, and hast prevailed: I am in derision daily, every one mocketh me.

8 For since I spake, I cried out, I cried violence and spoil; because the word of the LORD was made a reproach unto me, and a derision, daily.

9 Then I said, I will not make mention of him, nor speak any more in his name. But his word was in mine heart as a burning fire shut up in my bones, and I was weary with forbearing, and I could not stay.

10 For I heard the defaming of many, fear on every side. Report, say they, and we will report it. All my familiars watched for my halting, saying, Peradventure he will be

Jeremiah 1:9-10

9 Then the LORD put out his hand and touched my mouth; and the LORD said to me,
"Now I have put my words in your mouth.

10 See, today I appoint you over nations and over kingdoms,
to pluck up and to pull down,
to destroy and to overthrow,
to build and to plant."

Jeremiah 20:7-11

7 O LORD, you have enticed me,
and I was enticed;
you have overpowered me,
and you have prevailed.
I have become a laughingstock
all day long;
everyone mocks me.

8 For whenever I speak, I must cry out,
I must shout, "Violence and destruction!"
For the word of the LORD has become for me
a reproach and derision all day long.

9 If I say, "I will not mention him,
or speak any more in his name,"
then within me there is
something like a burning fire shut up in my bones,
I am weary with holding it in,
and I cannot.

10 For I hear many whispering:
"Terror is all around!
Denounce him! Let us denounce him!"
All my close friends

enticed, and we shall prevail against him, and we shall take our revenge on him.

11 But the LORD is with me as a mighty terrible one: therefore my persecutors shall stumble, and they shall not prevail: they shall be greatly ashamed; for they shall not prosper: their everlasting confusion shall never be forgotten.

Key Verse: **Then I said, I will not make mention of him, nor speak any more in his name. But his word was in mine heart as a burning fire shut up in my bones, and I was weary with forebearing, and I could not stay. (Jeremiah 20:9)**

are watching for me to stumble.
"Perhaps he can be enticed,
and we can prevail against him,
and take our revenge on him."
11 But the LORD is with me like a
dread warrior;
therefore my persecutors will
stumble,
and they will not prevail.
They will be greatly shamed,
for they will not succeed.
Their eternal dishonor
will never be forgotten.

Key Verse: **If I say, "I will not mention him, or speak any more in his name," then within me there is something like a burning fire shut up in my bones; I am weary with holding it in, and I cannot. (Jeremiah 20:9)**

As You Read the Scripture

Jeremiah 1:1. Jeremiah's family had been banished from Jerusalem several centuries earlier as the consequence of a power struggle following the death of King David. Jeremiah's ancestor Abiathar had preferred the rule of Adonijah to that of Solomon (1 Kings 2), and the latter had directed that Abiathar settle in the village of Anathoth. Jeremiah thus knew priestly lore from the "inside," and this may help to explain the candor with which he criticized that profession.

Verse 2. For King Josiah, see Lesson 8. His dates are 640–609 B.C.

Verse 3. The "captivity of Jerusalem" marks the beginning of the Exile, in 597 B.C., an event that Jeremiah escaped. He was subsequently taken by force to Egypt by a rebellious element of his own people (chaps. 43–44).

Verse 5. God had Jeremiah in mind even before his birth. The statement does not mean that Jeremiah existed before his birth, either as a discarnate "soul" or in a previous "incarnation."

Verse 6. In ancient Israel, wisdom was thought to characterize the aged, and thus youthfulness was to Jeremiah's disadvantage as far as prophetic effectiveness was concerned. His reluctance may be compared with that of Moses (Exodus 4:10-13) and contrasted with that of Isaiah (6:1-9).

Verse 9. For the symbolism of touching the prophet's mouth as a means of empowerment, see Isaiah 6:6-9 and Ezekiel 3:1-3.

8:22–9:3. The book of Jeremiah is not chronologically arranged, and thus it is sometimes difficult to date texts within the time of Jeremiah's ministry. Modern interpreters generally have suggested that this passage is from the reign of King Jehoiakim (609–598 B.C.), when the prophet was concluding that his society was doomed to destruction.

It is difficult to know who is speaking at a given sentence. It is clearly the deity in 8:13, the people in 8:14-15, and the prophet in 8:18, but what is the situation in 8:22–9:3? Interpreters disagree about this, but it may be argued that Jeremiah speaks in 8:22–9:1 and the deity thereafter. (In contrast to NRSV, note the wide space between verses 1 and 2 in REB and JB, signalling a transition.)

Gilead was noted for a tree that contained an aromatic gum that was used for medicinal purposes. For its export as far as Egypt, see Genesis 37:25.

Verse 3. The tongue, like a bent bow, shoots arrows of falsehood (see also v. 8).

20:7-13. Verses 7-12 are a poetic outburst of personal emotion, one of several that have come to be called "Jeremiah's Confessions." The others include 11:11-23; 12:1-6; 15:10-12, 15-21; 17:14-18; 18:18-23; and 20:14-18. In general, they seem to reflect the prophet's depression at the unresponsiveness of his society during the reign of King Jehoiakim, or perhaps during the even more desperate days of King Zedekiah (598–587 B.C.), which ended in the Exile.

Verse 7. The deception is apparently the easy task the deity outlined in the prophet's call: "Do not be afraid . . . for I am with you" (1:8).

Verse 8. In theory, the violence and destruction could be anticipated punishment on the society, or the prophet's characterization of his society's actions, or the abuse that Jeremiah's opponents heap upon him, or (and most likely) the abuse he feels the deity has caused him.

Verse 13. Because of the sudden swing in mood from lamentation to thanksgiving, some modern interpreters suppose that this verse is a later addition to the text. Such shifts, however, are often characteristic of biblical laments.

The Scripture and the Main Question

It is often a tough task to be called by God to speak. Jeremiah's spiritual crisis, reflected in his "Confessions," results from the contrast between the certitude of his commission from birth and his failure to bring about a transformation of his society. Indeed, the problem is more than his failure; it is the abuse that is heaped upon him because of his faithfulness to the commission.

Before You Were Born I Consecrated You

So compelling is the divine call, so certain of it is the young Jeremiah, that it can only be expressed as a vocation that God had in mind for him even before he was born. At this point, Jeremiah may have been influenced by stories of the child Samuel, who served in the temple at Shiloh (1 Samuel 1–3). Abiathar, Jeremiah's banished ancestor, had been the last functioning priest of Eli's line at that ancient temple. Thus Samuel may have served as a role model for the youthful Jeremiah.

I Am Only a Boy

Jeremiah's age is a contrast to what we know of the other prophets. Amos, for example, seems long established in farming and shepherding when the call comes for him to speak for the deity. Such youthfulness was to Jeremiah's disadvantage, since in his society it was age that brought wisdom and respect from one's audience. (This is in contrast to modern Western society, which caters to youth and lauds the "whiz kid," taking special notice of the child evangelist.) One can thus understand Jeremiah's reluctance to accept the divine commission, especially in view of its nature:

> "Today I appoint you over
> nations and over kingdoms,
> to pluck up and to pull down . . .
> to build and to plant." (1:10)

The deity, however, pays no attention to Jeremiah's protests and reassures him: "Do not be afraid . . . for I am with you to deliver you" (v. 8).

Such overwhelming assurance can only add to Jeremiah's spiritual crisis when the divine promise later does not conform to reality. This will lead to the accusation that the deity has deceived him (20:7), allowing instead "violence and destruction" to come upon him (20:8).

Is There No Balm in Gilead?

The young prophet began his ministry in an optimistic mood, during the reign of the pious King Josiah (who brought about a religious reformation in his society around 621 B.C.; see Lesson 8). His proclamation during this period is recorded primarily in chapters 1–6. The reformation, however, was temporary in its effect but nonetheless bred self-confidence in the people that they were righteous. Consequently, further exhortations by Jeremiah could be ignored as excessive and hyper-sensitive. Thereby Jeremiah's awareness of the depths of human sin and self-righteousness were greatly expanded. Thus, after the death of Josiah (609 B.C.), his accusations become increasingly sharp and aim at the country's leadership (whereas previously the aim had been at the average citizen). This will have the effect of focusing official displeasure upon him and ultimately lead to charges of sedition, thus inaugurating his spiritual crisis.

During the reign of King Jehoiakim, Judah became increasingly entangled in foreign intrigue—making alliances and then breaking them, seeking the favor alternatively of Babylonia and Egypt. The prophet concluded that such shifting loyalties, rather than ensuring the survival of his country, would lead to its destruction. The Babylonians would vent their wrath on Judah, and there would be no escape. He understands this to be more than a secular event; it is God's judgment upon a society that has betrayed its ancient ideals and thus has forsaken its religious commitment.

Why the members of his society (and especially its rulers) could not see what was about to happen, why they did not treasure the values and loyalties of the Mosaic faith, why they did not respond to the prophet's authentic proclamation, was a disappointment and mystery to Jeremiah. Societal and political healing, as readily available as is balm from Gilead for the physically injured, is being offered to no avail.

Not only was Jeremiah disillusioned with the ineffectiveness of his ministry, but he was also horrified by the fate that he anticipated for his society. "My eyes are a fountain of tears," he says (9:1). For this reason, he chooses to remain childless, believing this to be not only prudent but the will of God as well; his offspring would either be killed during the conquest by the Babylonians or would die of disease, and their dead bodies would be food for the birds and the beasts of the earth (see 16:1-4).

Jeremiah's agony is, he believes, like that experienced by the deity, who will allow destruction and exile as a means of transforming Israel. (In this regard he seems to have been a disciple of Hosea; see Lesson 11). Thus he reports the following divine reactions.

> "How can I pardon you?
>   Your children have forsaken me." (5:7)
> I have forsaken my house,
>   I have abandoned my heritage;
> I have given the beloved of my heart
>   into the hands of her enemies. (12:7)

Jeremiah's gloomy view of the future, as well as his personal attacks on the king, made it precarious for him to continue to speak in public. He apparently found it necessary to hide out for a while, and this added to his depression; it deprived him of the profession to which he had been called. It was a time of self-examination, of feeling that he had failed, of bitterness about his calling. It was during this time of turmoil, apparently, that he uttered his so-called confessions.

O Lord, You Have Enticed Me

Reading Jeremiah's "Confessions" (only one of which is part of the current lesson) is like stumbling across the prophet's personal diary. They are rare glimpses into the inner thoughts of a prophet, behind the barrage of confidence that they otherwise seem to have. Their sincerity and their trueness to life have led to their inclusion in Scripture, even though they do not report the Word of God (rather, the words of Jeremiah).

Jeremiah complains that he got into this prophet business when he was too young to understand its full implications. God had, in effect, taken advantage of his gullibility and, therefore, is responsible for the fact that he is "a laughingstock all day long" (20:7). Why not then surrender his prophetic commission and find a worthwhile profession? Because it is impossible. He has not only chosen to speak, but also has been called to do so:

> Within me there is
>   something like a burning
>   fire . . .
> I am weary with holding it in,
>   and I cannot. (v. 9)

This, then, is the prophet's dilemma: An irresistible urge to speak out is the cause of his suffering, but the cure (to remain silent) is worse than the disease!

Let Us Denounce Him!

As if the prophet's love-hate relationship with God were not sufficient for his misery, he must also worry about "all my close friends" (20:10). Their specific identities are not given, but his opponents elsewhere include prophets, priests, and government officials (see 26:10-11; 28:1-17). Presumably, they disagree with his analysis of what God has in store for the society and seek some basis for discrediting Jeremiah. Note 26:11, where "the priests and the prophets said to the officials and to all the people, 'This man deserves the sentence of death because he has prophesied against this city.'"

But the Lord Is with Me

Despite all the disillusionment and suffering that his relationship with the deity has caused, and despite all the resentment and plotting of his "friends," the prophet does not abandon his call and ultimate commitment. There is, after all, no one else to whom he can turn. Thus he will plunge doggedly ahead, trusting that it is all ultimately worthwhile. God's concern in the long run will compensate for the inadequacies of the present. Thus, as the prophet's "Confession" moves toward a conclusion, he breaks into a song of thanksgiving (20:13). Perhaps this is a pattern of worship (from lament to praise) that he has learned from the temple liturgy (now found in the book of Psalms: see, for example, Psalm 22).

Helping Adults Become Involved

Preparing to Teach

It may be helpful to have a general idea of the history of Judah, which forms the background for Jeremiah's long book. The major events are as follows.

628 B.C.: Judah begins to regain independence from Assyrian control, under King Josiah.

621 B.C.: Josiah's religious reform (see Lesson 8).

609 B.C.: Death of King Josiah in battle as he sought to prevent Assyria's Egyptian allies from coming to Assyria's aid (2 Kings 23:29-20; 2 Chronicles 35:20-24). He is succeeded by his son Jehoahaz. After three months of his reign, the Egyptians take control of Judah, replacing Jehoahaz with his more pliable brother Jehoiakim (Eliakim). He does not continue the reforming policies of his father, leading to condemnation by Jeremiah.

603 B.C.: Jehoiakim, sensing that the Babylonians will defeat the Egyptians, transfers his allegiance to the former (2 Kings 24:1).

601 B.C.: Encouraged by Egyptian success in repulsing a Babylonian invasion at its frontier, Jehoiakim again switches his allegiance (2 King 24:1). To the Babylonians, this was an unforgivable offense, and it was only a matter of time until they would invade Judah.

598–597 B.C.: Jehoiakim dies during the Babylonian siege and is replaced by his son Jehoiachin (Jeconiah/Coniah). After three months, Jerusalem surrenders. The king is taken into exile, along with a large number of prisoners and much booty. (See discussion of the setting of the Deuteronomic History in Lesson 3 under the heading "Developing the Lesson.") Judah thus becomes (again!) a vassal-state of Babylonia, and Zedekiah (the son of Josiah) is placed on the throne. For Jehoiachin, see Jeremiah 13:18-19 and 22:24-30.

598 B.C.: Restlessness among the states in Palestine, fueled by Egypt, leads to plans of revolt against the Babylonians. King Zedekiah is torn about what side to take and consults Jeremiah several times about it (Jeremiah 21:1-7; 37:1-10; 38:14-23). He finally joins the rebels, which is a fatal mistake.

588–587 B.C.: The Babylonian army destroys the major cities of Judah—including Jerusalem—exiles massive numbers of the population, and places the country under the governorship of Gedeliah (Jeremiah 39; 2 Kings 25).

Should you desire to read more about these events, the following articles in *IDB* will be helpful: "Jehoiachin" and "Jehoiakim," vol. 2, pp. 811-14; "Zedekiah," vol. 4, pp. 947-49. Much more brief is the "Introduction" to the book of Jeremiah in *IOCB*, pp. 372-73.

Should you desire an overview of Jeremiah's thought and of the book in which it is described, the following will be helpful: "Jeremiah the Prophet" in *IDB*, vol. 2, pp. 823-35. A section-by-section commentary may be found in *IOBC*, pp. 372-404. If it is available at your local library, excellent detail may be found in William Holladay, *Jeremiah: Spokesman Out of Time* (Philadelphia: Pilgrim Press, 1974).

Presentation to the class might take place under the following headings.

    I. What we know about the prophet's historical setting
   II. What we know about Jeremiah the person
 III. What we know about the book of Jeremiah
 IV. The text of the lesson

Introducing the Main Question

A pastor with whom I served as an associate in Iowa would regularly visit one of the farm families and spend a while driving whatever machinery was currently in use. When I asked him what his purpose was in doing so ("To appear to be a 'regular guy'?"), he replied that it was satisfying to see something concrete that he had accomplished that day. The goals of ministry are not so easily accomplished, and one can sometimes be discouraged at how slowly the gospel becomes normative in the lives of members of the congregation. To make matters worse, the more seriously one takes the gospel, the more likely one is to encounter determined resistance from powerful individuals or groups. Otherwise put, the ideals we may envision at the start of ministry (as clergy, teacher, laity), the way the Bible and preachers may lead us to believe things will be, sometimes are contradicted by harsh realities of disinterest, opposition, and failure.

Modern witnesses to the faith are not the only ones to experience disappointment and even anger at the deity for not bringing expectation to reality, thus seemingly allowing one to waste one's life in a useless cause. Such was the experience and reaction of one of the most famous of prophets, Jeremiah of Judah, around the beginning of the sixth century. His protests about this, so candid that they would shock a congregation if a pastor expressed them as his or her own in a service of worship, have nonetheless been treasured and preserved as part of Scripture.

Modern Christians will find kinship in Jeremiah's so-called Confessions, and possibly will gain the faith to continue.

Developing the Lesson

I. What we know about the prophet's historical setting
Sufficient information about this may have been provided above under the heading "Preparing to Teach."

II. What we know about Jeremiah the person
Some information has been provided as part of the topic "The Scripture and the Main Question." You may include the following data as well: (1) He

belonged to a priestly family (1:1), which may have led him to identify with the child Samuel. (2) He remained single out of fear for security of children (16:1-4). (3) He studied the prophets who preceded him, and Hosea in particular. (4) He had a friend and scribe named Baruch who helped to present and preserve his message (36:4-8; 32:12-15; 43:2-7). (5) He began his ministry as a mere youth (1:5-6). (6) He was willing to question his faith, for example, in his "Confessions."

III. What we know about the book of Jeremiah
This topic is optional, but it might be well to explain that the book is not chronologically arranged, and thus it cannot be read from start to finish with clarity as to progression of thought. Details of its organization may be found in the *IDB* article "Jeremiah the Prophet" (Section D, "The Book").

IV. The text of the lesson
Proceed under the divisions as outlined above in "The Scripture and the Main Question."

Helping Class Members Act

Discussion might include the following issues as the class members think about the implications of the lesson for their own lives.
1. Do you think that it is a proper role for clergy in the present to criticize the social, economic, and political policies of our country, as did Jeremiah in his society? Is it their task not merely "to build and to plant" but also "to pluck up and to pull down" (1:10)?
2. Are there modern equivalents of Jeremiah's choosing to remain childless out of concern for the fate of descendants? We live in an environment that is becoming increasingly hazardous—poisons in the air, the water, and the food. There is the possibility of biological, chemical, and nuclear warfare. In such circumstances, should we bring children into the world? Those who now feel this way will know something of Jeremiah's turmoil.
3. What are some of the tendencies of human beings and of our society in particular that you think discourage clergy, comparable to the despair Jeremiah felt? When he envisioned the destruction of his country (because of departures from the traditional faith and because no one would listen to his warnings), is he comparable to persons in the present who warn repeatedly of the horrors of nuclear war while there is still time and no one will listen?
4. Contrast Jeremiah's candid, passionate, angry outbursts with the unreality of modern liturgies that concern tragedy. Is anger at God a valid expression of religious faith? Ought it to be incorporated into a few of the liturgies of the Church, just as Jeremiah's "Confessions" are a part of Scripture? On what occasions would you find such expressions to be appropriate?

Planning for Next Sunday

Next Sunday, we move to the New Testament. Ask your class, "What would you say (after this study of the Hebrew prophets) is the 'good news' of the prophets?"

Good News for All

UNIT I: COMING OF THE GOOD NEWS
William and Patricia Willimon

FOUR LESSONS   DECEMBER 6–27

As the Christian Church moves through the Christian seasons of Advent, Christmas, and Epiphany, the lessons for this quarter all deal with different aspects of the good news, the gospel, which has come in Jesus Christ.

Unit I consists of four lessons that focus on key passages about the coming of Christ. Because the season of Advent, comprising those Sundays before Christmas, is the season of preparation for the birth of the Christ Child at Bethlehem, it is appropriate for this unit to be entitled "Coming of the Good News." All of the passages serve to build our expectancy of the arrival of the long-awaited Messiah.

The good news that arrives among us must then be enacted in our daily lives. On the first Sunday of the New Year, January 3, we begin a five-session exploration (Unit II) of the church as our means of "Living the Good News." In the church's liturgical year, Epiphany is January 6. *Epiphany* means "manifestation" or "revelation." When we in the church gather to pray, witness, and serve, we are the manifestation of the good news in our world.

Unit III completes our focus on the good news with four lessons on the theme of "Sharing the Good News." Once again, the tie with the church year is fortuitous. Epiphany is a traditional time to emphasize the spreading mission of the church throughout the world.

In his book *Overhearing the Gospel* (Nashville: Abingdon Press, 1977) Fred Craddock claims that many of us do not really hear the good news today because we have "overheard" the gospel—that is, we have heard it so many times that we have become dulled to its truth. "Ho hum, here we go again," we say as the stories, teachings, and precepts of the gospel are proclaimed to us for the fiftieth time.

May these key passages concerning the good news be an invitation for you and your adult class to hear the good news as if for the first time, to celebrate again, during these first Sundays of the new Christian year, the marvelous work of God which unfolds among us in Jesus the Christ.

LESSON 1   DECEMBER 6

God's Purpose Through Love

Background Scripture: Hebrews 1:1-4; Ephesians 1:3-14

The Main Question

Recently a friend and I were discussing an episode in my life. I had been through a small crisis at the chapel where I work. Fortunately, through an unexpected turn of events, things had worked out surprisingly well. Even though I had tried to make things work out through my own efforts, they had turned out well almost despite my efforts.

So I said to my friend, "The Lord was looking after us." My friend, who is a committed Presbyterian by denomination and a Calvinist in theology, said to me, "One of these days I am going to get you to admit to the truth of our doctrine of predestination!"

We laughed. I don't yet know whether I believe in predestination, the belief that God foreordains or predestines certain things to happen in certain ways in the future. Yet it is interesting how very often in life we are able to say, in all seriousness, "The Lord was looking after us."

To make that claim is to assert that God is still busy in human affairs, that laid over our human efforts to make history turn out right are God's efforts. Behind today's lesson is a good pre-Christmas question: How can we be assured of the purposes of God in our lives? "Long ago God spoke to our ancestors in many and various ways by the prophets, but in these last days he has spoken to us by a Son" (Hebrews 1:1-2).

Selected Scripture

King James Version

Hebrews 1:1-4

1 God, who at sundry times and in divers manners spake in time past unto the fathers by the prophets,

2 Hath in these last days spoken unto us by his Son, whom he hath appointed heir of all things, by whom he also made the worlds;

3 Who being the brightness of his glory, and the express image of his person, and upholding all things by the word of his power, when he had by himself purged our sins, sat down on the right hand of the Majesty on high;

4 Being made so much better than the angels, as he hath by inheritance obtained a more excellent name than they.

Ephesians 1:3-14

3 Blessed be the God and Father of our Lord Jesus Christ, who hath blessed us with all spiritual blessings in heavenly places in Christ:

4 According as he hath chosen us in him before the foundation of the world, that we should be holy and without blame before him in love:

5 Having predestinated us unto

New Revised Standard Version

Hebrews 1:1-4

1 Long ago God spoke to our ancestors in many and various ways by the prophets, 2 but in these last days he has spoken to us by a Son, whom he appointed heir of all things, through whom he also created the worlds. 3 He is the reflection of God's glory and the exact imprint of God's very being, and he sustains all things by his powerful word. When he had made purification for sins, he sat down at the right hand of the Majesty on high, 4 having become as much superior to angels as the name he has inherited is more excellent than theirs.

Ephesians 1:3-14

3 Blessed be the God and Father of our Lord Jesus Christ, who has blessed us in Christ with every spiritual blessing in the heavenly places, 4 just as he chose us in Christ before the foundation of the world to be holy and blameless before him in love. 5 He destined us for adoption as his children through

the adoption of children by Jesus Christ to himself, according to the good pleasure of his will,

6 To the praise of the glory of his grace, wherein he hath made us accepted in the beloved.

7 In whom we have redemption through his blood, the forgiveness of sins, according to the riches of his grace;

8 Wherein he hath abounded toward us in all wisdom and prudence;

9 Having made known unto us the mystery of his will, according to his good pleasure which he hath purposed in himself:

10 That in the dispensation of the fulness of times he might gather together in one all things in Christ, both which are in heaven, and which are on earth; even in him:

11 In whom also we have obtained an inheritance, being predestinated according to the purpose of him who worketh all things after the counsel of his own will:

12 That we should be to the praise of his glory, who first trusted in Christ.

13 In whom ye also trusted, after that ye heard the word of truth, the gospel of your salvation: in whom also after that ye believed, ye were sealed with that holy Spirit of promise,

14 Which is the earnest of our inheritance until the redemption of the purchased possession, unto the praise of his glory.

Jesus Christ, according to the good pleasure of his will, 6 to the praise of his glorious grace that he freely bestowed on us in the Beloved. 7 In him we have redemption through his blood, the forgiveness of our trespasses, according to the riches of his grace 8 that he lavished on us. With all wisdom and insight 9 he has made known to us the mystery of his will, according to his good pleasure that he set forth in Christ, 10 as a plan for the fullness of time, to gather up all things in him, things in heaven and things on earth. 11 In Christ we have also obtained an inheritance, having been destined according to the purpose of him who accomplishes all things according to his counsel and will, 12 so that we, who were the first to set our hope on Christ, might live for the praise of his glory. 13 In him you also, when you had heard the word of truth, the gospel of your salvation, and had believed in him, were marked with the seal of the promised Holy Spirit; 14 this is the pledge of our inheritance toward redemption as God's own people, to the praise of his glory.

Key Verses: **God, who at sundry times and in divers manners spake in time past unto the fathers by the prophets, hath in these last days spoken unto us by his Son, whom he hath appointed heir of all things, by whom also he made the worlds. (Hebrews 1:1-2)**

Key Verses: **Long ago God spoke to our ancestors in many and various ways by the prophets, but in these last days he has spoken to us by a Son, whom he appointed heir of all things, through whom he also created the worlds. (Hebrews 1:1-2)**

As You Read the Scripture

Hebrews 1. The Letter to the Hebrews was addressed to a dispirited early Church. An anonymous Christian writer used every literary and scriptural means to fill believers with hope.

Verse 1. The Old Testament prophets were God's spokespersons. As is sometimes said, the prophets were not so much "foretellers" (predicters of future events) as "forthtellers" (proclaimers of God's word). Through the prophets, God spoke to Israel in the past.

Hebrews 1:2. "In these last days" refers to the early Christian belief that they lived in the final days of history when the exalted Christ would soon return to his Church. The same God who spoke through the prophets now speaks by even more intimate, superior means—his very own Son. Jesus is not only God's Son, but was also present at creation, taking part in the formation of the world.

Hebrews 1:3. Christ was not only present at creation but continues to guide and uphold the universe through his power. That power is revealed by his being seated "at the right hand" of God. Kings in ancient times had their queens or heirs sit on their righthand side as a sign of sharing in the king's rule.

Hebrews 1:4. The power of Christ is superior to that of angels. Evidently, some persons in the early church honored or worshiped angels as powerful heavenly beings. The idea of angels as powerful demigods came from the religions of Persia.

Ephesians 1. The beautiful Letter to the Ephesians opens with a poetic doxology in which the author praises the greatness of Christ.

Ephesians 1:3. Like today's passages from the Letter to the Hebrews, Ephesians stresses the presence of Christ "in the heavenly places," seated next to and equal in power to God.

Ephesians 1:4-5. God has chosen us "before the foundation of the world" to be "his children." These verses have caused no end of debate among Christians over "predestination," the idea that God predetermines who will be saved and who will be excluded. I believe that the author's main point here is that our salvation is something willed by God, for all, from the very beginning of time.

Ephesians 1:6-10. The writer praises the extravagance, the lavishness, of God's grace upon us in Christ, asserting again (v. 10) that Christ is part of an eternal plan of God to "unite all things in him."

Ephesians 1:11-14. This whole passage is doxological. The Greek word *doxa* means "praise" and is the word from which we get our word *doxology*. The effect of these verses is like a great hymn, a shout of praise to the glory of Christ. The "seal" spoken of in verse 12 is probably the sign of the cross made on the forehead of a new Christian at baptism as a sign of the gift of the Holy Spirit.

The Scripture and the Main Question

"Don't tell me, show me," pleads a song in the musical *My Fair Lady*. It is a wonderful thing to say to someone, "I love you." But sometimes we need more than just words. That's why we communicate not only through words, but also by actions, symbols, and signs. "Actions speak louder than words," we sometimes say.

Fortunately for us, God understands this about us. In the Bible, God not only says "I love you" through the dramatic and poetic words of the prophets and the compelling words of the law delivered to Moses, but God's love is also demonstrated to us. "This will be a sign for you: you will find a child wrapped in bands of cloth and lying in a manger" (Luke 2:12). The babe at Bethlehem becomes a visible, in-the-flesh, irrefutable sign to us that God loves us.

If you think back over all of the Bible passages you have studied in your church and through these Bible lessons, you will have to say that God is an infinitely resourceful communicator. Through all the words of Scripture God continues to try to get through to us, to get our attention, to express love for us in ways that we can hear and understand. "Long ago God spoke to our ancestors in many and various ways by the prophets, but in these last days he has spoken to us by a Son," says the Letter to the Hebrews (1:1-2).

The faith of Israel is a faith that is born out of an encounter between a listening people and a loquacious God. Presumably, if God had been content to keep silent, had not had such desire to get through to his creatures, there would have been no Israel and, therefore, no church. "Faith comes from hearing," says Paul. We have come together as the Church because we claim to have heard something that much of the world has not yet heard.

The Bible is the long story of the eternal conversation between God and people. Time and again, we have closed our ears, turned the other way, and stopped listening. Fortunately for us, God did not stop talking. Again and again, God came back to us, found us, and resumed the discussion.

The writer to the Hebrews claims that the very summit of the conversation between humanity and God is Jesus the Christ. He is uniquely able to communicate the nature of God because Jesus fully shares in that nature. "He is the reflection of God's glory and the exact imprint of God's very being," says Hebrews 1:3.

Christians are those who believe that one finds out about God not by taking long walks in the woods or pondering deep thoughts in one's library or by rummaging around in the recesses of one's ego. We find out about God by looking at his Son, this Jesus who is "the exact imprint of God's very being." In Jesus, we Christians claim to have seen as much of God as we ever hope to see.

Thus the Church has historically been deeply suspicious of any claim about the attributes of God that did not square with what we have seen of God in the life, teachings, death, and resurrection of Christ. Any claim about God's nature must be measured by what we see of God in Christ.

Thank God that, when God came among us and revealed himself to us, God chose human form. God came among us as one who was born, lived, suffered, and died as a human being. This made the great, eternal God accessible and believable to us. Our God, revealed in Jesus, has an unmistakably human quality.

In our bleakest, most terrifying moments, this is our deepest human question: Is anybody up there? Does anybody up there care?

Somebody very close to God is closer to us than "up there." The Christ, the one who is God in the flesh, is *here.* In Christ, God comes to us—Immanuel, "God with us," beside us.

In many ways God tried to get through to us; now God has come to us as a Son.

Superior to Angels

All that may make all the more perplexing the next major claim of the writer to the Hebrews: "he sat down at the right hand of the Majesty on high, having become as much superior to angels" (1:3-4). You and I can relate to Jesus, who looks like us, feels like us, is tempted like us, and who suffers and dies like us. But what are we to do with this rather strange claim that Jesus also created the world and now sits "at the right hand of the Majesty on high"?

At the heart of the gospel is this paradox: Jesus was a baby born, as we shall celebrate in a few weeks, in a manger at Bethlehem. Yet, this little baby was also the one who was the King of kings, Lord of lords, Sovereign of the universe. Here, in the Christ, is combined the humanity and, therefore, the accessibility of one who is fully one of us with the majesty, power, and creativity of one who is fully God.

The *humanity of Christ* assures us that he understands what it is to live in this world, to ache where you ache, to cry when you cry, to feel what you feel. The *deity of Christ* assures us that he is able to do for us what we cannot, in our human weakness, do for ourselves.

It is some comfort for us to assure hurting persons on the basis of the story of Christ's nativity at Bethlehem, that God is here, in the flesh, among us, sharing our burdens and sorrows. But that comfort would be rather shallow were it not for the fact that our God is also "up there," "in the heavenly places" (Ephesians 1:3).

You Have Heard the Word of Truth

When I emerged from five years of seminary and graduate school and was serving my first parish in rural Georgia, I quickly found that many of my parishioners couldn't understand my sermons. My talk was full of technical theological terms, high-sounding ideas, quotations from learned theologians, name dropping from the books I had read. I eventually decided that, if I were going to preach so as to be heard, I would have to learn how to talk to people about spiritual realities through earthly means.

Today's Scripture from Hebrews and Ephesians claims that Jesus of Nazareth is God's supreme communicative act. Having tried so many ways to assure us of his love, to show us the way, God at last stole into human history in the form of a baby in a manger. In our times of struggle, when life leads us to clinch our fists and scream out, this one came and lived among us as God's most eloquent, loving, compelling response.

Helping Adults Become Involved

Preparing to Teach

Today's lesson deals with issues related to communication between God and humanity. The Scripture and your class study provide a wonderful opportunity to prepare for Christmas and the Incarnation.

First, read over the assigned Scripture passages from Ephesians and Hebrews. While some of the images that are presented by these early Christian writers may seem somewhat obscure, they compose some of the most beautiful portions of Scripture. You will probably find it most helpful not to bog down in intricate details of these passages. Your main emphasis is that Christ shares in the rule of God.

Read "The Scripture and the Main Question" and "As You Read the Scripture." Keep your main theme of divine-human communication before you as you plan your lesson.

In preparing your outline for presenting today's lesson, you might wish to keep in the back of your mind the following two questions in order to elicit illustrations of the Scripture from your own experience:

1. How has God communicated his love and power to me in my life?

2. In what ways does my relationship with Christ assure me that the love and power of God are available for my times of need?

Your experiences as a contemporary teacher may be shared with your class in order to depict the ways God speaks to us through the Christ.

Among the questions your adults might raise after hearing the assigned passages from Hebrews and Ephesians are: How can I be sure that God is speaking to me? Does God really speak to people today? How can Christ be more real for my life? According to the Bible, what is the purpose of life? With so many terrible things happening in the world, what evidence is there that God is good or that God really cares for us?

You might wish to prepare these questions for your class to ponder before and after they study today's Scripture in your adult class. Put them on newsprint or a chalkboard.

Introducing the Main Question

Read "The Main Question" a succinct presentation of the main question that lies behind today's Scripture.

"The Main Question" raises the issue of divine providence. Can it really be said that the Lord is looking after us? Many of your class members have probably read the morning newspaper before church this morning. There they read of all of the tragedies, wars, chaos, and confusion that infect the modern world. When Christians make the claim that God has overriding purposes for our world and that, in Christ, God is busy working out those purposes for us, some may be led to doubt on the basis of the lack of evidence.

Yet, that is the Christian claim. God is busy intruding upon the world, "blessing us in Christ" (Ephesians 1:3) in innumerable ways. Few of us would claim that God's work in the world is always immediately discernible. Yet, we believe that behind the headlines, sometimes on the backstage of human history, God is busy.

You begin today's lesson with the simple, honest admission that today's headlines tend to raise questions about the bold, extravagant claims for divine power that are made in Hebrews 1 and Ephesians 1. You might even collect an assortment of news headlines from your local paper and simply read them to your class at the beginning of the lesson to set the context for the Scripture. However, one of the purposes of today's Scripture (and this lesson) is to assert that while today's headlines tell the story of much of our world, they are not the whole story.

Here is the outline for today's lesson:

    I. Set the context for the passages from Ephesians and Hebrews.

    II. Note the many attributes the writers ascribe to Christ.

    III. Explore the relevance of Christ's nature for human need.

    IV. Describe the nature of God on the basis of what we know of God in Christ.

    V. Conclusion.

Developing the Lesson

I. Set the context for the passages from Ephesians and Hebrews.

After reading aloud today's assigned passages, set them in context by describing, in your own words, the situations of these early congregations. Then ask your group, "In what ways do contemporary Christians resemble the early believers? What questions within our own situation are similar to theirs?" Refer to the two questions in the section "Preparing to Teach," which you have written on the chalkboard or newsprint.

The passages from Ephesians and Hebrews are, in effect, answers to pressing questions. Your class ought to experience the questions before they will be able to grasp the answers.

II. Note the many attributes the writers ascribe to Christ.

Now lead your class back through the Scripture, noting the attributes of Christ that are presented as answers to the plight of the early believers. Among the attributes listed in Ephesians are that: Christ is God's way of blessing (Ephesians 1:3); Christ is the sign of God's choice of us as his people (1:4); Christ is proof that God loves us (1:5); our sins are forgiven (1:7); God's way is revealed to us (1:9); and Christ is God's means of uniting everyone to God (1:10).

Hebrews says that Christ shares in the Creator's power (1:3); Christ is superior, even to the angels in heaven (1:4-5).

In just a few verses, we have learned a great deal about Christ, and, in Christ, we have learned a great deal about God.

III. Explore the relevance of Christ's nature for human need.

You will want to explore with your group the relevance of all the divine attributes for human need. Refer back to the questions you and your group have listed. Ask them how Christ's nature and work address our human dilemma.

IV. Describe the nature of God on the basis of what we know of God in Christ.

Our theme is "God Speaks Anew in Christ." Having noted the attributes of Christ on the basis of today's Scripture and the way in which those attributes relate to human need, now lead your class in describing the nature of God on the basis of God's self-disclosure in Christ. In "The Scripture and the Main Question," it is said that Christ is as much as we ever hope to know of God. Have members of your class describe the attributes of God on the basis of what is revealed in Christ.

V. Conclusion.

Close today's study of Hebrews and Ephesians by reading aloud 1 John 1:1-4 to your class. Although this passage is not part of today's study, it provides a beautiful and fitting conclusion to our study today as well as a good way of moving us toward Christmas.

Helping Class Members Act

Ask the class members to suggest ways in which your church, in today's world, serves to reveal the nature of God in Christ, even as Christ reveals God to the Church.

Planning for Next Sunday

Most of us are already hard at work preparing ourselves and our families for Christmas. Ask, "What do you want for Christmas?" Then ask the class members to read Luke 1:5-17.

God's Promise to Zechariah

Background Scripture: Luke 1:1-25

The Main Question

"I am really frustrated," he said. "My little church is so traditionalistic. I don't think they want to try anything new."

"Tell me about the composition of your congregation," I said.

"Well, the main fact about them is that they are all older adults. I'd say that the median age is about sixty-five, or even older. And you know how older people are."

"How are older people?" I asked, probing to find out his opinions.

"Well, old. Conservative, traditional, clinging to the past, afraid of anything new."

"Are they?" I asked. I told him that I had just read an article about aging which noted that the majority of traumatic, difficult, demanding experiences a person goes through in life occur after the age of sixty-five. The loss of health, the loss of mobility, and the need to move to a nursing home are just some of the traumatic changes that older adults must confront.

It isn't that older adults refuse to change. They are already trying too much newness! They are holding on for dear life.

Today's Scripture from Luke centers on what happened to two faithful older adults when God surprised them by deciding to work some new thing for humanity through them.

Be careful, all those of you over sixty-five! Be careful what you pray for. No one is ever too old, too fixed in life to be immune to surprises of God.

What are some of the surprising ways God answers our prayers?

Selected Scripture

King James Version	New Revised Standard Version

Luke 1:5-17

5 There was in the days of Herod, the king of Judaea, a certain priest named Zacharias, of the course of Abia: and his wife was of the daughters of Aaron, and her name was Elisabeth.

6 And they were both righteous before God, walking in all the commandments and ordinances of the Lord blameless.

7 And they had no child, because that Elisabeth was barren, and they both were now well stricken in years.

8 And it came to pass, that while he executed the priest's office before God in the order of his course,

9 According to the custom of the priest's office, his lot was to burn incense when he went into the temple of the Lord.

10 And the whole multitude of the people were praying without at the time of incense.

11 And there appeared unto him an angel of the Lord standing on the right side of the altar of incense.

12 And when Zacharias saw him, he was troubled, and fear fell upon him.

13 But the angel said unto him, Fear not, Zacharias: for thy prayer is heard; and thy wife Elisabeth shall bear thee a son, and thou shalt call his name John.

14 And thou shalt have joy and gladness; and many shall rejoice at his birth.

15 For he shall be great in the sight of the Lord, and shall drink neither wine nor strong drink; and he shall be filled with the Holy Ghost, even from his mother's womb.

16 And many of the children of Israel shall he turn to the Lord their God.

Luke 1:5-17

5 In the days of King Herod of Judea, there was a priest named Zechariah, who belonged to the priestly order of Abijah. His wife was a descendant of Aaron, and her name was Elizabeth. 6 Both of them were righteous before God, living blamelessly according to all the commandments and regulations of the Lord. 7 But they had no children, because Elizabeth was barren, and both were getting on in years.

8 Once when he was serving as priest before God and his section was on duty, 9 he was chosen by lot, according to the custom of the priesthood, to enter the sanctuary of the Lord and offer incense. 10 Now at the time of the incense offering, the whole assembly of the people was praying outside. 11 Then there appeared to him an angel of the Lord, standing at the right side of the altar of incense. 12 When Zechariah saw him, he was terrified; and fear overwhelmed him. 13 But the angel said to him, "Do not be afraid, Zechariah, for your prayer has been heard. Your wife Elizabeth will bear you a son, and you will name him John.

14 You will have joy and gladness, and many will rejoice at his birth, 15 for he will be great in the sight of the Lord. He must never drink wine or strong drink; even before his birth he will be filled with the Holy Spirit. 16 He will turn many of the people of Israel to the Lord their God. 17 With the spirit and power of Elijah he will go before him, to turn the hearts of parents to their children, and the disobedient to the wisdom

17 And he shall go before him in the spirit and power of Elias, to turn the hearts of the fathers to the children, and the disobedient to the wisdom of the just; to make ready a people prepared for the Lord.

of the righteous, to make ready a people prepared for the Lord."

Key Verse: **But the angel said unto him, Fear not, Zacharias: for thy prayer is heard; and thy wife Elizabeth shall bear thee a son, and thou shalt call his name John. (Luke 1:13)**

Key Verse: **But the angel said to him, "Do not be afraid, Zechariah, for your prayer has been heard. Your wife Elizabeth will bear you a son, and you will name him John." (Luke 1:13)**

As You Read the Scripture

Luke 1:5-17. John the Baptist is reported to be the forerunner of Jesus. His story is told with remarkable similarity in all the Synoptic Gospels (Matthew, Mark, and Luke). Like the birth of Jesus, the birth of John is portrayed as an unusual and divinely initiated event. The hymn in honor of John (Luke 1:14-17) is possibly an early Christian hymn.

Verse 5. The citation of the reign of Herod the Great suggests that the births of John and Jesus were approximately 7–6 B.C. The "order of Abijah" is discussed in 1 Chronicles 24:10.

Verses 6-7. Although Elizabeth and Zechariah were "both righteous before the God," completely obedient to all the precepts of the faith of Israel, "they had no children." They were old and childless, a terrible condition for Near Eastern people, because this meant that their old age would be a time of poverty and great insecurity without children to care for them. Throughout the Old Testament, children are seen as evidence of divine favor.

Verses 8-9. Second Chronicles 31:2 and Exodus 30:1, 6-8 discuss the duties Zechariah was performing in the Temple.

Verses 14-15. John and his work are presented in this song. The reference to John's abstinence from "wine" and "strong drink" depicts John as a holy person, sanctified for holy duties as were Old Testament priests (Numbers 6:1-4). "Filled with the Holy Spirit" is a phrase that appears frequently in Luke to indicate that a person has been equipped by God for holy work.

Verses 16-17. John's main function will be that of a forerunner, someone to prepare "the people of Israel" for the reign of God, which is coming in the long-awaited Messiah. His ministry is portrayed in Luke 3:1-20. About this time, Israel practiced proselyte baptism in which Gentiles who wished to convert to Judaism were asked to bathe before circumcision. John requires even Jews to be washed as sign of repentance and preparation for the Messiah.

The Scripture and the Main Question

Elizabeth and Zechariah

Isn't it interesting how Luke chooses to begin his story of Jesus? The beginning of a story is either the time to catch the reader's imagination or an opportunity to give the reader a preview of what is to come. Why then begin the story of Jesus with these two unheard-of old people and their prayers?

Luke is trying to make an important point by beginning in this way. Who are the first to get the news of the birth of the Christ in Bethlehem? Two old people hanging around the Temple (Luke 1:5-25); a young, unmarried peasant woman named Mary (Luke 1:26-56); poor, lowly shepherds out in the fields watching their sheep (Luke 2:8-18).

Isn't it interesting that the news does not go to those in power in Jerusalem or Rome? No one up at the palace got the news. When God began to move in the Incarnation, God chose not to use the mighty and the exalted ones. Instead, God chose the angels. The messengers of God went to those persons on the bottom of society: an old, childless couple; a young, unmarried woman; poor shepherds.

Luke is teaching us something about the way God chooses to enter human history. God often bypasses those whom we regard as having such power and importance. And who is more powerless than elderly people? In that society, as in our society, the aging were often relegated to the bottom of the social ladder. Our culture values people who produce. But many older adults are past their ability to work and contribute, so society relegates them to the fringes. We institutionalize our elderly, putting them aside after a lifetime of contribution.

And, particularly in the context of the first century, who is more powerless than elderly people who have no children? In Near Eastern society, children were considered a blessing because they were the equivalent of our Social Security system. By having children, a person could ensure some security in old age. Without children, a person would almost surely die in great misery and even starvation.

So when our Bible tells us that Elizabeth was "barren," a rather harsh way of speaking of a childless woman, it means that she was barren in more than one way. Without children, she and her husband had no real future. They faced a future that was, well, *barren.*

To add even more tragedy to their tragic circumstances, in the Old Testament, childlessness was sometimes regarded as a sign of divine disfavor. If children were claimed as a blessing from God, then the absence of children was sometimes deemed a virtual curse from God. "Why am I childless?" Elizabeth must have asked herself. "What have I done wrong?"

Moreover, there were probably people in Jerusalem who asked these same questions about Elizabeth. "Her husband is a priest, a member of the clergy, but if they are such good people, then why don't they have a child?" "They are always down at the Temple working, but a lot of good it has done them. God has still refused to give them the one thing they want most in life." So the talk must have gone, the talk about childless old Elizabeth and Zechariah.

The question behind today's Scripture is one of the most perplexing ever asked by believers. Why is it that people can be good, do what is right, earnestly pray to God, and still not receive from God what they want?

Recently I talked with a couple, a comparatively young couple, who want a child more than anything else in life. They have prayed for a child, are willing to sacrifice anything for a child, would make perfect parents for a child. Still, in their early thirties, it appears they will not have a child. They have applied for adoption, but cannot be assured that even adoption will be a possibility for them.

Theirs is a sad, bleak—let us say *barren*—situation. Why has their prayer, their sincere, earnest, heartfelt prayer, gone unanswered?

I don't know. Yet, Luke says that the situation of Zechariah and Elizabeth was as bleak or more so. What happened to them?

Your Prayer Has Been Heard

I like to picture Elizabeth at home on the day Zechariah was visited by the angel Gabriel. Her arthritis was bothering her that day, and she suggested that Zechariah go on to the Temple without her. She would stay home and rest.

At her age, she had learned to pace herself; she had learned her limits. Age does that to us. We learn what can be done and what can't be done, and we adjust. She had adjusted to her circumstances—old, childless, futureless. A lifetime of prayers for a child had gone unanswered. She still hurt, but she had learned to adjust. She was now old, utterly without hope of a child.

Then her husband came home, led by the people. Poor old Zechariah was literally speechless (Luke 1:20-22). And why not? He had received some rather dumbfounding news.

The angel had said to him, "Do not be afraid, Zechariah, for your prayer has been heard. Your wife Elizabeth will bear you a son, and you will name him John" (Luke 1:13). For her part, Elizabeth was so shocked, so embarrassed, that she hid herself rather than go out and show all the neighbors the strange event that had come to pass at their house (1:24).

Does any of this remind you of another strange pregnancy? Remember the story of elderly, childless Abraham and Sarah (Genesis 12-17). God promised to bless Abraham by making him the father of a new, chosen nation. But Abraham and his wife, Sarah, were both very old. Sarah laughed at the idea, but, as things turned out, Sarah laughed all the way from the geriatric ward to the maternity ward. She gave birth to a son, whom she called Isaac, a name that means "laughter." Now, at the beginning of the story of Jesus, there is an equally surprising story of the birth of a child to equally unsuspecting parents.

I believe that Luke is making a claim with this strange birth story: With God, most anything is possible. Particularly in our lives when we are confronted with situations in which there appears to be no hope, no way out, no future, no possibility, with God there is a way. The story of Elizabeth and Zechariah reminds us that with God all is possible.

This does not mean that all of our prayers will be answered in exactly the way we want. After all, we are dealing with God here, not some cosmic Santa Claus, not some personal genie whom we can command. When God acts, it is not because we asked in the right way or prayed with proper technique. It is because it was God's own good time and was according to God's plan for the ages; our desires coalesced with God's desires for us and our world. Elizabeth and Zechariah were blessed as part of God's larger purposes for blessing the whole world through the Christ.

Above all, beyond the mystery of prayer, this story of the birth of John implies that our future is much more open-ended, possibility filled, and potentially blessed than we may dream. Just how full of possibility the future is would soon be revealed by a birth even more strange than that of John. The child of Mary (Luke 1:26–2:20) would be the supreme evidence that God answers our prayers, giving us answers more wonderful than we can imagine.

Helping Adults Become Involved

Preparing to Teach

Today's lesson is about God's answering of prayer. Perhaps more to the point of our text from Luke, today's lesson is about the people who pray. Realize, as you prepare your lesson, that we are walking over risky terrain when we discuss prayer. In your class there will probably be a number of people who have had difficult experiences with prayer.

Even though you may be somewhat hesitant to delve into such potentially painful events, today's Scripture offers a marvelous opportunity to do so. One reason why we study the Scriptures is for help with life's unanswered questions, for strength to live through life's difficult moments.

"Teach us to pray," the disciples asked Jesus (Luke 11:1). In response, Jesus gave them a model prayer, the prayer that we call the Lord's Prayer (Luke 11:2-4). Perhaps, at the beginning of this lesson on prayer, we should remind ourselves that the Lord's Prayer begins with, "Thy will be done." That sets the tone for all Christian prayer. Not our will, but God's will be done.

None of this answers the tough question of why some of our prayers are answered and some of them are not, why our desires, even when they are utterly noble and worthy, are not fulfilled in ways we expect. There is much that we do not know about prayer simply because we can't know everything about God or the working out of God's purposes.

Have you ever received a rather unexpected answer to a prayer? Have you personally had the experience of earnestly praying for something, never to receive what you prayed for? It might be helpful, in preparing for today's lesson, for you to recall those experiences.

There is much discussion in today's lesson about the plight of older people in our society. The age and situation of your adult class will affect the way you decide to present this material. If your class is composed of older adults, your group will have definite, personal feelings about this material. Perhaps your older adults do not like to think of themselves as powerless, in need of deliverance (as was the case of Zechariah and Elizabeth). Or perhaps, if your class is very young, you might have to present more material on the nature of aging and the plight of the elderly to help them see the biblical text in the human context.

Now read carefully "The Scripture and the Main Question" and "As You Read the Scripture." These provide you with a way into the biblical text as well as real-life, contemporary application of the text.

Here is the outline for today's lesson:

    I. Put the story of Elizabeth and Zechariah in context.
    II. Questions raised by this story.
    III. Conclusion.

Introducing the Main Question

To seize the attention of your class members, you might begin by retelling, in your own words, the introductory material in "The Main

Question." Do your class members believe that these attitudes about older people are prevalent in our society? Have any of your class members had experiences of caring for elderly family member?

List on a chalkboard or newsprint the class members' responses to the statement, "The worst part about growing old is. . . . "

Now read aloud today's Scripture. Does your class hear anything in Luke's account of the situation of Zechariah and Elizabeth that relates to their own feelings about the elderly?

Developing the Lesson

I. Put the story of Elizabeth and Zechariah in context.

Using the material found in "The Scripture and the Main Question," discuss what it means for Luke to begin his story of the birth of Jesus with God's messengers coming to old people, young unmarried women, and shepherds.

Discuss what it meant back then for Elizabeth to be barren, without child. Ask, "Can you think of people in similar circumstances in our society who would feel themselves to be 'barren' like Elizabeth?" For instance, how does someone feel who has never been able to find a decent paying job? A person who has a terminal illness?

II. Questions raised by this story.

Ask your group whether they think it is proper for someone in the situation of Elizabeth and Zechariah to pray for a child. Is it appropriate for us to pray to God for change in such "hopeless" circumstances?

We modern, scientific, skeptical people are prone to ask, when we hear a strange, miraculous story like that of Elizabeth's pregnancy, "Now, how did that happen?" Of course, the response is, "We don't know." An event is neither strange nor miraculous if it can be explained. But what if the most pressing question to ask of today's Scripture is not "How did that happen?" but "Why did that happen?" What is the meaning of this event for the story of the coming of Christ?

In "The Scripture and the Main Question" it is suggested that Christ came to open up the closed lives of many in the first century—elderly people like Elizabeth and Zechariah, poor people like the shepherds. Have any members of your class known people, in desperate and closed circumstances, for whom, through their prayer, God has opened up new futures?

Do your class members see any dangers in applying the story of Elizabeth and Zechariah and their answered prayer to the circumstances of their lives today? For instance, what do you say to the childless couple who earnestly pray for a child but never receive a child? The concluding paragraphs of "The Scripture and the Main Question" may be helpful.

Helping Class Members Act

Behind today's lesson are some tough questions. This Scripture may not explicitly tell us why some of our prayers are answered and why some are not. The main assertion is that, when God enters the world in Christ, the future is much more open than we ever imagined. Doors are opened by the coming of the Christ.

Ask everyone to bow in silence for prayer. First, say to the group, "Think of some circumstance in your life right now in which the door seems closed, the future looks bleak." Then say, "Now, ask God to help you to find an open door out of this particular situation."

Close by praying the Lord's Prayer.

Planning for Next Week

Next Sunday, the Sunday before Christmas, we will focus on Luke's story of the birth of Jesus, in Luke 2:1-40. Ask your class, during their preparations for Christmas, to read the second chapter of Luke.

LESSON 3   DECEMBER 20

God's Promise to the Gentiles

Background Scripture: Luke 2:1-40

The Main Question

"CHRISTMAS IS THE SEASON OF GIVING," says a large billboard alongside the highway I take to work each day. As a Christian, I can certainly affirm the truth of that claim. Christmas *is* a season of giving. But it is not a season of giving in the sense proclaimed by that billboard, which is only an advertisement for a local department store. The giving that the billboard is talking about is not the gift of the Savior at Bethlehem. It is the buying for our family and friends all of the expensive gifts that are currently on sale at that department store.

When we Christians speak of Christmas as a "season of giving," we mean something quite different from what the rest of the world may mean. The second chapter of Luke's Gospel, so beloved by us all, speaks of the gift God put on our doorstep that first Christmas, the gift of salvation.

Much of our energy is expended this time of the year in thinking up appropriate gifts to give our family and friends. Today's Scripture focuses on the great gift God has given us in the Christ Child.

What is the gift that was given to us at Bethlehem?

Selected Scripture

King James Version	New Revised Standard Version
Luke 2:1-7, 22-32	*Luke 2:1-7, 22-32*
1 And it came to pass in those days, that there went out a decree from Caesar Augustus, that all the world should be taxed.	1 In those days a decree went out from Emperor Augustus that all the world should be registered. 2 This was the first registration and was

2 (And this taxing was first made when Cyrenius was governor of Syria.)

3 And all went to be taxed, every one into his own city.

4 And Joseph also went up from Galilee, out of the city of Nazareth, into Judaea, unto the city of David, which is called Bethlehem; (because he was of the house and lineage of David:)

5 To be taxed with Mary his espoused wife, being great with child.

6 And so it was, that, while they were there, the days were accomplished that she should be delivered.

7 And she brought forth her firstborn son, and wrapped him in swaddling clothes, and laid him in a manger; because there was no room for them in the inn.

....

22 And when the days of her purification according to the law of Moses were accomplished, they brought him to Jerusalem, to present him to the Lord;

23 (As it is written in the law of the Lord, Every male that openeth the womb shall be called holy to the Lord;)

24 And to offer a sacrifice according to that which is said in the law of the Lord, A pair of turtledoves, or two young pigeons.

25 And, behold, there was a man in Jerusalem, whose name was Simeon; and the same man was just and devout, waiting for the consolation of Israel: and the Holy Ghost was upon him.

26 And it was revealed unto him by the Holy Ghost, that he should not see death, before he had seen the Lord's Christ.

27 And he came by the Spirit into the temple: and when the parents

taken while Quirinius was governor of Syria. 3 All went to their own towns to be registered. 4 Joseph also went from the town of Nazareth in Galilee to Judea, to the city of David called Bethlehem, because he was descended from the house and family of David. 5 He went to be registered with Mary, to whom he was engaged and who was expecting a child. 6 While they were there, the time came for her to deliver her child. 7 And she gave birth to her firstborn son and wrapped him in bands of cloth, and laid him in a manger, because there was no place for them in the inn.

....

22 When the time came for their purification according to the law of Moses, they brought him up to Jerusalem to present him to the Lord 23 (as it is written in the law of the Lord, "Every firstborn male shall be designated as holy to the Lord"), 24 and they offered a sacrifice according to what is stated in the law of the Lord, "a pair of turtledoves or two young pigeons."

25 Now there was a man in Jerusalem whose name was Simeon; this man was righteous and devout, looking forward to the consolation of Israel, and the Holy Spirit rested on him. 26 It had been revealed to him by the Holy Spirit that he would not see death before he had seen the Lord's Messiah. 27 Guided by the Spirit, Simeon came into the temple; and when the parents brought in the child Jesus, to do for him what

brought in the child Jesus, to do for him after the custom of the law,

28 Then took he him up in his arms, and blessed God, and said,

29 Lord, now lettest thou thy servant depart in peace, according to thy word:

30 For mine eyes have seen thy salvation,

31 Which thou hast prepared before the face of all people;

32 A light to lighten the Gentiles, and the glory of thy people Israel.

was customary under the law, 28 Simeon took him in his arms and praised God, saying,

29 "Master, now you are dismissing your servant in peace, according to your word;

30 for my eyes have seen your salvation,

31 which you have prepared in the presence of all peoples,

32 a light for revelation to the Gentiles and for glory to thy people Israel."

Key Verses: **And the angel said unto them, Fear not: for, behold, I bring you good tidings of great joy, which shall be to all people. For unto you is born this day in the city of David a Saviour, which is Christ the Lord. (Luke 2:10-11)**

Key Verses: **But the angel said to them, "Do not be afraid; for see—I am bringing you good news of great joy for all the people: to you is born this day in the city of David a Savior, who is the Messiah, the Lord." (Luke 2:10-11)**

As You Read the Scripture

Luke 2:1-7, 22-32. This is Luke's beautiful and beloved account of the birth of Jesus. Through this narrative, Luke attempts to give us a preview of Jesus and his work by highlighting how Jesus was born and who was told of his birth.

Verses 1-5. The date was around 6–5 B.C. Augustus was one of the most renowned of the Roman emperors, the founder of the great "Peace of Augustus," when all of the Roman Empire was at peace. Unfortunately, this peace was based on ruthless military might. Evidence of the military occupation of Judea is found in Luke's comment that an order had been issued for "all the world" to be "registered." Many Jews resisted such enrollment, because its purpose was to register all Jews in order to control them better. Everyone, even pregnant women like Mary, was forced to travel back to the originating city of the man's family in order to be registered.

Verses 6-7. Swaddling cloths were strips of cloth that Near Eastern mothers wrapped around their babies—a sort of primitive diaper. Many Near Eastern families lived with their valuable livestock, so the use of the manger is probably not so unusual.

Verses 22-24. Such purification after childbirth and thanksgiving for the birth of a child is prescribed in Leviticus 12:2-8 and Exodus 13:2, 12. Luke depicts Mary and Joseph as faithful, obedient followers of the faith of Israel.

Verses 25-28. Simeon, like anyone in the Gospel of Luke who is given special revelation of the purposes of God, is gifted with the Holy Spirit. Once again, as in the case of Zechariah and Elizabeth (Luke 1:1-25), an older person is set at the forefront of the story of Jesus, thus showing God's special concern, in the new inbreaking kingdom, for the vulnerable and the marginalized of society.

Verses 29-32. This is possibly an early Christian hymn, the "Nunc Dimittis," so-called because of the Latin translation of the first words of the hymn. Note that Simeon foresees that this new child shall be "a light for revelation to the Gentiles" as well as for Israel, a foreshadowing by Luke of a major purpose of his Gospel—to show that Jesus comes for Gentiles as well as for Israel.

The Scripture and the Main Question

I Am Bringing You Good News of Great Joy

For a child has been born for us,
    a son given to us . . .
    and he is named
Wonderful Counselor, Mighty God,
    Everlasting Father, Prince of Peace. (Isa. 9:6)

Have you had the experience of receiving a gift from someone you really don't know all that well? A gift just out of the blue. You casually know this person, but certainly do not consider this person one of your good friends. And he or she gives you a gift. To your consternation, it turns out to be a really nice gift, one that you didn't really want and certainly didn't ask for, but there it is—a really good gift from someone who is not a really good friend.

Now, what is the first thing that you do? Right. You try to come up with a gift to give the person in return. You want to give the person a gift in return, not out of gratitude (after all, you didn't ask for it) or out of friendship (after all, you hardly know the person), but *because you don't want to feel guilty.*

You don't want to be indebted to that person. That gift, you see, lays a claim on you—especially when it has come to you from someone you hardly even know. And you don't like that. It's hard to look the person in the face until you have somehow reciprocated, because suddenly, whereas there was absolutely nothing linking you together before, now you are indebted to this virtual stranger. This person, in giving you a gift, has power over you, having indebted you.

Unto You Is Born . . . a Savior

It may well be, in Jesus' mind, more blessed to give than to receive. But I'll tell you this: It is more difficult to receive. Watch how people blush when they are given compliments. And watch what we do to Christmas, the so-called season of giving. We enjoy thinking of ourselves as basically generous, beneficent, giving people. That's one reason why everyone, even the nominally religious, loves Christmas. Christmas has become a season to celebrate our alleged generosity. The newspapers keep us posted on how many needy families there are in our communities. The Salvation Army kettles enable us to be generous while buying groceries (for ourselves) at the supermarket or gifts (for our families) at the shopping malls. The people at the office, who usually balk at taking up a collection to pay for the morning coffee break, fall all over themselves to collect funds to make Christmas for some family who doesn't have any.

We love Christmas because, as we say, "Christmas brings out the best in us." Everyone becomes a giver at Christmas, even the stingiest among us. Probably, Charles Dickens's story of the transformation of Scrooge has done more to form our notions of Christmas than has Luke's story of the birth in the manger. Whereas Luke tells the tale of God's gift to us, Dickens tells us a story of how we can give to others. Dickens's *A Christmas Carol* is more congenial to our images of ourselves—Dickens suggests that, down deep, even the worst of us is capable of becoming a generous, giving person, just like Ebenezer Scrooge.

However, we are better givers than getters, not because we are generous people, but because we are also proud, arrogant people for whom it is easier to give than to receive.

The Christmas story, according to the Gospel of Luke rather than Charles Dickens, is not about how blessed it is for you and me to be *givers,* but how essential it is for you and me to see ourselves as *receivers.* If you have ever been given a gift, a really good gift, by someone who is a virtual stranger, you know what I mean.

We like thinking of ourselves as givers—powerful, competent, self-sufficient, capable people for whom goodness consists of our being motivated to employ a little of our power, competence, and gifts for the benefit of the less fortunate among us. That is in direct contradiction to the biblical account of the first Christmas. There the story is not about us as givers but our nature as receivers. Listen again to Luke's or Matthew's account of the nativity, and you will be struck with how the stories of Jesus' birth go to great lengths to demonstrate that we—our power, generosity, competence, capabilities—had little to do with God's work in Jesus. God wanted to do something for us so strange, so utterly beyond the bounds of human imagination, so foreign to human projection, that God had to resort to angels, pregnant virgins, and stars in the sky to get it done. We didn't think of it, understand it, or approve it. All we could do, at Bethlehem, was receive it—a gift from a God we hardly even knew.

This fact hit me a few years ago during a counseling session with a woman in my church. It was December. She was telling me about her worry and confusion over a number of problems in her life. Because I had several counseling courses in seminary, I knew how to be a good counselor—that is, I knew to keep quiet, to listen patiently, to ask questions, but not to offer her any direct guidance. After I had given her ample opportunity to "ventilate" her feelings, I spoke to her as I had been taught to speak. "Now, I believe that you have the solution to your problems within you. I believe that, down deep, you know what your real problem is and that you have the resources to handle it. You have, within you, the solution to what ails you."

And then it hit me. Wait a minute. It was the middle of December, late Advent. In less than two weeks I would be standing in front of a congregation, reading the nativity story as told in Matthew or Luke, demonstrating through a strange story of a virgin birth to a peasant couple in Judea, that the solution to what ails us has very little to do with us. After generations of our trying to cure what ails us, God reached for something strange, radical, inconceivable. God put a solution on our backdoor step that was so radical most people missed it—and still miss it.

The faith that arises from this strange story of a birth in Bethlehem is *training in how to be a good receiver.* The first word of the Church, a people born out of so strange a nativity, is that the most important thing to know about us is that we are getters rather than givers. Discipleship is training in the art of seeing our lives as gifts. And that's tough. It's tough because I would rather see myself as a giver. I want power to stand on my own. I don't like picturing myself as dependent, needy, empty-handed.

Being a part of a university, working with many students, I've decided that this lack of receptivity to gifts is a major reason why many children come to despise their parents. It's humbling to see that your life, your talents, your capabilities, values, weaknesses, and strengths have come to you as gifts from your parents. We would rather be self-made men and women, standing on our own feet, striding bravely into a totally new world of our own creation. It's humbling to look into the mirror at twenty-one and admit, "My God, I look just like my old man."

I suspect this is also why marriage has fallen on hard times. It's painful to be thrust into such close proximity to another human being, day after day, year after year, until we gradually come to see that we are what we are, to an alarming degree, because of what our spouse has given us. Marriage is an everyday experience of living our lives in the red—debtors to someone we have just begun to know.

It's tough to be on the receiving end of God's love. It requires that we see our lives, not as our possessions, but as gifts. It's tough to admit that the things we need most come, not as the result of our programs, projects, and striving but as a result of God's gracious giving.

One of the most familiar Christmas texts is Isaiah 7:14: "The Lord himself will give you a sign. Look, the young woman is with child and shall bear a son, and shall name him Immanuel." Less familiar is its context: Isaiah has been pleading with King Ahaz to put his trust in God's promise to Israel rather than in alliances with stronger military powers. Isaiah warns King Ahaz: "If you do not stand firm in faith, you shall not stand at all." And then Isaiah tells the fearful king that God is going to give him a baby as a sign. Isn't that just like God? Ahaz must have thought. What Ahaz needed, with Assyria breathing down his neck, was a good army, not a baby!

This is often the way God loves us—with gifts we thought we didn't need, that transform us into people we don't necessarily like to be. With our advanced degrees and armies and government programs and material comforts and self-fulfillment techniques, we assume that religion is about giving a little of that to confirm to ourselves that we are indeed as powerful and self-sufficient as we claim.

Then a stranger comes to us and blesses us with a baby, calling us to see ourselves for who we really are—empty-handed recipients of a gracious God who, rather than leave us to our own devices, gave us a gift.

Helping Adults Become Involved

Preparing to Teach

"The Main Question" reminds us that today's Scripture from Luke's Gospel is one of the most familiar and dearly beloved texts in the whole Bible. That is a great help to you as a teacher. Yet, as the introduction to today's lesson suggests, it is also a great challenge. Having heard this text so often, many in your class may need to hear it again with a new hearing. So one of your goals as a teacher of today's lesson will be to help your class members encounter today's text anew.

The aim of today's lesson is summed up in its title: "God Offers Salvation." Throughout the lesson you will hear it stressed that the Incarnation of Christ is God's gift to us, an act of God that transcends human efforts.

With this in mind, read carefully "The Scripture and the Main Question" and "As You Read the Scripture." Keep a pen and paper handy as you read so that you can jot down your own insights and ideas to use in the presentation of the lesson.

Today's lesson outline:

> I. Introduction.
> II. Jesus is God's gift to us.
> III. God is with us.
> IV. Conclusion.

Introducing the Main Question

A number of provocative ideas are presented in "The Main Question." Read that section now. Through these ideas, you will be highlighting some of the basic theological concepts that lie behind Luke 2.

You might introduce today's lesson by leading your group in a discussion of "the difficulties of being a good giver." Everyone in the class has been going through the trials and tribulations of buying gifts for others for Christmas.

Then, using the opening material in "The Main Question," in your own words introduce the idea that, while it is often said that it is more blessed to give than to receive, it is also tough to receive. Lead the class in a discussion of how they feel when they have received a gift from someone they hardly know or when they have received a great compliment from someone. Do they agree with the idea that receiving gifts can be as difficult as giving gifts?

Developing the Lesson

I. Introduction.

Have someone in the class read aloud today's selected Scripture from Luke 2. Using the material in "As You Read the Scripture," note those aspects in Luke's story that underscore the helplessness and utter need of those who are the participants in the nativity (residents of occupied Judea, poor Mary and Joseph, poor shepherds).

II. Jesus is God's gift to us.

The Christmas story is about God as a giver and humanity as receivers. Ask your group, "Is this a message we like to hear?" Using some of the material in "The Scripture and the Main Question," lead a discussion of how our image of ourselves as resourceful, achievement-oriented, competent people who would rather do things for ourselves contrasts with Luke's proclamation of the birth of Jesus as the supreme instance of God's giving to us. In what ways, despite the beauty of Luke's words, is this a threatening or disturbing message for us?

Thinking back over what you know of the Bible, are there any instances you can think of to illustrate the difficulty we have in being receivers of God's gifts? (In the Exodus, after liberation from Egyptian slavery, the Hebrews made their own false gods rather than trust the God who delivered them. Later, Jesus told his disciples repeatedly to trust him rather than themselves for their security and power.)

III. God is with us.

In "The Scripture and the Main Question," marriage and childbearing are used as examples of training to be a good receiver. Ask your group if any of them have experienced this difficulty in being a receiver of gifts in their own lives. Are there any ways in which your group feels that society is getting back to making Christmas a religious rather than merely a commercial holiday? Many families are consciously cutting back on their own Christmas expenses. Some people are learning the joy of making Christmas gifts rather than simply going to a store and buying them. Others donate to a charity in honor of a person the money they would have used to purchase a gift for that person. These are possible ways in which persons hope to recover the true spirit of Christmas giving.

IV. Conclusion.

Christmas is the celebration of the Incarnation. "This will be a sign for you," the angels told the shepherds (Luke 2:12). Jesus is our visible, tangible, in-the-flesh sign of God's determination to save us by God's means rather than our own.

"The Scripture and the Main Question" suggests that sometimes our giving to others is a subtle means of giving to ourselves. What does your group think of that idea? God's love, made flesh in the babe at Bethlehem, wants to make receivers of us all.

Helping Class Members Act

Only a few days lie between us and Christmas. Even in these few remaining pre-Christmas days, there is still time for us to experience and to demonstrate the gift of salvation, which the birth of Jesus brought to us. Suggest that members of the class might think of one person who, during the past year, has given them a gift—a teacher, a good friend, a pastor, a child. Ask members to take some time, during the next busy days before Christmas, to thank that person for the gift of his or her life. In this way, we acknowledge, in our life together, that we are more often receivers than givers.

Planning for Next Sunday

The next time we meet, Christmas will be two days past. Our Christmas celebration will be mostly over. Yet, our exploration of the meaning of the advent of Jesus into our world will just be beginning. Ask class members to read Matthew 3:16–4:11 in preparation for next Sunday's class.

Jesus Filled with the Spirit

Background Scripture: Matthew 3:1–4:11

The Main Question

We have entered the season of the Christian year called Christmas. In our International Lessons, this Sunday we enter the time of Jesus' ministry. Quite quickly the Gospel writers take us through Jesus' birth in Bethlehem, saying almost nothing about his childhood or young adult development, to the time of his baptism by John in the Jordan. His ministry is beginning.

On Christmas we celebrated the Incarnation, the truth that God is with us, Immanuel. Now we begin exploring the implications of that claim for us. The babe at Bethlehem is also the one empowered to represent the words and ways of God to humanity.

I work with young adults at a university. A frequent dilemma for young adults is what they should do with their lives. They are preoccupied with vocational questions. A major source of their dilemma is their lack of confidence that they have what it takes to perform a job.

"I like science, but do I have the patience to be a doctor?" they ask.

"I have always done well in school, and I like to study. But I'm not sure if that qualifies me to be a good high school teacher."

They wonder whether they have what it takes to get the job done.

At the beginning of his ministry, as a young adult, Jesus had his life's work before him. Surely he must have wondered, as any young adult would, whether he had what it takes to get the job done. How will Jesus face the great challenges that lie ahead? In his baptism, Jesus was given what it took to get the job done.

What does it mean to be strengthened by the Spirit? That's the question we shall explore together in today's lesson.

Selected Scripture

King James Version	New Revised Standard Version
Matthew 3:16-17	*Matthew 3:16-17*
16 And Jesus, when he was baptized, went up straightway out of the water: and, lo, the heavens were opened unto him, and he saw the Spirit of God descending like a dove, and lighting upon him:	16 And when Jesus had been baptized, just as he came up from the water, suddenly the heavens were opened to him and he saw the Spirit of God descending like a dove and alighting on him. 17 And a voice from heaven said, "This is my Son, the Beloved, with whom I am well pleased."
17 And lo a voice from heaven, saying, This is my beloved Son, in whom I am well pleased.	
Matthew 4:1-11	*Matthew 4:1-11*
1 Then was Jesus led up of the Spirit into the wilderness to be tempted of the devil.	1 Then Jesus was led up by the Spirit into the wilderness to be tempted by the devil. 2 He fasted

2 And when he had fasted forty days and forty nights, he was afterward an hungered.

3 And when the tempter came to him, he said, If thou be the Son of God, command that these stones be made bread.

4 But he answered and said, It is written, Man shall not live by bread alone, but by every word that proceedeth out of the mouth of God.

5 Then the devil taketh him up into the holy city, and setteth him on a pinnacle of the temple,

6 And saith unto him, If thou be the Son of God, cast thyself down: for it is written, He shall give his angels charge concerning thee: and in their hands they shall bear thee up, lest at any time thou dash thy foot against a stone.

7 Jesus said unto him, It is written again, Thou shalt not tempt the Lord thy God.

8 Again, the devil taketh him up into an exceeding high mountain, and sheweth him all the kingdoms of the world, and the glory of them;

9 And saith unto him, All these things will I give thee, if thou wilt fall down and worship me.

10 Then saith Jesus unto him, Get thee hence, Satan: for it is written, Thou shalt worship the Lord thy God, and him only shalt thou serve.

11 Then the devil leaveth him, and, behold, angels came and ministered unto him.

Key Verses: **And Jesus, when he was baptized, went up straightway out of the water: and, lo, the heavens were opened unto him, and he saw the Spirit of God descending like a dove, and lighting upon him: And lo a voice from heaven, saying, This is my beloved Son, in whom I am well pleased. (Matthew 3:16-17)**

forty days and forty nights, and afterwards he was famished. 3 The tempter came and said to him, "If you are the Son of God, command these stones to become loaves of bread." 4. But he answered, "It is written,

'One does not live by bread alone,
   but by every word that comes
     from the mouth of God.'"

5 Then the devil took him to the holy city and placed him on the pinnacle of the temple, 6 saying to him, "If you are the Son of God, throw yourself down; for it is written,

'He will command his angels
   concerning you,'
and 'On their hands they will
   bear you up,
so that you will not dash your foot
   against a stone.'"

7 Jesus said to him, "Again it is written, 'Do not put the Lord your God to the test.'"

8 Again, the devil took him to a very high mountain and showed him all the kingdoms of the world and their splendor; 9 and he said to him, "All these I will give you, if you will fall down and worship me." 10 Jesus said to him, "Away with you, Satan! for it is written,

'Worship the Lord your God,
   and serve only him.'"

11 Then the devil left him, and suddenly angels came and waited on him.

Key Verses: **And when Jesus had been baptized, just as he came up from the water, suddenly the heavens were opened to him and he saw the Spirit of God descending like a dove and alighting on him. And a voice from heaven said, "This is my Son, the Beloved, with whom I am well pleased." (Matthew 3:16-17)**

As You Read the Scripture

Matthew 3:16—4:11. Matthew's account of the baptism of Jesus by John and the subsequent testing of Jesus by Satan in the wilderness serve to give the reader important information about the nature of Jesus and his ministry.

Verses 16-17. John was practicing baptism as a rite that prepared converts for the new messianic reign. John is therefore surprised when Jesus comes for baptism (Matthew 3:13-15). Jesus explains to John that he has come to "fulfill all righteousness," to show people the way to become part of the new kingdom. Baptism, showing that everyone needs to repent (to change, to turn around), is the door to membership in the movement that begins in Jesus. The opening heavens and descent of the dove at Jesus' baptism separate his baptism from others.

Matthew 4:1. No sooner is Jesus baptized than he is tested out in the "wilderness." In the Old Testament, after Israel is liberated from Egyptian slavery, Israel faced severe trail and testing "in the wilderness." Time and again, Israel failed its testing in the wilderness. What will happen to Jesus?

Verse 2. Fasting was the traditional way to prepare oneself for holy work (see Exodus 34:28).

Verses 3-4. Satan uses food as a means of testing Jesus. Recall that Israel, in the wilderness during the Exodus, was tested with food because of hunger. "The tempter" (v. 3), the devil, and "Satan" (v. 10) are interchangeable names for that being who is actively opposed to the will of God. Jesus responds by quoting Scripture (Deuteronomy 8:3).

Verses 5-7. Next Satan tempts Jesus by suggesting that he use spectacular, miraculous shows of power to prove that he is who the voice at his baptism said that he was. Again, Jesus responds by quoting Scripture (Deuteronomy 6:16).

Verses 8-11. Finally Satan suggests that Jesus seize political power (which Satan says belongs to him!). Jesus rejects this as the way to his kingdom, quoting Deuteronomy 6:13. Luke thus shows that Jesus is quite knowledgeable and puts his trust in the Hebrew Scriptures. He also shows, through the temptation accounts, what this new kingdom will not be as well as what it will be.

The Scripture and the Main Question

"The Heavens Were Opened" (Matthew 3:16)

Let's be honest: The Sunday after Christmas is not a particularly great day to be at church. Many people use this weekend for travel to visit relatives, so expect attendance in your class to be down today. After all the energy and preparation and buildup for Christmas, it is inevitable that today, two days after Christmas, should seem a bit anticlimactic. On Christmas Eve in your church, the music, the preaching, and the fellowship of the Christmas service were wonderful. But that was Christmas—this is the Sunday after Christmas.

Life outside of church consists of peaks and valleys. Sometimes you are up, but more often you are down. In our day, religion is frequently reduced to an exercise in self-induced joy or peace. We say that we're in church to put ourselves "in the right frame of mind," to "give ourselves a lift."

The preacher and choir labor to "create a worshipful mood" in us. Why doesn't it last?

Self-induced religion is no match for the realities of life. Our moods and emotions are notoriously fickle. One moment we feel secure in our faith, strong and committed. The next moment we do not know what we believe.

We hear the beautiful poetry of the beloved Christmas carols, and we are sure of our belief, certain of our commitment to God. But then there is the Sunday after Christmas. The crowd is smaller. The choir has been given a vacation after their hard work for the Christmas cantata. Things are down.

What we need is some means of keeping us at discipleship even when we don't feel like it, even when it doesn't please us to be faithful. We need some power outside ourselves, better than ourselves, some strength greater than our own.

As Jesus began his ministry, he came to be baptized by John in the Jordan River (Matthew 3:16-17). The "heavens opened, and he saw the Spirit of God descending like a dove and alighting on him. Then a voice from heaven said, 'This is my Son, the Beloved, with whom I am well pleased'" (Matthew 3:17). Whatever fears Jesus might have had about his ability to accomplish his mission, whatever doubts he might have had about his own abilities, all of this was strengthened through the gift of the Spirit, through this public outpouring of the power of God on his life.

Here is our hope in our own times of difficulty and despair. Whenever we go through the valley, we can take heart in the fact that at our baptism, even as in Jesus' baptism, we are gifted with the empowering, enabling, strengthening Spirit.

The Spirit of God

How much do we talk today about God as a Spirit? That seems too strange, exotic, optional in a modern, thinking, whirring machine of a world where competent people are busy helping themselves, taking charge, looking out for themselves, shaping their destinies, determining their own future.

If you don't have spirit, then it's best to keep everything in your life manageable. Keep your goals easily attainable, your sights fixed clearly on the status quo. Just go ahead and be who you are without trying to be any better than you are. Without spirit, without some help, some prodding, some force behind you more significant than you, that's about the best you can expect of life.

Fortunately, according to today's Scripture, Jesus was given the Spirit. He moved from his baptism in the Jordan to his temptation in the wilderness. There Satan offered the young Jesus everything that is generally considered worth having in this life—bread (material blessings), the kingdoms of this world (political power), spectacular displays of divine power (miraculous religion)—and Jesus had the strength to turn his back on it all, to walk down the narrow path to which God had called him. This empowerment came through the gift of the Spirit.

In your life, too, because of baptism, you have spirit. You can attempt big things in your life, face the most tempting of temptations squarely in the face and still be able to resist. The same power that enabled Jesus to do God's will enables you to do God's will as well. You've got Spirit.

SECOND QUARTER

Descending Like a Dove

Our text occurs at the beginning of Jesus' ministry, with his baptism in the Jordan and his temptations in the wilderness. Later, as his earthly ministry ended, the Risen Christ came back to his disciples, telling them to wait in Jerusalem until they were given the same power Jesus has (Acts 1). Then on the day of Pentecost, the heavens opened again, with a rush of wind and tongues of fire.

That baptismal fire has, since Pentecost, spread like wildfire over the face of the earth so that there is no nation without people who are empowered with the same Spirit that inflamed Jesus. Across all boundaries—racial, national, political—leapt this fire; through all barriers has pushed this power so that, in every corner of the earth, there is someone who is able to rise up and say:

> The spirit of the Lord God is upon me,
>   because the Lord has anointed me;
> he has sent me to bring good
>   news to the oppressed,
>   to bind up the brokenhearted,
> to proclaim liberty to the captives. (Isaiah 61:1-2)

Jesus promised us, "Just wait. I'll give you the same power that encouraged me." He is talking about *you*. Now, anything can happen.

Helping Adults Become Involved

Preparing to Teach

In this lesson, using parts of the third and fourth chapters of Matthew, we explore the gift of the Spirit to Jesus at his baptism and then Jesus' empowerment by the Spirit to resist temptation in the wilderness. You might organize today's lesson in two main parts: (1) Jesus' empowerment with the Spirit at his baptism and its strengthening him to resist temptation, and (2) our empowerment by the Spirit at our baptism and the Spirit's strengthening us to resist temptation and to be faithful in our struggles.

Think about this suggested lesson plan as you read through the material in "The Main Question," "As You Read the Scripture," and "The Scripture and the Main Question." Jot down ideas, illustrations from your own life experience of the Holy Spirit, and other notes as you read.

Introducing the Main Question

Begin today's class by reading, or by simply paraphrasing in your own words, today's account from Matthew about Jesus' baptism and his temptation in the wilderness. Using the material in "As You Read the Scripture" and "The Bible and the Main Question," point out the significance of Jesus' baptism and the meaning of the three temptations Satan put before him in the wilderness.

Today's lesson outline:

    I. Introduction.
   II. The Spirit strengthened Jesus.
  III. The Spirit strengthens each of us.
  IV. Conclusion.

Developing the Lesson

I. Introduction.
Obtain a copy of your church's baptismal ritual. It may be contained in your church's hymnal, or your pastor may be able to provide you with a copy. Summarize its contents for your class. Find the point in the baptismal service when the Holy Spirit is mentioned.

II. The Spirit strengthened Jesus.
Note how Jesus, early in his adult life, had to face temptation. He was strengthened by the Spirit.

Recalling other episodes from Jesus' ministry, can your group think of other times when Jesus was strengthened by the Spirit? (Examples: in Nazareth, when Jesus preached his first sermon, saying, "The Spirit of the Lord is upon me to preach . . ." [Luke 4], when Jesus prayed in Gethsemane [Matthew 26:30-46], etc.).

III. The Spirit strengthens each of us.
Now move to the second major part of today's lesson, the application of our affirmation of the Spirit to our needs as contemporary disciples. Using the material in "The Scripture and the Main Question," as well as any experiences of the Spirit in your own life, lead your adults in a discussion of the way in which the Spirit provides us strength to resist our own temptations and to be faithful in our day. Of course, the Spirit, by its very nature, is undefinable, invisible (even though it took the form of a dove at Jesus' baptism), so our experiences of the Spirit will be varied.

Remind your class members of the temptations Satan offered Jesus. Using the discussion of the temptation in "The Scripture and the Main Question," ask them to list—as you write responses on a chalkboard or newsprint—some of the major temptations that are set before contemporary followers of Jesus. In "The Main Question," we note that young adults may face certain doubts and temptations. What are some of the greatest challenges facing young adults today? In other words, if Satan were tempting us today in the wilderness, which temptations might he offer us?

Can anyone in your class point to evidence that the Spirit is strengthening us to resist these contemporary temptations?

As discussed in "The Scripture and the Main Question," the church has been given the gift of the Spirit, even as individual Christians are gifted with the Spirit at our baptism. What evidence is there that, nearly two thousand years after Pentecost, we continue to be gifted with the Spirit as a Church?

Helping Class Members Act

Today's Scripture asserts that Jesus was gifted with the Spirit at the beginning of his ministry. Yet, Matthew 3:16–4:11 is not just an account of the gift of the Spirit. It is also a story of the use of the Spirit. No sooner had

Jesus received the Spirit than he went into the wilderness, where he relied on the Spirit to help him resist Satan's temptations.

Likewise, it is one thing for us to be gifted with the Spirit in our baptism, but it is another thing for each of us to rely on the Spirit to guide our lives. How often do we, when confronted with some perplexing decision in life, ask ourselves, "Where is the Holy Spirit attempting to lead me in this situation?"

Most of us, according to the discussion in "The Scripture and the Main Question," are accustomed to relying on ourselves rather than on the Spirit. We like to think of ourselves as competent, relatively self-sufficient individuals.

But for us to live the Christian faith boldly means that we will be boldly confronted by the powers of evil. No sooner have we finished celebrating Christmas than we reenter a world that mocks our Christmas cheer. No sooner have we been baptized and called "Christians" than we encounter a host of forces that try to erase that name from us. Ask the class members to suggest some of the forces that assault the church today, pressuring the church to become sidetracked from its divinely appointed mission (material success, popularity, anxiety over its own survival, etc.).

Close today's session by asking members of your class to sit quietly for a moment and ponder the working of the Spirit upon their lives, asking themselves, "Where is the Holy Spirit leading me today? In what ways can I be a better bearer of God's Spirit?"

Planning for Next Sunday

Next Sunday we will continue this exploration of the Spirit. While we have focused on the gift of the Spirit to individual Christians in today's lesson, next Sunday we shall explore the gift of the Spirit as a communal, ecclesial experience. The Spirit is not just given to individuals, it is given to the whole Church. Ask class members to read the account of Pentecost in Acts 2, asking themselves as they read, "What difference does it make that the church has received the gift of the Holy Spirit?"

UNIT II: LIVING THE GOOD NEWS

William and Patricia Willimon

FIVE LESSONS   JANUARY 3–31

There is an expression I have sometimes heard in the church in my part of the world: "Don't talk the talk if you don't walk the walk."

That is a rather down-home way of speaking about a central Christian belief. That is, don't transform the Christian faith into some intellectual "head trip," something you are to think about, to get straight in your head. Christianity, the gospel Jesus preached, is a "discipleship trip."

Edgar Guest said, "I'd rather see a sermon than hear one." He meant that he would rather see the faith embodied in a person's life rather than simply hear platitudes and intellectual assertions about the faith.

In previous lessons, we celebrated the coming of the good news in the birth of Jesus in Bethlehem and the descent of the Holy Spirit at Pentecost. But the good news is rather empty if it doesn't somehow issue forth in our lives. The good news of Jesus must not only be asserted, but it must be lived as well. Therefore, we now begin a series of lessons on "Living the Good News." These lessons will all explore the practical, daily (remember, Jesus told us to take up our cross "daily") implications of the good news of the gospel.

Exploring passages from the Acts of the Apostles as well as a number of the Epistles, we shall uncover implications not only for believing Jesus but also for following Jesus.

Please note that our organization of *The International Lesson Annual* always moves from study of the lesson to application of the lesson. The climax of each lesson is the last section, "Helping Adults Become Involved." That's where you come in. You are the teacher, who not only helps class members to think about Scripture, but also encourages them to live the Scripture, to become involved.

Don't talk the talk if you don't walk the walk!

The Coming of the Holy Spirit

Background Scripture: Acts 2

The Main Question

"Unless the LORD builds the house, those who build it labor in vain" (Psalm 127:1). The community, rather than taking matters into its own hands by organizing and venturing forth with banners unfurled, has withdrawn to wait and to pray. The next move is up to God. It is up to the risen Christ to make good his promise to bestow the Spirit and to restore the kingdom to Israel. In a sense, this is what prayer is—the bold, even arrogant, effort on the part of the community to hold God to his promises. In praying, "Thy kingdom come, thy will be done," we pray that God will be true to himself and give us what has been promised. Prayer is born out of confidence in the faithfulness of God to the promises God makes.

The Church still exists today in a situation of complete dependency upon God to empower it with the Spirit. Despite our hard work in the Church, if God doesn't want the Church, if God is unwilling to empower us with the gift of the Spirit, then there will be no church.

Here you are, probably late at night, preparing to teach this lesson for your adult class. This is hard work. Yet, the truth of the matter is that if God refuses to empower you to teach the word, all your hard work will be in vain. At least that is the implication of our scripture from Acts 2. In all that we do as Christians, we utterly depend on God's Spirit.

How is God's empowering Spirit received?

Selected Scripture

King James Version	New Revised Standard Version

Acts 2:1-7, 12-17a

1 And when the day of Pentecost was fully come, they were all with one accord in one place.

2 And suddenly there came a sound from heaven as of a rushing mighty wind, and it filled all the house where they were sitting.

3 And there appeared unto them cloven tongues like as of fire, and it sat upon each of them.

4 And they were all filled with the Holy Ghost, and began to speak with other tongues, as the Spirit gave them utterance.

5 And there were dwelling at Jerusalem Jews, devout men, out of every nation under heaven.

6 Now when this was noised abroad, the multitude came together, and were confounded, because that every man heard them speak in his own language.

7 And they were all amazed and marvelled, saying one to another, Behold, are not all these which speak Galilaeans?

....

12 And they were all amazed, and were in doubt, saying one to another, What meaneth this?

13 Others mocking said, These men are full of new wine.

14 But Peter, standing up with the eleven, lifted up his voice, and said unto them, Yet men of Judaea, and all ye that dwell at Jerusalem, be this known unto you, and hearken to my words:

15 For these are not drunken, as ye suppose, seeing it is but the third hour of the day.

16 But this is that which was spoken by the prophet Joel;

17 And it shall come to pass in the last days, saith God, I will pour out of my Spirit upon all flesh.

Acts 2:1-7, 12-17a

1 When the day of Pentecost had come, they were all together in one place. 2 And suddenly from heaven there came a sound like the rush of a violent wind, and it filled the entire house where they were sitting. 3 Divided tongues, as of fire, appeared among them, and a tongue rested on each one of them. 4 All of them were filled with the Holy Spirit and began to speak in other languages, as the Spirit gave them ability.

5 Now there were devout Jews from every nation under heaven living in Jerusalem. 6 And at this sound the crowd gathered and was bewildered, because each one heard them speaking in the native language of each. 7 Amazed and astonished, they asked "Are not all these who are speaking Galileans?"

....

12 All were amazed and perplexed, saying to one another, "What does this mean?" 13 But others sneered and said, "They are filled with new wine."

14 But Peter, standing with the eleven, raised his voice and addressed them, "Men of Judea and all who live in Jerusalem, let this be known to you, and listen to what I say. 15 Indeed, these are not drunk, as you suppose, for it is only nine o'clock in the morning. 16 No, this is what was spoken through the prophet Joel:

17 "In the last days it will be, God declares,

that I will pour out my Spirit upon all flesh."

Key Verse: **And they were all filled with the Holy Ghost, and began to speak with other tongues, as the Spirit gave them utterance. (Acts 2:4)**

Key Verse: **All of them were all filled with the Holy Spirit and began to speak in other languages, as the Spirit gave them ability. (Acts 2:4)**

As You Read the Scripture

Acts 2:1-7, 12-17a. The day of Pentecost was the day in which Israel celebrated the giving of the Law (found in the first five books of the Old Testament, the "Pentateuch"), seven weeks after Passover (see Leviticus 23:15-21). By placing the gift of the Spirit on this day, Luke links the gift of the Law to Israel with the Church's reception of the gift of the Spirit. Even as the Law empowered the religion of Israel, so also the Spirit empowers the religion of the Church.

Verses 1-5. John the Baptist had foreseen the gift of the Spirit and fire (see Luke 3:16). This dramatic event depicts the inbreaking of this holy fire. The other languages may be the ecstatic, charismatic speech that caused trouble in Corinth (1 Corinthians 14:1-33), or Luke may have in mind simply the speech of all the nations of the earth, which were said to be present at the Pentecost gathering (vv. 5-11). There is a wordplay at work here since Greek uses the same word (*pneuma*) to describe "wind" and "spirit."

Verses 6-12. Some have said that the real miracle of Pentecost was the gift of hearing rather than the gift of strange speech. The people are amazed that, even though there they are from "every nation under heaven" (v. 5), everyone is able to hear and to understand what is being said (unlike the gathering at the tower of Babel, where everyone's speech was confused [Genesis 11:1-9]). What does this strange phenomenon mean?

Verses 13-16. Peter responds, giving the young church's interpretation of the event, to the mocking crowd outside the room, who hear the strange noises and ascribe it to drunkenness. All of this is in gracious fulfillment of Joel's prediction that one day the Spirit would be given to all people (Joel 2:28-32).

Verse 17a. Previously, the Spirit was given only to certain individuals, the prophets, who were gifted with prophetic power through the Spirit. Now, after Pentecost, anyone is able to receive the Spirit in this new community of the Spirit. As Peter says at the end of his Pentecost sermon, "Everyone who calls on the name of the Lord shall be saved" (Acts 2:21).

The Scripture and the Main Question

When the Day of Pentecost Had Come

In telling the story of Christ, Luke, more than any of the other Gospels, expends great detail on Jesus' birth. In Luke's Gospel, the birth stories become a kind of vignette of the rest of the story. "In my beginning is my end," says the poet, T. S. Eliot. The start of a person's life indicates the direction his or her life will take. Much that will have significance later can be seen in our origins. Therefore, it is with great interest that we turn to Luke's account of the birth of the Church at Pentecost. (In fact, a comparison of the birth of Jesus in Luke with the birth of the Church in

Luke's second volume, Acts, yields fascinating parallels: Both stories begin with the arrival of the Spirit; in both, the period immediately before is not devoid of the Spirit's work; in both, the promise is contrasted with John the Baptist.) Knowing the way Luke handles a story, we can expect to learn much from this narrative of the infancy of the first Christian community.

It is popular to refer to Pentecost as the "birthday of the Church." At Pentecost the power of God, made manifest at the resurrection and ascension of Christ, is bestowed on the people of God. In reading the Pentecost account in the second chapter of Acts, we are part of an author's struggle to bring to speech something of the truth about the Church, something that cannot be known except by this story. Therefore, we shall pass over questions of probable historical context, possible psychological motives, or other questions that might interest us and let the story have its way with us. We shall let this story redescribe and create new reality for us, trying to uncover the answers to the questions the story would have us ask. The new community is revealed by a recounting of its origin in a powerful work of the Spirit.

They Were All Filled with the Holy Spirit

It is the dawn of the day of Pentecost, and the followers of Jesus are gathered to wait and to pray. The new day begins with an eruption of sounds from heaven and wind (2:2). Things are coming loose, breaking open. Can it be the same wind that, on the very first morning of all mornings, swept across dark waters—the wind of creation (Genesis 1)? The wind is once again bringing something to life.

What was first heard is then seen—tongues like fire (2:3). It is not until verse 4 that we learn that this strange eruption is none other than the promised Holy Spirit. John the Baptist had said that the Christ would "baptize you with the Holy Spirit and fire" (Luke 3:16). The first gift of the Spirit is the gift of speaking different languages. So we are hearing a story about the eruption of the Spirit into the community and the first fruit of the Spirit—the gift of proclamation.

The scene shifts from inside the upper room, where the disciples are gathered, to the street outside, where the gospel is already drawing a crowd. In the beginning of his Gospel, Luke characterizes John the Baptist as one who "will turn many of the people of Israel to the Lord their God" (Luke 1:16). But out in the street, "devout Jews from every nation under heaven" (Acts 2:5) for the first time confront the Church, and their response is bewilderment. The irruption of the Spirit leads to proclamation by the community, which leads to the bewilderment of bystanders. These "tongues" are obviously various languages of "every nation under heaven," since each foreigner exclaims, "We hear, each of us, in our own native language" (v. 8). No nationality of dispersed Jews is excluded from the proclamation, as Luke's roll call of the peoples makes clear.

Yet, nothing is clear to the bystanders, who are thoroughly "amazed and perplexed" by the whole episode, questioning, "What does this mean?" (v. 12). Some of the bystanders do not want to know. They have their own urbane, sophisticated, yet mocking, theory for such strange manifestations of religious enthusiasm: "They are filled with new wine" (v. 13). The world explains as mere inebriation the power that the church proclaims as gift of God.

The Spirit Gave Them Ability

The crowd's questions become a cue for one of the disciples to stand and speak; and Luke expends about twice as many verses interpreting the meaning of the ecstatic events as he does reporting the event itself. Who could have predicted the one who speaks? We have heard him speak before, in Acts 1:16-22. But then we could hardly hear Peter speak to the necessity of finding a replacement for the betrayer Judas, because of our still lingering memory of how Peter himself had proved quite capable of repeated betrayal when the going got rough (Luke 22:31-34, 54-62). It was Peter who only "followed at a distance," Peter whom the maid drove to utter the terrible words, "Woman, I do not know him" (Luke 22:57). We left him weeping in the courtyard, a disciple tested and found wanting.

This underscores the miracle that here, before the half-inquiring, half-mocking crowd, Peter is the first, the very first, to lift up his voice and proclaim openly the word, which only a few weeks before he could not speak even to a serving woman at midnight. In Genesis 2:7, the Spirit of God breathed life into dust and created a human being. In Acts 2:1-4, the Spirit has breathed life into a once cowardly disciple and created a new man, who now has the gift of bold speech.

One popular interpretation of Pentecost is that this story signifies that what happened at Babel has been reversed (Genesis 11:1-9). Human language, so confused at Babel, has been restored, and community, so scattered there, has been restored. It is doubtful that Luke had this in mind. The "mighty works of God" are proclaimed only to Jews at this point. The time is not yet ripe in the story for the division between Jew and Gentile to be healed. The miracle is one of proclamation. Those who had no "tongue" to speak of the "mighty works of God" now have the means to preach.

It is doubtful that Luke is describing ecstatic speech here, because that sort of speech needed translation in order for anyone to understand. Judging from the discussion of glossolalia in 1 Corinthians 14, it appears that the Spirit manifested its presence in a variety of ways in Paul's churches. Luke's concern is with the description of a Spirit-empowered, intelligible proclamation in foreign languages (2:6, 8).

To those in the Church today who regard the Spirit as an exotic phenomenon of mainly interior and purely personal significance, the story of the Spirit's descent at Pentecost offers a rebuke. Luke goes to great pains to insist that this outpouring of the Spirit is anything but inferior. Everything is consumed by wind and fire, loud talk, buzzing confusion, and public debate. The Spirit is the power that enables the church to "go public" with its good news, to attract a crowd, and, as we shall see in the next section, to have something to say that is worth hearing. A new wind is set loose upon the earth, provoking a storm of wrath and confusion for some, a fresh breath of hope and empowerment for others. Pentecost is a phenomenon of mainly evangelistic significance, as the central question of the crowd makes clear: *What must we do to be saved?* Whereas the crowd who heard Jesus' sermon in Nazareth sneered, "Is not this Joseph's son?" (Luke 4:22), Luke is delighted to report that Peter's Spirit-inspired sermon produced enthusiastic converts. Now "Jews from every nation under heaven" are coming to the good news.

Helping Adults Become Involved

Preparing to Teach

It seems fitting, on this first Sunday of 1993, that our biblical text should be from Acts 2, Luke's account of the first gathering of the Church. The beginning of the new year is a good time for us to remind ourselves of the basics, to get things in perspective, to get back in touch with our origins.

The discussion of Acts 2 in "The Scripture and the Main Question" suggests parallels between Luke's account of the birth of the Church in Acts 2 and his account of the birth of Jesus in the second chapter of his Gospel. Fortunately, you studied Luke 2 with your class a couple of Sundays ago. Since we are still in the period of Christmas, according to the calendar of the Church Year (Epiphany is not until January 6), you might make today's class a fitting culmination of the Christmas season.

The main assertion today's Scripture makes about the Church is that it is the creation of God, a result of the gracious outpouring of God's Spirit. Without that Spirit, there would be no Church. As the beloved hymn by Samuel J. Stone puts it:

> The church's one foundation is Jesus Christ her Lord;
> She is his new creation by water and the Word.

Read carefully "The Scripture and the Main Question" as well as "As You Read the Scripture." Here you will discover the main thrust of today's lesson as well as gain insights into the explication of the text. As you read, think about your own congregation. Ask yourself, "In what ways is my church the fulfillment of the nature of the Church as depicted in Acts 2? In what ways does my church today show the need to be open to the leading of the Holy Spirit?"

Have paper and pencils ready. Also, if you follow the suggestion of ending your class with one of the hymns of the Holy Spirit, you will need hymnals or copies of the hymn you plan to use.

Here is today's outline:

I. The story of the gift of God's Spirit
II. The implications of the gift of God's Spirit
III. Conclusion

Introducing the Main Question

"The Main Question" serves as an introduction to today's lesson. Read that section again, keeping in mind that the main concern is to present the Church as the gift of the Holy Spirit at Pentecost.

I. The story of the gift of God's Spirit
Begin today's class by reading aloud the text from Acts 2. Then, using the material in "As You Read the Scripture" as well as the commentary found in "The Scripture and the Main Question," lead your class through the text, pointing out ideas and insights you have learned about the text.

Tell your class about the connection between the Greek word for

150

"wind" (*pneuma*) and the Greek word for "Spirit" (*pneuma*). The connection between the Spirit or "wind" (which is mentioned in Genesis 1:2), and the "wind" or Spirit that blows in on Pentecost is a connection of creation. From nothing God creates something new. Whereas in Genesis 2 a new world was created, in Acts 2 a new people, the Church, is being created.

II. The implications of the gift of God's Spirit

Now, having gone through the biblical text itself, you are ready to lead your class in a discussion of the implications of the Scripture. Ask them, "What do we learn about the nature of the Church from this story its birth?" List responses on a chalkboard or newsprint. Some responses may be that we learn that the church is for all people, from all nations and that a major job of the Church is speaking, proclamation.

III. The need for the Spirit in the Church today

We spend all this time in the Acts of the Apostles looking at the Church of two thousand years ago in order to better see our Church today. Distribute paper and pencils to class members and ask them to think about the Church of today. Remembering Luke's account of the Church at Pentecost, they should write down what they think are the most pressing needs of today's Church for which we need the empowerment of the Holy Spirit.

For instance, my own denomination, like many mainline Protestant denominations, has lost many thousands of members over the last few decades. Our failure to evangelize the unchurched is accentuated by the account in Acts of Peter's bold preaching and its rather dramatic response. We need the gift of the Spirit for evangelism!

Give your class members a few minutes to think quietly about the question you have raised, then lead them in a discussion of the needs of your church for the strengthening of the Spirit.

Helping Class Members Act

In "The Main Question" we note how interesting it is that the disciples, after Jesus' resurrection and ascension, withdraw to pray. They don't act. They don't move forward, organize, form committees, take up an offering, begin a new program. They pray.

Remember: The Spirit is what we need, and it comes, not as our accomplishment, but as God's gift. The Spirit is a gift. Therefore, a good way to end today's class might be for class members to place themselves in a position similar to that of the Church before Pentecost. Having cited all the needs of our Church today for the Spirit, pray for the gift of the Spirit to empower us in our time and place.

Close by singing (or simply reading together) one of the church's great hymns about the Spirit. For instance, "Breathe on Me, Breath of God," "Spirit of Faith, Come Down," or "Spirit of God, Descend upon My Heart."

Planning for Next Sunday

We continue our unit on "Living the Good News" by studying our call to live holy lives. Ask everyone to read 1 Peter 1:13-25 in preparation for next Sunday's class.

A Call to Holy Living

Background Scripture: 1 Peter 1:13-25

The Main Question

"Be holy yourselves in all your conduct" (1 Peter 1:15). This verse is the crux of today's Scripture reading. When was the last time you heard someone urge others to be "holy"? I expect it has been a long time. As a youth, I remember someone pointing out a girl in our school who dressed in the old-fashioned mode, never curled her hair or wore make-up, and never attended school dances. "Her parents are members of a holiness church," someone explained. "Holiness" became, in my youthful mind, a synonym for someone who was out of step with modern ways.

A few generations ago, there was a very lively holiness tradition within American Protestantism. My own church was rooted in the holiness tradition and gave birth to a number of denominations that continued to stress personal and social holiness as a hallmark of Christian living.

When Methodists came to this country before the Revolutionary War, they had as a firm rule that no follower of John Wesley could hold slaves. Wesley himself was utterly opposed to what he called that "villainy of slavery." His last letter was written to the great English abolitionist Wilberforce to urge him on in his work to end the practice of slave trading.

Yet, after the American Revolution, the Methodist Church grew rapidly, making many new converts on the American frontier. This once-scorned English sect became a great success. As the Church grew, there was growing pressure to remove the prohibition on holding slaves. But one group within the Church continued to argue that it was utterly wrong for Christians to hold slaves. Eventually, when the sad day came that Methodists were allowed to hold slaves, this group withdrew and formed the Wesleyan Methodist Church, a great denomination that exists to this day.

The word *holiness* has an archaic, old-fashioned sound about it mainly because the church has made so many compromises with the world. Time and again we have decided to be successful rather than faithful, to get in step with modern ways rather than pursue the more narrow gospel way. Rather than make disciples who look and act different, we have been content to produce people who, although they are called Christian, look and act about like everyone else.

Against our accommodation and compromise, 1 Peter hurls a challenge to us today, "As he who called you is holy, be holy yourselves in all your conduct" (1 Peter 1:15).

What does it mean to be holy in our day?

Selected Scripture

King James Version	New Revised Standard Version
1 Peter 1:13-25	*1 Peter 1:13-25*
13 Wherefore gird up the loins of your mind, be sober, and hope to	13 Therefore prepare your minds for action; discipline your-

the end for the grace that is to be brought unto you at the revelation of Jesus Christ;

14 As obedient children, not fashioning yourselves according to the former lusts in your ignorance:

15 But as he which hath called you is holy, so be ye holy in all manner of conversation;

16 Because it is written, Be ye holy; for I am holy.

17 And if ye call on the Father, who without respect of persons judgeth according to every man's work, pass the time of your sojourning here in fear:

18 Forasmuch as ye know that ye were not redeemed with corruptible things, as silver and gold, from your vain conversation received by tradition from your fathers;

19 But with the precious blood of Christ, as of a lamb without blemish and without spot:

20 Who verily was foreordained before the foundation of the world, but was manifest in these last times for you,

21 Who by him do believe in God, that raised him up from the dead, and gave him glory; that your faith and hope might be in God.

22 Seeing ye have purified your souls in obeying the truth through the Spirit unto unfeigned love of the brethren, see that ye love one another with a pure heart fervently:

23 Being born again, not of corruptible seed, but of incorruptible, by the word of God, which liveth and abideth for ever.

24 For all flesh is as grass, and all the glory of man as the flower of grass. The grass withereth, and the flower thereof falleth away:

25 But the word of the Lord endureth for ever. And this is the word which by the gospel is preached unto you.

selves; set all your hope on the grace that Jesus Christ will bring you when he is revealed. 14 Like obedient children, do not be conformed to the desires that you formerly had in ignorance. 15 Instead, as he who called you is holy, be holy yourselves in all your conduct; 16 for it is written, "You shall be holy, for I am holy."

17 If you invoke as Father the one who judges all people impartially according to their deeds, live in reverent fear during the time of your exile. 18 You know that you were ransomed from the futile ways inherited from your ancestors, not with perishable things like silver or gold, 19 but with the precious blood of Christ, like that of a lamb without defect or blemish. 20 He was destined before the foundation of the world, but was revealed at the end of the ages for your sake. 21 Through him you have come to trust in God, who raised him from the dead and gave him glory, so that your faith and hope are set on God.

22 Now that you have purified your souls by your obedience to the truth so that you have genuine mutual love, love one another deeply from the heart. 23 You have been born anew, not of perishable but of imperishable seed, through the living and enduring word of God. 24 For

"All flesh is like grass
    and all its glory like the flower
        of grass.
The grass withers,
    and the flower falls,
25 but the word of the Lord
    endures forever."

That word is the good news that was announced to you.

SECOND QUARTER

Key Verse: **But as he which hath called you is holy, so be ye holy in all manner of conversation. (1 Peter 1:15)**

Key Verse: **Instead, as he who called you is holy, be holy yourselves in all your conduct. (1 Peter 1:15)**

As You Read the Scripture

1 Peter 1:13-17. This section might be summarized by the admonition in verses 14-15: "Do not be conformed to the desires that you formerly had in ignorance. Instead, as he who called you is holy, be holy yourselves in all your conduct." The letter is addressed to people who have just become Christians. Even though they are now baptized, some of their old habits crop up from time to time. Christ is holy, meaning that Christ is totally attuned in thought and deed to the will of God. The claim of the letter is that we have the same capability because of the gifts of Christ.

Verses 18-21. Our Scripture passage is in no way a call to self-righteous ethical heroism. We can be holy because we have been bought, ransomed (v. 18), by one who is holy. "Through him you have come to trust in God" (v. 21). Our hope is clearly not in ourselves and our innate goodness, as if we could become holy through our own devices. Rather, our hope is in the gift of the God who ransomed us and then gives us the gifts to be disciples. Christian behavior is responsive—that is, we love in a certain way because we have been loved. God gives us the means to be the people God calls us to be.

Verses 22-25. "You have been born anew" (v. 23). The reference is surely to baptism. In fact, many scholars believe that 1 Peter may be a very early instruction for performing baptisms. Those who go under the waters of baptism are "purified" (v. 22) from their "futile ways" (v. 18). This is an important claim. The basis of Christian behavior rests in the work God has done in us and (at times) despite us in baptism. Because we have been born anew, we have the means of acting like new persons. Thus in our living and acting, our "faith and hope are set on God" (v. 21).

The Scripture and the Main Question

In reading over today's selected scripture from 1 Peter, it strikes me that we are reading, among other things, a very straightforward, practical account of how believers in Christ ought to live. This is a very practical letter. Sometimes we Americans give the word *practical* a bad name. We are "practical," "utilitarian," "pragmatic" people, which means that we judge all persons and experiences on the basis of the question, What good will this do me? What practical, real-life consequences will this have for me? Practicality can be vulgarized into the notion that what works is what's best.

However, *practical* need not be defined so superficially. One reason why we study scriptures like 1 Peter and apply them to our Christian lives is that we believe our faith should be put into practice. Warmed hearts must become active hands. Christian study is mainly of interest in the service of Christian formation. When we discuss, ponder, research, read, and study as Christians, it is rarely for the purpose of simply thinking long thoughts about deep subjects. It is in the interest of transforming lives. Theology is to be lived.

Does this passage from 1 Peter sound practical? People often accuse the

154

Church, when it speaks out on some ethical issue, of being impractical. The Church ought to face facts and realize that teen pregnancy is an unavoidable "fact" of modern life, that drug abuse is something that is typical and understandable, that poverty is just the way things always have been and ever shall be, that family life isn't what it used to be and never will be again. In this climate, the words we are studying today from 1 Peter do sound impractical.

Are these words truly impractical, or does the world lack the spiritual and communal resources needed to put these words into effect? One of the claims of the Church is that, by the grace of God, we have been given the means to do God's will. God's will for the world is considerably more than the world is able to achieve when left to its own devices. Fortunately, we have not been left to our own devices. Christ has come to us and has given us the means to be holy.

Even people like us can be holy.

Making Disciples

Toward the end of Matthew's Gospel, Jesus gives his disciples their marching orders, telling them to, "Go therefore and make disciples of all nations, baptizing . . . teaching . . . " (Matt. 28:19-20).

Just in case anybody thought that following Jesus was something that comes naturally, an inborn inclination, a matter of nice people gradually becoming a bit nicer, Jesus settles all that in this Great Commission. Disciples are not born. Disciples are *made*.

The way Jesus invites us to walk is a narrow way, so against the stream, so uncommon that anything less than intentional, careful, formation will not do. If being a Christian were merely a matter of breathing the air and drinking the water, absorbing a little godliness by osmosis, then we wouldn't need the Church; we wouldn't need help from our friends. We could be Christian the same way people become Rotarians or members of the Women's Garden Club. We could hand them a membership card and a lapel pin rather than half drowning them by baptism.

From all that we know of Jesus and his demands of us, we know being a disciple of his is demanding, requiring more than the completion of a pledge card and the right hand of fellowship. Discipleship requires a lifetime of commitment, trial and error, struggle, correction, prayer, and a host of virtues that cannot be had simply by wanting them. The great God reaches out, grabs us, and accepts us just as we are, warts and all, even the part of us that we have never placed on public view, long before we get around to reaching out and accepting God (justifying grace). God wants serious, life-changing, total renovation when he comes after us (prevenient grace). When God begins working on us, what God has in mind is more than a paint job and a new front porch. God is planning a complete, basement to attic overhaul, which will cost us an arm and a leg (sanctifying grace).

This helps to explain why the word *disciple* is related to the much more troubling and decidedly old-fashioned word *discipline,* a word that evokes bad memories of your third-grade piano teacher, of Coach Smith with the whistle around his neck, and of boot camp at Fort Bragg. We're not much into discipline these days, are we?

But it is unimaginable that one could be a disciple, could follow a master whose name is Jesus, without discipline—the conscious, intentional submission of our feelings, time, talents, and projects to the will of God as revealed in Christ? Disciples are made, not born.

John Wesley gave ordinary people a vision of who they were called to be. He issued an invitation for them to come out of the cultural status quo of eighteenth-century England, to cast off the chains enslaving them, and to allow their lives to be disciplined to the way of the cross, promising that they really could become better people. They really could fashion for themselves lives of courage and hope.

So Wesley demanded that all theology, all hymnody, all church structure, and all preaching and teaching have as their function the making of disciples. The church is the place where you receive the equipment you need to live out the gospel wherever you live.

With a Little Help from Our Friends

The call to holiness of life, which we read in 1 Peter, would be unimaginable if disciples were on their own in the matter of discipleship. Fortunately, we are not on our own. We are all in this together. Together, in the church, we encourage and sustain one another. We study and grow together. Right now, in your adult class, Christians are busy obtaining the necessary equipment for discipleship, for living holy lives in an often unholy world.

Prepare your lesson well for this Sunday's class. You are about some serious business!

Helping Adults Become Involved

Preparing to Teach

At the beginning, let us admit to both the challenge and the promise of today's lesson. The challenge you have is to teach a biblical idea that may be foreign or even unwelcome to the members of your class—the idea of holiness. The words *holy* and *holiness* sometimes conjure up thoughts of people who are purists, self-righteous, aloof, morally condescending. What is the relevance of the biblical idea of holiness for us today?

Today's lesson on 1 Peter gives us the basis for Christian living, the bedrock of all Christian thinking and acting—namely, our inclusion into the Church as members of God's holy people. There may be those in your class who believe that being a Christian is mainly a matter of "trying to do what is right in daily life." Of course, that is a major concern of today's lesson. However, we act, not on the basis of our innate human goodness or our individual moral heroism, but rather on the basis of our being loved and saved by God in Christ. Because we are made, through baptism, into new people, we can act like new people.

Prepare by thinking about this important distinction and then by reading the material in "As You Read the Scripture," followed by the exposition in "The Main Question" and "The Scripture and the Main Question."

Here is today's class outline:

    I. Christians are not to be conformed to this world.
    II. God in Christ has a claim on our lives.
    III. The church is a primary means of helping us to be holy.
    IV. The disciplines of holiness.

Introducing the Main Question

Open your class by using the example that is given in "The Main Question." The early Methodists' accomodation to slavery is an example of how the Church sometimes compromises its beliefs about biblical holiness in order to be more accepted by the world and its values.

Can members of your class point to other historical instances when the Church has compromised its originating vision in order to conform itself to the world? For instance, the early Church forbade people to serve in the military. But by the early Middle Ages, one was forbidden to serve in the army unless one had been baptized! The Church had come a long way from its originating vision.

How can Christians keep from being compromised by the world and its values? Can the idea of holiness be a help to us in our struggles with the world? That is today's question. Have someone read the selected scripture from 1 Peter.

Developing the Lesson

I. Christians are not to be conformed to the world.

Verses 13-17 set the tone for today's lesson. Read them aloud again to your class, asking each person to imagine that these words are addressed specifically to him or to her. Christians are called to be different. What are some of our innate characteristics that lead us to fear being different? How do we get the courage to stand up for what we believe, even when others may ridicule our behavior? You might ask your group to discuss childhood or youthful memories of times when they were faced with this dilemma. What gives a child the courage to live a certain life-style even when the child's friends may be following a different path? More to the point of our situation, what gives an *adult* the courage to act in a way that is holy, even though that way may be different from the way the majority of people act? Such a discussion will begin your class in an honest, realistic way.

What do the members of your class think the writer of 1 Peter means when he uses the phrase "during the time of your exile" (v. 17)? Are there ways in which contemporary Christians may feel that they are in exile in American culture today? Share with your class the discussion (from "The Scripture and the Main Question") of the ways contemporary American Christian discipleship demands disciplined believers. An exile is a stranger in a strange land, with different values and customs. Ask members of the group to cite specific examples of ways the accepted and conventional values of modern life collide with traditional Christian values.

II. God in Christ has a claim on our lives.

Verses 18-20 explicate the basis for Christian behavior. Our behavior arises, not from our own attributes or characteristics, but on the basis of our being chosen and blessed by God in Christ. We have been "ransomed from the futile ways inherited from [our] ancestors" (v. 18). The image being used here is that of the purchase of freedom for a slave. We were in slavery, but Christ has purchased us and now has a claim on us.

Ask your class members to discuss how our realization of what God has done for us in Christ influences our behavior. How is gratitude a basis for behavior? Perhaps you might use the analogy of a child and a parent. As we

157

grow up and feel a sense of gratitude for what our parents have done for us, we want to please them and do well for them, not out of fear of them but out of love. Our parents have a claim on us, the claim of love. We act a certain way as thanksgiving for what they have done for us. In what way is this an analogy for our relationship to God?

When we were teenagers, our mother would not tell my sister and me what other parents might tell their children—to "act like you are somebody." She would say, "Remember, you *are* somebody." Our acting flows out of our being.

III. The church is a primary means of helping us to be holy.

Use the material in "The Scripture and the Main Question" to lead a discussion of the church as a means of helping us to be more disciplined and holy. Share some examples from your own life of ways your church has given you encouragement to live a more disciplined and faithful life. Ask members of the group to share their experiences of support by the church for more ethical living.

Can your group think of additional ways the church ought to be of more help to contemporary believers? For instance, does your church help you to think through difficult contemporary problems like abortion, nuclear power, pornography, and gambling? Have you ever heard any sermons on these subjects? Do members of your class think that such controversial issues are fit subjects for sermons? Do you ever discuss contemporary ethical issues like this in your adult class?

If the church is a safe haven from all difficult and controversial issues, how can the church help us to live more holy lives?

When people are in exile (v. 17), they often gather to sing the songs of their native land, to speak the old language, to tell stories, to identify one another, and to pass on the ways of their former country to the children they are raising in the land of their exile. In a way, that is not a bad image for what it feels like to be in the Church today. Does your church sufficiently appreciate how difficult it is to be a Christian in today's world?

IV. The disciplines of holiness.

As Christians, we are called to holiness. Ask your class to end its exploration of biblical holiness by brainstorming ways your church helps it members to lead more holy lives. Then ask your class members to think of some specific ways your church could encourage more holy living (such as classes for in business ethics, classes for youth in Christian attitudes toward human sexuality, discussions of your denomination's stand on various social issues, etc.).

Helping Class Members Act

As a pastor, when I have visited unchurched people and have encouraged them to become active in our church, I have frequently had them say to me, "We can't see the point of it. People in the church seem just about like everybody else. They have the same problems, the same weaknesses, the same miseries. What is the point of joining a church?"

Of course, church people do have the same challenges in life as people who are not in the church. Yet, none of that lets us church people off the hook of holiness. The world is quite right in judging the church on the basis of the sort of people we are able to produce. Each of us, in our daily lives, provides a positive or a negative witness to the formative power of Christ over a person's life.

Holiness, as discussed in today's Scripture, is an everyday, practical, visible testimony to what God can do once God gets in a person's life. Are you and I, in our daily living, examples of that testimony?

Planning for Next Sunday

After today's lesson, stressing the need for Christians to be holy, nonconformed to the world, and set apart, one might get the impression that the Christian faith is a matter for only the chosen few, select insiders. Nothing could be further from the truth, as we shall learn in next Sunday's lesson.

In preparation for that lesson, ask your class members to think about the ways the church, intentionally or unintentionally, builds barriers between people, erects walls to separate one person from another.

Today we have studied about how the love of Christ makes us holy people. Next Sunday we shall learn how the love of Christ forms us into inclusive, accepting people.

The Church Is for All People

Background Scripture: Acts 11

The Main Question

In the Church today, sometimes the question is asked, "Will the Jews be saved, even when they do not believe in Jesus?" The question is raised by one who perceives himself or herself to be an insider concerned about the fate of the outsider. From the standpoint of the Acts of the Apostles, it is a curious question. In Acts, the issue is not whether the Jews will be saved. That issue had already been decided, at the dawn of history, by the promises of God to Abraham—God will have this people as his own. Every act of God since then, including the gift of Jesus and the Holy Spirit, demonstrates God's fidelity to that promise. As Peter told the wondering crowd out in the street at Pentecost, "For the promise is for you, for your children, and for all who are far away, everyone whom the Lord our God calls to him" (Acts 2:39). The fidelity of God to his promise to Israel is the very foundation of the good news in Acts.

The question whose answer required massive argument and all of the theological and literary skills at Luke's disposal was this: "Will the *Gentiles* be saved, even if they believe in Jesus?" The answer was not self-evident, and the case could not be closed. Luke's church based its preaching on the truth and fulfillment of God's promises to *Israel*.

SECOND QUARTER

We build walls between people, separate out people on the basis of color or national origin or some other external characteristic. How is it possible to overcome our boundaries, to move toward people whom we had not expected to meet? That is the question we shall investigate in today's lesson.

Selected Scripture

King James Version

Acts 11:1-18

1 And the apostles and brethren that were in Judaea heard that the Gentiles had also received the word of God.

2 And when Peter was come up to Jerusalem, they that were of the circumcision contended with him,

3 Saying, Thou wentest in to men uncircumcised, and didst eat with them.

4 But Peter rehearsed the matter from the beginning, and expounded it by order unto them, saying,

5 I was in the city of Joppa praying: and in a trance I saw a vision, A certain vessel descend, as it had been a great sheet, let down from heaven by four corners; and it came even to me:

6 Upon the which when I had fastened mine eyes, I considered, and saw fourfooted beasts of the earth, and wild beasts, and creeping things, and fowls of the air.

7 And I heard a voice saying unto me, Arise, Peter; slay and eat.

8 But I said, Not so, Lord: for nothing common or unclean hath at any time entered into my mouth.

9 But the voice answered me again from heaven, What God hath cleansed, that call not thou common.

10 And this was done three times: and all were drawn up again into heaven.

11 And, behold, immediately there were three men already come unto the house where I was, sent from Caesarea unto me.

12 And the Spirit bade me go with them, nothing doubting. Moreover

New Revised Standard Version

Acts 11:1-18

1 Now the apostles and the believers who were in Judea heard that the Gentiles had also accepted the word of God. 2 So when Peter went up to Jerusalem, the circumcised believers criticized him, 3 saying, "Why did you go to uncircumcised men and eat with them?" 4 Then Peter began to explain it to them, step by step, saying, 5 "I was in the city of Joppa praying, and in a trance I saw a vision. There was something like a large sheet coming down from heaven, being lowered by its four corners; and it came close to me. 6 As I looked at it closely I saw four-footed animals, beasts of prey, reptiles, and birds of the air. 7 I also heard a voice saying to me, 'Get up, Peter; kill and eat.' 8 But I replied, 'By no means, Lord; for nothing profane or unclean has ever entered my mouth.' 9 But a second time the voice answered from heaven, 'What God has made clean, you must not call profane.' 10 This happened three times; then everything was pulled up again to heaven. 11 At that very moment three men, sent to me from Caesarea, arrived at the house where we were. 12 The Spirit told me to go with them and not to make a distinction between them and us. These six brothers also accompanied me, and we entered the man's house. 13 He told us how he had seen the angel standing in his house and saying, 'Send to Joppa and bring Simon, who is called Peter; 14 he will give you a message by which you and your entire household will be saved.' 15 And as I

160

began to these six brethren accompanied me, and we entered into the man's house:

13 And he shewed us how he had seen an angel in his house, which stood and said unto him, Send men to Joppa, and call for Simon, whose surname is Peter;

14 Who shall tell thee words, whereby thou and all thy house shall be saved.

15 And as I began to speak, the Holy Ghost fell on them, as on us at the beginning.

16 Then remembered I the word of the Lord, how that he said, John indeed baptized with water; but ye shall be baptized with the Holy Ghost.

17 Forasmuch then as God gave them the like gift as he did unto us, who believed on the Lord Jesus Christ; what was I, that I could withstand God?

18 When they heard these things, they held their peace, and glorified God, saying, Then hath God also to the Gentiles granted repentance unto life.

Key Verse: **When they heard these things, they held their peace, and glorified God, saying, Then hath God also to the Gentiles granted repentance unto life. (Acts 11:18)**

speak, the Holy Spirit fell upon them just as it had upon us at the beginning. 16 And I remembered the word of the Lord, how he had said, 'John baptized with water, but you will be baptized with the Holy Spirit.' 17 If then God gave them the same gift that he gave us when we believed in the Lord Jesus Christ, who was I that I could hinder God?" 18 When they heard this, they were silenced. And they praised God, saying, "Then God has given even to the Gentiles the repentance that leads to life."

Key Verse: **When they heard this, they were silenced. And they praised God, saying, "Then God has given even to the Gentiles the repentance that leads to life." (Acts 11:18)**

As You Read the Scripture

Acts 1-18. Today's selected scripture from Acts consists of Peter's defense, before the elders of the church at Jerusalem, for his baptism of Cornelius and his family, spoken of in Acts 10. Read through Acts 10 first in order to understand the reason for Acts 11:1-18.

Throughout Acts, Luke has been steadily leading us up to the point when the Gentiles are received into the Church. At the very beginning of Acts, the risen Christ had told his disciples, "You will be my witnesses in Jerusalem, in all Judea and Samaria, and to the ends of the earth" (Acts 1:8*b*). That promise is now fulfilled as the Church has moved from the baptism of those who stood in the street on Pentecost day in Acts 2, to Philip's baptism of the Samaritans (Acts 8:1-25), to the final, culminating act of the baptism of a Gentile named Cornelius.

Verse 1. The "apostles and the believers . . . in Judea" represent the core of the young Church. No move can be made without checking with the original leaders of the Church, who are still residing in Jerusalem. The faith that is taken to the Gentiles is the faith of Israel.

Verses 2-3. The "circumcised believers" were those in the early Church who contended that one could not become a Christian until having first become a Jew through the initiating rite of circumcision. Hebrew dietary laws prohibited the Jews from eating the improperly prepared food of Gentiles. (See Galatians 15:1-5.)

Verses 4-17. Luke repeats the story of the vision (Acts 10) in order to emphasize its importance in the unfolding narrative. The vision must be repeated to Peter three times because it is asking him to do something that is wholly against his instincts. The vision shows that the movement of the Church to the Gentiles is the result of divine command and initiative.

Verse 18. Peter's testimony thoroughly convinces the Jerusalem assembly, who state the main point of the whole narrative: "Then God has given even to the Gentiles the repentance that leads to life."

The Scripture and the Main Question

Even to the Gentiles

Will the Jews be saved, even though they have not recognized Jesus as their long-awaited Messiah?

As interesting as such questions may be for us, they are not Luke's questions. By Luke's day, Israel's verdict on Jesus had, for the most part, been delivered. A group that first thought of itself as a sect within Judaism was out of the synagogues and on its own. The Church was rapidly becoming a Gentile phenomenon, a fact that Luke, to his credit, could still ponder with amazement and gratitude for the graciousness of God toward the Gentiles rather than with our contemporary smugness. Amazement at the inclusion of the Gentiles, as well as the lingering questions such inclusion raised, not the fate of the Jews, was Luke's concern in Acts. The fate of the Jews rested, as it always had, in the hands of a faithful and just God, the same God who now, wonder of wonders, had made a place within his chosen family even for Gentiles.

The significance of how that came to be is the concern of the book of Acts, especially chapter 11. Peter's speech to the assembly at Jerusalem is one of the most decisive episodes in Acts. When we read Acts 11, we know that we are dealing with a crucial concern, a pivot for the entire book, a turning point in the long drama of redemption.

How did the Church arrive at a turning point where insiders were willing to include outsiders? Acts tells of this long journey in which the new Christians came to see that the same Christ who accepted them also accepted people who were not like them. Beginning in Jerusalem, the good news has been taken out into Samaria; then, with the conversion of the Ethiopian, to the very "ends of the earth" (1:8). What is more, Saul, a vile persecutor of the community, has now become Paul, God's chosen instrument. Where shall the gospel go next?

Chapter 10 of Acts tells of the spectacular conversion of Cornelius, who was a Roman army officer. What was a Roman army officer doing in Jerusalem? He was there with his soldiers enforcing the Roman occupation of Judea. And Cornelius became the very first Gentile convert.

If a man like Cornelius, a Gentile who made his living enforcing the laws of Caesar against the Jews, can be converted, then anybody can be converted! Anybody.

But when Peter got back to the church in Jerusalem, after baptizing Cornelius, he had some explaining to do. "What were you doing with people like Cornelius?" the other apostles wanted to know. "Is it true that you ate with him? Can it possibly be true that you baptized him?"

The Spirit Told Me to Go with Them

The story of Peter's vision in Joppa (11:5-17) is retold for emphasis. Luke, the writer of Acts, softens the resistance of the church by saying that table fellowship with Gentiles angered the saints at Jerusalem, but the baptism of a Roman was the probable root of their anger. (The two go together, because baptism would initiate someone into the table fellowship of the Church.) Is the table fellowship issue a matter of who shall eat at the Lord's Supper? Luke leaves it ambiguous, probably because Luke's church would know no distinction between "religious" meals and "nonreligious" meals. The question of who shall be admitted to the Church's table is a thoroughly religious question.

Peter now says that "the Spirit told [him] to go with them and not to make a distinction" (11:12). The Church's silence and then response shows that it realizes that a bold (and perhaps frightening) chapter has opened in the saga of the people of God. To Gentiles also has God granted the ability to turn toward life. The real "hero" of the story, the "star" of the drama, is not Peter or Cornelius, but the gracious and prodding One who makes bold promises and keeps them, who finds a way even in the midst of human distinctions and partiality between persons.

No Partiality

So is this a story about the conversion of a Gentile named Cornelius, or is it a story about the conversion of a group of people called the Church? Perhaps the most dramatic conversion occurred to Peter and to the Church when they realized that God's love would not be held by narrow, nationalistic or racial barriers. With God, there is no distinction.

Later, the Epistle to the Ephesians would remind Gentile Christians like Cornelius that they were

without Christ, being aliens from the commonwealth of Israel, and strangers to the covenants of promise, having no hope and without God in the world. But now in Christ Jesus you who once were far off have been brought near by the blood of Christ. For he is our peace; in his flesh he has made both groups into one and has broken down the dividing wall, that is, the hostility between us. (Ephesians 2:12-14)

This reminds us, all who sit in the adult class this Sunday, that if the Church had not followed the leadings of the Spirit when Cornelius was converted, we wouldn't be here! Because we feel gratitude that, even though we Gentiles were strangers, we were taken in, we are empowered to receive others, even as we have been received.

One of the first crises to hit the Church was the question of whether to receive the Gentiles into fellowship. Each generation confronts the Church with a new set of "Gentiles," a new set of strangers, asking the Church whether or not it should be able again to follow the leading of God and show acceptance of others as God has shown acceptance to us.

Who do you think are the "Gentiles" of our generation, standing at the door of the Church and asking, "Can I also be included?"

Helping Adults Become Involved

Preparing to Teach

Begin your preparation by reading the entire account of the conversion of the first Gentile, which is recorded in Acts 10–11. This will help to set in context your study of the crisis in the Church that is reported in Acts 11.

Throughout your preparation, keep in mind today's key question, as stated in "The Main Question." How is it possible to overcome our boundaries?

The learning activities for today's lesson are based on the assumption that, even as the church of Acts was challenged to follow the leading of the Holy Spirit over the boundaries between Gentile and Jew, so also our church is being challenged in our day to follow the Spirit across the boundaries we erect between people. If you want a simple outline for today's lesson, try this:

I. Retell the story of the crisis in the church, which was provoked by Peter's baptism and visit to Cornelius.
II. Discuss groups within our society today that are equivalent to the Gentiles in Luke's day.
III. Explore the ways your church can show God's acceptance of all people through acceptance of others.

Now read through the material found in "As You Read the Scripture" and in "The Scripture and the Main Question." Jot down your own impressions, questions, and ideas as you read.

Here is a suggested outline for today's class:

I. What about the Gentiles?
II. Today's "Gentiles."
III. Making disciples of all people.
IV. Conclusion.

Introducing the Main Question

I. What about the Gentiles?

You might begin by telling your group how so much of the Acts of the Apostles is concerned with the issue of the place of the Gentiles in God's plan of salvation. Did Jesus come for the Gentiles as well as for the Jews? That question occupies most of Acts. We care about the final resolution of this dilemma because, after all, we are all Gentiles! How did we get here?

Paraphrase Acts 10–11. Using the material in "The Scripture and the Main Question," underscore what a radical, potentially disruptive issue this inclusion of Gentiles was for the Church. Not only was Cornelius a Gentile, but also he was a Roman; not only was he a Roman, but also he was a Roman army officer. When Acts records Cornelius as the first Gentile convert, it is almost as if Luke wants to make this story as scandalous and controversial as possible. Major boundaries are being overcome here. If God's Spirit can convert a man like Cornelius, then almost anybody can be converted!

II. Today's "Gentiles."

Now lead your group in a discussion of contemporary groups or individuals in today's world who are excluded in ways similar to Cornelius's exclusion.

Our congregations like to think of themselves as friendly. Yet, I don't think I have ever been in a congregation where there were not some people, even within the congregation, who at times felt excluded.

What are some of the reasons why people sometimes feel excluded in even the "friendliest" of congregations? The predominant reason given by people who are asked why they are not members of a church is that no one has ever asked them to be members.

We say that we have an open-door policy at our church, that we are open and accepting of everyone. But few of our churches truly embody our claims. Like attracts like. We tend to congregate with people like ourselves. Few churches really draw their membership from across the strata of society, from more than one race, from a variety of educational and economic backgrounds.

Present some of these ideas to your group and ask them if they can think of any groups within our world of whom the Church has not shown true Christian acceptance. List their responses on newsprint or a chalkboard. For instance, how do we feel about people who have radically different life-styles from our own? Explore the specific ways your church can demonstrate God's acceptance of all people.

The church that tells the story of the conversion and baptism of Gentile Cornelius is the church that understands that God means for the good news of Christ to go to all people. If God can get Cornelius, God can get anybody.

III. Making disciples of all people.

Your group has identified those persons within our world who are in need of Christian acceptance. Now lead your group in a discussion of specific ways your church might be more hospitable toward today's "Gentiles."

A previous congregation I served became concerned that we were not growing. We thought of ourselves as an open, warm, and friendly church. Why did we not get more new members? We invited a church-growth consultant to help us. When he came to our church, he made a number of disturbing observations: We had no signs on nearby streets to tell people how to get to our church. We had no parking spaces set aside for visitors. There were no signs to the church office, to the children's nursery, or to the restrooms. Even the bulletin, listing the various acts of worship, was confusing to someone who was visiting our church for the first time. In other words, our church existed mainly for the folk who were already there. We needed to go through an act of conversion similar to the conversion that occured at the church in Jerusalem when it received Cornelius. We had to begin looking at our church through the eyes of visitors and outsiders rather than through the eyes of insiders.

SECOND QUARTER

IV. Conclusion.

In nearly every community there are people who are homeless, people who are down on their luck, confused people, lonely older adults. These ought to be people who are just perfect for the Church, because the Church is a place that specializes in providing a home, in supporting the downtrodden, in helping people make sense out of life, in offering friendship and fellowship. Do our churches really want to reach out to those who need us, or do we prefer to maintain a sort of club for those who are already there?

Helping Class Members Act

In today's lesson, by exploring Acts 11 and the story of the controversy that erupted over the conversion of the first Gentile, we have pondered the need for the Church to accept those who are often regarded as unacceptable. In your discussion of the implications of the Scripture for your church, you may have uncovered some potentially controversial feelings and attitudes. Just remember: Acts 11 reminds us that there is good precedent for the Church's being disturbed and prodded!

Having identified those individuals and groups who need the ministry of the Church today, as well as ways the Church might reach out to those persons, close today's session by identifying one way your church is reaching out and accepting persons in the name of Christ. Even as Acts 11 ends positively with the Church's having accepted the Gentiles, so also today's session ought to end with your claiming some way in which your church is responding to God's acceptance of us with our acceptance of others.

Planning for Next Sunday

How smart must you be to be a Christian? That's a provocative question! Does it help to have a high IQ? Ask your class to read 1 Corinthians 1:18-31 in preparation for next Sunday's session. It is Paul's answer to this provocative question.

LESSON 8   JANUARY 24

Learning God's Wisdom

Background Scripture: 1 Corinthians 1:1–2:13

The Main Question

In the university chapel where I work, we try to invite the greatest preachers in the country to preach in our pulpit. We want to expose our students who worship in our chapel to the greatest Christian communicators. This means that we have many sermons that are thoughtful and

166

profound. It is not unusual for someone to emerge from our chapel, at the close of the Sunday service, and request a recorded tape or a printed transcript of the sermon, "so that I can have more time to ponder its meaning."

But I will never forget one of the first visiting preachers we had when I came here. My predecessor had invited a relatively unknown bishop from the Church of England to be a guest preacher. I'd never heard of the man, nor had any in our congregation heard of him before he came to the chapel. All we knew was that he was the bishop and that he came from the Church of England.

On the Sunday when he was to preach, he marched in behind our chapel choir wearing his bishop's miter and flowing Episcopal robes. He really looked like a bishop! But how was a bishop supposed to preach? Would he give us a learned theological dissertation on some deep subject? Because he came from a church of another nation, would he make some comment on current political events?

To our surprise, he began his sermon this way: "I am not a clever man. I must confess that I do not have a sermon which is worthy of your magnificent and wondrous building. However, I do hope to say something to you today that will be helpful in your own spiritual life. I want to talk to you about prayer."

The bishop then talked to us, in a conversational, straightforward way, about the need to pray. He did not use fancy or eloquent language, nor did he talk of complex and abstract concepts. He talked to us as a pastor, as someone who had himself struggled with prayer and wanted to pass on his insights about prayer to us.

His sermon really had an effect on the congregation. I could tell that everyone was listening to him with great interest. I believe the thing that truly gripped them was not his eloquence, for he was not an eloquent speaker, but rather his straightforward sincerity, his simplicity and seriousness. He really conveyed to the congregation that he deeply cared about us and our struggles with prayer. His sermon will long be remembered by the people who were there that day as one of the most moving, helpful, and significant sermons we have heard.

Paul said to the Corinthians, "When I came to you, brothers and sisters, I did not come proclaiming the mystery of God to you in lofty words or wisdom" (1 Corinthians 2:1).

What does it mean to speak of "the foolishness of the gospel"? This is the question behind today's lesson.

Selected Scripture

King James Version

New Revised Standard Version

1 Corinthians 1:18-31

18 For the preaching of the cross is to them that perish foolishness; but unto us which are saved it is the power of God.

19 For it is written, I will destroy

1 Corinthians 1:18-31

18 For the message about the cross is foolishness to those who are perishing, but to us who are being saved it is the power of God. 19 For it is written,

the wisdom of the wise, and will bring to nothing the understanding of the prudent.

20 Where is the wise? where is the scribe? where is the disputer of this world? hath not God made foolish the wisdom of this world?

21 For after that in the wisdom of God the world by wisdom knew not God, it pleased God by the foolishness of preaching to save them that believe.

22 For the Jews require a sign, and the Greeks seek after wisdom:

23 But we preach Christ crucified, unto the Jews a stumblingblock, and unto the Greeks foolishness;

24 But unto them which are called, both Jews and Greeks, Christ the power of God, and the wisdom of God.

25 Because the foolishness of God is wiser than men; and the weakness of God is stronger than men.

26 For ye see your calling, brethren, how that not many wise men after the flesh, not many mighty, not many noble, are called:

27 But God hath chosen the foolish things of the world to confound the wise; and God hath chosen the weak things of the world to confound the things which are mighty;

28 And base things of the world, and things which are despised, hath God chosen, yea, and things which are not, to bring to nought things that are:

29 That no flesh should glory in his presence.

30 But of him are ye in Christ Jesus, who of God is made unto us wisdom, and righteousness, and sanctification, and redemption:

31 That, according as it is written, He that glorieth, let him glory in the Lord.

Key Verse: **For after that in the wisdom of God the world by wis-**

"I will destroy the wisdom of the wise,
and the discernment of the discerning I will thwart."
20 Where is the one who is wise? Where is the scribe? Where is the debater of this age? Has not God made foolish the wisdom of the world? 21 For since, in the wisdom of God, the world did not know God through wisdom, God decided, through the foolishness of our proclamation, to save those who believe. 22 For Jews demand signs and Greeks desire wisdom, 23 but we proclaim Christ crucified, a stumbling block to Jews and foolishness to Gentiles, 24 but to those who are the called, both Jews and Greeks, Christ the power of God and the wisdom of God. 25 For God's foolishness is wiser than human wisdom, and God's weakness is stronger than human strength.

26 Consider your own call, brothers and sisters: not many of you were wise by human standards, not many were powerful, not many were of noble birth. 27 But God chose what is foolish in the world to shame the wise; God chose what is weak in the world to shame the strong; 28 God chose what is low and despised in the world, things that are not, to reduce to nothing things that are, 29 so that no one might boast in the presence of God. 30 He is the source of your life in Christ Jesus, who became for us wisdom from God, and righteousness and sanctification and redemption, 31 in order that, as it is written, "Let the one who boasts, boast in the Lord."

Key Verse: **For since, in the wisdom of God, the world did not** dom knew not God, it pleased God by the foolishness of preaching to save them that believe. (1 Corinthians 1:21)

know God through wisdom, God decided, through the foolishness of our proclamation, to save those who believe. (1 Corinthians 1:21)

As You Read the Scripture

1 Corinthians 1:18-31. Paul's first letter to the Corinthians is one of the most valuable of all of his letters. It contains some of his most developed and well-thought out descriptions of the gospel. It also gives us a good picture, at least by implication, of some of the challenges of church life in an actual congregation in the first century. Corinth was a great center of the Mediterranean world. If you go there today, you can still see the ruins of an early Christian church, perhaps the same church Paul wrote this letter to. As an important trade center, Corinth was a sophisticated town. Perhaps its worldly sophistication led to some of the problems Paul addresses in today's Scripture passage.

Verse 18. Throughout his letters, Paul speaks of the theology of the cross. Whereas some Christian communicators (such as the writer of the Gospel of Mark) stress the power of Jesus, Paul stresses the cross. God's love is known to us, not through mighty and miraculous acts, but through his suffering love for us as shown on the cross. This love is sheer folly to most of the world, but it is at the heart of our gospel.

Verses 19-21. Paul now launches an attack against what he calls the "wisdom of the wise." It seems foolish that a mighty God should suffer, and yet that is what the gospel claims in Jesus Christ. Evidently, there were some in the church at Corinth who presumed to be sophisticated and wise, but Paul calls them very foolish because they do not understand the wisdom of the cross.

Verses 22-25. Paul admits that for Jews, who "demand signs," and Greeks, who "desire wisdom," the cross presents a great problem. But in the wisdom of God, what appears to be foolishness to the world is the very means of the world's salvation.

Verses 26-29. As an example of the foolishness of the cross, Paul points to the Corinthians themselves. He asks them to remember who they were before they were saved by the gospel. Most of them were probably rather lowly, insignificant people in the world's eyes. But God chose them to be the bearers of his saving gospel. Therefore, there is no ground for human boasting, since God has lifted up the lowly to be his chosen ones in the Church.

Verses 30-31. If there is any ground for Christian boasting, it is boasting in the grace of God. The sheer grace of God, not our own intelligence or achievements, saves us.

The Scripture and the Main Question

The Message of the Cross Is Foolishness

Sometimes you and I, who sit on Sunday mornings in churches that have brass crosses on the altars, who are so accustomed to seeing the cross adorning our hymnals, Bibles, and other objects of worship, fail to appreciate what an odd symbol the cross is. The cross was, in the Roman world, not the symbol of salvation, but signified the most degrading and cruel form of human punishment the world had devised. For Christians to take the cross as the symbol of salvation would be equivalent to some group's taking a hangman's noose or an electric chair as its symbol today.

Archaeologists have discovered a graffito, done by some forgotten Roman, to make fun of the Christians. It consists of a man bowing down before a cross on which is a man with a donkey's head. Underneath is a crude inscription, "He worships his God." This was what the Roman world thought of the cross of the Christians.

Despite our fashioning of beautiful crosses in gold and silver for our churches, the cross is still a stumbling block and a scandal for most of the world. We live in a world that worships power and success. There is a syndicated television program called "Lifestyles of the Rich and Famous." Each week the program takes viewers to the fabulous estates of very powerful and very successful people. To my knowledge, there is not a television program entitled "Lifestyles of the Suffering and the Lowly." That is because those who are crucified and lowly are still considered to be insignificant to the world.

Paul reminds the Corinthians that Jesus himself was considered lowly and insignificant. That is because, in Paul's words, "Jews demand signs and Greeks desire wisdom" (1:22). Most people want their religion to be significant and miraculous. We want God to come to us with a great show of power and glory, something we can see, some visible proof that God is truly God. And yet Jesus came to us as a baby born in a lowly manger. He was not a success by the world's standards, and he ended in a terrible death on a scandalous cross. Is this any way for a God to act?

What is more, is this any way for God's people to act? In many of our churches, the congregations are greatly flattered when some prominent and influential citizen joins the church. We take delight when some business executive or powerful person in the community chooses to join our congregation.

And yet, when Paul wrote to the Corinthians, he reminded them that not many of them fit our description of the "good" church member. Paul reminded them that "not many of you were wise by human standards, not many were powerful, not many were of noble birth" (1:26). And yet they were the ones to whom God had entrusted the saving gospel. They were God's own representatives to the rest of the world.

When one considers the sort of religion we value, as well as the sort of people we value getting for our churches, could it not still be said that the cross continues to be "folly" to some and a "stumbling block" to others?

Has Not God Made Foolish the Wisdom of the World?

The foolishness of the cross continues to be one of the great stumbling blocks to Christian proclamation. As you may know, I preach the gospel in a university chapel. People do not come to the university to look lowly, foolish, and ignorant. No, they come here to look wise and intelligent. They go to classes in the hope of obtaining advanced degrees to certify their wisdom. I suspect that my university congregation is not that much different from your congregation. I dare say that most of us probably think of religion as a way of making relatively powerful people even more powerful, relatively successful people even more successful.

When I watch so-called Christian television programs, I see that this seems to be the predominant theme. If you just give your life to Jesus, he will make you successful. Everything will turn out well for you. Jesus is the best deal a person ever had.

Undoubtedly, there were many in the church in Corinth who felt this way about Christianity. The Romans had many different religions, all promising to give their adherents power, immortality, material wealth, or some other sign of divine favor. There were probably people who had joined the church in Corinth, thinking that Jesus Christ was just another means to obtain all the world could offer. They were confused into thinking that Christianity was just another means of self-satisfaction.

To counter their misunderstanding, Paul told them: "When I came to you, brothers and sisters, I did not come proclaiming the mystery of God to you in lofty words or wisdom. For I decided to know nothing among you except Jesus Christ, and him crucified" (2:1-2).

Paul did not preach about the resurrection of Jesus, nor did he preach about the miracles of Jesus. He preached on the cross of Jesus as the ultimate sign of the peculiar nature of the Christian faith. Here is a God who saves through losing, a God who empowers by becoming powerless. In fact, as Paul tells us, the Church itself is a good illustration of the peculiar way in which God saves the world. After all, God shows the Corinthians!

To [Preach] . . . Jesus Christ, and Him Crucified

The story is told that one day a young pastor was showing the late Southern Baptist prophet Clarence Jordan around his expensive new church building. The young pastor was proudly showing Jordan the elegant fixtures of his newly built sanctuary. Pointing out the massive cross that was suspended over the altar, the young preacher said, "Would you believe that cross alone costs this church over $12,000?"

Jordan expressed amazement. Then he said, "Young man, I think you got took. Do you know that Christians used to be able to get those things delivered for nothing?"

In a church that often worships success and sometimes presents the Christian faith as just another comfortable, pleasing option that leads to power, prestige, and success, Paul's words on the peculiar wisdom of God are timely. Paul reminds us that Christianity is a very peculiar way of looking at life. We look at life through the lens of the cross. Having seen God come to us in the form of a crucified Savior makes us look upon the lowly of the world differently. Having been saved by a lowly God in our own lowliness, our vision is turned around. We expect to see God more often in lowly places than in high places, among those whom the world regards as foolish and of little account, rather than among those whom the world regards as important and mighty.

For us, this is true wisdom.

Helping Adults Become Involved

Today's lesson, from the first and second chapters of Paul's First Letter to the Corinthians, contains a foundational Christian truth: The cross is not only at the very heart of the Christian gospel, but it represents, as well, in the eyes of the rest of the world, a great scandal, a "stumbling block" or "folly," in the words of Paul. During this lesson, you will have an opportunity to explore this essential image of the Christian faith and its implications for our lives today.

Preparing to Teach

Begin by carefully reading the selected Scripture for today, making notes as you read about your own ideas and impressions of the biblical text. Next, read through the material in "The Main Question." This will serve as an introduction to the Scripture and as a means of linking the Scripture to everyday life concerns.

Use the material in "As You Read the Scripture" to help you understand various points of the selected scripture from 1 Corinthians. As you prepare, think of your own illustrations of ways in which the cross and the lowliness of both Christ and Christian believers is experienced today as a scandal and as a stumbling block.

Here is today's lesson outline:

     I. Introduce the main question.
    II. The wisdom of the world.
   III. The foolishness of the cross.
   IV. Consider your call.

Introducing the Main Question

You might open class discussion by sharing with class members your paraphrase of the material in "The Scripture and the Main Question." Ask the class what qualities they look for in a "good" sermon: eloquence or simplicity?

Developing the Lesson

I. Introduce the main question.

Today's lesson deals with a great paradox of the Christian faith. Ask class members to think of the story of Jesus. In what way can it be said that the story of Jesus illustrates the fact that God has "made foolish the wisdom of the world"? The Lord and Savior of the whole world comes to us as a baby born to poor parents. What a way for a messiah to begin!

II. The wisdom of the world.

Ask your class to ponder Paul's concept that the "wisdom of the world" is, in reality, foolishness. We live in a culture in which many people neglect their health and sacrifice their families and their own emotional well-being in order to earn more money. Is our "success" in reality our failure? Can anyone think of other examples of ways in which, when the world thinks it is being so smart, it is really being foolish?

Are there ways in which the Church is guilty of substituting some of the world's standards of wisdom for the foolishness of the gospel of Christ? For instance, is it not odd, in a gospel that begins with a poor baby, that the Church is so often a place of opulence and affluence?

172

III. The foolishness of the cross.

Using the illustrative material in "The Scripture and the Main Question," lead your class in a discussion of the notion of the foolishness of the gospel. In your own words, define how Paul can speak of the gospel of Christ as foolishness. In what ways do the principles of the gospel appear to collide with the wisdom of the world?

IV. Consider your call.

Paul says that the gospel of Christ looks like foolishness in the eyes of a "wise" world. Then he discusses the ways in which the followers of Christ also look foolish to the world. Lead class members in thinking of their own experiences of the church. Are there ways in which the ministry of the church, though appearing ineffective or unimportant to the world, is really a faithful response to the true wisdom of Christ?

Who comes to a church? The healthy, the secure, and the happy? Or the needy, the insecure, and the infirm? Who is the Church really for? Who best illustrates the Church as a "success" in its living out of the gospel? A wealthy, prosperous, self-assured church member? Or a member who is considered to be a "failure" in the world's eyes?

Have members of your class heard people sometimes criticize the Church for being ineffective or unimportant, when, in reality, that criticism showed that the Church was actually fulfilling its mandate to show that "God made foolish the wisdom of the world"?

Helping Class Members Act

The Church is commissioned to reach the world with the gospel of Jesus Christ. However, in its efforts to reach out, sometimes the Church becomes only a mirror for the world's values. Ask your class members to think of specific ways in which your church can affirm, in its proclamation and life together, that "God's foolishness is wiser than human wisdom, and God's weakness is stronger than human strength." The old image of the Church as a "hospital for the sick and sinful rather than a haven for the well and the righteous" may apply to your discussion.

I remember someone's describing a particular church as a place full of people who were old, some of whom were addicted or poor, most of whom were outcasts, failures, and has-beens. In short, that was a church in which Jesus would have felt right at home!

Planning for Next Sunday

In every church where I have served, unity was always a major concern. Every congregation has to struggle with actions, differing groups, and the possibility of division. When describing the Church, we often use words like *unity, fellowship,* and phrases like "just like a family." In reality, most congregations have their share of divisions. The good news is that this problem is not new. Ask everyone in your class to think about the problem of building a unified congregation as they read next Sunday's scripture, Ephesians 4, in preparation for the lesson.

173

One Body in Christ

Background Scripture: Ephesians 4:1-16

The Main Question

"This church loves to have a fight," the young pastor said of his new congregation. I have heard this complaint of congregations before. When the church ought to be struggling on behalf of the way of Christ against the world, so often it is divided against itself. And church fights can be the bloodiest fights of all.

From its beginning the Christian church has been deeply concerned with unity, community, and communion. A vision so bold as Christ's, a task so great as the one to which he assigned his disciples, a message so powerful as the one he preached can be sustained only by a body of believers who speak and act as one. On Pentecost, the Spirit descended on "[people] from every nation under heaven" (2:5). Despite great diversity, each person heard and understood every other person, and "all who believed were together and had all things in common" (2:44). This is a rosy picture of church unity. You need look no further than the letters of Paul to see that unity, oneness, and communion were often a goal or an ideal for New Testament churches, rather than an accurate description of the way things really were.

"When you come together as a church, I hear that there are divisions among you; and to some extent I believe it," says Paul in 1 Corinthians 11:18.

Unity in the church continues to be a problem. Whether in its worldwide or local form, the church seeks to convert people from all nations, races, ages, sexes, and economic situations. Yet, it also seeks to form them into a unified body of believers. It seeks to affirm the meek, God-given diversity of each person and yet to bind that diversity within a cohesive community of faith. It strives to be open to all and yet strives for the intimacy of a close family.

Is it possible for the church to fulfill its mission without thwarting the very unity that it seeks? How in the world, in which so many divisions and differences divide human beings, can our Church find the unity to live and work together in Christ?

Selected Scripture

King James Version

Ephesians 4:1-16

1 I therefore, the prisoner of the Lord, beseech you that ye walk worthy of the vocation wherewith ye are called,

2 With all lowliness and meekness, with longsuffering, forbearing one another in love;

New Revised Standard Version

Ephesians 4:1-16

1 I therefore, the prisoner in the Lord, beg you to lead a life worthy of the calling to which you have been called, 2 with all humility and gentleness, with patience, bearing with one another in love, 3 making every effort to maintain the unity of

3 Endeavouring to keep the unity of the Spirit in the bond of peace.

4 There is one body, and one Spirit, even as ye are called in one hope of your calling;

5 One Lord, one faith, one baptism,

6 One God and Father of all, who is above all, and through all, and in you all.

7 But unto every one of us is given grace according to the measure of the gift of Christ.

8 Wherefore he saith, When he ascended up on high, he led captivity captive, and gave gifts unto men.

9 (Now that he ascended, what is it but that he also descended first into the lower parts of the earth?

10 He that descended is the same also that ascended up far above all heavens, that he might fill all things.)

11 And he gave some, apostles; and some, prophets; and some, evangelists; and some, pastors and teachers;

12 For the perfecting of the saints, for the work of the ministry, for the edifying of the body of Christ:

13 Till we all come in the unity of the faith, and of the knowledge of the Son of God, unto a perfect man, unto the measure of the stature of the fulness of Christ:

14 That we henceforth be no more children, tossed to and fro, and carried about with every wind of doctrine, by the sleight of men, and cunning craftiness, whereby they lie in wait to deceive;

15 But speaking the truth in love, may grow up into him in all things, which is the head, even Christ:

16 From whom the whole body fitly joined together and compacted by that which every joint supplieth, according to the effectual working in the measure of every part, maketh increase of the body unto the edifying of itself in love.

the Spirit in the bond of peace. 4 There is one body and one Spirit, just as you were called to the one hope of your calling, 5 one Lord, one faith, one baptism, 6 one God and Father of all, who is above all and through all and in all.

7 But each of us was given grace according to the measure of Christ's gift. 8 Therefore it is said,

"When he ascended on high he made captivity itself a captive;

he gave gifts to his people."

9 (When it says, "He ascended," what does it mean but that he had also descended into the lower parts of the earth? 10 He who descended is the same one who ascended far above all the heavens, so that he might fill all things.) 11 The gifts he gave were that some would be apostles, some prophets, some evangelists, some pastors and teachers, 12 to equip the saints for the work of ministry, for building up the body of Christ, 13 until all of us come to the unity of the faith and of the knowledge of the Son of God, to maturity, to the measure of the full stature of Christ. 14 We must no longer be children, tossed to and fro and blown about by every wind of doctrine, by people's trickery, by their craftiness in deceitful scheming. 15 But speaking the truth in love, we must grow up in every way into him who is the head, into Christ, 16 from whom the whole body, joined and knit together by every ligament with which it is equipped, as each part is working properly, promotes the body's growth in building itself up in love.

Key Verse: **There is one body, and one Spirit, even as ye are called in one hope of your calling.** (Ephesians 4:4)

Key Verse: **There is one body and one Spirit, just as you were called to the one hope of your calling.** (Ephesians 4:4)

As You Read the Scripture

Ephesians 4:1-16. Paul's Letter to the Ephesians is one of his most beloved Epistles. Few of his writings reach the poetic heights of this letter. It seems to have been written when Paul was a prisoner (3:1), about the same time as his Letter to the Colossians. Our selected scripture for this Sunday comes from the section in the middle of the Letter to the Ephesians (chaps. 4–6) where Paul takes up practical questions of church life. Throughout this section, a chief concern is the unity of the church. The call for "unity of the Spirit" (4:3) is probably addressed to conflict between Jewish and Gentile Christians. Here were two groups that had been hostile to each other since the beginning of time. And yet, in Christ, Gentiles and Jews have been brought together as one in the Church, but not without difficulty.

Verses 1-3. In noting that he is a "prisoner in the Lord," Paul is claiming authority for what he is preparing to teach the Ephesians. He is paying for his faith with his own imprisonment. In referring to the "calling to which you have been called," Paul is probably referring to their baptism, the time when Christians are given the gift of the Spirit. For Paul, one of the chief gifts of the Spirit is the ability to work with other Christians in peace (vv. 2-3).

Verses 4-6. The Ephesian Christians can be one because they all are yoked, through baptism, to one Lord. Here are listed seven elements of Christian unity.

Verses 7-10. Unity within the church is not a human achievement. Rather it is a result of the grace given to each of us through the Holy Spirit in baptism. There is no urging here for the Ephesians to work hard to try to get along with one another. Rather, Paul is urging them to utilize the gifts that they have been given. Unity is a gift of the Spirit, not a human attainment. Paul cites Psalm 68:18 to claim that Christ, having defeated the enemies of his kingdom ("a host of captives"), reigns in glory on high. The power and authority of Christ empowers Christians to have unity in their churches.

Verses 11-12. Paul lists some of the leaders of the church, noting that all gifts for leadership have a single goal—"to equip the saints." Leaders in the church are not to lead for their own personal gain, but rather for "building up the body of Christ." Leaders in the church have significance only as they are able to "equip the saints."

Verses 13-16. In these verses, Paul seems to equate disunity in the church with spiritual immaturity. Immature Christians still live by the ways of the old order. Because of their superficial grounding in the faith, they are like children, "tossed to and fro," subject to manipulation by deceitful people. Paul urges the Ephesians "to grow up in every way" into Christ, who is the one head of the church.

Verse 16. Paul uses the human body in its unity of diverse parts as an analogy for the church. The human body needs each of its parts to work together in order to function. He makes a similar argument in 1 Corinthians 27:31.

The Scripture and the Main Question

Bearing with One Another in Love

First, the good news. I remember a young pastor complaining to me about the terrible divisions within her congregation. She actually had people who refused to sit on the same pew together, even to speak to each other, because of a dispute that had divided the congregation years before. Now, people had nearly forgotten what the original dispute was about, but they had not forgotten their divisions. She had tried everything to get them together, but their divisions seemed permanent.

"The good news," I told her, "is that this is nothing new. Pick up, for instance, Paul's First Letter to the Corinthians, or his Letter to the Ephesians. You will find that your problem is as old as the church itself. Fortunately, things have not gotten as bad at your church as they were in Corinth!"

Of course, the bad news is that, while we have perhaps made a number of advances in human life, it appears that we have not made many advances in the ability of humans to work together. As a character in one of Dostoevski's novels says, "Men have learned to swim through the water like fish, to move across the land like fast horses, or fly through the air like birds. When will they learn to live on the earth like men?" (*The Brothers Karamazov*).

Although we like to speak of our congregations as "friendly" churches, places "where we are all just like family," few churches really approximate this ideal. In reality, there are divisions.

In one church where I served, people were always bragging about what a friendly church we were. Then one new member told of her first couple of visits to our church. When she entered the hallway, on her way into the sanctuary to worship, everyone was standing around talking to one another, having a good time visiting. But no one spoke to her. Our church seemed friendly to us because we were all talking to each other, but we ignored our visitors. What we experienced as "friendliness" she experienced as a very exclusive, unfriendly group.

Paul urges the Ephesians to "bear with one another in love" (4:2). Life in the church does require us to bear with one another. After all, the church deals with important matters. Many times we deal with potentially threatening and controversial matters. No church can deal with the church's true business without the possibility of division. Therefore, we must learn patience and forbearance with differing opinions, deep feelings, and other points of view.

Take a moment and think about recent disputes within your congregation that may have caused controversy. Are any difficult issues being faced by your denomination that are causing the growth of different factions within your church?

One Body and One Spirit

"There is one body and one Spirit, just as you were called to the one hope of your calling, one Lord, one faith, one baptism, one God and Father of all, who is above all and through all and in all" (4:4-6). This is Paul's beautiful statement for the basis of Christian unity. The church does not base its unity on the fact that we all share a common race or a common heritage or a common economic background. In fact, the church would be wrong to seek its unity in such worldly characteristics. We have unity only because we have all been called forth by one Lord, have been initiated through one baptism, and share one hope. Any unity we have is, therefore, not of our own creation, but rather comes as an amazing gift of Christ and his amazing grace (4:7).

Requirements for Congregational Unity

From what I have observed of Christian churches, I have compiled six requisites for congregational unity. How does your church display these aspects of unity?

1. Common sense of identity. A church must know who it is and to whom it belongs. There must be some degree of "specialness" within the congregation's identity. I served a congregation at one time that took great pride in being "one of the most forward-thinking and youthful congregations in town." A church must be able to name itself.

2. Common authority. The congregation can articulate the gospel by which it is judged and by which it judges itself. There must be some creed, text, constitution, or person to which the congregation as a whole ultimately appeals in times of internal crisis. I am speaking of the guiding purposes and goals that name a congregation, that make a gathering a specifically *Christian* gathering. Without a commonly recognized source of authority, it is difficult for a congregation to deal constructively with differences of opinion within that congregation. If we cannot appeal to some commonly recognized source for reconciling our differing points of view, there is no way to settle and debate an argument within the congregation. About all a congregation can do is to keep everything superficial and polite. Unity becomes a matter of superficial congeniality rather than a matter of shared faith.

3. Common memory. The congregation must have a shared story, a common history through which it understands itself and its mission. Every unified church places great emphasis on its history. This may begin with older members talking about "the way things used to be." Early ordeals and struggles, founding fathers and mothers, will be treated with reverence. The shared story, a common history, gives a congregation its roots, its identity. We do not always value the past. Our lack of shared and known history is often a factor in our disunity and loneliness. In a mobile society, many congregations neglect or forget their past. As Christians, our past extends not only to our individual congregation but to our church as a whole. The study of the Bible is a way of enlarging our common memory.

4. Common vision. The congregation must share common goals and guidelines for which and by which it lives. Just as a common memory identifies where the congregation has been, so also a common vision identifies where the congregation hopes to be. Churches would do well to set specific goals and objectives, projecting themselves into the future and evaluating how well they are accomplishing their mission. Some of the most effective pastors are visionaries—dreamers and interpreters of dreams to the congregation. A good leader is one who says, "Here is my vision of where I think we ought to be going. Does anyone else share this with me?" "Where there is no vision, the people perish" (Proverbs 29:18 KJV).

5. *Common shared life together.* A congregation must share the intimacy and mutual feeling that is the visible sign to the world of the presence of the kingdom of God in our midst. Just before he died, the great modern theologian Paul Tillich noted that whereas the theology of the 1950s and the 1960s was concerned with questions of reconciliation and estrangement, the theology of the 1970s and 1980s would be primarily concerned with questions of meaning and community. Today's lessons suggest that community is perhaps *the* issue for congregations. In our culture there is a deep yearning for togetherness and community. But there is also, among many, a feeling of loneliness and fragmentation. Probably the ultimate test of a church's faithfulness to the Christian vision is when outsiders can look at us and exclaim, "See how they love one another."

6. *Common shared life in the world.* A Christian congregation is called to be more than an isolated enclave of like-minded friends. A church is called to be a visible witness to the kingdom of God in the world. When congregational togetherness becomes self-infatuation, something is wrong. The Church exists between the tension of being not of the world and yet also called to win and transform the world. A congregation's investment in the needs of the world can foster a new sense of congregational identity and unity. Some congregations may discover what it means to be a *Christian* congregation through actually trying to live as Christians in the world. Even when a congregation's involvement brings conflict, a congregation's response to the conflict can promote a more unified church. The conflict can provide an occasion for working through the congregation's faith.

A pastor once told me about a church I was moving to, "Those people love to fight. Your job will be to keep them fighting the world, or they are sure to fight one another."

Take a moment and rate your congregation on the basis of the six requisites for congregational unity. What are the areas on which you think your congregation needs to work in order to show forth the unity of life in the one Spirit?

Helping Adults Become Involved

Preparing to Teach

In today's lesson, you are leading your adults to consider one of the most persistent problems in the Church—congregational unity. The selected scripture from Paul's Letter to the Ephesians will serve as a catalyst for your class members to think about the subject of unity. Specific requisites for congregational unity will be discussed, using your own congregation as a case study in the possibilities and the problems in Church unity.

Prepare for the lesson by reading all of the material in "The Main Question" and "The Scripture and the Main Question." Study the selected scripture by reading it along with the material in "As You Read the Scripture." As you prepare, make notes to yourself on illustrations from your own experience that will help you to present the lesson.

Before the class, list the six requisites for congregational unity on a chalkboard or newsprint for your class to see when they arrive. The list of requisites are found in "The Scripture and the Main Question."

Here is a suggested lesson outline:

179

I. Characteristics of a unified congregation.
II. Is our church unified?
III. Ways to greater unity.

Introducing the Main Question

Present today's Scripture, using the material you find in "As You Read the Scripture" and "The Scripture and the Main Question."

I. Characteristics of a unified congregation.

After reading aloud today's selected scripture to the class, ask your class members to mention some essential characteristics of a unified church. Note that congregational unity must have been a problem for the Church from its very beginning.

Developing the Lesson

The main development of today's lesson will be a discussion of the six requisites for congregational unity, which are listed and discussed in detail in "The Scripture and the Main Question." You should list these six items on a chalkboard or newsprint before the class begins.

After having introduced the scripture from Ephesians and the main issue before you, now lead your group in a discussion of the requisites for unity within a congregation. You should thoroughly familiarize yourself with the discussion of these six requisites so that you will be able to lead your class in a discussion of these requisites in your own words.

After stating each requisite and discussing its meaning (using the material found in "The Scripture and the Main Question") ask your class to cite examples from your own congregation of ways in which your congregation succeeds or fails to fulfill this requisite within its life together.

For instance, requisite number one says that a unified congregation must have a strong sense of identity, it must know who it is. Does your congregation have a distinctive identity? How would the class members complete the phrase, "Our congregation is best known for its. . . "?

II. Is our church unified?

You will want members of your adult class to claim the ways in which your congregation is already demonstrating Paul's call to be unified in Christ as well as to be honest about the ways in which your church members could do a better job of loving one another in unity as Christ has loved us.

Helping Class Members Act

III. Ways to greater unity.

Within your discussion of the ways your congregation succeeds or fails to fulfill the six requisites for congregational unity, members of your class have undoubtedly been thinking of how your congregation could do a better job of being united in Christ.

Ask your group to return to the list of requisites for congregational unity and to suggest one specific program or action your congregation might take to foster more congregational unity. For instance, requisite number one speaks of the need for a congregation to have a good sense of its own identity. Perhaps your congregation needs a class for new members so that

new members could be instructed in the history and programs of your
congregation.

Planning for Next Sunday

Next Sunday we begin a new unit on "Sharing the Good News." Ask your
class members to prepare for next Sunday's lesson by thinking of the ways in
which the good news of Jesus Christ has been shared with them in their lives.

UNIT III: SHARING THE GOOD NEWS

William and Patricia Willimon

FOUR LESSONS   FEBRUARY 7–28

The final unit in this quarter is a three-session study on "Sharing the
Good News." In this unit we shall explore some key biblical texts that deal
with proclamation, service, and teaching as the Church shares the good
news of Jesus Christ in all the world.

The great preacher Harry Emerson Fosdick once compared the Sea of
Galilee to the Dead Sea. He noted that these two bodies of water are about
the same size and are located in similar geographical circumstances.
However, they are dramatically different: One body of water is a living lake.
It teems with wildlife and provides food for the inhabitants of the area. We
know from the Bible that the Sea of Galilee was an important part of the
lives of the people of the Holy Land from the dawn of history.

On the other hand, the Dead Sea is precisely that—dead. Its salt-laden
waters are unfit for any living organism or any life except for some
microorganisms. Why? Whereas the Sea of Galilee flows into other bodies
of water, the Dead Sea is a dead end for any water that flows into it. As
Fosdick noted, "One sea, the Dead Sea, lives only to receive. The other sea
lives to give. When we do not give and share, we die."

Sharing the good news is a life-and-death matter for the Church.

LESSON 10   FEBRUARY 7

Commissioned to Witness

Background Scripture: Luke 24:13-53

The Main Question

"You are [my] witnesses," the risen Christ tells his disciples toward the
end of Luke's Gospel as the risen Christ prepares to ascend to heaven.

Christians are those who witness to God's gift of the Christ. We use the
word *witness* in a dual sense. We say that someone was a witness to an

accident. By that we mean that someone has personally seen and experienced some event.

The word *witness* has another meaning as well. If someone has "witnessed" an accident, that person may be asked to come into a court of law and "witness" to what he or she has seen. Used in this way, the word *witness* means to testify to what has happened.

Throughout the Bible, the word *witness* is used in a similar twofold way. Luke says that Jesus' disciples have witnessed his life, teachings, ministry, death, and resurrection. Being with Jesus was not a matter of some inner, subjective experience they felt in their hearts. It was not something they dreamed up, some invisible, mystical phenomenon. Jesus was an event in their lives. He came to them and spoke to them. Even after the Resurrection, when they expected Jesus to remain only a sad memory, he came back to them, healed their doubts, and even encouraged them to touch him. They were witnesses in that they saw and experienced him. Then, he commissioned them to go to all the world and testify to what had happened to them. Those who had seen and heard something went into the world to witness to what they had seen and heard.

Behind today's lesson is this question: In what ways are we witnesses to what has happened to the world in Jesus Christ, and in what ways have we been commissioned to witness to the whole world about Christ?

Selected Scripture

King James Version

Luke 24:36-53

36 And as they thus spake, Jesus himself stood in the midst of them, and saith unto them, Peace be unto you.

37 But they were terrified and affrighted, and supposed that they had seen a spirit.

38 And he said unto them, Why are ye troubled? and why do thoughts arise in your hearts?

39 Behold my hands and my feet, that it is I myself: handle me, and see; for a spirit hath not flesh and bones, as ye see me have.

40 And when he had thus spoken, he shewed them his hands and his feet.

41 And while they yet believed not for joy, and wondered, he said unto them, Have ye here any meat?

42 And they gave him a piece of a broiled fish, and of an honeycomb.

43 And he took it, and did eat before them.

44 And he said unto them, These

New Revised Standard Version

Luke 24:36-53

36 While they were talking about this, Jesus himself stood among them and said to them, "Peace be with you." 37 They were startled and terrified, and thought that they were seeing a ghost. 38 He said to them, "Why are you frightened, and why do doubts arise in your hearts? 39 Look at my hands and my feet; see that it is I myself. Touch me and see; for a ghost does not have flesh and bones as you see that I have." 40 And when he had said this, he showed them his hands and his feet. 41 While in their joy they were disbelieving and still wondering, he said to them, "Have you anything here to eat?" 42 They gave him a piece of broiled fish, 43 and he took it and ate in their presence.

44 Then he said to them, "These

are the words which I spake unto you, while I was yet with you, that all things must be fulfilled, which were written in the law of Moses, and in the prophets, and in the psalms, concerning me.

45 Then opened he their understanding, that they might understand the scriptures,

46 And said unto them, Thus it is written, and thus it behoved Christ to suffer, and to rise from the dead the third day:

47 And that repentance and remission of sins should be preached in his name among all nations, beginning at Jerusalem.

48 And ye are witnesses of these things.

49 And, behold, I send the promise of my Father upon you: but tarry ye in the city of Jerusalem, until ye be endued with power from on high.

50 And he led them out as far as to Bethany, and he lifted up his hands, and blessed them.

51 And it came to pass, while he blessed them, he was parted from them, and carried up into heaven.

52 And they worshipped him, and returned to Jerusalem with great joy:

53 And were continually in the temple, praising and blessing God. Amen.

Key Verse: **And that repentance and remission of sins should be preached in his name among all nations, beginning at Jerusalem. (Luke 24:47)**

are my words that I spoke to you while I was still with you—that everything written about me in the law of Moses, the prophets, and the psalms must be fulfilled." 45 Then he opened their minds to understand the scriptures, 46 and he said to them, "Thus it is written, that the Messiah is to suffer and to rise from the dead on the third day, 47 and that repentance and forgiveness of sins is to be proclaimed in his name to all nations, beginning from Jerusalem. 48 You are witnesses of these things. 49 And see, I am sending upon you what my Father promised; so stay here in the city until you have been clothed with power from on high."

50 Then he led them out as far as Bethany, and, lifting up his hands, he blessed them. 51 While he was blessing them, he withdrew from them and was carried up into heaven. 52 And they worshiped him, and returned to Jerusalem with great joy; 53 and they were continually in the temple blessing God.

Key Verse: **And that repentance and forgiveness of sins is to be proclaimed in his name to all nations, beginning from Jerusalem. (Luke 24:47)**

As You Read the Scripture

Luke 24:13-53. The culmination of Luke's Gospel is the unexpected, glorious resurrection of Christ. That event, and the disciples' experience of the return of the risen Christ, is what produced the church. Indeed, it could be said that Christians are those who have witnessed the Resurrection.

Verses 13-35. Luke is one of the greatest storytellers in the Bible. In Luke 23 are the beloved parables of the prodigal son and the good Samaritan. These verses contain another of Luke's marvelously told stories, that of the journey to Emmaus. This story is playful, at times humorous (poking fun at the disciples' blindness to the fact of the Resurrection) and dramatic. One of the functions of this story is to show that the disciples in no way expected or hoped for the Resurrection. The Resurrection was God's way of surprising the despair of Jesus' followers. He came back to talk to them, to walk among them, to instruct them, and to eat with them. All of this happened "on the first day of the week" (v. 1)—that is, Sunday. So, in a way, the story of Emmaus is the story of Christians on every Sunday—the day when Christ comes to us, speaks to us, and eats with us.

Verses 36-47. The risen Christ ministers to the doubts of his disciples. He instructs them, basing his instruction on Scripture (vv. 44-46). Without the risen Christ, disciples would not be able to understand Scripture or its implications for their lives.

Verses 48-49. The story inspires its listeners to share it. Christ clearly commands his people to go forth and tell what they have seen. He gives them not only his command but also his Holy Spirit (v. 49), which will give disciples the encouragement and power to proclaim the gospel. This proclamation is not just for a few chosen, not just for one nation or race. The good news is to be "proclaimed in his name to all nations" (v. 47).

In just a few verses, here at the close of his Gospel, Luke is able to give us a mandate for the church. The church consists of those who are witnesses to the risen Christ, and they now are given the means to witness to that event to the whole world.

After writing his Gospel, Luke wrote a second volume, the Acts of the Apostles, in which he depicts the disciples obeying Jesus' mandate to witness "in Jerusalem, in all Judea and Samaria, and to the ends of the earth" (Acts 1:8).

The Scripture and the Main Question

How Did You Get Here?

We were sitting in the living room, discussing how we all got there. Looking around the room, anyone could see that we were different ages, spoke with different accents, came from different backgrounds, and had few things in common. However, we all had one thing in common: We all were Christians. How did we get to be that way?

"I suppose I have always believed in Jesus, ever since I can remember. In a way, I guess you could say that I was born a Christian. I can't remember a time when I didn't know that I was a believer," said Mary Smith.

John Jones's experience was a little different. "I was not raised in a Christian home, like Mary. I spent most of my adult life never really having heard the gospel. Occasionally, I attended church with some friends of mine when I was young, but that was about it. It was not until my late thirties that I was brought to Christ through the efforts of some faithful Christian friends."

Others in the group had similar experiences. Some came to Christ early, others arrived late. Yet, as they talked, a common theme ran through the discussion. Almost all of them had become Christians the same way—that is, someone had to tell them the story, had to live the faith before them in such a way that they wanted to embrace this faith.

Even the people who had claimed that they had been Christians all their lives knew enough about life to know that someone had to tell them the story, name the name, and live the faith before them so that they knew what Christianity was all about. Even those people who could say that they were born "into a good Christian home" did not arrive on this planet already knowing about Jesus. Someone, probably when these people were very young, had to tell them about Jesus.

So, in a way, to everyone's surprise, everyone had to admit that all of them were Christians as a gift. None of them were Christians by natural inclination. None of them had made this discovery alone. All of them had to receive this faith through the testimony, the witness, the encouragement, and the gifts of others who had witnessed to them.

At this realization, everyone in the room grew silent and thoughtful.

"I guess this means that if it hadn't been for other people," said Gladys Hart, "we wouldn't be here."

"We are all here as debtors," said Ray Block. "Every single one of us is indebted to somebody else for helping to make us a Christian."

The group was now silent and thoughtful because they all came to the realization that, as Christians, we are not only indebted to others for the gift of faith, but we also bear a great responsibility to share this faith with others. Although God can use many miraculous means to lead people to believe, according to the Bible, the means that God most often uses is people. Somebody else had to tell us the story.

You Are [My] Witnesses

So who is that somebody who has to tell the story of Christ to others? I think it is apparent: that "somebody" is usually a very ordinary, typical, everyday Christian. Most of us are influenced by people like ourselves, people with whom we come in contact in everyday life.

I am a preacher. I spend most of my time thinking about how to proclaim and witness to the gospel. And yet I know, from personal experience, that most of the gospel that gets shared is shared by people like you, not like me. Laypersons, in their daily lives, are most likely to influence other laypersons. *You* are a witness.

If you thumb through the pages of Luke's Gospel or Acts, you will see his intense concern for witnessing. It is fitting, therefore, that he concludes his Gospel with the call for us to be witnesses to the ends of the earth. Here is a gospel that is meant to be shared. The Resurrection has a way of exploding its power into every corner of the earth, producing its own witness. Whenever we share the story of Christ with others, in word or deed, we are participating in that great post-Easter explosion, which Luke depicts in his Gospel and in the book of Acts.

My own denomination, like many other mainline Protestant denominations, has been steadily losing members over the past couple of decades. Why? Are people less religious than they used to be as is sometimes claimed? Is God any less active in our world? The major reason for our decline in numbers, when the research has been done and all factors have been evaluated, appears to be that many of our churches have simply gotten out of the business of making new disciples. At some point, probably without any public decision or debate, we stopped sharing the good news in a vibrant, effective way. Now the statistics show our lack of witness.

So, in a rather odd way, the unimaginable has happened. A generation of Christians refuses to shoulder the responsibility of making new Christians.

SECOND QUARTER

Our membership declines because our determination to share the good news has declined. Fortunately, the statistics are not so dismal in every denomination or in every part of the Church. The Church is growing quite well on the continent of Africa and in South America. But the mainline Protestant church is not growing in the United States. Why? We have stopped sharing.

I am confident, on the basis of studying Luke's Gospel, that Luke would say that any church that stops sharing stops being the Church! That sounds hard, and it is meant to be, but I think such a statement can be defended on the basis of the story of Christ as Luke tells it. It would be inconceivable to Luke that something so stupendous, so amazing, so life-changing as the resurrection of Jesus could occur without also producing people who are obsessed with the desire to share what they have seen and heard. In fact, one of the most incontrovertible "proofs" for the resurrection of Jesus was the fact that a group of ordinary, everyday people (like you and me!) risked everything, braved every terror, to share the good news of what God had done in Christ. The vitality of the witness is itself proof of the validity of what is being witnessed.

"You are [my] witnesses of these things" (24:48).

To All Nations

Even as I write these words, great movements are taking place around the world. The former tyrannical government of Romania, a government that terribly persecuted its people for decades, fell in late 1989. No one predicted that such a change could occur. How did it begin?

It seems that the brutal state police tried to capture a Protestant pastor and take him to prison. People loyal to their pastor surrounded his house in order to block the way of the police. They were soon joined by others who, though they did not share the people's faith, shared their hatred for the government. Shots were fired, and many died. But that incident was the spark that ignited a revolution.

While it is still too early to tell what is ahead for the oppressed people of Romania, we know that things there will never be as they were before. A small group of people, loyal to a God whose dominion is greater than that of any nation, are busy turning a world upside down through their courageous witness. They are showing that the emperor is not God, that there are higher values than those of the modern state, that God will not forever be mocked, that when ordinary people are inflamed with extraordinary fire, something miraculous happens.

They are witnesses.

Helping Adults Become Involved

Preparing to Teach

In a very direct way, today's lesson will help members of your class to focus on the responsibility each of us has to share the good news, through word and deed, wherever we are. Prepare by reading over the Scripture for today, as well as the explanatory material within "The Main Question" and "The Scripture and the Main Question."

Here is an outline for today's class:

I. Sharing the good news is at the heart of the gospel.
II. The difficulties of being a witness.
III. Equipment for witness.
IV. Encouragement for witness.

Introducing the Main Question

"The Scripture and the Main Question" portrays a group of contemporary Christians discussing how each became disciples. You might introduce today's lesson by leading your class in a discussion of "How We Got Here (As Christians, That Is)."

Would you be willing to share with the group your own story of coming to faith? If not, begin by sharing someone else's story of becoming Christian. Then ask other members of the class whether their paths to discipleship were the same or different from the one you related.

The purpose of this exercise is similar to the material in "The Scripture and the Main Question." When we recall how significant other witnesses were in our own path to faith, we see how important it is for each of us to witness to others. Disciples are made because someone else, some witness, told us the story.

Developing the Lesson

I. Sharing the good news is at the heart of the gospel.

Having introduced the main theme of today's lesson from your own experiences as a Christian, now lead your class to today's scripture. Using the material in "As You Read the Scripture," discuss Luke 24:13-53. It is noteworthy that these are the words with which Luke concludes his Gospel. This is the last thing that Jesus told us before his ascension. These words are the climax of the gospel. Sharing the good news is not peripheral to the gospel. Witnessing is the very point of the gospel.

You might underscore the significance of witnessing by noting other occasions in Luke's Gospel, or in the book of Acts, in which witnessing is portrayed as a key activity of disciples.

II. The difficulties of being a witness.

Time for a little honesty. Jesus commanded us, at the close of Luke's Gospel, to be witnesses. We agreed that the call to evangelize, to show forth the gospel in word and deed, is at the heart of the gospel. Yet, here is a command that is not easy to fulfill. Our mainline denominations continue to lose members. How many new Christians has your congregation made in the past year? How many individuals have you personally brought to Christ and his church in the last few months?

Ask your group to ponder honestly some of t'.e reasons why it is difficult for us to obey the command of Jesus to be witnesses. You might list their reasons on a chalkboard or newsprint (for example, embarrassment, "people would think I was a religious showoff," "don't know how to talk about religion," "don't want to pry into other people's personal lives," etc.). You might refer back to Luke's Gospel or to Acts for examples of resistance to the spread of the gospel as biblical instances of the difficulty in being a witness.

III. Equipment for witness.

Having been honest about the difficulties in being witnesses today, ask your group to discuss ways in which the church could better equip each of us to be a witness. Perhaps your own adult class, in giving people an opportunity to talk about the Bible and their own faith, is a means of preparing people to witness.

IV. Encouragement for witness.

Today's lesson challenges the notion that witnessing is something only for professional clergy or for just a few particularly gifted Christians. All of us are called to be witnesses for Christ. Close your study of Luke 24 by giving examples of witnessing in daily life. Share some of your own experiences and encourage other members of the class to share also. When have you seen examples of people bringing others to the gospel through word and deed?

Helping Class Members Act

Ask the class members to think about their own contacts with people. Where they work or shop or play, there are people who are uninvolved in a church, people who have never had anyone openly discuss religion with them, people who may be eager for someone to care enough about them to reach out to them. Today's scripture is meant to encourage all disciples to be witnesses in every corner of the world.

Suggest that, this coming week, each member of the class share the gospel with one person with whom they come in contact. They don't have to tell the person's name. All they must do is to be intentional about witnessing to someone else in the coming week.

Planning for Next Sunday

If members of your class act on their intentions and share their faith with someone in the coming week, that will be excellent preparation for next week's lesson. Next Sunday, we will continue our exploration of sharing the good news with a study of the nature of Christian proclamation.

Ask the members of your class to ponder the questions, What is the best sermon you ever heard? What is the best sermon you ever *saw*?

Come back next week, and we'll share our responses!

LESSON 11   FEBRUARY 14

Proclaim the Gospel

Background Scripture: Romans 10

The Main Question

"Faith comes from what is heard," Paul wrote to the Romans (Romans 10:17). This is a rather bold claim for the power of proclamation. Paul says that the Christian faith is basically an auditory experience. Faith comes because someone has heard a voice.

As a preacher, I have always more or less believed this to be true. And in my present preaching assignment, I now know it to be true.

I preach within a university chapel. On Sunday mornings, my congregation is made up of a number of "regulars" and a good number of tourists, students, and people who just seem to be passing through town. For the first time in my ministry, I find myself preaching to a great many people who appear never to have heard very much about the gospel before. Many of them are not regular church members. Some of them have had religious experiences in their backgrounds, but have not been active in a church for a long time.

In these circumstances, where people are not coming to church out of habit or because all of their friends are in church or because this is the place where their family has always worshiped, there is little to unite us except the Word. Many within our Sunday morning congregation have never heard the gospel before. It comes to them new. It isn't something their parents told them. It isn't something they perceive to be the normal, expected, American thing to do. It comes to them quite fresh.

Yet, though they have had little preparation for the gospel, many of them believe. They talk to me at the church door after the service. Some of them make appointments to speak with me during the week. They want to know how they can hear more. Where can they go to explore the Christian faith in more depth?

I have absolutely no way of explaining their response except to refer to Romans 10:17. Paul was right. Faith really does come by hearing. Sometimes we come to this faith because we are attracted to it by our friends. Sometimes people join a church simply to participate in some of its fellowship activities. But for a surprisingly large number of people, faith comes simply by hearing. In the silence of their lives, a word is heard. Amid the confusing, jangling sounds of modern life, a clear note is sounded. They hear. They come forward. Their ears perk up, and they say yes.

Now the question is this: How can I, in my own life, proclaim this auditory faith to others?

Selected Scripture

King James Version	New Revised Standard Version
Romans 10:5-17	*Romans 10:5-17*
5 For Moses describeth the righteousness which is of the law, That the man which doeth those things shall live by them.	5 Moses writes concerning the righteousness that comes from the law, that "the person who does these things will live by them." 6 But the righteousness that comes from faith says, "Do not say in your heart, 'Who will ascend into heaven?'" (that is, to bring Christ down) 7 "or 'Who will descend into the abyss?'" (that is, to bring Christ up from the dead). 8 But what does it say?
6 But the righteousness which is of faith speaketh on this wise, Say not in thine heart, Who shall ascend into heaven? (that is, to bring Christ down from above:)	
7 Or, Who shall descend into the deep? (that is, to bring up Christ again from the dead.)	"The word is near you,

8 But what saith it? The word is nigh thee, even in thy mouth, and in thy heart: that is, the word of faith, which we preach;

9 That if thou shalt confess with thy mouth the Lord Jesus, and shalt believe in thine heart that God hath raised him from the dead, thou shalt be saved.

10 For with the heart man believeth unto righteousness; and with the mouth confession is made unto salvation.

11 For the scripture saith, Whosoever believeth on him shall not be ashamed.

12 For there is no difference between the Jew and the Greek: for the same Lord over all is rich unto all that call upon him.

13 For whosoever shall call upon the name of the Lord shall be saved.

14 How then shall they call on him in whom they have not believed? and how shall they believe in him of whom they have not heard? and how shall they hear without a preacher?

15 And how shall they preach, except they be sent? as it is written, How beautiful are the feet of them that preach the gospel of peace, and bring glad tidings of good things!

16 But they have not all obeyed the gospel. For Esaias saith, Lord, who hath believed our report?

17 So then faith cometh by hearing, and hearing by the word of God.

on your lips and in your heart" (that is, the word of faith that we proclaim); 9 because if you confess with your lips that Jesus is Lord and believe in your heart that God raised him from the dead, you will be saved. 10 For one believes with the heart and so is justified, and one confesses with the mouth and so is saved. 11 The scripture says, "No one who believes in him will be put to shame." 12 For there is no distinction between Jew and Greek; the same Lord is Lord of all and is generous to all who call on him. 13 For, "Everyone who calls on the name of the Lord shall be saved."

14 But how are they to call on one in whom they have not believed? And how are they to believe in one of whom they have never heard? And how are they to hear without someone to proclaim him? 15 And how are they to proclaim him unless they are sent? As it is written, "How beautiful are the feet of those who bring good news!" 16 But not all have obeyed the good news; for Isaiah says, "Lord, who has believed our message?" 17 So faith comes from what is heard, and what is heard comes through the word of Christ.

Key Verse: **So then faith cometh by hearing, and hearing by the word of God. (Romans 10:17)**

Key Verse: **So faith comes from what is heard, and what is heard comes through the word of Christ. (Romans 10:17)**

As You Read the Scripture

Paul's Letter to the Romans is one of the greatest of all Christian writings. In this letter Paul gives his most extended, coherent treatment of the major themes of Christian theology, such as the place of Old Testament law in Christian life, salvation by faith alone, and the place of the Jews in God's plan of salvation. This letter is obviously the product of a mature, experienced theological leader who seeks to offer careful guidance to young congregations.

Romans 10:5-9. Today's scripture comes at the conclusion of Paul's anguished discussion of the place of his fellow Jews within God's scheme of salvation. Paul wrote from within the context of the rejection of Jesus as God's promised Messiah by the people of Israel. This rejection was a source of "great sorrow and unceasing anguish in [his] heart" (Romans 9:2). Paul was convinced that, in God's great mercy, both Gentiles and Jews shall be brought to faith.

But how? That is the question of our scripture passage toda. How does faith arise in a person? Paul seems to believe that faith is a distinctly auditory phenomenon. Faith is a word that is near because it is "on your lips and in your heart" (v. 8).

Verses 10-13. For Paul, faith is something that must be expressed openly (see v. 10). Both the Jew and the Gentile have equal access to the salvation of God, offered in Christ, because both are able to call "on the name of the Lord" (v. 13). This is quite a claim, coming from a loyal son of Israel, that Gentiles can be saved, just by hearing and confessing Jesus.

Verses 14-16. After setting forth the basis for salvation for both Jews and Gentiles (Paul refers to Gentiles here as "Greeks"), Paul issues a ringing call to evangelization. How is the good news spread? Through preaching. By quoting a couple of verses from the Old Testament, Paul tries to ground his emphasis on the necessity of the spoken word within the tradition of Israel.

Verse 17. For Paul, faith is a great mystery. He does not know why two people hear the same proclamation and one believes and the other does not. Belief is a gift of God's mysterious grace, not a result of human striving. Yet, he does know that the primary source of our faith is our first hearing the gospel. Therefore, proclamation of the gospel is at the center of the church's task. Both Jews and Gentiles alike are frighteningly dependent, so far as their salvation is concerned, on the presence of someone who can preach the gospel.

The Scripture and the Main Question

How Shall They Believe?

Have you ever wondered why you are a Christian, and why so many others are not Christians? Why is it that this faith, which seems so real and true to you, does not seem so to everybody else? You may have friends, good friends you love dearly, who are so much like you in every way but in this way. Why is it that you and your friends can agree on so much, but cannot agree that Jesus Christ is Lord? This is a great mystery. Throughout his letters, Paul maintains that faith is a gift. It is not something we have earned or achieved or have figured out solely by ourselves. Faith is a gift of God, working through the testimony of others. But why is it that some seem to receive this gift and others have not? This was the great, mysterious, and deeply painful question that lay behind Paul's remarks to the Romans about the proclamation of the gospel. Behind every word of his letter to the Romans is Paul's own deeply painful experience of seeing his own family reject what had so changed his own life. Paul boasts that he was a Jew above all Jews. He was nurtured in the faith of Israel and knew its Scripture thoroughly, and yet found himself excluded from his own people because of his newfound Christian faith. Today's scripture from the tenth chapter of Paul's Letter to the Romans is part of Paul's painful thoughts on the matter of why some believe and some do not.

Paul claims that Moses clearly spoke of the righteousness of God (Romans 10:5). Paul could look through the Hebrew Scriptures and hear them pointing to the Christ (10:7-11, 13). Unfortunately, many of his fellow Jews looked at those same Scriptures and did not see or hear what Paul saw and heard, and that hurt him deeply.

Whatever we say about this matter of belief and non-belief, we should begin by saying that, if we believe, it is not from our own achievement. Faith has not been given to us because we are good or particularly intelligent or perceptive. It has come to us as a gift, as a mysterious act of divine grace. In last week's lesson, we noted how all of us are indebted to other people for having told us the story of Jesus. So there is no cause for pride or haughtiness on our part because we have believed. Our only stance can be one of gratitude for this gift.

Besides, even the firmest believers know what it means to doubt. Many things in life cause us to question our Christian belief. None of us can ever feel firm and completely certain. Therefore, we should have great empathy for those who find it difficult to believe, because we ourselves also experience difficulties from time to time.

Those Who Bring Good News

Paul says that "faith comes from what is heard" (Romans 10:17). At the heart of the Christian faith is the necessity for Christians to be tellers of the good news. We are commissioned to speak "good tidings of peace" wherever we find ourselves. People sometimes say, "I would rather see a sermon than hear one." We also say, "Practice what you preach." Statements like this imply that doing the good news is infinitely more important than speaking the good news. It is more important that we act and live out our faith than simply talk about our faith.

If these statements are true, they are true only up to a point. Through the spoken word, we communicate the truth of the gospel to one another. We catch a glimpse of the Christian vision. Our lives are put in perspective. We hear the story of Jesus, a story that becomes a "lens" through which Christians view the world.

Actions are fine as far as they go. But one of the reasons why a Christian's good works are different from good works done by others is that our good deeds arise as our response to the Christian story. Our hearing of words has led to our doing of deeds. Without the word, would we have acted?

In fact, one wonders today whether the Christian faith seems less influential over our lives because we are doing less speaking of the Word. I remember that my grandmother always used to say things like, "I will see you tomorrow—God willing." Of course, this was simply a little habit of hers, a conventional, everyday expression. However, it was also a way of bringing God's name to every affair of life, including our leave-taking and times of farewell. It was a gentle, ever-present reminder from her that our lives are held in God's care. It was a way of stating that, beyond our doing and willing, God is also willing. Her use of the expression "If God wills" was a small, but I think significant, means of being a bearer of the good news.

A while back I took a seat next to a man on an airline flight. He smiled pleasantly at me when I sat down, and then he continued whatever he was reading. During the flight, when the meals were given out, we began a conversation. He told me that he was in sales for a large eastern company. He told me about his family. Then, quite easily and naturally, he began talking about his church and how much he enjoyed being a part of his church. He taught a Sunday school lesson from time to time—by chance, he had taught from *The International Lesson Annual!*

Then he said something like, "You know, my faith means a great deal to me. If you are not a Christian, I would like to tell you more about what my faith means, if you would be willing."

I told him that I was indeed a Christian and that I was pleased that I could say that my faith also meant much to me.

"I didn't mean to intrude," he said.

"Oh, you didn't intrude," I responded. "In fact, I really appreciate your sharing this with me. I really admire the easy, natural way that you are able to speak about your faith, and I hope that you will do so with the next person you meet."

Glad Tidings of Good Things

Paul, in noting that our faith comes from hearing and in observing our utter dependency on others to tell us the story, breaks forth into a grand exclamation. Quoting from the Old Testament, he says, "How beautiful are the feet of those who bring good news!" (Romans 10:15). Even the feet are beautiful of those who are bold enough to preach good news. Even the feet! It is beautiful, even in a world in which so many forces work together to render us speechless and silent, that there are still those who dare to speak the good news. How beautiful it is that we have witnesses, people who proclaim the gospel wherever they are, to whomever they meet.

When was the last time you shared your faith with someone else?

Helping Adults Become Involved

Preparing to Teach

There are Sundays when the Scripture you must teach to your class deals with subjects that may be somewhat foreign and removed from your people. Today that is definitely not the case. Everyone in your class has had the experience of hearing the gospel preached. Everyone in your class has also probably had the exhilarating (or sometimes frustrating) experience of trying to share the faith with someone else.

Prepare yourself for today's lesson by reading over today's scripture, using the material in "As You Read the Scripture" to help you through today's passage from Paul's Letter to the Romans.

Recall instances when the Christian faith was made particularly real and believable to you through preaching. Perhaps you will remember some particularly moving sermon you have heard.

Now recall an instance when someone else, a layperson, not an ordained preacher, proclaimed the Christian faith to you in such a way that your own faith was strengthened.

SECOND QUARTER

Your aim is to help persons in your class to uncover their own experiences of the validity of Paul's claim that "faith comes from hearing."
Organize today's lesson as follows:

I. The gospel is for everyone.
II. Faith in the gospel comes from hearing the gospel proclaimed.
III. We have the responsibility of proclaiming the gospel.

Introducing the Main Question

Read through "The Main Question" section, which introduces today's lesson. This material should be helpful as you introduce today's theme to your class. You may use the illustration of the preacher in the university chapel, or you might choose to use one of your own illustrations of the power of preaching in proclaiming the gospel.

Ask members of your class to share their recollections of effective preaching. They may want to share their response to the question, "What is the best sermon you have heard?"

Developing the Lesson

I. The gospel is for everyone.
   A. The gospel is addressed to us as we are. Read Romans 10:5-13 aloud to your class, explaining the context of this passage within Paul's discussion of salvation for Jews and Gentiles. Even though Paul did not know precisely how faith occurred in some people and not in others, he was convinced that faith came as the result of their having heard the good news of Christ. This good news is not limited to a few but is available to all.

Note, in today's scripture, how Paul speaks about faith coming to both the Jews and the Gentiles as they are. A crucial aspect of any form of communication is that the communication be done in an accessible way so that everyone may hear. We must speak in a language and use thought forms that make sense to those listening.

Ask the class members if they can think of instances when someone attempted to communicate the Christian faith to them in a way that was incomprehensible to them. Perhaps the speaker "talked over my head" or was too dogmatic or too simplistic or the like.

   B. We must proclaim the gospel to people as they are. In what ways does our proclamation of the gospel today cause people to be turned off to the gospel? For instance, are we proclaiming the gospel to our youth in words they can understand?

Can members of your class think of examples of how the Church has reached out to speak to people in their own way, as they are? For instance, William and Catherine Booth became convinced that the Church in the nineteenth century had failed to reach out to the poor. They organized street bands and specialized in straightforward speaking in the language of the people of the streets. The Salvation Army was their way of reaching out to people where they were.

II. Faith in the gospel comes from hearing the gospel proclaimed.
   A. Biblical faith is auditory—it comes from speaking and hearing. Recall instances from Scripture when someone hears and believes. You might

194

mention such instances as the call of Abraham or Jacob in Genesis, the annunciation of the angel to Mary in Luke 2, and so on. Biblical faith seems to arise when someone is addressed by God in his or her own name.

B. *We do not always know why some hear and some do not hear.* Using the material in the middle section of "The Scripture and the Main Question," discuss the mystery of belief and disbelief. Paul struggled with this mystery in Romans. Have members of your class ever felt frustration in being unable to communicate with someone? Perhaps the person spoke another language or the person had a hearing disability or the person simply did not want to hear.

III. *We have the responsibility of proclaiming the gospel.*

A. *We are to find the words to express our faith.* Do members of your class think that their church gives them enough help and training in being able to share their faith with others? What are some ways your church could help its members to be better preachers of the gospel in their daily lives?

B. *We are to seek daily opportunities to proclaim the gospel.* Use the illustration of the person sharing his faith, which is found toward the end of "The Scripture and the Main Question." Ask members of the class whether they have had similar experiences of someone's sharing the faith in their daily lives.

C. *Ordinary Christians can be some of the most effective preachers.* Close today's lesson by discussing the importance of ordinary Christians' sharing their faith wherever they find themselves. Perhaps members of the class could offer examples of ways in which their own lives have been touched by another person's verbally sharing the faith with them.

Helping Class Members Act

Ask everyone in the class to think of one specific person, with whom they may come into contact during the next week, who might be receptive to a discussion of the Christian faith.

Planning for Next Sunday

Ask the class to prepare for next Sunday's lesson with this assignment: "Today we have spoken of sharing our faith by the proclamation of the gospel in our speech. Next week, we shall focus on the proclamation of the gospel through our actions. Think about one way the gospel has been proclaimed to you through the actions of someone else."

Serve and Honor

Background Scripture: Romans 15:1-13

The Main Question

For most of her adult life, Jane had been struggling with an alcohol problem. She had been encouraged by friends and family to get help for her illness. But it took her many years even to admit that she had a problem and many more years to get up the courage to think about doing something about her alcoholism. She realized that in confronting her alcohol problem she was facing a greater power than herself. How could she possibly summon up the strength to conquer this affliction?

She overlooked one thing. She did not have to face her alcoholism alone. When she told her husband, children, and friends at church that she was going to enter an alcohol treatment center, they swung into action. They had always been supportive of her during her need, and now they supported her during her treatment. A couple of people offered to help her with the expenses. Her Sunday school class volunteered to prepare meals for her husband and children while she was in treatment. Someone from the class took her two children every morning during the month of her treatment and picked them up every afternoon and cared for them. A number of people took her husband out to lunch during the month to provide him needed emotional support during her absence.

After her treatment, she was a new person. But she could not have been a new person without the sustenance of her church. Her story demonstrates the fact that one of the great resources we have as Christians is our fellow Christians. "We who are strong ought to put up with the failings of the weak, and not to please ourselves. Each of us must please our neighbor for the good purpose of building up the neighbor" (Romans 15:1-2). Thus Paul reminds the church at Rome that Christians exist to serve not themselves, but one another. The question behind today's Scripture is this one: How are you and I challenged to serve others in the name of Christ today?

Selected Scripture

King James Version	New Revised Standard Version
Romans 15:1-13	*Romans 15:1-13*
1 We then that are strong ought to bear the infirmities of the weak, and not to please ourselves.	1 We who are strong ought to put up with the failings of the weak, and not to please ourselves. 2 Each of us must please our neighbor for the good purpose of building up the neighbor. 3 For Christ did not please himself; but, as it is written, "The insults of those who insult you have fallen on me." 4 For whatever
2 Let every one of us please his neighbour for his good to edification.	
3 For even Christ pleased not himself; but, as it is written, The reproaches of them that reproached thee fell on me.	

196

4 For whatsoever things were written aforetime were written for our learning, that we through patience and comfort of the scriptures might have hope.

5 Now the God of patience and consolation grant you to be likeminded one toward another according to Christ Jesus:

6 That ye may with one mind and one mouth glorify God, even the Father of our Lord Jesus Christ.

7 Wherefore receive ye one another, as Christ also received us to the glory of God.

8 Now I say that Jesus Christ was a minister of the circumcision for the truth of God, to confirm the promises made unto the fathers:

9 And that the Gentiles might glorify God for his mercy; as it is written, For this cause I will confess to thee among the Gentiles, and sing unto thy name.

10 And again he saith, Rejoice, ye Gentiles, with his people.

11 And again, Praise the Lord, all ye Gentiles; and laud him, all ye people.

12 And again, Esaias saith, There shall be a root of Jesse, and he that shall rise to reign over the Gentiles; in him shall the Gentiles trust.

13 Now the God of hope fill you with all joy and peace in believing, that ye may abound in hope, through the power of the Holy Ghost.

Key Verses: **We then that are strong ought to bear the infirmities of the weak, and not to please ourselves. Let every one of us please his neighbour for his good to edification. (Romans 15:1-2)**

was written in former days was written for our instruction, so that by steadfastness and by the encouragement of the scriptures we might have hope. 5 May the God of steadfastness and encouragement grant you to live in harmony with one another, in accordance with Christ Jesus, 6 so that together you may with one voice glorify the God and Father of our Lord Jesus Christ.

7 Welcome one another, therefore, just as Christ has welcomed you, for the glory of God. 8 For I tell you that Christ has become a servant of the circumcised on behalf of the truth of God in order that he might confirm the promises given to the patriarchs, 9 and in order that the Gentiles might glorify God for his mercy. As it is written,

"Therefore I will confess you
    among the Gentiles,
    and sing praises to your name";
10 and again he says,
"Rejoice, O Gentiles, with his
    people";
11 and again,
"Praise the Lord, all you Gentiles,
    and let all the peoples praise
    him";
12 and again Isaiah says,
"The root of Jesse shall come,
    the one who rises to rule the
    Gentiles;
in him the Gentiles shall hope."
13 May the God of hope fill you with all joy and peace in believing, so that you may abound in hope by the power of the Holy Spirit.

Key Verses: **We who are strong ought to put up with the failings of the weak, and not to please ourselves. Each of us must please our neighbor for the good purpose of building up the neighbor. (Romans 15:1-2)**

As You Read the Scripture

Romans 15:1-13. In last Sunday's lesson, we were introduced to Paul's Letter to the Romans, one of his most complex and well-developed writings. After having treated such themes as the salvation of Gentiles and Jews, salvation by faith alone, and other great theological ideas, Paul turns to more practical concerns toward the end of this letter. Our scripture selection today comes from his discussion of issues within the congregation. Here Paul puts to rest the misconception that Christianity is mainly a matter of getting one's personal life in order without regard to the needs of anyone else.

Verse 1. In speaking of the "strong" and the "weak," Paul is probably referring to people within the congregation. Generally, Paul uses the term *weak* to refer to those people who lack a sure faith in Christ, people who follow the regulations of the Old Testament Law and insist that others do the same. In this verse he pleads for charity and understanding on the part of the strong with the limitations of the weak.

Verses 2-7. Paul bases his appeal to the stronger members of the congregation to show compassion toward the weaker members on their experience of Christ. Even as Christ showed more concern for his disciples than for himself, so we ought to place the needs of others above our own. Just as Christ was patient with us (vv. 4-5), so also we ought to be patient with others. The basic thrust of the passage is verse 7, that we should receive others in the same manner as Christ has received us.

Verses 8-15. In verses 8-12, Paul picks up the theme of the salvation of the Gentiles. Perhaps there were some newly baptized Gentiles in the congregations at Rome who felt superior to the (possibly poorer) Jewish Christians in the congregation. Paul reminds these Gentiles that they are recipients of the promises of God to Israel, that they have no claim upon the faith other than through the sheer grace of a loving God. Therefore, they are so to live that their lives will reflect their gratitude for the gift of salvation in Christ.

It is interesting that Paul links good works done by Christians to the Christians' praise of God (v. 11). In other words, when Christians do good work for others, they are doing the same sort of thing that they do when they pray or sing hymns of praise. They are rejoicing over the great gift that is theirs in Christ. Our worship and our service are related.

The Scripture and the Main Question

To Receive One Another

Old First Church has a grand history. In the 1920s and 1930s, it boasted the largest congregation of any church in the city. Its fine Neo-Gothic building was built by a world-renowned architect in the 1920s. Many distinguished leaders of the denomination came from old First Church.

But that was yesterday, not today. Today, old First Church still has its beautiful building, but now that building has become as much of a burden as a blessing. Today the congregation is only about one-fifth the size it was fifty years ago. Most of its members are older people, loyal members who grew up in old First Church and stayed with the church, even when many members left and moved to the suburbs. Now the congregation of old First

Church worships on Sunday morning, a small group of people huddled within a vast sanctuary.

And yet, these facts do not tell the whole story of old First Church. While old First Church has declined in numbers, it has not declined in commitment to the enactment of the Christian faith. Throughout its now troubled urban neighborhood, old First Church has the reputation of being a community-minded congregation. Its members not only keep a roof over their beautiful old building, but they also use their meager resources to provide a clothes closet and a food pantry for the poor. A part of old First Church is used each evening to provide shelter for the homeless within that part of the city, and two or three community organizations are given free office space in some of the vacant Sunday school rooms. Do you think old First Church has declined or grown?

Alas, too many of our churches put emphasis simply on membership statistics or the size of the budget. Today's scripture passage from the fifteenth chapter of Paul's Letter to the Romans reminds us that we should also put stress on the growth of our Christian commitment. Paul's words suggest that a church should be measured, not by the number of people on the membership roll, but by the Christian service performed by those people.

Take a moment to think about your own congregation. If there was some yardstick to measure evidence of Christian commitment through service to others, how would your church measure up?

As Christ Has Received Us

In the opinion of the community, old First Church is a "community-minded church." By this, most people who are not members of old First Church mean that the members of First Church show that they care about supporting the community in which they find themselves. However, the commitment that takes place at old First Church is considerably more than public-spirited activism. For the members of old First Church, their actions are their faithful reaction to the action of Christ upon their lives. They give because Christ has given so much to them. They care for others because they have experienced Christ's caring for them. Here is the root of all Christian service. We do not serve because we believe that in serving others they might in turn serve us. We do not serve because the Church is some sort of glorified civic club that exists to do a few nice things for the community.

Rather, the Church serves others as a visible outpouring of our faith in Christ. I think Paul puts it well in his Letter to the Romans when he tells them that Christians ought to receive one another "as Christ as received us" (15:6). Something has happened to each of us, and that makes us different people. There are people in our world who feel absolutely no responsibility for the needs of others. These people sometimes describe themselves as being self-made. They may tell you, "I worked for what I got." Or they may say, "I think we all ought to look out for ourselves."

These attitudes, although held by many people, hardly express the Christian point of view. We serve because, in Christ, God has served us. We receive the stranger (as old First Church gave food, clothing, and other aid to strangers) because Christ has received us.

Paul wrote his Letter to the Romans against a background of a church that had recently discovered that the good news was meant not only for

Jews, but also for Gentiles. Undoubtedly there were many Gentiles in the congregation of the church at Rome. So when Paul spoke of "receiving others as Christ has received you," they had concrete examples of this right within their own congregation. Of course, within our congregations today, we have plenty of examples—namely, all of us! All of us have been received by a gracious God. Our graciousness toward others is an expression of our gratitude for God's graciousness toward us. Our service is an expression of gratitude. I remember that, when I went as a new pastor to a congregation, on the first or second Sunday that I was there, one of the men in the congregation took me aside and said to me, "Preacher, I want you to know that if you ever have anybody come by the church who is hungry and needs a meal, for whatever reason, I want to personally provide that meal. All you have to do is let me know how much you spend for such help, and I will gladly repay you. I don't want this church to ever turn anyone away who needs food. Whether it's individuals or families, it doesn't matter. I want to provide them the food they need."

His offer impressed me greatly. I knew that, as a pastor, I would probably be asked for aid by numerous persons. I wondered why this seemed to mean to much to him. So I asked him. He answered, "One time in my life, many years ago, I was hungry. I was down on my luck, terribly embarrassed, and didn't ask anybody for help. A woman in the church quietly provided me food for a couple of months, until I found work. I swore then that, whenever I got on my feet again, I would do whatever I could to respond to others as that good woman responded to me."

This man's story, in which he provided help for other people as help had been provided to him, strikes me as a typically Christian experience of service to others. We love because we have been loved. We receive others because we never forget how God has received us.

Once again, Paul's life illustrates this truth. Although Paul was not a Gentile, he had been a terrible enemy of the Church. He personally led a bloody persecution of the Church. However, God found Paul, chose him to be an instrument on his behalf, and converted him to the gospel. Therefore, Paul probably looked on people whom the Church regarded as "strangers" or "outsiders" in a special way. He never forgot that he himself had been an outsider and a stranger (15:7-10).

Again, I Say, Rejoice

Do you find it interesting that today's scripture ends with Paul calling on the church at Rome to rejoice (15:10-12)? Paul has been talking about the necessity for Christians to receive one another and to serve others. What does this call to rejoice have to do with his call for them to serve others?

In the fifteenth chapter of Paul's Letter to the Romans, it is almost as if Paul can restrain himself no longer. He has been talking about service in a rather mundane and prosaic way. At last he can restrain himself no longer, and he overflows in a great symphony of praise, a great call to the Church to rejoice.

We ought to take our cue from Paul in this matter of service to others. Sometimes we speak of service to others as some sort of obligation, a duty that Christians must labor to fulfill. Paul hereby reminds us that we rejoice for the same reason that we sing hymns in church, for the same reason that we sometimes shout out "Amen!" Just as our singing in church is an overflowing of our gratitude and joy in response to what God has done for us, so also our deeds to others are our joyful response to the God who has responded so lovingly to us. We serve for the same reason that we sing.

Think a moment about your congregation, the way it spends its time and its money, the matters that are given emphasis in your congregational life. What sort of picture emerges of your congregation? A church that is turned in on itself? Or a church that reaches out in joyful service to others? What are some of the ways your congregation "rejoices" through its service to others?

Helping Adults Become Involved

Preparing to Teach

At the close of "The Scripture and the Main Question," it was suggested that we ought to look over our church's program and ask ourselves in what ways we "rejoice" through our service to others. Obtain a copy of your church's yearly budget. What does your budget tell you about the nature of your congregation and its values?

The aim of this lesson is to help the adults in your class to rediscover the joy that comes from service to others in the name of Christ.

Use the following lesson outline:

I. We are called to serve as Christ has served us.
II. We are called to receive others as Christ has received us.
III. In what ways could our church be a more joyful servant to others?

Introducing the Main Question

Using the explanatory material in "As You Read the Scripture," take your class through an overview of today's selected scripture from Paul's Letter to the Romans. You may also use some of the discussion of this passage, found in "The Scripture and the Main Question."

Developing the Lesson

I. We are called to serve as Christ has served us.

A. *A church is not a church if it does not reach out to others.* In your own words, retell the story of Jane, which is found in "The Main Question" section. Ask class members in what ways they see this story as an illustration of today's scripture from Romans 15. Of course, the story of Jane is a story of someone who is in the Church being served by fellow members of the congregation. We are called as Christians to reach out to those in need outside the Church as well.

B. *How does my church measure up in its service to others?* Paul says that we ought not to serve just ourselves, but we should serve others as well. Now hand out copies of your church's budget, which you obtained before today's class. Ask your class: "Do you see Paul's principle of Christian service reflected in the way our congregation spends its money? Does the budget show a great overflowing of joyful gratitude to God?" Jesus once said that where our treasure is, there is our heart also. Does your congregation's budget reveal where your congregation's heart is?

Discuss within your class ways in which the program and budget of your church could be more responsive to Paul's challenge for us to serve.

II. *We are called to receive others as Christ has received us.*

A. *Churches die when they become closed in upon themselves.* In your own words, retell the story of old First Church, which is told in "The Scripture and the Main Question." Ask members of the class whether they have had experiences with any churches similar to old First Church.

B. *A church that opens itself up to new life receives new life.* Jesus said that in giving we receive. Old First Church received new life by daring to reach out to those in need in its surrounding community. Perhaps members of your class have had similar experiences with the Church in which the Church's service to others resulted in new life for the congregation. Ask them to share these experiences with the class.

For instance, one congregation, which was made up mostly of older people, became concerned about the plight of the children in its neighborhood. While the members of the congregation had few children of their own, they felt there was a need that they could meet. They opened a day-care center, staffed by volunteers from the congregation. Young families in the neighborhood sent their children to the day-care center and thereby became acquainted with the people in the church. Many of these eventually began attending and even joined the church. Today, a congregation that was once made up of people over sixty has a wide array of ages because those people over sixty reached out.

III. *In what ways could our church be a more joyful servant to others?*

Using the illustration of the man who gave out of a sense of gratitude (found toward the end of "The Scripture and the Main Question") discuss ways in which our service is the result of our gratitude for what God has done for us. We love others because God has first loved us.

Lead your class in a discussion of specific ways your church could be a more joyful and responsive servant to others. List their ideas on a chalkboard or newsprint.

Helping Class Members Act

Will someone in your class take responsibility for presenting some of your class's service ideas to the official leadership of your congregation? Are there any good ideas for service that your class alone could undertake?

Planning for Next Sunday

Ask everyone to read 2 Timothy 2:14-26 in preparation for next week's lesson. Next Sunday's lesson should be particularly challenging to you as a teacher because it discusses ways we spread the gospel through the ministry of teaching.

Ask class members to ponder the question "What are the characteristics of a good teacher?"

Teach the Truth

Background Scripture: 2 Timothy 2:14-26; Titus 2

The Main Question

I work with young adults at a university. Since I was a college student, there has been a rather dramatic growth of a number of groups that have had an effect on undergraduate religious life. You have undoubtedly heard of the followers of Reverend Moon, the "Moonies," and their hold over their youthful converts.

For Christians, the growth of these groups is disturbing. We do not agree with many of their beliefs or with many of their tactics. Yet, time and again, as I have become acquainted with some young person who has become involved in these groups, I have had to ask myself, "What is the attraction of these sects? Why are they successful in luring away many of our youth?"

I have come to the conclusion that much of their success is evidence of our failure. And today's scripture reading from Paul's Second Letter to Timothy suggests that Paul would thoroughly agree with me. Young people are caught up in the beliefs of these sect groups because these youth have such a poor religious foundation of their own. Not knowing what they believe, they are susceptible to believing almost anything. They say that they reject Christianity, when what they are usually rejecting is a hodgepodge of misinformation, immature ideas, and superficial theology. What they reject is their own mixed-up brand of Christianity.

If we had done a better job of educating these young people when they were growing up in the Church, would we be loosing them to the cults?

What difference does it make, in the lives of our people, whether we are committed to teach?

Selected Scripture

King James Version

2 Timothy 2:14-26

14 Of these things put them in remembrance, charging them before the Lord that they strive not about words to no profit, but to the subverting of the hearers.

15 Study to shew thyself approved unto God, a workman that needeth not to be ashamed, rightly dividing the word of truth.

16 But shun profane and vain babblings: for they will increase unto more ungodliness.

17 And their word will eat as doth

New Revised Standard Version

2 Timothy 2:14-26

14 Remind them of this, and warn them before God that they are to avoid wrangling over words, which does no good, but only ruins those who are listening. 15 Do your best to present yourself to God as one approved by him, a worker who has no need to be ashamed, rightly explaining the word of truth. 16 Avoid profane chatter, for it will lead people into more and more impiety, 17 and their talk will spread like gangrene. Among them are

a canker: of whom is Hymenaeus and Philetus;

18 Who concerning the truth have erred, saying that the resurrection is past already; and overthrow the faith of some.

19 Nevertheless the foundation of God standeth sure, having this seal, The Lord knoweth them that are his. And, Let every one that nameth the name of Christ depart from iniquity.

20 But in a great house there are not only vessels of gold and of silver, but also of wood and of earth; and some to honour, and some to dishonour.

21 If a man therefore purge himself from these, he shall be a vessel unto honour, sanctified, and meet for the master's use, and prepared unto every good work.

22 Flee also youthful lusts: but follow righteousness, faith, charity, peace, with them that call on the Lord out of a pure heart.

23 But foolish and unlearned questions avoid, knowing that they do gender strifes.

24 And the servant of the Lord must not strive; but be gentle unto all men, apt to teach, patient,

25 In meekness, instructing those that oppose themselves; if God peradventure will give them repentance to the acknowledging of the truth;

26 And that they may recover themselves out of the snare of the devil, who are taken captive by him at his will.

Key Verse: **Study to shew thyself approved unto God, a workman that needeth not to be ashamed, rightly dividing the word of truth. (2 Timothy 2:15)**

Hymenaeus and Philetus, 18 who have swerved from the truth by claiming that the resurrection has already taken place. They are upsetting the faith of some. 19 But God's firm foundation stands, bearing this inscription: "The Lord knows those who are his," and, "Let everyone who calls on the name of the Lord turn away from wickedness."

20 In a large house there are utensils not only of gold and silver but also of wood and clay, some for special use, some for ordinary. 21 All who cleanse themselves of the things I have mentioned will become special utensils, dedicated and useful to the owner of the house, ready for every good work. 22 Shun youthful passions and pursue righteousness, faith, love, and peace, along with those who call on the Lord from a pure heart. 23 Have nothing to do with stupid and senseless controversies; you know that they breed quarrels. 24 And the Lord's servant must not be quarrelsome but kindly to everyone, an apt teacher, patient, 25 correcting opponents with gentleness. God may perhaps grant that they will repent and come to know the truth, 26 and that they may escape from the snare of the devil, having been held captive by him to do his will.

Key Verse: **Do your best to present yourself to God as one approved by him, a worker who has no need to be ashamed, rightly explaining the word of truth. (2 Timothy 2:15)**

As You Read the Scripture

2 Romans 2:14-26. Paul's Second Letter to Timothy is a moving letter from an older Christian missionary, Paul, to a younger associate, Timothy. Paul urges this younger man to have endurance in the face of the opposition and challenges to the gospel. Acts 16:1 says that Timothy was the son of a Greek Jewish woman. He was already a Christian when Paul came to where Timothy was living in Lystra, Asia Minor. From there, Paul took him as his helper in the work of spreading the gospel among the Gentiles. This session's scripture reading stresses not so much what the Christian teacher ought to teach but *how* Christian doctrine should be taught.

Verses 14-16. There is no way to be sure why Paul is concerned about Timothy's avoiding "disputing about words." Evidently, there was some sort of controversy at the church that Paul feels is fruitless and distracting. While it is important to be sure about the "word of truth" (v. 15), "godless chatter" about irrelevant minutiae of theology is pointless.

Verses 17-19. Evidently, some in Timothy's congregation, like Hymenaeus and Philetus, taught that the resurrection of the dead had already occurred and that believers had already achieved immortality of some sort. Paul encountered similar beliefs among the Corinthians. "Why should we conduct ourselves in an ethical manner," these supposedly resurrected people might have asked, "when we have already been raised to immortality?"

Verses 20-23. "In a large house," refers to the church (compare Romans 9:19-24). The writer urges Timothy to prepare himself for "any good work" through adhering to the highest standards of behavior (vv. 22-23) and by teaching the essentials of orthodox doctrine. A mark of a Christian teacher's work is that it edifies the "large house" of the church.

Verses 24-26. Even in the midst of important controversy over correct doctrine, disputants must remember that they are in the church and that they must conduct themselves accordingly, "correcting opponents with gentleness." Only through lovingkindness can the teacher hope that those who are taught will "repent and come to know the truth." The teacher adapts his or her words to the condition of the hearers that they might be attracted to correct teaching.

The Scripture and the Main Question

Rightly Handling the Word of Truth

In today's scripture, Paul, the older Christian, gives advice to Timothy, a younger Christian: "Do your best to present yourself to God as one approved by him, a worker who has no need to be ashamed, rightly explaining the word of truth" (2 Timothy 2:15).

It's tough out there, Paul seems to say. Don't go out unless you are suitably equipped, appropriately armed. A major means of Christian armament, it appears, is teaching and study.

"Have nothing to do with stupid and senseless controversies; you know that they breed quarrels" (2 Timothy 2:23). All of this is the sort of advice that wise teachers often give their students. But this teacher, Paul, is instructing his student, Timothy, for purposes more significant than obtaining a degree. Paul is busy giving Timothy what he will need to survive as a Christian. It's tough out there. We teach in order to equip persons for the challenges of faith in today's world.

Think of that as one of the major reasons why your class gathers today to study Scripture—to equip themselves to be strong followers of Jesus in a world that does not know Jesus Christ as Lord. You do important, life-or-death work in your adult class. Pray, as you prepare today's lesson, that you will "rightly [explain] the word of truth."

Remind Them and Warn Them Before God

When were you converted to Christ? That is not an easy question for me to answer, not because I am unable to point to certain times in my life when I have said yes to Christ, but because there have been a number of times when I could claim to have been "converted to Christ." But if you pushed me, I might respond that I was converted to Christ, of all places, in a college religion class.

By the time I was a senior in high school, I was beginning to question my faith. I was an inquisitive student who enjoyed learning new things and exploring different ideas. But these attributes did not seem to be required for being a Christian, at least that is what I thought I heard from some of our youth leaders. They told us to hold our questions, to be careful about our thoughts, and to guard against new ideas. I got the distinct impression that, in order to be a really firm Christian believer, one must first turn off one's brain, shut one's ears, and close one's eyes.

When I went off to college, I became an instant skeptic, thinking that, if my youth leaders back home were wrong about their narrow beliefs in so many matters, the Christian faith must be wrong about everything. Perhaps it was all just one big fairy tale, an ancient myth that modern humanity has now outgrown. Remember, I was a college freshman at the time.

It was about this time that I found myself in my first college religion class. There, I gained a whole new perspective on belief. For one thing, my notion that one had to be closed minded and intellectually dull in order to be a believer was disproved the minute I met the professor who was teaching the class. He was as sharp as anyone else on the faculty. Obviously, he was not letting any intellectual questions go begging in order to be a Christian.

The next thing I learned was that the Christian faith is not threatened by doubts and questions. It can stand on its own quite nicely, with no help from nervous youth leaders. In the religion class I learned for the first time what various troublesome passages in the Bible really mean to contemporary believers. In regard to the biblical miracles, I was moved from my rather adolescent preoccupations with "Did this really happen?" to the more important "Why did this really happen? What is the meaning of this event for faith?"

I found that it wasn't enough simply to affirm that the virgin birth of Jesus really occurred. It was even more important to know why the early Church believed that the virgin birth of Jesus was important.

Do you see what happened? In the weeks and days ahead, my faith came to be reconstructed. Rather than falling back into a defensive position of closing my ears and shutting off my brain, I went on the offensive, so far as my faith was concerned. I emerged from that first semester of serious religious study with a much deeper, more vibrant faith than when I began. That professor had, in effect, converted me to Christianity by convincing me that, as the truth, Christianity is not threatened by our questions. It thrives on our questions, has complex, true, real responses to our questions. So, although some persons claim that they lost their faith in college religion courses, I suppose that I could say that I found mine there.

Those courses were taught in a college that was founded many years ago by my denomination. My denomination felt, in the early days of this country, that it needed its own schools to train its youth in the faith. Rather than escaping from the tough questions raised by Christian belief, my church waded into the fray, did battle on behalf of Christian believing, and made education one of its special ministries.

That professor, through his lectures, assignments, discussions, and reading, fulfilled Paul's charge to Timothy to "remind them . . . warn them before God" (2 Timothy 2:14). There I was reminded of who I was as a follower of Christ, and I was charged to continue in that way throughout my adult life. In a classroom, I got converted.

By the way, I made an A in Introduction to the New Testament that year.

To Know the Truth

I wonder whether, in writing about the importance of teaching and learning in today's lesson, I am "preaching to the converted." As an adult teacher in the Church, you are already someone who is participating in the Church's commitment to teach.

Yet, all of us need reminding from time to time of the importance of our work. At one point a few years ago, because of the pressures of time and family commitments, I was forced to give up some of my activities. I chose to give up my writing for the *International Lesson Annual.* No sooner had I done so than it seemed as if I were besieged by classes who had used my material. Sometimes they wrote me with questions or disagreements. Their disagreements did not matter; what mattered was that they were using my work and learning from it.

So, here I am, writing another quarter's lessons in the *International Lesson Annual,* fulfilling my own commitment to the Church's teaching ministry.

And here you are, teaching another series of lessons, fulfilling your commitment to the teaching ministry.

In your own class, you have seen people probe, through their questions, to a firmer, more active faith. You have seen people grow beyond their inadequate, immature beliefs to more mature, more sure belief. You have experienced Christians' learning and exploring together, as we seek to uphold one another as contemporary disciples. All of this is holy work, part of the Church's teaching ministry, part of our effort to "rightly [explain] the word of truth," a ministry we share with teacher Paul and student Timothy.

This is holy work, worthy of our deepest commitment.

Helping Adults Become Involved

Preparing to Teach

During this series of lessons, we have been focusing on the means whereby we fulfill Christ's mandate that we should share the good news. We have focused, in previous lessons, on the need to share the good news through proclamation and service to others, and we close this series with a focus on sharing the good news through teaching.

In "The Scripture and the Main Question," it is suggested that this Sunday's lesson might be a matter of "preaching to the converted" in its stress on the need for Christian education. After all, you would not be reading this material if you were not preparing to educate Christians!

Today's lesson can be helpful in enabling your adults to see the importance of the time they spend in your adult class and in preparing themselves to study the Scripture.

Throughout your preparation to teach this Sunday's class, remember our main question: What difference does it make, in the lives of our people, whether we are committed to teach?

Some have said that Americans live in an anti-intellectual society, that we put great stress on practical, down-to-earth activity and tend to be somewhat suspicious of intellectual pursuit. This past year, Harvard biologist Stephen Jay Gould spoke at our university commencement on the decline of science in American society.

Gould asserted that the main reason why our nation is slipping behind in the sciences lies in the way our society treats people, from their earliest years of life, who excel in school. Children who show great academic ability are labeled by other children as "eggheads," called "geeks," "nerds," and other derogatory names. By contrast, said Gould, in a society like that of Japan, children who achieve in school are considered heroes and models by their classmates. This anti-intellectual bias, from the kindergarten to the university, is strangling our society and closing off our future options, said Gould.

The training of future scientists is not our concern this Sunday. The training of vibrant, committed Christian disciples is our concern. But there is a connection. Correct doctrine, orthodox believing, and scripturally based opinion are not minor concerns for the church. A church that fails to think clearly is a church that eventually pays dearly, at least that is the assertion in the illustration of young people and cult groups in "The Main Question." Read this material, along with the more extended discussion in "The Scripture and the Main Question," keeping this Sunday's main question in your mind as you read.

Here is an outline for today's class:

I. Paul urged Timothy to learn and to teach correct doctrine.
II. We also need to come to a more certain grasp of Christian doctrine.
III. As we learn, we ought to respect one another in our teaching and learning.

Introducing the Main Question

Use the material in "As You Read the Scripture" to study today's scripture from the Second Letter to Timothy.

I. Paul urged Timothy to learn and to teach correct doctrine.

Begin today's session by paraphrasing today's scripture passage. This is Paul's attempt to encourage Timothy to hold fast to correct doctrine and to teach that doctrine to others in the church who may be confused.

II. We also need to come to a more certain grasp of Christian doctrine.

Share with the class the illustration found in "The Main Question." Do members of your class feel that young people are getting a solid foundation in Christian education today? Ask them if they have had similar experiences, in their families or among their friends, of people who have been confused and led astray because they had an uncertain grasp of Christian doctrine.

In "The Scripture and the Main Question" there is a rather extended discussion of my experiences of high school doubts being healed in a college religion class. Retell this illustration to the class. Have you or they had similar experiences of being moved out of confusion and doubt through the work of a good teacher?

Can anyone in your group cite a similar personal experience of growth in faith that occurred within this class? Would they share the experience with the group?

III. As we learn, we ought to respect one another in our teaching and learning.

In the discussion of 2 Timothy 2:24-26 in "As You Read the Scripture," it is noted that Paul urges Timothy to deal with people, even when they are mistaken and confused about Christian truth, with Christian kindness and compassion. We can take issues of doctrine seriously, realizing that matters of great importance are at stake here, without losing our respect for one another.

More than one church has been split apart as people took some rather unchristian stands against one another over Christian issues. As Paul notes to Timothy, we will fail to persuade others if we deal with others in ways that hurt them. Ask your group, "What are important characteristics of a Christian teacher?"

Helping Class Members Act

In one sense, your class is already acting on today's lesson by being here in class! However, any of us can do a better job of growing in faith. As you close today's session, ask each person to resolve to do one of the following activities in order to grow in faith through learning:

• Set aside time each day for systematic Bible reading.
• Resolve to read a biography of some faithful Christian or some book of Christian inspiration within the next few weeks.

Planning for Next Sunday

Next Sunday begins a new unit of study on the Gospel of John. Ask everyone to prepare by reading John 1 in its entirety before next Sunday's class.

THIRD QUARTER
Believing in Christ
(The Gospel of John)

UNIT I: JOHN: THE WORD BECAME FLESH
Pat McGeachy

FOUR LESSONS   **MARCH 7–28**

"They that wait upon the Lord," promises the fortieth chapter of Isaiah, "shall mount up with wings like eagles." There is no part of the Christian Scriptures more likely to help us take off on such a venture than the Fourth Gospel. Indeed, in ancient art, John the Evangelist is sometimes depicted as an eagle. During this quarter, we will be privileged to taste some soaring spiritual ideas. But it will not be complicated or theologically difficult. It will be built around the person of Jesus of Nazareth, and particularly the last days of his life, in which he is revealed in simple concepts like bread and wine, water and light. Of such is our worship built and our spiritual life made whole.

Unit I, "John: The Word Became Flesh," consists of four lessons that describe Jesus in four one-syllable words: Word, Birth, Light, and Life. The most profound issues of our lives are struggled with here in the simplest terms, to start our thinking on high and holy matters as they relate to our everyday comings and goings.

Unit II, "John: The Great Love," continues our one-syllable pattern, dealing both with God's love for us and our love for God and one another. The four lessons include an Easter message, and they call us to translate our Resurrection faith into service to others. The last lesson, on bread, keeps us down to earth in our daily opportunities for duty.

Unit III, "John: Believe in Jesus," calls us to an act of faith. There are five lessons here, built around those persons whose lives were most directly affected by Jesus: John the Baptizer, Andrew, Peter, Philip, Nathanael, the Samaritan woman at the well, Nicodemus, and others, including some of Jesus' enemies. We end with the lovely devotion-like material in John 14, which calls us to our own trust in the one who is the Way, the Truth, and the Life and who calls us to eternal peace. Simple words, simple people, profound truths—it should be an exciting quarter.

This Quarter's Writer:

Leading us through this quarter's in-depth study of the Gospel of John will be someone who is no stranger to regular readers of *The International Lesson Annual*. The Reverend **Pat McGeachy** has written extensively, not only for many years with the *Annual* but also in a wide array of church publications. He serves as Associate Pastor, Downtown Presbyterian Church, in Nashville, Tennessee. An avid farmer, player of the guitar, and singer of folk music, Pat has done workshops around the country in preaching and worship as well as youth ministry and music ministry. Regular readers of *The International Lesson Annual* have come to know Pat as a lively, engaging interpreter of the Bible and the Christian faith. What better person to lead us through the Gospel of John than Pat McGeachy, who exemplifies, both in his ministry and in his writing, a life filled with the joyful, exuberant Spirit of Christ?

Life in Christ

Background Scripture: John 1:1-18

The Main Question

What's the bottom line? You can ask this question in lots of ways: What's the point of life? "What is the chief end of man?" (*The Westminster Catechism*). How can we make sense of things? Questions such as these are not easy for most of us, but, if we do not ask them, we will find ourselves spending all of our days living for the wrong ends, at cross purposes with ourselves, busy, but not productive, often frustrated, and rarely happy. Do you ever feel that way? If so, perhaps you are not stopping every morning before your bathroom mirror and asking: "Magic bathroom glass of mine, tell me what's the bottom line?" Of course, you don't get the answer to such questions from your mirror, but where do you get them?

The author of the Fourth Gospel reveals its purpose toward the end of the book (20:31). It was "written so that you may come to believe that Jesus is the Messiah, the Son of God, and that through believing you may have life in his name." The author possesses a powerful clue to the meaning of existence, and he wants to share that secret with us. What a momentous thing! We are about to be let in on something hidden from the sages of the world (see Luke 10:21 and 1 Corinthians 2:9). You and I are privileged to see a document that originated in the highest echelons of authority. We are about to learn the principle that lies at the heart of the universe. If we are willing to listen well and to respond wisely, we can discover how to live joyfully and victoriously (see Deuteronomy 30:19-20). The alternative is misery, a failure to live. What *is* that bottom line?

Selected Scripture

King James Version	New Revised Standard Version
John 1:1-18	*John 1:1-18*
1 In the beginning was the Word, and the Word was with God, and the Word was God.	1 In the beginning was the Word, and the Word was with God, and the Word was God. 2 He was in the beginning with God. 3 All things came into being through him, and without him not one thing came into being. What has come into being in him was life, and the life was the light of all people. 5 The light shines in the darkness; and the darkness did not overcome it.
2 The same was in the beginning with God.	
3 All things were made by him; and without him was not any thing made that was made.	
4 In him was life; and the life was the light of men.	
5 And the light shineth in darkness; and the darkness comprehended it not.	
6 There was a man sent from God, whose name *was* John.	6 There was a man sent from God, whose name was John. 7 He came as a witness to testify to the light, so that all might believe

7 The same came for a witness, to bear witness of the Light, that all *men* through him might believe.

8 He was not that Light, but *was* sent to bear witness of that Light.

9 *That* was the true Light, which lighteth every man that cometh into the world.

10 He was in the world, and the world was made by him, and the world knew him not.

11 He came unto his own, and his own received him not.

12 But as many as received him, to them gave he power to become the sons of God, *even* to them that believe on his name:

13 Which were born, not of blood, nor of the will of the flesh, nor of the will of man, but of God.

14 And the Word was made flesh, and dwelt among us, (and we beheld his glory, the glory as of the only begotten of the Father,) full of grace and truth.

15 John bare witness of him, and cried, saying, This was he of whom I spake, He that cometh after me is preferred before me: for he was before me.

16 And of his fulness have all we received, and grace for grace.

17 For the law was given by Moses, *but* grace and truth came by Jesus Christ.

18 No man hath seen God at any time; the only begotten Son, which is in the bosom of the Father, he hath declared *him*.

Key Verse: **And the Word was made flesh, and dwelt among us, (and we beheld his glory, the glory as of the only begotten of the Father,) full of grace and truth. (John 1:14)**

through him. He himself was not the light, but he came to testify to the light. 9 The true light, which enlightens everyone, was coming into the world.

10 He was in the world, and the world came into being through him; yet the world did not know him. 11 He came to what was his own, and his own people did not accept him. But to all who received him, who believed in his name, he gave power to become children of God, 13 who were born, not of blood or of the will of the flesh or of the will of man, but of God.

14 And the Word became flesh and lived among us, and we have seen his glory, the glory as of a father's only son, full of grace and truth. (John testified to him and cried out, "This was he of whom I said, 'He who comes after me ranks ahead of me because he was before me.'" 16 From his fullness we have all received, grace upon grace. 17 The law indeed was given through Moses; grace and truth came through Jesus Christ.

18 No one has ever seen God. It is God the only Son, who is close to the Father's heart, who has made him known.

Key Verse: **And the Word became flesh and lived among us, and we have seen his glory, the glory as of a father's only son, full of grace and truth. (John 1:14)**

As You Read the Scripture

John 1:1-18. In all of the Bible there is no more profound statement than these verses; yet, there is not a difficult word in them. It is as deep as the sea and as simple as a stream. It is eternal truth in daily language. It is "the Word become flesh."

Verse 1. "Word" here means just what you and I mean when we use the word *word* in its ordinary sense. But it also means "the rational principle at the heart of all things." Moreover, as we shall clearly see, it also means Jesus Christ. Note that this passage begins just as the Bible itself begins, "In the beginning." It is a mini creation story, and in it Christ is identified with the Creator.

Verse 2. Christ (the Word) existed with God before history began. (See John 8:58; Colossians 1:15; 1 Peter 1:20; Revelation 1:17-18.)

Verse 3. Christ (the Word) took part with God in the Creation. (See Proverbs 8:22-31; Colossians 1:16.)

Verse 4. Christ is the source of both life and light (understanding).

Verse 5. No matter how dark and chaotic things get, God's life in Christ continues to shine (Psalm 23:4; Isaiah 9:2).

Verses 6-8. These three verses are an aside to tell us about John the Baptist, the "forerunner" who introduces Christ, the true light.

Verse 9. Christ came for the whole human race. (See also 1 John 2:2.)

Verse 10. That Christ is the light should be obvious to us, for we were created in God's image, but sin prevents us from recognizing him (Romans 1:19-20).

Verse 11. Surely the children of Israel, the "chosen people," should recognize God's Messiah, but they did not accept Jesus. (See Mark 6:1-6.)

Verse 12. However, the Messiah is available to everyone who will believe. Those who do believe become part of God's family.

Verse 13. We belong to God's family, not simply because we were born into it by human birth (children of Abraham), but because we are reborn spiritually (see John 3:5 and Luke 3:8).

Verse 14. The "rational principle at the heart of the universe," the Word, became a human being, the historical person, Jesus. John speaks here as an eyewitness ("we beheld").

Verse 15. Another aside referring to John the Baptist (see 1:30).

Verse 16. Those who believe in Christ are given the ability to understand who God is and to receive God's gift of new life, "grace upon grace"—that is, a continual outpouring of that gift.

Verse 17. The Hebrew Scriptures (Moses) taught us the moral law, so that we all should know how we ought to live. But Christ gives us, as God's free gift, a deeper understanding of God, and power to keep the law and to change our lives from falsehood to truth.

Verse 18. Eternal truth cannot be understood by ordinary human minds (how could an ordinary mortal comprehend infinity?). But when the Word became flesh—that is, when God became a human being in Christ—we became capable of understanding. You can't see God, but you can see Jesus. The eternal Word, rationality itself, comes to us through a person.

The Scripture and the Main Question

The Truth at the Heart of All Truth

John 1:1-18 is an introduction to the deepest of life's questions: What does it all mean? John's words are simple, but their meaning is profound, so we must begin by defining his key word: *word*. Of course, *logos*, the Greek word used here, has its ordinary meaning, "word." But *logos*, like *word*, carries many meanings. Here are a few of them found in the New Testament itself:

sayings—Matthew 5:28; 19:1; 26:1; etc.
account—Matthew 12:36
report (rumor, KJV)—Luke 7:23
conversation (communications, KJV)—Luke 27:17
book (treatise, KJV)—Acts 1:1
word of mouth—Acts 15:17
the oracles of God (KJV)—Acts 7:38; Romans 3:2; Hebrews 5:12;
    1 Peter 4:11
In verb form:
consider (reckon, KJV)—Romans 8:18
reasoned (thought, KJV)—1 Corinthians 13:11
reckoned (imputed, KJV)—Romans 4:22-24
As an adjective:
spiritual (reasonable, KJV)—Romans 12:1

It is even found in one form that means "a dispute about words" in
1 Timothy 6:4 and 2 Timothy 2:14. (Look up *logomachy*.)

The root *logos* is very common in the English language, as this list of
examples shows: *logic, logical, logarithm, prologue* (a word at the beginning),
epilogue, apology (this does not always mean an "excuse," but sometimes a
"rational explanation," as in Plato's *Apology*), *doxology* (a word of praise), and
a whole host of words ending in *logy,* meaning "a study," such as *theology,*
paleontology, and *archaeology.* Then there are *analogy, decalogue, dialogue,* and
many others. If you like word meanings as much as I do, you may want to
look up some of these.

In the first century, when this Gospel was being written, *logos* would have
had special meaning for educated people throughout the known world. Of
course, it had its ordinary meaning (a word or thought), but among the
philosophers it denoted "the basic rational principle in the universe." With
some of them, especially among the Stoics, it almost seemed to mean a kind
of "secondary deity," the intermediate principle between the divine reality
and the human mind. Philo of Alexandria, who lived at the same time as
Jesus, spoke of the *logos* as the image of God, by whom God created the
world. So when John chose it as the key word for his introduction to Christ,
he would have had a possible bridge of understanding with the Gentile audience
for whom he was writing.

It would also have had a meaning for his Jewish readers. It is clearly
related to the Old Testament, beginning with God's act of creating by
speaking (Genesis 1:3, 9; Psalm 33:6). And how many times do you think
the phrase "the Word of the Lord" occurs in the history books and the
writings of the prophets? But there is one special place in Hebrew literature
that deserves a look when we are discussing John's prologue, and that is the
eighth chapter of Proverbs, to which we should now turn.

Creation Stories

This remarkable passage—Proverbs 8—was probably written rather late
in Hebrew history. It was included in the collection known as Proverbs when
it was put together during the Hellenistic period, shortly before the time of
Christ. Together with Job and Ecclesiastes (and the non-canonical books
Ecclesiasticus and the Wisdom of Solomon), Proverbs forms what is called
the Wisdom Literature of the Jews. These writings struggle with difficult
questions related to our main question: What is the meaning of life? Job, of
course, wrestles with the problem of pain and Ecclesiastes with life's

seeming meaninglessness. The Proverbs are usually thought of as fairly simple common-sense ways of applying faith to life, and many of them are. But, here and there in this book there are deep waters. (Look, for instance at the sense of mystery and wonder in Proverbs 30:18-19, or the serious-minded faith of 1:2-7.) In Proverbs 8, we find an exciting account that personifies wisdom almost as a co-creator with God.

If you read the context in which this mini creation story is placed, you will see that Wisdom is personified as a woman (8:1-21 and 8:32—9:6) who is contrasted with the wicked ways of Folly, another woman (7:6-27, 9:13-18). The two are introduced in 7:1-5. In chapter 8, Wisdom speaks in the first person, and in verses 22-31, she describes herself as participating with God in the vary act of creation itself. At the very least, Wisdom was God's architect (8:30). If we translate this personification into plain talk, we get a sentence that is a pretty good description of John 1:1-3: God created the universe through the Word, the rational principle at the heart of all things.

There are other creation stories in the Bible, of course: the evolutionist's account in Genesis 1:1-2:3; the creationist's account in Genesis 2:4-25; the poetic account in Job 38—41; the account of God as sustainer and supplier in Psalm 104; and the story of fallen creation in Romans 8:18-25. And see briefer accounts, such as Amos 4:13 and Psalm 148:5. In addition to our text for today, John 1:1-18, Colossians 1:15-20, makes it clear that Jesus Christ was in the beginning with God.

Christ the Creator

The doctrine of the Trinity is a mystery by which we sometimes separate God into functional parts: Creator, Redeemer, Sustainer. But our lesson for today makes it clear that such a division, however rational, doesn't tell the whole story. Jesus Christ is also involved in the Creation (look at Revelation 13:8). The God who made us is also the one who redeems us. The wonderful news of the Fourth Gospel is that the rational principle at the heart of all things has come to live among us, in flesh and blood (John 1:14). To know this is to be given a fresh and exciting view of life. To believe that Jesus is the Word of God (Revelation 19:13) is to believe that the Old Testament is fulfilled in Jesus, who transcends all the law and the prophets (Luke 9:28-36). To believe in Jesus (John 1:12) is to have new life, to become a part of the true Israel, the family of God. It is a secret worth sharing! When so many of the world's people are searching for meaning, there can be no more exciting Word.

Helping Adults Become Involved

Preparing to Teach

This is a tough lesson because it is somewhat philosophical or abstract. Our task is to help our adults get through the "head talk" to the heart's questions that lie behind it. Begin by asking yourself, "What is the point of life?" When you think you know the answer, see what John says.

It would be profitable to spend some time with a dictionary, investigating the meaning of the Greek word logos and its derivatives, and also in a search of biblical uses of the word. For this you really need a concordance that lists the words by their Greek roots, such as the Englishman's Greek Concordance or

Young's Analytical Concordance. But they probably aren't in your library, which is why I listed some meanings of the word for you in the first part of "The Scripture and the Main Question." You may want to look up the New Testament references cited; if you have time in class, this could be an exercise for class members.

In any event, come to class having carefully read John 1:1-18 at least three times, and try to determine for yourself what the author is saying. Then you can better help your class answer that question.

Here is a class outline:

I. The Word
II. The Word as Creator
III. The Word as Light
IV. The Word as Jesus Christ

Introducing the Main Question

Start by referring your class to John's statement of purpose in 20:30-31, because it sets the stage for what we are going to be doing this whole quarter. You will want to refer to it many times. Let the class reflect for a few minutes on it now.

Then give them pencils and three-by-five cards, or do this entirely on a chalkboard or newsprint easel. Ask them to fill in the blank in the following sentence, using, if possible, *only the word.*

"The most important thing in life is _____." There are other ways to word this, so you might try a different one, such as, "The bottom line for me is _____" or "The one thing I must remember each day is _____." You might even make an attempt at perking up interest by asking, "If you had a magic mirror, like the one the witch in *Snow White* had, what would you ask it every morning?" The main thing is to get your class thinking along the lines of John's prologue and to help them to be ready to deal with the sentence, "In the beginning was the Word."

Developing the Lesson

I. The Word

Start by making sure everyone understands the depth of meaning in this important word. I love words so much that I probably spend more time on this than you would, but you might enjoy trying to define it. At least look at a dictionary, preferably an unabridged one, and share what you have found there with your class. The 1935 Webster's Unabridged has a fine eighteen-line paragraph under "Logos."

II. The Word as Creator

It is also fun to see how many creation stories you can find in the Bible. This might get you off on a side-track between the "creationists" and the "evolutionists" in your class, which is hinted at in the distinction between Genesis 1 and 2 in the section called "Creation Stories." You may wish to avoid that, but your class members might find it interesting. Of course, it is most important for them to look carefully at Proverbs 8:22-31 and Colossians 1:15-20, which are directly related to our lesson. If your class can't think of many creation stories, introduce them to those listed here.

216

III. The Word as Light

There isn't much about this in "The Bible and the Main Question," but it is clearly there in John 1, and you might want to spend some time on this. If you do, some passages that you might want to look at are Genesis 1:3 (the "Big Bang"), Psalm 119:105, Isaiah 8:16–9:2, Isaiah 45:7, John 8:12 (which should be read along with Matthew 5:14-16), and 1 John 1:5-7. A concordance can lead you to others. Note that the light does more than shine; it "illuminates"—that is, it gives meaning and understanding to those in a dark, confusing world. Ask them if they know what an "Ah ha!" experience is. Or refer them to the hymn "Sometimes a Light Surprises."

IV. The Word as Jesus Christ

This, of course, is the heart of the lesson, where you will want to spend most of your time. Here are some questions that may help your class deal with this:

1. What is the difference between "the words of Jesus" and "Jesus the Word"?
2. In what ways is Jesus the Word of God?
3. If Jesus is the Word of God (Revelation 19:13), what is the Bible? (It may help to distinguish between "the written word" and the "Living Word.")
4. What does it mean to say "the Word became flesh"? Look up the meaning of the word *incarnation*.
5. How has Christ made God known (John 1:18)?

Helping Class Members Act

It's not easy to move from a philosophical discussion about such things as "word" and "light" and "grace and truth" to the business of everyday living, but move we must if Christ is to be incarnate in us and we are to be the lights of the world in our own generation. I think this is summed up for us by Jesus in the Sermon on the Mount, Matthew 5:16: "Let your light so shine. . . ." Here Jesus equates light with works. We, too, are to be God's word to others.

I once saw written on a church bulletin board these words: "You may be the only Bible that someone will read." That places a pretty strong responsibility on us, doesn't it? Another way of saying this is a sentence attributed to Augustine: "A Christian should be an Alleluia from head to toe!" To translate that into John's language: If your life is a doxology ("a word of praise"; note the word *logos* hiding in there), or if you "flesh out" your faith, will others be able to see Christ in you? The best evangelism is not so much the words we speak, but our actions, which speak louder still. Here is one final question for your class: "If you believe that you have the power to become a child of God (John 1:12), and so become a light to the world, what will you do first, when you leave this class today?" (You don't even have to leave, you can start doing it right this minute!)

Preparing for Next Sunday

The phrase "born again" is heard often these days. Ask your class to bring next time their definitions of what those words mean.

Necessity of the New Birth

Background Scripture: John 3:1-21

The Main Question

"Are you saved?" You have probably been asked that question by someone—a street-corner evangelist, a radio preacher, or a friend. I have been asked it many times, but vividly remember the first. I was a freshman in a small rural college, hitchhiking to a nearby city, in search, I suppose, of bright lights and excitement. The man who gave me a ride, I discovered, was a fundamentalist preacher who made a practice of picking up college students, so he could ask them that question. But I was unprepared for it. I stammered some sort of reply. "Ah . . . I hope so," I said. "Then you aren't," he told me. "If you were saved, you would know it." And he began to quote Scripture to me.

I don't remember the texts he used. They were not unfamiliar to me, because, in spite of my awkward reply, I was not biblically illiterate. My father was a minister, and I had been to church twice a Sunday and once a Wednesday all of my young life. I had a string of Sunday school attendance pins, and I had once won first prize in a Bible trivia contest. But all my "knowledge" seemed to fail me in this conversation. That preacher quoted rings around me, and when he let me out at my destination, he left me wondering, "Was I *really* saved?"

Perhaps that preacher was presumptuous and intolerant. Certainly he was imperious and judgmental. But for all his gall, I have never forgotten the favor he did me that day. He forced me to ask myself aloud a question about something I had always taken for granted. I was born and baptized into the Church. I don't even remember not being a Christian. But had I been born again? Have you?

Selected Scripture

King James Version	New Revised Standard Version
John 3:1-17	*John 3:1-17*
1 There was a man of the Pharisees, named Nicodemus, a ruler of the Jews:	1 Now there was a Pharisee named Nicodemus, a leader of the Jews. 2 He came to Jesus by night and said to him, "Rabbi, we know that you are a teacher who has come from God; for no one can do these signs that you do apart from the presence of God." 3 Jesus answered him, "Very truly, I tell you, no one can see the kingdom of God without being born from above." 4 Nicodemus said to him, "How can anyone be born after having grown old?
2 The same came to Jesus by night, and said unto him, Rabbi, we know that thou art a teacher come from God: for no man can do these miracles that thou doest, except God be with him.	
3 Jesus answered and said unto him, Verily, verily, I say unto thee, Except a man be born again, he cannot see the kingdom of God.	

4 Nicodemus saith unto him, How can a man be born when he is old? can he enter the second time into his mother's womb, and be born?

5 Jesus answered, Verily, verily, I say unto thee, Except a man be born of water and of the Spirit, he cannot enter into the kingdom of God.

6 That which is born of the flesh is flesh; and that which is born of the Spirit is spirit.

7 Marvel not that I said unto thee, Ye must be born again.

8 The wind bloweth where it listeth, and thou hearest the sound thereof, but canst not tell whence it cometh, and whither it goeth; so is every one that is born of the Spirit.

9 Nicodemus answered and said unto him, How can these things be?

10 Jesus answered and said unto him, Art thou a master of Israel, and knowest not these things?

11 Verily, verily, I say unto thee, We speak that we do know, and testify that we have seen; and ye receive not our witness.

12 If I have told you earthly things, and ye believe not, how shall ye believe, if I tell you of heavenly things?

13 And no man hath ascended up to heaven, but he that came down from heaven, even the Son of man which is in heaven.

14 And as Moses lifted up the serpent in the wilderness, even so must the Son of man be lifted up:

15 That whosoever believeth in him should not perish, but have eternal life.

16 For God so loved the world, that he gave his only begotten Son, that whosoever believeth in him should not perish, but have everlasting life.

17 For God sent not his Son into the world to condemn the world; but that the world through him might be saved.

Key Verse: **Jesus answered and**

Can one enter a second time into the mother's womb and be born?" 5 Jesus answered, "Very truly, I tell you, no one can enter the kingdom of God without being born of water and Spirit. 6 What is born of the flesh is flesh, and what is born of the Spirit is spirit. 7 Do not be astonished that I said to you, 'You must be born from above.' 8 The wind blows where it chooses, and you hear the sound of it, but you do not know where it comes from or where it goes. So it is with everyone who is born of the Spirit." 9 Nicodemus said to him, "How can these things be?" 10 Jesus answered him, "Are you a teacher of Israel, and yet you do not understand these things?

11 "Very truly, I tell you, we speak of what we know and testify to what we have seen; yet you do not receive our testimony. 12 If I have told you about earthly things and you do not believe, how can you believe if I tell you about heavenly things? 13 No one has ascended into heaven except the one who descended from heaven, the Son of Man. 14 And just as Moses lifted up the serpent in the wilderness, so must the Son of Man be lifted up, 15 that whoever believes in him may have eternal life.

16 "For God so loved the world that he gave his only Son, so that everyone who believes in him may not perish but may have eternal life.

17 "Indeed, God did not send the Son into the world to condemn the world, but in order that the world might be saved through him."

Key Verse: **Jesus answered him,**

said unto him, Verily, verily, I say unto thee, Except a man be born again, he cannot see the kingdom of God. (John 3:3)

"Very truly, I tell you, no one can see the kingdom of God without being born from above." (John 3:3)

As You Read the Scripture

John 3:1-17. There is no more familiar story in the New Testament than these verses. Just *because* it is so familiar, we must be sure we are listening to it.

Verse 1. The Pharisees were highly respected Jewish leaders, in spite of the negative image we may have of them. (See Jesus' criticism in Matthew 23. Their potential was great; therefore, their sin was the greater [see Luke 12:48b].) Moreover, Nicodemus was a "leader"—that is, a member of the Sanhedrin, their highest court.

Verse 2. Cautious (he came by night) and polite (he began with a compliment), Nicodemus was impressed by Jesus' "signs" (remarkable deeds).

Verse 3. May be translated "born again" or "born from above."

Verse 4. Nicodemus took Jesus to mean literally that one must have a physical rebirth.

Verses 5-6. Jesus makes it clear that he means a spiritual rebirth. "Spirit" (*pneuma*) may mean either that or "wind" or "breath."

Verses 7-8. Jesus plays on the double meaning of the word. As the wind comes from who knows where, so the Spirit is a gift of grace, "out of the blue," so to speak.

Verses 9-11. Jesus calls Nicodemus to open his eyes, to see beyond the traditional teaching in which he has been trained, and accept the good news of something new and different. Note the "we" in verse 11. This is not only Jesus speaking, but John and the Gentile Christians.

Verse 12. If Nicodemus and the Pharisees are not able to accept the need for a radical renewal of Judaism, they will not be able to receive the further truth that Jesus has to give them.

Verse 13. Nicodemus may see the need for political change (earthly things) but has not yet caught the vision of those things that come from heaven, which can be understood only through special revelation, by one who has been there—namely, Jesus (see Ephesians 4:7-10).

Verses 14-15. This reference to Numbers 21:4-9 is used by Jesus as an illustration of his crucifixion. As the raised serpent gave healing to physical illness, so the raised cross promises eternal life to those who have the spiritual vision to see it.

Verse 16. This is, as most would agree, the great verse, the text of texts. It may be worth noting that editors disagree as to whether the quotation marks should end with verse 15. Some feel that the rest of this section is not Jesus, but our author speaking. The powerful truth is valid in either case. Let's break the verse down.

God so loved the world—not just Israel or the Church.

. . . *that he gave his only Son.* Perhaps it is not irreverent to think of the Hallmark slogan: "to care enough to send the very best." God's own heart, the heart of reality (remember John 1), the deepest truth in the universe, is a gift in Jesus, born of God's love.

. . . *that everyone who believes in him.* To be born again is to come to the realization (intellectual acceptance) that God really does love us and to trust God and live accordingly (commitment of the will).

. . . *may not perish but may have eternal life.* We may still die physically; even Jesus did. But all will be well.

Verse 17. This is good news, not bad news.

The Scripture and the Main Question

Confession

Approaching this passage is a little like walking into a great cathedral; one wants instinctively to hush and be still in the presence of holiness, or to take off one's shoes, like Moses did at the burning bush. We must tread carefully here, but we dare not refuse to enter. Like Nicodemus by night, we must tiptoe reverently into the Presence, for there awaits us a great gift.

Let's begin with confession, as did Isaiah (6:5) and Simon Peter (Luke 5:8). Let's confess that we are Pharisees, like Nicodemus. The "liberal" in me will want to confess that I have been trying all along to save myself by good works. I have helped the poor; I have fed the hungry; I have supported the church; I have visited the sick and those in prison; and so on, and so on. Yet I will need to hear Jesus say, "Not enough. You must be born again." The "conservative" in me will want to confess that I have been trying all along to save myself by my piety. I have kept myself unspotted from the world; I have read my Bible faithfully; I have prayed until dawn; I have increased my faith; and so on, and so on. Yet I will need to hear Jesus say, "Not enough. You must be born again."

What a blow to my ego! I have done all these things, and you tell me, "Not enough!" What more can I do? But there is a catch: Jesus is not asking us to do more. This is not bad news but good news (look again at v. 17). Jesus is asking us to let *him* do something—to blow on us with the breath of new life, that we may turn loose of our self-saving efforts, our attempts to make God love us, and to discover that God already loves us, so much that God's own Son, the heart of God, has been sent as a gift to us. Why is this so hard to do? How is it that our own goodness stands between us and eternal life?

The Wonderful Wind

Let's play with Jesus' metaphor. In both Hebrew and Greek the words for "spirit," "wind," and "breath" are the same. In the Ezekiel 37, there is a wonderful story about new life coming to dry bones, in which all three forms are used: "Come from the four *winds, O breath,* and breathe upon these slain, that they may live" (v. 9, italics added); "I will put my *spirit* within you, and you shall live" (v. 14, italics added). This is the same word that is found in Genesis 1:2: "A *wind* from God swept over the face of the waters" (italics added).

In our passage for today, Jesus is making an obvious play on the double (triple?) meaning of the word *spirit (pneuma).* He said, in effect, "Unless you are born of water and wind, you cannot enter the kingdom." And then he adds, "No one knows where the wind comes from; it blows where it wants to, and so the Spirit (God's wind) comes as a gift."

As a boy, I was a sailor. We had a sixteen-foot racing sloop (a Snipe for those who identify boats by class) and looked forward to spending summer days on the water. On the west coast of Florida, where I grew up, you could almost count on being becalmed just at sundown, when your mother called you for supper, for the wind would cease as it changed directions, because of the difference in temperature between the land and the water. When this happened, the sails hung limp, and we would watch with hungry anticipation for the least sign of a ripple, meaning a breeze was coming. Otherwise, it was paddle, paddle, paddle, lest you get caught out in the dark and miss your supper.

I used to beg my father for a motor boat. "They're noisy, and they smell bad," he would say. "And you're always shearing a pin or running out of gasoline." "We run out of wind more often," I would argue. "Yes," he would counter, "but the wind always comes again; the gas never does." So it is with the Wind of God.

When I think of the Spirit as wind, I think of myself sitting becalmed. The voyage is long, and paddling is largely hopeless; that is our piety and our works. But the wind *will* come, as sure as the promises of God, and our task is to set and trim the sails, what our ancestors used to call "the means of grace," prayer, the sacraments, Bible study, and the Christian life. We must go on doing them, faithfully and patiently, but we do not know when the wind will blow. When it does, we will be ready.

The Grand Miracle

To be born again means to come to the realization that John 3:16 is true. Not simply to know it in my mind, as I know that $2 + 2 = 4$, but to know it in my deepest and inmost being, and to commit my life to it. As one who grew up in the Church, I have always "known" that Jesus is my Lord and Savior. I have always been a "believer," in that sense. But "belief" in the Christian sense is more than the acceptance of a truth; it is the discovery that truth is *really* true. *Faith* is really a verb as well as a noun. When we use the words *belief* and *believe,* we often imply a little doubt. Consider the following sentences:

> "Is the doctor in?" "I believe so." (But maybe not.)
> "I believe the train will be here at 6:00." (If it isn't delayed.)
> "I believe my spouse loves me." (That's a good bit stronger.)
> "I believe that God loves me." (How strong is that?)

There is an old story about a missionary who was searching for a word for "believe" to translate Acts 16:31 into the language of a Polynesian tribe that had few abstract concepts. A native runner came panting into the missionary's hut with a message, flinging himself on a bamboo couch and saying in his language, "I lean my whole weight on this couch." That is what the verse means: "Lean your whole weight on Jesus Christ, and you will be saved."

To do this is to be born again. It is one thing to be able to quote the Bible, but it is another to live a life in the confident assurance that God loves the world and sent the Son, not to condemn me but to save me. When I *know* that and live like that, when anyone asks me whether I am saved, I will not have to hem and haw. I will be able to answer with utter simplicity: "Yes."

Helping Adults Become Involved

Preparing to Teach

The great question of this lesson is this: "Have you been born again?" We had better not set out to teach others if we have not asked ourselves that question. Some of us may be able to put an actual time and place on what we might call a "born-again" experience. For me, it took place on a certain New Year's Eve, long ago, when I had the responsibility of preparing a watchnight worship service for my church. I remember confronting, as though I had never noticed it before, the passing of the innumerable centuries since the creation of the world. At first, I responded skeptically. "What does the death of a man nearly two thousand years ago have to do with me in this modern age?" Then there came to me, as if by a voice or a spirit or a breath or a wind), the text from 2 Peter 3:8 (and Psalm 90:4), "With the Lord one day is like a thousand years, and a thousand years are like one day." At that moment, it began to dawn on me that all rational attempts to explain eternity are a failure, and I decided to trust God, not my own philosophy.

For others, the experience may have happened over and over again. It happens to me almost every Sunday, during the service of worship, when we say to one another, "Friends, believe the good news of God: in Jesus Christ, we are forgiven."

Still others may say, "I have always been born again." This may be the best answer of all. I don't remember my physical birth, and I don't remember my spiritual birth. I have grown up surrounded by the love of God in Jesus Christ.

I'm not saying that you must define your rebirth the way I do. I'm saying you will want to define it the way *you* do, as you set out to talk to others about it.

Here is a suggested class outline:

> I. The wind of God
> II. A summary of all scripture
> III. Being born again

Introducing the Main Question

Start your class with slips of paper containing the following statement: "A born-again Christian is. . . . " When all have been given time to complete that statement to their own satisfactions, ask those who will to share their answers with others. It is important here not to force folks to talk about their deeply held religious convictions unless they feel comfortable in doing so, and it is important not to hold their opinions up to ridicule when they are expressed.

Perhaps more than one of your class members may say, "I don't know what the expression means," or "I don't know if I have been born again." That is your cue to move toward the answer by turning to the Scriptures to ask what it does mean. Be careful not to assume that your understanding of

223

Scripture is the only correct one. We are dealing here with deep matters, and we will only partly comprehend them.

I. The wind of God

Spend some time developing the meaning of the word that is translated "wind," "breath," or "spirit." You may want to tell the class that the Hebrew word used is *ru-ach,* an onomatopoetic word, which sounds like blowing or breathing. The Greek root for "spirit" is *pneuma,* from which we get the English word *pneumatic.* But the important point is that the whole idea of wind, breath, and spirit is life itself (see Genesis 2:7). You might even enjoy making some of your own "plays" on this word. Here are a couple of mine: (1) A man with bad breath (Mark 1:23). (2) More seriously, what about spiritualizing a line such as that in the popular song, "You are the wind beneath my wings" (Isaiah 40:31)? In the main, you want the class members to feel comfortable with Jesus' own wordplay on "wind," "breath," and "spirit." Ask: "In what sense is the Holy Spirit the Wind of God?"

II. A summary of all Scripture

When you get to John 3:16, you are on your own. So much has been written and sung about this great verse that my words will not add much. You might simply ask class members to say the verse together, three times, committing it further to memory and starting their thinking on its deep meaning. In my childhood Sunday school classes, we used to sing it to the chorus of "Love Lifted Me": "When nothing else could help, John 3:16." Or you may ask the adults to put it in their own words. It helps me to point out how important the seventeenth verse is. It is John's way of saying what Paul said in Romans 8:1.

Helping Class Members Act

III. Being born again

Here is a long list of questions that I would want my class to take a look at as they go forth from this session:

1. What difference will it make in your life when you come to the realization that you are born again? Or when you can say that you truly believe the message of John 3:16? (You will see that I think those two questions are basically the same.)
2. Does the phrase "born-again Christian" arouse a positive or a negative feeling in you? If negative, is that because it has been misused by some Christians? How can we think of it in a positive way?
3. How should a born-again Christian act? Is there a difference between a Christian and a born-again Christian? Or should all Christians think of themselves as born again?
4. How should a Christian respond if a street-corner evangelist asks, "Are you saved?"
5. Am I a Pharisee? Can a Pharisee be born again? Will that person still be a Pharisee afterwards? A different sort of Pharisee?
6. How can we lift up Christ as Moses lifted up the bronze serpent? (See John 12:32 and Matthew 5:16.)
7. What is the relationship between being born again and living a life of service to others? Which comes first?

Preparing for Next Sunday

Next week our lesson is about Christ, "the Light of the world." We have already done some thinking about light; it is a favorite word for John. This time we will be seeing it through the eyes of a blind man, and "not seeing" it through the eyes of the religious leaders of Jesus' day. Ask your class members to read the ninth chapter of John and to ask themselves to determine whom they identify with in the story. (There are a good many characters in it.) If your class enjoys singing "Amazing Grace," ask them to look for any similarity between that song and next week's scripture reading.

LESSON 3   MARCH 21

Light of the World

Background Scripture: John 9

The Main Question

A tourist stood at the reflecting pool on Florida's Iron Mountain, listening with rapt attention to the magnificent carillon in the Bok Tower. Moved by the moment, he turned to a stranger sitting on a park bench, reading a newspaper. "Isn't that heavenly music!" Receiving no response, the tourist repeated what he had said. "Sorry," said the stranger, "I can't hear you. Those confounded bells are making too much noise."

There are times when, even with all of our senses functioning, we can miss out on wonderful things going on around us. It is as the Lord said to Isaiah the prophet:

> Keep listening, but do not comprehend;
> keep looking, but do not understand.
> (Isaiah 6:9; see also Mark 4:12)

In today's lesson we are called to sharpen our eyesight in order that we may see the obvious. Once our two-year-old daughter, who was something of a climber, found it pleasurable to walk up the *outside* of the banisters on our front hall stairs, out of reach of her mother. As a defensive action, we wired the card table to the stairs so she couldn't get her little hands around the banisters, and her mother relaxed. Well, a couple of years later, we needed a card table for some reason, and had to borrow one because we couldn't find it! There it was in the front hall, right where I looked at it every time I entered the house, but it had ceased to be a card table. It had become a child-restraint device.

Jesus Christ is the Light of the world. But it is possible to look straight into the light and not see it. How can we be so blind?

Selected Scripture

King James Version

John 9:1-12, 35-41

1 And as Jesus passed by, he saw a man which was blind from his birth.

2 And his disciples asked him, saying, Master, who did sin, this man, or his parents, that he was born blind?

3 Jesus answered, Neither hath this man sinned, nor his parents: but that the works of God should be made manifest in him.

4 I must work the works of him that sent me, while it is day: the night cometh, when no man can work.

5 As long as I am in the world, I am the light of the world.

6 When he had thus spoken, he spat on the ground, and made clay of the spittle, and he anointed the eyes of the blind man with the clay,

7 And said unto him, Go, wash in the pool of Siloam, (which is by interpretation, Sent.) He went his way therefore, and washed, and came seeing.

8 The neighbours therefore, and they which before had seen him that he was blind, said, Is not this he that sat and begged?

9 Some said, This is he: others said, He is like him: but he said, I am he.

10 Therefore said they unto him, How were thine eyes opened?

11 He answered and said, A man that is called Jesus made clay, and anointed mine eyes, and said unto me, Go to the pool of Siloam, and wash: and I went and washed, and I received sight.

12 Then said they unto him, Where is he? He said, I know not.

....

35 Jesus heard that they had cast him out; and when he had found

New Revised Standard Version

John 9:1-12, 35-41

1 As he walked along, he saw a man blind from birth. 2 His disciples asked him, "Rabbi, who sinned, this man or his parents, that he was born blind?" 3 Jesus answered, "Neither this man sinned nor his parents sinned; he was born blind so that God's works might be revealed in him. 4 We must work the works of him who sent me while it is day; night is coming when no one can work. 5 As long as I am in the world, I am the light of the world." 6 When he had said this, he spat on the ground and made mud with the saliva and spread the mud on the man's eyes, 7 saying to him, "Go, wash in the pool of Siloam" (which means Sent). Then he went and washed and came back able to see. 8 The neighbors and those who had seen him before as a beggar began to ask, "Is this not the man who used to sit and beg?" 9 Some were saying, "It is he." Others were saying, "No, but it is someone like him." He kept saying, "I am the man." 10 But they kept asking him, "Then how were your eyes opened?" 11 He answered, "The man called Jesus made mud, spread it on my eyes, and said to me, 'Go to Siloam and wash.' Then I went and washed and received my sight." 12 They said to him, "Where is he?" He said, "I do not know."

....

35 Jesus heard that they had driven him out, and when he found

him, he said unto him, Dost thou believe on the Son of God?

36 He answered and said, Who is he, Lord, that I might believe on him?

37 And Jesus said unto him, Thou hast both seen him, and it is he that talketh with thee.

38 And he said, Lord, I believe. And he worshipped him.

39 And Jesus said, For judgment I am come into this world, that they which see not might see; and that they which see might be made blind.

40 And some of the Pharisees which were with him heard these words, and said unto him, Are we blind also?

41 Jesus said unto them, If ye were blind, ye should have no sin: but now ye say, We see; therefore your sin remaineth.

Key Verse: **As long as I am in the world, I am the light of the world. (John 9:5)**

him, he said, "Do you believe in the Son of Man?" 36 He answered, "And who is he, sir? Tell me, so that I may believe in him." 37 Jesus said to him, "You have seen him, and the one speaking with you is he." 38 He said, "Lord, I believe." And he worshiped him. 39 Jesus said, "I came into this world for judgment so that those who do not see may see, and those who do see may become blind." 40 Some of the Pharisees near him heard this and said to him, "Surely we are not blind, are we?" 41 Jesus said to them, "If you were blind, you would not have sin. But now that you say, 'We see,' your sin remains."

Key Verse: **As long as I am in the world, I am the light of the world. (John 9:5)**

As You Read the Scripture

John 9. Of all the stories about Jesus' miracles, this one is the most informative, including the psychology of both the man who is healed and the crowd around him. We can learn much from it about our own reaction to Christ and his offer of wholeness.

Verses 1-3. Although, according to the Bible (and common sense), *some* human suffering is related to human sin (see Leviticus 26; Psalm 103:3; Luke 5:23-24), we are here clearly told that this is not true in all cases. (See also Luke 13:1-5 and Matthew 5:45.)

Verses 4-5. The man's blindness provides an opportunity for Jesus to demonstrate something about the nature of God as light. This is a genuine healing, but it is more than that; it is also a sign. This is not the only time Jesus has called himself the light of the word (see John 8:12 and 12:46; also Matthew 5:14). Indeed, the idea of Christ as light is at the heart of John's writings (John 1:4-5; 9:5; and 1 John 1:5-7).

Verses 6-12. This is one of only a few cases in which Jesus uses medicinal aids in his healing work (see Mark 7:33 and 8:23). Saliva was thought by the ancients to have healing power, and, indeed, it is a fairly bland saline solution, though in today's medicine, bodily fluids are considered somewhat dangerous. Compare this washing with the story of Naaman the leper in 2 Kings 5, where Naaman's willingness to follow instructions is an indication of his faith. Although the blind man in John 9 really doesn't know much about Jesus, he does have enough trust to obey Jesus' orders.

Verses 13-17. The Pharisees, in their righteous zeal, were more concerned with sabbath observance than with healing. (See Mark 2:23–3:6; and many other such references.) But the man himself called Jesus a prophet.

Verses 18-23. The man's parents are too afraid to testify.

Verses 24-34. The authorities engage in what logicians call *argumentum ad hominem*, "argue to the man." Rather than face the obvious truth that an astonishing healing has happened, they first call Jesus a sinner and then cast out the former blind man with the same charge. Their logic is that one must be born in sin if one is born blind. Meanwhile, the man stubbornly persists in believing in the obvious, like the little boy who saw at once that the emperor had on no clothes. The most famous line in the paragraph is the one quoted in the hymn "Amazing Grace": "I was blind, now I see." Note that the leaders fully believe that they are giving "glory to God" (v. 24) and defending the Scriptures (vv. 28-29). But sometimes even the Scriptures can stand between us and our conversion.

Verses 35-41. It is made clear that the blind man really did not know who had healed him. Of course, he had never seen Jesus before. He had never seen anyone before. But now he sees and believes. The Pharisees, on the other hand, although they can see with their eyes, cannot see with their hearts. They claim to be righteous, to know the truth, so their guilt remains. "If we say that we have no sin, we deceive ourselves, and the truth is not in us" (1 John 1:8). The repentant prodigal knows that he has been forgiven; the "faithful" elder brother does not (Luke 15:11-32).

The Scripture and the Main Question

The Cast of Characters

This is an interesting chapter about all sorts of people. Do you see yourself in the story? Here are the characters in the order of their appearance:

Jesus, who "passes by," performs an act of healing, then disappears to return at the end of the chapter with a final message;

the man born blind, who moves, step by step, from blindness to faith;

neighbors and acquaintances, who failed to recognize the man in his new state of seeing;

the religious leaders who cannot see the goodness of this act of healing, because of their preoccupation with the rules and their eagerness to find blame;

the parents, who are afraid to support the testimony of their own eyes, but "pass the buck" to their son.

Do you identify with any of these people? Like the blind man, has your faith developed over the passing of time? Like the neighbors, have you known someone to be so changed by faith as to be unrecognizable? Like the Pharisees, have you ever stubbornly stuck to a principle, only to miss the principal point? Like the man's parents, have you occasionally lacked the courage to speak up for what you know to be the truth? I guess I see something of myself in all of these folks. But what about Jesus? Can we dare to identify with him in some small way? Do we have the power to help others see? (See John 14:12.)

Spiritual Blindness

There is blindness in differing degrees in every person in this story—except Jesus. And there is blindness in every one of us. Look at the following markings:

Some of us, seeing the strange characters, have a hard time discovering what they mean. Others see the meaning instantly. If you haven't spotted it, take a couple of pieces of paper, or two business cards, and place them directly above and below the drawing, and the meaning will probably jump out at you. This is what artists call a field and ground reversal. The dark lines are not code symbols, but spaces between the letters.

In a similar way, the mysterious person Jesus passes through the pages of the New Testament. Sometimes he is impossible to see (Matthew 25:37-39; Luke 4:30; 24:31). At times his identity is uncertain (Mark 6:49; Luke 24:16; John 20:14; Acts 9:5). And at other times he is as clear as the sun at noonday (John 20:18, 29; Mark 8:29; 1 Corinthians 13:12; Revelation 1:17).

In our daily lives, there are times when Jesus is more clear to us than at others. Can you say that you have seen Jesus? When is the vision of him most clear? We need to see him in order to be able to see God (John 1:18; 14:9).

What prevents us from seeing Jesus? The Pharisees in our story were so wrapped up in the details of their religion that they couldn't see the forest for the trees. On another occasion, Jesus called them "blind guides" (Matthew 23:16-24; see also Luke 6:39). What blinds us? For the Pharisees, it was what was most precious to them, their legalism. What things are precious to us? Money? Family? Position? Our nation? All these things, wonderful in themselves, when worshiped as gods blind us to the true God and often lead us astray. It has been said of all idols (which are themselves blind) that, though they do not have the power to save, can destroy.

Progress Toward the Light

The blind man in this story did not achieve full faith all at once. He does say, however, "I was blind, now I see" (v. 25). But that sight is only partial at first. He is like another blind man (Mark 8:22-26), who first saw "men as trees walking" and saw clearly only after a second touch from the Master. Some experiments by psychologists indicate that those who have had their sight restored by some medical "miracle" after having been sightless since birth cannot at first distinguish shapes, but see only a shapeless mass of color. They have learned to associate shape with touch, but not yet with sight. I do not know about that, but I can testify in the realm of spiritual blindness that I have seen people (myself included) who have looked straight at the truth and failed to see it.

Look at the steps through which the sightless blind man moves:

> Total blindness (v. 1);
> Sight, but ignorance of his healer (vv. 7-12);
> Realization that Jesus is a prophet (v. 17);
> Stubbornly sticks to the fact of his new sight (v. 25);
> Able to argue with the authorities (vv. 30-33);
> Seeing Jesus for the first time (vv. 35-37);
> Filled with belief and reverence (v. 38).

Perhaps we are only a part of the way on our faith journey and need to move to another level of belief.

The Law of Readiness

We can't make belief happen. It comes as a gift. Note that Jesus sought the man out (v. 35) and, having found him, Jesus revealed himself to the man. We can seek Jesus (John 12:21), but we will not find him until he is ready to be found or until we are ready, which is much the same thing. It is like the wind of the Spirit, blowing when it wills. But when that wind *does* blow, pray that your sails are set. At least three or four times in my ministerial career someone has come to me and said, "I have just discovered the wonderful truth that I have been saved, not by my own works, but by the grace of God! Why has no one told me this before?" "I have said that at least twice in every sermon I have preached," I reply. "Well, I never heard you say it," is the usual response. It seems that some things are so obvious, like my card table in the front hall, that they are invisible. How can we keep ourselves from being blind to such truths? The only answer I can give is that you must go about doing good, search the Scriptures, gather with fellow Christians for the Word and Sacrament, keep on praying, and one day Jesus will spit in your eye and tell you to wash. By all means, do it!

Helping Adults Become Involved

Preparing to Teach

Unless we are to be the "blind leading the blind" we must sharpen our own eyesight. It used to be believed that eating carrots made one's night vision more acute. If that is so, what "carrots" should we consume before going into the classroom? The following is a list of rules I like to require of myself before I teach any passage of Scripture:

1. *Read the passage yourself.* This sounds obvious, but, especially with familiar passages, we may think we know what the Bible says and yet be blind to the real meaning. Almost without exception, when I seriously reread a Bible passage I see something that I had never noticed before. To test what I suggest, I just this minute looked at John 9 again, and verses 8-9 jumped out at me with a question I had never thought about before: How does a sighted person look different from a sightless person? Is it something about the eyes? Or is it something in me? You can see your mail carrier every day and recognize that person in uniform, but when you encounter him or her out of context, say in a supermarket check-out line, you have trouble remembering where you have seen that person. Do people look different after their eyes have been opened spiritually (Acts 4:13)?

2. Be sure that you understand what the passage means. Go over the verses as outlined in "As You Read the Scripture," making notes. If anything is unclear to you, consult a commentary or a dictionary. If you still don't understand the passage, let your class members help.

3. Boil down the content of the passage to one or more simple truths. Here's my attempt at reducing John 9 to its essentials:

Jesus can give sight to the physically blind.
Jesus can give insight to the spiritually blind.
Our own strongly held convictions can blind us.
It takes courage to face the light (truth) and grow toward it.

The lesson outline:
I. Telling the story of John 9
II. Looking at our own blindness
III. Growing toward the light

Introducing the Main Question

Ask the class members to share examples of obvious truth that is hard to see. You may have access to some good "optical illusions" that you could use as illustrations. You might use the field and ground reversal illustration from the section called "Spiritual Blindness" above. Make a copy of it to use in your class. But better than actual show-and-tell by the teacher would be stories brought by class members, like mine about the disappearing card table.

Developing the Lesson

I. Telling the story of John 9
After introducing the question of spiritual blindness, lead your class through a brief telling of the story. One way to keep their interest is to ask them whether they see themselves in any of the characters as the story unfolds.

II. Looking at our own blindness
In the section titled "Spiritual Blindness," I have raised the question, "What prevents us from seeing Jesus?" The Pharisees in the story are deeply religious people, but their very dogma keeps them from the truth. Ask your class members to look at ways our preciously held beliefs can blind us to what God is trying to tell us. I know a woman who gets upset when a stranger sits in her favorite pew at church. Is she being blinded to the opportunities for witness that God is trying to send to her?

III. Growing toward the light
Finally, let the class members have a go at discussing how we can grow in our ability to see spiritually. In what sense must we move from our spiritual birth (in the last lesson) to spiritual maturity? (See Ephesians 4:11-16 and Colossians 1:28.) All of the Christian life is a movement from decreasing blindness to increasing insight. Most plants grow toward the light. As the man in this story in John 9 deepens in relationship to the One who healed him, so should we.

Helping Class Members Act

As the lesson comes to a close, encourage the class to develop a list of daily rules for "stepping in the light" (1 John 1:7). Theirs and yours might be different from mine:

> Keep your spiritual eyes open.
> Remember that the truth is your friend.
> Look for Christ in others.
> Do more listening than talking (I don't do this one well).

Be a constant skeptic. The root from which the word *skeptic* comes means "to look for," as in *telescope* and *microscope*. True Christians, like true scientists, should constantly question the things that might be blinding us to the truth, that we may be open to the new light that Christ is waiting to give us.

Planning for Next Sunday

In three weeks it will be Easter. On that day we will be looking at the Great Resurrection, begun in Christ (1 Corinthians 15:22). But before that great event, there is the story of another resurrection, that of an ordinary man. Have your class read that story in John 11, asking themselves, as they read, Is there resurrection in *my* life?

LESSON 4   MARCH 28

Coming to Life

Background Scripture: John 11:1-44

The Main Question

> If it is cut down, that it will sprout again. . . .
> If mortals die, will they live again? . . .
> For there is hope for a tree,
>   if it is cut down, that it will sprout again. . . .
> But mortals die, and are laid low.
> (Job 14:14, 7, 10)

The speaker in the passage above is Job, suffering with disease and anguishing over the calamities that have befallen him. He seems to be saying, "I could stand all this pain, if I had some assurance that death is not the end." I have heard a modern Job, head buried in his hands, grieving over the untimely death of his wife and daughter, say much the same thing: "It all seems so useless."

Death is not the worst thing there is—not by a long shot. A "heroic" death for one's kin or country sometimes gives one noble status, and peaceful death at the end of a long illness sometimes is called a blessing. But there is a finality about death that brings us at best a sense of wondering despair. Job's question may very well be the main question, not only of this lesson, but of life itself. Indeed, as Hamlet said, that *is* the question.

Certainly it is something we all must face. It is our last great adventure, and we must do it all by ourselves, no matter how many Marys and Marthas may be gathered around our bedside when the time comes. In this lesson we encounter our Lord, weeping in death's presence, but by no means defeated by it. If we take the Scripture passage from Job seriously, we will confront the question of our own mortality, and, thanks to the Lord of life, we will find an answer to it.

Selected Scripture

King James Version	New Revised Standard Version

John 11:1-4, 21-44

1 Now a certain man was sick, named Lazarus, of Bethany, the town of Mary and her sister Martha.

2 (It was that Mary which anointed the Lord with ointment, and wiped his feet with her hair, whose brother Lazarus was sick.)

3 Therefore his sisters sent unto him, saying, Lord, behold, he whom thou lovest is sick.

4 When Jesus heard that, he said, This sickness is not unto death, but for the glory of God, that the Son of God might be glorified thereby.

....

21 Then said Martha unto Jesus, Lord, if thou hadst been here, my brother had not died.

22 But I know, that even now, whatsoever thou wilt ask of God, God will give it thee.

23 Jesus saith unto her, Thy brother shall rise again.

24 Martha saith unto him, I know that he shall rise again in the resurrection at the last day.

25 Jesus said unto her, I am the resurrection, and the life: he that believeth in me, though he were dead, yet shall he live:

26 And whosoever liveth and believeth in me shall never die. Believest thou this?

John 11:1-4, 21-44

1 Now a certain man was ill, Lazarus of Bethany, the village of Mary and her sister Martha. 2 Mary was the one who anointed the Lord with perfume and wiped his feet with her hair; her brother Lazarus was ill. 3 So the sisters sent a message to Jesus, "Lord, he whom you love is ill." 4 But when Jesus heard it, he said, "This illness does not lead to death; rather it is for God's glory, so that the Son of God may be glorified through it."

....

21 Martha said to Jesus, "Lord, if you had been here, my brother would not have died. 22 But even now I know that God will give you whatever you ask of him." 23 Jesus said to her, "Your brother will rise again." 24 Martha said to him, "I know that he will rise again in the resurrection on the last day." 25 Jesus said to her, "I am the resurrection and the life. Those who believe in me, even though they die, will live, 26 and everyone who lives and believes in me will never die. Do you believe this?" 27 She said to him, "Yes, Lord, I believe that you are the Messiah, the Son of God, the one coming into the world."

27 She saith unto him, Yea, Lord: I believe that thou art the Christ, the Son of God, which should come into the world.

28 And when she had so said, she went her way, and called Mary her sister secretly, saying, The Master is come, and calleth for thee.

29 As soon as she heard that, she arose quickly, and came unto him.

30 Now Jesus was not yet come into the town, but was in that place where Martha met him.

31 The Jews then which were with her in the house, and comforted her, when they saw Mary, that she rose up hastily and went out, followed her, saying, She goeth unto the grave to weep there.

32 Then when Mary was come where Jesus was, and saw him, she fell down at his feet, saying unto him, Lord, if thou hadst been here, my brother had not died.

33 When Jesus therefore saw her weeping, and the Jews also weeping which came with her, he groaned in the spirit, and was troubled.

34 And said, Where have ye laid him? They said unto him, Lord, come and see.

35 Jesus wept.

36 Then said the Jews, Behold how he loved him!

37 And some of them said, Could not this man, which opened the eyes of the blind, have caused that even this man should not have died?

38 Jesus therefore again groaning in himself cometh to the grave. It was a cave, and a stone lay upon it.

39 Jesus said, Take ye away the stone. Martha, the sister of him that was dead, saith unto him, Lord, by this time he stinketh; for he hath been dead four days.

40 Jesus saith unto her, Said I not unto thee, that, if thou wouldest believe, thou shouldest see the glory of God?

41 Then they took away the stone from the place where the dead was

28 When she had said this, she went back and called her sister Mary, and told her privately, "The Teacher is here and is calling for you." 29 And when she heard it, she got up quickly and went to him. 30 Now Jesus had not yet come to the village, but was still at the place where Martha had met him. 31 The Jews who were with her in the house, consoling her, saw Mary get up quickly and go out. They followed her because they thought that she was going to the tomb to weep there. 32 When Mary came where Jesus was and saw him, she knelt at his feet and said to him, "Lord, if you had been here, my brother would not have died." 33 When Jesus saw her weeping, and the Jews who came with her also weeping, he was greatly disturbed in spirit and deeply moved. 34 He said, "Where have you laid him?" They said to him, "Lord, come and see." 35 Jesus began to weep. 36 So the Jews said, "See how he loved him!" 37 But some of them said, "Could not he who opened the eyes of the blind man have kept this man from dying?"

38 Then Jesus, again greatly disturbed, came to the tomb. It was a cave, and a stone was lying against it. 39 Jesus said, "Take away the stone." Martha, the sister of the dead man, said to him, "Lord, already there is a stench because he has been dead four days." 40 Jesus said to her, "Did I not tell you that if you believed, you would see the glory of God?" 41 So they took away the stone. And Jesus looked upward and said, "Father, I thank you for having heard me. 42 I knew that you

laid. And Jesus lifted up his eyes, and said, Father, I thank thee that thou hast heard me.

42 And I knew that thou hearest me always: but because of the people which stand by I said it, that they may believe that thou hast sent me.

43 And when he thus had spoken, he cried with a loud voice, Lazarus, come forth.

44 And he that was dead came forth, bound hand and foot with graveclothes: and his face was bound about with a napkin. Jesus saith unto them, Loose him, and let him go.

always hear me, but I have said this for the sake of the crowd standing here, so that they may believe that you sent me." 43 When he had said this, he cried with a loud voice, "Lazarus, come out!" 44 The dead man came out, his hands and feet bound with strips of cloth, and his face wrapped in a cloth. Jesus said to them, "Unbind him, and let him go."

Key Verse: **Jesus said unto her, I am the resurrection, and the life: he that believeth in me, though he were dead, yet shall he live. (John 11:25)**

Key Verse: **Jesus said to her, "I am the resurrection and the life. Those who believe in me, even though they die, will live." (John 11:25)**

As You Read the Scripture

John 11:1-2. It's a little difficult to piece together the Mary/Martha stories of the Gospels. Lazarus is mentioned no place but here (the Lazarus in Luke 16 is not the same man). They were clearly Jesus' friends and were apparently his disciples. The account of Mary's anointing of Jesus is anticipated (it actually comes in 12:1-8) and may have been mentioned here by John because it was a well-known story in the early Church. It takes other forms in Mark (14:3-9), Matthew (26:6-13), and Luke (7:37-38) and may be an entirely different incident. It was probably to these friends that Jesus withdrew just before the Crucifixion.

Verses 3-6. It was natural that these friends would send for Jesus, knowing that he was a healer. His reluctance to go seems at first uncaring, but it is similar to what he said about the man's blindness in 9:3. Jesus seems to know that something great is going to come of this illness.

Verses 7-10. Notice how Jesus seldom does what other people think he ought to do. He is, we would say, highly self-motivated. And yet he is clearly doing what he has to do, when the time is right. Especially in John's Gospel, we find Jesus using expressions like, "My hour has not yet come" (2:4) and knowing that "his hour had come" (13:1). To us he seems unpredictable, but he is following his own inner timetable. It seems that the message took about a day to get to Jesus, then he delayed two days, then it took them a day to get there—hence the four days. Lazarus must have died about the time the messenger left to find Jesus; in that sub-tropical climate, as in many lands, one did not leave a corpse unburied for long.

Verses 11-16. Again, Jesus makes it plain that the death of Lazarus has a purpose. Note that it is "doubting" Thomas who displays the most courage in this story. Although, like the other disciples, Thomas lacks understanding, he does not lack commitment.

Verses 17-27. Martha fusses at Jesus for being late, and she doesn't seem to understand what he means to do, even when he tells her that he *is* the resurrection. But at least she knows something of who he is: the Christ of God.

Verses 28-32. Next comes Mary, also upset with Jesus. Her tears move him to tears, but they are not for Lazarus. Jesus' tears are his identification with us in our grief and his sorrow over our lack of faith.

Verses 38-44. Now that he is ready to make his move, Jesus is a commanding presence. His orders are obeyed, even though they seem illogical. (Who would open the tomb of a decaying corpse?) His prayer is not for power to do the miracle; he knew he already had that. His prayer is to include those who stood there, and us, that we may believe. He speaks in an authoritative voice, calling to the man who had been dead, and sets him free from the binding grave clothes to live a normal life again. Here is supreme evidence of the fulfillment of the promise of our author's purpose (see John 20:31).

The Scripture and the Main Question

The Importance of Friends

Most of us can say, "I have lots of friends, but only a few *friends.*" You can count on your fingers those wonderful persons with whom, when you meet after a long absence, you can begin a conversation almost as though you had never interrupted it. It was to these that Jesus turned on the eve of the last passionate week of his life. And it was here that lived the only man mentioned by name in the Gospel of John as one whom Jesus loved (see vv. 3, 5, 11, and 36). At least one scholar (Floyd V. Filson, in *The Layman's Bible Commentary* [Richmond: John Knox Press, 1970], pp. 21-25) makes the case that Lazarus must have been "the disciple whom Jesus loved" (see 13:23; 19:26-27; 20:2-10; and 21:7, 20-24), rather than John, as is commonly held. Whether that is true or not, Lazarus (whose name in Hebrew, Eleazar, means "God has helped") was certainly a special person in Jesus' life. Fully incarnate in our human lives (1:14) and sharing our human frailties (4:6; 11:33; 19:28; etc.), Jesus had a deep need for human companionship, and especially for friendship (15:13-15). He found that friendship equally well with both male and female acquaintances, of whom all three of these Bethany residents are our best examples. Wouldn't it be something to be able to say that Jesus needed you, that you had befriended him? Does God need friends (see 2 Chronicles 20:7; Isaiah 41:9; James 2:23)?

Though he needs his friends, is moved by their grief, and is concerned for their concerns, Jesus has his own agenda. Throughout this chapter, we see him moving on his own schedule, almost ignoring their pleas, giving orders with authority. Neither fear of death nor compassion for others keeps him from the completion of his task on his own terms. There is a calling higher even than friendship.

Resurrection

John 11 is one of two great resurrection chapters in the New Testament; the other is 1 Corinthians 15, at which we will briefly look. The doctrine of resurrectiom is shadowy in the Hebrew Scriptures, though not entirely absent. Such pessimism as that of Ecclesiastes 9:10 and 11:8 is offset by the hopefulness of Isaiah 26:19, Ezekiel 37, Daniel 12:2-3, and Job 19:23-27. By the time of Jesus, belief in life after death had become common; the Pharisees held it firmly, and the Sadducees denied it (Mark 22:23). But it was only after Christ's own resurrection, joyfully acclaimed by his followers, that belief in resurrection became firmly fixed. Christians to this day celebrate on the first day of the week because of Jesus' resurrection on that day; every Sunday is a little Easter.

Belief in resurrection is not the same as the Greek doctrine of the immortality of the soul. This belief was held by many Greek philosophers before the time of Christ, and it marked a kind of dualism between the natural world and the spiritual world. The body, which is of the physical world, may decay. But the soul, a kind of invisible, indestructible thing from the eternal world, lives on. Such a distinction is not found in the Bible. Both body and soul face death (Matthew 10:28), and, like the phoenix of Egyptian mythology, both rise again. Jesus uses the metaphor of a seed (John 12:24), which must die in order to come to new life in its fruit. This is implicit in many of his sayings (Luke 9:24, for example). And Paul uses the same idea in 1 Corinthians 15:37.

By the time we get to Paul, the doctrine of the resurrection has become essential to basic faith (1 Corinthians 15:17). Many of us say every Sunday in the Apostles' Creed, "I believe in the resurrection of the body." A basic affirmation of our faith is that death, though it may be the last enemy, does not have the last word. "Thanks be to God, who gives us the victory through our Lord Jesus Christ" (1 Corinthians 15:57). The story of Lazarus is a vivid introduction to what is to become the great promise of the Christian faith.

Jesus Wept

If you grew up, as I did, in a family where it was the custom to have everyone take turns saying a Bible verse, you know that John 11:35 was a life-saver for a biblically illiterate child. It is, of course, the shortest verse in the Bible. (The longest, if you are wondering, is Esther 8:9). But there is more theology in the two words *Jesus wept* (KJV) than first meets the eye. Jesus' tears are a brief enactment of God's compassion for us, the divine identification with our human condition. I do not weep easily (except at the wrong times, in B movies, at overly sentimental things), but this is a fault in me. It is a virtue of our Lord, a strength if you will, that he knows and shares the pain of living. This is not the only time he wept (see also Luke 19:41; Hebrews 5:7). Our anguish is God's anguish (Isaiah 16:9; Jeremiah 48:32). The unique gift of the Christian gospel to the religions of humankind is our awareness that the God of the universe is not some immovable, invulnerable distant deity but one who shares our sorrows and knows our discontent. There is no corner of the human spirit that escapes the divine notice. We don't know exactly *why* Jesus wept. It could have been his identification with the weeping Mary, his grief over the lack of the faith of his disciples, or even his sorrow at having to bring Lazarus back from the very brink of heaven. But the point is that he did weep. He knows our frame; he remembers that we are dust (Psalm 103:14). In Jesus, God enters completely into our human condition.

THIRD QUARTER

Lazarus

What would it be like to die and then be brought back to life? Some have suggested that Lazarus was really the first martyr; having passed through death, he now has it to do all over again. But others theorize that, having once tasted of the borders of that heavenly country, Lazarus would have been able to live for the rest of his life with a calm assurance. Having come to know with a certainty that death can be borne and that eternal life is a reality, he is now free to live. After all, Jesus did promise that whoever loses his or her life for Christ's sake would find it (Luke 9:24); those who have undergone near-death experiences almost universally report that the experience was not unpleasant. A friend of mine who narrowly survived a fatal auto accident says that for him the deepest result of the calamity has been a renewed confidence in God. I think Lazarus would agree.

Helping Adults Become Involved

Preparing to Teach

It is always difficult to discuss death. As a pastor, I find that many otherwise thoughtful married couples neglect to talk about death with each other, with the result that they sometimes have inadequate insurance programs, and fail to prepare wills. When death comes, the survivor—usually the wife—is unprepared for the important decisions that must be made. There seems to be a sort of this-won't-happen-to-us attitude. And I have found it difficult to persuade young adults to begin to look at the important issues related to their own mortality. In recent years there has been a rise of interest in courses on death and dying, but I still think it is true that we are dealing with a taboo subject. For this reason, you will want to make special preparation to help your class "open up" on the essential matter of this week's lesson.

Begin by asking yourself what *you* feel about your own death. Perhaps you or someone in your class has had a recent grief experience and can bring fresh insights to your class. Below are three questions you might ask yourself, and then, if you like, use at the beginning of your class period to raise the consciousness of your group:

1. Do you find it difficult to talk about death with those closest to you?
2. Have you made out a will?
3. Does your Christian faith make a difference in the way you feel about such questions?

Read carefully through John 11:1-44 with those questions in mind, and prepare yourself to talk frankly, openly, and confidently with your class about this difficult, but important, matter.

Here is today's outline:

> I. Jesus and his friends
> II. Jesus' reluctance
> III. The doctrine of the resurrection
> IV. Jesus' compassion

238

Introducing the Main Question

Because talking about death is a difficult matter, I'd suggest that you begin your class by raising a question not directly related to it. Ask whether anyone has ever thought about the shortest verse in the Bible, "Jesus wept." Why did Jesus weep? Some possible answers:

Jesus wept because of the lack of faith of his friends.
Jesus wept because he was deeply moved by Lazarus' death.
Jesus wept because he understood his friend's tears and empathized with them in their grief.

Verse 33 indicates to me that the last stated reason is the most likely. If your class members agree with this, you can start the lesson by saying something like this: "Because we know that God understands our fear of death and sympathizes with us in our grief, we can face death with courage and be free to talk openly and honestly together about it."

Developing the Lesson

I. Jesus and his friends

Introduce the class to the other scripture passages (Luke 10:38-42 and John 12:1-8) that tell us about the two sisters. Discuss the importance of Jesus' friends to him and his importance to them. I once heard a Protestant minister and a Roman Catholic priest discussing their friends. The pastor said, "I envy you because you are free from family ties. You can take a courageous stand on an issue, knowing that you are not putting your family in jeopardy." The priest answered, "I envy you because you have someone to come home to, who can support and comfort you when you have taken a courageous stand on an issue." Why do you think Mary and Martha were important to Jesus? Why do you suppose our author tells us more than once that Jesus loved them (vv. 3, 5, 36)? Does God need friends?

II. Jesus' reluctance

Discuss with your class the way in which Jesus delays his visit to Mary and Martha. What does he know that they don't know? Do we sometimes feel that God is slow in acting when we need help?

III. The doctrine of the resurrection

You may wish to spend considerable time on this, looking back at the suggested Old Testament Scripture. Ask about the importance of the doctrine of resurrection in the lives of your class members. There is a legend as old as the Crusades about an Arab woman carrying a yoke with a brazier of coals on one end and a bucket of water on the other. She said, "I carry the fire to burn up heaven and the water to quench hell, so that people will worship God, neither for hope of reward nor for fear of punishment, but because God is God." Would it be possible to be a Christian without believing in the resurrection? See what Paul has to say in 1 Corinthians 15:12-19.

How would you evaluate the following statement by a layperson? "I don't understand the doctrine of the resurrection, but I think it is God's way of telling us not to worry, that no matter what happens, all will be well for those who love God." See Romans 8:28, 38-39.

IV. Jesus' compassion

At the end of the lesson you should return to what is, for some, the most important point of this chapter: that God hurts with us in our grief experiences and that because God shares our pain it is easier for us to bear. Most of the time Jesus does not come and raise our Lazaruses from the grave. We have to go on dealing with our grief. In a way, Jesus says about us something like what he said to Thomas in John 20:29: "Blessed are those who have not seen and yet have come to believe."

Helping Class Members Act

The last words of this passage, in the King James Version, are Jesus' instructions concerning Lazarus: "Loose him, and let him go." There is a sense in which this story liberates us, turns us loose, to live different lives because we believe in the power of God to raise the dead and to make things right. Your class members should go from this lesson feeling that they can face the burden of daily living, and even their own mortality, because of what they know about Jesus' power and about Jesus' caring compassion for us in our human hurt.

Planning for Next Sunday

Ask the class members if they would like to have a foot-washing next Sunday. Their answer will help you to decide how to prepare. Tell them to be sure to read John 13:1-20.

UNIT II: JOHN: THE GREAT LOVE

FOUR LESSONS   APRIL 4–25

Whereas Unit I is about vertical matters—our relationship to God—Unit II is about our horizontal relationships, modeled after Christ. It is a fleshing out of the command in 1 John 4:11: "Beloved, since God loved us so much, we also ought to love one another." Lesson 5 deals with our Lord's example as a servant who washes the feet of others, and the lesson explores the concept of service in our time. Lesson 6 falls on Easter Sunday. We turn to look at Mary Magdalene in the garden and, through her weeping eyes, examine our own understanding of the Resurrection. Lesson 7 deals with a post-Resurrection appearance of Christ at a seaside breakfast, where we learn with Simon Peter of our calling to feed God's sheep. And Lesson 8 invites us to eat of the bread to which Jesus calls us—not the manna of the wilderness, but the costly bread that is his broken Body, the Church. All of these lessons lead us to serve one another in love.

Do as I Have Done

Background Scripture: John 13:1-20

The Main Question

Jesus was a master teacher. Not only did he make wonderful use of his literary gifts (illustrations from nature, irony and invective, humor, exaggeration, and all sorts of rhetorical skills, including his special gift, the parable), but also he supremely taught by example. In John 13 we see him employ "show and tell," complete with visual aids: a towel and a basin. So real are they to many Christians that these objects take on a sacramental nature. In addition to the bread and wine of the Lord's Supper and the water of baptism, the towel and basin are used by some as a regular part of worship. What was Jesus trying to get across to us by using them?

Sometimes when I teach on the foot washing in John 13, I think it would be more effective to *do* it than to talk about it—actions speak louder than words. I have never been involved in a foot washing (or a hand washing, which some Christians practice) that has not remained vivid in my memory, though I cannot tell you much of what was said at the time. However, Jesus has given us permission to talk about the ritual, for he had words to say on the subject himself. And those words are the key to our main question. "I have set you an example," he said, "that you also should do as I have done to you" (John 13:15).

When we put Jesus' statement into question form, we must ask: How should we behave toward one another? And the answer, of course, is as servants. But what does this mean? How do twentieth-century Christians effectively engage in service to one another?

Selected Scripture

King James Version

John 13:1-16

1 Now before the feast of the passover, when Jesus knew that his hour was come that he should depart out of this world unto the Father, having loved his own which were in the world, he loved them unto the end.

2 And supper being ended, the devil having now put into the heart of Judas Iscariot, Simon's son, to betray him;

3 Jesus knowing that the Father had given all things into his hands, and that he was come from God, and went to God;

New Revised Standard Version

John 13:1-16

1 Now before the festival of the Passover, Jesus knew that his hour had come to depart from this world and go to the Father. Having loved his own who were in the world, he loved them to the end. 2 The devil had already put it into the heart of Judas son of Simon Iscariot to betray him. And during supper 3 Jesus, knowing that the Father had given all things into his hands, and that he had come from God and was going to God, 4 got up from the table, took off his outer robe, and tied a towel around himself. 5 Then

4 He riseth from supper, and laid aside his garments; and took a towel, and girded himself.

5 After that he poureth water into a basin, and began to wash the disciples' feet, and to wipe them with the towel wherewith he was girded.

6 Then cometh he to Simon Peter: and Peter saith unto him, Lord, dost thou wash my feet?

7 Jesus answered and said unto him, What I do thou knowest not now; but thou shalt know hereafter.

8 Peter saith unto him, Thou shalt never wash my feet. Jesus answered him, If I wash thee not, thou hast no part with me.

9 Simon Peter saith unto him, Lord, not my feet only, but also my hands and my head.

10 Jesus saith to him, He that is washed needeth not save to wash his feet, but is clean every whit: and ye are clean, but not all.

11 For he knew who should betray him; therefore said he, Ye are not all clean.

12 So after he had washed their feet, and had taken his garments, and was set down again, he said unto them, Know ye what I have done to you?

13 Ye call me Master and Lord: and ye say well; for so I am.

14 If I then, your Lord and Master, have washed your feet; ye also ought to wash one another's feet.

15 For I have given you an example, that ye should do as I have done to you.

16 Verily, verily, I say unto you, The servant is not greater than his lord; neither he that is sent greater than he that sent him.

Key Verse: For I have given you an example, that ye should do as I have done to you. (John 13:15)

he poured water into a basin and began to wash the disciples' feet and to wipe them with the towel that was tied around him. 6 He came to Simon Peter, who said to him, "Lord, are you going to wash my feet?" 7 Jesus answered, "You do not know now what I am doing, but later you will understand." 8 Peter said to him, "You will never wash my feet." Jesus answered, "Unless I wash you, you have no share with me." 9 Simon Peter said to him, "Lord, not my feet only but also my hands and my head!" 10 Jesus said to him, "One who has bathed does not need to wash, except for the feet, but is entirely clean. And you are clean, though not all of you." 11 For he knew who was to betray him; for this reason he said, "Not all of you are clean."

12 After he had washed their feet, had put on his robe, and had returned to the table, he said to them, "Do you know what I have done to you? 13 You call me Teacher and Lord—and you are right, for that is what I am. 14 So if I, your Lord and Teacher, have washed your feet, you also ought to wash one another's feet. 15 For I have set you an example, that you also should do as I have done to you. 16 Very truly, I tell you, servants are not greater than their master, nor are messengers greater than the one who sent them."

Key Verse: For I have set you an example, that you also should do as I have done to you. (John 13:15)

As You Read the Scripture

John 13:1-20. Our story evidently takes place in the "upper room" (Mark 14:15), during (or possibly just at the beginning of) what we have come to call the Last Supper. John omits the familiar details of the sacrament, but he gives us events that the other writers do not mention: the foot washing and the wonderful farewell discourses of chapters 14–17.

Verses 1-3. These verses are a very long, involved explanatory lead-in to Jesus' actions: (1) Jesus' time had come, and he knew it. (2) Jesus' love had never slackened. (3) Judas's impatience with Jesus had come to the breaking point. Jesus was supremely confident that he was in God's hands.

Verses 4-5. Foot washing was an entry rite, usually performed by a slave when guests arrived. Its neglect would be remarked upon (see Luke 7:44). None of the disciples had volunteered to do it, perhaps because they didn't want to be seen as inferiors (see Luke 22:24-27). Jesus seized this moment to make his point dramatically.

Verses 6-9. Peter's reluctance is understandable. If you have ever taken part in a foot washing, you will have noticed that, for some strange reason, it is much easier to kneel down and wash someone else's feet than it is to sit there and let someone wash yours. It is embarrassing; you don't know which way to look or what to do with your hands. Peter's last words, "Then wash all of me!" are like the punch line of a joke: If washing my feet will save me, then what if you wash me all over?

Verses 10-11. There is definitely a relationship between this washing and the symbolism of baptism, which means, among other things, entering with Christ into his passing (see Mark 10:38-39; Luke 12:50; and 1 John 1:7). Jesus may be saying here, "When you have been baptized with me, you will be truly clean." But the outward symbol is not enough, for in Judas's case it did not take effect.

Verses 12-15. Jesus explains his action and calls his disciples to live as servants to one another. It is right to be a leader, but the true Leader leads by example and by service, not by imperious order. This counsel is not confined to John's Gospel; for other references, see Matthew 10:24; Luke 6:40; 22:27; and 1 Peter 2:21.

Verse 16. The word translated "servant" here, and almost everywhere else in the New Testament, really means "slave." In Roman times, foot washing was typically a slave's duty.

Verse 17. This beatitude has the same message as the parable of the two houses (Matthew 7:24-27).

Verse 18. The reference is to Psalm 41:9, the cry of one who is lonely, betrayed by his friends, but still confident in God.

Verse 19. Jesus doesn't want his disciples to be completely disconcerted when the betrayal takes place.

Verse 20. Jesus gives his followers the authority of his own evangelistic invitation. It is similar to the promise to Peter in Matthew 16:19. (See also Matthew 10:40; 18:5; Mark 9:37; Luke 9:48; 10:16.) True evangelism is not the preacher's saying, "Come up with me," but one beggar saying to another, "I have found some bread."

The Scripture and the Main Question

A Rite of Entry

What do you routinely do when visitors come to your home? Take their hats and coats? Ask them (euphemistically) if they want to "wash up"? Offer them something to drink? Invite them to have a seat, to "make themselves at home"? In Jesus' day, in a well-to-do home a servant would take and put away the guests' sandals and wash the dust of the road from the persons' feet. (There are negative references to sandal dust elsewhere in Jesus' teaching; see Mark 6:11.) Such acts are ways of saying, "Welcome! Consider yourself a part of the family." Today, the last vestige of foot washing is the familiar doormat (which may have WELCOME printed on it) for the cleaning of visitors' feet. People in certain parts of the country also provide boot scrapers for visitors. But, by and large, we leave people's feet alone.

Perhaps the closest thing to foot washing that is left in our society is the shining of shoes, and this is done either at a barber shop, where one pays to have it done, or at home, by the person himself or herself. The posture of the shoeshiner is kneeling, a humble position, not unlike that of the foot washer, but the job of shoeshining is fast disappearing. Certainly we no longer offer to do it in our homes, though some hotels still offer it as part of their extra services.

All of this talk is just to try to make us feel as familiar as possible with the strange practice in which Jesus engaged in this story. We need to understand that foot washing was not unusual in his day, and clearly it was an act of humility and graciousness, usually done by the lowest person on the social totem pole. It is no wonder that the disciples, who seemed to be continually vying for position, did not think of performing the ritual on one another. To their embarrassment, their Lord and Master stooped to the task.

Follow My Example

Here we have clear instructions from Jesus that we "ought to wash one another's feet" (v. 14). Why do we not all practice foot washing as a sacrament? Is this command no less clear than, "Do this in remembrance of me"? Of course, some branches of the Church—Primitive Baptists and some Lebanese Christians, for instance—do it regularly, and they should be respected for it; it is a meaningful ritual. We might stop for a moment to ask ourselves how an act gets to be a sacrament in the first place. The word *sacrament* means, obviously, a "sacred act," and it can stand for anything one does out of a sense of worship or religious duty. As such, a sacrament is an outward, visible, sign of an inward, spiritual, reality. Even so simple an act as shaking hands, then, may be considered sacramental. The outward sign, offering my open hand to you without fist or weapon, points to an inward reality, I love you and desire to act toward you in peace and good will.

Historically, the Church began to recognize as many as seven acts as sacred rites: baptism, confirmation, the Lord's Supper, marriage, ordination, penance (an act expressing contrition for sins), and extreme unction (anointing of the dying). When, at the time of the Reformation, Church scholars asked themselves which of these acts could clearly be demonstrated as sacraments in the New Testament, only two, baptism and the Lord's

Supper, met these conditions: (1) They are specifically commanded by Jesus. (2) They were later practiced by the early Church.

In the case of baptism, we have the specific command to be baptized (Matthew 28:19) and many evidences of its being obeyed (see Acts 8:38; 1 Corinthians 1:16). For the command to celebrate the Lord's Supper, see Matthew 26:26-29; Mark 14:22-25; Luke 22:17-19; and 1 Corinthians 10:16 and 11:23-26. For its being carried out, see Acts 2:42 and 1 Corinthians 10:16 and 11:28. Though Christ clearly commanded the disciples to wash each other's feet, there is no evidence in the Bible that the Church continued this practice. We may conclude, then, that Jesus' words, "You ought to wash one another's feet," were meant for those in the upper room only.

A Society of Foot Washers

Does that argument hold truth? Would Jesus have given a commandment to the Twelve that might not apply to the rest of us? We can be certain that, even if Jesus did not mean the act to become a permanent ritual, he *did* mean for us to adopt the attitude of service to one another as a lasting life-style. Dozens of New Testament verses give evidence to the fact that members of the early Church were (or ought to have been) given over to serving one another. (Consider a few verses: Acts 2:44-45; 4:32; 6:1-6; Romans 12:3-21; and Hebrews 13:1-3.) It is clear that our Lord asks us to follow his own example (Matthew 10:45) by serving one another.

But how shall we do this? Thomas Keefer, a character in Herman Wouk's novel *The Caine Mutiny*, defends the need for a peacetime Navy, saying, "Suppose all of a sudden the whole survival of America hung on shining shoes. Never mind how. Suppose it did. What would happen? All of us would become shoeshiners, and the professional bootblacks would take over the country." Well, what if the survival of humanity hung on the washing of feet? In fact, it does. If we professional foot washers—that is, the disciples of Jesus Christ—don't do our job and teach the world how to love, then humanity may destroy itself. But how can we accomplish such a task? Jesus' dramatic illustration, complete with basin and towel, clearly means more than that we should be polite, opening doors for one another, saying "please" and "thank you." Certainly we should do those things, but above and beyond the superficial niceties of politeness, Jesus calls us to lay down our lives for one another (John 15:13). When the day comes that we are truly willing to go the second mile for each other, then our witness for Christ will have the evangelical effect we all dream of.

Ernest Gordon, in his autobiographical story *Through the Valley of the Kwai*, recounts how the Christians among his fellow prisoners massaged his gangrenous feet and legs until life was restored in them; they eventually won his heart for Christ. In less dramatic fashion, but just as surely, we need to offer our best "foot-washing" acts to one another and so fulfill the law of Christ (see Galatians 6:23). In a society of servants, we would all reign like kings and queens.

Helping Adults Become Involved

Preparing to Teach

In addition to a careful reading of the text for this Sunday, I would do two things to prepare for the teaching experience. First, I would find a basin and a towel, preferably a plain pottery basin and a simple white towel, and take them to church with me, placing them on a low table at the front of the classroom. I would put water in the basin. I probably wouldn't use them during the class, because that would be too complicated. There would be too much of a problem with shoes and stockings. But I want the water basin and the towel to be in the classroom because they are named in the Bible and will help to keep the reality before us. Also, I want the class members to be a little nervous all during the period; footwashing is an embarrassment.

The other thing I would do is to search for another entry rite that is common in today's society and use it to welcome persons to the class to drive home the point of what it means to make people welcome. Maybe I'll bring a doormat to class. If I don't come up with anything concrete, I'll start off by asking the class members to help me.

Today's lesson outline:

I. Getting into the Bible story
II. Symbol or Sacrament
III. Living as servants to one another

Introducing the Main Question

Introduce the main question by asking how, in our society, we welcome others and make them feel a part of our home. If Jesus did not mean for us literally to wash each other's feet, what did he mean? Here are some servant roles that have occurred to me. You and your class will think of others:

Introducing newcomers
Swapping pictures
Listening to each others' stories
Finding out basic data: where people are from, what they do for a living, etc.
Telling jokes

All of these are fairly superficial, but they are the necessary steps we must go through before we can get to deeper servanthood and the bearing of each others' real burdens (Galatians 6:2).

Developing the Lesson

I. Getting into the Bible story

Have your class read John 13:1-20 aloud, either together or taking turns. Then try to imagine the physical setting. There may not have been a table, as in Leonardo da Vinci's painting. They could have been seated or lying (see 13:23), supported on one elbow, in a U shape or semi-circle. If your class chooses not to wash each others' feet (and I don't think my class is going to want to), you might consider having one person simply go around the room and kneel before the other members of the class. If the class is small enough, each person could take a turn doing this. Even this simple act would help them get a feel for the awkwardness of assuming the posture of servanthood in the presence of others.

Go over any difficulties that you or any class members may have in understanding the text. Make sure each person understands Peter's reluctance in verses 6-9.

II. Symbol or Sacrament

Discuss the relationship between foot washing and the sacraments of baptism and the Lord's Supper. Ask whether any members of your class grew up in a community where foot washing is considered to be a sacrament. If class members agree that we shouldn't practice foot washing on a regular basis, do they think it might be a good thing to do on some occasions? Discuss the two conditions that Protestants have traditionally claimed a sacrament must meet. (See the section titled "Follow My Example.") Ask the class members if they think their marriage is a sacrament.

III. Living as servants to one another

This is, of course, the most important part of the lesson. How did Christ serve us (Matthew 10:45)? How should we serve one another? (Look at the texts listed in the section called "A Society of Foot Washers.") Ask your class members to list ways in which we can truly serve one another in our day-to-day relationships. Try to go beyond mere politeness. You may want to point out that the word usually translated "servant" in the New Testament literally means "slave."

Helping Class Members Act

Establish a list of rules for good servants. Suggest that the class members think of these rules as guidelines they can practice until the rules become automatic. Below is starter list; use some of the suggestions if you want to get the discussion going, but it will be best if you can elicit ideas from the class.

1. I will learn to quit talking so much and do a better job of listening. And I'll try to listen with a spiritual ear—that is, I will listen not only to the words that are being said, but also to the deepest feelings that are being expressed.
2. I won't ask anyone, "How are you?" unless I am really willing to listen to all of his or her troubles.
3. I will say to myself at least once a day, "How can I help?" and then try to do it.
4. I will try to make all the people I meet feel that I respect them as persons by spiritually washing their feet—that is, making them welcome.
5. I will mentally carry a towel and basin with me—that is, I will keep in mind constantly the fact that the role of servant is honorable. I will not grovel, but will be eager to help.

Planning for Next Sunday

Next Sunday is Easter, the celebration of the Lord's resurrection. Ask your class to read the account of Mary Magdalene in the garden and to think about this question: "Do I really believe in the Resurrection?" If the answer to that question is yes, then ask the next question: "Why am I not a more joyful person?"

"He's Back!"*

William H. Willimon

You know, don't you, that there are people who argue that we gather in our churches on Easter morning out of a collective wish projection. Here's how the argument goes: We just can't accept the fact that creatures so wonderful as us should die, that there will be a day when we, as well as all those we love, will be no more. So we fantasize about some inexplicable reversal of everything we know about life (namely, that it is terminal), which enables people who have once lived and died to live again. We want to live forever, so we project our wish as reality.

I call this idea, propagated with great subtlety by philosophers like Feuerbach, "The Tinkerbell Theory of Religion." Do you remember how, in the stage version of *Peter Pan,* Tinkerbell for some reason fades away and can be resuscitated only if all the people in the theater close their eyes and believe very hard in fairies?

"Do you believe in fairies, boys and girls? Say you do," pleads Peter Pan. "Believe in fairies, and they will be true."

Thus someone has called the resurrection the most selfish of all Christian doctrines. We Christians just cannot get it through our heads that we shall die. So we close our eyes and, with the aid of Matthew, believe in the resurrection.

Yet that is not at all what we claim to be celebrating on Easter, and if nonbelievers are going to dismiss us, they at least ought to do us the courtesy of rejecting what we claim to believe rather than in wasting time disbelieving what we don't believe in anyway.

Easter is not just a celebration of a general resurrection of dead people. It is certainly not about the immortality of the soul or the eternal return of the robin in the spring or other such drivel. No, Easter is about a dead Jesus, whom we helped to condemn, humiliate, torture, nail to a cross, and finally kill. This dead Jesus, who was taken down from the cross, wrapped in linen, and entombed, this Jesus come back to us risen—risen indeed.

Jesus did not come back to us as a disembodied, ethereal "soul." He came back to us as *Jesus;* the same person who troubled us before Good Friday came back to us on Easter. His physical appearance had changed, and some people did not recognize him at first. But once the disciples had been with him a while, they agreed with the women who had run back from the cemetery: He's back. Jesus has come back for us.

If we were wishing for something, would we have wished for that? After all, Jesus gave us enough challenge in the three or four years we knew him; he said things that shook us up, so why would we have wanted *him* back? There are those who claim that the resurrection of Jesus was a myth propagated by his disciples, who had worked themselves up into such grief over his death that they just couldn't bear to let him go. So they got together and imagined that he never really died.

That's not how the story goes. He was dead. The disciples knew that he was as dead as dead.

"We weren't really all that near," said Matthew and Mark. "We told the

* Adapted from *Best Sermons 4,* James W. Cox, ed. (New York: HarperCollins Publishers, 1991), pp. 64-68.

women to go on up to the front where they could see better, but even from where we were, at the back, we could see he was dead."

More than that, the Gospels agree that all of his followers accepted his death. On Sunday, the women went out to dress Jesus' body with spices. They did not go in the hope that his death was just a bad dream or that in some way he would live on in their memories.

It was the first day of the week. People were back at work. The Jesus movement, begun with such promise, was over. None of the disciples really expected him back; what is more shocking, none of them appear to have *wanted* Jesus back. It would have been fine to have had back some disembodied phantom who murmured soothing clichés like "consider the lilies," but they had on their hands the one who worked into his sermons stuff like, "Go, sell what you have and give it to the poor" and "Anyone who loves father or mother more than me is not worthy of me." To have *that* once-dead man back on your hands on a Sunday morning was something else again. Is that why the risen Christ keeps saying to his astonished disciples, "Do not fear" and "Peace be unto you"? Isn't it interesting that the predominant emotion on the first Easter was not joy? It was *fear*. Earlier they had said, "He's dead. Now what's to become of us?" After Easter, they said, "He's back! Now what's to become of us?"

The resurrected Jesus is not a Santa Claus, returning to pat us on the head and give us what we want. But that isn't Jesus before Easter. Plenty of folk agreed with the troubled man who shouted, upon meeting Jesus for the first time, "Get out of here, Jesus of Nazareth. What have you to do with us?" And if you've been here in church on Sundays other than Easter and heard the stories about the pre-Easter Jesus, you know enough to empathize with disciples who were less than pleased to go out to the cemetery to visit the grave of a dead man, only to be encountered there by the not-at-all-dead post-Easter Christ. They were scared.

Wish projection, my eye. The real comfort comes not from believing in the resurrection of Jesus of Nazareth, but from believing that he is gone. After a decent period of mourning, we can proceed right on with business as usual, free now to be as cynical or as naively optimistic or whatever we choose to be. It really doesn't matter, because we're on our own anyway. Now, it's all up to us to figure out what to do on Monday, since our world with Jesus ended on Friday.

Let's get back to the good old status quo, back to the comfort of things as they had always been before Jesus intruded on our settled arrangements and conventional judgments. We can go on killing in El Salvador, separating the races in South Africa, having sex with other people's spouses, and all of our other death-loving ways, and who would there be to stop us, judge us, call our hand?

But if the women are right, if this thing isn't over but is just beginning, if it's Jesus again, then. . . .

> Where can I go from your spirit?
>   Or where can I flee from your
>   presence? . . .
>   If I make my bed in Sheol, you are there.
>   If I take the wings of the morning
>   and settle at the farthest limits
>   of the sea. . . .   (Psalm 139:7-9)

Surprise!

If there is one thing we fear more than the death of God, it's the fear of a god who won't stay dead, who keeps following us, hounding us, coming back to us. The disciples had come all the way out to the cemetery to show some respect for poor, dead Jesus, only to be told that he had beaten them back to town and was even now prodding and nagging them just as in the old days.

"He isn't here," said the angel. "He is risen."

I remember, as a student, seeing a play that depicted a troubled man who had spent his whole life tormented by thoughts of God, by feelings of his own inadequacy, obsessed by guilt. Finally, he determined to end it all, to at last put a stop to the voices, dreams, late-night visions, and inner torment. In the last scene, raving mad, he grabs a pistol and puts a bullet through his head.

The audience hears the explosion of the shot, and the stage goes totally dark. Then the lights come back on. The man is sprawled in the middle of the stage, pistol nearby. Behind him a man sits at a desk, and he speaks: "Gabriel, bring me the file on Smith. That's J. A. Smith."

The dead man struggles to his feet. The man at the desk speaks to him now: "Well, Mr. Smith, so much for the theatrics. Now let's get down to business. We've got all the time in the world." And the play ends.

What if the real hell of life is not that we are without God, but that we can't be rid of God? What if our business with God isn't over until he says it's over? "If I make my bed in Sheol. . . . If I take the wings of the morning . . . you are there." That is our hope. God won't leave us be in our lives—we know that.

On Easter, we know—to our surprise and even sometimes fear—that he has no intention of leaving us in death. He has come back and will come back whenever we get caught, back against the wall, dead end, whether it be all the dead ways we attempt to deal with death on our own, the dead habits and social arrangements, lies and deceits, or whether it be the death that comes on the last day of life.

"He's back!"

LESSON 6   APRIL 11

I Have Seen the Lord

Background Scripture: John 20:1-18

The Main Question

The main question for this lesson is "Why are you weeping?" It is Easter morning! Weeping itself is not a bad thing. No, God gave us tears. There is a time to weep. Jesus set the example, as we have seen. In the presence of grief, our Gospel reading tells us with the Bible's shortest sentence (John 11:35), God identified with us in our sorrow: Jesus wept. He wept when he topped the hill and saw the city (Luke 19:41), which he would have gathered under his wings as a mother hen gathers her chicks. He wept in blood in the garden (Luke 22:44; Hebrews 5:7). There is a time to weep—for Jeremiah and his kin; whenever injustice reigns, and the poor are trampled underfoot; whenever Rachel remembers her children (Matthew 3:18). It is even all right to weep for yourself and your own grief. Did not Jesus say it to the women along the Via Dolorosa: "Daughters of Jerusalem, do not weep for me, but weep for yourselves and for your children" (Luke 23:28)? There is a time for the strong to weep. Did not Jesus say, "Blessed are you who weep" (Luke 6:21)? Yes, there is a time to weep.

But this is not that time. This is Easter morning. The moon of wintertime has become the moon of the vernal equinox. The sap with which the world was made is rising once more, beyond belief, out of death, out of darkness, out of doubt, out of despair. The spoiling evolution of injustice and greed has been halted in its tracks, and time is working backward. What could not have happened has happened. This is the one day (should it not be true every Lord's day?) when we must ask ourselves and everyone who has seen the Lord, "Why weep?"

Selected Scripture

King James Version

John 20:1-16

1 The first day of the week cometh Mary Magdalene early, when it was yet dark, unto the sepulchre, and seeth the stone taken away from the sepulchre.

2 Then she runneth, and cometh to Simon Peter, and to the other disciple, whom Jesus loved, and saith unto them, They have taken away the Lord out of the sepulchre, and we know not where they have laid him.

3 Peter therefore went forth, and that other disciple, and came to the sepulchre.

4 So they ran both together: and the other disciple did outrun Peter, and came first to the sepulchre.

5 And he stooping down, and looking in, saw the linen clothes lying; yet went he not in.

6 Then cometh Simon Peter following him, and went into the sepulchre, and seeth the linen clothes lie,

7 And the napkin, that was about his head, not lying with the linen clothes, but wrapped together in a place by itself.

New Revised Standard Version

John 20:1-16

1 Early on the first day of the week, while it was still dark, Mary Magdalene came to the tomb and saw that the stone had been removed from the tomb. 2 So she ran and went to Simon Peter and the other disciple, the one whom Jesus loved, and said to them, "They have taken the Lord out of the tomb, and we do not know where they have laid him." 3 Then Peter and the other disciple set out and went toward the tomb. 4 The two were running together, but the other disciple outran Peter and reached the tomb first. 5 He bent down to look in and saw the linen wrappings lying there, but he did not go in. 6 Then Simon Peter came, following him, and went into the tomb. He saw the linen wrappings lying there, 7 and the cloth that had been on Jesus' head, not lying with the linen wrappings but rolled up in a place by itself. 8 Then the other disciple, who reached the tomb first, also went in, and he saw and believed; 9 for as yet they did not understand the scripture, that he must rise from

8 Then went in also that other disciple, which came first to the sepulchre, and he saw, and believed.

9 For as yet they knew not the scripture, that he must rise again from the dead.

10 Then the disciples went away again unto their own home.

11 But Mary stood without at the sepulchre weeping: and as she wept, she stooped down, and looked into the sepulchre,

12 And seeth two angels in white sitting, the one at the head, and the other at the feet, where the body of Jesus had lain.

13 And they say unto her, Woman, why weepest thou? She saith unto them, Because they have taken away my Lord, and I know not where they have laid him.

14 And when she had thus said, she turned herself back, and saw Jesus standing, and knew not that it was Jesus.

15 Jesus saith unto her, Woman, why weepest thou? whom seekest thou? She, supposing him to be the gardener, saith unto him, Sir, if thou have borne him hence, tell me where thou hast laid him, and I will take him away.

16 Jesus saith unto her, Mary. She turned herself, and saith unto him, Rabboni; which is to say, Master.

Key Verse: **Mary Magdalene came and told the disciples that she had seen the Lord, and that he had spoken these things unto her. (John 20:18)**

the dead. 10 Then the disciples returned to their homes.

11 But Mary stood weeping outside the tomb. As she wept, she bent over to look into the tomb; 12 and she saw two angels in white, sitting where the body of Jesus had been lying, one at the head and the other at the feet. 13 They said to her, "Woman, why are you weeping?" She said to them, "They have taken away my Lord, and I do not know where they have laid him." 14 When she had said this, she turned around and saw Jesus standing there, but she did not know that it was Jesus. 15 Jesus said to her, "Woman, why are you weeping? Whom are you looking for?" Supposing him to be the gardener, she said to him, "Sir, if you have carried him away, tell me where you have laid him, and I will take him away." 16 Jesus said to her, "Mary!" She turned and said to him in Hebrew, "Rabbouni!" (which means Teacher).

Key Verse: **Mary Magdalene went and announced to the disciples, "I have seen the Lord"; and she told them that he had said these things to her. (John 20:18)**

As You Read the Scripture

John 20:1. Three of the Gospels mention that Mary Magdalene was at the cross (Matthew 27:56, 61; Mark 15:40, 47; and John 19:25), and all four place her at the empty tomb (Matthew 28:1; Mark 16:1 [and maybe 16:9], and John's verse here). She had been an early disciple (see Luke 8:2) and has sometimes been identified with the sinful woman of Luke 7:36-50, though there is absolutely no biblical evidence for this. Her name simply means that she was from Magdala, a town near Tiberius on the western shore of the Sea of Galilee.

Verse 2. She ran to tell Peter and John what she had seen. The word *we* indicates that she was not alone, as attested by the other Gospels.

Verses 3-4. There was a lot of running that morning! They were obviously and quite properly excited.

Verse 5. But when they arrived, they were understandably reluctant to enter the tomb.

Verse 6. Not surprisingly, the impetuous Simon was the first to enter.

Verse 7. The arrangement of the grave clothes may indicate that Jesus had simply "disappeared" out of them, leaving the head linen in its logical place. This seemed to make no impression on Peter.

Verse 8. But when John saw it, he was moved to believe.

Verse 9. They had not yet seen the meaning of the Scriptures that foretold the Resurrection (see 2:22 and 12:16).

Verse 10. So they went home, apparently deeply moved but also deeply puzzled.

Verse 11. Mary, ever faithful, could not bring herself to leave her Master's grave.

Verse 12. Matthew and Mark mention only one angel, but Luke's account agrees with John.

Verse 13. Here, for the first time, our main question is asked, "Why are you weeping?" Some believe that angels cannot empathize with human emotions.

Verse 14. Was Jesus' resurrected body somehow different from his earthly one? Or did God purposely dim the disciples' spiritual vision? This is not the only place where Jesus is unrecognizable. (See Luke 24:16; John 21:4.)

Verse 15. Again our question is asked. But surely Jesus *does* understand Mary's grief. He is calling her to faith.

Verse 16. There are only two words in this conversation, but they are the words of mutual recognition, all the dialogue that is needed.

Verse 17. Apparently Jesus had not yet assumed the bodily form that he would use later to present himself to Thomas (v. 27), although we are not told that Thomas actually touched him, or to eat breakfast (21:9-13), although we are not told that Jesus actually ate anything. The notion of a resurrected body is bound to be mysterious to us. Look at the trouble Paul has in speaking of it in 1 Corinthians 15:35-50. (The body of the risen Christ may be different from the body of a Resurrected Christian.)

Verse 18. Some say that Mary Magdalene was the first apostle—that is, the first eyewitness to the Resurrection and the first to tell others of the good news (Acts 1:22),

The Scripture and the Main Question

Grief

It is gray and cold in the garden, and there is a woman there, weeping. Her name is Mary, and weeping is nothing new to her. For most of her bitter young life she has known tears: the tears of madness—rage against the inner injustice of adolescence, perhaps, or the outer injustice of a brutal society in which everyone strained under the burdens of a cruel legalism, especially a woman, even one as attractive as Mary of Magdala. Valued a little more than property, condemned to drudgery, declared "unclean"

253

once a month simply for going through her natural cycle, with a life expectancy of less than thirty years and very likely to die before then in the agony of childbirth, a woman of those days had much to weep over and little to cheer. It is no wonder that Mary fell prey to "seven demons," and that weeping so filled her days that her very name, Magdalene, became, by the mysterious process of etymology, our word *maudlin*, meaning "tearful, lugubrious, lachrymose." Medieval painters always depicted her with red and swollen eyes.

For one brief, shining moment all that had seemed to be over and gone. Out of nowhere her shining knight had come, Jesus of Nazareth. From him had come the power to rid her of the plaguing demons, and from his tenderness had come a new self-respect, for he had treated her as no man had before, as though she were a person of worth. The burden of her guilt had been lifted, and she had loved him as much, or more perhaps, as any woman had ever loved. She had poured out her life savings in expensive ointment on his feet and wiped them with her hair. (No one knows for sure that the woman of Luke 7:36-50 was Mary Magdalene, but I like to believe it.) For a few short days she had known an ecstasy that was almost enough to make up for the grief of her early years.

But now that too is gone. "I knew it," she must be saying to herself. And the old anguish overwhelmed her once more in the dark garden where she and some other women had gone to pay their last respects to their fallen Lord. Indignity had been heaped upon her heartache; not only was he dead, but the dear body was gone too, spirited away she knew not how, and there was no tangible way for her to express the outpouring of her broken heart. There was no more precious ointment to offer, only the acid of her tears.

Friends Can't Really Help

She had run for the only friends she knew: first Peter, for he had the strength, then John, for he would understand. And they too ran to see for themselves. John, the younger, arrived first at the dark maw of the tomb, but could not bring himself to go in. Peter, panting but impetuous, pushed past him into the sepulcher and saw that Mary was right—the body was gone. John, getting up his courage at last, also entered and saw—but saw more: that the grave clothes were undisturbed, as they surely would have been if the body had been carried out. By what strange sublimation had the solid flesh been spirited away? John believed—but what? Whatever their own thoughts, Peter and John were no help to Mary. They went home, leaving her there alone, Maudlin Mary, weeping her heart out in the graying garden.

The Old Demon Tries to Return

O broken soul, what will you do now? You had almost found the secret to unlock the prison against which your maddened heart now beats in vain. You had almost followed the "Pied Piper" into paradise, but the rocks have crashed together, and you are once more left outside. You had almost flown with "Peter Pan" to Never Never Land, but the magic dust has blown away, and you have landed with a thud in the mean streets. Like Cinderella, your carriage has turned once more into a pumpkin, and your proud horses have scurried away like rats in the underbrush. It's over now, you foolish dreamer. And once again the seductive fingers of the old demons clutch at you, to draw you back, to turn you once again into Mad Mary. To hell with it—*toujours gai*—there's life in the old dame yet. Dry your tears and return to reality; you have been following a phantom.

But the Truth Will Not Desert Her

Silent as dawn, and brighter, two angels are suddenly sitting in the tomb, looking at her. "Woman, why are you weeping?" they ask, in their bloodless incorporeal voices. Mary is not afraid. What are a couple of angels to one who has been possessed by seven devils? She responds almost as though it were a close encounter of the most ordinary kind: "Why do you think? Because they have taken away my Lord, and I do not know where the have laid him." And she turns to walk away into the adequate mercy of her solitude. But there is somebody else—another angel? No, a human form, probably the gardener. And he asks her the same question: "Woman, why are you weeping?" Will they not leave her alone to weep? "Look, if you know where his body is, tell me, and I'll take care of it." Still the mist of misery is in her eyes, and she is blind to her one best hope.

But then, one word, her name—the old voice, the best voice, the dead and silenced voice, alive and vibrant with the same tones that loved her once from madness loves her now from her blindness and her grief. Her heart stops for an eternity, and in the wonder of that silence she too speaks one word, a Hebrew word, "Rabboni," my dear teacher. And the tears are gone forever. When we last see her, she is moving again. Running? Skipping? Dancing? Mounting with wings like eagles? Walking without fainting, the first apostle, to sing to all the world, "I have seen the Lord."

In some Christian traditions, on Easter day there is no prayer of confession in the order of worship. For once we are forbidden to wallow in our guilt. Listen, Mary, the demons are gone. And just for today we are commanded to feel what no mortal has felt since our first ancestors fell: unequivocal, unadulterated, unqualified, unmistakable, clear, decisive, and absolute joy. We are waking from our demonic nightmare and are to process singing, as the psalmist promised:

> When the LORD restored the fortunes of Zion,
>   we were like those who dream.
> Then our mouth was filled with laughter,
>   and our tongue with shouts of joy. . . .
> Those who go out weeping,
>   bearing the seed for sowing,
> shall come home with shouts of joy,
>   carrying their sheaves.
>   (Psalm 126:1-2, 6)
> Weeping may linger for the night,
>   but joy comes with the morning.
>   (Psalm 30:5)

There *is* a time for weeping, but Easter is not the time.

THIRD QUARTER

Helping Adults Become Involved

Preparing to Teach

How do you feel about Easter? Some people dislike it because the celebration began as a pagan holiday, an old rite for the spring equinox, celebrating the goddess of the dawn. It does have some negatives attached to it, but eggs and bunny rabbits and new hats have nothing to do with us. Just as we baptized the winter solstice feast and made it Christ's birthday, so also we have made a Christian festival out of Easter. I prefer not to call this day "Easter," but "The Resurrection of the Lord."

Still others (a lot of them clergy) seem to get disgruntled at this time of the year because of all the busy activities. But that seems as silly to me as a farmer being disgruntled about harvest time! What do we think we're here for?

Let's make a covenant not to weep at Easter this year. As you prepare to teach, think of the Lord's question to Mary. Instead of being upset about next Sunday's lesson, think of it as a great glad day! We'll be better teachers if we live the thing we're trying to get across.

Follow this outline for your lesson:

> I. Mary Magdalene
> II. The evidence at the empty tomb
> III. The best news ever

Introducing the Main Question

One of the best ways to get a good discussion going on this subject is to bring up the parental admonishment, "Big girls and boys don't cry," to which most of us were subject at one time or another. Is that good counsel? Who suffers most from this, boys or girls? (We *all* suffer when emotions are repressed.) Ask the class what makes them cry, now that they are adults. Then discuss the question of appropriate versus inappropriate tears. What would your class think of my proposal for a new Sunday blue law: "Thou shalt not weep on the Lord's Day?" My point is that there should be a time when Christians can rejoice without reservation.

Developing the Lesson

I. Mary Magdalene

The "weeping saint" is an interesting character, and it would be worth some class time to reintroduce her to class members. If you have access to a good encyclopedia, you might enjoy seeing what traditions have grown up about her since the time of the New Testament. There are colleges named after her at both Oxford and Cambridge, and C. S. Lewis taught at both of them. There are towns named after her in both Mexico and New Mexico, and in Bolivia she is a river, a state, and a city. There's an island named Magdalena off the coast of Chile, and a whole group of islands in the Gulf of St. Lawrence. Authors and artists have been fascinated by her. In the musical *Jesus Christ, Superstar* she is an important character, who sings the well-known song "I Don't Know How to Love Him." Her feast day as a saint in the Roman Catholic Church is July 22.

You might ask your class members how they feel about calling her the first apostle.

II. The evidence at the empty tomb

The four Gospel writers agree on the importance of the empty tomb as being central to the faith; all four give it considerable space (see Matthew 27:57–28:10; Mark 15:42–16:8; and Luke 23:50–24:11). In order to get the whole story, we have to piece together the four accounts. In spite of some differences in detail, the stories together make a dramatic whole that, if you have time, is worth looking at. A good question for starting discussion on this might be: "In most of our churches the central visible object is a cross. Is this the most important symbol of our faith? Which is more important, the cross or the empty tomb? In other words, should we emphasize Good Friday or Easter?"

What about the reaction of the various disciples to the discovery of the empty tomb? Is there something about Mary's response to it that gives her special importance? John's account helps us to see that, of all the witnesses, she is the one who, in spite of her tears, clings most tenaciously to hope. Something about her makes me think of the verse, "Therefore, I tell you, her sins, which were many, have been forgiven; hence she has shown great love" (Luke 7:47).

III. The best news ever

Like the blind authorities in John 9:40, we fail to recognize Jesus when he is standing in our midst. Help the class to deal with those things that blind us from joy on Easter morning: Cynicism? Intellectual barriers? Preoccupation with the things of this world? The seemingly unsolvable burdens of our daily lives? Other promises that have disappointed us? Stubborn refusal to let God rule our lives?

Ask your class to say, perhaps three times to drive it home, the ancient Easter greeting:

> Leader: The Lord is risen!
> People: He is risen indeed.

Helping Class Members Act

I don't know if we can help people to act joyfully. They either will or won't. But it sometimes helps me to sing a song, such as "Rejoice, Rejoice, Believers" or "Rejoice, Ye Pure in Heart" or "Rejoice, the Lord is King." Maybe just this once we could spend the whole class period singing songs of joy. At least that would send the class members out the door rejoicing, and maybe they would keep it up for a while.

Or maybe you can get them to write down and remember the little JOY acrostic to help keep their spirits in an Easter mode:

Trust **J**esus	Love **J**esus
Trust **O**thers	Love **O**thers
Trust **Y**ourself	Love **Y**ourself

Planning for Next Sunday

Next week we will be dealing with one of the post-Resurrection appearances of our Lord. I call it "Breakfast with Jesus." Ask your class to read John 21 and then to consider the question: Have you ever experienced the presence of Jesus? And the follow up: What difference did that experience make in your life?

LESSON 7   APRIL 18

To Love Is to Serve

Background Scripture: John 21

The Main Question

Have you ever wished that you could meet Jesus personally, face to face? John 21 brings to my mind a fantasy that I should like to live out. It begins in the cold, pre-dawn air on a silent beach. To the east, across the water, just over the distant hills, a thin line of salmon-colored light is beginning to form; the day is about to break. As I look northward along the shore, I think that I can see the twinkle of firelight in the distance, and my pace quickens as I begin to walk toward it. Sure enough, as I draw closer, I can see a fire, and something is cooking on it. As the light increases, I see that there is a boat drawn up on the sand and that figures are standing around the fire, warming their hands and watching while fresh-cooked fish sizzle on the coals.

The smell of frying fish and fresh bread fills my nostrils. Everyone in the group turns to look at me as I approach. One of them speaks. "Come and have breakfast," he says. I dare not say anything. Though I have never met him before, I know who he is. It is a face that I have seen a thousand times in my prayers. It is like, but somehow not like, every attempt by an artist to portray him. It is that face upon which to look is joy itself, that fills me with such love that I know that whatever commands he makes of me I will do. I wonder what he will ask.

I said that this is a fantasy, but actually it isn't. Everyone who truly wants to see Jesus *will* see him (see Jeremiah 29:13; Luke 2:29-30; John 12:21). To look on the face of Jesus is to be filled with love, and to be filled with love is to be moved to act. What will he ask of you?

Selected Scripture

King James Version

John 21:12-22

12 Jesus saith unto them, Come and dine. And none of the disciples durst ask him, Who art thou? knowing that it was the Lord.

13 Jesus then cometh, and taketh bread, and giveth them, and fish likewise.

New Revised Standard Version

John 21:12-22

12 Jesus said to them, "Come and have breakfast." Now none of the disciples dared to ask him, "Who are you?" because they knew it was the Lord. 13 Jesus came and took the bread and gave it to them, and did the same with the fish. 14 This was

14 This is now the third time that Jesus shewed himself to his disciples, after that he was risen from the dead.

15 So when they had dined, Jesus saith to Simon Peter, Simon, son of Jonas, lovest thou me more than these? He saith unto him, Yea, Lord; thou knowest that I love thee. He saith unto him, Feed my lambs.

16 He saith to him again the second time, Simon, son of Jonas, lovest thou me? He saith unto him, Yea, Lord; thou knowest that I love thee. He saith unto him, Feed my sheep.

17 He saith unto him the third time, Simon, son of Jonas, lovest thou me? Peter was grieved because he said unto him the third time, Lovest thou me? And he said unto him, Lord, thou knowest all things; thou knowest that I love thee. Jesus saith unto him, Feed my sheep.

18 Verily, verily, I say unto thee, When thou wast young, thou girdedst thyself, and walkedst whither thou wouldest: but when thou shalt be old, thou shalt stretch forth thy hands, and another shall gird thee, and carry thee whither thou wouldest not.

19 This spake he, signifying by what death he should glorify God. And when he had spoken this, he saith unto him, Follow me.

20 Then Peter, turning about, seeth the disciple whom Jesus loved following; which also leaned on his breast at supper, and said, Lord, which is he that betrayeth thee?

21 Peter seeing him saith to Jesus, Lord, and what shall this man do?

22 Jesus saith unto him, If I will that he tarry till I come, what is that to thee? follow thou me.

Key Verse: **He saith unto him the third time, Simon, son of Jonas, lovest thou me? Peter was grieved because he said unto him the third**

now the third time that Jesus appeared to the disciples after he was raised from the dead.

15 When they had finished breakfast, Jesus said to Simon Peter, "Simon son of John, do you love me more than these?" He said to him, "Yes, Lord; you know that I love you." Jesus said to him, "Feed my lambs." 16 A second time he said to him, "Simon son of John, do you love me?" He said to him, "Yes, Lord; you know that I love you." Jesus said to him, "Tend my sheep." 17 He said to him the third time, "Simon son of John, do you love me?" Peter felt hurt because he said to him the third time, "Do you love me?" And he said to him, "Lord, you know everything; you know that I love you." Jesus said to him, "Feed my sheep. 18 Very truly, I tell you, when you were younger, you used to fasten your own belt and to go wherever you wished. But when you grow old, you will stretch out your hands, and someone else will fasten a belt around you and take you where you do not wish to go." 19 (He said this to indicate the kind of death by which he would glorify God.) After this he said to him, "Follow me."

20 Peter turned and saw the disciple whom Jesus loved following them; he was the one who had reclined next to Jesus at the supper and had said, "Lord, who is it that is going to betray you?" 21 When Peter saw him, he said to Jesus, "Lord, what about him?" 22 Jesus said to him, "If it is my will that he remain until I come, what is that to you? Follow me!"

Key Verse: **He said to him the third time, "Simon son of John, do you love me?" Peter felt hurt because he said to him the third** time, Lovest thou me? And he said unto him, Lord, thou knowest all things; thou knowest that I love thee. Jesus saith unto him, Feed my sheep. (John 21:17)

time, "Do you love me?" And he said to him, "Lord, you know everything; you know that I love you." Jesus said to him, "Feed my sheep." (John 21:17)

As You Read the Scripture

John 21. Chapters 1–20 constitute a whole, and the last two verses of chapter 20 serve as a fitting conclusion. Chapter 21 seems to be an addition, perhaps by the same author, told to confirm the pastoral appointment of Peter and to correct a misunderstanding about the fate of "the beloved disciple."

Verse 1. The Sea of Galilee (see 6:1) had begun to be called The Sea (or Lake) of Tiberius by the end of the first century because of the city of Tiberius, built on the southwest shore by Herod Antipas in honor of Tiberius Caesar, who ruled from A.D. 14–37.

Verses 2-3. It was natural that Peter would turn to his old trade during this time of uncertainty. What were the leaderless disciples to do next, not having received their commission? It was natural also that his seven friends should go with him. The two who are not named may have been disciples who were not counted among the Twelve. Biblical scholar Floyd Filson thinks that one of them was Lazarus, "whom Jesus loved."

Verse 4. Perhaps because of the faint light at dawn, and perhaps because of the same spiritual blindness that affected Mary Magdalene (20:14) and the two on the Emmaus road (Luke 24:16), the fishermen did not recognize the Lord.

Verse 5. Jesus calls them children and greets them with the standard greeting we give to every angler we meet: "Doing any good?"

Verse 6. This reminds us of Luke 5:3-7.

Verse 7. With the great catch, the light begins to dawn, first on "the disciple whom Jesus loved," who tradition says was John. Impetuous as always (see Matthew 14:28-29), Peter takes up his outer garments, which he had set aside for work, and swims to shore.

Verse 8. The others take their time with the boat.

Verses 9-14. Though there was food already on the shore, it wasn't enough for the whole group, so they added some that they had caught. The figure 153 has been played with by numerologists (Augustine noted that it is the sum of the numbers 1 through 17 and suggested that it is symbolic of the Old Covenant [10 commandments] plus the New [7 gifts of the Spirit]), but I wouldn't make too much of that sort of thing. It probably just means that there was a heck of a lot of fish!

Verses 15-17. Peter is ordered to be a pastor (one who cares for sheep). Jesus uses the words *agapao* ("to have charity for") and *phileo* ("to love as a friend") interchangeably.

Verses 18-19. Jesus foretells Peter's martyrdom.

Verses 20-23. The writer corrects the false impression that Jesus had predicted that the beloved disciple would never die. (Perhaps he *had* died at the time of this writing, and some were wondering about the accuracy of Jesus' prophecy.)

Verse 24. A scribe (most of the New Testament books were written by stenographers) or later editors confirm the accuracy of John's testimony.

Verse 25. This secondary conclusion (in addition to 20:30-31) makes it clear that the Gospels were not intended to be complete biographies, but were to set forth certain facts about Jesus that would serve to convert their hearers from unbelief to faith.

The Scripture and the Main Question

Experiencing the Lord

You could almost have predicted that Peter and his friends would have toiled all night without catching any fish. After all, this was not the first time that had happened. If we put the Gospels of Luke and John together, we will see that this happened both at the beginning and at the end of the story of Peter and Jesus. The first fish story (Luke 5:1-11) is a brief worship experience, like the call of Isaiah (Isaiah 6:1-10). Here's how I like to outline these stories, alongside the fundamental outline of Christians at worship. The acrostic derived from the outline is **GRACE.**

The Experience of Worship	Isaiah's Experience (Isaiah 6:1-10)		Peter's Experience (Luke 5:1-11)	
G **Give** glory to God	1-4	Experiencing the glory	1-7	The miraculous catch
R **Repent** of your sin	5	Acknowledge your guilt	8	"Depart from me, sinner"
A **Announce** God's absolution	6-7	Being forgiven	10a	"Don't be afraid"
C **Hear** God's call	8a	"Whom shall I send?"	10b	"Fish for folks"
E **Enlist** in God's service	8b	"Here I am, send me!"	11	They left everything

So much am I convinced that this mini-order of worship is a true description of the best experience of the holy that we can have that I use it a lot in my everyday devotions.

Without stretching it too much, this little outline can also be superimposed on the events of John 21, so that Peter's relationship with Jesus both begins and ends with a deep religious experience.

Glory to God	*Verses 1-14.* Not only does Peter experience anew the miraculous catch of fish, but this time there is added to it the even more stupendous miracle of the resurrected Christ.
Repentance	*Verse 17.* Grieved over Jesus' triple repetition of the phrase "Do you love me?" Peter is conscious of his threefold denial of his Lord.
Absolution and Call	*Verses 15-19.* Jesus, in saying three times to Peter, "Feed my sheep," grants him a threefold pardon and once again calls him into service. This call is reemphasized in the closing verse and is repeated in verse 22: "Follow me!"
Enlistment	Although there is no specific statement at the end of the Fourth Gospel about Peter's reenlistment in the service of his Lord, we have only to turn one more page in the New Testament to find, in the early chapters of the book of the Acts, clear evidence of his obedience.

All through our lives, Christ's faithful are required to repeat this pattern. We do it ritually in our church services (compare your church bulletin with this formula), and we do it daily in our going from one life experience to another, from a night with no fish to a breakfast with Jesus.

The Coming Death

One clue that we have to Peter's enlistment is Jesus' prediction concerning Peter's martyrdom. According to some traditions he was crucified in Rome, in an upside-down position, believing himself to be unworthy to die in a manner similar to that of Jesus. It has always seemed to me that John 21:18 is a good example of a verse that *can* be quoted out of its context and still make its point. It is a good verse for those of us who are getting along in years and need to face with humility our own declining powers. Someday, my children may have to put me in a nursing home, even though I may not want to go. I hope that, if that time comes, I can remember Jesus' warning to Peter.

What Is It to You?

Another sentence that will bear repeating in many other places than its context is the last part of verse 22: "What is that to you? Follow me!" That could have been said to the workers who were paid different wages in the parable in Matthew 20:1-15. Or it could have been said to one of the dinner guests who got a better seat at the banquet (Luke 14:7-11). Or to the disciples squabbling about one who would sit on Jesus' right hand in the kingdom (Matthew 20:20-28). But most of all it should be said to you and me when we have the least tinge of jealousy over some status or reward that one of our friends may receive. I think I may paste it over my mirror: "What is that to thee? Follow thou me" (KJV).

I'd be a better Christian if I thought of it every day.

"Feed My Sheep"

On second thought, I think I'll paste that verse on my mirror, for surely those words apply not only to Peter but to all of us. The bumper sticker shouldn't say, "Honk if you love Jesus." It should say, "Feed the lambs if you love Jesus." All that this wonderful Fourth Gospel has to say about the Word who is the Light of the World must ultimately be translated into our shepherding one another. It is unfortunate that we call our professional clergy pastors, which means "shepherd." There is only one true Shepherd (Psalm 23; John 10:16), and we all are called to the shepherding task. The same thing goes for the word *minister*, meaning "servant," for surely we are all called to serve. We must have professional pastors and shepherds, I suppose, as long as we live in an imperfect world, but we ought to try to put them out of their jobs by seeing to it that they are unnecessary. We should all "feed the sheep."

And that means, of course, more than providing pasture. It is a metaphor referring to all manner of things that we can do, from taking meals to shut-ins to teaching a person to read. Three times, Jesus asks each of us, "Do you love me?" If we answer in the affirmative, I hear him saying, "Then get to work." Ever since I was a small boy I have disliked those words. They smack of chores, jobs, duty, responsibility, homework, and obedience. But they are good words. And, once we set about doing them, we discover that they are fun and satisfying. I hope that when the Lord comes I will be found doing my duty (Luke 17:10).

Helping Adults Become Involved

Preparing to Teach

Read carefully through the twenty-first chapter of John, trying to picture it as an actual event. I've done something of that sort in my fantasy under "The Main Question." What sounds, sights, smells, and the like come to your mind? Ask yourself if you have ever experienced the presence of Jesus in your life. What were the circumstances? This week you are going to encourage your class members to think of their own encounters with the Lord and the consequences of those meetings. It will help for you to do your thinking about this ahead of time.

Today's lesson outline:

> I. Grace
> II. Christ's commands to us
> III. To follow Jesus

Introducing the Main Question

Some class members have a hard time talking about anything so intimate as an experience with the Lord. I have found that they can be eased into it by giving them something a little more comfortable to deal with first.

Divide the class into twos, preferably so that people are paired with those they may not know well. Ask them to take one minute each to tell each other why they have come to the class today. Then, when the two minutes are up, spend a few minutes getting the pairs to report, in one word or phrase, while you write on the board, their reasons for being there. You might get answers like: "My children made me come"; "I need to do regular Bible study"; "I like the fellowship of this class"; "It's a life-long habit."

After they have broken the ice, so to speak, with this sharing, ask them to share a time when they have felt that Jesus or God or the Holy Spirit was very close to them. Then share in a word or two with the whole group those situations. Answers such as these might surface: "At a special conference or worship experience"; "During a time of great tragedy in our family"; "When I was in the armed services"; "During a walk through the woods."

Finally, ask them these questions: "What difference did that experience make in your life? How were you changed by it?"

This exercise will take approximately fifteen minutes. Use the rest of your time dealing with the study outline below.

Developing the Lesson

I. Grace

I like my little five-step outline for summarizing an encounter with the Lord, but you don't have to use it. If you do, you may want to make copies of the outline under "Experiencing the Lord" and let your class see if it applies at all to their own experiences. It is not necessary for all these steps to be present or for them to happen exactly in the order I have outlined, but something of God's greatness, our inadequacy, and our empowerment ought to be present. Perhaps one of the many experiences your class members have had will serve as a model on which you can spend a good bit of discussion time.

II. Christ's commands to us

A. *Feed my sheep.* The most obvious of the commands, repeated three times to Peter, is "Feed my sheep." In what sense are we all called to be pastors or shepherds? Do we leave this too much to our professional shepherds? What does it mean to feed the lambs of God? Ask your class members for suggestions here, but be prepared to offer some of your own. The most obvious one that comes to me is *literal* feeding. In what ways are your class members involved in this? Feeding their own children? Serving meals at the church? Feeding the poor? Taking meals to shut-ins?

After you have discussed actual acts of feeding, ask if the class thinks Jesus meant these instructions to Peter in a broader, spiritual sense. How can we feed people with something other than food? You may want to look at some of the discussion of the Bread of Life in chapter 6. Here are a few tips about feeding:

> speaking a good word about Jesus;
> teaching the Scriptures;
> being a loving and supportive friend;
> calling on those in need;
> simply being a Christian, living like Christ in the midst of the world, through your life-style, attitude, and example.

B. *Follow me.* This command is given twice to Peter, once meaning simply, "Walk down the beach with me a little way; I want to talk to you privately" (v. 19). The second time Jesus clearly refers to Peter's responsibility to do his duty no matter what others may be doing or what rewards they may appear to be receiving (v. 22).

III. To follow Jesus

In discussing this subject, you may find it helpful to ask your class, "Have you ever felt that you didn't get the recognition you deserved for some act of faithfulness on your part? If so, what should your response be?" (Some wag has suggested that happiness is doing a good deed and not telling anybody about it, but having everybody find out about it anyway.) The old Sunday school question is worth asking one more time, for we need to think of it daily: What does it mean to follow Jesus?

Helping Class Members Act

In a way, this section is superfluous this week because the whole point of the lesson is to help class members act. Maybe this week you and your class would like to consider planning a joint project that will enable you to follow Jesus and to feed his sheep. Is there a program in your community for feeding the homeless? Could you take part in it? Could you start one? Your class may have ideas.

Planning for Next Sunday

Next week's lesson has to do with feeding ourselves on the Bread of Life. We must do this before we can feed others. Ask class members to read John 6 with these questions in mind: "Would I have been one of those who wanted that Bread always? Would I have been one who found Jesus' saying too hard? Would I have stuck with Jesus, as the Twelve did?"

LESSON 8   APRIL 25

The Bread of Life

Background Scripture: John 6

The Main Question

"Well, what are you hanging around for?"

There is a scene in Herman Wouk's novel *The Caine Mutiny* in which Willie Keith, a ship's executive officer, has taken over the ship following an enemy attack that caused the captain to abandon ship.

Only Ensign Farrington remains on the bridge, leaning against the flagbag, wiping his eyes with his sleeve. Willie says harshly, "What's holding you back?"

"After you, sir." The ensign's pale face was smeared with black, and he grinned half in fright and half in boyish enjoyment.

There are times when it doesn't pay to desert your leader.

I am continually impressed, in writing these introductions called "The Main Question," at how often the question itself is asked in the Scripture passage, plainly and simply. In the case of John 6, it is Jesus who asks the question of the disciples, and so, ultimately of us: "Do you also wish go away?" (v. 67).

To that, Simon Peter answers, "Lord, to whom can we go? You have the words of eternal life" (v. 68). What will we answer? What if everybody in the world deserted the Church? Would you stick around? What if the going all of a sudden became tougher than you had ever believed it would? What if God (unmistakably) appeared before you and said, "My child, I'm a failure after all," would that be a time to desert? Where else could we go? The Scripture calls us to make our ultimate commitment. How shall we answer?

Selected Scripture

King James Version	New Revised Standard Version
John 6:35-51	*John 6:35-51*
35 And Jesus said unto them, I am the bread of life: he that cometh to me shall never hunger; and he that believeth on me shall never thirst.	35 Jesus said to them, "I am the bread of life. Whoever comes to me will never be hungry, and whoever believes in me will never be thirsty.

36 But I said unto you, That ye also have seen me, and believe not.

37 All that the Father giveth me shall come to me; and him that cometh to me I will in no wise cast out.

38 For I came down from heaven, not to do mine own will, but the will of him that sent me.

39 And this is the Father's will which hath sent me, that of all which he hath given me I should lose nothing, but should raise it up again at the last day.

40 And this is the will of him that sent me, that every one which seeth the Son, and believeth on him, may have everlasting life: and I will raise him up at the last day.

41 The Jews then murmured at him, because he said, I am the bread which came down from heaven.

42 And they said, Is not this Jesus, the son of Joseph, whose father and mother we know? how is it then that he saith, I came down from heaven?

43 Jesus therefore answered and said unto them, Murmur not among yourselves.

44 No man can come to me, except the Father which hath sent me draw him: and I will raise him up at the last day.

45 It is written in the prophets, And they shall be all taught of God. Every man therefore that hath heard, and hath learned of the Father, cometh unto me.

46 Not that any man hath seen the Father, save he which is of God, he hath seen the Father.

47 Verily, verily, I say unto you, He that believeth on me hath everlasting life.

48 I am that bread of life.

49 Your fathers did eat manna in the wilderness, and are dead.

50 This is the bread which cometh down from heaven, that a man may eat thereof, and not die.

51 I am the living bread which came down from heaven: if any man

36 But I said to you that you have seen me and yet do not believe. 37 Everything that the Father gives me will come to me, and anyone who comes to me I will never drive away; 38 for I have come down from heaven, not to do my own will, but the will of him who sent me. 39 And this is the will of him who sent me, that I should lose nothing of all that he has given me, but raise it up on the last day. 40 This is indeed the will of my Father, that all who see the Son and believe in him may have eternal life; and I will raise them up on the last day."

41 Then the Jews began to complain about him because he said, "I am the bread that came down from heaven." 42 They were saying, "Is not this Jesus, the son of Joseph, whose father and mother we know? How can he now say, 'I have come down from heaven'?" 43 Jesus answered them, "Do not complain among yourselves. 44 No one can come to me unless drawn by the Father who sent me; and I will raise that person up on the last day. 45 It is written in the prophets, 'And they shall all be taught by God.' Everyone who has heard and learned from the Father comes to me. 46 Not that anyone has seen the Father except the one who is from God; he has seen the Father. 47 Very truly, I tell you, whoever believes has eternal life. 48 I am the bread of life. 49 Your ancestors ate the manna in the wilderness, and they died. 50 This is the bread that comes down from heaven, so that one may eat of it and not die. 51 I am the living bread that came down from heaven. Whoever eats of this bread will live forever; and the bread that I will give for the life of the world is my flesh."

eat of this bread, he shall live for
ever: and the bread that I will give is
my flesh, which I will give for the life
of the world.

Key Verse: **I am the living bread
which came down from heaven: if
any man eat of this bread, he shall
live for ever: and the bread that I
will give is my flesh, which I will
give for the life of the world. (John
6:51)**

Key Verse: **I am the living bread
that came down from heaven. Whoever eats of this bread will live
forever; and the bread that I will
give for the life of the world is my
flesh. (John 6:51)**

As You Read the Scripture

John 6:1-13. This passage should be compared with other accounts of this
event, or others like it, in Matthew 14:13-21; 15:32-39; Mark 6:32-44;
8:1-10; and Luke 9:10-17. The feeding of the multitude is one of only a few
stories about Jesus that are found in all four of the Gospels. It is Passover
time (v. 4), and, for once, Jesus has not chosen to celebrate it in Jerusalem.
At the next Passover, he *will* go there and face the end of his life. The
multitude has followed him because of the healings he has performed.

Jesus tests Philip and the others by asking a simple question: "How can we
feed this crowd?" In reply, Philip points out that they do not have the money
to handle such a multitude. Two hundred denarii is a difficult amount for
us to translate into contemporary dollars. The New Revised Standard
Version indicates that a denarius was the usual day's wage for a laborer (see
Matthew 20:1-16). In the United States, as I write this, a day's pay at
minimum wage would be around thirty-four dollars before taxes. So Philip
is talking about a lot of money. He's saying, in effect, "You couldn't feed this
crowd for six thousand dollars!" It's doubtful that there was enough money
in the disciples' purse (John 13:29) for such an undertaking.

Andrew's suggestion that "there is a boy here . . . " is, on the face of it,
equally useless. But Jesus does not hesitate. Instead, he multiplies the gifts
of the boy into plenitude, so much so that there is a considerable surplus left
over (v. 13).

Verses 14-15. The reaction of the crowd is to identify Jesus with the
expected prophet, like Moses (see the promise in Deuteronomy 18:15-18)
or like Elijah (Malachi 4:5). Surely Jesus is feeding them much the same as
Moses fed their ancestors (Exodus 16). They try to make him king, for there
were also political expectations of the promised one, who would be not only
like Moses but also like David, as the promised Messiah/King of Psalm 2 and
numerous other references (such as Zechariah 9:9).

Verses 16-20. Another supernatural event (see Matthew 14:22-27 and
Mark 6:45-51).

Verses 22-25. Because of Jesus' signs, the crowd continues to grow.

Verses 26-34. Jesus perceives that they are following him for the physical
food and that they miss the spiritual significance.

Verses 35-40. Jesus explains what the true Bread means.

Verses 41-51. Again taken literally, Jesus repeats that "the bread of life"
refers to something deeper than mere manna.

Verses 52-59. Still they take him literally and interpret what he says about

267

eating his flesh as a kind of cannibalism. By now, the running argument has moved indoors to the Capernaum synagogue.

Verses 60-66. Even some of the disciples find this talk of eating flesh and drinking blood too hard.

Verses 67-71. When the question is put to the Twelve, Peter, their spokesman, makes a confession of faith (see Matthew 16:16; Mark 8:29; John 1:41), and the faithful few, including Judas, continue to stick by their leader.

The Scripture and the Main Question

Free Bread

Most of us grew up singing the old gospel song "Guide Me, O Thou Great Jehovah," with the earnest repeated line, "Bread of heaven, feed me till I want no more." And we love to picture the Shepherd leading us to green pastures and beside still waters. But do we really want the diet that our Savior plans for us? (See Matthew 20:22-23.) Like the multitude in John 6, James and John don't fully realize what following Christ will lead to. The crowd is thinking of free bread; Jesus knows that the cross is just around the corner.

Throughout the Gospel of John, Jesus is at pains not to attract too much attention to himself with his miracles, lest people follow him for the wrong reasons (see Luke 5:14-16 and many other such accounts). As children, we may have a naïve view of God as a kind of security blanket or umbrella to whom we turn in stormy times. Of course, we should turn to God when times are tough and ask for help whenever we need it. But sometimes the tough times come from God, who calls us to walk not only in the green pastures, but also through the valley of deep darkness. It is one thing to follow the gentle Jesus, friend of children, and quite another to eat the solid food of Christian maturity (see Hebrews 5:14). The diet to which Christ calls us may be more than we have bargained for.

When Jesus first entered Jerusalem, "the large crowd was listening to him with delight" (Mark 12:37). However, at the end of that week, when he faced the hostility of the authorities, these same people were calling for his crucifixion (Mark 15:13). We must be careful that we follow Jesus for something more than a miraculous handout.

Literalism

There is nothing more difficult to talk about than literalism, for we are almost certain to be misunderstood. Consider the following dialogue between a seminary professor and a student:

Professor: I believe in the virgin birth, but I do not think that such a miracle can be reduced to purely biological terms.
Student: I don't see how you can say you don't believe in the virgin birth when. . . .

The student heard exactly the opposite of what the teacher was saying. Perhaps there is no way the two of them will ever understand each other.

This is always a problem when we deal with matters so high that they transcend human understanding. How can we expect to put such concepts as the creation, the Trinity, the virgin birth, or the mystery of bread and wine made into Christ's body and blood into language that will easily communicate between us? Not even Jesus could do it. Notice that three times in John 6 Jesus is taken literally when he meant to be understood spiritually. (Please note that Jesus *did* mean his literal words to be true, but that there was more truth in them than the people realized.)

	What the People Heard	What Jesus Meant
Verse 31	Jesus can multiply bread!	I have given you a sign.
Verse 41	He claims to have come directly from heaven.	I have spiritual bread to give you.
Verse 52	He wants us to eat him!	I am the living bread; and I will die for you.

Of course, we are to take Jesus literally, but we need not think that we have understood what he has said to us if we do not take him spiritually as well.

A profound thought is present in this chapter, as profound as the mysterious talk about Jesus as Word in John 1—and that is the thought of Jesus as Bread. The two thoughts are found in the same sentence, spoken by Jesus to the tempter in Matthew 4:4 (see also the source of Jesus' quote, Deuteronomy 8:3). We are not to live by mere words, but by the living Word, Jesus Christ, and not by mere bread, but by the Bread of Life, Jesus Christ.

Many Christians see in the several stories of Jesus' feeding of the multitude a reference to the Lord's Supper (note the careful taking up of leftovers in vv. 12-13, like the pastor's handling of any remaining consecrated elements). In one sense all meals are sacraments; certainly any meal with Jesus is (see Luke 24:30-35 and John 21:9-12). But this act of multiplying the loaves and fish is more than a miraculous event; it is a sign of greater things to come, of a growing Church, motivated and empowered by the nourishment of Jesus, the Bread of Life.

Enlistment

There are times in all our lives when choices are to be made. We symbolize such a time with the act of confirmation, or "joining the church." It's easy to make such a commitment when we are young and inspired. We have to be careful not to encourage young people too much at such times, lest they commit themselves to grand schemes for their lives that they will later regret. But the commitment of Peter and the other disciples does not come at an easy time; it comes at a hard moment, when everybody else is deserting the ship. And the voice of Jesus comes, almost pleading, "Are you going to leave me, too?"

Such a time, for adults, may come only once or twice: a career decision or church leadership role decision or a decision to undertake a difficult or even perilous action in civic life. When such a time comes to us, we need to remember not only the challenge to which Christ calls us, but also the promises he makes.

Read again to verse 35: "I am the bread of life. Whoever comes to me will never be hungry, and whoever believes in me will never be thirsty."

And verse 51: "I am the living bread that came down from heaven. Whoever eats of this bread will live forever; and the bread that I will give for the life of the world is my flesh."

And verses 55-56: "For my flesh is true food and my blood is true drink. Those who eat my flesh and drink my blood abide in me, and I in them."

As hard as the saying about "flesh" and "blood" is, to those who believe it is a great comfort. We are called upon to enlist in the service of the one who has power to overcome the world. It is a challenge we dare not refuse. Jesus can take our limited resources and talents, five barley loaves and two fish, and work wonders with them. Human resources alone are meager, but the resources of God know no limits. Besides, where else can we go? Jesus alone has the words of eternal life.

Helping Adults Become Involved

Preparing to Teach

There is difficult material in this chapter, but it is not beyond our understanding. It is important that we see more than the crowds did. They were limited to a literal interpretation of the events. They saw free bread and a popular leader whom they would make king. But we must see the true bread and the true kingship of Christ, whose kingdom is not of this world. As you prepare to teach this lesson, ask yourself the question Jesus asked the Twelve: "Will you also go away?" If you are ready, as teacher, to say yes to this question, you will be more effective in asking others to give a positive answer.

The outline for today's class:

I. The feeding of the multitude
II. Taking things literally
III. Enlistment

Introducing the Main Question

I think I would start teaching this chapter from the end—that is, to begin with verses 66-71. You might briefly tell a few of the other Gospel stories that have to do with enlisting in Jesus' service, enabling your class members to take seriously the issue of commitment. You might use the events in Lesson 7 (John 21), with the commands "Feed my sheep" and "Follow me." Also remind the class of the rich young man in Mark 10:17-22, ending with its imperatives: "Go, sell, give, come, follow me." Or Luke 9:57-62, which concludes, "No one who puts a hand to the plow and looks back is fit for the kingdom of God." Or the list of excuses in Luke 14:15-24. Or Mark 1:17. There are lots of opportunities for enlistment.

After discussing the subject of loyalty with the class, perhaps by using some of the preceding stories, ask them the main question, "Will you also go away?" Point out that Jesus asked this question of his disciples, not at the beginning of his ministry, but toward the end, when his popularity had begun to wane, the conflicts with the authorities were on the increase, and the cross was becoming more and more imminent. It was one of those situations where somebody might say, "When the going gets tough, the tough get going." That's when it's hard to stick with the ship.

Developing the Lesson

I. The feeding of the multitude

The simple point of this wonderful story is that God takes our limited human resources (a few loaves and fish) and uses them to do wonderful things. Can you and your class think of examples of this in their own lives, or that of your congregation? I knew of two college students who wanted to make a real change in the life of their institution. They covenanted to pray together at a certain time and place each week. In a few weeks the number of those coming to pray had increased dramatically, and a considerable revolution eventually took place among the student body. When the church that I serve was founded, its attendance consisted of five women and one man. Eventually it grew to be the largest congregation in the denomination. (It isn't anymore; everybody has moved to the suburbs, but that's beside the point.) Is this the sort of thing that the feeding of the multitude means to your class?

II. Taking things literally

Free bread is wonderful, but this story is about more than bread. Helping your class to move beyond literalism is not going to be easy, but if you are to be true to the spirit of John 6, you need to attempt it. You might get at it by talking about Holy Communion in your church. In what sense do we *really* feed on the body and blood of Jesus Christ when we receive the elements of the Eucharist? At the time of the Reformation, the theologians got into some heavy discussions about what it meant to say of the bread, "This is the body of Christ." Some Christians take a very literal view of it and are very protective of the elements themselves, especially after they have been served, lest Christ's body be profaned. Others think of it as merely a memorial service in which the elements are purely symbolic. Most Protestants hold to a view somewhat in between these, called by some "The Doctrine of the Real Presence," meaning that Christ is really present somehow, though not physically, in the bread and the cup. How would your class members interpret this?

In the section titled "Literalism," I have suggested what I think Jesus was trying to say in his discourses about the Bread of Life. Ask your class what Jesus' words mean, particularly in verses 27, 33, 35, and 51. What is the food that perishes, and what is the food that endures? What is the bread that comes down from heaven? Is it really true that if we believe in Jesus we will never hunger or thirst?

III. Enlistment

All this time we have been talking about how things are getting difficult and how everybody seems to be deserting the ship. And we seem to be asking ourselves to make a *hard* commitment. But is it really all that hard? When I got married, I made a pretty tough promise to stick by my wife "in joy and in sorrow, in plenty and in want, in sickness and in health." At the time, I thought I was making a great sacrifice. But the truth is that I was receiving a great blessing. As I look back on our nearly forty years of marriage I am certain that what I thought was a sacrifice was really a gift.

I think that is what Jesus is telling us here. He *has* given us a hard saying. But his promises are true, and his rewards are great.

Helping Class Members Act

Close the class this week by saying a prayer of dedication based on Peter's confession. Here's my attempt at writing one:

Lord Jesus, to whom shall we go? You have the words of eternal life, and we have believed and have come to know that you are the Holy One of God. We commit ourselves to you and to your service. Feed us, we pray, on the living Bread. Slake our thirst with living Water. Empower us to live as you would have us live, to follow you, to feed your sheep, and to serve you all the days of our lives. Amen.

Feel free to use that prayer. Better still, have your class adapt it to fit your needs, or write another. Then pray it together as an act of enlistment in Christ's service.

Planning for Next Sunday

Ask the class members to read John 1:19-34, keeping in mind the question, "To whom (or what) does my life point?"

UNIT III: JOHN: BELIEVE IN JESUS

FIVE LESSONS   MAY 2–30

This last unit helps us to deepen our belief as we see Jesus through the eyes of those with whom he came in contact. Lesson 9 describes the actions and words of John the Baptist, who serves as a model, pointing not to himself but to Christ. In Lesson 10 we are taught how to be natural witnesses in our daily lives, through the example of some of Jesus' first followers, who invited others to "come and see." Lesson 11 introduces us to a familiar figure: the woman at the well, who helps us to look at how we react to the Lord when we encounter him in our daily tasks. Lesson 12 helps us to deal with opposition to our faith, through Jesus' own example and that of Nicodemus, whose discipleship proves costly. Finally, in Lesson 13 we deal with what is the favorite passage in all the Bible for many people. We conclude our study with a chance to deepen our faith and to learn what it means to have the genuine peace that passes all understanding.

The Witness of John the Baptist

Background Scripture: John 1:19-34

The Main Question

A few years ago, a full-page advertisement, consisting of only two things, appeared in a national magazine: a photograph of a very expensive bottle of whiskey and the caption beneath it, "Honor thyself." Disregarding the use of King James-sounding language, which makes the ad sound a little like a biblical injunction, consider the philosophy that lies behind such an appeal. It is what we may call the attitude of "looking out for number one." There is a prooftext for such a philosophy in the non-existent Heretic's Bible: "Those who toot not their own horns hear no tooting thereof" (Hezekiah 4:32).

There is no question that we live in a society that has a me-first attitude. People are enjoined to win friends and influence people by wearing the latest designs, using the proper sprays and colognes, and attending all the right seminars on assertiveness training. On a local radio station I periodically hear an ad for a restaurant that uses a jingle proclaiming, "I want to be seen at the (name of restaurant deleted)." We want to be noticed, admired, loved, and paid well. If we don't look out for number one, who will?

Of course, there is a kind of self-assertion that is worthwhile. It *is* important for us to feel good about ourselves. Some minority groups or labor unions *ought* to be more aggressive in standing up for their rights. But fundamentally, the best heroes point not at themselves, but at someone else. John the Baptist, hero of today's lesson, tells us that there is someone who ranks before him. He points not to himself, but to another. And that is our question: To whom do we point?

Selected Scripture

King James Version

John 1:19-34

19 And this is the record of John, when the Jews sent priests and Levites from Jerusalem to ask him, Who art thou?

20 And he confessed, and denied not; but confessed, I am not the Christ.

21 And they asked him, What then? Art thou Elias? And he saith, I am not. Art thou that prophet? And he answered, No.

22 Then said they unto him, Who

New Revised Standard Version

John 1:19-34

19 This is the testimony given by John when the Jews sent priests and Levites from Jerusalem to ask him, "Who are you?" 20 He confessed and did not deny it, but confessed, "I am not the Messiah." 21 And they asked him, "What then? Are you Elijah?" He said, "I am not." "Are you the prophet?" He answered, "No." 22 Then they said to him, "Who are you? Let us have an answer for those who sent us. What

art thou? that we may give an answer to them that sent us. What sayest thou of thyself?

23 He said, I am the voice of one crying in the wilderness, Make straight the way of the Lord, as said the prophet Esaias.

24 And they which were sent were of the Pharisees.

25 And they asked him, and said unto him, Why baptizest thou then, if thou be not that Christ, nor Elias, neither that prophet?

26 John answered them, saying, I baptize with water: but there standeth one among you, whom ye know not;

27 He it is, who coming after me is preferred before me, whose shoe's latchet I am not worthy to unloose.

28 These things were done in Bethabara beyond Jordan, where John was baptizing.

29 The next day John seeth Jesus coming unto him, and saith, Behold the Lamb of God, which taketh away the sin of the world.

30 This is he of whom I said, After me cometh a man which is preferred before me: for he was before me.

31 And I knew him not: but that he should be made manifest to Israel, therefore am I come baptizing with water.

32 And John bare record, saying, I saw the Spirit descending from heaven like a dove, and it abode upon him.

33 And I knew him not: but he that sent me to baptize with water, the same said unto me, Upon whom thou shalt see the Spirit descending, and remaining on him, the same is he which baptizeth with the Holy Ghost.

34 And I saw, and bare record that this is the Son of God.

Key Verse: And I saw, and bare record that this is the Son of God. (John 1:34)

do you say about yourself?" 23 He said,

"I am the voice of one crying out in the wilderness,

'Make straight the way of the Lord,' "

as the prophet Isaiah said.

24 Now they had been sent from the Pharisees. 25 They asked him, "Why then are you baptizing if you are neither the Messiah, nor Elijah, nor the prophet?" 26 John answered them, "I baptize with water. Among you stands one whom you do not know, 27 the one who is coming after me; I am not worthy to untie the thong of his sandal." 28 This took place in Bethany across the Jordan where John was baptizing.

29 The next day he saw Jesus coming toward him and declared, "Here is the Lamb of God who takes away the sin of the world! 30 This is he of whom I said, 'After me comes a man who ranks ahead of me because he was before me.' 31 I myself did not know him; but I came baptizing with water for this reason, that he might be revealed to Israel." 32 And John testified, "I saw the Spirit descending from heaven like a dove, and it remained on him. 33 I myself did not know him, but the one who sent me to baptize with water said to me, 'He on whom you see the Spirit descend and remain is the one who baptizes with the Holy Spirit.' 34 And I myself have seen and have testified that this is the Son of God."

Key Verse: And I myself have seen and have testified that this is the Son of God. (John 1:34)

As You Read the Scripture

John 1:19. For more about John the Baptist, read Mark 1:1-11 and the corresponding passages in Matthew and Luke. John's Gospel often uses the name "the Jews" in a special sense. In its usual meaning the name (which means "those of the tribe of Judah" or "inhabitants of Judea") refers to all the citizens of Israel. In that sense, John, Jesus, and their disciples were all Jews. But here, and in most places, the author of the Gospel of John uses the name to mean the Jewish authorities. We might translate verse 19 to read: "When the authorities in Jerusalem sent. . . . " The priests and Levites (assistants to the priests) were the logical people to conduct such an investigation. It is no wonder that the authorities were curious; John is a curious person. According to the other Gospels, he dressed like a "hippie"—that is, he rebelled against the typical social order. His clothing was coarse camel's hair, in contrast to the soft wool of societal dress, and his meals were a simple high protein and natural sweet diet of grasshoppers and honey. He ranted and raved in the wilderness and called for repentance. No wonder the authorities were saying, "Who is this person?"

Verses 20-21. John refuses to apply to himself either the title of Messiah (Christ)—that is "the anointed one"—or prophet (Deuteronomy 18:15) or Elijah (Malachi 4:5).

Verses 22-23. Instead, he identifies himself with the "wilderness voice" of Isaiah 40:3, who is calling us to prepare the way. In other words, he is the forerunner of the Messiah.

Verses 24-28. Asked to be more specific, John the Baptist turns from his own ministry to point to another, who is greater than himself. He compares his own act of baptizing, simply one of repentance and cleansing, to a more spiritual baptism, which that other one will offer (see Matthew 3:11).

Verses 29-30. Now John specifically names Jesus (this is the first use of that name in the Gospel of John) as the one to whom he refers.

Verse 31. Probably John does not mean that he had never met Jesus, for, as Matthew 3:14 implies, he seems to know him. After all, they were cousins, and John was only about six months older than Jesus (see Luke 1:36-56). Perhaps he means that at first he did not recognize the truth of Jesus' Messiahship, but that it has now been revealed to him.

Verses 32-34. This spiritual insight is confirmed by the visible sign of the descending dove (the Holy Spirit), so that John is now able to say confidently, "This is the Son of God." It is remarkable that John could so identify Jesus, because in many ways the two men were very different. John and his disciples lived an ascetic and almost antisocial life, in contrast to the genial social habits of Jesus, who came "eating and drinking," and freely associating with people of all classes (See Matthew 9:14 and Luke 7:33-35). Later (Luke 7:18-23), John seems to have had some doubts about Jesus, but Jesus has strong good words to say about John (Luke 7:24-30). He even identifies John with Elijah (Matthew 11:14) in spite of John's refusal to give that title to himself (John 1:21). The fact is that the two men played off each other in a powerful and creative way. Ultimately they both died for their faith, and they are remembered because both pointed beyond themselves.

THIRD QUARTER

The Scripture and the Main Question

A Wild Man

In one sense, John the Baptist is a hard person to like. He thunders and rails in the desert. He sternly demands repentance on the part of common people and rulers. (Repentance means more than mere sorrow for one's sins; it means a complete turning around of one's life.) He called the Pharisees and Sadducees (who, to their credit, came to him to be baptized) a "brood of vipers" (Matthew 3:7). You wouldn't want John for a nextdoor neighbor. But then, he wouldn't have been, for he chose the desert as his home, eschewing the comforts of civilization, preferring to live a hermit's existence and demanding that the world come out to see him.

Yet, his popularity was so great that the authorities feared to deny his authenticity (see Matthew 21:26). People went out in droves to hear this wild man preach (Matthew 3:4) and to submit to his strange rite of baptism (Matthew 3:5). He didn't invent baptism; ceremonial rites of washing were frequent among the Jews, some of them prescribed in the Old Testament (Exodus 29:4, for example), and there is evidence that in later Judaism it was the practice to baptize converts. But it was a new thing for John's day, as was his revival of the old custom of prophesying, and it caught on. There must have been a heavy load of guilt pressing down upon the people in those days, along with the oppressive load of the Roman conquerors. People were saying to one another, "We are doing something wrong. We need to change." The country was ripe for revival. Now comes this desert denouncer, and his words of judgment strike a chord in the troubled people. There is a great buzz among them. "Can this really be the Christ? Has God at last sent the great prophet? Let us go and see."

True Greatness

John illustrates well the strange paradox in life that I call Catch One. He is at once visible and invisible. He is visible in the sense that he dresses funny and attracts attention way out in the wilderness. But he is invisible in that he has no press agent and does no image building. He doesn't honor himself at all. His wild behavior would more likely repel than attract. His strength is that he does not rely on his own strength. His popularity arises from the fact that he points, not to himself, but to another.

As a longtime critic of "televangelism" and a dedicated prophet watcher, I can almost offer a sure-fire method of telling a false prophet from a true one. One good question to ask is this: "How much money does the televangelist charge for services?" This is merely a roundabout way of getting to the deeper question: "Is the evangelist pointing to self or to Christ?" One of the things that have kept Billy Graham going strong for forty years has been his consistent refusal to claim power for himself. "I don't heal people, God does. I didn't write the message; I'm just the delivery boy," he has said.

Catch One comes from the fact that you can't deliver the message without ringing the doorbell. You must call attention to yourself to some extent, even if it only means putting on a messenger's uniform. But uniforms don't mean importance. The doorkeeper at a fancy hotel may wear an admiral's hat and a lot of gold braid, but he or she doesn't own the hotel, but just opens the door for you and tells you where to park your car (see Psalm 84:10). The ecclesiastical dress of clergy could be thought of in something of the same way—not as a sign of authority, but as a description of function: doorkeeper or messenger. So John's camel's hair clothing does attract attention, but it is meant to point to something/someone else.

If Jesus were standing outside a window, and you wished to point him out to another, you would, of course, have to point to the window also. So John does point to himself, but beyond himself as well. So also does the Bible. We are not to worship it, but to see in it, or through it, the living Word to whom the written word points. Even Jesus points beyond himself. "Why do you call me good?" he asked the rich young man. "No one is good but God alone" (Mark 10:18). And again he said, "I do not speak on my own; but the Father who dwells in me does his works" (John 14:10). Catch One is the fact that true greatness is ultimately true humility. "The Son of Man came not to be served but to serve, and to give his life a ransom for many" (Matthew 20:28).

Pointing to Christ

Our task, then, is to aim beyond ourselves. Like John the Baptist, we are to say, "Don't look at me; look beyond me at another." We are to be like the angel of Revelation 19:10, who said, when the Evangelist fell down to worship him, "You must not do that! I am a fellow servant with you and your comrades who hold the testimony of Jesus. Worship God!" We must point beyond ourselves to Jesus.

First, we must get the attention of those we want to aim in Christ's direction. We will not do that by beating our own drum but by becoming good listeners to the people around us. Evangelism ought to be the most natural thing in the world. It should come because, in our day-to-day contact with people, we learn to share their hurt and to know their hopes and dreams. When, in this process, it becomes appropriate for us to speak openly about Jesus it will come naturally and easily. Most people would be repelled if you came up to them as a stranger, whipped out your Bible, and began making judgments about them. For John the Baptist this may have been necessary. And no doubt we need folks who dress in ways that go against contemporary fashion and who live on peculiar diets and cry in the wilderness. But, ultimately, the task of one who points to Christ is to enter into the world of others, to nurture them to the point of repentance, when they ask, as the Philippian jailer did, "What must I do to be saved?" (Acts 16:30). Then we can speak the name of Jesus.

This tactic is not meant to be manipulative. We are not to sneak slyly up on people's blind side and trick them into following Christ. Rather, like John the Baptist, we are to be an honest breath of fresh air, speaking the truth in love (Ephesians 4:15) and by our words and example offering them what they have been longing to hear. To paraphrase Ralph Waldo Emerson: If you can point people to the truth, even if you build your house in the woods or go out and preach in the desert, the world will beat a path to your door.

Helping Adults Become Involved

Preparing to Teach

Once, when I was a young preacher, I was asked to speak in a little country church in the mountains. I was pretty full of myself and had a manuscript full of erudite things that I had learned in seminary that I hoped would impress those people. But, when I walked up to the pulpit, I noticed that someone had lovingly carved into the wood, just where the minister's notes would be placed, the words of John 12:21 (KJV): "Sir, we would see Jesus." I took a deep breath, discarded my notes, and spoke for a while about what Jesus meant to me. I will never know whether that sermon was better than the one I had prepared, but ever since then, I have tried to remember that the people who come to church aren't looking to see me; they're looking to see the One toward whom I point.

That is also true of our role as Sunday school teachers. You can best prepare yourself to teach this lesson by making sure that, in presenting it, you point beyond yourself to another, whose sandals no one is worthy to unlatch. This does not mean that you aren't to do your best, you just need to remember where you are pointing. Begin by pointing to John the Baptist; if you follow him correctly, you will end by pointing to Jesus.

It would help to read all the accounts in the Gospels about John the Baptist. In addition to John 1:19-34, read 3:22-30 and 10:40-42. Then read Matthew 3:1-17; 11:1-19; 14:1-12; 17:9-13; 21:23-27; Mark 1:1-11; 6:18-29; Luke 1:5-23, 57-80; 3:1-20; and 7:18-35. If you don't have time to read all of these, at least read the selections in Matthew.

Here is an outline for this lesson:

I. Getting people's attention
II. Starting where they are
III. Pointing to Christ

Introducing the Main Question

If you try to point out something to a dog (even a pointer), the dog usually will not look in the direction you are pointing, but at your finger. The teacher or preacher who tries to point to the Scriptures in an especially interesting way is faced with the same experience. People get interested in your illustrations, or they say, "Isn't she a good teacher?" That is great, but not if the class members miss the point. Get the point? In other words, what's a good way to point to John the Baptist without pointing at yourself? You have one thing going for you here: John is a very interesting person, a real character. One method you might employ is to assign each member of your class one of the passages listed in "Preparing to Teach" above (perhaps adding Mark 11:27-33; Luke 5:33; and John 5:31-36), with instructions to look for characteristics that might describe the Baptizer. Then list on the chalkboard what the class discovers. If you have an artist or a cartoonist in your class, it would be fun to draw a picture of John. If not, you might be able to locate a picture from the children's department. The main thing is to get people to think about the wild desert man who points beyond himself to Jesus.

Developing the Lesson

I. Getting people's attention

We have already drawn a verbal picture of John. Was he showing off? Of course he did call attention to himself at first, but that was only to get their attention. It's a little like the initial words on the public address system, "May

I have your attention, please," or "Now hear this." And it's like the old joke about the veterinarian who, when asked to help break a mule, knocked it out with a two-by-four. "In dealing with mules," he explained, "you first have to get their attention."

But now that John has their attention, what does he tell them? Ask those who have been searching the Scriptures about the Baptist to deal with this. What are his basic teachings? What references can they discover in which he points beyond himself to Christ?

How should we in the Church point beyond ourselves? What methods of advertising are appropriate? Neon signs? Newspaper advertisements? What would you think of a church that advertises with a slogan like, "The Church Where You Can Feel at Home"? Should a church advertise?

II. Starting where they are

We must begin with the needs of the people. John's popularity was based on his recognition that something was wrong with the society in which he lived. As a prophet, he saw that the whole nation was in great need of repentance. Look at what we are told about John's preaching in Luke 3:10-14. When the ordinary people, disturbed by his message, asked what they should do, John gave them ordinary advice: Share your goods with the poor, be honest in your business dealings, behave ethically toward others, don't be greedy. In other words, do your best to live a morally responsible life. John's teachings are not very different from those of Jesus or from the basic rules for living found in the Old Testament. What's so special about him then? He provides his hearers with a means to change their ways, to repent and be baptized and turn to God and, more specifically, to turn to God's promised one, the Messiah. Likewise, we cannot point people to Christ until we have come to know them, gotten down in life's ditch with them, and established a trust relationship with them, so that we can then point them in the right direction.

III. Pointing to Christ

The lesson should not end with John the Baptist. Your class members should leave looking, not at themselves and not at John, but at Jesus. A dramatic ending to the class session would be to place a good picture of Jesus beside a picture of John. Then you might point to the picture of Jesus and say, "Behold, the Lamb of God who takes away the sin of the world." If you don't have a picture, you can do this with words.

Helping Class Members Act

Ask the class members to plan, during the week to come, to make an extra effort to be good inviters. This may mean inviting people to church, but surely it will mean inviting them, both by your words and your deeds, to walk in the light of Jesus Christ. Evangelism should be a natural part of our daily lives. In our day we wouldn't dress in camel's hair (although my father did when he was young), but in a way that demonstrates our true priorities. What are they?

Planning for Next Sunday

Ask the class to read John 35:1-50. Ask them to be prepared to discuss the question, "How did you first hear about Jesus Christ?"

We Have Found Him

Background Scripture: John 1:35-40

The Main Question

Have you ever been a member of a nominating committee? Or a search committee, seeking, for instance, a new director for the local Chamber of Commerce or a non-profit agency? Or have you tried to hire a new secretary? Or moved to a strange town and had to locate a physician for your family? Or served as casting director for a community play? Or needed a plumber? If so, you know how difficult it is to find the right person for a particular purpose. Many branches of the Church find their pastors through nominating committees. How would you go about such a task?

There are many standard models for finding the right person for the right job. Look in the Yellow Pages. Advertise in the newspaper. Get a list from a trade group, like the American Medical Association. But I have served on dozens of such task forces (and sometimes looked all by myself), and I am convinced that none of those standard methods is very effective. There is one method, however, that in the long run almost always has to be employed, and that is what we call "word of mouth." Even if you get a lot of applications for the job, you will still want to use the word-of-mouth method, by making contact with the applicants' references or by calling friends who might know them. There is no substitute for personal testimony, especially from someone you can trust.

How then, would a person find Jesus? That is our question for this lesson, and we will find that, one way or another, it happens through word of mouth.

Selected Scripture

King James Version	New Revised Standard Version
John 1:35-40	*John 1:35-40*
35 Again the next day after John stood, and two of his disciples;	35 The next day John again was standing with two of his disciples, 36 and as he watched Jesus walk by, he exclaimed, "Look, here is the Lamb of God!" 37 The two disciples heard him say this, and they followed Jesus. 38 When Jesus turned and saw them following, he said to them, "What are you looking for?" They said to him, "Rabbi" (which translated means Teacher), "where are you staying?" 39 He said to them, "Come and see." They came and saw where he was staying, and they remained with him that day. It was
36 And looking upon Jesus as he walked, he saith, Behold the Lamb of God!	
37 And the two disciples heard him speak, and they followed Jesus.	
38 Then Jesus turned, and saw them following, and saith unto them, What seek ye? They said unto him, Rabbi, (which is to say, being interpreted, Master,) where dwellest thou?	
39 He saith unto them, Come and see. They came and saw where he	

dwelt, and abode with him that day: for it was about the tenth hour.

40 One of the two which heard John speak, and followed him, was Andrew, Simon Peter's brother.

Key Verse: **He first findeth his own brother Simon, and saith unto him, We have found the Messias, which is, being interpreted, the Christ. (John 1:41)**

about four o'clock in the afternoon. 40 One of the two who heard John speak and followed him was Andrew, Simon Peter's brother.

Key Verse: **He first found his brother Simon and said to him, "We have found the Messiah" (which is translated Anointed). (John 1:41)**

As You Read the Scripture

John 1:35. John is, of course, John the Baptist, who had disciples, just as Jesus did. One of the two disciples mentioned here was Andrew (v. 41), and the other is traditionally identified as John, the author of this Gospel, the brother of James. If the second disciple is the author of this Gospel, he modestly refrains from identifying himself. It is too early in the story for him to use the characteristic expression "the disciple whom Jesus loved" (13:23; 19:26; 21:2, 7, 20, 24). If he was in fact John, that would account for the calling of James, so that this chapter covers half of the eventual Twelve.

Verse 36. John repeats his designation of Jesus as the Lamb of God (v. 29). It is as though he is encouraging his own followers to leave him and follow another.

Verse 37. This, in fact, they did. The Fourth Gospel's account of these disciples' early encounter with Jesus helps to explain why they responded so quickly when he called them (Matthew 1:20; Mark 1:20; and Luke 5:11).

Verse 38. Jesus, aware of them, turns and asks what they seek. They call him "Rabbi" (literally "My great one"), and ask where he is staying. According to verse 28, this would have been Bethany (not the one near Jerusalem [see chap. 11]), a site east of the Jordan.

Verse 39. "That day" was really "that evening" from about four o'clock until bedtime.

Verses 40-42. Andrew becomes the prototype of the Christian witness in calling his brother, Simon Peter. *Cephas* is the Aramaic, and *Peter* the Greek, form of our word "rock" (see Matthew 16:18).

Verse 43. Jesus decides to go to Galilee. All of the disciples mentioned in this section are from there. That they had crossed the Jordan to be with John indicates something of his appeal and of their need to search for a leader. Philip was probably one of John's disciples also.

Verse 44. Peter and Andrew lived at Capernaum, according to Mark 1:29, but here, along with Philip, they are listed as being from Bethsaida.

Verses 45-46. Nathanael (traditionally identified with Bartholomew) was from Cana (21:2). He regarded Nazareth as an insignificant town. His question, "Can anything good come out of Nazareth?" may have been a common saying in his day; it has certainly become one since then.

Verses 47-49. Nathanael continues his skepticism until Jesus reveals that he knows all about him (he does the same thing with the Samaritan woman; see 4:39), but afterwards he ecstatically gives Jesus the highest possible titles: Son of God and King of Israel.

Verse 50. "There's more to me than a little mind-reading," Jesus says in effect. In the next verse he makes reference to the story of Jacob's ladder (Genesis 28:12), and, perhaps in response to the kingly titles Nathanael gives him, he uses his favorite title for himself: Son of man, as recorded by all four Gospel writers, emphasizing his humanity.

John the Baptist has appeared at the beginning of the story, like a master of ceremonies, and has raised the curtain on Jesus, the star performer. Now John disappears from the stage. He makes one more brief appearance in the Fourth Gospel (3:22-30) and is mentioned in 4:1; 5:33-36; and 10:40-42. But he has done his work. Now he must decrease so that Jesus can increase.

The Scripture and the Main Question

Searching for Jesus

The quest takes as many forms as there are people, for we are all different. I have heard it expressed in such ways as, "I need to find meaning and purpose in my life," or "I want to change my ways and get right with God." Often it is not stated that clearly. It may simply be the recognition by someone that something is wrong. "I don't know where to turn." "I feel guilty." "My life has become unmanageable." Or simply the vague statement, "I'm not happy." Sometimes it isn't stated at all. There are people who need Jesus but do not even know that they are missing him.

The disciples we meet in John 1:35-50 are clearly already in a search mode. They have begun to follow John the Baptist. They are young men, and some of them, we know from other Gospel accounts, are fishermen. We can surmise from what we know about the history of the little nation in which they lived that the times were hard economically and politically. They were suffering under an oppressive regime, the conquering Roman Empire, which taxed its conquests excessively. Like residents of one of the Third World countries today, they may very well have been jealous of what they saw in other cultures that they did not have in their own. It was natural that they would be dissatisfied with their lot in life and were seeking someone to deliver them.

Moreover, as good Jews, they were believers in God and knew something of the promises of Scripture concerning their nation. They longed for the coming of the promised Messiah, foretold in their traditions. It was not only the poor fishermen who felt this way but even the Jewish leaders were looking for a deliverer and had gone out into the wilderness to see if John the Baptist could be that person (1:19). The whole nation was in a state of dissatisfaction, longing for deliverance.

The world into which Jesus came has been called by some historians "the Hellenistic era." It was a confusing and unsettling time, not unlike our own. In 334 B.C., Alexander the Great undertook the greatest military conquest up to his time. He died as a very young man, and his empire was divided among his lieutenants, but he succeeded in spreading Greek culture everywhere. Greek became the nearest thing to a universal language, much as English has become in our time due to the expansion of the British Empire in the last century. Little nations like Israel had long existed in a relatively simple environment. Of course, life had not been all *that* simple. Israel had been taken captive by other nations: Egypt, Assyria, Babylon, to name a few. But Alexander's conquests involved a shakeup of the whole known world. The new philosophies of Plato and Aristotle were spread abroad and were argued about by everyone. Mysterious religions abounded: astrology, fertility cults, Greek and Roman polytheism, and others. If you were a pious young Hebrew, it would be difficult for you to know what to believe.

During this period, that part of the Hebrew Bible known as the Wisdom Literature was collected. The Proverbs were designed to help the young stay on the straight and narrow against all these tempting ideas. The book of Job struggles with the problem of human suffering. Ecclesiastes agonizes over the apparent meaninglessness of the modern world. People needed all the help they could get, and it seems that almost everyone, especially the young disciples of John the Baptist, was searching with all his or her heart for answers to life's basic questions.

These same problems confront us today. The church that I serve is located in the heart of a city of diverse cultures, and we are busy all day long trying to help people who are searching. Not a day passes that someone does not ask for help. Sometimes the problems are easily diagnosed: poverty, drugs, mental illness, ignorance, or loneliness. But these problems are not so easily solved. How can we help these persons?

Spreading the Word

It is clear that the task of the Church is the same as that of John the Baptist and of Andrew and of Philip. Like John, we are to point to Jesus, and say "Look, here is the Lamb of God, who takes away the sin of the world." Like Andrew, we are to find our sisters and brothers, and say, "We have found the Messiah." Like Philip, we are to seek out the Nathanaels around us and say, "We have found him of whom Moses in the law and also the prophets wrote."

We cannot do this simply by shouting at them about Jesus. We cannot do it from "the top down." Evangelism is not a preacher calling down from the podium for people to come up on a level with him. It is more like one beggar saying to another, "I know where there is some bread." We are to share our bread with such seekers. In order to do this, we must become good listeners. We must identify with them in their hurt and get to know them as friends, so that they can believe us when we tell them that we have found the One who will answer their deep and disturbing questions.

How do you find Jesus? Someone tells you about him, and you must then go and see. Look at the Simons around you. Jesus can take them in their instability and give them a new name: Rock. Look at the Nathanaels around you. Jesus can show them things far more marvelous than they would have believed. And what about you and me? Who are we in this story? Are we John or Andrew or Philip, bearers of the good news? Some of the time. But we are also Simon and Nathanael, those who need a good word from a friend. That is why the Church exists, so that we can constantly be saying to one another, "Behold, the Lamb."

We will do this through the traditional methods of worship and the sacraments of prayer and preaching and Bible study. But we will also do it by going to look for people where they are. They are searching for Jesus, even if they may not know it or be able to say it. They need to hear that their sins have been forgiven, that there is great potential for good in them, that they do not have to live in the confusion of a world without direction. We will not have trouble finding them. They are our children, our nextdoor neighbors, the persons in the pew next to us, and those who knock on the church door. They sit beside us on the bus, in the next desk in school or at the office. We meet them at civic clubs and baseball games. Through the natural process of being servants to one another, we can introduce them to One who can give them a vision of angels ascending and descending the ladder that God has placed between heaven and earth.

Who Is Really Doing the Searching?

There is one other method of finding Jesus besides hearing about him by word of mouth. And it will happen no matter what you and I do. Look again at verse 43. *Jesus found Philip.* And if we will open our eyes, he will find us and say, "Follow me."

Helping Adults Become Involved

Preparing to Teach

Begin with an assumption: All the members of the class will be here this week because they are looking for something. You don't have to motivate them to want to deepen their relationship with Christ, because, if they are normal Christians, they already want to, even if they might not say so. Like Andrew and Peter and Philip and Nathanael and John and James, they are searchers. If we can bring something to them this Sunday, they will be eager to receive it. What, then, do we have to offer them?

Read the lesson for this week again. As you go over it, look for what will speak to the needs of your class. And the best way to look for that is to look for what speaks to your own needs. You might use the following suggestions or think of some of your own:

1. I am grateful to the many people who have said to me, in one way or another: "Behold, the Lamb." They include my parents, my grandparents, my pastors and teachers, my friends in Sunday school, my spouse and children, my parishioners, and the people who have come to me for counseling. There are John the Baptists and Andrews and Philips everywhere, and I am grateful for them.
2. Jesus has given me a new name (Revelation 2:17). He changed Simon's name to Peter, and he has made me into a different person. I'm willing to bet he has a new name for you. What is it?
3. Jesus knows more about me than I know about myself. As he saw Nathanael under the fig tree, he saw me before I saw him. Getting to know Jesus has helped me to understand myself better than I ever did before.

You will find other things here that speak to your condition. I think that as you begin to teach this lesson, your class will make some discoveries, too.

Today's lesson outline:

I. The basic desire of the human heart.
II. Does Jesus meet our needs?
III. Jesus calls us.

Introducing the Main Question

I have said that the main question is How can we find Jesus? Furthermore, our lesson tells us that for most disciples, someone else initially points the way. Begin by calling the attention of your class to the three introductions:

> John's: "Look, here is the Lamb of God."
> Andrew's: "We have found the Messiah."
> Philip's: "We have found him of whom Moses wrote."

Point out to the class Jesus' own invitation: "Come and see." Then let them take part in a discussion based on the question you asked them at the end of Lesson 9: "How did you first find out about Jesus?"

Developing the Lesson

I. The basic desire of the human heart.

"You have made us for yourself, O God," Augustine prayed, "so that our hearts are restless, till they rest in you."

"Our whole being," wrote C. S. Lewis, "by its very nature is one vast need . . . crying out for Him who can untie things that are now knotted together and tie up things that are still dangling loose" (*The Four Loves* [New York: Harcourt, Brace, and World, 1960], chapter 1).

"My soul thirsts for God," sang the psalmist (42:2).

You might share the preceding quotations and others that come to your mind, and then ask your class for their ways of expressing the need that lies at the heart of all of us. (In a previous lesson, I suggested that you ask your class members why they have come to Sunday school today. This would be one way of getting at our question.) After they have had a chance to talk about their needs, discuss with them the needs of the young men who became Jesus' disciples. For what had they been searching? Why had they gone out after John the Baptist? Why do you think they so quickly deserted him for Jesus? What was there in the Galilean that so appealed to them that they simply dropped their fishing nets and went with Jesus?

II. Does Jesus meet our needs?

Does Jesus speak at all to the sorts of needs the class members indicated? Are there some nets that we need to drop? In what ways can contemporary Christians turn loose of some things and follow Jesus? If the class is unable to answer that question specifically, then you may suggest to them that, for the time being, we will simply have to follow Jesus' request that we "come and see." Continue to learn more and more about the Lord by studying the Scriptures, by participating in the life of the church, by your own personal lives, and by serving him in the world. We will learn through service to him who he is.

III. Jesus calls us.

One person witnesses to us besides other disciples. That person is Jesus himself. There is a wonderful hymn that you and your class might like to sing to help drive home this truth:

> I sought the Lord, and afterward I knew
> He moved my soul to seek him, seeking me;
> It was not I that found, O Savior true;
> No, I was found of thee.

How does one find Jesus? One answer is "Wait."

Helping Class Members Act

Before sending your class members home this week, ask them to consider the role each one of them should play in pointing others to Christ. One of my congregations had an "Andrew" club, which was made up of those who regularly called on newcomers and invited them to church. In a five-year period, they found over 300 new members. But that should not be an exclusive club. We all ought to be Andrews and Philips. This will have been a successful class period if only one person leaves here and, during the week ahead, says to one other person, "Come and see." Why not challenge them with this?

Planning for Next Sunday

Next week's lesson is about a chance encounter between a man and a woman at a well. The results of that meeting completely changed the woman's life, we can surmise, and even altered the point of view of a whole town. Ask your class, as they get ready to study John 4, to be on the alert for experiences they may have in meeting people during the week. Ask them to be prepared to report on any living Water shared.

LESSON 11   MAY 16

Encountering Christ

Background Scripture: John 4:1-42

The Main Question

Brother Lawrence, it is said, felt closest to God when he was washing dishes in the monastery kitchen. In this lesson we have the story of a woman who was going about an ordinary task, carrying a water jug (and probably a considerable length of cord), to get water for the man she was living with. We do not know what thoughts may have been going through her mind; perhaps they were not too healthy, for she had a somewhat spotty past. But they may have been pious thoughts, for she was interested in the religion of her people and knew something about it. But I doubt that she was thinking much of religion at the time; probably her thoughts were the sort one usually has when going about the familiar hum-drum duties of the day. But her life is about to be changed. (By the way, can you think of another woman in the Bible who had an encounter at a well that completely changed her life? See Genesis 24:15 and the story in which it occurs.)

Jesus also is not doing anything particularly important. He is tired from a long journey and simply rests by the well. What thoughts may have been going through his mind we also do not know. He may have been praying; he may have been planning strategy for his ministry in Galilee, where he is headed. Or maybe he was just letting his mind rest, thinking about nothing in particular. But one of the special characteristics of our Lord is his ability to relate instantly and deeply to people he meets in all sorts of situations.

Have you ever met Jesus? What will happen if you do? How do you think you would react? Will you know him when you see him?

Selected Scripture

King James Version

New Revised Standard Version

John 4:7-15, 20-26

7 There cometh a woman of Samaria to draw water: Jesus saith unto her, Give me to drink.

8 (For his disciples were gone away unto the city to buy meat.)

9 Then saith the woman of Samaria unto him, How is it that thou, being a Jew, askest drink of me, which am a woman of Samaria? for the Jews have no dealings with the Samaritans.

10 Jesus answered and said unto her, If thou knewest the gift of God, and who it is that saith to thee, Give me to drink; thou wouldest have asked of him, and he would have given thee living water.

11 The woman saith unto him, Sir, thou hast nothing to draw with, and the well is deep: from whence then hast thou that living water?

12 Art thou greater than our father Jacob, which gave us the well, and drank thereof himself, and his children, and his cattle?

13 Jesus answered and said unto her, Whosoever drinketh of this water shall thirst again:

14 But whosoever drinketh of the water that I shall give him shall never thirst; but the water that I shall give him shall be in him a well of water springing up into everlasting life.

15 The woman saith unto him,

John 4:7-15, 20-26

7 A Samaritan woman came to draw water, and Jesus said to her, "Give me a drink." 8 (His disciples had gone to the city to buy food.) 9 The Samaritan woman said to him, "How is it that you, a Jew, ask a drink of me, a woman of Samaria?" (Jews do not share things in common with Samaritans.) 10 Jesus answered her, "If you knew the gift of God, and who it is that is saying to you, 'Give me a drink,' you would have asked him, and he would have given you living water." 11 The woman said to him, "Sir, you have no bucket, and the well is deep. Where do you get that living water? 12 Are you greater than our ancestor Jacob, who gave us the well, and with his sons and his flocks drank from it?" 13 Jesus said to her, "Everyone who drinks of this water will be thirsty again, 14 but those who drink of the water that I will give them will never be thirsty. The water that I will give will become in them a spring of water gushing up to eternal life." 15 The woman said to him, "Sir, give me this water, so that I may never be thirsty or have to keep coming here to draw water."

Sir, give me this water, that I thirst not, neither come hither to draw.

....

20 Our fathers worshipped in this mountain; and ye say, that in Jerusalem is the place where men ought to worship.

21 Jesus saith unto her, Woman, believe me, the hour cometh, when ye shall neither in this mountain, nor yet at Jerusalem, worship the Father.

22 Ye worship ye know not what: we know what we worship: for salvation is of the Jews.

23 But the hour cometh, and now is, when the true worshippers shall worship the Father in spirit and in truth: for the Father seeketh such to worship him.

24 God is a Spirit: and they that worship him must worship him in spirit and in truth.

25 The woman saith unto him, I know that Messias cometh, which is called Christ: when he is come, he will tell us all things.

26 Jesus saith unto her, I that speak unto thee am he.

Key Verse: **And [they] said unto the woman, Now we believe, not because of thy saying: for we have heard him ourselves, and know that this is indeed the Christ, the Saviour of the world. (John 4:42)**

....

20 Our ancestors worshiped on this mountain, but you say that the place where people must worship is in Jerusalem." 21 Jesus said to her, "Woman, believe me, the hour is coming when you will worship the Father neither on this mountain nor in Jerusalem. 22 You worship what you do not know; we worship what we know, for salvation is from the Jews. 23 But the hour is coming, and is now here, when the true worshipers will worship the Father in spirit and truth, for the Father seeks such as these to worship him. 24 God is spirit, and those who worship him must worship in spirit and truth." 25 The woman said to him, "I know that Messiah is coming" (who is called Christ). "When he comes, he will proclaim all things to us." 26 Jesus said to her, "I am he, the one who is speaking to you."

Key Verse: **They said to the woman, "It is no longer because of what you said that we believe, for we have heard for ourselves, and we know that this is truly the Savior of the world." (John 4:42)**

As You Read the Scripture

John 4:1-6. Jesus was not yet ready to confront the Pharisees; he still had work to do in educating his disciples and preparing himself for the great events, so he decided to leave Judea, where John the Baptist had been persecuted. He had to pass through Samaria, whose people were somewhat related to the Jews and followed many of their customs, including circumcision and the Jewish feasts and ordinances. However, there had been "bad blood" between the two cultures for a long time, so that Jews had no dealings with Samaritans. This hostility made Jesus' parable of the good Samaritan (Luke 10:29-37) all the more effective. (For a negative saying about these people, see Matthew 10:5, but for positive dealings with them, see Luke 17:11; Acts 1:8; and 8:5-8.) Unlike the Jews, the Samaritans accepted only the first five books of the Old Testament, and understood it to command the erection of a temple on Mt. Gerizim (Deuteronomy 11:29 and 27:12).

Jesus suffered human infirmities just as we do. (See John 11:35, 38; 19:29.)

Verses 7-15. Jacob's well is still located in the same spot; I have drunk water from it, but it wasn't easy. The level of the water is more than forty feet below ground, and one needs a pail on a long cord to get to it. Jesus fell into conversation with the Samaritan woman on the question of natural water, but what he had in mind was a deeper matter: eternal life. (*Eternal* does not mean simply "endless," but "supernatural" or "spiritual.") However, the woman takes Jesus literally.

Verses 16-18. As he had with Nathanael (1:48), Jesus gives evidence of second sight. If she will not respond to his words about the water of life, he will give her a spiritual shock by telling her the truth about herself.

Verses 19-26. Perceiving that Jesus has prophetic powers, and possibly to change the subject, the woman asks him to comment on the principal dispute between Jews and Samaritans. But he will not be drawn into it. Again he tries to lead her from the idea of a physical place of worship to the deeper concept of spiritual worship. He identifies himself as the Messiah.

Verses 27-37. The return of the disciples causes the woman to go into town, where she cannot keep the news to herself. The disciples, though astonished that Jesus should be talking with a woman (let alone a Samaritan), do not upbraid him for it. Instead they encourage him to eat and get from him a sermonette on the true harvest. Though the actual harvest is still four months off, Jesus calls them to lift up their eyes and look across the fields. He sees the Samaritans coming and knows that the gospel will spread to them.

Verses 39-42. Jesus' prediction proves true; the Samaritans are truly moved by the woman's testimony, and they beg him to stay longer, which he does. Almost, it seems, against his own best judgment (Matthew 10:5), he finds it necessary to spread the word to these semi-Gentiles. Compare his encounter with this woman to another in Matthew 15:21-28, who helped Jesus sharpen and broaden his approach. But the woman in this story has now faded into the background, and Jesus is ministering directly to the inhabitants of Sychar.

The Scripture and the Main Question

A "Chance" Encounter

We should not debate whether or not everything that happens is part of a complex divine design. One part of me says that nothing happens by accident; another part says, "God sends the sun and the rain on the good and the evil alike" (see Matthew 5:45). But this is certainly what I would call a "happening." At first, only two characters are present. (How did the disciples come to know of this conversation? Did Jesus summarize it for them when they got back? Or did John, who seemed to have a special place with Jesus, wait with him and remain silent throughout the subsequent talk? We don't know.)

I have such encounters all the time. I work in the inner city, and I have found that one of the characteristics of the city is a lot of bumping of elbows. I meet people in the post office, in the pharmacy, on the steps of the church. They encounter me when I'm out changing the letters on the bulletin board or trying to negotiate in and out of our tiny parking lot. Many times they recognize me as someone connected with the church and start a conversation with me.

A woman in line at a check-out counter in the drugstore smiled at me, so I smiled back and asked, "How are you?" She said, "Terrible! I wore the wrong color shoes this morning, and my son is in the hospital, and they don't know what is wrong with him, and they may be coming today to repossess my house." How would you have replied? "At least you have your priorities in order"? I'm ashamed to say that I was late for an appointment, so with barely appropriate words of sympathy, I made my excuses and left.

A little later, the cashier where I bought my sandwich for lunch, asked, "What's this I see in the papers about them trying to organize one super church amongst all the Protestants? Isn't that of the antichrist?" I didn't feel like arguing while my sandwich got cold. "Bullfrog burgers!" I said, or something like that. "I know those people in the Consultation on Church Union personally, and they are simply trying to help us quit fighting each other so we can get on with the business of fighting the devil." And I went out into the sunlight with my sandwich.

The drugstore and the lunch counter are the modern equivalents of the village well. I had two brushes with two human beings who had deep questions on their minds. The woman in the drugstore was simply overwhelmed by the burdens of her troubled life; the restaurant cashier was wondering, "On which modern mountain should I worship God?" Like Jesus, I was weary of my comings and goings, but, unlike Jesus, I didn't stop to listen to the voices of their hearts. I snapped answers and went about my business. I had safely avoided intimacy with two troubled people.

But that's not a very good way for a Christian to be. You never know when, as the writer of the Letter to the Hebrews said (13:2), you may be entertaining "angels unawares." I wish now that I had stayed a moment longer, and tried, to the best of my knowledge, to hear the inner cry of their souls. Just as we ought to "stop and smell the roses," so also we ought to stop and commune with Lazarus at our doorstep (Luke 16:20) or with the woman who gives us a drink of water. (By the way, did you notice that Jesus never got his drink?)

Who's Helping Whom?

One of the main reasons we need to learn to stop and listen to others is that we will be helped. You see, in this story, we are not Jesus; we are that woman. Jesus is the stranger who needs water, the woman in the drugstore, the clerk in the cafe. I can testify that when I *do* take time to stop and listen to people, when I *do* ask God to help me understand what their hearts are asking for, invariably I have been helped. Consider the story in today's Scripture passage from this reverse angle for a moment. Identify, not with Jesus, but with the woman.

She speaks: "Let me tell you what happened! I went to the well to get water, and there was a man there, and he said, 'I'm thirsty; give me a drink.' So I argued with him for a while because I could tell he was a Jew. And do you know what happened? Before I knew it he had given me something more than water, something that he called living water. I didn't understand him at first, but the more I think about it, the more I realize that, although he was asking me for something, he's the one that gave me something. My life hasn't been the same since."

Encounters with Jesus happen all the time, and we just don't notice them. There is a song about this story that has the line, "Jesus met the woman at the well." I suggest that we ought to sing, "The woman met Jesus at the well." If we want to meet Jesus, we must keep our eyes open wherever we go.

Spirit and Truth

We must not miss the theology of this chapter, which is summed up in verse 23. I divide this verse as follows:

The hour is coming, and is now. . . . In every moment, in both the present and the future, there is an opportunity for us to glorify God, no matter where we are. There is a sense in which we can never purely glorify God until the future hour comes, but there is another sense in which we must seize the day, for the hour is at hand (2 Corinthians 6:2).

When the true worshipers will worship the Father. . . . Christians are forever debating over who the true worshipers are. Sometimes we split over what constitutes the marks of the true Church. I'd like to suggest that true worshipers are those who don't waste time arguing over their own purity, but drink deeply of the pure living water that Christ gives. What difference does it make whether we get it from a faucet or a spring or a baptismal font or a river?

Will worship the Father in spirit and truth. Is this "doctrinal" truth of which Jesus is speaking? I don't think so. The woman at the well wants to argue over which is the proper mountain on which to worship. Jesus isn't concerned about that. He's concerned about whether or not we have the Spirit. And the fruit of the Spirit is love, joy, and peace (see Galatians 5:22-23).

Helping Adults Become Involved

Preparing to Teach

Jesus has a way of not answering people's questions. Consider his response to Nicodemus in John 3:3, or to those who followed him to the other side of the sea in 6:26. Instead of replying directly to the words of the Samaritan woman in this story, Jesus replies directly to the questions her heart is asking. In teaching this lesson, you should be very sensitive to the "heart questions" your class members may have. So as you prepare for this week, you might use the following prayer:

Lord, give me spiritual ears this Sunday, that I may hear the hearts of those in my class. And help me to hear my own heart, too. Grant that I may not so much seek to answer questions as to fulfill longings. Give me living water that I may drink it and thirst no more and that I may share it with those for whom I am responsible.
Amen.

Reread John 4 with an ear to the deep questions it is asking and to the deep questions your class may have.

THIRD QUARTER

Today's class outline:

I. Samaritans
II. Living water
III. Spirit and truth

Introducing the Main Question

I indicated that I think the main question for this lesson is "Will you know Jesus when you see him?" Another way to ask this question is to put it in the positive: Jesus is present in every encounter I have. In what sense is Jesus present in the encounter between teacher and class in this lesson? In the encounters between members of the class? In Matthew 25:40, Jesus says, "As you did it to one of the least of these . . . you did it to me." It is a logical step to say, "Whenever I meet one of the least of my fellow class members, I am meeting Jesus."

You might try this exercise with your class: Ask them to sit very quietly at the beginning of the period and reflect on the question "Is Jesus in this room today?" After a while, ask them what they have concluded. Some of them may suggest that he is present spiritually. Others may say, "I feel him in my heart." I think we reach our most mature Christian position when we realize that Jesus is in the person next to us. If you and your class agree with this, ask them to think about it during the lesson period and see what Jesus will have to say to you through one another.

Developing the Lesson

I. Samaritans

The term *Samaritan* has come to mean certain things to us because of our familiarity with the parable we call "the good Samaritan" (Luke 10:29-37). We need to realize that both there and in the story for today, the nationality of the main character is significant because in Jesus' time there was a strong prejudice against Samaritans. Whether there was any justification for this behavior is almost beside the point. The point for us is that not only must we expect our fellow class members to minister to us today, but also we must expect the help to come where we least expect it. Who is the most despised person in your class? (Maybe you'd better not ask that question out loud, but I'm willing to bet that somebody in your group qualifies.) *That's* the person you will want to listen to today, one of the "least of these."

It might sharpen the story for you to substitute a word for *Samaritan* in the story. You must be careful here, because it would defeat the purpose if you should mention a group and call them despised, even if they are. But, in our society, there are people we look down upon, joke about, and even discriminate against. Is there a safe way to talk about this? Perhaps you could get at it by taking a humorous approach. For instance, if you, the teacher, belong to a particular group, you could make light of your own background. If I were doing it, I could say, "Well, you Samaritans are going to have to listen to a Scot this morning." But if you're uneasy about trying this, forget it. At least help them to feel that they have much to learn from persons they may have not expected much of.

292

II. Living water

Do we really have something as precious as that to offer one another? I think we do. Every person I meet has something to offer me that is of infinite value. It may begin when that person asks me for help, saying, "Give me a drink." What's the usual response to such a question? Running to get a drink of water? Or saying, "Sorry, I've got a Sunday school class to teach"? Perhaps between the two there is a response that we can give that will indicate a genuine interest, such as, "You must be very thirsty." The first step is to identify with the person in his or her need. From that we can move to dealing with what really matters to both of us.

In the story for today, the conversation went swiftly from talking about water to speaking of the Holy Spirit. Jesus and the woman began with well-water, moved to living water, and from that to the realization that God wants us to worship in "spirit and in truth." You might read to the class my account of the two brief encounters I described in the section called "A 'Chance' Encounter" and ask them what they think I should have said in response to what was said to me. To be even more effective, ask class members to share any experiences they may have had as they considered the assignment made at the end of the last lesson. Even if none of them remembered to do this, they will have had plenty of encounters that they could share with the group now. Why not give them a chance to do this?

III. Spirit and truth

Conclude the lesson by having the class say together John 4:23. Ask them to consider what this profound statement means to them as a class and as individuals. (See my analysis of the verse in "The Scripture and the Main Question.") Help them to see that every time human beings bump into each other there are lively possibilities for the coming of the kingdom of God.

Helping Class Members Act

Well, it's time to go out into the world again. We will be meeting each other at community watering holes. Will we meet Jesus in others there? Will others meet Jesus there in us? Encourage your class to expect this to happen. If they expect it, it will.

Planning for Next Sunday

Tell them to read John 7:37-52. Point out that the living water theme will be continued there. Ask them to read it with two questions in mind: "Who is Jesus Christ?" and "Is he both Savior and Lord to me?"

Confronting the Galilean

Background Scripture: John 7:37-52

The Main Question

I would like to think that, had I lived in first-century Palestine, I would have recognized Jesus as the Messiah immediately. What if someone appeared today in your community and claimed to be the Messiah? Usually when this happens we say such folks are crazy. How, if we had been there, would we have made the decision that the Jewish authorities had to make in the story for today? By what criteria do we decide that someone is a true prophet?

Jesus had some things to say about false prophets (Matthew 7:15; 24:11, 24). In our day, we must constantly make decisions about prospective leaders. Electing a bishop, voting for a president, or selecting a teacher all involve our being able to evaluate the gifts of other persons. By what standards do we make such judgments?

Once we have decided to put our trust in someone, what are our obligations to stand up for that person when he or she is under hostile attack? Just as I like to think that I would have recognized Jesus immediately, so also I like to think that I would have stood by him courageously. But again I have to wonder. Unfortunately, like Peter, I have denied Jesus many times in my life.

The main question for us in this lesson is not so much about putting our lives on the line for Jesus as it is about our daily affirmation of Jesus' lordship in our lives. How shall we measure up?

Selected Scripture

King James Version	New Revised Standard Version

John 7:37-52

37 In the last day, that great day of the feast, Jesus stood and cried, saying, If any man thirst, let him come unto me, and drink.

38 He that believeth on me, as the scripture hath said, out of his belly shall flow rivers of living water.

39 (But this spake he of the Spirit, which they that believe on him should receive: for the Holy Ghost was not yet given; because that Jesus was not yet glorified.)

40 Many of the people therefore, when they heard this saying, said, Of a truth this is the Prophet.

41 Others said, This is the Christ.

John 7:37-52

37 On the last day of the festival, the great day, while Jesus was standing there, he cried out, "Let anyone who is thirsty come to me, 38 and let the one who believes in me drink. As the scripture has said, 'Out of the believer's heart shall flow rivers of living water.' " 39 Now he said this about the Spirit, which believers in him were to receive; for as yet there was no Spirit, because Jesus was not yet glorified.

40 When they heard these words, some in the crowd said, "This is really the prophet." 41 Others said, "This is the Messiah." But some

But some said, Shall Christ come out of Galilee?

42 Hath not the scripture said, That Christ cometh of the seed of David, and out of the town of Bethlehem, where David was?

43 So there was a division among the people because of him.

44 And some of them would have taken him; but no man laid hands on him.

45 Then came the officers to the chief priests and Pharisees; and they said unto them, Why have ye not brought him?

46 The officers answered, Never man spake like this man.

47 Then answered them the Pharisees, Are ye also deceived?

48 Have any of the rulers or of the Pharisees believed on him?

49 But this people who knoweth not the law are cursed.

50 Nicodemus saith unto them, (he that came to Jesus by night, being one of them,)

51 Doth our law judge any man, before it hear him, and know what he doeth?

52 They answered and said unto him, Art thou also of Galilee? Search, and look: for out of Galilee ariseth no prophet.

asked, "Surely the Messiah does not come from Galilee, does he? 42 Has not the scripture said that the Messiah is descended from David and comes from Bethlehem, the village where David lived?" 43 So there was a division in the crowd because of him. 44 Some of them wanted to arrest him, but no one laid hands on him.

45 Then the temple police went back to the chief priests and Pharisees, who asked them, "Why did you not arrest him?" 46 The police answered, "Never has anyone spoken like this!" 47 Then the Pharisees replied, "Surely you have not been deceived too, have you? 48 Has any one of the authorities or of the Pharisees believed in him? 49 But this crowd, which does not know the law—they are accursed." 50 Nicodemus, who had gone to Jesus before, and who was one of them, asked, 51 "Our law does not judge people without first giving them a hearing to find out what they are doing, does it?" 52 They replied, "Surely you are not also from Galilee, are you? Search and you will see that no prophet is to arise from Galilee."

Key Verse: **Others said, This is the Christ. But some said, Shall Christ come out of Galilee? (John 7:41)**

Key Verse: **Others said, "This is the Messiah." But some asked, "Surely the Messiah does not come from Galilee, does he?" (John 7:41)**

As You Read the Scripture

John 7:37. The feast (see v. 1) was Sukkot, the Feast of Booths or Tabernacles. It was instituted, according to Deuteronomy 16:13-15, in the days of Moses and served as a reminder to the people of Israel of their nomadic origin. No matter how permanent their society became, when they built houses and other buildings, they were, at least once a year at harvest time, to dwell in temporary housing, to remember that they owed everything to the grace of God, not to the labor of their hands. Some very conservative groups within Israel, such as the Rechabites (Jeremiah 25), took vows *never* to live in permanent dwellings (see Jeremiah 25:8-9). God had led them from oasis to oasis in the wilderness in the days of Moses, and they believed in trusting in God alone for their security. Jesus' reference to spiritual thirst shows that he understood the meaning of this feast.

Verse 38. Jesus continues the reference to God's living water (see also 4:13-14). It is not clear what Scripture he is quoting here. There are references to the idea in Isaiah 58:11 and other texts, such as Isaiah 44:3 and 55:1 as well as Ezekiel 47:1. The word translated "heart" is really "belly" (see KJV; it is translated "womb" in John 3:4). The belly, or bowel, in Hebrew thinking was considered the seat of the emotions. Could Jesus here be likening himself to the Temple, from which water flowed (see also Revelation 22:1)?

Verse 39. Whatever the bodily image, what Jesus is speaking of is not a literal but a spiritual gift that is to come.

Verse 40. Jesus' words impress some. The prophet was regarded as a forerunner of the Messiah (see Deuteronomy 18:15).

Verse 41. Others grant Jesus the ultimate accolade, but still others claim that Galilee is not mentioned in prophecy. (However, see Isaiah 9:1 and Matthew 4:15.)

Verse 42. They were right. (See Micah 5:2; Matthew 1:1; and Luke 2:4.)

Verses 43-44. They can't decide whether or not to arrest Jesus.

Verse 45. Without having heard Jesus, the authorities condemn him.

Verse 46. Do the officers speak of Jesus' manner or of his words? (See Matthew 7:29.)

Verses 47-49. Again the authorities argue not on the merits of Jesus, but on the credibility of the witnesses. (Compare this with their attitude toward the newly sighted blind man in 9:34.)

Verses 50-51. Nicodemus, whom we know from chapter 3 had been impressed with Jesus early, has the courage to point out what we have been saying: "You're judging without evidence." The Jewish law supports Nicodemus (see Exodus 23:1 and Deuteronomy 19:15). Nicodemus began to sneak out to see Jesus after dark (3:2); now, albeit somewhat hesitantly, he speaks out on Jesus' behalf and at the end gives evidence of total commitment as a disciple (19:39).

Verse 52. The authorities accuse Nicodemus of being a Galilean. This same charge was laid on Simon Peter (see Mark 14:70). Of course, with regard to Nicodemus, it is meant sarcastically. (By the way, there *was* a prophet from Galilee, Jonah, who was from Gath-hepher, a Galilean city; 2 Kings 14:25.)

The Scripture and the Main Question

Camping Out

The Feast of Tabernacles does for the religious life of Israel what a summer camping trip does for us in our secular life. A camping trip forces us to remember how dependent we are on things beyond ourselves: thermostats, frozen foods, microwave ovens, mattresses, screen wire, indoor plumbing, and an endless list. My father once warned me not to marry a woman until I had been on a camping trip with her. He said, "Things are one way on formal dates, eating in restaurants, and when all is well. You need to know how you will get along with each other when the bacon falls in the fire and the smoke gets in your eyes." The Feast of Tabernacles forces us to remember that we live by grace, not by our skills as farmers, carpenters, masons, and merchants. A severe earthquake could teach us the same lesson, but fortunately God doesn't often get our attention with such violence.

In the end, the Christian gospel teaches us that God's tent will be pitched in our midst (Revelation 21:3). In that city there will be no temple (Revelation 21:22). Just as in the days when the portable tabernacle went with the wandering nomads through the desert, God will be in our midst, wiping away our tears. The furniture in the old tabernacle had rings on it, through which poles could be thrust for carrying (Exodus 25:12). Contrast this with our present-day massive pulpits and altars and our pews that are bolted to the floor. (And sometimes the people are bolted to the pews.) Do you think we ought to have a Feast of Booths today? Or at least a camping trip?

In our lesson, Jesus' Galilean ministry is over. His death is impending. He has cut his roots with his family and has left the place of his childhood and youth. There has begun to take place the falling away of the crowds who once followed him (6:66) and the increasing hostile attacks from his critics among the Pharisees. From now until the end, Jesus will be more and more alone, until we find him at last, praying in the solitude of the garden while his friends sleep, and then, forsaken by all of them (Mark 14:50). So, although Jesus went to this feast, he went privately, almost reluctantly (7:8-10). But, vulnerable as he was, he spoke the truth with courage. Although his own throat may have been dry, he promised living water from his heart. And those around him, the crowds, his disciples, and the authorities had to decide once and for all what to make of him and to do with him. And so must we.

How to Spot a True Prophet

I have devised a list of ways to spot false prophets:

> Those who charge money for their prophecies (Acts 8:20).
> Those who point more to themselves than to God (Luke 3:16).
> Those who pretend to be righteous (Matthew 7:15).
> Those who are mean, not loving (Matthew 7:16).
> Those who pretend to have the secret of truth when it is really as plain as the nose on your face (Matthew 24:11, 23-27) for all to see (Matthew 11:25).

But how do you recognize a true prophet? This brief encounter, on the last day of the Feast of Tabernacles, gives us insight into a few ways we can test the validity of those who claim to have good news for us.

True prophecy will satisfy my thirst. Jesus' promise of living water (vv. 37-38) can easily be tested. Nobody needs to offer a discourse on the value of water to a thirsty desert traveler. The need is there, and the solution is obvious. Now a false prophet can *pretend* to offer what will slake your thirst. Saloon-keepers make such promises. But only the true water satisfies in the long run.

True prophecy speaks to the inner soul. I demand of the prophet that more than my head be converted. My heart (belly, bowel) has to be involved (v. 38). Not by logic or by clever tricks, but by the language of the depths of my being am I changed. This does not mean that prophecy must be illogical or irrational. Far from it. It must be *so* logical and *so* rational that it goes deeper than mere head knowledge. To use two contemporary expressions: "True prophecy moves both halves of my brain"; and "True prophecy gives me both an understanding and a gut feeling."

True prophecy is spiritual. This concept isn't so easy to handle because the word *spiritual* has so many interpretations. Not every voice that speaks to you in the night is the Holy Spirit of God. There are evil spirits as well. But the Holy Spirit can be known, just like false prophecy, by the fruit that is produced. Once a man came into our church and demanded a dollar for lunch. We might have given it to him, but this was not his first visit, and one of the officers said to him, "It would be better for you to get a job so you can feed yourself" (2 Thessalonians 3:10). With this, the man flew into a rage and cursed, shouting, "I am an angel of God! I am filled with the Spirit! How dare you refuse me?" But a woman who stood nearby said in a soft voice: "You don't sound like the Spirit to me. 'The fruit of the Spirit is love, joy, peace, patience, kindness, goodness, faithfulness, gentleness, self-control' " (see Galatians 5:22-23). And the man's anger subsided.

True prophecy rings true. Jesus *sounded* true (vv. 40, 46). Sometimes when you're fishing, you think you have a bite. But when you do have a bite, you don't think so—you know it.

Loyalty

I am so proud of Nicodemus! He began his acquaintance with Jesus in secret (3:2), but now he is developing the courage to put himself on the line (v. 50). In a way, the last true test of prophecy is not whether it satisfies one's thirst or speaks to one's heart or moves one's spirit, but whether or not one is willing to bet one's life on it. It was said of Polycarp (A.D 70–56), bishop of Smyrna, that when he stood before his captors in Rome and was told, "You are an old man. All you have to do is say of the Christians, 'Away with the atheists!' and you will be spared." So, indicating the huge crowd of Roman citizens, he said, "Away with the atheists." "No, no," they cried. "You must denounce the Christians." "Eighty and six years have I served the Lord," he said. "How then can I deny my king, who saved me?" And so he passed through death into life.

Helping Adults Become Involved

Preparing to Teach

As usual, you will have carefully read the Scripture for this week, John 7:37-52. These fifteen verses are packed full of challenge for us. We are up against the supreme question of life: What are we to make of Jesus Christ?

It has been said that while many Christians, grateful for the grace of God's forgiveness in Jesus, are eager to accept him as Savior, many of us have a hard time acknowledging him as Lord. We find it easy to say, "Thank you, Jesus, for forgiving my sins," but we do not easily say, "Lord, put me to work." I'm not sure about that. In fact, I know many Christians who are eager to be given jobs to do. But they have a hard time admitting that they need a Savior. Let's just say that *both* affirmations come hard to most of us. As a teacher, you must ask yourself at the beginning of each class, "Do I really believe?" If you do, then you will be able to help others to come to the same faith. If you don't, then they will probably see through you.

Think about each of your class members by name. Don't stand in judgment of them, but ask yourself what you can do to help them strengthen their commitment to the Lord?. First of all, you can read the Scripture passage for today; having drunk of the living water there, you will have a river of water in your own heart (gut?) to share.

The lesson outline:

I. Jesus' unpopularity
II. A true prophet
III. Loyalty

Introducing the Main Question

How much do we trust Jesus? I'd suggest that the best way to begin this class is to introduce the class members to Sukkot, the Feast of Booths. (You might invite a local rabbi to visit with your class and tell how that feast is celebrated in contemporary Judaism; that would liven things up a little.) The heart of that holiday is a realization that, no matter how accustomed we become to ordering the affairs of our own lives, we need to remind ourselves that ultimately we are entirely dependent on God. Who can add time to his or her span of life? Or keep the heart beating? Or preserve children from calamity? Or alter the stock market? Or inflation? A camping trip every now and then might help us urban types remember how much we need to implore divine help. Tell your class about Sukkot and set them searching today's lesson for answers to the question "Do we indeed affirm Jesus' lordship in our lives?"

Developing the Lesson

I. Jesus' unpopularity

During the 1940s and 50s, when I began the practice of ministry, there was a general "revival" of interest in the church in America. Membership, attendance, and contributions were up, and there was a kind of euphoria among young clergy. But, after the unsettling 1960s, things have changed. Most of the "mainline" churches in our country are experiencing decline. The me-first generation hasn't much interest in religion. Rich young dinks (double income, no kids) are so wrapped up in computers and investments that they don't seem to have time for church, and the very poor are so busy simply trying to provide food and shelter for their families that they have little leisure for theology. What are we to make of this?

Jesus, by the time we get to John 7, was no longer the popular folk hero of Mark 12:37. When his sayings were too hard, many of his disciples fell away (John 6:66). And the criticism of the authorities, who were perhaps encouraged by this, became stronger. Some of them "conspired against him, how to destroy him" (Matthew 12:14). It would not have been a happy time for Nicodemus and others like him, who had to ask themselves, "What do I really believe about this man?"

Ask your class whether it is easy, in your community, to be a committed Christian. Are there many temptations to fall away? Does Jesus really fill a great need in their lives? John 7:43 says, "There was a division in the crowd because of him." Is there such a division in our time?

II. A true prophet

In such times, prophets are put to the test. But how do you test a prophet? I have listed some tests in the section entitled "How to Spot a True Prophet," which your class may want to react to. Would they disagree with some of them? Would they like to add other tests? For me, it really boils down to a very pragmatic question: Does it work? I dislike putting my faith in Jesus into such a mundane way of speaking, but, having lived in part of eight decades I have come to the conclusion that one of the reasons I cling to my faith is that *it works!* In all of my life, whenever I have faithfully obeyed Jesus Christ as Lord, things have gone well for me, and whenever I have disobeyed him, I have gotten into trouble. Would your class members agree with this? Ask them how they put God to the test (see Malachi 3:10 and 1 John 4:1). Can we depend on Jesus? (See the words of Polycarp above.)

III. Loyalty

At the close of this lesson, tell the story of Nicodemus again, citing the three references to him in the Gospel of John. Show how he grew from timid inquirer to bold supporter to, at last, committed mourner. Ask the class to consider their own loyalty. It is ourselves we need to test, not Christ (2 Corinthians 13:5).

Helping Class Members Act

As a closing exercise, ask each member of the class to write on one side of a card (which will not be shown to anyone else) an answer (there could be many) to this question: "What does Jesus Christ mean to me?"

On the other side, they are to write the answer to this question: "In the light of what Jesus means to me, what shall I do?"

Encourage the class members to carry their cards with them for a while and see what comes of their answers.

Planning for Next Sunday

Next week's scripture passage, John 14, is many people's favorite. Encourage the class to enjoy reading it.

LESSON 13   MAY 30

The Promise of the Spirit

Background Scripture: John 14

The Main Question

One of my sons, who is a professional actor and singer, graduated from college and received a fellowship to teach first-year English at the same university, while he worked on a graduate degree. "How," I asked him, "will you be able to go from being a student one semester to being a teacher the next? Will your students respect you?" "Don't worry, Dad," he told me. "I'm a theater major. I'll *act* like a teacher!" I have since been told by other teachers that they all have to pretend to be teachers for the first few years until they begin to realize that they really are.

In fact, the same thing goes for brand-new physicians, clergy, baseball players, and auto mechanics. And for new Christians. It is one thing to walk in the presence of Jesus, to study about Jesus in Sunday school and maybe learn to give the right answers there. But it is quite another to be out in the world, attempting to live the Christian life on our own.

This wonderful chapter is Jesus' last word to us on the matter. He is leaving his disciples, and they will be on their own. But the point of his parting words is to reassure them that they (and we) will not be strictly own their own. In Matthew's telling of the story, Jesus' last words are, "And remember, I am with you always." Here Jesus tells us how that will be. It is his answer to our human question (I remember asking it of my father), "How will I know what to do when you are gone?" "You'll know," is the reply. "You'll do even greater things than I did. Because, the truth is, I won't be gone at all."

Selected Scripture

King James Version

John 14:15-27

15 If ye love me, keep my commandments.

16 And I will pray the Father, and he shall give you another Comforter, that he may abide with you for ever;

17 Even the Spirit of truth; whom the world cannot receive, because it seeth him not, neither knoweth him: but ye know him; for he dwelleth with you, and shall be in you.

18 I will not leave you comfortless: I will come to you.

19 Yet a little while, and the world seeth me no more; but ye see me: because I live, ye shall live also.

20 At that day ye shall know that I am in my Father, and ye in me, and I in you.

21 He that hath my commandments, and keepeth them, he it is that loveth me: and he that loveth me shall be loved of my Father, and I will love him, and will manifest myself to him.

22 Judas saith unto him, not

New Revised Standard Version

John 14:15-27

15 "If you love me, you will keep my commandments. 16 And I will ask the Father, and he will give you another Advocate, to be with you forever. 17 This is the Spirit of truth, whom the world cannot receive, because it neither sees him nor knows him. You know him, because he abides with you, and he will be in you.

18 "I will not leave you orphaned; I am coming to you. 19 In a little while the world will no longer see me, but you will see me; because I live, you also will live. 20 On that day you will know that I am in my Father, and you in me, and I in you. 21 They who have my commandments and keep them are those who love me; and those who love me will be loved by my Father, and I will love them and reveal myself to them." 22 Judas (not Iscariot) said to him, "Lord, how is it that you will reveal yourself to us, and not to the

Iscariot, Lord, how is it that thou wilt manifest thyself unto us, and not unto the world?

23 Jesus answered and said unto him, If a man love me, he will keep my words: and my Father will love him, and we will come unto him, and make our abode with him.

24 He that loveth me not keepeth not my sayings: and the word which ye hear is not mine, but the Father's which sent me.

25 These things have I spoken unto you, being yet present with you.

26 But the Comforter, which is the Holy Ghost, whom the Father will send in my name, he shall teach you all things, and bring all things to your remembrance, whatsoever I have said unto you.

27 Peace I leave with you, my peace I give unto you: not as the world giveth, give I unto you. Let not your heart be troubled, neither let it be afraid.

world?" 23 Jesus answered him, "Those who love me will keep my word, and my Father will love them, and we will come to them and make our home with them. 24 Whoever does not love me does not keep my words; and the word that you hear is not mine, but is from the Father who sent me.

25 "I have said these things to you while I am still with you. 26 But the Advocate, the Holy Spirit, whom the Father will send in my name, will teach you everything, and remind you of all that I have said to you. 27 Peace I leave with you; my peace I give to you. I do not give to you as the world gives. Do not let your hearts be troubled, and do not let them be afraid."

Key Verse: **But the Comforter, which is the Holy Ghost, whom the Father will send in my name, he shall teach you all things, and bring all things to your remembrance, whatsoever I have said unto you. (John 14:26)**

Key Verse: **But the Advocate, the Holy Spirit, whom the Father will send in my name, will teach you everything, and remind you of all that I have said to you. (John 14:26)**

As You Read the Scripture

John 14:1-30. There is no better place for us to conclude this study of the Fourth Gospel, for this is a favorite chapter of many persons, and certainly it is rich with more than we can deal with in one lesson.

Verses 1-3. Jesus comforts his disciples with the promise that there is a place for them in heaven. The word translated "mansions" in the King James Version and "dwelling places" in the NRSV comes from a root meaning "to remain," "to dwell," or "to abide." It also occurs in verse 23: We will "make our *home* with them," but nowhere else in the New Testament. This reminds us of another gracious promise, in Micah 4:4, that asserts that one day everyone will have a vine and a fig tree, in a secure place without fear.

Verses 4-7. Thomas (see John 11:16 and 20:25) is no doubter, nor does he lack courage. But he is a literalist, and he expects an earthly manifestation of the kingdom. Jesus helps him to see that the dwelling of which he speaks is a spiritual dwelling in heaven, not on earth, and that the *way* there is through Jesus himself. To get there, one must live by the example of, in the spirit of, and through faith in Jesus. For some time in the early days of Christianity, the movement was simply called "The Way" (see Acts 9:2; 19:9, 23; 22:4; and 24:22). John 14:26 has been used by some Christians to describe the exclusiveness of the gospel, but its intent is to open doors for us.

Verses 8-11. Jesus identifies himself with God. We cannot see the invisible God (1:18), but we can see Jesus (see also 16:38 and 15:24) and truly know what the invisible God is like.

Verses 12-13. The more we enter into the spirit of Christ, the more we too can show God to others and do great deeds.

Verse 15. Faith is translated into works, belief into ethics.

Verses 16-17. "Comforter" or "counselor" literally means "advocate" (see Romans 8:26-27).

Verses 18-24. Judas (Thaddaeus or Lebbaeus, Matthew 10:3), like Thomas and Philip, is looking for a literal manifestation, but verse 23 makes it clear that the Father, Son, and Spirit will dwell within us in the ethical and moral life of the Christian.

Verses 25-27. Though we can see neither God nor Jesus, we can and will experience the Spirit. This will bring us peace with a literal manifestation that the world cannot give. The poise and confidence with which Jesus lived, acted, and spoke can be our poise and confidence. Jesus repeats his counsel that we lift up our hearts and turn away from fear. The world cannot stop us (Matthew 16:18).

Verses 28-31. There is nothing to do but rise and get on with the business of life (v. 30b). Jesus will no longer be here in the flesh, but the world and its ruler (Satan) cannot stop him from succeeding. And insofar as we are in Christ, we will prevail. As Jesus says in John 16:33, "In the world you have tribulation; but be of good cheer, I have overcome the world."

The Scripture and the Main Question

The Peace That Passes Understanding

In Exodus 17:1-7, at a place that came to be called "Meribah" (Contention), the people found fault with Moses for bringing them out into the wilderness "to kill us with thirst." They grumbled, asking, "Is the Lord among us or not?" It was there that Moses struck the rock with his rod and brought forth a spring of water. The spring of Moses is still there, along the "King's Highway" in Jordan (I have drunk from it). I know how the Israelites felt. In the wilderness wandering that is our daily lives, we constantly wonder whether the Lord is with us.

In John 4, Jesus promised the woman at Jacob's well that he could offer her "living water" (4:10). I also understand that woman. She had lived a life of doubtful value and wondered about its purpose. In the weariness of our daily lives, we constantly wonder whether the Lord is with us.

But Jesus is Immanuel, God with us (Isaiah 7:14; Matthew 1:23), and the certainty of this fact is what makes it possible for us to keep on keeping on. If we know that God is for us, we know that whatever is against us can be overcome (Romans 8:31, 38-39). In Romans 5:1-5, Paul describes our relationship with God, through Christ, as being solid ground on which to stand, so that we can rejoice in the tribulations of life, "because God's love has been poured into our hearts through the Holy Spirit that has been given to us" (Romans 5:5). Paul summarizes this by saying, "Since we are justified by faith, we have peace with God" (v. 1).

But that peace is not the peace of this world (John 14:27). It is the peace of God, which passes all understanding (Philippians 4:7). It is, Jesus says, "My peace." The peace that the world gives, we all know and long for: freedom from fear, freedom from want, freedom of speech and religion. You will recognize those as the famous "Four Freedoms," delineated by Franklin Roosevelt during World War II to help Americans understand why we were fighting. Norman Rockwell created four famous paintings to commemorate them. However, it is said that when the president asked a group of religious leaders to comment on the four freedoms, one of them said, "Nero had them all." The Emperor Nero had religious freedom; he ordered others to worship him. He had freedom from want; he had slaves to serve him. He had freedom of speech; the emperor can say whatever he wants. And he had freedom from fear, for he was in command of the world's mightiest army. Meanwhile, the followers of Jesus could not speak their faith in public, and, like their Lord, many of them had no place to lay their heads. They experienced want and persecution and eventual martyrdom.

The world's peace means cessation of hostilities and plenty on the table. But God's peace means a relationship with Jesus Christ, who goes with us on the way, so that we can "boast in our sufferings, knowing that suffering produces endurance, and endurance produces character, and character produces hope, and hope does not disappoint us" (Romans 5:3-5). Such peace passes the world's understanding. But to those who have discovered that Jesus is the way, the truth, and the life, it is the only peace worth having.

Experiencing the Spirit

Sometimes we make the doctrine of the Holy Spirit far too complicated. It seems to worry many people. I remember a young seminarian saying to his teacher in a theology class, "I think I understand and believe in God, and I think I understand and believe in Jesus, but I don't understand the Holy Spirit." The professor said, "So you believe in a binity, then?" The young man shook his head and said, "I guess so, whatever one of those is." But the Holy Spirit is not a theological doctrine; the Holy Spirit is a person.

When I think of God the Creator and Parent of us all, the image that I have in my mind is a magnificent one. All the galaxies of the universe spread out toward infinity, all the subatomic particles spreading in toward utter minuteness, and all the exotic beings in between: mountains and fruit trees, horses and humpback whales.

When I think of God the Savior, Jesus Christ, my image is more personal. There is a face and a voice, there are words and deeds, images of a life lived at once in utter self-confidence and humility, the hero-servant. And there is also a picture of a cross and of an empty tomb.

But when I think of God the Holy Spirit, the image ceases almost altogether to be a visual one. I see neither the immensity of the universe nor a human face. I see—rather I feel—the sense of a Presence, the rustle of a breeze, invisible, from a far country, carrying with it the scent of an unnameable thing, for which I am filled with desire—sweeter than sweetness, stronger than strength, hotter than heat—the wind of God.

But that is poetic imagery, and what I am talking about is plainer than poetry, just as it is plainer than theology. I cannot put it into words, not because it is irrational, but because it is *too* rational to be pinned down by mere terminology. It is the *logos*, the word that was in the beginning, the Wind that brooded upon the waters (Genesis 1:2).

Let me try to picture it using the simplest words: Sometimes, when I am working on a difficult task, trying hard to be a good Christian, with all my limitations, a verse in the Bible or a phrase in a prayer or the touch of a friend will give me just the affirmation and support I need to enable me to go ahead and do my duty, however imperfectly. When that happens, something in me says, "God's Spirit is at work." I dare not take pride in it myself, as though it were *my* spirit. It (or better, he or she, for the Spirit is a person, not a thing) is God's Spirit, and all I can do is rejoice. The Holy Spirit is *God present* in you and me.

Helping Adults Become Involved

Preparing to Teach

Victor Frankl survived the Nazi Holocaust to become a brilliant psychiatrist. He asked himself all during his imprisonment, "What keeps me going? Why do I continue to live, with neither pleasure nor pride, when others, healthier and stronger than I, are dying?" (see Victor Frankl, *Man's Search for Meaning: An Introduction to Logotherapy* [New York: Pocket Books, 1963], p. 16). Frankl came to the conclusion that his faith in God, in the meaning and purpose of life, was what kept him going. He began to speak of "the will to meaning," and he founded a school of psychiatry called "logotherapy." Frankl said, "We can stand anything, if we understand why."

I'd like to suggest another way of putting the same thing, which I think is a clue to finding peace in the "holocaust" of our daily lives. John 14 tells us that we can stand anything, if we know Who—that is, we can overcome the world when we are not cut off from God, when we know that Jesus is with us in our tribulation (John 16:33). As you prepare to teach this final lesson on John, "the Gospel of the eagles' wings," meditate for a while on the Spirit, God with us in our daily lives (John 14:16), helping us in our prayers (Romans 8:26), convicting us of sin (John 16:8), and teaching us all that we need to know (John 14:25). Ask the Spirit to be with you as you read the Scripture, as you prepare your lesson, and as you teach the class.

Introducing the Main Question

The main question is "How can we survive in the world without Jesus?" And the answer is that we can't, but we don't have to. Start the lesson in an unexpected place. Discuss one who, like Victor Frankl, found himself cut off from all hope, the singer of Psalm 22. A psychologist once said to me, "That psalm contains all the symptoms of clinical depression." And so it does. But it also contains an affirmation of faith. Even though the psalmist feels forsaken by God, still the ringing promise comes (vv. 27-28):

> All the ends of the earth shall remember
>   and turn to the Lord;
> and all the families of the nations
>   shall worship before him.
> For dominion belongs to the Lord,
>   and he rules over the nations.

Jesus knew this scripture passage so well that he cried it out when he was dying on the cross. But he also spoke from another Psalm (31:5): "Into your hand I commit my spirit."

How could both of these words come from the same dying person? How could Psalm 23 follow immediately on the heels of Psalm 22? How is it that the people of God can know both despair and hope at the same time? Ask these questions of your class and help them to see that the answer is the Spirit, who is with us both in joy and in sorrow.

Developing the Lesson

I. Peace with God

After facing the question "How can we live in a world without Christ?" we need to ask, "How is Christ present with us?" The answer to that is tied up with our understanding of what genuine peace means. Someone once asked an African religious leader, whose country was going through perilous times, "How can you, a Christian pacifist, justify the violence that your people are engaged in?" He answered, "I am not a pacifist, I am a peace lover." I am not sure what he meant by that, but I know what I mean by it. Sometimes there *is* violence in the world, and poverty and pain and sadness. Indeed there always is. But that does not keep peace from being present. The peace that God offers is not of this world. It is not the absence of conflict. It is not a chicken in every pot. It is not escape or nirvana. Such peace is sought by substance abusers, ostriches, slug-a-beds, and suicides. God's peace is trust in the midst of tribulation.

Ask your class what peace means to them. Ask them what Jesus meant when he said, "My peace is not of this world." You might get at this by writing the word *peace* on a chalkboard or newsprint and seeing how many definitions your class will come up with. In the long run, they will have to agree that Jesus' definition is something other than ours. In verse 17 he tells us that the world is incapable of receiving the Spirit. That is why the world does not know the peace of God that passes all understanding.

II. The Holy Spirit

You might also have your class try to define what the Spirit is; write answers on the chalkboard. Each of us needs to know what the Spirit means to us. My own simplistic definition of the Trinity goes like this: The Father is God above us. The Son is God beside us. The Spirit is God within us.

I have seen a stained-glass window that has on it a design something like this (the words are in Latin, but I put them in English):

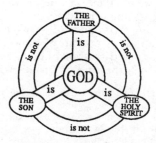

That doesn't explain anything, but it helps me think about it.

Helping Class Members Act

The action that your class members need to take in response to this lesson is actually more passive than active. They need to open themselves to the Spirit. Return to Lesson 2 (esp. John 3:8), with its metaphor of the Spirit as God's Wind. Ask whether anyone knows how to set sails. You don't have to know anything about sailing to discuss this. Just ask the class members what one needs to do to catch the wind. The means of grace are as old as the Church, but we need to hear them fresh each day: prayer, Bible reading, the sacraments, the fellowship of believers, the life of Christian service. If we do all those things, when the wind comes we will be ready.

Planning for Next Sunday

Next Sunday, your class begins a four-lesson study of Paul's Letter to the Philippians. Ask class members to begin reading this beautiful biblical book. It is not a long book, but it is full of inspiration for today's Christians.

FOURTH QUARTER
Following God's Purpose

UNIT I: JOY IN SERVING CHRIST
William H. Smith

FOUR LESSONS   JUNE 6–27

Philippians is Paul's most personal letter. As he writes to beloved friends in Christ he reveals the depths of his soul. But instead of depression, there is joy; in place of uncertainty, there is the confident affirmation that God is at work in the seemingly overwhelming events of this world: "Therefore, my brothers and sisters, whom I love and long for, my joy and crown, stand firm" (4:1). Nothing, not even the threat of death, can daunt his spirit. There is more here than the mere power of positive thinking. Paul bids his readers to "rejoice *in the Lord* always" (4:4; italics added). He who has come to us "in the form of a servant, who became obedient unto death, even death upon a cross," is the One whose glorious resurrection gives hope and courage to all who trust him. Is it any wonder that this epistle, written from prison, has become for many the favorite of Paul's letters? As the Quakers would say, "It speaks to our condition." Perennially so. And that is why in these latter days we turn to it again.

This Quarter's Writer:
Leading us through this quarter's study on selected Epistles is the Rev. Dr. William E. Smith. Dr. Smith is uniquely qualified to write this series of lessons. He is Professor of the Practice of Christian Ministry at Duke Divinity School, Durham, North Carolina, where he teaches courses in Parish Administration, Preaching, and the Church's Ministry.

Dr. Smith is a graduate of Western Maryland College and Boston University. His doctoral work was in the area of New Testament. He has taught at Boston and American Universities and Wesley Theological Seminary, where he was Vice President for four years.

Most of Dr. Smith's professional life has been spent as a campus pastor and as a parish pastor. He has served parishes in Massachusetts and in Maryland. From 1965 to 1982 he was Senior Minister of the three thousand member North Broadway United Methodist Church in Columbus, Ohio. He was later District Superintendent of the Columbus South District of the West Ohio Annual Conference of The United Methodist Church, in which he gave direction to some eighty churches and eighty-five pastors.

His writing has appeared in a number of church publications and professional journals. Dr. Smith and his wife, Mary Lou, now live in Pinehurst, North Carolina.

A Worthy Life

Background Scripture: Philippians 1:3-14, 27-30

The Main Question

Is it possible that the main threat to a vital Christian faith comes not from the outside, but from within, and that too many of us are content with casual discipleship?

In his Letter to the Philippians, Paul is writing to a community of Christians of whom he is especially fond. The Philippians were the first Europeans to be converted to Christ by Paul (Acts 16:11-15), and so close bonds were formed. Paul and his co-workers, Timothy and Titus, visited the Philippians on their travels through Macedonia. The Philippians had provided financial support for Paul's ministry in Thessalonica and Corinth. Learning of his imprisonment, they sent Epaphroditus as their personal representative with gifts to ease his burdens and companionship to comfort him. Now Epaphroditus is returning home, bringing with him this most personal of Paul's letters.

Because Paul's future is so uncertain, this may be the last time he will write to them. What do you say to dear friends in the faith whom you may never see again?

The central theme is a joy that has its foundation in Jesus Christ: "Rejoice in the Lord always; again I will say, Rejoice" (4:4). There is also a deep concern for Christian morality. They are a tiny minority in a predominantly pagan society. There are also the dangers of false teaching and internal dissension, which could further weaken their witness as Christian disciples.

We also live in a predominantly secular world where casual sex, violent crime, drug dependency, racism, and greed threaten to destroy the moral fabric of our society. The challenge of Paul is clear: Are our lives worthy of the gospel? How we answer that question, not simply in words, but in daily living, makes all the difference in the world.

Selected Scripture

King James Version	New Revised Standard Version
Philippians 1:3-14, 27-30	*Philippians 1:3-14, 27-30*
3 I thank my God upon every remembrance of you,	3 I thank my God every time I remember you, 4 constantly praying with joy in every one of my prayers for all of you, 5 because of your sharing in the gospel from the first day until now. 6 I am confident of this, that the one who began a good work among you will bring it to completion by the day of Jesus Christ. 7 It is right for me to think this way about all of you, because
4 Always in every prayer of mine for you all making request with joy,	
5 For your fellowship in the gospel from the first day until now;	
6 Being confident of this very thing, that he which hath begun a good work in you will perform it until the day of Jesus Christ:	
7 Even as it is meet for me to think	

309

this of you all, because I have you in my heart; inasmuch as both in my bonds, and in the defence and confirmation of the gospel, ye all are partakers of my grace.

8 For God is my record, how greatly I long after you all in the bowels of Jesus Christ.

9 And this I pray, that your love may abound yet more and more in knowledge and in all judgment;

10 That ye may approve things that are excellent; that ye may be sincere and without offence till the day of Christ;

11 Being filled with the fruits of righteousness, which are by Jesus Christ, unto the glory and praise of God.

12 But I would ye should understand, brethren, that the things which happened unto me have fallen out rather unto the furtherance of the gospel;

13 So that my bonds in Christ are manifest in all the palace, and in all other places;

14 And many of the brethren in the Lord, waxing confident by my bonds, are much more bold to speak the word without fear.

....

27 Only let your conversation be as it becometh the gospel of Christ: that whether I come and see you, or else be absent, I may hear of your affairs, that ye stand fast in one spirit, with one mind striving together for the faith of the gospel;

28 And in nothing terrified by your adversaries: which is to them an evident token of perdition, but to you of salvation, and that of God.

29 For unto you it is given in the behalf of Christ, not only to believe on him, but also to suffer for his sake;

30 Having the same conflict which ye saw in me, and now hear to be in me.

you hold me in your heart, for all of you share in God's grace with me, both in my imprisonment and in the defense and confirmation of the gospel. 8 For God is my witness, how I long for all of you with the compassion of Christ Jesus. 9 And this is my prayer, that your love may overflow more and more with knowledge and full insight 10 to help you to determine what is best, so that in the day of Christ you may be pure and blameless, 11 having produced the harvest of righteousness that comes through Jesus Christ for the glory and praise of God.

12 I want you to know, beloved that what has happened to me has actually helped to spread the gospel, 13 so that it has become known throughout the whole imperial guard and to everyone else that my imprisonment is for Christ; 14 and most of the brothers and sisters, having been made confident in the Lord by my imprisonment, dare to speak the word with greater boldness and without fear.

....

27 Only, live your life in a manner worthy of the gospel of Christ, so that, whether I come and see you or am absent and hear about you, I will know that you are standing firm in one spirit, striving side by side with one mind for the faith of the gospel, 28 and are in no way intimidated by your opponents. For them this is evidence of their destruction, but of your salvation. And this is God's doing. 29 For he has graciously granted you the privilege not only of believing in Christ, but of suffering for him as well— 30 since you are having the same struggle that you saw I had and now hear that I still have.

Key Verse: Only let your conversation be as it becometh the gospel of Christ: that whether I come and see you, or else be absent, I may hear of your affairs, that ye stand fast in one spirit, with one mind striving together for the faith of the gospel. (Philippians 1:27)

Key Verse: Only, live your life in a manner worthy of the gospel of Christ, so that, whether I come and see you or am absent and hear about you, I will know that you are standing firm in one spirit, striving side by side with one mind for the faith of the gospel. (Philippians 1:27)

As You Read the Scripture

Philippians 1:1-2. The salutation is warm and friendly. Paul writes on behalf of both himself and Timothy, fellow "servant" (in Greek the word means "slave") of Jesus Christ. *Saints* ("holy ones") is a term Paul uses in all his letters to refer to those who are called by and deeply committed to Christ. Bishops (overseers) and deacons suggest a well-organized congregation.

Verses 3-5. Several times Paul refers to "my God," reflecting the loneliness of his confinement and the intensity of his prayers. When he remembers the Christians at Philippi, however, joy and thanksgiving flood his soul. They are "partners in the gospel," not only because of their commitment, but because of their witness to Christ.

Verse 6 (also v. 10). "The day of Jesus Christ" is the day he will return and the present age will end. First-generation Christians held a lively hope that Christ would come again soon.

Verses 7-11. "All of you share in God's grace with me." Despite persecution and imprisonment, Paul speaks of grace—the forgiving love of Christ, which the Philippians fully share. Because they are partners, his life and theirs are inextricably united. His love for them is as strong as Christ's. He prays that they may in turn love others "with knowledge and full insight"—that is, with deliberate forethought and clear intention of turning believers into disciples.

Verses 12-13. By the grace of God, Paul's imprisonment has strengthened, rather than weakened, the cause of Christ. The "whole imperial guard" refers to Roman soldiers who were assigned to guard this controversial prisoner. It was Christ who held him captive; in that was his freedom, and the soldiers knew it. Furthermore, his courage inspired others to speak the word of God without fear. We do not know for sure where Paul was imprisoned when he wrote this letter. It could have been written from Rome at the close of his life, or earlier in Ephesus or Caesarea. We know from Acts that Paul was imprisoned briefly in Philippi, was arrested in Jerusalem, and was moved under the protection of Roman troops to Caesarea and later to Rome, where, according to tradition, he met his death during Nero's persecution in A.D. 64. There may well have been imprisonments about which we do not know. The place, however, is not most important. That he wrote the prison epistles, giving eloquent testimony to his indomitable spirit and inspiring countless Christians to stand firm in the faith, is what makes Paul more than conqueror through him who loves us (Romans 8:37). In any case, for Paul his imprisonment is "for Christ" and the final outcome is in God's hands.

Verses 27-30. Worthiness suggests merit, character, value: "Be sure that your life measures up to the high standards of the gospel of Christ." Philippi was a Roman colony that expected exemplary conduct of its citizens. Christians are answerable to an even higher ethic. United in heart and mind, the Philippian saints are to strive together in witnessing for the faith, without fear of opposition. There are allusions here of being prepared for combat (as in Ephesians 6:10-20). Such unity in Christ will be a clear token or sign that they are on the side of God, which leads to salvation, while those who oppose the gospel are headed for destruction, which in a very real sense they bring upon themselves. The powers of evil do not give up without a fight! Those who stand firm for the way of Christ inevitably encounter resistance. That is why Paul is in prison. That is why the Philippians can expect costly conflict. No cross, no crown.

The Scripture and the Main Question

Life Worthy of the Gospel of Christ

I had always heard of atheistic communism, but I also knew that there were Christians in the Soviet Union, for I met a Russian Orthodox priest here in the United States. On a visit to Russia in the mid-1980s I had the rare privilege of being reunited with a dear friend and worshiping in the Cathedral of St. Peter and St. Paul, where he is the presiding pastor. I will always remember the faces of the people as they stood, packed into the cathedral. There were both joy and awe before the presence of God. And the music, hauntingly beautiful, rose from the depths of their souls. I came away with the indelible impression that religion is indeed alive in that communist land. More recently President Mikhail Gorbachev had an audience with Pope John Paul II, whom he addressed as "Your Holiness" and declared freedom of religion to be "indispensable" for the renewing of the Soviet Union.

Early one spring physician friends of my wife and me made a professional visit to China. They insisted, over the strong objections of their tour guide, on attending a church on Easter Sunday. They were given strict instructions: They would arrive for the five A.M. service, sit in a specially reserved section of the balcony, and not make any verbal or physical contact with the Chinese. Tears ran down their faces as they heard a choir hidden from view singing, "Were you there when they crucified my Lord? . . . Were you there when they laid him in the tomb? . . . when he rose up from the grave?" The singing was in Chinese, and our friends did not understand a word, but from that moment until the "Hallelujah Chorus" at the end they celebrated with a Christian congregation in China the resurrection of Jesus Christ. As they left, those who recognized them as Americans and could speak English reached out to welcome them. "God bless," they said. "We love you." No casual Christians there.

Does Christianity thrive best in a hostile environment? So it seems. Yet the threat that Christianity is only one generation away from extinction is very real, regardless of the environment.

Paul was very conscious of the dangers of trying to witness to the Christian faith in a pagan world. Imprisoned "for Christ's sake" and faced with the real possibility of death, he wrote to the Philippians to encourage them to stand firm in the faith: "Live your life in a manner worthy of the gospel of Christ."

By contrast, how easily we assume the responsibilities of Christian discipleship. Dietrich Bonhoeffer, who died a martyr for Christ in Hitler's Germany, wrote in *The Cost of Discipleship* that most of us live by "cheap grace": "The preaching of forgiveness without requiring repentance, baptism without discipline, Communion without confession, absolution without contrition. Cheap grace is grace without discipleship, grace without the cross, grace without Jesus Christ, living and incarnate" ([New York: Macmillan, 1948], p. 38).

Partakers of Grace

We make a mistake, however, if we reduce Paul's admonitions and Bonhoeffer's judgment to a set of do's and don'ts. Outward behavior is important, but just saying no to drugs, not watching pornographic movies, and staying within the speed limit do not make me a Christian. Something very important has to happen within my soul, and keep on happening, if I am to be an "ambassador for Christ" (see 2 Corinthians 5:20).

Paul never ceases to give thanks for the transforming love of Christ in his own life and in the lives of his converts: "All of you share in God's grace with me." This is costly grace. No one could have hated the Christians more vehemently than did Saul (Paul's Hebrew name), agent of the Jewish hierarchy in hunting down and arresting the "heretic" followers of Christ. Yet it was this hate-filled zealot whom Christ confronted on the Damascus Road and called to be his apostle to the Gentiles (Acts 9:1-15). This dramatic conversion completely turned Paul around and made him into a bold, tireless witness to the love of Christ. Amazing grace! This is where morality begins—not with rules, but with a heart reconciled to God. The estrangement is over; forgiven, we are welcomed home with loving embrace, and a whole new life begins, not of servitude but joyous freedom in which, to use Paul's language, we become "slaves of righteousness." That's what Paul shared with the Philippians, and for this we rejoice.

But we do not live the Christlike life alone and detached. "There is no such thing as a solitary Christian," declared John Wesley. Our identity as Christians has its source in the community of believers we call the church. "To all the saints in Christ Jesus who are in Philippi," Paul writes—and in Atlanta, Detroit, and San Diego. A congregation is always greater than the sum of its parts. The spirit of Christ is always there, comforting, inspiring, and strengthening. Paul wanted the Philippians to know the unity in Christ that is essential to a vital church in a pagan society: "So that, whether I come and see you or am absent and hear about you, I will know that you are standing firm in one spirit, striving side by side with one mind for the faith of the gospel."

No, casual Christianity will not do. In Latin America Christians gather in hundreds of "base communities." They are very poor, and most are uneducated. They have no church building, but their meeting together in a home or a thatched-roof community center provides strength and hope to carry on. Usually one of the literate members reads a passage from the Bible. Then they discuss its meaning for their lives. Before they close they pray for one another, for the sick, and for those in jail or in any other difficulty. A priest comes every few weeks to visit and offer the sacraments. This is the Church, the Body of Christ, as it was meant to be.

FOURTH QUARTER

Witness in the World

Live your life in a manner worthy of the gospel of Christ. Transformed by the love of Christ, strengthened by our fellowship together in Christ, we are now prepared for witness in the world. It is not easy, for there is always the temptation to put ourselves first and others last. *Hubris*, the sin of pride, is as old as the Garden of Eden. Even James and John, two of Christ's most trusted disciples, were eager advocates of "me first." But then there are the Jimmy Carters of this world, building homes for Habitat for Humanity, and the Mother Teresas, reaching out in mercy to the poor and dying, and the Bishop Oscar Romeros, giving their lives for the sake of human justice. "He has graciously granted you the privilege not only of believing in Christ, but of suffering for him as well."

Central Methodist Mission in Johannesburg, South Africa, is an inter-racial church, a mix of black and white and brown South Africans—a sign of God's alternative to apartheid. On the altar at every service is the candle of Peace and Justice, twelve inches or so high, with a single strand of barbed wire encircling it. The barbed wire is a harsh reminder of those who have suffered for the sake of righteousness and of the power of evil that fans the fires of hatred and bitter prejudice in that strife-torn land. But the light of the candle is undimmed: "The light shines in the darkness, and the darkness did not overcome it" (John 1:5). "Let your light so shine. . . ."

Helping Adults Become Involved

Preparing to Teach

Since the four lessons in June are based on Paul's Letter to the Philippians, it is very important, in preparing for the first meeting of the class, to do some reading and reflection in advance. First, I recommend reading the Philippian letter in its entirety, without the help of a concordance or study guide. Simply read all four chapters in one sitting. In the New Revised Standard Version it is less than five pages long. This will give you a sense of the whole and demonstrate how the themes of joy, gratitude, and loving concern for others permeate Paul's letter. You will also find memorable passages that are among the most beautiful and profound Paul wrote, such as 2:5-9; 3:12-16; and 4:8-9.

It will also be helpful to read as background information the story of Paul's first visit to Philippi. It is told with vivid excitement by Luke in Acts 16:6-40, beginning with a vision that came to Paul, urging him to leave Asia Minor (modern Turkey), cross the Aegean Sea and "come over to Macedonia and help us." The very first community he visited was Philippi. Your Bible may have a map of the New Testament world, including Paul's missionary journeys, which will provide the geographical context. Lydia and her household were the first converts, followed by the jailer and his family. Even in jail amazing things happened! Here was the first beachhead of Christianity established by Paul in Europe. The citizens of Philippi were given Roman citizenship, as were the citizens of Tarsus, Paul's hometown. That was another bond they shared. Any pastor will tell you that his or her first church was very special. Deep friendships were formed that last a lifetime. There was the excitement of new beginnings. So it was with Paul.

You will also want to read the devotional lesson 2 Corinthians 5:1-15.

314

Although addressed to a different congregation and under different circumstances, it provides a window into the soul of Paul.

The outline for presenting today's lesson:

> I. Being Christian in a hostile world
> II. Stages in Christian maturity
> III. Being Christian today

Introducing the Main Question

As the class begins, place the two passages to be considered at the forefront of the people's minds. One person may read the text, pausing for another to read the commentary in "As You Read the Scripture." Then "The Main Question," which rises out of the lesson, should be read. The thrust is both institutional (addressed to a congregation) and individual. We do not have not pretend that the letter is addressed to us. The fact is that contemporary American society is much like that at Philippi.

It is important that members of the class become involved in a dialogue with Paul. For that reason you should resist the temptation of doing all the talking and, instead, encourage participation. The main strength of "The Scripture and the Main Question" is that it relates Paul's message to today and to experiences with which all of us can relate. In your own words, summarize its contents for your class. The purpose of this summary is to prepare for discussion.

Developing the Lesson

Probably some questions will come to mind as you read the lesson in advance. And it is certain that an alert class will raise unanticipated ones! My questions, listed below, are not meant to be exhaustive and do not have to be rigidly followed. Their purpose is to generate reflection and the sharing of ideas.

1. Is it easier or harder to be a Christian in a hostile environment such as the Soviet Union (prior to Gorbachev) or China?
2. The religious landscape in the United States is rapidly and dramatically changing. We are told that in Chicago, which is considered the heartland of America, there are now more Moslems than Methodists, more Buddhists than Presbyterians, more Hindus than Congregationalists. What implications do these changes have for Christians and for our nation?

The obvious implication is that we need more than casual Christians if the Christian faith is to be a formative power in our lives and in the lives of our neighbors. Note that a central argument in "The Scripture and the Main Question" is that the Christian life is not first of all a matter of rules, but of relationships—with Christ and others. For our lives to be transformed by Christ there must be growth, change, and development: "I do not consider that I have made it on my own; but this one thing I do: . . . I press on" (Philippians 3:13, to be considered more fully on June 20).

M. Scott Peck, author of *The Different Drum* (New York: Simon and Schuster, 1987), maintains that there are four stages of human development. He calls Stage I "Chaotic, anti-social." People in this stage seem generally incapable of loving others. Their relationships with others are "essentially manipulative and self-serving." Stage II is "Formal, institutional." People in this stage cling to the status quo. They become upset when the order of worship is changed or the pastor moves. They long for permanency. Stage III is "Skeptic, individual." These are the "doubting Thomases" who begin to question even the most sacred tenets of the faith. Some may become practical atheists or at least agnostics. Unless they are handled with care, they are likely to leave the church. But those who keep on maturing enter Stage IV: "Mystic, communal."

Among human beings they are the ones most aware that the whole world is a community and realize that what divides us into warring camps is precisely the *lack* of this awareness. Having become practiced at emptying themselves of pre-conceived notions and prejudices and able to perceive the invisible underlying fabric that connects everything, they do not think in terms of factions or blocs or even national boundaries; they *know* this to be one world.

Ask the class and yourself: In what stage are you? Where should you be? Is it possible that you may revert back to earlier stages occasionally, especially when life is uncertain and the world you once knew is no longer there?

Can you name someone who touched your life in a very special way, reaching out to care for you when you needed it most, so that you saw glimpses of Christ in that self-emptying love? What do you remember most about that experience?

Helping Class Members Act

Are there people you need to reach out to: lonely, troubled, anxious? One lady felt so forsaken that she put an advertisement in the local paper: "My telephone hasn't rung in weeks. Is there anyone out there who cares?"

How are we to combat racism in our community, or the kind of hostility that pits Arab against Jew or white South Africans against black? (See especially Philippians 2:29-30.)

Planning for Next Sunday

Ask the class members to read and reflect at home on Philippians 2:1-16. Urge them to bring to class examples of models we tend to imitate in our society, such as movie and television celebrities and rock stars. How can we model Christ in a secular society? Does it mean being "different"? If so, how?

Christ, Our Model

Background Scripture: Philippians 2:1-18

The Main Question

Paul provides a powerful model for Christians to follow. If Paul's model was contrary to the prevailing morality in the first century, it is even more so today. Even among professing Christians, Christ is more to be admired than imitated. People often profess to live by the Ten Commandments and the Sermon on the Mount while worshiping money and the things money can buy ("You shall have no other gods before me" [Exodus 20:3]) and having trouble loving their family and friends, to say nothing of loving their enemies (Matthew 5:43-44). Are we serious about following Christ and making him the model of our lives? *If not Christ, who?* That is the question implicit in today's lesson.

There is, however, a more insidious problem here. It is primarily internal. The Philippian church was beset by problems of *conceit* and *spiritual pride*, which led to selfishness and divisiveness that broke the spirit of fellowship and good will that had been so evident at the beginning. Before we can model Christ in the world, we need to model him as members of his body, deeply dependent upon God's grace and very much concerned for one another.

We are fond of singing, "They'll Know We Are Christians by Our Love." But if, in fact, we are split apart by petty jealousies and political power plays, that factionalism will not only be sensed by those we would like to attract to our fellowship, but it could lead to our destruction as a Christian community as well.

How to live harmoniously as a congregation called to be the Body of Christ (1 Corinthians 12:27) and to be *in* the world with all its temptations, but not *of* it is the double challenge we face.

Selected Scripture

King James Version	New Revised Standard Version
Philippians 2:1-16	*Philippians 2:1-16*
If there be therefore any consolation in Christ, if any comfort of love, if any fellowship of the Spirit, if any bowels and mercies,	1 If then there is any encouragement in Christ, any consolation from love, any sharing in the Spirit, any compassion and sympathy, 2 make my joy complete: be of the same mind, having the same love, being in full accord and of one mind. 3 Do nothing from selfish ambition or conceit, but in humility regard others as better than yourselves. 4 Let each of you look not to your own interests, but to the interests of
2 Fulfil ye my joy, that ye be like minded, having the same love, being of one accord, of one mind.	
3 Let nothing be done through strife or vainglory; but in lowliness of mind let each esteem other better than themselves.	
4 Look not every man on his own	

317

things, but every man also on the things of others.

5 Let this mind be in you, which was also in Christ Jesus:

6 Who, being in the form of God, thought it not robbery to be equal with God:

7 But made himself of no reputation, and took upon him the form of a servant, and was made in the likeness of men:

8 And being found in fashion as a man, he humbled himself, and became obedient unto death, even the death of the cross.

9 Wherefore God also hath highly exalted him, and given him a name which is above every name:

10 That at the name of Jesus every knee should bow, of things in heaven, and things in earth, and things under the earth;

11 And that every tongue should confess that Jesus Christ is Lord, to the glory of God the Father.

12 Wherefore, my beloved, as ye have always obeyed, not as in my presence only, but now much more in my absence, work out your own salvation with fear and trembling.

13 For it is God which worketh in you both to will and to do of his good pleasure.

14 Do all things without murmurings and disputings:

15 That ye may be blameless and harmless, the sons of God, without rebuke, in the midst of a crooked and perverse nation, among whom ye shine as lights in the world;

16 Holding forth the word of life; that I may rejoice in the day of Christ, that I have not run in vain, neither laboured in vain.

Key Verse: **Let this mind be in you, which was also in Christ Jesus. (Philippians 2:5)**

others. 5 Let the same mind be in you that was in Christ Jesus,

6 who, though he was in the form of God,
did not regard equality with God
as something to be exploited,
7 but emptied himself,
taking the form of a slave,
being born in human likeness.
And being found in human form,
8 he humbled himself
and became obedient to the point of death—
even death on a cross.
9 Therefore God also highly exalted him
and gave him the name
that is above every name,
10 so that at the name of Jesus
every knee should bend,
in heaven and on earth and under the earth,
11 and every tongue should confess
that Jesus Christ is Lord,
to the glory of God the Father.

12 Therefore, my beloved, just as you have always obeyed me, not only in my presence, but much more now in my absence, work out your own salvation with fear and trembling; 13 for it is God who is at work in you, enabling you both to will and to work for his good pleasure.

14 Do all things without murmuring and arguing, 15 so that you may be blameless and innocent, children of God without blemish in the midst of a crooked and perverse generation, in which you shine like stars in the world. 16 It is by your holding fast to the word of life that I can boast on the day of Christ that I did not run in vain or labor in vain.

Key Verse: **Let the same mind be in you that was in in Christ Jesus. (Philippians 2:5)**

As You Read the Scripture

Philippians 2. Paul is deeply concerned about the church's falling apart because of internal strife. He speaks directly to that concern in the first half of this chapter.

Verse 1. There are four conditional clauses: (1) "If there is any encouragement in Christ"—Paul wants the Philippians to know they are a community loved by Christ. (2) "[If there is] any consolation from love"—because they are loved by Christ they are able to love one another. (3) "[If there is] any sharing in the Spirit"—because they were baptized into one body, no earthly power can tear them apart. (4) "[If there is] any compassion and sympathy"—Christ is deeply affected by and sympathetic toward their personal (internal) problems.

Verse 2. The Philippians are a source of joy. Paul will refer to them later as "his joy and crown" (4:1). Now he asks that by responding to his appeals in verse 1, they will be one in both head and heart and have the same love toward one another as Christ has for them.

Verse 3. Now the truth comes out: *selfishness* exhibited by those who wish to promote themselves instead of Christ is causing dissension as well as *conceit*, vain, empty glory that makes one a rival of God (!) and destroys community life. To be humble is often regarded as being a wimp. Humility was equally scorned in Paul's day. Paul urged the Philippian Christians, in the spirit of Christ, to consider others as better than themselves, which is a positive force of loving concern for others.

Verses 5-11. They are to let their behavior toward one another arise out of their life in Christ Jesus. This is the famous "kenotic" passage, from the Greek word *kenoun,* meaning "to empty," "to reduce to nothing," "to annihilate." Although Christ was divine, he did not take advantage of his exalted status, but emptied himself, a free and deliberate act on his part. He was a servant (the Greek word Paul used is *doulos,* meaning "slave"), the lowest form of humanity with no rights or privileges. The phrase "in human form" refers to Christ's complete identification with us, with all our frailties and sins. His ultimate humiliation was death on a cross. It was impossible to sink any lower. But God exalted him above all creatures through the Resurrection and Ascension, giving him the "name" (the glory and authority) that is above all names, so that the entire cosmos might exclaim, "Jesus is Lord." Commentators suggest that Paul is quoting here an early hymn of the Church, possibly used at baptism, in which the candidate symbolically dies to sin as the waters close over him or her and the person is raised to newness of life in Christ. By dying himself and being raised by God, Christ is able to offer us eternal life.

Verses 12-13. These words are addressed to the Church as a whole. Paul does not advocate that we earn our salvation by accumulating merit points. That is completely antithetical to his theology. Rather, in the light of Christ's death and resurrection on our behalf, we are to make him our model, with "fear and trembling," for it is a huge assignment if left on our own. But we are not alone. "God . . . is at work in [us]."

Verses 14-16. These are continued moral admonitions that are understood as arising out of our life in Christ, enabling us to be children of God in the midst of a "crooked and perverse" generation. "The day of Christ" is the consummation of history in which Paul hopes that his confidence in them will be vindicated.

The Scripture and the Main Question

How to live a Christian life in an unchristian world is a concern of Paul's and of contemporary Christians as well. Paul told the Philippians to "be blameless and innocent, children of God without blemish in the midst of a crooked and perverse generation, in which you shine like stars in the world."

If Not Christ, Who?

I watched a television drama depicting a true story of a terrible tragedy that tore a family apart. They had been so very happy: a father and mother and three sons who lived comfortably and with high hopes for the future. The mother was murdered, and her husband was the leading suspect. I wondered as they went through the long, drawn-out trial how the family survived without belief in a caring God or a high, compelling standard of morality. The father was convicted not only of the murder, but, in the words of the prosecuting attorney, of gross immorality (he was having an extra-marital affair) and greed (he had recently taken out a huge life insurance policy on his wife). A closing scene showed the sons emerging from a cemetery where they had interred the ashes of their mother. (Was no minister present?) Unquestionably the father's selfishness became his undoing and devastated his family. Had he no conscience? Was there no remorse? He tried to reassure his sons that he loved them. But did he really understand what love means? And where, in all this, was God?

One hardly expects to find God on a television screen. Yet, strangely enough, God appears in the most unlikely places. A leading article in *The Atlantic Monthly* was entitled "Can We Be Good Without God?" That a purely secular magazine should raise such a religious question is unusual, to say the least. It turned out to be a short course in Christian theology: "inclination toward evil" is primarily an inclination to exalt ourselves rather than allowing ourselves to be exalted by God. The author of the article claimed: "We exalt ourselves in a variety of ways: for example, by power, trying to control all the things and people around us; by greed, accumulating an inequitable portion of the material goods of the world; by self-righteousness, claiming to be wholly virtuous, and so forth."

At the center of life, however, we find God's *agape* ("self-giving love") which "raises all those touched by it into the community brought by Christ, the Kingdom of God. . . . The Lord of all time and existence has taken a personal interest in every human being, an interest that is compassionate and unwearying. The Christian universe is peopled exclusively with royalty!" Clearly we do need God who has come to us supremely in Christ: "If we turn away from transcendence, from God, what will deliver us from a politically fatal fear and faintheartedness?" ("Can We Be Good Without God?" *The Atlantic Monthly* [December 1989]: 72, 77, 85).

Looking Out for Number One

Surely Christians are aware of transcendence—God's presence in the seemingly mundane experiences of life. And as followers of Christ our moral standards stand in sharp contrast to the world's. Unfortunately we have to say no to both assumptions. Nothing could be more mundane than a young man's learning to be a carpenter and dying on a cross. Many still find it hard to believe that God was deeply involved in the life and death of an obscure Galilean carpenter, and the Resurrection continues to be a scandal. As for a higher morality, the fact is that sin flourished in Philippi. Selfishness and conceit—looking out for number one—were all too prevalent. Not only were these negative forces undermining the spirit of unity, but also they betrayed a serious lack of commitment to Christ.

We should not be shocked to find conflict in the Church. "In the real world . . . congregations are made up of imperfect persons who live in an imperfect world. We Christians (and other humans) vividly demonstrate the doctrine of original sin in the workings of the institutions we establish" (Robert D. Dale, *Pastoral Leadership* [Nashville: Abingdon Press, 1981], p. 159). Conflict, while signaling trouble, can be the means of reaching new understanding and closer relationships, provided, of course, that the conflict is handled creatively. Antagonism, however, is unhealthy conflict and is usually caused by those who "go out of their way to make insatiable demands, usually attacking the person or performance of others. These tacks are selfish in nature, tearing down rather than building up, and are frequently directed against those in a leadership capacity" (Kenneth C. Haugk, *Antagonists in the Church* [Minneapolis: Augsburg, 1988], pp. 21-22).

As a pastor I can testify to having been caught between opposing factions in the Church, a most uncomfortable place to be. I can also testify that I have had to examine my own motives to make sure I was not further poisoning the atmosphere by insisting on my way: "Not thine, but mine be done!" If we are honest with ourselves and with God we can only exclaim, "Lord, have mercy upon me, a sinner."

He Humbled Himself

The only way to overcome sin, having confessed our transgressions to God, is to model our lives after Christ, who, though divine, chose to empty himself of all godly attributes and live among the lowly and powerless. When evil people, including some of his most trusted followers, conspired against him, he "humbled himself," choosing to die like a common criminal. "Therefore God also highly exalted him. . . . "

Christian conduct is not so much a matter of obeying rules as having "the mind of Christ." It is not looking to one's own interest, but to the interests of others, humbly regarding the personal concerns of others as important as one's own.

God Is at Work

Who is sufficient for this? Even if one sincerely desires to follow Christ, can one possibly measure up to such high standards? Paul recognizes the dilemma. "I find it to be a law that when I want to do what is good, evil lies close at hand" (Romans 7:21). Therefore, we work out our salvation with "fear and trembling," knowing that even our best intentions are often flawed by self-interest and pride. "God . . . is at work in you. . . . " That may seem a paradox: God at work, even in the lives of sinners?

That, indeed, is the great miracle of our faith. Seriously flawed people have always been used as the channels of God's grace. Consider Peter, swearing in the high priest's courtyard that he never knew Jesus, and Paul, a self-righteous fanatic consumed by hate. Yet God was at work in them.

Can we believe that God can use us for his great purposes and trust God's grace to work so powerfully in our lives that others may see Christ in us? A little boy, seeing impressive figures in stained-glass windows for the first time, was told they were saints. As he was being put to bed that evening his mother and he reflected on the highlights of the day. "I know who saints are," he exclaimed. "They're people who the light shines through." So it is for those who model their lives after Christ.

Helping Adults Become Involved

Preparing to Teach

In preparing yourself for today's lesson, read the Philippians passage, 2:1-16. I highly recommend as a personal exercise the reading of "As You Read the Scripture" first, so that the message might be firmly fixed in your mind. Then read "The Main Question." You will also find inspiration by reading John 14:1-14. Note Verse 7: "If you know me, you will know my Father also." The model Paul bids us follow is none other than God incarnate in the life of God's Son.

Everyone needs a model. A child will model the behavior of his or her parents or whomever the child spends much time with. One of the most devastating problems for black youth in our nation's inner cities is that a large percentage live in homes where there is no father to provide a healthy role model. Many youth who fall victim to drug crimes come from broken families. Because family love and support are missing in their lives, they seek answers to their unhappiness in destructive behavior. Good modeling, therefore, is absolutely indispensable to wholesome living.

Use this outline to present today's lesson:

I. Models of goodness.
II. Christ as our model.
III. God is at work in you.

Introducing the Main Question

It is appropriate for you as the teacher to introduce the main question. You may wish to read it in full or summarize it in your own words. While we do not want to stress hypocrisy, the fact is that we so easily *say* that Christ is our model, but there is a big gap between our words and our actions. It will be helpful to discuss the problem of "modeling" in general before focusing on the problem of disharmony in the Church.

Developing the Lesson

Having introduced the main question, "If not Christ, who?" invite the class to name some models in secular society and the influence they have on people. (Class members were asked last week to bring names of secular models to this class session.) For example, Elvis Presley continues to affect thousands with his emotional music, his addictive and flamboyant life-style, and his mysterious death. There have even been reports of Elvis' returning from the dead! What are the consequences of idolizing such people? Can we use them as models and still be committed to Christ?

Such a discussion will be good preparation for focusing on the text. Again, you may wish to have someone read the text, pausing while another reads the commentary "As You Read the Scripture."

Remind the class that in the Letter to the Philippians Paul is writing to very close personal friends. Yet, at the same time, he minces no words about their sins: *selfishness* and *conceit*. Are any of us guilty of those same sins? Is our life as a congregation less than perfect? How well do we handle controversy as individuals and as a congregation? What might we do to reduce the tensions and be "of the same mind, having the same love, being in full accord" (2:3)? Does it mean becoming a spineless wimp?

Now hold up the model of Christ, who "emptied himself, taking the form of a slave." Will that kind of behavior be admired in our aggressive, greedy, success-oriented world? Or is it meant to be a pattern for the worldly type? That is a crucial point. You may well want to ask the question: "Whom did Paul expect to live the self-emptying life?" The answer is clear: not everyone in general, but Christians in particular—those who name the Name and confess that Jesus Christ is Lord. What is said by their lips is demonstrated by their lives.

Several additional questions are suggested by the text: What does it mean to "work out your own salvation"? Can we, by our good deeds, earn God's forgiving grace? I once knew a young man who claimed to have been "saved." He said that because of his new relationship with Christ it was impossible for him to sin. Can we, by strong intentions and unreserved dedication, reach perfection in this life, as my friend claimed?

Later in the letter (3:16) Paul makes it clear that salvation is not a one-time event, but a continual process. Does Paul seem to contradict himself by adding: "God . . . is at work in you, enabling you both to will and to work for his good pleasure"? The entire sentence, verses 12 and 13, must be seen as a whole. Then it becomes clear that when we turn our lives over to God, seeking to do God's will above all, we will experience an infusion of power and determination that will enable us to overcome every obstacle. We will feel upheld by God. We will know that even when we fail, God's grace is greater than our sin. Thus the transforming Spirit of God, revealed in Christ, will guide, uphold, and empower us as we seek to work out our salvation.

Can we influence those outside the Body of Christ (2:14-15)? How can we shine as lights in a "crooked and perverse generation"?

Beside famed Copley Square Episcopal Church in Boston is a statue of Phillips Brooks, beloved pastor, powerful preacher, and author of "O Little Town of Bethlehem." Behind him stands the figure of Christ, his hand raised to bless. The symbolism is unmistakable: In Philips Brooks—his preaching, his pastoral care—people saw Christ. Is not that our call in a "crooked and perverse" generation?

Helping Class Members Act

To bring the lesson to a memorable close it would be helpful to enlist some class members to model several famous Christians. Have them simply stand and talk very briefly about these persons, not mentioning their names—and possibly speaking in the first person: "I." When they have finished, the rest of the class members are to guess who they are. For example:

Martin Luther King, Jr., who gave his life in a controversial but non-violent struggle to provide dignity and freedom to minorities, especially black people. He was a Nobel Prize winner.

Mother Teresa, a humble Roman Catholic nun who felt called to leave her convent in Calcutta to minister to the poor and dying. She founded the Missionaries of Charity, who follow her example in cities around the world. She also was a recipient of the Nobel Peace Prize.

Abraham Lincoln, the sixteenth president of the United States, issued the Proclamation of Emancipation, forever freeing American slaves and died in the attempt to bring restoration and healing to a broken nation.

Saint Francis of Assissi, born in twelfthth-century Italy, the son of a wealthy merchant. He led a care-free life until on several occasions he heard Christ calling him. One such instance was when he was praying in a crumbling church. "Francis," came the call, "rebuild my church." He forsook his father's wealth and lived in poverty, attracting many disciples and founding a Catholic order named after him. He ministered extensively to the poor, especially lepers, and was a joyous proclaimer of the good news. He wrote: "Lord, make me an instrument of thy peace." You and/or the class may think of others who have modeled Christ.

Planning for Next Sunday

Have the class members read Philippians 3:1-16. Ask them to think about "the good old days." What must happen for the future to be even better?

LESSON 3   JUNE 20

Keep On Keeping On

Background Scripture: Philippians 3:1-16

The Main Question

Paul was continually hounded by those who openly attacked him and questioned his credentials as an apostle of Christ. The result is that occasionally Paul is put on the defensive. Clearly that is the case in Philippians 3. What we find here, however, is not only a response to those who would undermine his ministry, but mighty affirmations of faith.

Essentially the question being addressed is this: Who are the true Christians, Paul or his enemies? It is a familiar conflict. Jesus told of two men going into the Temple to pray: one a Pharisee, a respected member of a prominent religious party, and the other a tax collector, regarded as a sinner because he collaborated with the hated Romans. Each one said his prayers, the Pharisee reminding God of how faithfully he had lived up to the law, and the tax collector, burdened by guilt, pleading for mercy. Which one, asked Jesus, went to his home justified (approved by God)? To the utter amazement of his hearers, Jesus commended the sinner (Luke 18:9-14).

The lesson is clear: We need to be careful when making judgments about people; those we condemn may well be accepted by God. Moreover, we must resist the temptation to establish our own definitions of sainthood and declare ourselves charter members! Here is the source of much divisiveness: Protestants versus Catholics, fundamentalists against liberals, Orthodox against Reformed. Your church does not practice foot washing? Then you are not among the elect. You do not ordain women? Does that mean God speaks only through men? Churches have been divided and denominations formed over matters less weighty.

Selected Scripture

King James Version

Philippians 3:1-16

1 Finally, my brethren, rejoice in the Lord. To write the same things to you, to me indeed is not grievous, but for you it is safe.

2 Beware of dogs, beware of evil workers, beware of the concision.

3 For we are the circumcision, which worship God in the spirit, and rejoice in Christ Jesus, and have no confidence in the flesh.

4 Though I might also have confidence in the flesh. If any other man thinketh that he hath whereof he might trust in the flesh, I more:

5 Circumcised the eighth day, of the stock of Israel, of the tribe of Benjamin, an Hebrew of the Hebrews; as touching the law, a Pharisee;

6 Concerning zeal, persecuting the church; touching the righteousness which is in the law, blameless.

7 But what things were gain to me, those I counted loss for Christ.

8 Yea doubtless, and I count all things but loss for the excellency of the knowledge of Christ Jesus my Lord: for whom I have suffered the loss of all things, and do count them but dung, that I may win Christ,

9 And be found in him, not having mine own righteousness,

New Revised Standard Version

Philippians 3:1-16

1 Finally, my brothers and sisters, rejoice in the Lord. To write the same things to you is not troublesome to me, and for you it is a safeguard.

2 Beware of the dogs, beware of the evil workers, beware of those who mutilate the flesh! 3 For it is we who are the circumcision, who worship in the Spirit of God and boast in Christ Jesus and have no confidence in the flesh—4 even though I, too, have reason for confidence in the flesh.

If anyone else has reason to be confident in the flesh, I have more: 5 circumcised on the eighth day, a member of the people of Israel, of the tribe of Benjamin, a Hebrew born of Hebrews; as to the law, a Pharisee; 6 as to zeal, a persecutor of the church; as to righteousness under the law, blameless.

7 Yet whatever gains I had, these I have come to regard as loss because of Christ. 8 More than that, I regard everything as loss because of the surpassing value of knowing Christ Jesus my Lord. For his sake I have suffered the loss of all things, and I regard them as rubbish, in order that I may gain Christ 9 and be found in him, not having a righ-

which is of the law, but that which is through the faith of Christ, the righteousness which is of God by faith:

10 That I may know him, and the power of his resurrection, and the fellowship of his sufferings, being made conformable unto his death;

11 If by any means I might attain unto the resurrection of the dead.

12 Not as though I had already attained, either were already perfect: but I follow after, if that I may apprehend that for which also I am apprehended of Christ Jesus.

13 Brethren, I count not myself to have apprehended: but this one thing I do, forgetting those things which are behind, and reaching forth unto those things which are before,

14 I press toward the mark for the prize of the high calling of God in Christ Jesus.

15 Let us therefore, as many as be perfect, be thus minded: and if in any thing ye be otherwise minded, God shall reveal even this unto you.

16 Nevertheless, whereto we have already attained, let us walk by the same rule, let us mind the same thing.

Key Verse: **I press toward the mark for the prize of the high calling of God in Christ Jesus. (Philippians 3:14)**

teousness of my own that comes from the law, but one that comes through faith in Christ, the righteousness from God based on faith.

10 I want to know Christ and the power of his resurrection and the sharing of his sufferings by becoming like him in his death, 11 if somehow I may attain the resurrection from the dead.

12 Not that I have already obtained this or have already reached the goal; but I press on to make it my own, because Christ Jesus has made me his own. 13 Beloved, I do not consider that I have made it my own; but this one thing I do: forgetting what lies behind and straining forward to what lies ahead, 14 I press on toward the goal for the prize of the heavenly call of God in Christ Jesus. 15 Let those of us then who are mature be of the same mind; and if you think differently about anything, this too God will reveal to you. 16 Only let us hold fast to what we have attained.

Key Verse: **I press on toward the goal for the prize of the heavenly call of God in Christ Jesus. (Philippians 3:14)**

As You Read the Scripture

Philippians 3:1. Paul is about to end his letter when his mind takes another direction. Although he has repeatedly warned his friends against those who mutilate the flesh, he needs to do it again, and in no uncertain terms. So, after the call to rejoice—a major theme of the letter—he launches into a sharp condemnation of their enemies and a long and eloquent defense of his own faith and practice.

Verse 2. Usually those who kept the law referred to those who did not as "dogs" because they were "unclean." Paul turns the tables and calls his legalistic critics by the same epithet. They are "evil workers" because they are in league with Satan and insist that one can be a Christian only if one is circumcised.

Verse 3. The true disciples of Christ do not practice circumcision as a sacred rite; it is at best an external ordinance. True Christians worship God in spirit: "A person is a Jew who is one inwardly, and real circumcision is a matter of the heart—it is spiritual and not literal" (Romans 2:29).

Verses 4-6. Paul now becomes unashamedly personal. If these Judaizers wish to compare credentials, he can outrank them all. Born a Jew, circumcised according to the law on the eighth day, he was a member of the tribe of Benjamin, named after the second son of Jacob and Rachel, as was Saul, the first king of Israel. Although he lived in a hellenistic society (as a resident of Tarsus), he remained faithful to the Hebrew law and, in fact, became a Pharisee, the party within Judaism known for its scrupulous observance of the law. With great zeal he persecuted the Christian church, demonstrating his unwavering devotion to the law by which he was judged blameless.

Verses 7-11. Why should a high-ranking, widely respected Jew give up all these gains? For one reason only: because of the "surpassing value of knowing Christ Jesus my Lord." "Knowing" Christ is more than intellectual knowledge. "To know Christ is to love and to serve him and to identify our lives with his" (*IB*, vol. 11, p. 85). "For his sake I have suffered the loss of all things, and regard them as rubbish [bodily waste consigned to the garbage heap!]." Here is a strong combination of a mystical union with Christ and a willingness to sacrifice both possessions and power for his sake. Note the emphasis on faith in Christ from which true righteousness springs (v. 9). When one has risen to new life in Christ, one is then prepared to share his sufferings and thus "attain the resurrection from the dead."

Verses 12-16. It is quite possible that some members of the Philippian church had fallen into a mood of self-complacency. They argued that since Christ had saved them there was no need for any further effort. They were in full possession of the Christian life and thus "had it made." If that were the case, they were more spiritually advanced than Paul! He had not reached perfection; rather, he forgot the past, straining forward into the future. "I press on," he wrote, "to make it my own." Paul is comparing the Christian life to running a race. In ancient times the prize was placed in a prominent place where the race was going to end. The sight of it roused the competitors to strain every nerve and to forget everything but that one object. The "heavenly call" is God's summons to inherit eternal life. As the runner crosses the finish line he or she bears the victor's welcome: "Well done, good and faithful servant, enter into the joy of the Lord." Paul invites all who are "mature" to think of the Christian life in this way. John Wesley would say, "We are going on to perfection." Only in death is the race over.

The Scripture and the Main Question

The debate between Paul and his critics is not over. It may be expressed in different terms, and the context in which the debate is waged is radically different. Still the question implied throughout this entire passage is still being debated: "Who is the true Christian?"

Paul's answers, directed both to the Christians at Philippi and to his opponents seeking to undermine his ministry, are as valid today as they were then.

First, *true Christians are those who worship God in spirit* (3:3). Jesus entered into a fascinating conversation with a woman of Samaria (John 4:7-42) in which the subject of worship came up. The Samaritans believed that God was to be worshiped on Mt. Gerizim, while for Jews Mt. Zion was the holy hill on which their beloved Temple, the center of Hebrew worship, was built. Jesus expanded this vision by saying that worship must not be limited to a certain place: "God is spirit, and those who worship him must worship in spirit and truth" (John 4:24).

Outward Show or Inner Encounter?

There were people in Jesus' time who loved to parade their piety, wearing their prayer shawls in public, calling attention to themselves as God's chosen ones (see Matthew 23:1-12). Jesus' condemnation of them was withering: "Woe to you, scribes, Pharisees, hypocrites!" Worship is not an outward show, but an inward encounter. Serious differences in theology, worship, and church governance separate Christians today and will more than likely remain, despite improved ecumenical relationships. But both Jesus and Paul remind us that these outward differences are ultimately of secondary importance. True Christians are those who "worship in the Spirit of God and boast in Christ Jesus" (3:3).

While We Were Still Sinners

Again, *true Christians believe in salvation by faith, rather than by works* (3:9). This is where the Judaizers were guilty of misleading the people. Dependence on outward deeds, rather than the inner experience of Christ's forgiving grace, makes us responsible for our own salvation. That is wrong. It is Christ who rescues us from ourselves: "While we were still sinners Christ died for us" (Romans 5:8).

By "faith" Paul means *active trust.* Trust, we are told, is formed, or not formed, in our very first year of life, depending on how much we are loved and how well we are treated. A baby is completely dependent on a parent to provide food and care for the baby's every need. Likewise we are to trust the One who loves us so much that he sent his Son to be our savior.

Faith is also *confession*: "If you confess with your lips that Jesus is Lord and believe in your heart that God raised him from the dead, you will be saved" (Romans 10:9). We often read a confession of faith in a Sunday worship service. It reminds us of the major elements of our faith: "I believe in God the Father Almighty . . . . and in Jesus Christ his only Son our Lord . . . . in the Holy Spirit, the holy Catholic Church, the communion of saints, the forgiveness of sins, the resurrection of the body, and the life everlasting." But confession is more than repetition. It is total commitment to One who accepts us even though we are unacceptable. Thus we are saved, not by our works, but by his mercy.

Keep On Growing

Not only do true Christians worship God in spirit and believe in salvation by faith, rather than works, but *they also keep on growing as long as they live*: "Not that I have already obtained this or have already reached the goal, but I press on to make it my own, because Christ Jesus has made me his own"

(3:12). Again, "forgetting what lies behind and straining forward to what lies ahead, I press on toward the goal for the prize of the heavenly call of God in Christ Jesus" (3:13-14). Have you heard the advice about what to do when you're at the end of your rope? Tie another knot and hang on. But what if there is no more rope, and you are completely exhausted by your efforts to save yourself?

Paul revels in the fact that Jesus Christ rescued him from a life of self-centeredness and pride and that his own worthiness had nothing to do with it. God took the initiative through Christ, who called Paul to be an apostle. Answering that call was, and continued to be, the most important thing in his life. He was willing to turn his back on the past—which was no small thing, for he was a "Pharisee of the Pharisees," a key figure in the power structure of Judaism. Now he looked forward, with eager anticipation, to receiving the prize of the upward call of God.

The Forward Look

The most exciting Christians I have known were and are those with a forward look. I remember a nationally prominent pastor walking down the aisle of the auditorium where he had just received his certificate of retirement. I reached out my hand to congratulate him, and he said, "Bill, pray for me." I was stunned. He wanted me to pray for him, who stood as a spiritual giant among us? He could not live in the past; it was over. He had only the future, and it was a bit frightening. Yet, very typically, he was soon engaged in new creative ministries of teaching and counseling theological school students, helping to shape these young people for the ministries to which they were called. His reliance on Christ increased, his faith deepened, and he began to look forward to the future, rather than fearing it. He never stopped growing.

I will never forget a dear friend in Christ who became my spiritual adviser. Her husband of many years had recently died. Her children were all grown and were making their way in the world. It was a time for self-pity, for looking back into the past. That is how some express their grief—leaving a room in the house exactly was it was when the person was alive. But not Anna. Her final years were the most exciting. She had a large network of friends who loved her dearly and maintained close contact. She counseled people of all ages. Young people especially looked to her for wisdom. And she was a continual source of inspiration for me. She was constantly sending clippings and books for me to read. And when I made a pastoral call on her, it took practically all afternoon. What wonderful, mind-stretching conversations we had!

As she neared death, she said confidently, "I'm not sure when the Lord will call me, but I'm ready: my bags are packed. Straining forward, I press on toward the goal." She was quite feeble the Sunday we asked her to give her testimony of faith at an early service. But when she began to speak, her voice was strong, and her witness to Christ was deeply moving.

The last time I visited her in the hospital, expecting her to breathe her last breath, she was writing vigorously in bed with her Bible beside her. "What are you writing?" I asked. "I'm writing a commentary on my favorite psalm for my grandchildren."

Here, I submit, is a glimpse of a true Christian.

FOURTH QUARTER

Helping Adults Become Involved

Preparing to Teach

Paul is deeply distressed by the vulnerability of the Philippian church to those who impugn him personally and accuse them of not being truly Christian. It is a serious threat, calling forth a passionate personal defense and an urgent plea to "join in imitating me" (v. 17).

As you prepare to teach I urge you to read Romans 15:1-13, the recommended devotional reading, in which Paul tells of God's deliberate plan of sending Christ as a "servant to the circumcised" (the Jewish nation) and "in order that the Gentiles might glorify God" (Romans 15:8-9). This is needed perspective, helping us understand that Paul was not a narrow sectarian battling for his point of view simply for the sake of argument. Rather, he deeply believed that he had been called as an ambassador to the Gentiles so that both Jews and non-Jews might be won to Christ. You will also find it helpful to read the entire fifteenth chapter of Romans in which he becomes, as in his letter to the Philippians, very autobiographical.

You will note that while "keep on keeping on" has a strong contemporary appeal, the deeper issue in Philippians 3:1-16 is the question of who is a true Christian. That focus should be maintained. You will want to read "As You Read the Scripture" and "The Main Question," making notes and jotting down thoughts to emphasize in class.

The outline for today's lesson:

I. Who is a true Christian?
II. Growing as Christians.
III. Staying in the race.

Introducing the Main Question

Ideally the members will have read the passage before coming to class. That, incidentally, should be a weekly assignment. Some will undoubtedly consult a commentary and be prepared to delve quite deeply into the subject, and those persons need to be encouraged. At the same time we must not neglect those who are not so motivated and have little to say in class. They must not be left out!

I recommend that you first read the commentary in "As You Read the Scripture," alternating the text with commentary. Then "The Main Question" will make more sense.

Some general comments about conflict in the Church may well be in order. When good but misinformed people suggest that everything in today's churches would be solved if we could only return to biblical times, they need to read Paul's letters, which remind us of how seriously the saints were divided. Only by God's grace did they survive.

Developing the Lesson

There are two issues here. The larger one is the question of who is the true Christian. The other, less significant, but very relevant one is this: "Is it possible to get stuck in the past, or were the 'good old days' really that good?"

330

One way to get people immediately involved is to ask them to define a true Christian. No peeping at Paul's answers; no reading from a commentary—just a candid and open discussion, possibly writing down the answers on a chalkboard or newsprint for all to see.

This can be followed by summarizing "The Scripture and the Main Question." Be careful not to put down anyone for the suggestions made. Please do not imply that while someone's comments are appreciated, the lesson for the day is infallible and no questions are to be asked. Invite discussion, even disagreement if it is done in a good spirit. Questions like these will stimulate discussion: (1) The author maintains that being a Christian is first of all a personal relationship with Christ, an inner, rather than an outward experience. Do you agree? (2) What does it mean to be saved by faith rather than works? (3) Don't good works (deeds) count for something?

The section titled "Keep On Growing" should lead to the most lively discussion. Why do some people (all of us at times) want to remain in the past? Isn't it an understandable tendency, and don't we all enjoy leafing through picture albums or showing slides of our trip to the Grand Canyon ten years ago? Surely we would not deprive the elderly of their treasured memories of days gone by. The past is the only thing they have left—or so it seems.

What is the alternative? How does Paul deal with that problem? What does he say about "keep on keeping on"? If the discussion falters, have someone read "Keep On Growing" and have the class react.

Helping Class Members Act

Today's lesson calls for personal reflection. Before rushing out to help others, we need to get our own spiritual house in order. The class should be encouraged to reflect on two questions: (1) What am I looking forward to? and (2) How can I continue to grow? These are serious issues, especially as we grow older. Some people simply cannot deal with the prospect of old age. They either work themselves to death or do not live very long after retirement. It is helpful, of course, to have hobbies and to give ourselves in volunteer service to others. But basically the problem is one of trust in God, who has come to us supremely in Christ and who calls us to "press on toward the goal for the prize of the heavenly call."

The race is not over. God expects our best. John Wesley sang on his deathbed the words of Isaac Watts:

> I'll praise my Maker while I've breath;
> And when my voice is lost in death,
> Praise shall employ my nobler powers.

Can we strive to win the prize of eternal life and in confidence, with Paul, leave the rest to God?

A pastor I know takes time out, even in the busiest seasons of the year, to be with his grandchildren. His reason is like a confession: "I neglected my family when they were growing up, and I'm not going to let that happen to my grandchildren." Why is it that volunteers in a regional hospital in my community seem always to be smiling? Because they are too busy to spend time in self-pity and because, though they may not say it, they have discovered the truth that it is in dying to self that we are born to eternal life.

Planning for Next Sunday

Read the lesson. What is the source (or sources) of true happiness in life? Might happiness ("don't worry, be happy") become an escape from the harsh realities of life, or is it a prescription for overcoming them? Think about it. Be prepared to discuss.

LESSON 4   JUNE 27

Rejoice in the Lord

Background Scripture: Philippians 4

The Main Question

The next-to-the-last decade of the twentieth century has been called "The Roaring Eighties." The reference is not so much to a collapsing morality, though it is implied, as to be a gold-rush culture consumed by "vanity, ego and greed" (*Time*, February 26, 1990). Epitomizing the glittering life-style of the era were Donald and Ivana Trump of New York, "awash in power and glitz," whose divorce made international headlines and whose most pressing concern was how to settle the estate estimated at $2.6 billion. Meanwhile, financial disaster claimed some of the most powerful and greedy corporate raiders on Wall Street. It was a time of unease.

That raises a compelling question: What is the source of true happiness? Surprisingly, the same question is implied in our text for today: "Rejoice in the Lord always; again I will say, Rejoice" (Philippians 4:4). Is our highest happiness to be found in the Lord?

There are many prescriptions for worldly satisfaction: "Don't worry, be happy," an entertainer sings to persons seeking escape from the proverbial "rat race." *Looking Out for Number One* was a bestseller few years ago. Self-centeredness is in! Then there are a number of quasi-religious books that appeal to one's quest for inner peace: *How to Make Positive Imaging Work for You* and *The Be Happy Attitudes*. These books tell us that happiness is within reach of everyone, provided we learn the rules of the game. We can win if we try.

Another way to put it is to ask this question, "Can we be happy without God?" It is one of life's most urgent questions.

Selected Scripture

King James Version	New Revised Standard Version
Philippians 4:4-20	*Philippians 4:4-20*
4 Rejoice in the Lord alway: and again I say, Rejoice.	4 Rejoice in the Lord always; again I will say, Rejoice. 5 Let your

5 Let your moderation be known unto all men. The Lord is at hand.

6 Be careful for nothing; but in every thing by prayer and supplication with thanksgiving let your requests be made known unto God.

7 And the peace of God, which passeth all understanding, shall keep your hearts and minds through Christ Jesus.

8 Finally, brethren, whatsoever things are true, whatsoever things are honest, whatsoever things are just, whatsoever things are pure, whatsoever things are lovely, whatsoever things are of good report; if there be any virtue, and if there be any praise, think on these things.

9 Those things, which ye have both learned, and received, and heard, and seen in me, do: and the God of peace shall be with you.

10 But I rejoiced in the Lord greatly, that now at the last your care of me hath flourished again; wherein ye were also careful, but ye lacked opportunity.

11 Not that I speak in respect of want: for I have learned, in whatsoever state I am, therewith to be content.

12 I know both how to be abased, and I know how to abound: every where and in all things I am instructed both to be full and to be hungry, both to abound and to suffer need.

13 I can do all things through Christ which strengtheneth me.

14 Notwithstanding ye have well done, that ye did communicate with my affliction.

15 Now ye Philippians know also, that in the beginning of the gospel, when I departed from Macedonia, no church communicated with me as concerning giving and receiving, but ye only.

16 For even in Thessalonica ye sent once and again unto my necessity.

17 Not because I desire a gift: but

gentleness be known to everyone. The Lord is near. 6 Do not worry about anything, but in everything by prayer and supplication with thanksgiving let your requests be made known to God. 7 And the peace of God, which surpasses all understanding, will guard your hearts and your minds in Christ Jesus.

8 Finally, beloved, whatever is true, whatever is honorable, whatever is just, whatever is pure, whatever is pleasing, whatever is commendable, if there is any excellence and if there is anything worthy of praise, think about these things. 9 Keep on doing the things that you have learned and received and heard and seen in me, and the God of peace will be with you.

10 I rejoice in the Lord greatly that now at last you have revived your concern for me; indeed, you were concerned for me, but had no opportunity to show it. 11 Not that I am referring to being in need; for I have learned to be content with whatever I have. 12 I know what it is to have little, and I know what it is to have plenty. In any and all circumstances I have learned the secret of being well-fed and of going hungry, of having plenty and of being in need. 13 I can do all things through him who strengthens me. 14 In any case, it was kind of you to share my distress.

15 You Philippians indeed know that in the early days of the gospel, when I left Macedonia, no church shared with me in the matter of giving and receiving, except you alone. 16 For even when I was in Thessalonica, you sent me help for my needs more than once. 17 Not that I seek the gift, but I seek the profit that accumulates to your

I desire fruit that may abound to your account.

18 But I have all, and abound: I am full, having received of Epaphroditus the things which were sent from you, an odour of a sweet smell, a sacrifice acceptable, well-pleasing to God.

19 But my God shall supply all your need according to his riches in glory by Christ Jesus.

20 Now unto God and our Father be glory for ever and ever. Amen.

account. 18 I have been paid in full and have more than enough; I am fully satisfied, now that I have received from Epaphroditus the gifts you sent, a fragrant offering, a sacrifice acceptable and pleasing to God. 19 And my God will fully satisfy every need of yours according to his riches in glory in Christ Jesus. 20 To our God and Father be glory forever and ever. Amen.

Key Verse: **Rejoice in the Lord alway: and again I say, Rejoice.** (Philippians 4:4)

Key Verse: **Rejoice in the Lord always; again I will say, Rejoice.** (Philippians 4:4)

As You Read the Scripture

Philippians 4:1. Paul has written a very personal letter to the Philippians. He ends with words of deep affection and strong admonition. The very first verse sets the theme: "Stand firm in the Lord in this way, my beloved."

Verses 4-7. Paul is addressing the entire congregation. His appeals to joy are not based on sheer optimism ("behind every dark cloud is a silver lining") or openness to the future, somehow hoping that things will turn out all right. The key to his exhortation is *in the Lord.* Here is more than simple encouragement. It is, above all, an appeal to faith.

Paul calls for their forbearance (KJV; "gentleness" in the NRSV). *Forbearance,* according to Ralph P. Martin (*Philippians,* New Century Bible Commentary [Grand Rapids: Eerdman's, 1976], pp. 154-55), is "a disposition of gentleness and fairmindedness to other people in spite of their faults, and inspired by the confidence Christians have that after earthly suffering will come heavenly glory" (see 3:20).

The Lord was expected soon, *at hand.* This is a familiar theme in Paul's letters and a strong belief among first-century Christians.

They were to have no anxiety. How can that be? In everything we are to bare our souls to God, giving thanks that God not only hears but also cares deeply. When we place our lives in God's care with complete trust, then we will know the peace of God which passes all understanding, which is literally beyond all human comprehension. God's peace will guard our hearts and minds—outside Christ there is no safety.

Verses 8-9. Paul encourages the Philippians to live up to the highest ideals—whatever is true in speech and fact, just, right, and fair. They must be pure—one must cleanse oneself of all that debases both one's body and one's soul; pleasing—attractive, winsome; commendable—literally fair sounding; excellence—the highest of moral achievement; worthy of praise—merit, respect; think about these things. These universal virtues are to be emulated by all.

For the Christian, however, life is modeled after the example of those who live in the manner of Christ, and Paul provides that model. That is why he can say, in effect, without boasting, "Do as I do, and God's peace will be yours."

Verses 10-20. Again Paul thanks his friends for their deep concern for his welfare. Note that he had not complained; he had learned under all circumstances to be content. The Greek words he uses suggest someone who is self-sufficient. But Paul was Christ-sufficient: "I can do *all things.*"

Had it not been for the Philippians Paul would not have been able to fulfill his mission. Repeatedly they came to his rescue with financial aid and other support, the sending of Epaphroditus being the latest. The "fruit" of their labors will not go unnoticed. Their gift to Paul is a fragrant offering, acceptable and pleasing to God. They will be rewarded! Their every need will be supplied.

Always he points upward: "To our God and Father be glory forever and ever. Amen."

The Scripture and the Main Question

What is the source of true happiness? This soul-searching question is answered persuasively by Paul in today's Scripture passage: "Rejoice in the Lord always."

In Spite of Blessings

The joy of which Paul speaks is given not because of blessings, but in spite of them. Paul is writing from prison. His freedom is restricted, and he may well receive the death sentence. There is very little chance that he will ever see the Philippians, or any other congregation he established, again. Yet he bids them rejoice!

Can we rejoice even when things do not go our way? We do not know why bad things happen to good people, except that no one is exempt from suffering. As a pastor I have seen people emerge from tragedy stronger in the faith, chastened but confident of God's unfailing love.

African Americans who endured the unspeakable hardships of slavery sang of the faith that sustained them in bitter times: "Nobody knows the trouble I've seen, nobody knows but Jesus. Glory Hallelujah!" They were joyful in spite of blessings.

What Must I Do?

Again, Paul's joy is rooted not in what he can do, but what God in Christ has done for him. We are not saved by self-promotion.

Christians are just as tempted as anyone else by the lure of financial security. We dream of having enough money to have a comfortable home, a good education for our children, fine cars, and enough savings to enjoy some luxuries and protection for a "rainy day." But the more we have, the more we want, and the more we concentrate on our own needs, the less compassion we have for others.

As Jesus was on his way to Jerusalem and certain death, a rich young man ran up, knelt before him, and asked with a sense of urgency: "Good Teacher, what must I *do* to inherit eternal life?" In the ensuing conversation it was clear that the man had been a faithful Jew, obeying all the commandments. Mark reports that "Jesus looking upon him loved him." By all conventional standards he was a good person. Yet, something was missing. He was looking to Jesus to provide a quick fix: "Tell me what I should do, and I'll do it." But when Jesus told him to sell his possessions and give to the poor, he "went away sorrowful." Gold had become his god, and he could not receive the gift of salvation, which is always free, until he was willing to part with what separated him from God (see Mark 10:17-21). True happiness cannot be bought.

A pastor had a life-long ambition to become a bishop. When he was finally elected and assigned an episcopal area, he found the job to be very lonely. The intimacy one enjoys with a congregation and the joy of preaching to the same people every week and growing with them in the faith were gone. He had reached the top rung of the religious ladder, but he was miserable. Happiness is not gained by self-seeking.

New Life in Christ

The rejoicing and the happiness that Paul knew and commended to the Philippians has its source "in the Lord." In other letters Paul speaks of being "in Christ": "If anyone is in Christ, there is a new creation: everything old has passed away; see, everything has become new!" (2 Corinthians 5:17). This intimate relationship is not earned; it is bestowed.

Hannah Whitall Smith, that wonderful Quaker author of the last century, wrote in her best-seller *The Christian's Secret of a Happy Life* ([New York: Fleming H. Revell, 1952], p. 45): "This blessed life must not be looked upon in any sense as an attainment, but as an obtainment. We cannot earn it, we cannot climb up to it, we cannot win it; we can do nothing but ask for it and receive it. It is the gift of God in Christ Jesus." To enter this "blessed life of rest and triumph," wrote Hannah Smith, we should repeat four words, emphasizing each time a different word:

Jesus saves me now—It is He.
Jesus *saves* me now—It is His work to save.
Jesus saves *me* now—I am the one to be saved.

I remember reading about a remarkable experience by Norman Vincent Peale during the Vietnam War. He was asked by then President Richard M. Nixon to go to Vietnam to speak to the American troops and visit the wounded in military hospitals. Dr. Peale was hesitant; it was not a popular war. Besides, there was an age difference of forty years between most of the troops and himself. Yet he felt compelled to go.

When he arrived he was greatly impressed by the dedication of the military chaplains. A Roman Catholic priest told of going twenty miles into the jungle twice a week to give "the blessed sacrament." "Isn't it dangerous?" asked Dr. Peale. "Yes," the priest replied, "but I have been called to serve God's children wherever and whatever their need." Dr. Peale wondered whether anything he might say would touch as deeply the lives of frightened soldiers.

He was taken to a jungle clearing where a large number of men were waiting for him to speak. He was not sure he was up to it and expressed his feelings to the commanding general. The general replied in words that became a spiritual mandate: "Just speak to them about Jesus Christ and

immortality, and speak to me about him, too. This may be the last time we
will hear about Christ."

When the service was over Dr. Peale was escorted to a waiting helicopter.
Every soldier, including the general, was standing at salute. "Why are they
saluting?" he asked. "I'm only a civilian pastor." Then it dawned on him:
they were showing profound respect and deep gratitude for the gospel they
had heard, assuring them of the deathless love of Christ and the confident
hope of immortality.

"Rejoice in the Lord always." Here is the source of true happiness; not
what I have done or earned or think I deserve in life, but what God has done
by coming to us in Jesus Christ and giving his life for our sake. When in
response to his love for me I give myself to him, especially by serving others,
I discover deep within the "peace which passes all understanding."
Through Christ there is joy in this life and hope for the life to come.

Helping Adults Become Involved

Preparing to Teach

This final passage may be Paul's last opportunity to communicate with the
Christians at Philippi. There is an urgency, an intensity to his words that
fasten one's attention. These are also some of the most sublime words the
apostle ever wrote.

It is important, as you prepare, to spend some time in reflection. First,
you should read, as an act of personal devotion, Romans 5:1-11. Note the
same concepts and even the same words found in Philippians 4: "Since we
are justified [accepted] by *faith* [not by works!], we have *peace* with God
through our Lord Jesus Christ. . . . While we were still weak, at the right
time Christ died for the ungodly. . . . *Boast* in God through our Lord Jesus
Christ" (Romans 5:1, 6, 11; italics added).

Second, it will be helpful to review the earlier chapters of Philippians,
lifting up the major themes in the previous three lessons. Having studied
them in detail, your reading them again will make them much more
meaningful and will provide a broad perspective—we need to see the woods
as well as the trees.

Third, as a teacher you need to take seriously Paul's admonition to pray
for understanding and guidance as you prepare to teach. That is a
prescription for a peaceful relationship with God, free of anxiety (4:4-7).
The person who does not pray is lacking in faith. Conversely, faith cannot
be deepened without prayer and trusting God unreservedly with the full
expectation that our prayers will be answered.

Here is the outline for this lesson:

> I. The setting of Philippians.
> II. Rejoicing in an anxious world.
> III. God strengthens us.

Introducing the Main Question

How we may find happiness is a major concern for most people, young
and old, rich and poor. I recommend that you read "The Main Question"
first, then pause for a brief discussion. Is this a fair portrayal of North

American society? Do we "nod to God" on Sundays and worship other gods (money, fame, success) the rest of the week? Be careful about pointing fingers at others whose excesses are obvious. What does this say about *you?*

Developing the Lesson

Moving now to the heart of the lesson, you should have a student read the text in sections (vv. 4-7, 8-9, 10-20), pausing after each section for another person to read "As You Read the Scripture." This will help provide the context in which the passage is to be understood.

Again for purposes of review, ask the class members to recall the conditions under which Paul wrote the letter. Be sure to remind them, if they do not mention it, of the very personal relationship Paul had with this congregation.

Then move to modern concerns. What does it mean to rejoice? Should we tell a homeless alcoholic, trying to keep warm on a grate in the sidewalk, to rejoice? Or is Paul speaking to those who have a special relationship with Christ? Might our being joyful cause us to be more sensitive toward the homeless person on the sidewalk?

Why are we anxious? Only personal and very honest answers are accepted! Because of the personal nature of the question, it would be helpful, if there are more than a dozen people present, to form small groups in which people will feel more comfortable talking about their personal feelings. You may ask them to discuss not only the kinds of anxiety we encounter in our pressure-packed, tension-filled world, but also ask them to deal with a natural follow-up: What is Paul's cure for anxiety? How do we know the "peace of God that passes all understanding"? Give the class fifteen minutes to do this activity and have a person from each group report to the entire class (not mentioning names!). It will be interesting to see whether the answers are similar or different.

Verse 8 reflects Paul's respect for high moral standards that can be found in a secular society like our own. The whole world is not going to the dogs!

But what about verse 9? Is it not a dangerous thing to hold oneself up as a moral example? Does this mean that Christians are to be "in the world but not of it"?

If there are persons in your class of unusual spiritual depth and strong faith, have them reflect in advance on what verses 11 and 13 mean to them and have them give their personal testimonies. Such a personal witness will enable the class to see that all of us, some more than others, have had experiences when the grace and power of God have sustained us through difficult days and that in witnessing to these experiences, we are not boasting (nor was Paul), but simply giving thanks for God's unfailing love.

Most adults have gone through hard times at one point or another. Our son was stricken with bone cancer and died just before his fourteenth birthday. You can imagine the grief that caused our family, our friends, and our church. The doctor in charge told my wife and me that we must do our best to carry on with our normal routine, as calmly and deliberately as possible. I can only witness to the fact that the gospel never meant so much to me and to my family as it did then. We discovered that marvelous preposition *in:* "We know that *in* all things God works for good with those who love him" (Romans 8:28 GNB). Paul understood that the conditions that crush us are also opportunities to discover as never before the limitless love of God. That is why he could rejoice in his suffering. That is why he could honestly say, "I can do all things through him who strengthens me."

Those who have gone through the valley of the shadow know, as only they can, that God is with them (see Psalm 23). That is why Paul's words mean so much to the Philippians, who are faced with their own special forms of danger—the danger of giving up their faith, of sliding back into their former pagan life-styles, of reckoning that the price of discipleship is too high and that caving in to their critics may be the easiest road to peace. They need a model, and Paul provides it both in word and deed. We, too, need Paul's words, and we need as well models who will inspire us to rejoice in the Lord.

Finally, there is the note of thanks, very personally expressed, in verses 14-20. What kind of "riches" is Paul referring to in verse 19?

Where *is* happiness to be found? The quotations from Hannah Whitall Smith, above, provide a fitting close.

Helping Class Members Act

We must not leave this lesson in a mood of spiritual self-satisfaction. Beyond the issue of personal happiness rooted in our relationship to Christ is this question: How do we model what we believe?

Planning for Next Sunday

Next Sunday we will begin Unit II, "Christ Above All." Ask the class to read Colossians 1 and to reflect on this question: If this passage provided the only information we have about Christ, who would we understand him to be?

Paul's Letter to the Philippians*

Fred B. Craddock

There is no indication that the writer or readers of Philippians ever thought it would be published, much less as sacred Scripture! No, Philippians is a letter in the commonly accepted sense of the term. As such it opens a window upon a relationship between the writer and the readers, a relationship which, by means of the letter, is remembered, enjoyed, nourished, and informed. A letter was the next best thing to being there, and we ought to try to make our reading of it the next best thing to having heard it read in the church at Philippi. We might be helped toward that end if we reflect briefly upon what it means to say Philippians is (a) a letter, (b) of Paul, (c) to a church.

* Adapted from Fred B. Craddock, *Philippians* (Atlanta: John Knox Press, 1985), pp. 2-8.

FOURTH QUARTER

A Letter

Much of Paul's ministry was by mail, and, for all the anxieties which that fact created for Paul and the churches, we are the richer because of it. Letters were not an invention or improvisation of Paul; they were quite common in Paul's time with many letters from the Greco-Roman world still extant. The term *epistle* referred to brief personal notes as well as to formal essay-like correspondence. In Paul's day, epistles had come to have a rather standard form consisting of three major parts: salutation, body, and farewell, with variations within that structure occurring due to factors such as haste or leisure, crisis or concord, intimacy or distance, privacy or publicity. Then, as now, letters served the general purpose of bridging a distance, usually geographical, and providing a kind of presence of the writer with the reader. This is obviously true also of Paul's letters, but as will be discussed below, the presence offered by Paul's letters was far more significant than was common to the correspondence in his culture.

Of Paul

That Philippians is a letter of Paul himself is undisputed. In fact, among students of Paul there are only two continuing debates touching Philippians as a letter. One has to do with whether or not the phrase "with the bishops and deacons" (1:1) is Paul's or is an addition from a later period in the church's life. . . . The other debate concerns the unity of the letter. Is our present Philippians a composite of two or three notes sent by Paul to the church at Philippi? This question has been fueled not only by a comment of Polycarp, early second-century Bishop of Smyrna, in a letter to the Philippians ("Paul, when he was absent, wrote letters to you" [3:2]), but by abrupt breaks in the flow of the letter itself. Note the unusual shift in both mood and thought in 3:1. . . . It might be well to remind ourselves that Paul comes to us in a body of letters written to the church, preserved by the church, transmitted by the church. Paul's letters were assembled and circulated as authoritative quite early (2 Peter 3:15-16), but that was no small task. Some of his correspondence was never recovered (1 Corinthians 5:9), and of what we possess, there is evidence of efforts to reconstruct letters by inserting fragments that still bear the marks of fragments. The most notable example is 2 Corinthians 6:14–7:1. Second Corinthians reads more smoothly and clearly without that unit. Also, if the process of transmitting Paul's letters in and for the church involved some editorial additions, as some claim of Philippians 1:1, our judgments about such matter should rest upon textual and historical evidence and not upon sentiment or preference. The point is that, whatever our conclusions in each case, the investigations are designed neither to reinforce nor to weaken confidence in the text as Scripture. On the contrary, one healthy result would be increased appreciation for the church that received and then passed along these letters. Paul's letters are documents in and for and to the church. Private reading, private assessment, and private interpretation, with a relationship to the church regarded as optional, could never have been imagined by Paul.

Paul had to write. His missionary style of establishing congregations in major urban centers and moving on (according to Acts, he was never in one place longer than two years, three months) dictated some type of ministry in absentia. Paul chose to write letters, perhaps because that form was closest to the oral.

To a Church

Paul's letters are personal but not private; he wrote to "all the saints." Even Philemon, which by its title gives the impression of being to an individual, is actually to Philemon and Apphia and Archippus and "the church in your house" (vv. 1-2). The congregation that received a letter from Paul very likely was a house church, the most common form of Christian assembly in the New Testament. We can safely assume that "house church" is not simply a term to designate where the Christians met but that the structure and behavior of the household as a social institution had a major influence in shaping the young churches. Most likely the congregation received that letter while assembled for worship. Paul was certainly aware that his words would be read in a worship setting and so filled his epistles with confessions, hymns, doxologies, eulogies, prayers, and benedictions. A writer at worship addressing a group at worship is a fact not to be missed by all others who read the letter, including ourselves. When the conditions of writer and reader are similar, new dimensions of understanding are opened. A letter from a soldier on a battlefront, written during a brief late-night respite from bombardment, is not best understood if read at the beach while partying with friends. More than dictionaries and commentaries are needed if midnight and high noon are to communicate. Nowhere in Paul's writing to Corinth does he better express the communicative distance between himself and that church than when he says; "You are wise, we are fools; you are rich, we are poor; you are kings, we are slaves; you are strong, we are weak; you are held in honor, we are garbage" (see 1 Corinthians 4:8-13). It was not so, however, between Paul and Philippi; they have been partners in giving, receiving, working, and rejoicing. Even now, the same agony Paul knows is what they also are experiencing. This fact more than any other accounts for what some call the beauty, others the simplicity, others the warmth, and yet others the spirituality of the letter.

Very likely all of these factors related to this particular correspondence have served to give Philippians so central a place in the reading of Scripture in Christian worship. All lectionaries use well over 50 percent of Philippians and some as much as 85 percent. Philippians 1:3-11 is often an Advent reading, and Philippians 2:5-11 is always the Epistle for Palm Sunday.

To say a letter of Paul was read in an assembly of Christians at worship is also to be reminded that the congregation received it by the ear, not by the eye. This is assuming that the practice of reading aloud Paul's letters (1 Thessalonians 5–27; Colossians 4:16) was a general one. After all, there was only one copy. This being the case, we may be sure that Paul would write for the ear. This means that the contents would be framed so as to be understood and remembered from having heard it. We would expect, therefore, that Paul would follow a pattern of letter writing familiar to his readers, that he would use some materials already known to them, such as hymns, confessions, and good conduct lists, and that he would employ such rhetorical devices as would aid a listener. In the commentary to follow, we shall have occasion to notice many such features in Philippians.

Finally, to say that a letter is to a church is to become very aware of that church: its circumstances, its work, its strengths, its problems. Paul wrote letters to congregations, not to the church universal; and whatever timelessness there was to his letters was a matter for others to discern and immortalize. Paul wrote no third-class circulars addressed to "Occupant, Greco-Roman World." His ministry was to particular groups trying to live out the gospel in concrete ways. So important to him were the crises and shifts of circumstances in the churches that Paul would send much-needed aides for news or even interrupt his own mission in order to learn how it was with a troubled congregation (2 Corinthians 2:1-13). His effort as preacher and teacher was to effect an indigenous hearing of the gospel. He did not, of course, wait until he arrived in a city to discover what to preach; he brought with him the tradition. The categories, the accents, the contours of his message, however, were appropriate to the condition of his hearers. To appreciate this feature of Paul's letters one has only to look at the later epistles of the New Testament. In them both writer and reader lose addresses and identities in epistles that go out to all of like faith (2 Peter), to the twelve tribes of the dispersion (James), to all Christians scattered throughout Asia (1 Peter). Not so with Paul. Mixed in the chemistry of his letters one finds always some of the local soil. Any interpreter who would be true to Paul will do the same thing, when bringing one of his letters to a new address.

UNIT II: CHRIST ABOVE ALL

FOUR LESSONS   JULY 4–25

Who is Christ for you? Is he a figure from the distant past to be revered but kept at arm's length? That is who he is for vast numbers of people, even some who attend church regularly, but who segregate work from worship. This was also the situation in the eastern Asia Minor city of Colossae, where Christianity was in danger of becoming just one more religious cult among many. Paul, writing from his prison cell, was deeply concerned that the Colossians understand who Christ is "the image of the invisible God. . . . For in him all the fullness of God was pleased to dwell" (Colossians 1:15, 19). But faith must lead to transformed lives: "As you therefore received Christ Jesus the Lord, continue to live your lives in him, rooted and built up in him and established in the faith" (2:6-7). Thus Paul devotes more than half of his letter to morality and the question of how one is to live the Christian life in a pagan world. (How, for example, will Philemon receive his recently converted slave? As a brother in Christ or as a piece of property?) We live in a different world, but the questions remain: How deep is my commitment to Christ? Does being a Christian make a difference? Do not read any further unless you are willing to deal with these questions.

The Preeminent Christ

Background Scripture: Colossians 1

The Main Question

The Letter to the Colossians is meant to counteract powerful influences that are corrupting the young Christian congregation. Three heretical doctrines threaten the truth about Christ and the Christ-like life.

First is the belief that Christ is one savior among many and that, therefore, Christianity is simply one more religion competing against a host of rivals.

Second is the idea that all that is physical or material is evil. Therefore, a pure and holy God would not stoop so low as to appear in the flesh. The tremendous gap between heaven and hell is filled with intermediary beings, but God dwells in "unapproachable light."

Third is the belief that the religious life as communicated to the Colossians through Epaphras, a "faithful minister of Christ on [Paul's] behalf," is incomplete. There are "festivals, new moons, and sabbaths [holy days]" (2:16) that must be observed if one is to be holy. These are a mixture of Jewish and pagan practices. "Paul sees clearly that all such views are incompatible with belief in a loving and personal God, such as is revealed to us in the face of Jesus Christ" (Stephen Neill, *Paul to the Colossians* [New York: Association Press, 1964], p. 14).

Is it so different in our time? Not only are Moslems, Hindus, and Buddhists growing in record numbers in traditionally Judeo-Christian areas of the country, but we have also witnessed a remarkable growth of cults like Zen Buddhism, I Ching, Hare Krishna, and the Unification Church of Sun Myung Moon, all of which challenge traditional faith. The question for the Colossians—and for us—is this: Is Christ just one god among many, or is Christ Lord of all?

Selected Scripture

King James Version	New Revised Standard Version
Colossians 1:3-5a, 11-23	*Colossians 1:3-5a, 11-23*
3 We give thanks to God and the Father of our Lord Jesus Christ, praying always for you,	3 In our prayers for you we always thank God, the Father of our Lord Jesus Christ, 4 for we have heard of your faith in Christ Jesus and of the
4 Since we heard of your faith in Christ Jesus, and of the love which ye have to all the saints,	love that you have for all the saints, 5 because of the hope laid up for you in heaven.
5 For the hope which is laid up for you in heaven.	
....	....
11 Strengthened with all might, according to his glorious power,	11 May you be made strong with all the strength that comes from his

unto all patience and longsuffering with joyfulness;

12 Giving thanks unto the Father, which hath made us meet to be partakers of the inheritance of the saints in light:

13 Who hath delivered us from the power of darkness, and hath translated us into the kingdom of his dear Son:

14 In whom we have redemption through his blood, even the forgiveness of sins:

15 Who is the image of the invisible God, the firstborn of every creature:

16 For by him were all things created, that are in heaven, and that are in earth, visible and invisible, whether they be thrones, or dominions, or principalities, or powers: all things were created by him, and for him:

17 And he is before all things, and by him all things consist.

18 And he is the head of the body, the church: who is the beginning, the firstborn from the dead; that in all things he might have the preeminence.

19 For it pleased the Father that in him should all fulness dwell;

20 And, having made peace through the blood of his cross, by him to reconcile all things unto himself; by him, I say, whether they be things in earth, or things in heaven.

21 And you, that were sometime alienated and enemies in your mind by wicked works, yet now hath he reconciled

22 In the body of his flesh through death, to present you holy and unblameable and unreproveable in his sight:

23 If ye continue in the faith grounded and settled, and be not moved away from the hope of the gospel, which ye have heard, and which was preached to every crea-

glorious power, and may you be prepared to endure everything with patience, while joyfully 12 giving thanks to the Father, who has enabled you to share in the inheritance of the saints in the light. 13 He has rescued us from the power of darkness and transferred us into the kingdom of his beloved Son, 14 in whom we have redemption, the forgiveness of sins.

15 He is the image of the invisible God, the firstborn of all creation; 16 for in him all things in heaven and on earth were created, things visible and invisible, whether thrones or dominions or rulers or powers—all thing have been created through him and for him. 17 He himself is before all things, and in him all things hold together. 18 He is the head of the body, the church; he is the beginning, the firstborn from the dead, so that he might come to have first place in everything. 19 For in him all the fullness of God was pleased to dwell, 20 and through him God was pleased to reconcile to himself all things, whether on earth or in heaven, by making peace through the blood of his cross.

21 And you, who were once estranged and hostile in mind, doing evil deeds, 22 he has now reconciled in his fleshly body through death, so as to present you holy and blameless and irreproachable before him— 23 provided that you continue securely established and steadfast in the faith, without shifting from the hope promised by the gospel that you heard, which has been proclaimed to every creature under heaven. I, Paul, became a

ture which is under heaven; whereof I Paul am made a minister.

servant of this gospel.

Key Verse: **And he is before all
things, and by him all things
consist. (Colossians 1:17)**

Key Verse: **He himself is before
all things, and in him all things
hold together. (Colossians 1:17)**

As You Read the Scripture

Colossians 1. Paul is writing to the "saints and faithful brothers and
sisters in Christ at Colossae." Colossae was one of three cities about one
hundred miles east of Ephesus, all lying close together in the valley of the
River Lycus. Laodicea and Hierapolis are both mentioned in the letter
(4:13), and Laodicea is one of the seven churches to which the Revelation to
John is addressed (3:14). It was a generally prosperous area with chalk and
wool as the main exports, and there was a large Jewish population there.

We do not know whether Paul personally visited Colossae. During his
third missionary journey he spent three years in Ephesus (see Acts 18 and
19), during which Epaphras may have heard Paul and was converted. He
then returned to Colossae to found a Christian congregation. Paul gives frequent references to being in prison (4:3, 10, 18) in either Ephesus or Rome.

Verses 1-2. A very traditional and warm Pauline greeting.

Verses 3-5a. Immediately following the greeting is an expression of
thanksgiving to God, "the Father of our Lord Jesus Christ," woven around
three words: *faith, love,* and *hope* (1 Corinthians 13:13). *Faith* is the utter trust
of sinner in a Savior who died to redeem them. *Love (agape)* is the ethical side
of faith. This is the love that "dissolves animosities and forgives injuries and
forges a true fellowship of the spirit" (*IB*, vol. 11, p. 151). *Hope,* founded on
Christ's resurrection, is fixed on "an inheritance that is imperishable,
undefiled, and unfading, kept in heaven for you" (1 Peter 1:4).

Verses 11-14. Following a prayer that the Colossians may be filled with
the knowledge of God's will and lead a life worthy of the Lord, "bearing
fruit in every good work and increasing in the knowledge of God" (see vv.
9-10), Paul continues in the mood of supplication, asking that they be
strengthened—a steady accession of strength, which is a gift of God—and
for endurance and patience: "May you be made strong with all the strength
which comes from [God's] glorious power, so that you may be able to endure
everything with patience" (vv. 11-12 GNB). The "inheritance of the saints"
is the eternal abiding place in the presence of God—the abode of those
whose spiritual warfare has ended. We are already delivered from the
"dominion of darkness" where evil holds sway, and we belong to the
"kingdom of his beloved Son" who redeems and forgives us.

Verses 15-23. This is the great christological passage that is the
theological foundation of both this letter and Paul's faith. A. M. Hunter
divides the first five verses into two sets of theological statements:

1. Christ and Creation (1:15-17)
   1. Christ is God manifest.
   2. In time and dignity he is prior to all creation.
   3. In him absolutely everything in the universe has been created, and
      not only is he God's mediator in creation, but he is creation's goal.
   4. It is to him that all things owe their coherence.

FOURTH QUARTER

Christ and the Church (1:18-20)
1. Christ is the Head of the Church, his Body.
2. As death's first conqueror, he is the sovereign Lord of a great risen host.
3. God in his fullness chose to dwell in him, and through him to reconcile to himself the whole universe.
4. The instrument of reconciliation is the Cross.
   (A. M. Hunter, *The Layman's Bible Commentary*, vol. 22 [Atlanta: John Knox Press, 1959], p. 123)

Verses 21-23. Those who were estranged have, through Christ's death, been reconciled to God. But they must remain stable and steadfast, not straying from the universal gospel they first received and of which Paul is Christ's servant.

The Scripture and the Main Question

Idolatry

Is Christ one divine being among many, or is he "Lord of all"? This question is not academic but, rather, very real.

Monotheism, belief in one God, is a distinctive contribution of the Judeo-Christian tradition: "Hear, O Israel: The LORD is our God, the LORD alone" (Deuteronomy 6:4). Yet how easily we compromise our faith. All of us are tempted by lesser gods. We may repeat the Apostles' Creed: "I believe in God, the Father, Almighty. . . . " but actually give our highest allegiance to money, material possessions, sports, success, and power. No one is free from the temptation to worship these powerful, but lesser, gods. Even Jesus had to struggle in the wilderness with Satan, who slyly suggested that if Jesus would only worship him, he could rule the world (Matthew 4:9).

At the heart of this struggle is the sin of *hubris*, pride. We see it in the Garden of Eden, where Adam and Eve were given all they possibly could want to make life pleasant. But they were fascinated by the forbidden fruit of the tree in the middle of the garden. Satan, who appeared in the form of a talking serpent, made evil positively attractive: "Go ahead and eat the fruit. You will not die; in fact, you will be like God" (see Genesis 3:4-5). That was the fatal blow. They ate, disobeying God's clear command, thereby severing the very special relationship between Creator and creature. When God is displaced by lesser gods, the results are always the same: estrangement, disruption of vital relationships, and the feeling that at the very core of life something is terribly wrong. The Bible has a very simple word for this rebellion: *sin*.

The Cults Are Coming

Not only is our faith weakened by idolatry, but in recent decades there has been an enormous rise in religious cults claiming a monopoly on divine truth. The Hare Krishnas, transcendental meditation, the Moonies, founded by Sun Myung Moon, I Ching, as well as witchcraft and Satanism, have become household words. Why do we have all these curious cults in an enlightened age and a scientifically advanced culture such as ours?

Interest in Eastern religions surfaced during World War II, especially among American troops serving in the Pacific. The wars in Korea and Vietnam brought further contact with Asian religions. With ever faster means of transportation and instant global communication, cultures once insulated are now open, with a consequent exchange of religious beliefs and practices.

Also, during the 1960s there was a profound reaction against the values of Western society, led by young people revolting from the beliefs and values of their parents. Retaining young people as active church members, at least in mainline churches, is difficult in any era. Keeping central their commitment to Christ in a polytheistic world (a world of many gods) has been especially difficult.

The Ultimate Commitment

We may dismiss the reading of horoscopes as being trivial and insignificant. How can a constellation of stars possibly affect our future? But most cults demand more than incidental allegiance. In 1978 a cult that began in San Francisco and relocated in Central America was the subject of a congressional investigation that focused mainly on their charismatic leader, Jim Jones. As "outsiders" closed in on the group's compound, Jones ordered his entire community of several hundred persons of all ages to commit suicide. It was a bizarre and tragic end to a strange and misled community. This is not to suggest that all cults are dangerous to your health. They do, however, pose a serious challenge to Christian faith and practice.

When the Center No Longer Holds

Strong forces are at work in our society that have made us vulnerable to strange and esoteric cults. One is the growing revulsion against a technological society and a life-style of material consumption. The cults offer an opportunity to withdraw from a greed-oriented, competitive world and focus on the things of the spirit.

There has also been amazing tolerance for new ideas and practices. This is especially true on college campuses, where eager young converts are made at a very formative time in their lives. The result is a kind of relativism that says that one religion is as good as the next; it doesn't make any difference what you believe as long as you are sincere! When all beliefs are considered true, nothing is exclusively or uniquely true. For Christians, this puts the truth of God revealed supremely in Jesus Christ in jeopardy.

Howard Wilson sums up the situation in these words: "It is a terrible thing to live without a center. Everyone needs a single truth around which to order life. It is one of the marks of our times that people feel fragmented, pulled in all directions by the competing forces and influences of modern life" (*Invasion from the East* [Minneapolis: Augsburg Publishing House, 1978], p. 121).

Put Christ in the Center

This is precisely the situation Paul addressed in his Letter to the Colossians. There was an attempt to blend Christian faith and practice with strange taboos—Do not handle; do not taste; do not touch (see 2:21)—and

347

the observance of "festivals, new moons, and sabbaths" that had no relationship with the Christian faith. The result was an amalgamation of Christian, Jewish, and pagan practices that threatened the very existence of the Church.

Paul responded to these dangers, which he had apparently learned about from Epaphras, by affirming the supremacy and uniqueness of the Christian faith: "[Christ] is the image of the invisible God, the firstborn of all creation. . . . He himself is before all things, and in him all things hold together. . . . In him all the fullness of God was pleased to dwell" (1:15, 17, 19).

He then spelled out in no uncertain terms how those who believe deeply in Christ should have no dealings with fads about foods or holy days or petty prohibitions against this practice or that. These are only "shadows." The substance, the reality, belongs to Christ (2:16-23). The last two chapters deal in detail with Christian morality, which flows from our being "raised with Christ" (3:1–4:6).

What does all this have to do with Christians living in the last decade of the twentieth century? First, it reminds us that we are to have no other gods (see Exodus 20:3). Second, we are not to water down the Christian faith by mixing it with alien beliefs and practices. Finally, we must be careful about slipping into the salvation-by-works mentality. Nothing we do can restore our broken relationship with God. The amazing good news is that we who were once estranged have been reconciled by the death of Christ, in whom there is new life indeed.

Helping Adults Become Involved

Preparing to Teach

This is the first of three lessons on Paul's Letter to the Colossians. It is not as personal as the Letter to the Philippians, but it is just as intense. It is important that you read the letter as a whole, without the aid of a commentary, so that you may become acquainted with both the major content and the tone of the epistle.

Last week, in "Planning for Next Sunday" you asked the class, "If the letter to the Colossians were the only source of knowledge we have about Christ, who would we understand him to be?" This is not a trick question, and the answer is not difficult. The first two chapters of Colossians are, in fact, mostly theological, pointing up the supremacy of Christ. There are parallels in the statement of his arguments with Ephesians, which we will be studying next month.

One way to highlight what Paul says about Christ is to list the theological references, beginning with "his beloved Son, in whom we have redemption, the forgiveness of sins" (1:13-14), and continuing at least through 3:4. That is quite an impressive list! At the time of the writing of this letter (roughly A.D. 61–63, at the latest) there was no such thing as a body of knowledge called Christian theology. Paul was not only writing an urgent letter to young believers, but also he was creating Christian theology at the same time.

The challenge for modern Christians is to discover what Paul has to say to us today. I believe the class will find it more relevant than it may first appear.

Today's lesson outline:

     I. The challenge of cults.
    II. Why are people attracted to cults?
  III. What difference does Christ make in our lives?

Introducing the Main Question

It is very important to understand the context in which Paul wrote Colossians. Chapter 19 of Acts highlights some memorable moments in his life in Ephesus. But there is no mention of Colossae or a letter written to the Christians there. We have to depend on the internal evidence of the letter itself for information about why it was written and what were the conditions which Paul addressed.

"The Main Question" is, therefore, very important. It summarizes the competing philosophies and practices that threatened to change the very character, if not the existence, of the Church. In order to get this before the people, the letter should be read in its entirety. If you have a chalkboard or newsprint, you might write the three "heretical doctrines" (see "The Main Question") for all to see.

Developing the Lesson

As in previous lessons, you may wish to begin with "As You Read the Scripture," by having one person read the text and another the commentary. Then follow with "Introducing the Main Question." In any event it is important that the class understand the major thrust of the letter and the context out of which it came.

The attraction of cults in our society raises some very interesting questions, such as: Why are these strange religions, with their odd beliefs and strict mandates concerning moral behavior, so appealing? Has anyone personally had experiences with cult members? How should we to deal with them?

This may prove to be embarrassing if any members of your class or their families have had unfortunate experiences with cults. If so, then you will want to shift to a more general question, such as, "Who or what are Christianity's main competitors in today's society?" The class should come up with several thought-provoking answers, such as those mentioned in the section on idolatry at the beginning of "The Scripture and the Main Question." That could lead to a discussion of what we can do about it (how we should respond to our competitors). Finish on a positive note with a refocus on the christological passages (esp.1:15-23).

Here is some additional information on religious cults which I hope will be both helpful and appropriate. I am grateful to an excellent resource, *The Cults Are Coming,* by Lowell D. Streiker (Nashville: Abingdon Press, 1978). Although a bit dated, the information is still very accurate:

A cult is a movement of social protest and personal affirmation. It offers a total way of life to those who are alienated from their families and the attitudes by which their families and their society attempted to prepare them for successful adulthood. Cults attract the dispossessed, the bored, the lonely. . . .

The tenets [beliefs] of a cult are set forth by a founder-prophet [like Sun Myung Moon]. Cult members are highly dependent upon their leader [who has absolute authority over the cult]. . . . They represent a definite break with prevailing religions.

For example, the Children of God was originally a Fundamentalist-Pentecostal sect. . . .

Krishna Consciousness is a manifestation of traditional Hinduism. . . .

Cults flourish in an atmosphere of stress and rapid social change. . . . If life is too easy, if the individual has neither purpose nor direction, if there is no ordeal ahead to test courage and ideals—at these times, cults are indispensable. . . .

. . . The hunger that drives men and women toward novel, difficult, self-abnegating paths is seldom born of economic need. On the contrary, a hallmark of the cults is their repudiation of the competitive, acquisitive materialism of our society. . . . [Once admitted to the cult,] you belong to the chosen, the elite, those set apart from ordinary mortals. (pp. 9-10)

Those in a cult are members of a new family in which they find a new sense of identity and purpose, and their conduct at all times is determined by harsh and very strict standards of discipline.

Are we as committed to Christ as the "Moonies" are to Sun Myung Moon? Here is a real Christian heresy. The teachings of the Moonies, writes Dr. Streiker, are "a blend of Christian theology, Korean folk religion, confused speculations, social activism, and heretical innovations" (p. 39).

Use these observations about cults to lead a discussion that includes these questions: Is Christ really preeminent? If so, what difference does it make in our lives?

Helping Class Members Act

Too many of us are uninformed and, therefore, may miss the challenge that Paul presents. It will be helpful for you to recommend books that provide information about cults and, to counteract them, books that focus on the central beliefs of Christianity. Your pastor should be a helpful resource person.

Planning for Next Sunday

Paul speaks in a very direct and personal way in Colossians 2:5-19: Is Christ my personal Savior, or am I among his admirers, but not his followers? We continue with the question, "Who is Christ for me?"

The Sufficient Christ

Background Scripture: Colossians 2

The Main Question

What More Do We Need?

For many people the claims of the Christian faith are literally too good to be true. They cannot accept that God forgives all our sins, even our worst, and that as unacceptable as we may be, God loves us and asks that we put our complete and utter trust in God. How do we know this? As Christians we believe that Christ is the incarnation of God, who loved us so much that he was willing to die when it was we who deserved the death penalty. He offers us eternal life that begins not in the hereafter, but in the here and now.

But guilt has a powerful hold over the human psyche. We may believe in our minds that the past is over and gone and that Christ had accepted us as we are, but in our heart of hearts we fear that it may not be so. So Martin Luther, on his way to becoming an Augustinian monk, flogged himself until he was nearly unconscious, because of imaginary sins. Many perfectionists demand such high standards of themselves that they can never rest; they are constantly aware of doing what they should not have done and not doing what they should do, and they cannot forgive themselves. Thus the peace of God eludes them.

Clearly that was the situation in Colossae—only it was even more serious because they were a young church. Being Christians was new to them, and it was so easy to lose their way. Besides, they were constantly bombarded by critics who insisted that they still observe a mixture of Jewish and pagan rituals. Paul's response is to affirm the sufficiency of Christ. What more do they need? It is our question as well.

Selected Scripture

King James Version	New Revised Standard Version
Colossians 2:5-19	*Colossians 2:5-19*
5 For though I be absent in the flesh, yet am I with you in the spirit, joying and beholding your order, and the stedfastness of your faith in Christ.	5 For though I am absent in body, yet I am with you in spirit, and I rejoice to see your morale and the firmness of your faith in Christ.
6 As ye have therefore received Christ Jesus the Lord, so walk ye in him:	6 As you therefore have received Christ Jesus the Lord, continue to live your lives in him, 7 rooted and
7 Rooted and built up in him, and stablished in the faith, as ye have been taught, abounding therein with thanksgiving.	built up in him and established in the faith, just as you were taught, abounding in thanksgiving.
8 Beware lest any man spoil you through philosophy and vain deceit,	8 See to it that no one takes you captive through philosophy and

351

after the tradition of men, after the rudiments of the world, and not after Christ.

9 For in him dwelleth all the fulness of the Godhead bodily.

10 And ye are complete in him, which is the head of all principality and power:

11 In whom also ye are circumcised with the circumcision made without hands, in putting off the body of the sins of the flesh by the circumcision of Christ:

12 Buried with him in baptism, wherein also ye are risen with him through the faith of the operation of God, who hath raised him from the dead.

13 And you, being dead in your sins and the uncircumcision of your flesh, hath he quickened together with him, having forgiven you all trespasses;

14 Blotting out the handwriting of ordinances that was against us, which was contrary to us, and took it out of the way, nailing it to his cross;

15 And having spoiled principalities and powers, he made a shew of them openly, triumphing over them in it.

16 Let no man therefore judge you in meat, or in drink, or in respect of an holyday, or of the new moon, or of the sabbath days:

17 Which are a shadow of things to come; but the body is of Christ.

18 Let no man beguile you of your reward in a voluntary humility and worshipping of angels, intruding into those things which he hath not seen, vainly puffed up by his fleshly mind,

19 And not holding the Head, from which all the body by joints and bands having nourishment ministered, and knit together, increaseth with the increase of God.

Key Verse: **As ye have therefore received Christ Jesus the Lord, so walk ye in him. (Colossians 2:6)**

empty deceit, according to human tradition, according to the elemental spirits of the universe, and not according to Christ. 9 For in him the whole fullness of deity dwells bodily, 10 and you have come to fullness in him, who is the head of every ruler and authority. 11 In him also you were circumcised with a spiritual circumcision, by putting off the body of the flesh in the circumcision of Christ; 12 when you were buried with him in baptism, you were also raised with him through faith in the power of God, who raised him from the dead. 13 And when you were dead in trespasses and the uncircumcision of your flesh, God made you alive together with him, when he forgave us all our trespasses, 14 erasing the record that stood against us with its legal demands. He set this aside, nailing it to the cross. 15 He disarmed the rulers and authorities and made a public example of them, triumphing over them in it.

16 Therefore do not let anyone condemn you in matters of food and drink or of observing festivals, new moons, or sabbaths. 17 These are only a shadow of what is to come, but the substance belongs to Christ. 18 Do not let anyone disqualify you, insisting on self-abasement and worship of angels, dwelling on visions, puffed up without cause by a human way of thinking, 19 and not holding fast to the head, from whom the whole body, nourished and held together by its ligaments and sinews, grows with a growth that is from God.

Key Verse: **As you therefore have received Christ Jesus the Lord, continue to live your lives in him. (Colossians 2:6)**

As You Read the Scripture

Colossians 2:5. Paul believed that absence in body need not mean absence in spirit. On the contrary, he believed in a spiritual fellowship that transcends time and space (see 1 Corinthians 5:3-5).

Verses 6-7. Verse 6 is connected in thought with 1:21-23. Now he reinforces his plea with a fresh statement of the preeminence of Christ and the vital relation with him into which they have entered. Once they have received him as Lord, Christ becomes the foundation and vital center of all existence.

Here is an appeal to the experience of Christ, which is the beginning of a new spiritual life. They have received him not as a system of ideas, but as a person. Fellowship with Christ is the surest protection against false doctrines and demonic powers.

Verse 8. Paul sternly warns against heretics who capture the unsuspecting with false philosophies and "empty deceit." Their great error is believing that Christ is only one among many "elemental spirits," or mediators, between God and the world.

Verses 9-10. Christ is the incarnation (enfleshment) of God. The "whole fullness of deity" is incorporated in his life, death, and resurrection. You need look no further for salvation, for you have come to "fullness of life" in the one who is supreme over all earthly powers.

Verses 11-15. In Christian baptism one dedicates one's whole being to God. This dedication in the realm of the spirit is more binding than a mere physical mark on one's body (circumcision):

> For when you were baptized, you were buried with Christ, and in baptism you were also raised with Christ through your faith in the active power of God, who raised him from death. You were at one time spiritually dead because of your sins and because you were Gentiles without the Law. But God has now brought you to life with Christ. God forgave us all our sins.

> (Colossians 2:12-13 GNB)

Christ's death on the cross canceled the bond that stood against us—literally, our debts, our "IOUs," which we could never repay, for there is no way we can satisfy all the requirements of the law! Christ not only paid what we owe by his death, but also he disarmed the "rulers and authorities" (the hierarchy of spiritual beings believed to exist between God and the world, as in v. 8). Here is another military metaphor. Christ, having vanquished his foes and disarmed them of any weapons, leads them in a military parade as he enters the capital city in triumph. This is an obvious reference to the triumphant victory parades of conquering heroes, except that Christ's victory is cosmic in that he has defeated all the unseen forces in the cosmos that bedevil our lives.

Verses 16-19. There will be those who tell you that you are still imperfect, that you need to observe some festival and abstain from certain foods. These are trivialities, "a shadow of what is to come." Christ is the one Reality we need—the true and perfect sacrifice for all.

Those who insist on these strange rituals are "puffed up" with their own importance and are not connected with Christ, the Head, without whom neither growth nor life itself is possible. Christ alone is sufficient.

FOURTH QUARTER

The Scripture and the Main Question

Visitors

As I drove into the driveway around ten o'clock at night they were waiting for me on the front steps. Two young men, clean-cut and soft-spoken. While I was startled to see them there (today we would probably call the police!), any fears I had were soon banished by their friendliness. Who were they, and what did they want?

They were members of The Church of Jesus Christ of Latter-day Saints, Mormons. They had spent the day in the New England village where I was pastor and needed a place to stay overnight. Someone had told them that I was single and that there was plenty of room in the house where I was living that summer while the owners were on an extended trip. It was very thoughtful of my friends to offer my hospitality!

This was my first personal encounter with Mormons. I welcomed them into my temporary home, and we had a long conversation that lasted until midnight. The next morning I was up "bright and early" and made a quick run to the store to get some coffee, only to discover, when my visitors came down to breakfast, that they did not drink coffee or any other "stimulant."

Before leaving, they presented me with the Book of Mormon, and we had a prayer together, giving thanks for our fellowship and asking God's blessing on our ministries. Soon my phone began to ring with parishioners wanting to know about the Mormons. That prompted me to change my sermon title for the next Sunday in order to answer their questions.

Strange Doctrines

I want to make it very clear, before continuing these comments, that I have the highest respect for the Mormon people I know. They are deeply dedicated to their church. They give at least 10 percent of their income to it every year. They adhere to high moral standards and stress the importance of a strong family life. Most important, they send their young people out as missionaries for two years to witness to the faith, going from house to house to win new converts. Because of this strong missionary thrust the Mormon Church is one of the fastest growing religious sects in America.

What surprises me is how people in our enlightened age can accept Mormon doctrines. Mormon beliefs arise from Joseph Smith of Seneca County, New York, who as a teenager in the early 1800s had a vision of God and his Son, Jesus Christ. This revelation continued the divine theophanies contained in the Old and New Testaments. Soon afterward a heavenly messenger appeared, giving his name as Moroni and revealing the existence of a record engraved on gold plates, hidden in a hill between Palmyra and Manchester. New York. Four years later the plates were delivered into Joseph's hands along with the ability to translate them. They allegedly contained the "fulness of Christ's Gospel" as made known by the "risen Redeemer" to the ancient inhabitants of America. The "translation" became the Book of Mormon (named after the father of Moroni, who as a mortal had concealed the golden tablets in the hill). While no one else has ever seen the tablets, these "scriptures" were believed to be authoritative and became the basis of a new religious sect.

The Church of Jesus Christ of Latter-day Saints recognizes two sources of doctrine: the written word of God (the Scriptures) and direct revelation from God. Their scriptures include the Old and New Testaments, the Book of Mormon, the Doctrine and the Covenants, a collection of revelations given in the present day chiefly through Joseph Smith, and the Pearl of Great Price, a collection of fragments from the writings of Moses and Abraham that are not found in the Bible, but were revealed to Joseph Smith. The president of the church is God's prophet, seer, and revelator who speaks for God.

Old Heresies in New Forms

In the opinion of many, Mormonism is a contemporary example of an ancient heresy that reduces Christ from the ultimate revealer of divine truth to one among several. It also contradicts the Scripture it professes to uphold: *In [Christ] the whole fullness of deity dwells bodily.*

Today's passage from Colossians also challenges all of those who still believe we can earn salvation. Protestants should know better. Martin Luther, plagued by guilt, rediscovered the central core of Pauline theology: "The one who is righteous will live by faith" (Romans 1:17), not by artificial laws governing human behavior. Again, Paul says, "Having been set free from sin, [we] have become slaves of righteousness" (Romans 6:18). We will say more about this in next Sunday's lesson.

Paul's ultimate appeal is to personal experiences of the redeeming grace of Christ: "You have come to fullness in him . . . you were buried with him in baptism, you were also raised with him through faith in the power of God, who raised him from the dead. . . . God made you alive together with him, when he forgave us all our trespasses" (Colossians 2:10, 12-13).

To Experience Christ's Love

The most important thing about our relationship with Christ is not our belief in the forgiveness of sins, but our *experience* of God's forgiving grace. In a wonderfully vivid story told by Luke (7:36-50), Jesus is the guest in the home of a prominent Pharisee, known for his meticulous obedience to the law. During dinner a woman of the streets entered the dining room and, standing behind Jesus (who was reclining at a table as was the custom), wet his feet with her tears, wiped his feet with her hair, and kissed his feet and anointed them with ointment. It was a shocking demonstration, for sinners were not permitted inside the home of the righteous. Moreover, by receiving a forgiven sinner and rejecting a self-righteous Pharisee, Jesus reversed the assumptions of conventional morality.

Her bold visit gave Jesus an occasion to teach Simon—and us—a lesson about love and forgiveness: "I tell you, her sins, which were many, have been forgiven; hence she has shown great love. But the one to whom little is forgiven, loves little" (Luke 7:47).

Have we experienced new life in Christ? Have we known the joy of being accepted by him even though, by the standards of many, we are unacceptable? Paul's concern is that we come to know that God through Christ loves us with a love that will not let us go. Let us "hold fast to the Head," therefore, in the firm faith that as members of his body we will find all that is needed to make our lives complete.

FOURTH QUARTER

Helping Adults Become Involved

Preparing to Teach

This is a difficult passage. Paul assumes that the Colossians understood terms that are difficult for us, such as his use of the word *circumcision* three times in verse 11, each with its own special nuance.

Verse 6 is, however, the key to the passage, and you will want to make sure, in dealing with the passage, that you return to that central theme.

I recommend that you read a modern translation, if available, such as the New Revised Standard Version or the Good News Bible, which are very reliable translations and are easier to understand.

You will find Hebrews 10:11-25 to be an excellent parallel passage in which Christ is seen as the great high priest whose offering of himself was sufficient for all our sins: "Where there is forgiveness . . . there is no longer any offering for sin" (Hebrews 10:18).

Today's lesson outline:

I. The problem of heresy
II. Christ in you
III. Focus on Christ

Introducing the Main Question

This week I recommend that you read "The Main Question" first in class. It will help the members to focus on the central theme and will provide a better understanding of Paul's message as it is presented in "As You Read the Scripture."

Developing the Lesson

A review of last week's "The Main Question" through point 3 will recall the context in which the letter was written. This is very important for everyone, and especially so for any who were not present last Sunday. Then summarize with these important points:

1. Paul is writing to a congregation that "has not seen [his] face." Therefore, the Letter to the Colossians lacks the personal touch so characteristic of Philippians.
2. Epaphras is Paul's pupil and apprentice in the faith and his special representative to the congregation at Colossae.
3. There is a great danger that the new Christian congregation will accept uncritically the demands that they observe a combination of pagan and Jewish rules and regulations, resulting in an amalgamation that has little resemblance to faith in Christ alone for salvation.

This week part of our focus is on heresy, defined as any belief or theory that is strongly at variance with established beliefs or mores. Ask the class this question: "Can anyone think of a contemporary sect that may loosely be called Christian but does not regard Christ as supreme?"

Someone may suggest the Jehovah's Witnesses. Here is a strongly fundamentalist sect who regard both Roman Catholic and Protestant churches as being misguided by Satan. The one true God, the Witnesses believe, is Jehovah as revealed in the Old Testament. The righteous in the Bible, from Abel on, testify to the setting up of the Rule of God, a theocracy in which God rules supreme. That is why Jehovah's Witnesses do not pledge allegiance to any national flag. For them it is putting country before God. Jesus Christ is perfect man, not God, and is God's agent in establishing the theocracy. The Witnesses do not believe in hell; the wicked are destroyed here on earth. That should be enough for the class members to discuss for a while!

You may wish to present my comments about the Mormon faith in "The Scripture and the Main Question." In both examples—the Mormons and the Jehovah's Witnesses—Christ is not considered sufficient in the traditional, biblical sense.

Make it very clear, however, that your class is not to criticize others in order to make themselves feel better. Then you all would be guilty of the same self-righteousness displayed by the Pharisee in Luke's story (7:36-50). You are simply drawing upon modern parallels to the situation in Colossae. This should not dominate the discussion, but it should be clear that the problems at Colossae are still with us!

Be sure to save plenty of time to explore the major theme: "As you therefore have received Christ Jesus the Lord, continue to live your lives in him." What does it mean to live "in Christ"?

Maxie Dunnam provides some splendid answers in his *Workbook on Becoming Alive in Christ* (Nashville: The Upper Room, 1986). It is one of several workbooks by him designed to strengthen our spiritual life.

The first chapter is entitled "The Indwelling Christ." That is the theme of the entire first week. He begins by quoting Colossians 1:24-29. The key verse is 1:27: "The secret is simply this: *Christ in you!* Yes, Christ in you bringing with him the hope of all the glorious things to come" (p. 15).

Dr. Dunnam tells of counseling a young woman who was very nervous, anxious, and uncertain. She spoke haltingly and in jerky phrases, but managed to communicate the fact that she had heard of the church's mission emphasis, particularly the work in Mexico, and she wanted to share in it. If she couldn't go personally, at least she could provide financial support. "The amount she mentioned was astronomical in relation to what I thought she must be earning."

Time went by. She dropped in occasionally for counseling, but it proved unsatisfactory. There were still hurts and deep feelings that she kept hidden.

Then one day she walked into the office smiling. Could it be the same person? She was certainly not the "frustrated do-gooder [Dunnam] had known three months ago." What happened?

Her story is a classic one of personal transformation. She had tried to do good so that God would accept her; she never felt "holy enough" or "righteous enough." She poured her resources into helping others. Hoping to feel better, she tried to get her life in order so that God would notice, but she couldn't bring it off. Then she learned that God loved her just as she was. She didn't earn that love, nor could she. She couldn't buy it or ever deserve it. Yet, she was loved and accepted.

Dunnam writes that she used a marvelous symbol to explain her experience: "I was trying to pry open the window to get in the house when all the time the door was open, and I had only to walk in" (pp. 16-17).

That is the beginning of new life "in Christ." But how do we sustain it? How do we continue to live in him? In the chapter on "Dying and Rising with Christ," Dunnam emphasizes that we must die if we want to live. In marriage we die to our own selfish desires in order to meet the needs of our mates. In all relationships we die to our own pride of identity in order to live in mutual friendship. To become a Christian we die to sin and our own efforts to save ourselves, and we come alive to Christ's forgiving grace. To become more Christian we die daily to all that separates us from God and others, and we come alive to Christ's presence, who leads us through death to resurrection. Dying, we live! The way is clear: "Unless a grain of wheat falls into the earth and dies, it remains just a single grain; but if it dies, it bears much fruit" (John 12:24; see also Dunnam, p. 56).

If only we can focus on Christ, instead of ourselves, and accept this unconditional acceptance of us, we will find, time and time again, that he is indeed the sufficient Christ!

Helping Class Members Act

We have no right to criticize others unless we take a real hard look at ourselves. We must not concentrate on the speck in our neighbors' eyes and miss the log in our own (Luke 7:41). Have someone read the material quoted from *Becoming Alive in Christ*; invite members to share any personal experiences or to cite how they have seen Christ in others. Are there clues here as to how we should live?

Planning for Next Sunday

The lesson for next Sunday focuses on the ethical life of the Christian. What difference does it make if we truly live in Christ? Ask the class to read the Scripture selection (Colossians 3:1-17) and ponder that question.

LESSON 7   JULY 18

Life in Christ

Background Scripture: Colossians 3

The Main Question

In this week's lesson, Paul moves from primarily theological concerns to moral behavior. This is where, as they say, "the rubber hits the road." In 2:20 he asked: "If with Christ you died to the elemental spirits of the universe, why do you live as if you still belonged to the world?" The battle to be won at Colossae is not only theological, but moral as well. Thus Paul devotes a major portion of his letter to the behavior of those whose lives are "hidden with Christ in God" (3:3).

Who was it who said that humankind is inflicted with "endemic cussedness"? This is the idea that evil abounds, not only because it is habit-forming and therefore hard to overcome, but also because we *enjoy it!* Besides, in a predominantly pagan culture these young Christians were assaulted by temptations on every side. That was brought home to me on a visit to the ruins of ancient Corinth a few years ago. Overlooking the site of that city, which once teemed with life, is a high promontory on which stood a temple to Aphrodite, the goddess of love and beauty, where "sacred" prostitutes were available for every sensual pleasure.

Christian morality should be different from—higher than—that of non-Christians. But how can we reach such a lofty goal?

Selected Scripture

King James Version

Colossians 3:1-17

1 If ye then be risen with Christ, seek those things which are above, where Christ sitteth on the right hand of God.

2 Set your affection on things above, not on things on the earth.

3 For ye are dead, and your life is hid with Christ in God.

4 When Christ, who is our life, shall appear, then shall ye also appear with him in glory.

5 Mortify therefore your members which are upon the earth; fornication, uncleanness, inordinate affection, evil concupiscence, and covetousness, which is idolatry:

6 For which things' sake the wrath of God cometh on the children of disobedience:

7 In the which ye also walked some time, when ye lived in them.

8 But now ye also put off all these; anger, wrath, malice, blasphemy, filthy communication out of your mouth.

9 Lie not one to another, seeing that ye have put off the old man with his deeds;

10 And have put on the new man, which is renewed in knowledge after the image of him that created him:

11 Where there is neither Greek nor Jew, circumcision nor uncircumcision, Barbarian, Scythian,

New Revised Standard Version

Colossians 3:1-17

1 So if you have been raised with Christ, seek the things that are above, where Christ is, seated at the right hand of God. 2 Set your minds on things that are above, not on things that are on earth, 3 for you have died, and your life is hidden with Christ in God. 4 When Christ who is your life is revealed, then you also will be revealed with him in glory.

5 Put to death, therefore, whatever in you is earthly: fornication, impurity, passion, evil desire, and greed (which is idolatry). 6 On account of these the wrath of God is coming on those who are disobedient. 7 These are the ways you also once followed, when you were living that life. 8 But now you must get rid of all such things—anger, wrath, malice, slander, and abusive language from your mouth. 9 Do not lie to one another, seeing that you have stripped off the old self with its practices 10 and have clothed yourselves with the new self, which is being renewed in knowledge according to the image of its creator. 11 In that renewal there is no longer Greek and Jew, circumcised and uncircumcised, barbarian, Scythian, slave and free; but Christ is all and in all!

bond nor free: but Christ is all, and in all.

12 Put on therefore, as the elect of God, holy and beloved, bowels of mercies, kindness, humbleness of mind, meekness, longsuffering;

13 Forbearing one another, and forgiving one another, if any man have a quarrel against any: even as Christ forgave you, so also do ye.

14 And above all these things put on charity, which is the bond of perfectness.

15 And let the peace of God rule in your hearts, to the which also ye are called in one body; and be ye thankful.

16 Let the word of Christ dwell in you richly in all wisdom; teaching and admonishing one another in psalms and hymns and spiritual songs, singing with grace in your hearts to the Lord.

17 And whatsoever ye do in word or deed, do all in the name of the Lord Jesus, giving thanks to God and the Father by him.

12 As God's chosen ones, holy and beloved, clothe yourselves with compassion, kindness, humility, meekness, and patience. 13 Bear with one another and, if anyone has a complaint against another, forgive each other; just as the Lord has forgiven you, so you also must forgive. 14 Above all, clothe yourselves with love, which binds everything together in perfect harmony. 15 And let the peace of Christ rule in your hearts, to which indeed you were called in the one body. And be thankful. 16 Let the word of Christ dwell in you richly; teach and admonish one another in all wisdom; and with gratitude in your hearts sing psalms, hymns, and spiritual songs to God. 17 And whatever you do, in word or deed, do everything in the name of the Lord Jesus, giving thanks to God the Father through him.

Key Verse: **And [put] on the new man, which is renewed in knowledge after the image of him that created him. (Colossians 3:10)**

Key Verse: **And [clothe] yourselves with the new self, which is being renewed in knowledge according to the image of its creator. (Colossians 3:10)**

As You Read the Scripture

Colossians 3. Paul's letters usually follow the same pattern: first a theological section and then an ethical one. The two sections belong together as do different sides of the same coin, for Paul's moral imperatives ("You should . . . ") flow out of his theological convictions ("You are . . . ").

Verses 1-4. The moral conduct of a Christian is not the *means* by which one earns God's salvation, it is the *consequence* of the new relationship with God.

Verse 1 might better be translated, "Because you have been raised with Christ. . . . " The mystical rising to new life in Christ is an accomplished fact, not some future blessing.

Verse 2 might be translated: "Your treasure, Christ, is now enthroned in the heavenly world, and your thoughts and aspirations should be there, too."

In verses 3-4 there is a certain hidden quality about life in Christ. It is not paraded or flaunted. As Christ dwells with God, so your life is grounded in him and is neither seen nor understood by non-Christians. But when Christ comes in final victory, you will appear with him and share his triumph. At the end, as at the beginning, the Christian believer is one with Christ.

Verses 5-11. One whose life is incorporated in Christ will no longer indulge in fleshly passions, such as fornication, impurity, and greed, for greediness is a form of idol worship. Such sins incur God's wrath. *Wrath?*

It represents a holy God's inevitable reaction to evil. . . . It is not, as anger so often is with us, the emotional reaction of an irritated self-concern. We conceive it best if we imagine the horror a good person feels in the presence of stark evil, and then multiply by infinity.
(Archibald M. Hunter, *The Layman's Bible Commentary* [Atlanta: John Knox Press, 1959], p. 137)

Also put away all sins of mind and mouth. *Anger* is the sudden outburst of fury. *Wrath* is hateful feelings. *Malice* is animosity, enmity. *Slander* is the defamation of a person's character. And *abusive language* should never come from our lips. Telling the truth is an obvious result of a renewed life. Verses 9 and 10 recall Genesis 1:26-27, where humanity is created in God's image. Now God designs, in Christ, to restore humanity to its former blessed state. In this redeemed humanity there will be no distinctions of race (Greek or Jew) or of culture (Greek or barbarian—or Scythian, considered the most uncivilized of persons) or of social standing (slave and free). These social divisions no longer matter. Christ is all that matters.

Verses 12-17. In contrast to pagan vices, Paul now names distinctive Christian virtues. All are social virtues, bearing on the Christian's relation to others. *Love,* the highest of all, is the self-denying principle that brings all other virtues together in perfect harmony.

The "word of Christ" is the word he preached and incarnated (John 1:14). That word is to make its home among them fully as they counsel one another in wisdom and sing hymns of thanksgiving to God. Hymn singing is essential to Christian worship; it has been so from the very beginning.

"Do everything in the name. . . . " All Christian activities should be undertaken with prayer, invoking the presence and aid of our Lord in everything. Then we should act under the authority of Jesus. Even our thanks to God should be offered through Jesus, since he is the one true Mediator, representing God to us and us to God.

The Scripture and the Main Question

Paul was deeply concerned about the moral behavior of new Christians. In the third chapter of Colossians he vividly describes the outward changes that result from inward transformation.

As One Redeemed

It is important that we understand the context out of which Paul speaks. In the first place, he is writing autobiographically. When he urges his readers to "put to death" whatever is "earthly" in them, he is recalling his own experience as a self-righteous legalist, alienated from God because of real and imaginary sins. When he advises them to have "as God's chosen ones, holy and beloved," qualities that demonstrate the "peace of Christ" at work in their hearts, it is his own transformation as one redeemed by Christ to which he refers.

The Seriousness of Sin

Second, Paul is aware, and wants his readers to be aware, of the seriousness of sin. Sin is alienation from God either because of our deliberate and willful disobedience, or because we are subject to, and bound by, the powers of evil. Jews and Gentiles alike are equally condemned, and our good intentions for reforming ourselves, like New Year's resolutions, are doomed to fail.

Paul frequently uses the word *flesh* to refer to humanity's "lower nature." "The works of the flesh are obvious: fornication, impurity, licentiousness. . . . Those who belong to Christ Jesus have crucified the flesh with its passions and desires" (Galatians 5:19, 24).

Yet, in spite of our sin, God loves us! That is the amazing good news that spread over the Mediterranean world in the wake of Christ's coming: "God so loved the world that he gave . . . " (John 3:16). "While we were still sinners Christ died for us" (Romans 5:8). "If anyone is in Christ, there is a new creation: everything has become new! All this is from God, who reconciled us to himself through Christ, and has given us the ministry of reconciliation" (2 Corinthians 5:17-18). In the language of Colossians: "You have come to fullness in him, who is the head of every ruler and authority. . . . You were buried with him in baptism, you were also raised with him through faith in the power of God, who raised him from the dead" (2:10, 12).

"By Grace You Have Been Saved"

We are, therefore, to take seriously the power of sin in our lives. But even more seriously, we are to give thanks that through the cross of Christ—his death and resurrection—Christ has conquered the power of sin, both in the universe, disarming the "principalities and powers," and in our own lives, if we will only believe and accept his gracious promise of salvation. "For by grace you have been saved through faith, and this is not your own doing; it is the gift of God" (Ephesians 2:8).

The crux of Paul's message to the Colossians is this: If your inward life has truly been transformed by the forgiving grace of Christ, your outward life will reflect the change. Once you were the embodiment of sin. Now you have become "new creatures in Christ." You are to "put on the Lord Jesus Christ" (Romans 13:14) and thus be in practice what you already are: "God's chosen ones" (3:12). This means putting to death the vices of fornication, impurity, passion, and so forth and putting on compassion, kindness, humility, and love (see 3:5, 12). Clearly Christian moral behavior is to be higher—much higher—than that of non-Christians.

How are we to "put to death" evil habits and "put on" higher ones? Is Paul slipping back into the old legalism from which he came, which said: "Do this; don't do that, and you will be saved"? Is there a contradiction here?

Christ Within

Not if we have, indeed, been raised with Christ. Christ's presence within us is the secret: "I have been crucified with Christ; and it is no longer I who live, but it is Christ who lives in me" (Galatians 2:19-20a).

Christ within as a sanctifying presence. He enables us to live a "holy" life; not one, however, that is free from struggle. Far from it! Even Paul himself admitted to a continuing battle with the powers of darkness and temptation within himself (Romans 7:14-20). But, as John Wesley said shortly after his heart-warming experience that forever changed his life, "Whereas before I was conquered, now [by God's grace] I am conqueror." We do not lapse back into the old effort to win our own salvation, when we put on compassion, kindness, and humility. It is *Christ within* who strengthens me (see Philippians 4:13).

A Guiding and Creating Presence

Christ within also becomes a *guiding and creating presence.* A pastor friend of mine was confronted with a major decision concerning the direction of his ministry. He went through all the struggles that most people experience when confronted by change: Is it time to move? Is this the right move, or should I wait for another opportunity? Is this a good change for my family? What are the long-range implications? What is God's will? The pastor told of the wonderful sense of peace that came as his wife and he communicated as never before about their life together and together prayed for guidance. When the decision was made, their minds were at peace.

A Uniting Presence

Finally, *Christ within as a uniting presence:* "Let the peace of Christ rule in your hearts, to which indeed you were called in the one body" (3:15). Christ not only dwells within us as individuals, but also by the power of his Spirit unites all believers, regardless of race or social status, to one another and to himself. Here in nascent form is the concept of the Church as the body of Christ, later to be developed in 1 Corinthians 12 and Ephesians 4.

We cannot possibly live the good life by ourselves. But, then, Christ is with us—within us—always.

> Christ be with me, Christ within me,
> Christ before me, Christ beside me.
> Christ to win me,
> Christ to comfort and restore me,
> Christ beneath me, Christ above me,
> Christ in quiet, Christ in danger,
> Christ in hearts of all that love me,
> Christ in mouth of friend and stranger. Amen.
> (from *Saint Patrick's Breastplate*)

Colossians 3:16-17 reminds us of Philippians 4:4: "Rejoice in the Lord always; again I will say, Rejoice." There is also that unforgettable scene in Philippi where Paul and Silas are arrested for disturbing the peace, beaten and put in solitary confinement, their feet in the stocks: "About midnight Paul and Silas were praying and singing hymns to God, and the prisoners were listening to them" (Acts 16:25). O for a thousand tongues to sing!

FOURTH QUARTER

Helping Adults Become Involved

Preparing to Teach

This is a delightful passage in which Paul spells out in vivid detail the life in Christ, in contrast to the pagan life out of which the Colossians have come.

It is not an easy transition! One does not suddenly change bad habits into good ones. An alcoholic or chain smoker can testify to that. Yet, change we must, if we are truly to be God's chosen ones.

In your own preparation it is important to have this passage of Scripture clearly in mind. Verses 1-4 serve as an introduction to the main theme: "If you have been raised . . . seek. . . . " Verses 5-11 describe the unregenerate life, and verses 12-17 describe life in Christ.

You will also find 1 Corinthians 12:12-26 to be extremely helpful. Here Paul expands the concept of "one body" in 3:15. The body of Christ, of which we are all members, each playing an indispensable part in its function, is a major Pauline theme.

Today's lesson outline:

I. Christian legalism, past and present
II. Motivation for Christian life
III. Christ dwelling in us

Introducing the Main Question

As the class begins, either read yourself or have someone else read "The Main Question." Be sure the class members understand that sin was not just an ancient problem, but that it is still very much with us and shows up in our own behavior. How are we to be different from those who do not profess Christ? Some have claimed that they have not joined the church because of all the hypocrites in it. Must we be perfect to join the church or remain in it? That should not distract us from the central issue: What we do inevitably reflects who we are.

Developing the Lesson

If you have older persons in your class, you might begin by having them recall the strict upbringing many of them experienced. Someone might even remember Prohibition days when the sale of liquor was banned. Clearly, the temperance people were, for a time at least, in charge. I grew up in a family where liquor was strictly forbidden, except for "medicinal purposes." My uncle used it for a "heart condition." It was never quite clear what the "condition" was.

The sabbath was strictly observed. The stores were closed. No one worked in yards. We had moved beyond the Puritan period when even games were prohibited. Still, one must be circumspect. I remember a hot Sunday afternoon when all was still and my father was taking a nap. My sister and I decided to play a game of croquet in the side yard where, we hoped, our father would not see or hear us. Imagine our surprise to see him appear on the porch. We were surely in for it. Then he asked, "Mind if I join you?" Amazing grace!

I also remember my first Sunday movie. Some have referred to a first attendance at a movie theater on Sunday as an experience of lost innocence. My conscience bothered me a bit, but not enough to prevent my going. Besides, it was a top motion picture! It was all a part of a changing moral climate, a disquieting time for those who felt that people who did such things were literally going to hell.

Ask the class this question: Are we as Christians better or worse for having been liberated from the 1930s and 1940s type of Christian legalism? How important is it to display good behavior? If, as someone suggested, the only difference between Episcopalians and Methodists is that the Methodists play cards with the blinds down, are Methodists worse or better?

We must go deeper. The sins Paul enumerates are serious, including not only blatant immorality, but also the sins of the heart: passion, evil desire, and greed (3:5). That covers a lot of territory! A former President of the United States confessed that he at times looked at women with lust in his heart. And he was a Baptist! Sin is serious: "All have sinned and fall short of the glory of God" (Romans 3:23).

If it is true that all are sinners ("None is righteous, no not one"; Romans 3:10), how are we to be delivered? I encourage you to ask that question and see what answers may be given in the light of the text. You may wish, at some point, preferably toward the end of the discussion, to introduce the main points in "The Scripture and the Main Question" and invite a response. Ask the class, "Do you believe this is true? Is it possible for Christ to dwell in us, guiding and empowering us, even though we may not be perfect?"

Helping Class Members Act

Not only must we monitor our own behavior, humbly seeking Christ's direction and forgiveness when we fail, but also—if we are to take this passage seriously—we need to be sensitive to those who may be going through tough times. I remember an alcoholic who came to our church, hungry for companionship and inner peace. She lived by herself, her husband having died several years before, and her son did not care whether she lived or died. When, in a visit to her home, I learned for the first time how serious her problems were, I was both shocked (I hope I was able to hide it!) and overcome with sympathy. What else is the Church for, if not to reach out and bring such persons into a life-changing experience of the grace of Christ?

There is a tendency, unfortunately, for churches to become closed societies, projecting the attitude, at least to some, that they are not welcome. In contrast, if a church takes its evangelistic task seriously, it will not only open its doors to all for whom Christ died but actively seek to bring them in as well.

George Hunter tells about a church that learned that the secret to growth is for all its members to become evangelists. One member brought to church a young woman who worked as a waitress in a nearby restaurant. She responded to the invitation to discipleship, and a time was set for her baptism by immersion. The friend who had brought her to the church sent engraved invitations to the service, and on the night of her baptism there were several rows of "strangers," including a bartender, several waiters and waitresses, and others who ordinarily would not step foot in the church. After the service there was a party in her honor, and the minister made a welcoming speech in which he said that all were truly welcome in their fellowship. For six Sunday evenings afterward, the woman accompanied one of her friends to the altar where each committed himself or herself to Christ.

How can we become the channels of God's redeeming grace?

Planning for Next Sunday

Urge the class to read Philemon and to reflect on this question: "What is our responsibility toward the people of the world who are enslaved by poverty, prejudice, and hopelessness?"

LESSON 8   JULY 25

Christ Unites

Background Scripture: Philemon

The Main Question

The Letter to Philemon presents an interesting ethical dilemma: What shall be done with a runaway slave? The issue is somewhat involved. Onesimus, slave to Philemon, a leading Christian in Colossae, escaped and went to Rome. There he came to know Paul (it would be interesting to know how that happened) and was converted to Christ. The relationship between them became like that of a father and son.

Legally, however, Onesimus belonged to Philemon and, therefore, Paul had no right to keep him, as much as he would like to have Onesimus minister to his needs in prison. So he decides to send Onesimus back along with a personal message addressed to his master. In it Paul appeals to Philemon's compassionate spirit to receive Onesimus back, not as a slave, but as a "beloved brother." It is a daring move, with no guaranteed outcome. To this day we do not know how the story ended.

Slavery has long since been prohibited in this country, but the subjugation of the weak by the strong continues. As the 1980s ended, the shackles of communist tyranny were being broken in country after country in Eastern Europe and in Latin America. Freedom, based on the inherent dignity of every single human being on earth, was spreading like a prairie fire. Even in South Africa, that bastion of racial segregation, there was movement toward accommodation.

Philemon's moral responsibility seemed clear. What of our responsibilities toward those who still suffer injustice, prejudice, and poverty? If Paul were to write a letter to us, what would he ask?

Selected Scripture

King James Version

New Revised Standard Version

Philemon 4-21

4 I thank my God, making mention of thee always in my prayers,

5 Hearing of thy love and faith, which thou hast toward the Lord Jesus, and toward all saints;

6 That the communication of thy faith may become effectual by the acknowledging of every good thing which is in you in Christ Jesus.

7 For we have great joy and consolation in thy love, because the bowels of the saints are refreshed by thee, brother.

8 Wherefore, though I might be much bold in Christ to enjoin thee that which is convenient,

9 Yet for love's sake I rather beseech thee, being such an one as Paul the aged, and now also a prisoner of Jesus Christ.

10 I beseech thee for my son Onesimus, whom I have begotten in my bonds:

11 Which in time past was to thee unprofitable, but now profitable to thee and to me:

12 Whom I have sent again: thou therefore receive him, that is, mine own bowels:

13 Whom I would have retained with me, that in thy stead he might have ministered unto me in the bonds of the gospel:

14 But without thy mind would I do nothing; that thy benefit should not be as it were of necessity, but willingly.

15 For perhaps he therefore departed for a season, that thou shouldest receive him for ever;

16 Not now as a servant, but above a servant, a brother beloved, specially to me, but how much more unto thee, both in the flesh, and in the Lord?

17 If thou count me therefore a partner, receive him as myself.

Philemon 4-21

4 When I remember you in my prayers, I always thank my God 5 because I hear of your love for all the saints and your faith toward the Lord Jesus. 6 I pray that the sharing of your faith may become effective when you perceive all the good that we may do for Christ. 7 I have indeed received much joy and encouragement from your love, because the hearts of the saints have been refreshed through you, my brother.

8 For this reason, though I am bold enough in Christ to command you to do your duty, 9 yet I would rather appeal to you on the basis of love—and I, Paul, do this as an old man, and now also as a prisoner of Christ Jesus. 10 I am appealing to you for my child, Onesimus, whose father I have become during my imprisonment. 11 Formerly he was useless to you, but now he is indeed useful both to you and to me. 12 I am sending him, that is, my own heart, back to you. 13 I wanted to keep him with me, so that he might be of service to me in your place during my imprisonment for the gospel; 14 but I preferred to do nothing without your consent, in order that your good deed might be voluntary and not something forced. 15 Perhaps this is the reason he was separated from you for a while, so that you might have him back forever, 16 no longer as a slave but more than a slave, a beloved brother—especially to me but how much more to you, both in the flesh and in the Lord.

17 So if you consider me your partner, welcome him as you would

18 If he hath wronged thee, or oweth thee ought, put that on mine account;

19 I Paul have written it with mine own hand, I will repay it: albeit I do not say to thee how thou owest unto me even thine own self besides.

20 Yea, brother, let me have joy of thee in the Lord: refresh my bowels in the Lord.

21 Having confidence in thy obedience I wrote unto thee, knowing that thou wilt also do more than I say.

Key Verse: If thou count me therefore a partner, receive him as myself. (Philemon 17)

welcome me. 18 If he has wronged you in any way, or owes you anything, charge that to my account. 19 I, Paul, am writing this with my own hand: I will repay it. I say nothing about your owing me even your own self. 20 Yes, brother, let me have this benefit from you in the Lord! Refresh my heart in Christ. 21 Confident of your obedience, I am writing to you, knowing that you will do even more than I say.

Key Verse: So if you consider me your partner, welcome him as you would receive me. (Philemon 17)

As You Read the Scripture

Philemon. The context, character, and content of Philemon make it one of the most fascinating documents in the New Testament. Barely one page in length, it was written by Paul from prison to an individual, not to a church. Its content, unlike his other letters addressed to one or more congregations, is very personal and extremely important. The fate of "my child, Onesimus," is at stake.

Onesimus, a slave owned by Philemon, a leader in the church at Colossae, had escaped and ended up in Rome. What better place to change his identity and lose himself than in the teeming streets of that cosmopolitan center? But somehow he came to know Paul and was converted to Christ. Paul would have liked to keep Onesimus in his service (Paul lived in Rome under house arrest; see Acts 28:16, 30), but he could not harbor a fugitive. Besides, Paul had a responsibility to Philemon, a "beloved fellow worker." As a Roman citizen Paul understands that a slave owner has absolute authority over the person and life of a slave. It is a risky venture to interfere with Philemon's personal affairs. Yet, Onesimus has become like a son to Paul. So Paul takes the risk, appealing to Philemon's Christian compassion to receive Onesimus no longer as a slave but as a beloved brother (see v. 16). It could cost Onesimus his life. On the other hand, it might unite all three men as brothers in Christ. Written in Rome between A.D. 60 and 63, the same time as the letter to the Colossians, the Letter to Philemon was sent with Onesimus and Tychius, who together returned to Colossae.

Verses 4-7. Following a traditional greeting, Paul expresses deep thanks for Philemon's love and faith, which he has generously shared with others.

Verses 8-9. With tact, but also with directness, Paul moves to the issue at hand. Although he could have exercised apostolic authority and commanded Philemon to do what ought to be done, Paul preferred instead to appeal to Philemon's Christian compassion: "Because I love you, I make a request instead" (GNB).

Verses 10-11. Note the very personal references: "my child, Onesimus, whose father I have become"; "my own heart" (v. 12). Verse 11 is a play on words; the name Onesimus means useful or beneficial.

Verse 13. It has been suggested that Paul's real wish is to keep Onesimus, but he would not do it without Philemon's approval. The rest of the letter, however, argues for a permanent return of Onesimus to Philemon's home without penalty.

Verses 15-16. Paul suggests that divine providence has ordained that Onesimus should return not as a slave, but as a "beloved brother" who will be loved not simply as a man but "in the Lord."

Verse 17. The Greek for "partner" is a business term, implying that Paul and Philemon have exceedingly important business to transact. "Welcome him back just as you would me."

Verse 18. It was customary when the possession of a slave was passed from one person to another or when the slave was freed for any debts or penalties to be assumed by the slave himself or by the new owner. Paul personally takes full responsibility for these debts.

Verse 19. Who owes whom, and how shall they repay? Paul gladly assumes Onesimus's debts to Philemon. Philemon owes the fact that he is a Christian ("your very self") to Paul. That is a greater debt!

Verse 20. "I am asking this favour of you as a fellow-Christian; set my mind at rest" (REB).

Verse 21. This is a gracious compliment: "I am confident that you will joyfully, lovingly, and by your own free will do even more than I ask." How could Philemon refuse?

The Scripture and the Main Question

Slavery

Slavery seems far removed from the 1990s. Yet it was only 130 years ago that slavery was practiced in the United States. A terrible war that bitterly divided the nation was fought over the issue. The slaves were freed, but the degradation African Americans have experienced since then makes us wonder who really won.

We are deeply impressed by Paul's loving concern for Onesimus and by the risks Paul took in sending him back to his master. It is especially noble of him to beg Philemon to receive Onesimus not as a slave, but as a brother in Christ. Christ does, indeed, unite disparate people. His love has broken every barrier down, and we rejoice that it is so.

But there is a deeper issue here. Paul says nothing about the institution of slavery itself. Was he not aware that it was one of the greatest evils in the Roman Empire? Did he not know of thousands of conquered people herded into the slave markets of Roman cities as spoils of victory? Might he have seen slaves beaten unmercifully as examples to those who might harbor visions of freedom? Instead of attacking the system, he offers moral instructions to slaves that they should obey their masters, and to masters that they should treat their slaves justly and fairly (see Colossians 3:22; 4:1; Ephesians 6:5-9).

Seeds of Love and Justice

It has been suggested that under the circumstances Paul could not attack slavery without putting Onesimus in even greater danger. Paul's greatest concern at the moment was for the freedom of that one slave. Moreover, Paul was convinced that Jesus would soon return and make earthly institutions irrelevant. Again, by attacking slavery, Paul would have brought Christianity into severe danger as a subversive movement. That would no doubt please his enemies, but bring great harm to his friends. Most important, the Letter to Philemon establishes a new model for relationships between masters and their slaves, a relationship based on Christian love. Thus, as Edward W. Bauman has pointed out, Paul did not openly attack slavery, but planted the seeds of love and justice, which made its downfall inevitable (see Bauman, *An Introduction to the New Testament* [Philadelphia: The Westminster Press, 1961], p. 71).

Slavery has disappeared from most countries, but poverty, prejudice, and oppression abound, not just in the Third World among the poorest of the poor, but in our own country where drug-infested ghettos breed crime and despair. Young people with little hope for the future drop out of school, bear unwanted children, and fall victim to drugs and crime.

Rural areas practice their own types of oppression. Thousands of migrant workers move across the land, harvesting crops, barely surviving on minimum wages, and living under dreadful conditions with little hope of ever breaking out of the system.

Compassionate Concern

It is difficult to fight institutional injustice. The problems are deep seated and complex. But, like Paul, we can help these persons, for whom Christ also died, on a personal basis.

Because I lived in Washington, D.C., and was an administrator in a theological school, I was sometimes requested to do personal favors. One August I received a call from a pastor in a university town in the Midwest, asking me to meet a young man who was coming to Washington as a first-year medical student at a local university. He was from Africa and knew no one in Washington. Could I welcome him and see that he was comfortably settled? The young man arrived late one evening. He was somewhat overwhelmed by the transition he was making from college to medical school, and by the city of Washington, D.C. It was a beautiful, moonlit night. We drove to the Lincoln Memorial to see its famous statue of our sixteenth president. To the east beyond the Washington Monument, we could see the lighted capitol building. He was deeply impressed.

My family and I did our best to acclimate him to his new environment. We had him as a guest in our home several times, and I was able to find a church that agreed to sponsor him financially and receive him as a Christian brother and friend. I was not exactly a Philemon, but at least I was able to be an intermediary on the young man's behalf. Twenty years later when we traveled to Africa I was able to see the conditions out of which he had come and to which, much to his credit, he returned. One has to see the living conditions of the poor in Third World countries to believe them. I continue to be troubled by those memories.

As concerned as we may be about the plight of the underprivileged, we must be careful about making judgments. I discovered while in Kenya that the indigent Christians, in spite of their squalor, were joyful about their faith. That is why Christianity is growing so rapidly there.

What Shall We Do with Onesimus?

Robert Coles, Harvard faculty member and noted child psychiatrist, writes with great poignancy of his encounters with children in the Third World. In Rio de Janeiro he climbed up the slopes of a famous *favella* ("shanty town") where the poorest people in the city live and yet, ironically, have the best view. Atop another of Rio's many hills is the *Monumento de Cristo Redentor,* the famed monument to Christ the redeemer. One twelve-year-old girl said, "My day begins when I go outside and look at Jesus. I tell him good morning. My day ends when I say good night to Jesus. I am sure He wants everyone to sleep well. We are lucky He chose us to live! We'll be seeing him soon!"

Her mother was not so sanguine. She was especially critical of the rich who own several homes and big cars and have no concern whatsoever for the poor. "I clean for them, the big shots. I know how much they own. There is only one piece of property they don't own: Heaven! God came to us as a poor man . . . and that means a lot."

In New Orleans, after school desegregation had become the law of the land, Coles talked with Ruby, a six-year-old African American girl who was heckled and threatened every day by hate-filled white parents of children who attended her newly integrated school. As a trained pediatrician, child psychiatrist, and psychoanalyst Coles wanted to know how her mind and body were responding to an extremely stressful time. Ruby's mother said, "My husband and I were talking the other night, and we decided that you ask our daughter about everything except God" (Robert Coles, *Harvard Diary: Reflections on the Sacred and the Secular* [New York, Crossroad, 1988], pp. 16-17, 135).

We have much to learn from the Onesimuses of this world. They are God's children, too. Money, race, and social position do not give us the right to look down on anyone. Christ died for all. He was one of them. What shall we do with Onesimus?

Helping Adults Become Involved

Preparing to Teach

First Peter 2:4-10 is a call to faith and courage in the face of persecution that is sure to come to Christians in Asia Minor. Verses 9 and 10 are a stirring affirmation of their true identity: "You are a chosen race, a royal priesthood, a holy nation." This is very appropriate devotional reading as you prepare to teach Philemon, reminding Christians then and now who we are.

You will need to read carefully all the material provided for the lesson. Although brief, Philemon addresses serious issues that are still with us. Here is an outline for today's lesson:

I. The problem of Onesimus the slave.
II. Contemporary parallels.
III. Christians respond to injustice today.

Developing the Lesson

A good way to begin to lead this week's lesson is either summarizing "The Main Question" or to read it in full. It helps to focus on the central theme.

Then have someone read the text, pausing for another to read the commentary in "As You Read the Scripture."

It is interesting that in this drama involving three persons Paul is the only one who speaks. You might wish to ask your class to speculate on how Onesimus felt in returning to his master. Was he afraid? Was he grateful for what Paul was doing, or trying to do, on his behalf? Or was he anxious, knowing that his life was literally placed in Philemon's hands? Did he worry about how his new relationship with Philemon, if his master responded favorably, might affect his standing with the other slaves in the household? If he could have spoken, what would he have said to Paul and to Philemon?

What will Philemon's response be when he reads the letter? Will he (a) excuse Paul for interfering with his private affairs? Or (b) decide that he cannot possibly free Onesimus and let him remain in the household while the other slaves remain bound? Or (c) will he bow to Paul's persuasive arguments, freely and generously granting his request and be willing to face the consequences?

Now restate the two questions in the final paragraph of "The Main Question" and have the class respond. Some may speak of the racial problems in our society or problems in our urban and rural ghettos. Some may have traveled in Third World countries and can speak to the issue of Christian responsibility in our "global village." In any event, it is very important to relate Philemon to today's world. In so doing we will find it painfully relevant.

A Historic Footnote

While we do not know for certain what action Philemon took in response to Paul's letter, there are strong reasons to believe that Onesimus eventually became an influential Christian. Fifty years after Paul wrote to Philemon, one of the early Church leaders, Ignatius of Antioch, sent a letter to the church in Ephesus in which he speaks a great deal about their bishop Onesimus, whom he describes in glowing terms and implores his people to live worthily because they have so noble a bishop. We cannot be sure that this is the same Onesimus, but it is an interesting possibility. Imagine a runaway slave, Paul's "son" becoming the leader of one of the strongest churches in the first century.

Another possibility is that Onesiphorus, mentioned in 2 Timothy, may in fact be Onesimus. Since Silas is referred to as Silvanus, Prisca as Priscilla and perhaps Epaphras as Epaphroditus, then why should we not assume that Onesimus's name is changed also? If so, we have a very warm commendation of him in Paul's words: "May the Lord grant mercy to the household of Onesiphorus, because he often refreshed me and was not ashamed of my chain; when he arrived in Rome, he eagerly searched for me and found me—may the Lord grant that he will find mercy from the Lord on that day! And you know very well how much service he rendered in Ephesus" (2 Timothy 1:16-18). Again, at the close of the letter he is mentioned: "Greet Prisca and Aquila, and the household of Onesiphorus" (4:19). Scholars admit that the identification here is somewhat more strained, but in any event, there are reasons to believe that Onesimus was freed from slavery and became an important leader in the early Church. (See *IDB*, vol. 3, p. 602.)

I also recommend a historical novel, *Onesimus,* by Bishop Lance Webb

(Nashville: Thomas Nelson Publishers, 1980). It is out of print now, and you may have difficulty finding it, but it is a fascinating and "sweeping drama of danger, intrigue, and love." Those who read it, however, need to remember that it is purely fictional. Nevertheless, Bishop Webb, a dear personal friend and predecessor as pastor of a church I served in Columbus, Ohio, writes with such vivid imagination and attention to detail that one is led to believe it is all very real.

Helping Class Members Act

What of our responsibilities to those who suffer injustice, prejudice, and poverty? What shall we do with Onesimus?

The class might well speculate on conditions in your community that need understanding, compassion, and help. Never underestimate what just a few people can do. I know of one Sunday school class in a quite conservative church that became deeply concerned about the homeless in their community. They decided they could not ignore the plight of their neighbors. They went to work on several fronts, challenging the city council to free up new money for a shelter, asking other churches to join them in providing food and personal assistance, and even opening their own church as an emergency shelter, carefully and lovingly supervised when needed. Their action galvanized their own congregation, other churches, and the community into action.

The problems of poverty, racism, and drug abuse are not "out there"; they are on our own doorstep. To use another biblical metaphor: shall we ignore the nameless victim lying in the ditch and pass by on the other side, or shall we stop and become involved?

Planning for Next Sunday

Next Sunday we begin a five-part study of Ephesians. This letter is regarded by many as the most sublime of all of Paul's writings, and it is important that we become immersed in its thoughts. Urge the class to read the entire epistle if they can, but definitely read 1:1–2:10 and 3:14-19.

UNIT III: NEWNESS THROUGH CHRIST

FIVE LESSONS   AUGUST 1–29

Are there tensions in your church? Are certain people in the community not welcome? Are you tempted by the glitter and success of a secular world where "nice guys finish last"? Do you sometimes feel victimized by the power of evil in the world and within your own soul? Then Ephesians is for you. If by some historic accident most of the epistle were lost and only 2:1-10 were preserved, it would be worthy of inclusion in the New Testament canon: "For by grace you have been saved through faith, and this is not your own doing; it is the gift of God" (2:8). But there is much, much more from that venerable "prisoner for the Lord" to disturb and bless our lives. Read, ponder, and be thankful.

373

New Life

Background Scripture: Ephesians 1:15–2:10; 3:14-19

The Main Question

Ephesians has been called "the Queen of the Epistles." Written during Paul's imprisonment in Rome (about A.D. 61–63), it is believed to have been a circular letter, or encyclical, sent not only to Ephesus, but to all the churches of Asia Minor as well.

In this encyclical the Apostle, having just written Colossians, and with all the Gentile Christians of Asia in his mind, sets down for his readers his profoundest and maturest thoughts about the role of Christ and his Church in God's great purposes for men, his aim being to confirm them in their faith, widen their spiritual horizons, and draw them closer in their bonds of Christian unity and brotherhood. (A. M. Hunter, *The Layman's Bible Commentary*, vol. 22 [Atlanta: John Knox Press, 1959], p. 45)

Ephesians 2:1-10 reads like a doxology, praising God who, "rich in mercy," out of his "great love . . . made us alive together with Christ." The transformation that is at the heart of the Christian's relationship with Christ is absolutely central for Paul. It reflects his own personal experience; it is available to all; it is a gift of God.

In 3:14-19 Paul prays that the Christians of Asia Minor may be strengthened by the spiritual presence of Christ in their hearts, that they may not only comprehend with their minds his divine nature, but also know the love of Christ that surpasses knowledge.

Why can't we accept God's grace, which is freely given? Why do we insist on earning our own salvation, even though it can't be done?

Selected Scripture

King James Version

Ephesians 2:1-10

1 And you hath he quickened, who were dead in trespasses and sins;

2 Wherein in time past ye walked according to the course of this world, according to the prince of the power of the air, the spirit that now worketh in the children of disobedience:

3 Among whom also we all had our conversation in times past in the lusts of our flesh, fulfilling the desires of the flesh and of the mind; and were by nature the children of wrath, even as others.

New Revised Standard Version

Ephesians 2:1-10

1 You were dead through the trespasses and sins 2 in which you once lived, following the course of this world, following the ruler of the power of the air, the spirit that is now at work among those who are disobedient. 3 All of us once lived among them in the passions of our flesh, following the desires of flesh and senses, and we were by nature children of wrath, like everyone else. 4 But God, who is rich in mercy, out of the great love with which he loved us 5 even when we were dead through our trespasses,

4 But God, who is rich in mercy, for his great love wherewith he loved us,

5 Even when we were dead in sins, hath quickened us together with Christ, (by grace ye are saved;)

6 And hath raised us up together, and made us sit together in heavenly places in Christ Jesus:

7 That in the ages to come he might shew the exceeding riches of his grace in his kindness toward us through Christ Jesus.

8 For by grace are ye saved through faith; and that not of yourselves: it is the gift of God:

9 Not of works, lest any man should boast.

10 For we are his workmanship, created in Christ Jesus unto good works, which God hath before ordained that we should walk in them.

Ephesians 3:14-19

14 For this cause I bow my knees unto the Father of our Lord Jesus Christ,

15 Of whom the whole family in heaven and earth is named,

16 That he would grant you, according to the riches of his glory, to be strengthened with might by his Spirit in the inner man;

17 That Christ may dwell in your hearts by faith; that ye, being rooted and grounded in love,

18 May be able to comprehend with all saints what is the breadth, and length, and depth, and height;

19 And to know the love of Christ, which passeth knowledge, that ye might be filled with all the fulness of God.

Key Verse: **For by grace are ye saved through faith; and that not of yourselves; it is the gift of God. (Ephesians 2:8)**

made us alive together with Christ—by grace you have been saved— 6 and raised us up with him and seated us with him in the heavenly places in Christ Jesus, 7 so that in the ages to come he might show the immeasurable riches of his grace in kindness toward us in Christ Jesus. 8 For by grace you have been saved through faith, and this is not your own doing; it is the gift of God— 9 not the result of works, so that no one may boast. 10 For we are what he has made us, created in Christ Jesus for good works, which God prepared beforehand to be our way of life.

Ephesians 3:14-19

14 For this reason I bow my knees before the Father, 15 from whom every family in heaven and on earth takes its name. 16 I pray that, according to the riches of his glory, he may grant that you may be strengthened in your inner being with power through his Spirit, 17 and that Christ may dwell in your hearts through faith, as you are being rooted and grounded in love. 18 I pray that you may have the power to comprehend, with all the saints, what is the breadth and length and height and depth, 19 and to know the love of Christ that surpasses knowledge, so that you may be filled with all the fullness of God.

Key Verse: **For by grace you have been saved through faith, and this is not your own doing; it is the gift of God. (Ephesians 2:8)**

FOURTH QUARTER

As You Read the Scripture

Ephesians 2:1-10. This is a splendid summary of Paul's teaching about what it means in one's own personal life to be a Christian. The first three verses tell of the terrible predicament of life without Christ. The remaining verses describe the transformation that Christ brings.

Verses 1-3. The Greek word for *trespass* means literally "to slip" or "to fall." The word for *sin* means "to miss the target." "The great central idea of sin is failure, failure to hit the target, failure to hold to the road, failure to make life what life was capable of becoming" (William Barclay, *The Letters to Galatians and Ephesians*, The Daily Study Bible [Philadelphia: The Westminster Press, 1958], p. 113).

Death is an apt description of the results of sin: a certain callousness toward others and a lack of awareness of the deterioration in one's own character. This moral degeneration robs persons of a sense of God's nearness and love. Once this was true of those for whom Ephesians was written. They were conformed to a world alienated from God, hostile to him, and poisoned with evil. They were under the influence of Satan, "prince of the air," who inhabits the space between heaven and earth.

Passions of our flesh refer not only to the "physical appetites"—such as gluttony, drunkenness, and fornication—but also to "the human impulse to self-aggrandizement, the rivalries and hostilities which result when this is thwarted: selfish ambition, envy, jealousy, fits of rage, a contentious temper which erupt into quarrels, dissensions, and party intrigues" (C. Leslie Mitton, *Ephesians*, The New Century Bible Commentary [Grand Rapids: Eerdmans Publishing Company, 1973], p. 85).

Wrath is God's persistent opposition to sin, which has been described as "an inevitable process of cause and effect in a moral universe: 'we reap what we sow' " (C. H. Dodd, quoted by Mitton, *Ephesians*, p. 86).

Verses 4-10. God, whose mercy and love are without limit, caused the resurrection of Christ to happen all over again in our lives, even though we were spiritually dead. Now, with Christ, we are members of God's household and are continually in God's presence. This transformation of our lives will be repeated in the lives of others for ages to come. So God's grace and "kindness in Christ Jesus" will be known again and again.

Verse 8. This has been called Paul's theology in a nutshell. One cannot improve on Paul's own words!

The sense of verse 10 is that faith is not real unless it "works through love" (Galatians 5:6). As newly formed Christians we will give ourselves gladly and totally to the fulfillment of God's will. We will do so not out of duty, but as an expression of the love with which we are loved.

Verses 3:14-19. This is a moving and eloquent prayer that may have been used in the early Church for liturgical purposes, possibly for baptisms. Paul's prayer is directed to God the Father "of whose fatherhood all fatherhood in heaven and upon earth is a copy" (Barclay, p. 153). There are three petitions: that the Holy Spirit may give you inner strength (3:16); that "Christ may dwell in your heart through faith" (3:17); that you may be "rooted and grounded in love" (3:17). This is the key to unlocking the deep things of God, whose nature is love. Then we will comprehend "with all the saints" the redemptive power of God in all its dimensions (breadth, length, height, depth) and "know" the love of Christ, which surpasses knowledge (a reference to those who put knowledge above all else), and we will be "filled with all the fullness of God," our highest goal and richest blessing.

The Scripture and the Main Question

Crisis

The woman on the phone was very upset. Her husband had tried to commit suicide and had been found near death by his son. He was on the critical list at a local hospital. Would I please visit him? I remember how, on my way to the hospital, I tried to recall his face. All I could remember was that he was a peripheral member. Neither his wife nor he attended services except, perhaps, at Christmas and Easter. He had once been a deputy sheriff of the county. Beyond that meager information, I knew nothing.

When I entered his room it was evident how very serious his condition was. I called him by name and tried as best I could to communicate, but was not sure I was getting through. However, when I took his hand and prayed, he slightly squeezed my hand. That was encouraging. Nevertheless, when I walked out of that room I frankly doubted that he would make it.

In fact, things went from bad to worse. His wife broke under the strain, had a heart attack, and was rushed to the same hospital. For several days it was not certain whether either would survive.

Christ Who Smiles

Then it happened. I walked into the man's room one morning and found him sitting up in bed and looking very cheerful. "What on earth happened?" I asked, unable to hide my amazement. "Jesus came and stood by my bed last night and smiled. You know, all my life I have seen only solemn pictures of Christ. Never has he been someone I could relate to. But his appearance last night has changed that image forever. If Jane and I survive, I am going to have an artist paint a picture of the smiling Christ, because that is who he really is. He has brought new life to me!"

It was wonderful to see the healing power of Christ work through the lives of those two people. They were healed not only physically, but spiritually as well. They had been very unhappy—they quarreled frequently; he had lost his job and his self-esteem; she was hyper-critical. He had tried to get back at her by ending his life ("She drove me to it") and had failed. He was at rock bottom. But now they were on the mend. They were reconciled to each other and to God. They were released from the hospital on the same day and soon were in church every Sunday. A short time later a local artist painted a picture of the smiling Christ, which hangs in a central place in the church for all to see. And, as long as he lived, that man told of the gift of new life he had received to scores of congregations throughout the region.

By Grace You Have Been Saved

It almost seems as if Paul had that man in mind when he wrote, "By grace you have been saved through faith." Grace? That is indeed what he received: the "utter generosity, unselfish, spontaneous, recklessly prodigal

377

generosity, which acts wholly out of loving concern for the other's need, even if he is completely unworthy of the love and help thus offered to him" (C. Leslie Minton, *Ephesians*, New Century Bible Commentary [Grand Rapids, Eerdmans, 1981], p. 92).

Prior to this experience his life was in shambles. He was a child of wrath, like the rest of humankind (2:3). "But God, who is rich in mercy"—that's the key; God made the first move. "Grace is God's initiative. Faith is man's response" (Minton, p. 93).

You have been saved. The Greek text refers to something that has taken place at a definite point in time but is now continuing: "You have been and you will continue to be." That is why Christ is smiling!

Obviously, "this is not your own doing," since you had virtually shut God out of your life. "It is the gift of God." Amazing grace!

A Nation of Mystics

While the man discussed above had a remarkable experience, it is by no means isolated. I have been impressed, over nearly forty years in pastoral ministry, by the number of people who have had life-transforming experiences. They were not all alike. Some were more dramatic than others. Some happened within a worship service; others outside. But the results were similar: They were surprised by grace; they had the assurance of Christ's forgiveness and unquestioned acceptance. It was like a resurrection. In the words of a favorite song our children's choir used to sing: "Every morning is Easter morning from now on."

Andrew Greely, the well-known and widely published Roman Catholic priest and sociologist, surveyed some fifteen hundred people to determine whether they ever had "ecstatic experiences"—moments when they were lifted out of themselves and felt a powerful surge of joy, light, warmth, and peace. He concluded that two out of five persons have had some kind of mystical experience not once, but many times, which led him to ask in his book *Death and Beyond*, "Are we a nation of mystics?"

> The kingdom of heaven is a perpetual spring festival, celebrating, as do all spring festivals, the persistence of life as life, triumphing, however painfully, over death.
> And blessed are you who celebrate despite your tears, for yours is the Kingdom of Heaven. (Andrew Greely, *Death and Beyond* [Chicago: Thomas More Press, 1976]: pp. 136-37)

All of this moves one to ask, in the words of Paul from another epistle: "If God is for us, who is against us? . . . Who will separate us from the love of Christ?" (Romans 8:31, 35).

But God, Who Is Rich in Mercy . . .

Later, as we will discover next week, Paul refers to Gentiles and Jews alike as being alienated from God. The law of Moses did not save, but served to condemn, the Jews. Worship of dozens of deities in the Greco-Roman world had not brought peace to the heart of the Gentiles. "But God, who is rich in mercy" has made us "alive together with Christ . . . and raised us up with him" (Ephesians 2:4-6).

There is a universality here that must not be overlooked. God's grace is not the exclusive gift to either Jew or Gentile. God's love and grace embrace us all. Neither can we earn it by good works, "so that no one may boast" (2:9). We stand before God as guilty as Lady Macbeth pleading that the imaginary spots of blood on her hands be removed. "But God, who is rich in mercy. . . . "

Because of the possibility that our lives and the lives of all who turn to Christ can be transformed, we join Paul in prayer that Christ may indeed "dwell in our hearts through faith," that we may know "the love of Christ which surpasses knowledge," and "be filled with all the fullness of God." We don't have to deserve these blessings. We could never, ever pay for them. We have only to accept them as free gifts from a gracious God. As the suicidal man said, "Christ smiled at me." And that was the beginning of new life.

Helping Adults Become Involved

Preparing to Teach

This is the first of five lessons on Ephesians. There is both a similarity and marked differences between this and previous Pauline letters we have studied, especially Colossians. The style of Ephesians is more complex, the concepts more highly developed, and it lacks the personal touch so prominent in Philippians and Philemon.

Yet it is a magnificent document. There is always more meaning to be discovered, though it may be read hundreds of times. It not only summarizes major theological concepts of Paul, but addresses issues, both theological and practical, that are still very much with us.

I urge you to read the entire epistle in one sitting, without reference to a commentary or study guide. Do not worry if you get lost now and then. For example, 1:15-23 (eight verses) are all one sentence! Rather, look for wonderful phrases that suddenly make sense, providing both insight and inspiration: "For by grace you have been saved through faith" (2:8); "For he is our peace; in his flesh he has made both groups into one and has broken down the dividing wall, that is, the hostility between us" (2:14); "Therefore be imitators of God" (5:1); "Finally, be strong in the Lord" (6:10). These are among the most sublime passages Paul wrote.

The devotional reading is Ephesians 1:3-14. It provides a sweeping view of God's plan of salvation "that he set forth in Christ . . . to gather up all things in him, things in heaven and things on earth" (1:9-10). These verses provide a helpful overview of what is to follow.

Read carefully "The Main Question" and "The Scripture and the Main Question." These provide both the foundation and the focus for today's lesson.

This is the outline for this lesson:

      I. Introduction to Ephesians
     II. Salvation in Ephesians
    III. Saved by God's grace

FOURTH QUARTER

Introducing the Main Question

In order to provide a brief introduction to Ephesians and to introduce the main question, either read or summarize in your own words "The Main Question."

Then have two persons share the responsibility preparing to read the text for the class, one reading the scripture passages and pausing while the other reads the appropriate comments from "As You Read the Scripture."

Developing the Lesson

It is important to involve the class early. Invite them, either as an entire class or in smaller groups, to respond to the following questions:

1. Is it possible to become so absorbed in the "passions of our flesh" that we lose all sense of the holy? (Be sure the meaning of that phrase is clearly understood.)
2. Why do we feel guilty? Jean-Paul Sartre and other secular philosophers speak of humankind as "fallen," even though they do not believe in God. Is guilt God's punishment for our trying to ignore him? Then why do we still feel guilty after we have done everything possible to please God?
3. Grace (God's undeserved and limitless love) is central to Paul's theology. Does God compromise his own moral standards when he accepts us just as we are, "warts and all"?
4. Is there any way to escape God's wrath?
5. Must we hit rock bottom before being rescued?
6. Why do we resist God's grace? Is it because of stubbornness, pride, embarrassment?

Let the discussion be free-ranging. Some of the remarks may be off the wall, as we sometimes say. Others will be most revealing, both about the class members' understanding of Paul and about the state of their own souls.

Be sure to encourage the timid and to discourage the pious from making judgments on those who may not be as spiritually developed as they. Nothing can ruin a good discussion faster than comments from a self-righteous person to the effect that if you don't see things their way, you're on the side of Satan rather than God!

Now introduce the story about the man who tried to commit suicide and his wife (in "The Scripture and the Main Question"), either by reading it or by summarizing it in your own words. You may want to pause after the section "By Grace You Have Been Saved" to ask: (1) Do you see yourself in the story? (2) What does it tell us about grace—our need of it and God's granting it? (3) Who seeks whom first?

It is important to have the members understand that God's grace is always available to everyone. We experience it in numerous ways. In any event, it is essential that we understand we are talking about ourselves and not "them."

Helping Class Members Act

It is not enough to talk about the new life that Christ brings. What we all need is to experience it personally. We are at various spiritual levels, of course, and yet all of us can benefit from the following suggestions:

Consciously and intentionally seek to improve your own self-image. Most of us are harder on ourselves than God is. We feel inferior; we tell ourselves that we cannot become the kinds of persons we ought or want to be. Change the "you" to "I" in 2:8 and repeat many times each day: "By grace *I* have been saved through faith, and this is not *my* doing; *it is the gift of God.*" Add from time to time that great affirmation: "I can do *all things* through him who strengthens me" (Philippians 4:13). That is called positive imaging, and it works.

Take very seriously the sacrament of the Lord's Supper. I am discovering new life in the divinity school where I now teach through the weekly observance of the Eucharist. The words of the liturgy always reassure me: "Christ died for us while we were yet sinners; that proves God's love toward us. In the name of Jesus Christ, you are forgiven." Christ died that we might live. The story of our redemption needs to be acted out, celebrated, and believed!

If you do not now belong to a spiritual formation group, think seriously about starting one. I strongly recommend the books *Workbook of Living Prayer, Intercessory Prayer, On Spiritual Disciplines,* and *Becoming Alive in Christ,* all by Dr. Maxie Dunnam, available, along with other spiritual resources, from The Upper Room, 1908 Grand Avenue, P. O. Box 189, Nashville, Tennessee 37202-0189.

This is not a retreat into self-centeredness. Far from it:

> By giving expression to the indwelling Christ I mean actually reflecting his life within us in our daily living; living out of his presence so that his Spirit will be expressed through us. Then that fantastic and thrilling rubric for our lives will become a viable possibility: *we will be Christ to, and/or receive Christ from every person we meet.* (Maxie Dunnam, *The Workbook on Becoming Alive in Christ* [Nashville: The Upper Room, 1986], p. 27).

Planning for Next Sunday

Urge your students to read Ephesians 2:11–3:6 as a background for next week's lesson. Ask them to reflect on these questions: "Is our church truly open to all? If not, who would not be welcome? Why? What would have to happen for us to become a more inclusive fellowship?"

LESSON 10   AUGUST 8

New Fellowship

Background Scripture: Ephesians 2:11–3:6

The Main Question

How can there be divisions in the Church when Christ, "who is our peace," has made us one and has broken down the dividing wall of hostility? It is an embarrassing question.

On a typical Sunday morning white residents in a community will go to their church while black citizens go to another. In Salem, Massachusetts, which was once predominantly Protestant but now has a majority of Roman Catholic citizens, you may observe some people going to Irish, French, Polish, and Italian Catholic churches. Meanwhile, Protestant divisions continue. Ethnic ties are strong, and cultural roots run deep.

A recent listing of denominations in the United States counted twenty-seven different Baptist bodies and twenty-five who used Methodist in their title, each one claiming special distinctiveness to justify separation.

There has been a proliferation of ethnic groups in predominantly white America. That predominance, in fact, is coming to an end. "In the twenty-first century—and that's not far off—racial and ethnic groups in the United States will outnumber whites for the first time. The 'browning of America' will alter everything in society, from politics and education to industry, values and culture" (*Time*, April 9, 1990, p. 28).

Will the Christian Church continue to reflect deep divisions in society, or will we be able to rise above racial, cultural, and doctrinal differences to claim our unity in Christ?

Selected Scripture

King James Version

Ephesians 2:11-22

11 Wherefore remember, that ye being in time past Gentiles in the flesh, who are called Uncircumcision by that which is called the Circumcision in the flesh made by hands;

12 That at that time ye were without Christ, being aliens from the commonwealth of Israel, and strangers from the covenants of promise, having no hope, and without God in the world:

13 But now in Christ Jesus ye who sometimes were far off are made nigh by the blood of Christ.

14 For he is our peace, who hath made both one, and hath broken down the middle wall of partition between us;

15 Having abolished in his flesh the enmity, even the law of commandments contained in ordinances; for to make in himself of twain one new man, so making peace;

16 And that he might reconcile both unto God in one body by the cross, having slain the enmity thereby:

17 And came and preached peace

New Revised Standard Version

Ephesians 2:11-22

11 So then, remember that at one time you Gentiles by birth, called "the uncircumcision" by those who are called "the circumcision"—a physical circumcision made in the flesh by human hands—12 remember that you were at that time without Christ, being aliens from the commonwealth of Israel, and strangers to the covenants of promise, having no hope and without God in the world. 13 But now in Christ Jesus you who once were far off have been brought near by the blood of Christ. 14 For he is our peace; in his flesh he has made both groups into one and has broken down the dividing wall, that is, the hostility between us. 15 He has abolished the law with its commandments and ordinances, that he might create in himself one new humanity in place of the two, thus making peace, 16 and might reconcile both groups to God in one body through the cross, thus putting to death that hostility through it. 17 So he came and proclaimed peace to you who were far off and peace to those who were near; 18 for

to you which were afar off, and to them that were nigh.

18 For through him we both have access by one Spirit unto the Father.

19 Now therefore ye are no more strangers and foreigners, but fellowcitizens with the saints, and of the household of God;

20 And are built upon the foundation of the apostles and prophets, Jesus Christ himself being the chief corner stone;

21 In whom all the building fitly framed together groweth unto an holy temple in the Lord:

22 In whom ye also are builded together for an habitation of God through the Spirit.

Key Verse: **Now therefore ye are no more strangers and foreigners, but fellowcitizens with the saints, and of the household of God. (Ephesians 2:19)**

through him both of us have access in one Spirit to the Father. 19 So then you are no longer strangers and aliens, but you are citizens with the saints and also members of the household of God, 20 built upon the foundation of the apostles and prophets, with Christ Jesus himself as the cornerstone. 21 In him the whole structure is joined together and grows into a holy temple in the Lord; 22 in whom you also are built together spiritually into a dwelling place for God.

Key Verse: **So then you are no longer strangers and aliens, but you are citizens with the saints and also members of the household of God. (Ephesians 2:19)**

As You Read the Scripture

Ephesians 2. From this memorable passage it becomes clear that the Christian community has accomplished what no other social institution has been able to do. Jews and Gentiles, who were considered totally incompatible, have been incorporated into one body *in Christ Jesus* in which the distinctions between the two races have been completely removed.

Verses 11-12. The spiritual plight of the Gentiles (the uncircumcision) before becoming Christians was grim: separated, alienated, strangers, hopeless, and without God.

Verse 13. But now *in Christ Jesus* their fate has been radically changed. *Far off* and *near* are not geographical but spiritual realities; because of the sacrifice of Christ there is now one gospel for Jews and Gentiles alike.

The phrase "in the blood of Christ" is used because Christ is the Messiah; his blood (his life offered in sacrifice) provides the possibility of communion with God.

Throughout the epistle the messianic office of our Lord is viewed as having universal significance; he is not Messiah for Israel alone. So, too, the effects of his death extend beyond the redemption of the people which had been taught to look for him; see John 11:51-52, "He prophesied that Jesus should die for the nation, and not for the nation only, but to gather into one the children of God who are scattered abroad." (*IB*, vol. 10, p. 655)

Verses 14-18 are a parenthetical insertion in which Paul describes the reconciling work of Christ. He is our *peace*; we who were divided have become *one*. The phrase "the dividing wall" refers to an actual wall that divided the inner court of the Temple, open only to Jews, from the outer court to which Gentiles were admitted. There were bilingual inscriptions (Latin and Greek) warning Gentiles not to enter the inner court. Those who broke that law paid with their lives! The wall of hostility between Jews and Gentiles throughout the Greco-Roman world was just as divisive. The breaking of the wall, therefore, meant the abolishing of all external customs and taboos of Judaism (commandments and ordinances) and the creation of a *new person* instead of two ("there is neither Jew nor Greek . . . slave nor free . . . for you are all *one* in Christ Jesus"; Galatians 3:28), so making *peace*. This is not a victory of Judaism over the Gentiles or vice versa; it is the incorporation of both into a completely new reality: *one body through the cross.* The unity of Christians is not mechanical or external, the Spirit of Christ holds it together. Through the Spirit we have direct access to God the Father.

Verses 19-22. "Strangers" and "sojourners" are like "resident aliens," who have only a temporary visa, not full citizenship. But now Gentiles are "[fellow] citizens with the saints," fully enfranchised members of God's family.

"The household of God" is a metaphor for the Church of Christ. Its foundation consists of apostles and prophets, leaders in the early Christian community who provide a link with the historical Jesus. But Christ Jesus himself is the cornerstone, the stone to which all others are aligned. Gentiles are now an integral part of the structure. Wherever this temple is to be found, there is the "dwelling place of God."

The Scripture and the Main Question

By the time Paul wrote the Letter to the Ephesians there were more Gentile than Jewish Christians. In previous letters Paul was concerned about the attempt to blend Jewish and pagan practices (Colossians 2:20-23) and the insistence that Gentiles must become Jews before they could be Christians (Philippians 3:2-7).

Now the tables are turned. No longer are Gentiles compelled by Jews to be circumcised or to observe Jewish dietary laws. The difficulty now is that the Gentiles, clearly in the majority, are questioning the value of maintaining strong ties with the Jewish past. How to forge a new identity while still holding on to the past is clearly a complex and delicate problem.

The Scandal of Division

This passage speaks with disturbing relevance to the Christian Church in the final decade of the twentieth century. Despite ecumenical break-throughs in recent years (including interdenominational dialogue, actual mergers of church bodies, and the emphasis on shared heritage and theological convictions), the scandal of division continues. We are fond of quoting the high priestly prayer of Jesus: "I ask not only on behalf of these, but also on behalf of those who will believe in me through their word, that they may all be one. As you, Father, are in me and I am in you, may they also be in us, so that the world may believe" (John 17:20-21). But when it comes to surrendering our own traditions and practices in order to enter into a greater unity, negative reactions set in and we settle for the status quo. Not that merger into some form of super-church will resolve our problems. It is simply that in the eyes of the world divided Christendom has a credibility problem: How can we preach reconciliation and not practice it ourselves?

The "Browning of America"

We are also confronted with developing changes in the racial complexion of America. In some places in America "beyond the melting pot" has already arrived. In New York State some 40 percent of elementary and secondary school children belong to an ethnic minority. By the year 2000 the proportion is expected to approach 50 percent. In California white pupils are already a minority. Hispanics account for 31.4 percent of public school enrollment, blacks add 8.9 percent, and others amount to 11 percent—for a non-white total of 51.3 percent. In San José bearers of the Vietnamese surname Nguyen outnumber the Joneses in the telephone directory fourteen columns to eight. If present trends continue, by 2056 whites will be a minority in America ("Beyond the Melting Pot," *Time*, April 9, 1990, pp. 28-29). What are the implications for the Christian Church?

Life in the Global Village

Meanwhile population explosion is proving deadly for the planet earth.

Americans are aware of global warming, acid precipitation, ozone depletion, loss of biological diversity, deforestation, desertification, the garbage crisis and increased vulnerability to epidemics. But most have yet to recognize that these are all symptoms of one potentially lethal disease: the expansion of human numbers and the human economy. (Paul R. Ehrlich and Anne H. Ehrlich, "Observations: A Collection of Notable Quotes," *The Charlotte Observer*, April 8, 1990, C-1)

Does this mean we will have to control population growth in order to survive? The implications are staggering.

The key verse points the way toward new patterns of relationships that are essential if we are to meet the challenges before us: "You are no longer strangers and aliens, but you are citizens with the saints and also members of the household of God" (Ephesians 2:19).

Members of the Same Household

Here is an appeal to unity that rises above all ecclesiological differences. Some say "debts" instead of "trespasses" when they repeat the Lord's Prayer; the Baptists insist on baptism by immersion; the Roman Catholics forbid birth control and are ultimately subject to the pope; the Pentecostals "speak in tongues" as a sign of the presence of the Holy Spirit; United Methodist pastors are appointed by a bishop; United Church of Christ pastors are "called" by the local congregation. And yet, as followers of Jesus Christ and members of his body, which we call the Church, we are all "citizens with the saints and also members of the household of God." How can we so model unity that the world may believe?

Bond of Love

Not only must we reclaim our essential unity amid diversity, but we must also encourage cross-cultural experiences among Christians in a world grown smaller. My life has been enriched by worship in black churches, by inspired African-American music, and by Spirit-filled preaching. It was also my privilege to be the pastor of a church that welcomed a Korean congregation into its midst, providing Korean children a chance to attend our Sunday school (which also helped them with their English) and a place where the Koreans could gather to worship in their native language. There were many opportunities for all to worship and enjoy fellowship together. Later, as a supervising pastor for some eighty-five churches, I enabled other congregations to enter into similar arrangements with Christians of different cultures. I especially remember a farewell party given by Laotian Christians meeting in a United Methodist Church. We sang, first in Laotian, then in English:

> We are one in the bond of love,
> We are one in the bond of love,
> We have joined our spirits with
> The Spirit of God,
> We are one in the bond of love.

As members of the "household of God" we must also take better care of this fragile planet on which we live. "The earth is the LORD's and all that is in it" (Psalm 24:1). Stewardship of the limited resources entrusted to our care is ultimately a religious responsibility, since God is the owner and we are the caretakers. How can we both preach and practice conservation and the distribution of precious natural resources so that more may live? "From everyone to whom much has been given, much will be required" (Luke 12:48).

He Is Our Peace

However, there is a real sense in which this unity we seek has already been given us by a gracious God: "But now in Christ Jesus you . . . *have been brought near.* . . . For he is our peace; *in his flesh he has made us both groups into one* and *has broken down the dividing wall*" (2:13-14; italics added). What we were unable to do by our own efforts, God has done for us through the sacrificial death of Christ. It is immensely important to know that the person who does not like me need not "get under my skin." To be honest, I may not like him or her very much either. But Christ is our peace and has made us both *one* that we might be reconciled with God and with each other. Thank God for God's grace!

Helping Adults Become Involved

Preparing to Teach

I am convinced that Ephesians is as relevant today as when it was first written. Paul wanted to convince the Ephesians that the wall of hostility that divided Jews and Gentiles had been abolished—as surely as the Berlin Wall, which separated East and West Germany, was demolished in 1989. He also challenged the new Christian communities of Asia Minor to live this new life of reconciliation for all the world to see. This was and is a new kind of fellowship made possible by the transforming love of Christ.

You will want to be well prepared for what promises to be an exciting class. Be sure to read the background scripture as well as the printed text. "As you Read the Scripture" provides a brief commentary. "The Main Question" asks whether the Church can rise above the divisiveness of society to demonstrate a unity that embraces the alienated and broken segments of society.

The devotional reading (Hebrews 13:1-7) offers simple, direct moral mandates: Do not neglect to show hospitality; remember those in prison, and the assurance of God's protecting care.

Here is today's class outline:

I. A new community of Jews and Gentiles in Ephesus.
II. Divisions and prejudice in our world.
III. Christ has broken down every barrier.

Introducing the Main Question

Please read this introductory section in class yourself or have a class member do so. Notice that it deals entirely with the present. You may wish to pause after introducing the main question to reflect on why we have so many divisions—in the Church as well as in society. Is there a basic need to be with people who are most like ourselves? Why do we shut out people who are not like ourselves? Let it be a tentative, preliminary discussion. But it will get the people involved early in the session, which is always desirable.

Developing the Lesson

Now move to the commentary in "As You Read the Scripture," asking two members to alternate the reading of the text and the commentary. Be sure to help the class see that what has happened in the Christian community in Ephesus is truly remarkable. Whereas close relations between Jews and Gentiles were virtually impossible because of deep-seated prejudices and taboos, Christ has created a new community in which Jews and Gentiles are on equal footing, and the hostility that formerly separated them is gone.

Prejudice runs deep throughout our society. Recently an Asian man was brutally murdered outside a shopping mall in suburban Raleigh, North Carolina. The murderer mistook him for a Vietnamese person. Since his brother was killed by the North Vietnamese in the Vietnam War, he took revenge for his brother's death on a helpless young man with different skin.

White firefighters in Birmingham, Alabama, sued city officials for promoting blacks to positions of leadership for which white employees felt they were better qualified. They claimed to be victims of "reverse discrimination."

Some white Christians were relieved when Martin Luther King, Jr., was assassinated because they believed he was "going too far too fast" and was "stirring up trouble."

Do our divisions as Christians reflect the social and racial barriers in our community? Is that why so many churches in inner cities have closed their doors? They simply were not able to relate to the people in the community who were different. Instead of opening the doors to all, they froze out people who were not like themselves. The problem now is that increasingly their "own kind" have moved out to the suburbs and drive in on Sundays to attend a church that, as far as people in the community are concerned, is closed to them. It is a losing proposition for everyone.

There are actually so-called experts in evangelism who contend that the most effective way for a church to grow is for church members to seek persons in the community who are most like themselves and invite them into their fellowship. This is called the principle of homogenization. It may work, but it is unchristian!

> In Christ there is no east or west,
> In him no south or north;
> But one great fellowship of love
> Throughout the whole wide earth.
> (John Oxenham)

How can we build bridges across the gulfs that separate us? What can we do to demonstrate that Christ is our peace, who has made us both one?

Recently I attended an evening worship service conducted by one of my divinity school students. It was held in a public housing project where she serves as a part-time chaplain. All the residents are living on public welfare. Theirs, at first glance, is not a happy lot. But they are racially integrated. And they sang joyfully of the love of Christ. I was seated beside an elderly lady from Cleveland who used a cane and had trouble getting around. But there was nothing wrong with her brain! When the hymn was announced, I offered to share a hymnal. She thanked me and added that she did not need it because she knew the song by heart, and she proceeded to sing every verse. The service was upbeat, and the sermon, which centered on the encounter of Jesus and the Samaritan woman (John 4:4-42), was inspiring. But the fellowship afterward truly knit us together. I do not recall a group where there were so many hugs and warm handclasps. There were differences in age, in physical condition (several were severely handicapped), and race. But that did not really matter. Christ had broken down every barrier.

Helping Members Act

Reflect on the questions asked at the end of last week's lesson: Are there people not welcome in our church? If so, why? What would have to happen for them to feel welcome? This may be painful for some to discuss openly. But it is important that Christians talk about very specific ways the "dividing wall of hostility" has been or can be broken down. Who are the alienated ones in our community? (There are many forms of alienation: race, sex, age, social status.) Are we going to be inclusive or exclusive? Are we going to lead or follow?

If the discussion falters, you may refer to "The Scripture and the Main Question," but you probably will not have to.

Planning for Next Sunday

Strongly recommend that the class members read Ephesians 5:1-20 in advance and reflect on the question, "Is it possible for human beings like us to imitate God?"

New Behavior

Background Scripture: Ephesians 5:1-20

The Main Question

On the surface it seems impossible, if not downright ludicrous. How can any mortal, including high-minded and well-intentioned Christians, be "imitators of God"? To suggest such a thing simply confirms what outsiders surmise, that some Christians are smug and legalistic and, yes, self-righteous. Is this where "imitation" leads?

Perhaps the Greek word *mimetai* meant something different from "imitate" back then. That is a familiar ploy, but it does not work. The best, most accurate, translation is "imitate." The *Living Bible*'s paraphrase, "Follow God's example in everything you do" waters down the original meaning. The NRSV has it right: "Be imitators of God."

If only we could dismiss this high command. The contexts, after all, are different; the contrasts in our culture between Christians and nonchristians are less clear. That's the point! Unless we imitate God, we will imitate the world and all its evils.

Why recoil at this command? Is it because God's image is not all that clear and, therefore, it is not easy to know how we are to imitate? Is it because "my thoughts are not your thoughts, nor are your ways my ways, says the Lord" (Isaiah 55:8)? And does it not strike you as the height of presumption that a mere mortal would try to become like his or her maker, as clay would strive to be like the potter who shapes it?

What is needed, obviously, is more understanding of this amazing passage in Ephesians—the context in which it was written, its meaning for those who first read or heard it and, most important, its meaning for us today.

Ultimately what is at stake here is the question "Are Christians supposed to be different?" If so, how? It is, I submit, a very timely question.

Selected Scripture

King James Version	New Revised Standard Version
Ephesians 5:1-20	*Ephesians 5:1-20*
1 Be ye therefore followers of God, as dear children;	1 Therefore be imitators of God, as beloved children, 2 and live in love, as Christ loved us and gave himself up for us, a fragrant offering and sacrifice to God.
2 And walk in love, as Christ also hath loved us, and hath given himself for us an offering and a sacrifice to God for a sweetsmelling savour.	
3 But fornication, and all uncleanness, or covetousness, let it not be once named among you, as becometh saints;	3 But fornication and impurity of any kind, or greed, must not even be mentioned among you, as is proper among saints. 4 Entirely out of place

4 Neither filthiness, nor foolish talking, nor jesting, which are not convenient: but rather giving of thanks.

5 For this ye know, that no whoremonger, nor unclean person, nor covetous man, who is an idolater, hath any inheritance in the kingdom of Christ and of God.

6 Let no man deceive you with vain words: for because of these things cometh the wrath of God upon the children of disobedience.

7 Be not ye therefore partakers with them.

8 For ye were sometimes darkness, but now are ye light in the Lord: walk as children of light:

9 (For the fruit of the Spirit is in all goodness and righteousness and truth;)

10 Proving what is acceptable unto the Lord.

11 And have no fellowship with the unfruitful works of darkness, but rather reprove them.

12 For it is a shame even to speak of those things which are done of them in secret.

13 But all things that are reproved are made manifest by the light: for whatsoever doth make manifest is light.

14 Wherefore he saith, Awake thou that sleepest, and arise from the dead, and Christ shall give thee light.

15 See then that ye walk circumspectly, not as fools, but as wise,

16 Redeeming the time, because the days are evil.

17 Wherefore be ye not unwise, but understanding what the will of the Lord is.

18 And be not drunk with wine, wherein is excess; but be filled with the Spirit;

19 Speaking to yourselves in psalms and hymns and spiritual songs, singing and making melody in your heart to the Lord;

20 Giving thanks always for all

is obscene, silly, and vulgar talk; but instead, let there be thanksgiving. 5 Be sure of this, that no fornicator or impure person, or one who is greedy (that is, an idolater), has any inheritance in the kingdom of Christ and of God.

6 Let no one deceive you with empty words, for because of these things the wrath of God comes on those who are disobedient. 7 Therefore do not be associated with them. 8 For once you were darkness, but now in the Lord you are light. Live as children of light— 9 for the fruit of the light is found in all that is good and right and true. 10 Try to find out what is pleasing to the Lord. 11 Take no part in the unfruitful works of darkness, but instead expose them. 12 For it is shameful even to mention what such people do secretly; 13 but everything exposed by the light becomes visible, 14 for everything that becomes visible is light. Therefore it says,
"Sleeper, awake!
    Rise from the dead,
and Christ will shine on you."

15 Be careful then how you live, not as unwise people but as wise, 16 making the most of the time, because the days are evil. 17 So do not be foolish, but understand what the will of the Lord is. 18 Do not get drunk with wine, for that is debauchery; but be filled with the Spirit, 19 as you sing psalms and hymns and spiritual songs among yourselves, singing and making melody to the Lord in your hearts, 20 giving thanks to God the Father at all times and for everything in the name of our Lord Jesus Christ.

things unto God and the Father in the name of our Lord Jesus Christ.

Key Verses: **Be ye therefore followers of God, as dear children; And walk in love, as Christ also hath loved us, and hath given himself for us an offering and a sacrifice to God for a sweet-smelling savour. (Ephesians 5:1-2)**

Key Verses: **Therefore be imitators of God, as beloved children, and live in love, as Christ loved us and gave himself up for us, a fragrant offering and sacrifice to God. (Ephesians 5:1-2)**

As You Read the Scripture

Ephesians 5:1-2. These verses continue the thought of 4:32 in which Paul speaks of Christlike virtues that overcome mean and unworthy vices. As "God in Christ" forgave you, so you are to be "kind, tenderhearted, forgiving one another." Christ is the model. In him we see God's nature revealed. In this context the demand to "be imitators of God" becomes more reasonable. Besides, we are to imitate God as "beloved children." It doesn't make sense to command rank unbelievers to imitate God. But those who have received God's reconciling love into their hearts know themselves as God's children, younger brothers and sisters in the same family as Jesus. That is, "You are to pattern your behavior after the highest you know, Jesus, in whom God is supremely made known." It is a high calling, but the children of God will aim at nothing less.

Paul uses a metaphor that relates to the primitive notion that animal sacrifices to the deity actually smell good (fragrant) to say that we are to model our lives after One who, in the giving of his life for us, pleased God.

Verses 3-5. The Greek word for fornication (*porneia*) covers a wide range of sexual evils, including adultery and prostitution. *Impurity* refers to various sexual perversions; *covetousness* implies sexual indulgence with a "callous disregard for the welfare of others" (C. Leslie Mitton, *Ephesians,* The New Century Bible [Grand Rapids: Eerdmans, 1981], p. 178). These blatantly pagan practices are not even to be mentioned.

There is to be no *filthiness,* anything shameful; *silly talk,* the talk of a fool; *levity,* "clever witticisms with nasty insinuations that raise a laugh at the expense of others." Instead, let there be thanksgiving for sexual intimacy within a faithful and enduring marriage relationship. Admittedly, this interpretation is based on implication; yet the point is well made. We are to conduct our lives as Christians so that we may be able to give thanks for all things and not be ashamed of any. (Mitton, *Ephesians,* pp. 178-79.)

Verses 6-14. Christians must not be "deceived by empty words." It is suggested that the immoralities referred to were indulged in by Gnostics, who claimed that only the soul is important and that whatever one does with one's body is unimportant. The danger is that otherwise committed Christians would be corrupted by this heresy (adultery, prostitution, and homosexuality need not damage the soul). On the contrary, Christianity holds that both the body and the soul are important—God created both, Jesus Christ took the form of a human being, the body is the temple of the Holy Spirit, and God is concerned about the salvation of the whole person.

Christians are not to associate with those who would corrupt the innocent. Christians are not only to abstain from sin, but also are to actually expose sin wherever it occurs. One cannot be neutral in this world. One must belong to either the light or the darkness; there is no middle ground. The quotation in verse 14 is from Isaiah 60:1 and may be associated with the rite of baptism. As the "sleeper" rises from "the dead," Christ becomes his or her light: "I am the light of the world. Whoever follows me will never walk in darkness but will have the light of life" (John 8:12).

Verses 15-20. Apparently those who advocated sexual freedom also advocated freedom with regard to the use of wine. Paul was distressed to learn that some Corinthian Christians got drunk when they celebrated the Lord's Supper (1 Corinthians 11:21). He warns the Ephesians that drunkenness can lead to debauchery (excess indulgence in sensual pleasure). It is better to be filled with the Spirit than with spirits! And let there be hearty singing with one persistent theme: "giving thanks to God the Father at all times and for everything in the name of our Lord Jesus Christ."

The Scripture and the Main Question

Let us explore further the theological implications of the word *imitate.* Ephesians 5:1 follows 4:32 and is a continuation of the thoughts expressed there: "Be kind to one another, tenderhearted, forgiving one another, as God in Christ has forgiven you. Therefore be imitators. . . . " Our relationships are to be shaped by God's relationship with us. We are to be imitators as *beloved children* who need a model by which to pattern our lives. As imitators we do not cease to be children. The distance between God and human beings is firmly maintained. "There can be no possible reference to an imitation whereby we become similar or equal to the model. To take God as a model means . . . to bear constantly in mind that as His children we live wholly by His love and forgiveness" (Gerhard Kittel, ed., *Theological Dictionary of the New Testament,* vol. 4 [Grand Rapids: Eerdmans, 1967], p. 671).

Echoes

Letty Russell writes in her excellent study on Ephesians, *Imitators of God* (published by the Women's Division, General Board of Global Ministries, The United Methodist Church, 1984) that in this demanding phrase she hears echoes of deep and central biblical themes. The first is *made in God's image,* as expressed in the creation story in Genesis 1:26-27. Both women and men have been created in God's image. The emphasis is not on appearance, but on the relationship of human beings to God. "Genesis seems to be saying that God is uniquely represented in creation by human beings who are related to God as partners in caring for the earth and for one another" (Russell, p. 2).

Another "echo" is *Christian perfection.* "Be perfect, therefore, as your heavenly Father is perfect" (Matthew 5:48). Russell cites John Wesley, who, in his *Plain Account of Christian Perfection,* stated that perfection does not mean that we are free from error, infirmity, or temptation but rather that the gift of the Holy Spirit makes it possible for us to grow continually in grace (Russell, p. 3).

John Wesley meant for preachers to be models of Christlikeness. Even today candidates for admission into the United Methodist ministry are asked:

1. Have you faith in Christ?
2. Are you going on to perfection?
3. Do you expect to be made perfect in love in this life?
4. Are you earnestly striving after it?
(*The Book of Discipline of The United Methodist Church* [Nashville: The United Methodist Publishing House, 1988], p. 232)

It may seem presumptuous to make such demands, but Wesley understood that basic to the Christian life is the principle of spiritual growth based on imitation of the highest we know. Our model is Christ; our goal is continued growth as long as we live.

The third "echo" is *God's covenant faithfulness*. The people of Israel were a covenant community, bound to God and to one another by an agreement to obey and serve God. God, in liberating Israel from Egyptian slavery and choosing them to be God's special people, promised them his steadfast love. In the New Testament community the covenant was renewed through the life, death, and resurrection of Christ: "This cup . . . is the new covenant in my blood" (Luke 22:20). At the center of these covenants is God's loving concern for all persons. When we work for human dignity and justice, we become bearers of God's *shalom*, God's peace, for all people (see Russell, pp. 4-5).

Whatever Happened to Sin?

Paul's condemnation of sexual sins is both clear and strong. Fornication (extramarital intercourse; in the Old Testament, "whoredom") and every kind of sexual perversion or indulgence for one's own selfish pleasure with "callous disregard for the welfare of others" are strictly forbidden. "The *porneia* of individual members makes the whole church unclean and threatens the whole work of the apostle, which is to present pure communities to Christ" (Kittel, p. 593). Those who are guilty will not enter the kingdom of Christ and of God!

Some years ago a psychiatrist of national stature wrote a book entitled *Whatever Happened to Sin?* How little we hear about it from mainline pulpits these days. Have we been taken in by the relativistic ethics and self-centered "life-styles of the rich and famous"?

One problem is that we talk about sin in the abstract; we do not make it explicit as Paul does in this passage. Meanwhile our society is saturated with sex; pornographic literature and X-rated movies portray sex as physical lust devoid of love. Magazine and television commercials push to the limits standards of decency, using sex as a means to boost sales in a blatant exploitation of women.

Is it any wonder that there is such a high incidence of rape and child molestation in our society, or that women are battered and exploited even within the marriage bond?

The Unholy Trinity

When sexual license is combined with illicit drugs, destructive forces are unleashed that claim hundreds of thousands of victims, including crack-addicted babies, the most pitiful of all who are born only to die. Unbridled sex, drug addiction, and drug-related crimes combine to make an unholy trinity whose worshipers are condemned to a fate worse than death. Unless they turn to God for mercy, they are without hope. No one, not even the "vilest offender," is beyond the reach of God's forgiving grace. The lesson, however, is painfully clear: When we ignore God for whatever reason, we bring destruction upon ourselves.

The Christian View of Sex

Therefore be imitators of God. What does this mean for contemporary Christians? It means that we are to regard our bodies as temples of the Holy Spirit, given to us by God (see 1 Corinthians 6:19). We are to keep our bodies pure from illicit sex, alcohol, and drugs. Paul said that he pummeled his body into submission lest in preaching to others he himself would be disqualified (see 1 Corinthians 9:27).

We must also regard sex as a beautiful gift of God, which provides us with possibilities of loving relationships. With the widespread threat of AIDS, as well as unwanted pregnancies, promiscuity is being seen for what it is: uncontrolled passion offering momentary ecstasy, but devoid of lasting satisfaction, in which one or both are exploited or hurt. For Christians sex and love go together. "Safe sex" may prevent the further spread of deadly disease and provide contraception. But only those who are committed to each other "until death us do part" can know the deeper joys of giving themselves to the other in love. And no one is exploited!

Finally, we must understand that the high demands of Paul are not impossible. Christ is our model, who "in every respect has been tested as we are, yet without sin" (Hebrews 4:15). Furthermore, God is faithful and will not "let you be tested beyond your strength" (1 Corinthians 10:13). As members of the Body of Christ, intimately related to Christ and to each other, we shall be given strength to conquer evil in every form. *Therefore be imitators.* For Christians there is no other way.

Helping Adults Become Involved

If anyone doubts whether the church has anything to say about burning issues of the day, let him or her read what Paul says in this passage from Ephesians. Here we are given not only timeless theological principles but also very explicit instructions about contemporary morality.

Preparing to Teach

Read carefully Ephesians 5:1-20. You might begin with the devotional reading (Ephesians 4:25-32), which provides a good lead-in for Ephesians 5. Paul wrote earlier: "Now this I affirm and insist on in the Lord: you must no longer live as the Gentiles live" (4:17). That is the key to all that follows.

It is extremely important that you read all of the lesson material in advance, keeping in mind two goals: an understanding of what Paul means by the command "be imitators of God" and helping people to confront serious ethical issues in our society, especially the abuse of sex and the pressure to use illegal drugs.

Here is the outline for this session:

    I. Ephesians as a call to Christian maturity.
   II. Are we growing as Christians today?
  III. Ways in which our church can help us grow in the faith.

Introducing the Main Question

You should begin the class by personally introducing the main question, either by reading it or by summarizing it in your own words. Make it very clear that Paul is speaking forcefully to us and not simply to the Christians of ancient Ephesus.

Developing the Lesson

Then present the passage to the class by using the familiar pattern of having two persons read—one from the scriptural text and the other from "As You Read the Scripture."

You might then begin with a general question: "How well is the Church doing in the development of moral character? Is it a major force in shaping people's lives?"

After a brief preliminary discussion, read the following:

In March of 1990 findings from "Effective Christian Education: A National Study of Protestant Congregations" were made public. According to the study 36 percent of all adults and 64 percent of youth surveyed lack "maturity of faith" in which persons "exhibit a vibrant, life-transforming faith marked by both a deep, personal relationship to a loving God and a consistent devotion to serving others."

Instead, they have what the report terms "undeveloped faith," resulting in part from lack of involvement in Christian education. Forty-five percent of the adults in a major mainline denomination reported being involved in forty or more hours of Christian education yearly. Fully one-third spend a mere ten or fewer hours yearly!

Four out of every ten youth surveyed in a major denomination reported involvement in three or more "at-risk behaviors," such as alcohol and drug use, depression, suicidal thoughts, binge drinking, sexual intercourse, theft, aggression, or trouble at school. More than half "report fewer than five hours of instruction or discussion at church, at any time in their lives, in such areas." ("North Carolina Christian Advocate," April 10, 1990, p. 4)

Ask the following questions:

  1. Why is the Church not addressing these issues of life and death?
  2. Has the Church in effect abdicated its moral responsibility and through benign neglect contributed to the deterioration of the moral climate of the nation?
  3. In what specific ways are Christians to be "different" from others? (Be sure to refer to the passage from Ephesians.)

Helping Class Members Act

Does the preceding discussion suggest any specific actions that you as a class or as a congregation might take? For example:

1. Is it possible for your class to initiate a dialogue with the youth of your church in an effort to understand the incredible pressures they are under to yield to all kinds of temptation? This would be a very sensitive and delicate venture, and in no way must the youth get the impression that they are under investigation. Instead, it would be an attempt by your class to understand what problems youth face and how youth and adults together can create a climate of understanding and support.

A very real challenge is finding adults of high moral integrity and strong commitment to Christ to serve as models. The youth will more readily imitate God, whom they cannot see, if they are attracted to godly persons they can see.

2. In what ways do we need to clean up our own act? A dynamic speaker, whose life had been transformed by the love of Christ, conducted a retreat for deacons of a local church. On the opening evening he spoke very explicitly about sexual sins. At the end of the message the pastor upbraided him for his plain speaking. These men, after all, were leaders in the community, of unquestioned moral character. But the speaker did not get much sleep that night because of deacons who came to his room to confess their sins and ask God's forgiveness.

3. How can we teach the Christian view of sex? (See "The Scripture and the Main Question.")

4. Is it possible, perhaps through the headquarters of your denomination, to support local churches that are providing spiritual help for people who are coming off drugs and offering a safe haven for battered women and a loving environment for crack-addicted babies? How can we share compassionate concern?

5. How can we make sure that our services of worship are truly Spirit-filled, that there are opportunities for people of all ages to commit themselves to Christ who "loved us and gave himself up for us"? Does our Sunday music lead us joyfully to give thanks "to God the Father at all times and for everything in the name of our Lord Jesus Christ"?

We are speaking of nothing less than a moral reformation: "Therefore be imitators of God, as beloved children." Let it begin, here and now.

Planning for Next Sunday

Have the class members read Ephesians 5:21–6:4 before next Sunday's class. Are Paul's rules for the Christian family still relevant?

New Family Order

Background Scripture: Ephesians 5:21–6:4

The Main Question

I remember with some embarrassment using today's passage from Ephesians for a homily in a wedding service. It was during a moment when the pastor speaks to the couple from God's Word. I had some doubts about the appropriateness of the passage, but still believed there were enough positive points to outweigh the negative. As hard as I tried, however, the nuances were those of male superiority: "Wives, *be subject* to your husbands as you are to the Lord. For the husband is the head of the wife just as Christ is the head of the church" (Ephesians 5:22-23; italics added). However pious the language, the damage was done. The difference between "be subject to" and "love" is considerable.

I ended up on the defensive: "Jeff and Ellen, in spite of the tone of male dominance, which is not surprising considering the context out of which Paul spoke, mutual respect and love, the same love that Christ has for his church, are the bonds that hold a marriage together."

Why was I uncomfortable? First, I do not believe God is a male chauvinist. God created both the male and the female (Genesis 1:27). They both were the crown jewels of God's creation; they both reflected God's image. Second, Paul has an even clearer word on our unity in Christ in his letter to the Galatians: "There is no longer Jew or Greek, there is no longer slave or free, there is no longer male and female; for *all of you are one in Christ Jesus*" (Galatians 3:28; italics added).

It is exciting to realize that Paul was shaping a new morality for family life that contrasted sharply with pagan life-styles. Yet one has to admit that in this passage the woman is subordinate to the man. So the risky question becomes: Are these rules still relevant?

Selected Scripture

King James Version

Ephesians 5:21–6:4

21 Submitting yourselves one to another in the fear of God.

22 Wives, submit yourselves unto your own husbands, as unto the Lord.

23 For the husband is the head of the wife, even as Christ is the head of the church: and he is the saviour of the body.

24 Therefore as the church is subject unto Christ, so let the wives be to their own husbands in every thing.

New Revised Standard Version

Ephesians 5:21–6:4

21 Be subject to one another out of reverence for Christ.

22 Wives, be subject to your husbands as you are to the Lord. 23 For the husband is the head of the wife just as Christ is the head of the church, the body of which he is the Savior. 24 Just as the church is subject to Christ, so also wives ought to be, in everything, to their husbands.

25 Husbands, love your wives, even as Christ also loved the church, and gave himself for it;

26 That he might sanctify and cleanse it with the washing of water by the word,

27 That he might present it to himself a glorious church, not having spot, or wrinkle, or any such thing; but that it should be holy and without blemish.

28 So ought men to love their wives as their own bodies. He that loveth his wife loveth himself.

29 For no man ever yet hated his own flesh; but nourisheth and cherisheth it, even as the Lord the church:

30 For we are members of his body, of his flesh, and of his bones.

31 For this cause shall a man leave his father and mother, and shall be joined unto his wife, and they two shall be one flesh.

32 This is a great mystery: but I speak concerning Christ and the church.

33 Nevertheless let every one of you in particular so love his wife even as himself; and the wife see that she reverence her husband.

1 Children, obey your parents in the Lord: for this is right.

2 Honour thy father and mother; (which is the first commandment with promise;)

3 That it may be well with thee, and thou mayest live long on the earth.

4 And, ye fathers, provoke not your children to wrath: but bring them up in the nurture and admonition of the Lord.

Key Verse: **Submitting yourselves one to another in the fear of God. (Ephesians 5:21)**

25 Husbands, love your wives, just as Christ loved the church and gave himself up for her, 26 in order to make her holy by cleansing her with the washing of water by the word, 27 so as to present the church to himself in splendor, without a spot or wrinkle or anything of the kind—yes, so that she may be holy and without blemish. 28 In the same way, husbands should love their wives as they do their own bodies. He who loves his wife loves himself. 29 For no one ever hates his own body, but he nourishes and tenderly cares for it, just as Christ does for the church, 30 because we are members of his body. 31 "For this reason a man will leave his father and mother and be joined to his wife, and the two will become one flesh." 32 This is a great mystery, and I am applying it to Christ and the church. 33 Each of you, however, should love his wife as himself, and a wife should respect her husband.

1 Children, obey your parents in the Lord, for this is right. 2 "Honor your father and mother"—this is the first commandment with a promise: 3 "so that it may be well with you and you may live long on the earth."

4 And, fathers, do not provoke your children to anger, but bring them up in the discipline and instruction of the Lord.

Key Verse: **Be subject to one another out of reverence for Christ. (Ephesians 5:21)**

As You Read the Scripture

Ephesians 5:21–6:4. This passage is set over against the condemnation of Gentile immorality (esp. 5:3-12). How does one's acceptance of Christ as

Lord affect relations between husband and wife, parents and children, slave and master? Paul is laying out a new ethic based on the principle of self-giving love that has its source in Christ, who "loved us and gave himself up for us." (Similar instructions are found in Colossians 3:18–4:1; 1 Peter 2:18–3:7; and 5:1-5.)

Verse 21. This is the principle of subordination, which is a major theme in Pauline ethics: "In humility regard others better than yourselves" (Philippians 2:3). Self-centeredness is to give way to concern for the well-being of others. Note that the principle of *mutual* subordination is being urged, *out of reverence for Christ,* literally translated: "out of the *fear* of Christ." Christ is our judge as well as our redeemer. "The first requirement of Christians, therefore, is to be obedient to God as we know him in Christ, so that at the last we may hear from him words of commendation, not condemnation" (C. Leslie Mitton, *Ephesians,* The New Century Bible Commentary [Grand Rapids: Eerdmans, 1981], pp. 196-97).

Verses 22-24. In the ancient Near East a wife had no legal rights and was absolutely dependent upon her husband to do with her as he pleased. The Greek world was no better. Demosthenes wrote: "We have courtesans for the sake of pleasure; we have concubines for the sake of daily cohabitation; we have wives for the purpose of having children legitimately and of having a faithful guardian of all our household affairs." As for Romans, "it is not too much to say that the whole atmosphere of the ancient world was adulterous" (William Barclay, *The Letters to Galatians and Ephesians,* The Daily Bible Series [Philadelphia: The Westminster Press, 1958], pp. 201-2).

Surely Christians gave to women a higher place in life than did their pagan counterparts. Yet, in spite of the new freedom women enjoyed within the Christian community and of the transformation this would ultimately bring to Christian marriage, "it is probable that Paul continued to feel that obedience was the proper attitude of the Christian wife to her husband" (Mitton, p. 198). Note, however, the qualifications: "as Christ is the head of the church . . . as the church is subject to Christ." This is not ruthless domination but a relationship based on respect (5:33) both for each other and for Christ, the "head of the church."

Verses 25-31. The Greek word used to mean "love" here is *agape,* the highest form of love: "God so loved *(agapesen)* the world that he gave his only Son" (John 3:16). The love of husbands for wives must be a *sacrificial love*: "as Christ loved the church and gave himself up for her." It must be a *purifying* love. Careful bathing was part of a bride's preparation for marriage, so the Church is prepared for Christ by the cleansing of baptism and the Word, which is the spoken witness of the convert: "If you confess with your lips that Jesus is Lord and believe in your heart that God raised him from the dead, you will be saved" (Romans 10:9).

It must be a *caring* love: "Husbands should love their wives as they do their own bodies." Again Christ is our model. As he nourishes and cherishes the Church, a Christian husband should care most of all for the happiness of his wife.

It is an *unbreakable* love. So intimate and lasting is the bond between them that they become "one flesh." They have left their parents and have forged a new identity. Genesis 2:24 clearly states that this is the will of God and has been since Creation.

This is a *great mystery*—that two separate people should become one. And this is exactly what the Church is: a varied collection of people from different backgrounds who become one. This unity, in Christian marriage and in Christ's relation to his church, is indeed a profound mystery.

Ephesians 6:1-4. The thoughts parallel Colossians 3:20-21. Obedience to one's parents is based on the fifth Commandment: "Honor your father and your mother" (Exodus 20:12). At the same time, children have rights also. They should neither be abused nor neglected.

The Scripture and the Main Question

The Way We Were

I grew up in a patriarchal family. My father was the head of the household; there was no doubt about it. He ran the family business, managed the finances, and made crucial decisions in which we all might have input, but the last word was his.

Yet, as I look back on those early years I do not think of our family life as being oppressive. My mother seemed fulfilled as wife, mother, and homemaker. There were two major influences at the center of our lives: one was the church. Both parents taught Sunday school and were otherwise active in leadership positions. We followed their example. More important, Bible reading and prayer were central in their lives. I carry a treasured picture in my memory of my parents kneeling in prayer before going to bed. The second influence was their own deep commitment to each other. They may have had conflicts, but they were quietly resolved. When state and national elections drew near my parents had spirited conversations, because each belonged to a different political party, but there was never any acrimony.

The Way We Are

Times have drastically changed. Fewer than 40 percent of our nation's families are "nuclear"—that is, with one parent, usually the father, being the sole breadwinner, while the other is the homemaker and keeper of the family hearth. Increasingly both parents work, nurseries and day-care centers are full, and there is a growing number of latch-key children who come home after school to empty houses. This change of roles, this increased freedom for women to pursue their own careers, this striving toward greater equality, has produced many advantages, but there are still many problems. Family income has increased; women have made their mark in the major professions, including the military, proving that they are just as capable as men. But divorce has been steadily on the rise for several decades, resulting in severe emotional stress on the family. And women are still exploited. Few receive salaries equal to their male counterparts, and they are still considered sex objects by some men. Hence the increase in violent crime, including rape, against women. Even within marriage there is a distressing incidence of violence against both women and children. Despite our affluence and sophistication, the end of the twentieth century is an unhappy time for too many families.

A colleague at Duke maintains that marriages these days are suffering from an "overdose of secular values." He mentions three in particular: (1) "Self" is sacred. "Much of our culture is designed to enhance self-development, or to put *me* at the center of the universe. So there's a tendency when we get married to ask 'what's in it for me?' and that can be a deadly attitude." (2) Marriage remains only an option and, therefore, is always expendable. Some may choose not to get married but to enjoy many of its privileges—the advantage, they reason, is that it's easier to break up if things don't work out. Others take the traditional walk down the aisle, but the prospect of a divorce does not daunt them. They look upon a divorce as a natural passage of life, which puts marriage in the category of another disposable commodity. (3) Marriage is just an emotional sideline. "The matrimonial bond becomes an emotional and sexual convenience, not a relationship that can bring true character and meaning into your life" (Paul A. Mickey, *Tough Marriage: How to Make a Difficult Relationship Work* [New York: William Morrow and Company, 1986], pp. 175-76).

Tough marriage, according to Mickey, is severely at odds with these secular notions. "Marriage is a sacred union, a uniting of two as one. Most important of all, it's conceived and sanctioned by God himself. So marriage isn't there just as a convenience or to make you feel good. It isn't intended as a commodity you try on for size or throw away when it wears out."

Another therapist and educator who works with individuals, couples, and families distinguishes between what he calls the unconscious and the conscious marriage. A conscious marriage

fosters maximum psychological and spiritual growth; it's a marriage created by becoming conscious of and cooperating with . . . fundamental drives: to be safe, to be healed, to be whole. . . . As a part of your God-given nature, you have the ability to love unconditionally and to experience unity with the world around you. . . . As you gain a more realistic view of love relationships you realize that a good marriage requires commitment, discipline, and the courage to grow and change; marriage is hard work. (Harville Hendrix, *Getting the Love You Want* [New York: Henry Holt and Company, 1988], pp. 75, 77)

The Way We Should Be

Let us return to the passage from Ephesians. Does it seem less objectionable? Despite the themes of male dominance and female subordinance, are there principles here that still apply? If I were to give another wedding homily based on these memorable rules for a new family order, I would make the following points:

1. Marriage is sacred. It unites two people in an intimate and holy relationship. Paul compares marriage to the holy bond between Christ and his Church and, quoting the passage in Genesis which Christ also used in speaking of the permanence of marriage (Matthew 19:3-5), Paul affirms that it is the will of God that one should leave one's parents and be joined to another, "and they become one flesh" (Genesis 2:24).

2. The secret to a truly harmonious marriage is self-giving love. Again, Christ is our model: "Be subject to one another out of reverence for Christ"; "Husbands, love your wives [and, wives, love your husbands!] just as Christ loved the church and gave himself up for her." Always one's main concern must be "What can I do to make you happy?"

3. This self-giving love extends to all family relationships. Discipline is needed (I question whether undisciplined children are truly loved!), but love is needed even more. At a recent memorial service for a very distinguished leader the most touching testimony came from a granddaughter, speaking for all the grandchildren. She said, "We don't think of him as a famous person. He was just our granddad. He put up tents in the yard for us to sleep in. He took us swimming and bought us ice cream. He wrote us notes, and he always had time to listen. That's because he loved us." Will our grandchildren, if God gives them to us, say the same about us?

Helping Adults Become Involved

Preparing to Teach

This is another lesson that speaks with amazing relevance to our times. You should prepare for lively participation by the members of your class, especially as you deal with the differences in the instructions for wives and husbands.

You will need to read very carefully the Scripture text and the appropriate materials in today's lesson. You will also find Colossians 3:12-21 helpful not only because there are parallel instructions, but also there is a listing of the qualities of Christian character: "lowliness, meekness, patience . . . and above all, love."

Today's class outline:

> I. Husbands and wives in Ephesians
> II. Subject to one another in Christ
> III. Christian marriage and family life today

Introducing the Main Question

There may be some who are shocked at the very notion that there may be conflict between what the Scripture says and how we should live our lives. They support without question the bumper sticker that reads: "GOD SAID IT; I BELIEVE IT; THAT SETTLES IT." And you will undoubtedly have some male chauvinists in your class who don't want to be challenged. But there will also be those who are quick to detect male domination and do, indeed, have questions as to what this passage says to Christian families in the last decade of the twentieth century.

I suggest that either you or a class member, carefully chosen, read aloud "The Main Question" in full.

Developing the Lesson

You will then want to let Paul speak by reading the text and the commentary, "As You Read the Scripture," using the same pattern suggested before: with one person reading the text and another the commentary. Now you are ready for discussion.

You will need to guard against a long and fruitless argument about Paul's position—was he or wasn't he a male chauvinist? It is possible to make a case for either side. Some will undoubtedly quote 1 Timothy 2:12: "I permit no woman to teach or to have authority over a man." Or they will quote 1 Corinthians 14:34-35: "Women should be silent in the churches. . . . If there is anything they desire to know, let them ask their husbands at home." Then what shall be do with a passage like Galatians 3:28: "There is no

402

longer Jew or Greek . . . slave or free . . . male or female; for all of you are one in Christ Jesus." The truth is that some of Paul's most trusted co-workers were women (see Romans 16:1, 3). And in a time when the husband was considered lord and master of the wife, one is surprised to read in 1 Corinthians 7:4: "For the wife does not have authority over her own body, but the husband does; likewise the husband does not have authority over his own body, but the wife does." If that is not equality, what is?

This, however, is almost beside the point. The key verse sets the theme of the lesson and is the key to all Christian relationships: "Be subject to one another out of reverence for Christ" (Ephesians 5:21). A more fruitful discussion, therefore, should proceed along these lines:

1. We need to be reminded that this passage is a continuation of the chapter that begins, "Therefore be imitators of God," a theme discussed last week. Midway through the chapter is the injunction: "Do not be foolish, but understand what the will of the Lord is" (v. 17). The larger theme here is "holy living appropriate for the people of God."

2. Apart from the obvious differences in instruction (which one can understand because of the cultural conditions out of which this epistle comes), what are some basic principles suggested for a wholesome Christian family life? It would be helpful at this point to use a chalkboard or newsprint to list the answers to these questions: What is to be the relationship between wives and husbands? Between parents and children?

3. Now comes the all-important question: Are these rules still relevant? You should encourage the class to discuss problems that modern families confront. If the conversation falters, you can refer to Paul Mickey's observation that many marriages these days are suffering from an "overdose of secular values" (in "The Scripture and the Main Question"). Allow plenty of time for an open and frank discussion about recent trends: the alarming rise in divorce rates, the break-up of the traditional family, and the effects all this has on morality, on crime, and on drug trafficking (especially among poorer, minority families) and other social consequences of the assault on family values. Possibly these issues should be discussed first. That should certainly be a live option; then list what Paul says about the new family order.

Be sure to stress that the patterns for Christian family life were, in fact, new. These were first-generation Christians, some with Jewish backgrounds, but most by this time were Gentiles raised in a thoroughly pagan environment. They needed strong guidance in shaping their lives in a distinctly Christian manner. Paul did not disappoint them.

Helping Class Members Act

Invite the pastor to discuss premarital counseling. How does the pastor help the couple prepare for a Christian marriage? Explore what Christian-oriented counseling resources for problem marriages are available in your community. Plan some workshops, possibly in cooperation with neighboring churches, on the dynamics of a healthy Christian home. Resource persons from your denomination can help you find leaders and audio-visual resources. One of the areas that usually needs attention is communication, not only between spouses, but between parents and children. Because better communication will likely uncover problems, how can they best be handled? Here, again, you may need professional guidance. This is not to suggest that your class take total responsibility for these ventures, but at least you can be the catalyst for providing opportunities for strengthening Christian family life.

Planning for Next Sunday

Urge all class members to read Ephesians 6:10-20 and be prepared to discuss what is meant by "rulers . . . authorities . . . cosmic powers of this present darkness . . . the spiritual forces of evil in the heavenly places." Could Paul have foreseen the mess our world is in?

LESSON 13   AUGUST 29

New Strength

Background Scripture: Ephesians 6:10-20

The Main Question

A special commission, acting on behalf of the entire denomination, was planning a new hymnal. They hoped to draw not only upon the great hymns of the past, but also upon those hymns that have become meaningful to a varied and pluralistic membership. The commission made every effort to communicate with the "grass roots," who, after all, would be the ones to use the hymnal for the next twenty-five years.

Unfortunately, word got out that one of the hymns that would not be included in the new hymnal was "Onward, Christian Soldiers." It was too militaristic, some said: "Like a mighty army moves the church of God." And it was sexist: "Brothers, we are treading where the saints have trod." Then the "grass roots" spoke up. They shouted: "That's one of our most beloved hymns; keep it in!" The commission heard and responded, and the hymn was retained. Sentiment prevailed over ostensibly high taste.

Why do people love "Onward, Christian Soldiers"? And why do we find the metaphor of Christians as soldiers girding for battle so inspiring? Is it not a vision of victory that lies ahead, that will not come easily, but, by the power of God, we will win?

The deeper question, however, is over who is the enemy. Who, or what, are the "principalities, the powers and the world rulers of this present darkness"? If we could understand who the enemy is, we would be better prepared for battle.

We do get the sense at times that evil is out of hand. Forces beyond our control wreak death and destruction on humankind. Why, for instance, should an innocent eighteen-year-old boy die of AIDS because of a contaminated blood transfusion?

But there is also evil within ourselves. Like Paul, we find that when we want to do right, "evil lies close at hand" (Romans 7:21). How shall we deal with the principalities and powers?

Selected Scripture

King James Version	New Revised Standard Version

Ephesians 6:10-20

10 Finally, my brethren, be strong in the Lord, and in the power of his might.

11 Put on the whole armour of God, that ye may be able to stand against the wiles of the devil.

12 For we wrestle not against flesh and blood, but against principalities, against powers, against the rulers of the darkness of this world, against spiritual wickedness in high places.

13 Wherefore take unto you the whole armour of God, that ye may be able to withstand in the evil day, and having done all, to stand.

14 Stand therefore, having your loins girt about with truth, and having on the breastplate of righteousness;

15 And your feet shod with the preparation of the gospel of peace;

16 Above all, taking the shield of faith, wherewith ye shall be able to quench all the fiery darts of the wicked.

17 And take the helmet of salvation, and the sword of the Spirit, which is the word of God:

18 Praying always with all prayer and supplication in the Spirit, and watching thereunto with all perseverance and supplication for all saints;

19 And for me, that utterance may be given unto me, that I may open my mouth boldly, to make known the mystery of the gospel,

20 For which I am an ambassador in bonds: that therein I may speak boldly, as I ought to speak.

Key Verse: **Finally, my brethren, be strong in the Lord, and in the power of his might. (Ephesians 6:10)**

Ephesians 6:10-20

10 Finally, be strong in the Lord and in the strength of his power. 11 Put on the whole armor of God, so that you may be able to stand against the wiles of the devil. 12 For our struggle is not against enemies of blood and flesh, but against the rulers, against the authorities, against the cosmic powers of this present darkness, against the spiritual forces of evil in the heavenly places. 13 Therefore take up the whole armor of God, so that you may be able to withstand on that evil day, and having done everything, to stand firm. 14 Stand therefore, and fasten the belt of truth around your waist, and put on the breastplate of righteousness. 15 As shoes for your feet put on whatever will make you ready to proclaim the gospel of peace. 16 With all of these, take the shield of faith, with which you will be able to quench all the flaming arrows of the evil one. 17 Take the helmet of salvation, and the sword of the Spirit, which is the word of God.

18 Pray in the Spirit at all times in every prayer and supplication. To that end keep alert and always persevere in supplication for all the saints. 19 Pray also for me, so that when I speak, a message may be given to me to make known with boldness the mystery of the gospel, 20 for which I am an ambassador in chains. Pray that I may declare it boldly, as I must speak.

Key Verse: **Finally, be strong in the Lord and in the strength of his power. (Ephesians 6:10)**

As You Read the Scripture

Ephesians 6:10-20. Life for first-century citizens of the Greco-Roman world was much more terrifying than it is for us today. They believed in demons, "spiritual forces of evil," and evil spirits. They believed the air was filled with these demonic creatures, all determined to bring harm and destruction upon human beings. For Paul also the whole universe was a battleground. Christians must be prepared to do battle against all the "hosts of wickedness."

Verses 10-11. *Be strong* is better translated "Be made strong" or "Find your strength in the Lord" (REB). God offers us his power. It is up to us to put on—clothe ourselves with—that power. The *whole armor* means the soldier's total equipment against the wiles of the devil, otherwise known as Satan. We may speak of the personification of evil. For the ancients the devil, a being possessing cosmic power, was very real.

Verse 12. Here the enemies are more explicitly described. They are not human beings (flesh and blood) but authorities and powers; these spirits were believed to have dominion over human life. "Cosmic powers of this present darkness" is probably reference to the gods of the Roman Empire, malignant spirits of great power. "Spiritual forces of evil" is "a comprehensive designation for all the classes of hostile spirits with whom the Christian must contend" (*IB*, vol. 10, p. 738).

Verse 13. The equipment that God can provide will enable the Christian to withstand even when the powers of evil seem overwhelming. God's power is greater than all the demonic forces combined. When the smoke of battle clears, the Christian, armed with the power of God, will be standing firm.

Verses 14-17. *The Interpreter's Bible* (vol. 10, p. 740) lists in detail the heavy armor worn by the Roman spearman. There are six essential pieces of armor the Christian needs in the battles against "the spiritual forces of evil": for your belt, truth; for your breastplate, righteousness. The breastplate was worn to protect the heart and lungs. Righteousness is total obedience to the will of God. Any divergence might leave a weak spot, which the enemy might penetrate and mortally wound.

For footwear, we need the gospel of peace. The Christian must be ready to go into the world to proclaim the gospel. As a shield, we need faith. Flaming darts, dipped in pitch and set ablaze, were deadly. Only a large, thick shield provided ample protection. A firm faith is the best answer to temptation from within and the threat of violence from without. For a helmet, we have salvation, "the glad awareness of having been put right with God, and the inward sense of 'wholeness,' peace and vitality which this brings" (C. Leslie Mitton, *Ephesians,* The New Century Bible [Grand Rapids: Eerdmans, 1981], p. 227). For your sword, take the word of God, which the Spirit will provide.

Verse 18. Pray at all times in the Spirit. The soldier of Christ is strong only as he or she maintains close communion with God. The Spirit "helps us in our weakness" and even "intercedes for us" (Romans 8:26). Such prayer must not be casual or careless. We are to pray "at all times" with perseverance—disciplined, determined, sustained. We are to make supplication for all the saints, praying for others more than for ourselves and letting God become the channel of our compassionate concern.

Verses 19-20. Finally, Paul asks for prayers for himself, that he may be given courage to witness to the "mystery" of the gospel, the unbelievable truth that in Christ there is salvation for all people everywhere. Even though in chains, Paul is still an ambassador for Christ (2 Corinthians 5:20). His greatest concern is not for personal safety or even release, but for courage, under all circumstances, to proclaim the "unsearchable riches of Christ" (3:8).

The Scripture and the Main Question

Authorities and Powers

"The rulers . . . the authorities . . . the cosmic powers of this present darkness" are reminders of how powerful and pervasive are the forces of evil. One recalls the Jewish Holocaust during World War II in which over six million victims in Central Europe were exterminated in Nazi gas chambers. And what about Nazism itself, led by an egomaniac who dreamed of a Third Reich that would last a thousand years? Imagine, if you can, millions of innocent lives lost because otherwise sensible people put their trust in a mad man.

The Soviet Union was labeled the "Evil Empire" by an American president who capitalized on that concept to justify a military budget that required a reordering of the nation's priorities, resulting in an enormous debt. Then, in one of history's greatest ironies, the head of the "Evil Empire" and the President of the United States became friends, and the threat of war subsided. The character of communism also changed. There were even profound apologies by a new East German parliament to Jews for Nazi atrocities and by the Soviets for the death of thousands of Polish officers at the hands of Joseph Stalin.

Atrocities are hardly new. Within a few years of the writing of Ephesians a great fire in Rome burned out of control for six days, devastating large areas of the city. When Emperor Nero (whom some believe started the fire himself) looked for scapegoats, he decided to blame the Christians, who were convicted and persecuted to death, not on grounds of clear evidence, but on the grounds of sullen hatred of the human race. It is believed that both Peter and Paul met their deaths at the hands of Nero. Later, Emperor Domitian, who adopted for himself the title "Lord and God," demanded allegiance throughout the empire. Christians who refused to pay tribute, including those in Asia Minor, paid with their lives. Later New Testament writings, especially 1 Peter, Hebrews, and Revelation, reflect the threat of imminent persecution.

Spiritual Forces of Evil

Clearly all the evils cited thus far are "man made." Yet, so entrenched and pervasive are such evils that they seem super-human. Perhaps Satan is real after all and has no lack of loyal, even fanatic, followers. That is surely implied in the language of Ephesians: "against the spiritual forces of evil."

Martin Luther King, Jr., who died a martyr for the cause of racial justice, was acutely aware how insidious is the power of hatred to distort, alienate, and incite fear and anger in otherwise sane and well-intentioned people. Prejudice, wherever found, is one of evil's most persistent powers. Only the power of love can overcome such hatred.

Demons are present at the beginning of the gospel story, just as a snake (representing Satan) inhabits the Garden of Eden. In his first full day of ministry in Capernaum Jesus was challenged by "an unclean spirit," who saw Jesus as the embodiment of God's power, and the battle was joined between good and evil. Jesus commanded the spirit to come out of the man, and he was healed, to the amazement of all who witnessed the miracle (Mark 1:21-28).

Even today, we sometimes blame bad behavior on demons: "I don't know what got into me." "The devil made me do it!"

In the Heavenly Places

There is also reflected in the New Testament a widespread belief in the influence of stars on human behavior. Pagan religions could only encourage people to accept their fate, regarding as unalterable the destiny written in the stars. Astrology is as ancient as recorded history and as recent as today's newspaper, where I am told, as a Pisces, that I should anticipate a new and exciting romance! No less than a former president's wife consulted an astrologer, who advised her about the most opportune time, determined by the stars, for her husband to embark on history-making ventures. The "principalities and power" are still with us.

It is in the spiritual realm that the battle against the powers of evil is to be fought and won. That is why the "whole armor of God" is needed, with truth as a belt, righteousness as a breastplate, the gospel of peace for our feet, faith as a shield, salvation as a helmet, and the word of God as our sword. Armed with the power of God we will be able to face all enemies, without and within.

Be Strong in the Lord

In many ways the enemies within are the most intense. I tried as best I could to minister to a clergyman dying of AIDS. He was depressed much of the time. I tried to lead him to confession so that we could claim the forgiving grace of Jesus Christ: "If we confess our sins, he is faithful and just, and will forgive our sins and cleanse us from all unrighteousness." But he was unwilling to admit the true nature of his illness, and he died, carrying his "secret" to the grave. I have seen what alcohol and drug addiction can do to a human body and, worst of all, to a human soul. It is in the realm of the spirit that the enemy is to be confronted. It is a deadly, and sometimes losing, battle!

But it does not have to be. We must believe that with the help of God victory is possible if we are fortified from within. God's limitless power is always available. We have only to receive and claim it as our own to "withstand on that evil day, and having done everything, to stand firm."

> Soldiers of Christ, arise, and put your armor on,
> Strong in the strength which God supplies thru his eternal Son;
> Strong in the Lord of Hosts, and in his mighty power,
> Who in the strength of Jesus trusts is more than conqueror.
>
> (Charles Wesley)

Helping Adults Become Involved

Preparing to Teach

This is the final lesson on Ephesians, and it is fitting that it should focus on a truly inspiring passage that may seem at first out of date. But the more one thinks about the nature and power of evil, the more one sees that it becomes very relevant indeed.

It is important that you read all of the lesson material designed to make clear the meaning of the text. You will also find a parallel passage in 2 Timothy 2:1-13, which will be helpful to you as a devotional reading: "Share in suffering like a good soldier of Christ Jesus" (2:3).

You may want to invite a retired military person or, better yet, someone presently in the military service to speak to your class. It would be fascinating to discuss with a soldier the importance of having the proper kind of equipment. Superior equipment was a decisive factor for American and Coalition forces in the war with Iraq (Operation Desert Storm) in early 1991. It included individual gas masks, which, fortunately, were not needed.

Besides preparing the actual equipment, how does a soldier prepare for battle? How does one overcome fear? What is the role of prayer? What if anyone questions, as many did during the conflict in Vietnam, whether he or she should be in battle? Such a conversation should not detract from the central theme, which is a challenge to put on the "whole armor of God." But it might just serve to make the lessons very relevant for the 1990s.

Here is today's lesson outline:

I. Ephesians and the equipment of early Christians.
II. The need for Christians equipment today.
III. How can we be better equipped as Christians?

Introducing the Main Question

In "The Main Question" I tried to demonstrate that there is a deep attachment to the military language in hymns like "Onward, Christian Soldiers." Many people do not think of this hymn as glorifying war; rather, they speak of victory over all the forces of evil. There are times when we need very much to be assured that the cause of Christ will prevail.

You should introduce "The Main Question" yourself, either by reading it or by stating the essential thoughts in your own words. Note the importance of the deeper question, "Who is the enemy?" Who or what are the principalities, the powers, and the world rulers of this present darkness?

Developing the Lesson

Again, I suggest that you have two members of the class read alternately the text and the commentary in "As You Read the Scripture." It would be good at this point to have a soldier (or sailor) describe the importance of being properly armed, both in terms of personal gear and weapons, as well as having the appropriate frame of mind.

With this as background, now ask the class to respond to this question in two parts: Who are our enemies (1) according to Paul and (2) in our contemporary world?

Have the class members define what or who are the devil and the principalities without spending too much time giving elaborate definitions. The important thing is to see that for Paul and the early Christians evil was a very powerful force; the heavens and the earth were inhabited by demons who were bent on opposing good at every turn, and because they were threatened by Christ, they fought all the more intensely.

As far as contemporary "enemies" are concerned, encourage your class to think of the forces that threaten the well-being of humankind: nuclear war, violence between races, pollution of the environment, pornography and sexual exploitation (see Lesson 11). List their answers on a chalkboard or newsprint for all to see.

Now comes the all-important question: How are we to do battle against these evils? It is crucial for your students to understand that Paul is using military armor as a metaphor. The "equipment" needed is not physical, but spiritual: truth, righteousness, peace, faith, salvation and the word of God.

Be sure to end the discussion on a positive note. Consider Martin Luther, tormented by doubt and fear resulting from his battles with the hierarchy of the medieval church, yet believing profoundly that our ultimate authority is the Word of God and that the "just shall live by faith" (Romans 1:17). The devil was so real to him that at one point Luther reportedly threw an inkwell at the devil. Yet his faith was stronger than his fear:

> And though this world, with devils filled,
> Should threaten to undo us,
> We will not fear, for God hath willed
> His truth to triumph through us.
> The Prince of Darkness grim,
> We tremble not for him;
> His rage we can endure,
> For lo, his doom is sure;
> One little word shall fell him.
> (Martin Luther, "A Mighty Fortress Is Our God")

Helping Class Members Act

Most Christians have favorite passages of Scripture they use to equip themselves for Christian defense. Perhaps the class members might be willing to make a list of some of their favorite passages, along with a brief statement as to why each one is helpful. Several will undoubtedly name Psalm 23 and other Psalms, Isaiah 40, the sayings of Jesus in the Gospels, and passages from Paul, such as the one today. If the class is relatively small and there is enough time, you may wish to share these Scripture passages. You may also wish to compile them into a "spiritual resource" book to be used by the members and even by others in the congregation.

Do you know people who are going through a hard time? Perhaps they have been recently divorced or have lost a loved one. Possibly someone is struggling to overcome addiction. How can you show care and encourage these persons to be strong in the Lord?

Planning for Next Sunday

Next Sunday we begin a new unit on Old Testament personalities. Ask members to come to class prepared to share their response to this question: "Who is a prophet?"

About Our Editors

William and Patricia Willimon live with their two children, Harriet and William, ages fifteen and seventeen, in Durham, North Carolina. Will is Dean of the Chapel and Professor of Christian Ministry at Duke University. Patsy is manager of the Cokesbury Bookstore at the Duke Divinity School.

Their first book together was *Turning the World Upside Down*, a juvenile biography of the Grimke sisters, nineteenth-century activist social reformers in South Carolina.

Will is the author of over thirty books and numerous articles. His books have sold over a half a million copies. He has been a frequent contributor to *The International Annual Lesson* over the years, writing exposition sections. In addition to his joint editorship of *The International Lesson Annual*, Will is on the editorial boards of *The Christian Century, Quarterly Review, Preaching*, and *Pulpit Digest*.

Will holds degrees from Wofford College, Yale Divinity School, Emory University, and an honorary doctorate from Westminster College. Patsy has degrees from Winthrop College and Southern Connecticut State University.

Patsy comes from a long line of United Methodist pastors. Her grandfather, grandmother, and father were all pastors in South Carolina. Will is a member of the South Carolina Annual Conference of The United Methodist Church and, before coming to Duke, served pastorates in Georgia and South Carolina. At Duke he directs the ministry of the Duke University Chapel and teaches courses in the Divinity School.

What Do You Think Of

The International Lesson Annual?

Please help us by taking a moment to complete this questionnaire and return it to:

Dr. Ronald P. Patterson
Senior Editor
Abingdon Press
P.O. Box 801
Nashville, TN 37202

About you:

Age: (18-25) _____
(26-35) _____
(36-45) _____
(46-55) _____
(56-65) _____
(over 65) _____

State or province in which you live: _____

Name of your church or denomination: _____

Years you have been teaching an adult class: _____

Sex   (M) _____   (F) _____

Total years of formal education: _____

How many Sundays per year do you usually teach? _____

How many hours a week do you usually spend in preparation of your

lesson? _____

About your class:

Average age of members of your class: _____

Average number of participants in your class: _____

Is your class predominantly: Male _____

Female _____

About equally mixed _____

How long is your average class period? _____

Do you usually teach by:

Lecture _____

Discussion _____

A mix of lecture and discussion _____

Other means _____

Your responses to *The International Lesson Annual:*

What does your class like best about the ILA?

_____

_____

What does your class like least about the ILA?

_____

_____

How would you evaluate your class members' response to each quarter in this year's ILA on a scale of 1 to 10, with 1 being lowest and 10 being highest?

First Quarter _____

Second Quarter _____

Third Quarter _____

Fourth Quarter _____

If you do one thing to change the format, content, or presentation of the ILA what would that be?

_____

_____

Where did you or your church purchase your copy of the ILA?

_____

_____

Thank you for taking the time to respond.

The Editors